글로벌 英語略字 大辭典

韓美敎育硏究院 編

東洋書籍

머 리 말

　오늘날 과학 기술의 급격한 발달로 모든 면에서 초첨단화 되어감에 따라 영어약자의 홍수시대에 살고 있다.
　신문 잡지뿐만 아니라 라디오와 TV뉴스 등에 끊임없이 영어약자가 등장하고 있다. 약자는 이미 알고 사용하는 사람에게는 편리할 수 있으나 처음 대하는 사람에게는 답답한 일이다. 따라서 자기 전문분야의 약자는 잘 알지라도 기타 분야의 약자에 대해 궁금해 하고 알고자하는 사람들을 위해 여러 약자를 모아 참고했고, 특히 최근에 여러 언론매체에 등장하는 시사약어용어를 모아 편집한 것이 본 약자사전이다.
　약자는 알파벳 순으로 배열하였으며 같은 약자이지만 다른 의미로 사용되는 경우에는 ①, ②, ③, … 등으로 표기하여 구분하였다.
　본 사전은 약자때문에 답답해하시는 분들에게 좋은 안내서가 되기를 바라면서 앞으로 수요자 여러분과 함께 계속 수정 보완 추가하여 그 때마다 완벽한 약자사전으로 개편해 나가고자 한다.
　끝으로, 약어(略語)와 약자(略字)는 말과 글자를 줄인다는 뜻으로 본 사전에서는 차별화를 두고자 약자(略字)라 명명하였음을 밝혀두는 바이다.

2009년 1월 25일
한미교육연구원
글로벌영어약자대사전 편찬위원 일동

목 차

A	9	N	318
B	63	O	345
C	83	P	358
D	122	Q	384
E	144	R	387
F	168	S	403
G	191	T	434
H	206	U	452
I	218	V	467
J	257	W	476
K	263	X	486
L	277	Y	488
M	291	Z	490

A ① abnormal 이상(異常)의, 불규칙한, 변태의, 병적(病的)인
② ampere 암페어 [전류, 전기량의 단위]
③ alpha [cell] 알파세포
④ argon [=Ar.] 아르곤
⑤ 아토 [군입]
⑥ Atto 계량보조단위 접두어

A angstrom (unit), angstrom unit 옹스트롬 단위, 1Å=10⁻¹m길이, 1억(100,000,000)분의 1cm

A2b AT&T사에서 개발한 오디오 압축 기술.0

A-4 Attack Aircraft ; Sky Hawk 공격기

A-6E All Weather Attack Aircraft Intruder 전천후 공격기

A2C2 Army Airspace Command and Control 육군 공역지휘 및 통제

AA ① Alcoholics Anonymous 알코올 중독 환자 자조 그룹.
② American Airlines 아메리카 항공.
③ Anti aircraft 대공(對空)
④ Asian African : Afro-Asian 아시아 아프리카의.
⑤ automatic approval 자동승인.
⑥ Automobile Association (영) 자동차협회.
⑦ absolute altitude 절대고도
⑧ accompanied by an adult (영) 15세 이하의 어린이는 어른이 동반하지 않으면 볼 수 없는 영화.→R
⑨ advance attrition (군사) 항공기 손모(損耗)예상.
⑩ affirmative action (미) 차별철폐조치.
⑪ acetic acid 아세트산, 초산
⑫ achievement age 교육연령, 성취연령, 달성연령, 지능연령, 취학연령, 학력연령
⑬ active avoidance 능동(적)회피, 적극(적)회피
⑭ acupuncture analgesia 침술 진동, 침술마취
⑮ acute abdomen 급성복통(急性腹痛)
⑯ abandoned aircraft 폐기 항공기(廢棄航空機)
⑰ airborne alert 공항비상대기
⑱ arrival angle 착륙각도

AA Group Asian African Group 아시아·아프리카 그룹.

AA System automatic approval system 수입(輸入) 자동 승인제.

AA Conference Asian African Conference 아시아·아프리카

AAA

회의. 반등회의.

AAA ① Amateur Athletic Asso-ciation 아마추어 체육협회 ② American Automobile Association 미국 자동차협회 ③ Anti Aircraft Artillery 고사모부대. ④ [미] 프로야구 마이너 리그 최상위 계급. ⑤ Agricultural Adjustment Act [미] 농업조정법. 1933년 제정, 1935년 폐지. ⑥ Agricultural Adjustment Administration [미] 농업조정국. ⑦ American Anthropological Association 미국 인류 학회. ⑧ Associated Actors and Artists of America 아메리카 예능인 연합. ⑨ anti aircraft artillery 대공포, 고사 ⑩ Act Against AIDS 에이즈퇴치운동<실천요강> ⑪ acute anxiety attack 급성불안발작 ⑫ Ambulance Association of America [=AA of A] 미국구급차협회 ⑬ American Academy of Allergy 미국알레르기학회 ⑭ American Academy of Audiology 미국 오디올로지학회, 미국청각(의)학회 ⑮ American Association of An atomists 미국해부학회

AAAA ① Amateur Athletic Association of American 미국 아마추어 운동 경기 협회. ② American Association of Advertising Agency 미국 광고 대리점 협회. * 1917년 설립. ③ Asian Amateur Athletic Association 아시아 육상 경기 연맹

AAAC all aluminum alloy cable 고강력 알루미늄 합금 케이블.

AAAHE American Association for the Advancement of Health Education 미국 보건 교육 진흥 협회

AAAI American Association for Artificial Intelligence 아메리카 인공 지능 협회

AAAL ① American Association for Arts and Letters 미국 예술학원. 현재는 AALAL로 개칭. ② American Association for Artificial Intelligence 아메리카 인공 지능 협회. ③ American Association for Applied Linguistics 미국 응용 언어 학회.

AAAM American Association for Aircraft Manufacturers 미국항공기 공업회.

AAAS ① American Association for the Advancement of Science 미국 과학진흥협회. ② American Academy of Arts

and Sciences 미국 학사원.
③ American Academy of Asian Studies 미국 아시아 학회

AAB ① Agency Administration Board [항공] 대리점 관리위원회.
② army air base 육군항공기지

AABB American Association of Blood Banks 미국혈액은행협회

AABC American Amateur Baseball Congress 미국아마추어 야구 협회.

AAC ① Asian African Conference 아시아·아프리카 신흥 19개국 정부 대표가 1955년 4월 인도네시아 반둥에서 개최한 국제 회의.
② Association of American Colleges 미국 대학 협회.

AACF Asian American Cultural Foundation 아시아 문화 재단

AACM Afro Asian Common Market 아시아·아프리카 공동시장.

AACN American Association of Colleges of Nursing 미국간호대학협회

AACP advanced airborne command post [군사] 전진 기상 지휘소(前進機上指揮所)

AACR ① American Association for Cancer Research 미국 암 연구 학회

② American Association of Clinical Research 미국임상의학회

AACS Airways and Air Communication Service [항공] 항공로 보안 관제 및 통신 작업 부대.

AAD ① analog audio disc 종래의 레코드 = AD
② antiaircraft defense 대공방어

AAE ① affirmative action employer [미] 차별철폐 고용주.
② American Association of Engineers 미국 엔지니어 협회.

AAEC Australian Atomic Energy Commission 호주 원자력 위원회.

AAED Academic American Encyclopedia Database [미] 아카데믹 아메리칸 백과사전에 의한 데이터베이스.

AAEE American Association of Electric Engineers 미국 전기 기술자 협회.

AAES American Association of Engineers Societies 미국 공학회 연합회.

AAF ① Army Air Forces (美) 육군항공대
② American Advertising Federation 미국 광고 연맹.
③ army air forces 육군항공부대
④ army airfield 육군비행장

AAFP American Academy of Family Physicians 미국가정의

AAGC

학회

AAGC American Association of Gifted Children 미국재능아(才能兒)협회

AAH advanced attack helicopter 신형 공격 헬리콥터.

AAHA ① American Association of Homes for the Aging 미국양로원협회
② American Association of Hospital Accountants 미국병원계리사 협회

AAHC American Association of Hospital Consultants 미국 병원고문 협회

AAI Ansar Ar Islam 안사르 알 이슬람 : 이라크

AALAL American Academy and Institute of Arts and Letters 미국 예술원. 옛 명칭은 AAAL

AAL ① aircraft approach light 항공기 진입등(進入燈).
② additional authorized list 추가인의 목록

AALA Asian-African Latin American People's Conference 아시아 · 아프리카 · 중남미 국가들의 인민 연대 회의.

AALCC Asian-African Legal Consultative Committee 아시아 · 아프리카 법률 자문 위원회.

AAM ① Air to Air Missile 공대지 유도탄(=ASM). 지대공 유도탄 (=SAM)
② American Association of Museums 미국박물관협회
③ American Academy of Microbiology 미국 미생물학회
④ American Association of Microbiology 미국 미생물학협회

AAMT American Association for Music Therapy [=NAMT] 미국음악요법학회

AAO approved area of operation 작전 인가 지역

AAOG American Association of Obstetricians and Gynecologists 미국산부인과학회

AAOU Asian Association Open Universities 아시아 원격 교육 협의회

A&M art and mechanical (광고) 예술적 센스를 요하는 일과 기계적 작업.

AAP ① Association of American Publishers 미국 출판사협회. 1970년 설립.
② Australian Associated Press 오스트렐리아 AP통신
③ acceptable alternate product 대체품(代替品)
④ (affirmative action plan) 승인된 시행계획
⑤ allied administrative publication 연합 행정 간행물

AAPE American Academy of

Physical Education 미국 의학 교육 학회

A&P The Great Atlantic and Pacific Tea Company 미국의 슈퍼마켓 회사.

AAPOR American Association of Publc Opinion Research 미국 여론 조사 협회.

AAPS American Association for the Promotion of Science 미국 과학진흥 협회.

AAPSO Afro Asian Peoples' Solidarity Organization 아시아·아프리카 인민 연대 기구.

AAPSS American Academy of Political and Social Science 미국 정치사회 학회.

AAQG American Aerospace Quality Group 항공우주 부품의 제조 및 서비스에 관한 품질경영 시스템 규격인 AS 9000 인증제도를 마련하고 운영할 목적으로 설립된 SAE의 위원회

AAR ① aircraft accident report 항공기사고보고(서)
② army area representative 육군지역대표
③ against all risks (해상보험) 전 위험담보.
④ Asiana Airlines 아시아나 항공.
⑤ air-to-air rocket 공대공 로켓.
⑥ antigen antibody reaction 항원 항체 반응.
⑦ Association of American Railroads 미국 철도 협회.

A&R assembly and repair 조립과 수리.

AARP American Association of Retired Persons 전미 퇴직자 협회.

AAS ① (라) Academiae Americanae Socius (= Fellow of the American Academy) 미국 학사원 회원.
② All America Selections 전 미국 화훼 심의회.
③ American Astronautical Society 미국 우주 항행 학회.
④ American Astronomical Society 미국천문 학회.
⑤ Association for Asian Studies 아시아 연구 협회.
⑥ ambient air standard 대기오염허용한도<치>
⑦ American Academy of Sanitarians 미국위생사학회
⑧ American Academy of Sciences 미국과학원(美國科學院), 미국과학아카데미
⑨ American Analgesia Society 미국 통증 치료<무통법>학회
⑩ American Auditory Society 미국청각학회
⑪ aneurysm of atrial septum 심방 중격동맥류
⑫ anthrax antiserum 탄저항혈청(炭疽抗血淸)
⑬ aortic arch syndrome 대동맥궁 증후군
⑭ atomic absorption spectrophotometry 원자 흡

광 측광법(測光法)
⑮ automatic addressing system 자동수신시스템.

AASB American Association of Small Business 미국 중소기업 협회.

AASCU American Association of State Colleges and Universities 미국 주립 대학 협회.

AASO American Association of Ship Owners 아메리카 선주(船主) 협회.

AAT Academic Aptitude Test 수학 능력 평가 수능시험

AATC automatic air traffic control 자동 항공 관제.

AATM American Academy of Tropical Medicine 미국 열대 의학회

AATP American Academy of Tuberculosis Physicians 미국 결핵 전문 의학회

AAU Amateur Athletic Union 미국 체육 협회.

AAUP ① American Association of University Professors 미국 대학 교수 연맹.
② Association of American University Presses 미국 대학 출판국 협회.

AAUW American Association of University Women 미국 대학 여성 협회.

AAW anti-air warfare 대(對) 항공전.

AAWS automatic attack warning system 자동 공격 경계 시스템.

ab. abbreviation ; about ; abridgment ; absent ; airborne.

a.b. (times) at bat (야구) 타수.

AB ① air base 공군기지.
② able-bodied seaman 숙련된 선원, 영국 해군 1등 수병.
③ Alberta (캐나다) 앨버타 주.
④ American Bureau of Shipping 미국 선급(船級) 협회 = ABS.
⑤ (러) artium baccalaureus (= bachelor of arts) (미) 문학사.
⑥ at bat (야구) 타수.
⑦ amphibious brigade 상륙여단
⑧ arm band 완장(腕章). armored brigade 기갑여단(機甲旅)
⑨ army band 육군군악대(軍樂隊). artillery brigade 포병여단(砲兵旅).
⑩ atomic bomb 원자폭탄(原子爆彈)
⑪ available budget 가용예산
⑫ air base 비행장

ABA ① Amateur Boxing Association (영) 아마추어 복싱협회.
② American Bankers Association 미국 은행 협회.
③ American Booksellers Association 미국 서적상(書籍商) 협회.

④ American, British, Australian 미국, 영국, 호주

A.B.A American Bar Association 미국 변호사협회.

ABAA Antiquarian Booksellers Association of America 미국 고서적상(古書籍商) 조합.

abb. abbess ; abbey ; abbot.

abbr. abbrev ; abbreviated ; abbreviation(s) 약어.

abby 여자이름. abigail의 애칭.

ABC ① aggressive, balance, cooperation 공격적, 침착, 협조.
② alcoholic beverage control 알코올 음료 제한.
③ American Broadcasting Company (미) ABC방송.
④ Argentine, Brazil, Chile 아르헨티나, 브라질, 칠레.
⑤ atomic, biological, chemical weapons 원자력, 생물, 화학 병기.
⑥ Audit Bureau of Circulations 신문잡지 발행부수 심사기관.
⑦ automatic background control 팩시밀리에서 원고배경과 기록된 정보의 농도차를 보정하는 회로.
⑧ automatic boiler control 보일러 자동제어.
⑨ automatic brightness control (텔레비전) 자동휘도 조절.
⑩ American-born Chinese 미국 태생의 중국인.
⑪ American Bowling Congress 미국 볼링 협회.
⑫ Arab Banking Corporation 아랍 은행.
⑬ Arab Boycott Committee 아랍 보이콧위원회.
⑭ Asahi Broadcasting Corporation (일) 아사히(朝日) 방송.
⑮ Australian Broadcasting Commission 오스트레일리아 방송 회사.

ABCC Atomic Bomb Casualty Commission 원폭 상해 조사위원회 미일 공동의 원폭 조사기관.

ABCDEF automation, biochemical, computer, do-it-yourself, energy, fine chemical 자동화, 생화학, 컴퓨터, 일요목수, 에너지, 파인 케미컬 신 생장(新生長) 산업. → SCRAP.

ABCS automatic broadcasting control system 자동방송관리시스템. 텔레비전, 라디오의 영상, 음성송출자동화 시스템.

ABC warfare atomic, biological and chemical warfare 원자력·생물·화학병기전쟁.

ABC weapons atomic, biological and chemical weapons 원자력·생물·화학 병기.

abd. abdicated ; abdomen ; abdominal.

ABD

ABD all but dissertation 필요한 단위는 취득했으나 박사학위는 못 받은 수업 연한이 지난 만기 퇴학자(滿期退學者).

ABD air base defense 공군기지 방어

Abe 남자이름. Abraham의 애칭.

ABECOR Associated Banks of Europe Corporate 유럽은행 연맹. 본부 브뤼셀. 1971년 설립

ABEDA Arab Bank for Economic Development in Africa 아프리카 경제개발 아랍은행.

ABEND abnormal end of task (컴퓨터) 작업의 이상종료.

ABF ① Asia Boxing Federation 아시아 권투연맹.
② Asian Baseball Federation 아시아 야구연맹
③ Asian Bowling Federation 아시아 볼링연맹

ABL Allied Bank of Pakistan Limited 파키스탄 합동 은행

ABM ① anti-ballistic missile 탄도탄 요격 미사일.
② asynchronous balanced mode (컴퓨터) 비동기 평형 모드.

ABMC American Battle Monuments Commission (미) 아메리카 전적(戰績) 위원회.

ABN airborne 항공기의.

ABO ABO형 혈액형 분류방식의 하나. A형, B형, AB형, O형으로 분류.

A-bomb atomic bomb 원자폭탄.

abp. archbishop.

abr. abridged ; abridgment.

ABRES advanced ballistic reentry system = ABRS (미) 고성능 탄도 재돌입 시스템. 탄도요격 미사일을 회피하기 위하여 미국에서 연구되고 있는 종래 이상으로 기동성을 가진 탄도탄.

abs. absent ; absolutely ; abstract

ABS ① absolute function 절대치 관수.
② acrylonitrile butadiene styrene copolymers 아크릴로니트릴·부타디엔·스티렌 수지 충격, 저온에 강하며 내열성, 내약품성이 우수하다.
③ alkyl benzene sultanate 합성세제의 주성분.
④ American Bureau of Shipping 미국 선급 협회.
⑤ antiskid brake system 옆으로 미끄러지는 것을 방지하는 브레이크.
⑥ Antilock Brake System(자동차의 제동력이 뛰어난 잠김 방지 제동장치)
⑦ Asset Backed Securities 자유유동화증권 (금융기관이나 기업이 대출자산 및 부동산 어음 등 보유자산을 담보로 발행하는 채권)

Abscam Arab scam (미) 1980년 FBI 수사원이 아랍의 부호와 그 대리인으로 꾸미고, 미끼수사를 펴 국회의원이 뇌물을 받는 사실을 적발한 사건.

abt. about

ABT American Ballet Theater 미국 발레단.

ABTA Association of British Travel Agents 영국 여행 대리점 협회.

ABU ① Asian Broadcasters Union 아시아 방송연합.
② Asia-Pacific Broadcasting Union 아시아 태평양 방송연합.

ABWR advanced boiling water reactor 신형비등수형원자로.

ac. acre ; account.

Ac actinium 악티늄. 원자번호 89.

AC ① adaptive control (컴퓨터) 적응제어장치. 이 장치를 가진 공작기계를 AC공작기라고 한다.
② Advertising Council (미)광고 협의회.
③ alternating current 교류.
④ analog computer 아날로그 · 컴퓨터.
⑤ anchor coat 초벌칠.
⑥ area code (전화) 시외국번.
⑦ Atlantic Charter 대서양헌장.
⑧ author's correction 저자정정.
⑨ Administration Committee (한) (국회의) 행정위원회.
⑩ aero club (영) 비행 클럽.
⑪ Air Canade 국영 캐나다 항공.
⑫ air corps 항공대
⑬ alpine club 산악회
⑭ (라) ante cibum (=betore meals) 식사전.
⑮ army corps 군대.
⑯ athletic club 운동 클럽.
⑰ Acguisition Cost 취득원가.

ac Acre (면적을 나타내는 계량단위, 1ac = 4,046.86㎡ 40.468 = 1,224평)

A.C. ante Christum(before christ) 서기 기원전.

A/C ① account 계정, 구좌.
② account current 당죄계정, 경상계정, 당좌적금.
③ aircraft 항공기.

ACA ① American Camping Association 아메리카 캠핑 협회.
② Antique & Classic Automotive, Inc. (미) 클래식 카 전문 자동차 메이커.
③ Asian Cooperation Association 아시아 협력협회.
④ Associate of the Institute of Chartered Accountants (영) 공인 회계사 협회 준회원.
⑤ Arms Control Association 군측 운동 연합 ; NGO

ACAA Agricultural Conservation and Adjustment Administration (미) 농업보호 조정국.

ACAP ① advanced composite airframe program (항공기) 선

17

ACAS

진 복합 재료체 구조계획. 항공기의 기체구조를 선진 복합재료로 만들려는 미국의 계획.
② Association of Consumers Affairs Professionals (일) 소비자 관련 전문가회의. 기업 내에서 소비자 대책을 담당하고 있는 전문가의 단체.

ACAS ① Advisory, Conciliation and Arbitration Service (영) 조언, 화해, 중재기관. *노사 분쟁 해결을 위하여 의회가 만든기관.
② airborne collision avoidance system 항공기 충돌방지 시스템.

ABC Air Circuit Breaker 기중차 단기(氣中遮斷機)

ACC ① Administrative Committee on Coordination (유엔) 행정조정위원회
② Agricultural Credit Corp. (미) 농업금융공사.
③ Air Coordinating Committee (미)항공정책위원회. 1962년 해산
④ Arab Cooperation Council 아랍 협력 회의.
⑤ area control center 항공로 관제센터.
⑥ automatic combustion control system 자동 연소제어장치.

ACCLRM accelerometer 가속도계.

ACCS (Association of Copyright for Computer Software) 컴퓨터 소프트에어 저작권 협회.

ACCU Asian Culture Center of UNESCO (일) 유네스코·아시아 문화센터

accy. accessory 장식품, 부속물

ACD ① Automatic call distribution 자동 전화 착신 분배.
② American College Dictionary 미국 대학 사전.

ACDA ① Arms Control and Disarmament Agency (미) 군비 군축 관리국.
② Asian Center for Development Administration 아시아 개발행정 센터.
③ (프) Action Concert'ee pour le Developpement Afrique (=Concerted Action for the Development in Africa) 아프리카 개발조정활동.

AC/DC alternating current, direct current
① 직류·교류양용
② 동성도 이성도 성행위의 대상으로 할 수 있는 것.

ACE ① active, creative efficient 적극적·창조적·능률적.
② Allied Command Europe 유럽연합군.
③ Aurally Coded English 발음으로 찾는 사전.
④ automatic calling equipment (전화) 자동호출장치.
⑤ adrenal cortical extract 부

신피질엑스(원액)
⑥ alcohol-chloroform-ether mixture 알코올 클로로포름 에테르 혼합 마취제.
⑦ American Council on Education 미국 교육 협의회.
⑧ Awards for Cable Excellence (미) 유선 TV 우수상.

Ac-Em actinium emanation 악티늄. 라돈의 방사선.

ACES ① Affluent college-educated seniors 대학교육을 받은 유복한 노인.
② annual cycle energy system 연간순환 에너지·시스템

ACF Army Cadet Force (영) 영국 후보생 군대.

ACGB Arts Council of Great Britain 영국 예술 평의회.

ACH ① automated clearing house 자동어음교환소.
② acetylcholine 아세틸콜린. 혈압 하강제.
③ adrenal cortical hormone 부신 피질 호르몬.
④ (러) Agentstvo Sovite Njus (=Soviet News Agency) (일)주로 모스크바 방송을 수신하여 뉴스를 제공하는 기관.

ACI ① acoustic comfort index 음향쾌적지수 * 항공기의 객실 내의 잡음의 정도를 나타내는 지수.
② automatic car identification 자동 자동차 식별.

③ (프) Agence Congolaise d'Infor - mation (= Congo Information Agency) 국영 콩고 통신.
④ Airports Council International 국제공항협회 1991 창설된 국제기구, 본부 스위스 Geneva 소재.

ACIA asynchronous communications interface adapter (컴퓨터) 비동기 통신용 인터페이스장치.

acidhead LSD상용자. LSD는 환각제의 이름.

ACII Associate of the Chartered Insurance Institute (영) 면허보험 협회 회원.

ack. acknowledge ; 승인하다 acknowledgment 승인

ACK acknowledge character (컴퓨터) 긍정(肯定)응답문자. 데이터가 정확히 전송되었다는 것을 알리는 부호.

ACL ① allowable cabin load 여객 기의 허용객실 적재량.
② Atlantic Container Line 유럽 컨테이너 전용선(專用船)그룹.

ACLANT Allied Command Atlantic 대서양연합군.

ACLD air-cooled 공기냉각(의)

ACLS American Council of Learned Societies 미 국제학회 평의원회.

ACLU American Civil Liberties Union 미국 자유 인권 협회.

ACM ① advanced composite material 선진복합재료. 섬유와 플라스틱을 복합하여 만든 신소재.
② advanced composite material 고등순항미사일.
③ African Common Market 아프리카공동시장.
④ anti armor cluster munitions 대장갑 클러스터탄.
⑤ Arab Common Market 아랍공동시장.
⑥ asbestos covered metal 석면피복금속.
⑦ Association for Computing Machinery (미) 컴퓨터학회.
⑧ Average Cost Method 평균원가법

ACME advanced computer for medical research (스탠퍼드대학) 의학연구용 고급컴퓨터.

ACMI air combat maneuvering instrumentation 공중 기동 전투용 계기(計器)

ACMRR Advisory Committee Experts on Marine Resources Research 해양자원 조사전문가 자문위원회.

ACMT advanced cruise missile technology (미) 고등순항 미사일기술.

ACN asynchronous control network (컴퓨터) 비동기(非同期) 제어망.

ACO action cut out ; automatic cut out 자동조종장치가 이상 작동하였을 때 이것을 알리는 보호 기능.

AC of S assistant chief of staff 참모장 보위관.

ACP ① African, Caribbean and Pacific Countries 아프리카, 카리브, 태평양지역제국.
② Airline Control Program (일) 교통공사의 항공권 예약 시스템.
③ acid phosphatase 산성인산분해효소.
④ American College of Pathologists 미국 병리 학회.
⑤ American College of Physicians 미국 내과 의사회.

ACR airfield control radar 공항 감시 레이더.

ACRR American Council on Race Relations 미국 인종 문제 협의회.

ACRS ① accelerated cost recovery system (미) 가속상각제도.
② Advisory Committee on Reactor Safeguards (미) 원자로 안전자문 위원회.

ACS ① Advanced Communi-cation Service (미) ATT의 고도데이터통신서비스.
② alternating current synchronous 교류동기.

③ approach control service 진입 관제 업무. 진입 관제구 내의 비행기에 여러 가지 지시를 하는 업무.
④ autonomous control system 자율 제어시스템.
⑤ Agricultural Cooperative Service (미) (농무성)농업협동 조합국.
⑥ American Cancer Society 미국 암 학회.
⑦ American Chemical Society 미국 화학 학회.
⑧ American College of Surgeons 미국 외과 의사회.

A.C.S American Cancer Society 미국 암 학회.

ACSA Acquisition and Cross Servicing Agreement 물품역무(役務)상호융통협정. 미군과 우호국 군대가 공동훈련 등을 실시할 때 통신, 수송등의 역무, 식량, 연료 등의 물품을 상호 융통하는 협정.

ACSR aluminum cable steel reinforced 강심(鋼心) 알루미늄선.

ACST access time (컴퓨터) 호출시간.

ACT ① active control technique 능동제어기술. 항공기의 비행 제어.
② algebraic compiler and translator (컴퓨터) 대수적 연산과 해석.
③ automatically controlled transportation system 자동 제어 교통시스템.
④ American College Test 미국 대학 입학 능력 테스트.
⑤ Action for Children's Television (미) 어린이의 텔레비전 프로의 정화단체.
⑥ (공군) air control team 항공 통제반.
⑦ Association of Container Transportation (영) 컨테이너 수송 협회.

ACTH adrenocorticotropic hormone 부신 피질 자극 호르몬.

ACTU Australian Council of Trade Unions 호주 노동 조합 협의회.

ACTV advanced compatible television 고품위 텔레비전 고선명 텔레비전(HDTV)의 일종. 현행의 NTSC와 호환성이 있으며, 16:9의 화면비와 증가된 수평 및 수직 해상도를 가지고 있다.

ACTWU Amalgamated Clothing and Textile Workers Union (미) 합동 의복·섬유 노동 조합.

ACU ① arithmetic and control unit (컴퓨터) 연산제어장치.
② Asian Clearing Union 아시아 청산동맹.
③ Asian Currency Unit 아시아 통화단위.
④ automatic calling unit (전화) 자동호출장치.

ACUS Administrative Conference

of the United States 미국행정회의.

ACV ① actual cash value 현금환산 가치, 시가.
② air control valve 공기제어판.
③ air cushion vehicle 에어쿠션정(艇), 호버크라프트(상품명)

ACW ① access control word (컴퓨터) 액세스제어.
② aircraft control and warning 항공기제어경보.
③ alternating continuous wave 교류연속전파.

ACWL Advisory Center WTO Law 세계보건기구 법률자문센터

ad. advertisement 광고

a.d. after date (어음)일부후(日付後).

AD ① action direct (프) 프랑스의 국제혁명 행동 그룹에서 파생한 극좌 게릴라조직.
② active duty (군) 현역.
③ addict of a drug 마약중독자.
④ airworthiness directive 내공성(耐空性)개선통보. 항공기의 결함 개선을 명령하는 항공국이 발행하는 문서.
⑤ analog disc 종래의 레코드.
⑥ analog to digital (컴퓨터) 아날로그에서 디지털로.
⑦ Anno Domini (in the year of our Lord) (라) 서력기원.
⑧ assistant director 연출조수.
⑨ assured destruction 확실파괴전략. 선제 핵 공격을 받았을 때 적에게 궤멸적인 손해를 줄 수 있는 핵전력을 보유하는 전략.
⑩ automated design 자동설계.
⑪ automatic depositor 현금자동 예입기.
⑫ average deviation 평균편차.
⑬ Accreditation 인가증, 출입증
⑭ Action Date 행동개시일
⑮ Anno Domini 서기(A.D)

A.D. (라) Anno Domini (=in the year of our Lord) 서력 기원.

A/D analog to digital conversion 변환 아날로그량(量) (연속하는 물리량 전압·전류등)을 디지털량(불연속량 계수형·숫자형의 량)으로 변환하는 것. 이의 반대는 D/A변환이라고 한다.

ADA ① action data automation (영해군) 전술정보처리시스템.
② American for Democratic Action 민주적 행동을 위한 미국인 시민지도자, 학자 등으로 결성된 정치단체.
③ Atomic Development Authority 원자력개발기관.
④ automatic data acquisition (컴퓨터) 자동데이터수집.
⑤ air defense artillery 방공포
⑥ American Dental Association 미국 치과 의사회.
⑦ American Dietetic Association 미국 영양 학회.

ADAM areal dental artillery munition (미) 지역 통과 거부 야포탄(野砲彈)

ADAPSO Association of Data Processing Service Organization (컴퓨터) 데이터 처리업 협회.

ADAPT adaptation of automatically programmed tool NC 공작기계의 제어테이프를 작성하는 번역 프로그램.

ADAPTS air deliverable antipollution transfer system 공중 투하식 해상 유출 석유 확산 방지 회수 설비.

ADB ① African Development Bank 아프리카 개발은행.
② Asian Development Bank 아시아 개발은행.

ADC ① analog to digital converter (컴퓨터) 아날로그 디지털 변환기.
② Aid to Dependent Children (미) 모자가정 보조제도.
③ Aerospace Defense Command (미) 우주항공 방위군(사령부).
④ aide-de-camp 부관.
⑤ air data computer 항공 데이터 컴퓨터.
⑥ Air Defense Command [일 자위대] 항공 사령부.
⑦ amateur dramatic club 아마추어 연극 클럽.
⑧ assured destruction capability 확증 파괴 능력.

ADCC air defense control center 방공관제소.

ADCCP advanced data communication control procedure (미) ANSI가 정한 동기식 전송제어 프로시저.

ADCIS Association for the Development of Computer - Based Instruction System (미) 컴퓨터원용교육개발협회.

ADCON Address Constant (컴퓨터) 번지상수. 기억장치의 번지를 계산하는데 사용되는 값 혹은 그 값을 표현하는 식.

A/D converter :
analog-to-digital converter (전자공학) AD콘버터. 아날로그 신호를 이에 해당하는 디지털표현으로 변환하는 전기적 장치.

ADCS advanced defense communications satellite 신형 방위 통신 위성.

add address 주소.

ADD ① American Dialect Dictionary 미국 방언 사전. Harold Wentworth편, 1944년 간행.
② Agency for Defense Development 국방과학연구소

ADDC air defense direction center 항공 사령 센터.

ADE ① automated design engineering 자동설계공학.
② air defense emergency (미) 방공 비상 사태.

ADEA

ADEA Age Discrimination in Employment Act (미) 연령에 의한 고용관계 차별금지법.

ADELA Atlantic Community Development Group for Latin America 대서양 공동체 중남미 개발그룹. 중남미 대서양 공동 개발 그룹.

ADEOS Advanced Earth Observing Satellite (일) 대형 지구 관측 위성. 신 지구 관측 위성.

ADES automatic data editing system 자동 데이터 편집 시스템.

ADESS automatic data editing and switching system (일) 기상자료 자동 편집 중계 시스템.

ADF ① African Development Fund 아프리카 개발기금.
② Asian Development Fund 아시아 개발기금.
③ automated design facility 자동설계 소프트웨어. 미국 MBA사의 상품명.
④ automatic direction finder 자동방향탐지기.
⑤ Arab Deterrent Forces 아랍 평화 유지군. 1976년 아랍 수뇌 회의 결의에 의해 설립.

ADFAED Abu Dhabi Fund for Arab Economic Development 아랍 경제 개발 아부다비 기금.

ADH antidiuretic hormone 항이뇨 호르몬.

ADHD Attention Deficit Hyper-activity Disorder 주의력 결핍 과잉 행동 장애.

ADI ① acceptable daily intake 1일 섭취 허용량.
② Air Defence Initiative 항공 전력방위구상.
③ altitude direction indicator 고도방향지시계. 항공기의 기체의 자세·속도등을 표시하는 계기.
④ anti-detonation injection 수(水) 알코올 분사.
⑤ area of dominant influence 특정의 텔레비전(또는 라디오) 프로가 가장 잘 시청되고 있는 지역.
⑥ attitude direction indicator 자세 표시기.

ad inf. ad infinitum(to infinity) (라) 무한히, 영원히.

ADIPA Association of Development Research and Training Institutes of Asia and the Pacific 아시아 태평양 개발 조사 연수기관협의회.

ADIZ air defense identification zone (미) 방공식별권. 이권내에 영공 침범의 우려가 있을 때 전투기가 긴급 발진한다. 영토의 외측 400~500km권.

adj. adjective (문법) 형용사.

Adjt. Adjutant 부관

ad lib (라) ad libitum (=at one's pleasure) 애드 리브.

ADL ① activities of daily life 일상생활동작.
② the advance decline line (증권) 등락주선.

ADLA Atlantic Community Development Group for Latin America 대서양공동체 라틴 아메리카 개발그룹, 아델라라고 함. 라틴 아메리카 대서양 공동체 개발 그룹.

ADF Automatic Direction Finder 자동방향탐지기.

ADIS Air Defence Identification Zone [군] 방위식별단. 한국전쟁당시 제일 미군이 일본영토를 3구역으로 나누어 관제를 설치하여 날라오는 항공기의 기종이나 소속을 식별한 체제의 뜻.

ADLOG advance logistical command 전진 병참 사령부.

adm. administration 관리, 행정 ; administrative 관리상의 administrator 행정관, 관리자 admiral 1군대장 (제독) ; admiralty 해군제독의 직위 admitted 인정된 admission 허가, 가입

ADM ① adaptive delta modulation (컴퓨터) 적응델타변조.
② air-launched decoy missile 공중발사 속임수 미사일.
③ atomic demolition munitions 폭파용 핵 자재.

ADMA Abu Dhabi Marine Areas 아부다비 근해 지역 석유회사.

ADMD Association for Dignified Mental Death 존엄사(尊嚴死)의 권리를 위한 협회.

ADMS automatic dyestuff mixing system 자동염료(染料)조합시스템.

ADN ① Allgemeiner Deutscher Nachrichtendienst (독) 전 독일 통신사. 동독의 국영 통신사.
② (스) Alianza Democratica Nacionalista (=Nationalist Democratic Alliance) (볼리비아) 민족 민주 동맹.

ADP automatic data processing (컴퓨터) 자동 데이터 처리.

ADPC Abu Dhabi Petroleum Company 아부다비 석유 회사.

ADPCM adaptive differential pulse code modulation (컴퓨터) 적응차분(差分) 펄스부호변조.

ADPE automatic data processing equipment (컴퓨터) 자동데이터 처리 장치.

ADPS automatic data processing system (컴퓨터) 자동 데이터 처리 시스템.

ADR ① advance decline ratio (증권) 등락비율.
② American Depositary Receipts 미국예탁증권.

ADS ① Assured Destruction Strategy 확증 파괴 전략.

25

② atmospheric diving suit 대기압 잠수복.
③ automatic diagnostic system 자동 진단 시스템.
④ automatic door seal 자동 도어실.

ADSM air defense suppression missile 방공제압미사일.

ADT ① American District Telegraph (미) 도난경보시스템.
② Anti-Dumping Tariff 덤핑관세율.

ADU automatic dialing unit 자동 다이얼 장치.

ad. val. ad valorem (according to the worth) = AV (라) 가격에 따른, 가격의.

ADX air defense exercise 방공 연습.

AE ① acoustic emission 음향방출. 물체에 힘이 가해져 물체 중에 균열이 퍼질 때 방출되는 음파.
② aeronautical engineering 항공공학.
③ atomic energy 원자력.
④ automatic exposure (카메라) 자동노출조정.
⑤ account executive 광고 대리점에서 광고주와 연락을 담당하는 사람.
⑥ Air Efficiency Award (영) 항공 능률상(賞)
⑦ aeronautical engineer 항공기사.

⑧ air entraining agent 공기연행제. 콘트리트가 갈라지는 것을 방지하는 콘크리트 혼입재.

AEA ① Adult Education Association (미) 성인교육협회.
② American Economic Association 미국 경제학회.
③ American Electronics Association 미국 전자공업협회.
④ American European Associates 구미의 전직 또는 은퇴를 앞둔 최고 경영자가 주주가 되어 도산 직전 상태에 있는 중소기업들을 사들여 회사를 다시 일으켜 세워 되팔거나 주식시장에 공개하는 방법을 통하여 막대한 수익을 올리고 있는 투자클럽.
⑤ Atomic Energy Authority (영) 원자력공사.

A.E and P. Ambassador Extraordinary and Plenipotentiary 특명전권대사.

AEB ① Atomic Energy Board (남아프리카) 원자력 위원회.
② American Embassy 미 대사관.

AEC ① Atomic Energy Commission (미) 원자력 위원회.
② automatic exposure control (카메라) 자동노출조정.

AECB Arms Export Control Board (미) 무기 수출 관리국.

AECL Atomic Energy of Canada Limited (캐나다) 원자력공사

AEDS Association for Educational Data System (미) 교육 데이터 시스템 협회.

AEETC Asian-Europe Environmental Technology Center (ASEM) 아시아·유럽환경 기술센터

AEIL American Export Isbrandtsen Lines 미국 해운 회사명

AEF American Expeditionary Force (미) 해외 파견군.

AEG Allgemine Elektrizitats Gesellschaft Telefunken (General Electric Company Telefunken) (독) 서독종합전기(電機)회사.

AEI ① American Enterprise Institute for Public Policy Research 미국국책연구회. 공화당의 싱크탱크.
② Associated Electrical Industries 영국 최대의 전기기기 제조회사.
③ average efficiency index 평균 효율 지수.

AEIBC American Express International Banking Corporation (미) 아메리칸·익스프레스·인터내셔널은행.

AEIMS Administrative Engineering Information Management System 설계개발 관리 정보시스템.

AEIS aeronautical en route information service 항공로 정보제공업무. 항공로상의 항공기에 대하여 필요한 기상정보를 제공하는 업무.

AEP Advanced Energy Project 첨단에너지·프로젝트.

AERA automated en route air traffic control 자동항공로 관제시스템.

AERE Atomic Energy Research Establishment (영) 원자력 연구소.

AEROFLOT Aero Flotilla 소련 항공

AEROSAT aeronautical satellite 항공위성. 지상과 항공기 사이의 통신에 사용하는 위성.

AES Apollo Extensions System (미) 아폴로 확대 계획. NASA의 인류 월면 착륙후의 우주개발계획.

AETN American Educational Television Network 미국 교육 텔레비전 망.

AEW airborne early warning 공중조기경계기 대형레이더를 탑재하여 적기를 발견한다.

AEW&C airborne early warning and control 공중조기경계관제.

AF ① adventure fiction 모험소설.
② air force 공군.
③ Air France 프랑스항공.
④ Anglo-French 영불(의).
⑤ audio frequency 가청주파수.
⑥ auto focus camera 자동초점

27

카메라.
⑦ automatic focusing (카메라) 자동초점조정.

AFA ① Advertising Federation of America 미국 광고연맹. ② Amateur Football Association 아마추어 축구연맹. ③ automatic fund allocation 수입 자동 할당제.

AFAG Air Force Advisory Group 공군 고문단

AFAK Armed Forced Assitance to Korea 대한 군사 원조

AFAP artillery fired atomic projectile 포 발사 원자포탄.

AFB ① air force base 공군기지. ② air freight bill 공수 화물 증권.

AFC ① automatic fidelity control 자동 충실도 제어. ② automatic flight control 자동 비행 제어장치 ③ automatic frequency control 자동주파수제어. ④ automatic fuel control 자동 연료관제장치. ⑤ Air Force Cross (영) 공군 십자 훈장. ⑥ air / fuel ratio control 공기/연료/ 비율 제어. ⑦ American Conference (미) 프로 축구 리그. → NFL, NFC

AFCET Association Francaise pour ls Cybernetique, Economique et Technique (French Association for Cybernetics, Economics and Technics) (프) 프랑스 인공두뇌 경제기술협회.

AFCS automatic flight control system (항공) 자동비행제어 (자동조종) 시스템. 비행기의 자세, 고도, 속도 비행방향 등을 일정하게 유지하는 장치.

AFDB African Development Bank = ADB 아프리카 개발은행.

AFDC Aid to Families with Dependent Children (미) 모자 (母子) 가정원조법.

AFDF African Development Fund 아프리카 개발기금. AFDB를 보조하는 기금.

AFDTS automatic faults diagnostic test system 자동고장진단시스템.

AFEB authorized foreign exchange bank 공인 외국환은행.

AFESD Arab Fund for Economic & Social Development 아랍경제사회개발기금.

aff. affirmative 긍정.

Afg. Afghanistan 아프가니스탄

AFGE American Federation of Government Employees 미국공무원연합.

AFI American Film Institute (미) 미국 영화연구소.

AFIPS American Federation of Information Processing Societies 미국 정보처리학회 연합회.

AFJ Advertising Federation of Japan 전 일본 광고 연맹.

AFKN American Forces Korea Network 주한 미군방송.

AFL ① A Fundamental Language (컴퓨터) 간이 프로그램 언어. ② Aeroflot 소련항공.

AFLC Air Force Logistics Command 항공 병참군(사령부).

AFL-CIO American Federation of Labor and Congress of Industrial Organization 미국 노동 총 동맹 산별(産別)회의.

AFL-UK American Football League, United Kingdom 영국 미식 축구 연맹.

AFM American Federation of Musicians 미국 음악가 연맹.

AFN American Forces Network 미군 방송.

AFNOR Association Franchise de Normalisation (Standards Organization of France) (프) 프랑스 규격협회.

AFNORTH Allied Forces Northern Europe 북유럽연합군.

AFP ① Agence France Presse (French Press Agency) (프) 프랑스 국영 통신. ② alphafetoprotein 알파페토프로테인. 양수 속에 있는 태아에 의해서만 생산되는 유일한 단백질.

AFPEL Anti-Fascist People's Freedom League (미얀마) 반파시스트 인민 자유 연맹.

AFR ① accident frequency rate 사고발생빈도. ② Air France 프랑스항공.

AFRA Average Freight Rate Assessment 평균 운임 요율.

AFRASEC Afro Asian Organization for Economic Cooperation 아프리카·아시아 경제협력기관.

AFRC aramid fiber reinforced concrete 아라미드 섬유 강화콘크리트.

AFRP aramid fiber reinforced plastic 아라미드 섬유 강화 플라스틱.

AFRS Armed Forces Radio Service (미) 해외주재 미군방송.

AFRTS Armed Forces Radio and Television Service 미군 라디오. 텔레비전 서비스.

AFS ① aeronautical fixed service 항공의 안전을 위하여 특정 지점간에서 제공되는 전기통신업무. ② American Field Service (미)

AFSA

국제장학금을 만들어 각국의 고교생의 교환유학을 추진하는 민간단체.

AFSA American Foreign Service Association (미) (국무성과 미국 홍보·문화 교류청의) 외교 사무 직원 단체.

AFSARC Air Force System Acquisition Review Council (미) 공군 시스템 취득 검토 평의회.

AFSATCOM Air Force Satellite Communications System (미) 공군위성통신시스템.

AFSC ① American Friends Service Committee 미국 프렌드 봉사단.
② American Forces Staff College (미) 군참모대학.

AFSCME American Federation of State, Country and Municipal Employees 미국 주·군·시 직원 연맹.

AFSOUTH Allied Forces Southern Europe 남유럽 연합군.

AFT American Federation of Teachers 미국 교원연맹.

AFTA ASEAN Free Trade Agreement 아세안자유무역협정

AFTAK Association of Foreign Trading Agents of Korea 한국무역대리점협회.

AFTAX aeronautical fixed telecommunication automatic exchange 항공고정전기통신자동 중계시스템. 국제민간항공의 안전운항에 필요한 정보를 중계·교환하는 시스템.

AFTN aeronautical fixed telecommunications network 항공 고정 전기 통신망.

AFTRA American Federation of Television and Radio Artists 미국 텔레비전·라디오 예능인 연맹.

AFV armored fighting vehicle 장갑 전투차.

ag. agriculture 농업.

Ag Agargentum (silver) (라) 은. 원자 번호 47.

Ag. August 8월 (=Aug)

AG Aktiengesellschaft (joint stock company) (독) 주식회사.

AG antigen 항원.

A.G Attorney General (미) 법무장관, 검찰총장.

A/G air to ground 공대지. 항공기 또는 공중에서 지상의 목표를 공격하는 경우를 말함.

AGA ① aerodromes, air route and ground aids 항공로 및 지상원조 시설.
② American Gas Association 미국 가스협회.

AGARD Advisory Group for Aerospace Research and

Development (NATO) 항공우주 연구개발 고문단.

AGB Audits of Great Britain, Ltd. 영국 텔레비전 방송 시청률조사 기관.

AGC ① Apollo Guidance Computer 아폴로 유도 컴퓨터. NASA의 시설.
② automatic gain control (컴퓨터) 자동출력제어. 전파의 강약에 관계없이 출력을 일정히 하는 장치. 텔레비전과 전화 등에 사용.

AGCA automatic ground controlled approach 자동지상 관제진입.

AGCL automatic ground controlled landing 자동지상 관제착륙.

AgCL Silver Chloride 염화은(鹽化銀)

AgCN Silver Cyanide 시안화은

AGE aerospace ground equipment 항공우주용지상장치. 로켓과 인공위성의 정비·점검 등을 위한 장치·기기류.

Agerpress Romanian News Agency 루마니아 국영 통신.

AGET Advisory Committee on Electronics and Telecommunications 전자통신 자문위원회. IEC의 자문기관.

AGF Asian Games Federation 아시아 경기연맹. 1982년에 OCA로 개조.

AGI ① adjusted gross income (미) 수정 총수입.
② Alliance Graphique Internationale (International Graphic Alliance) (프) 국제그래픽·디자인 연맹.
③ Silver Iodide (노란색의 작은 분말모양 결정. 감광성이 크고 특히 자외선에 예민하게 반응하며, 자외선을 쬐면 황색에서 회록색으로 변함. 녹는점 552℃, 끓는점 1,506℃, 비중 5.67), 요오드화은

AGIP (이) Azienda Generale Italiana Petroli (=Italian Petroleum Enterprise) 이탈리아 국영 석유 회사.

AGL above ground level 지면으로부터의 고도.

AGM ① air-launched guided missile 공중발사 유도미사일.
② air-to-ground missile 공대지 미사일.
③ annual general meeting 연차총회.

AGMA American Guild of Musical Artists 미국 음악 예술가 조합.

AGN again 다시 한번 해주시오. 텔렉스의 약어.

AGP Arbeitsgemeinschaft zur Forderung der betrieblichen

31

AGR

Partnerschaft (독) 경영제휴 촉진협회. (서독) 신뢰관계를 만드는 수단으로 노사협동체를 채용한 협회.

AGR advanced gas-cooled reactor 개량형 가스냉각원자로.

AGRIS International Information System for the Agricultural Science and Technology 국제농업과학기술정보시스템. FAO가 운영하는 세계의 농림수산관계의 조사·연구문헌을 수집, 처리, 제공하는 시스템.

AGS ① abort guidance system NASA의 로켓보조유도시스템. 우주선의 주유도시스템에 이상이 생겼을 때 사용하는 것. ② alternating gradient synchrotron 강집속(强集束) 싱크로트론. 브룩크헤이븐 국립연구소에 있는 입자가속기. ③ American Geographical Society 미국 지리학회.

AGT agent 대리인

AGT ① advanced gas turbine 고성능가스터빈. ② automated guideway transit 자동 운전 궤도 교통 기관. ③ aviation gas turbine 항공용 가스 터빈.

AGV automated guided vehicle (로봇) 자동유도이동체. 자력선이나 백선 등으로 유도되는 이동체.

AGVA American Guild of Variety Artists 미국 버라이어티 예능인 조합.

AGVS automatied guided vehicle system 자동유도장치를 장비한 교통기관,

AGZ actual ground zero (군) 실제로 지점. 실폭심의 직하·직상의 지(수) 표면의 점.

AH airfield heliport 비행장겸 헬리콥터 발착장.

Ah Ampere Hour 암페어시 [單位] (1A의 전류가 1시간 도체에 흐를 때 그 도체의 단면을 통하는 전기량의 총량, 1Ah = 3,600C)

AH&LA American Hotel & Lodging Association 미국호텔숙박협회.

AHA ① American Heart Association 미국 심장병학회. ② American Hospital Association 미국 병원 협회. ③ American Hotel Association 미국 호텔 협회.

AHAM Association of Home Appliance Manufactures (미) 가정용 전기제품 공업회.

AHC acute hemorrhagic conjunctivitis 급성 출혈성 결막염.

AHD audio high-density disk 홈이 없는 정전용량방식의 디스크. DAD방식의 하나.

AHH anti-helicopter helicopter 전투헬리콥터를 격파하는 전투

헬리콥터.

AHL American Hockey League 미국 하키연맹.

AHR aqueous homogeneous reactor 수균질원자로.

AHRC Asian Human Rights Commission 아시아 인권위원회.

AHRS attitude and heading reference system 자세방위(方位)기준장치. 비행·항법계기의 기준이 되는 시스템.

AHSR air height surveillance radar 비행고도감시레이더.

a.i ad interim (temporary) (라) 임시의.

AI ① Air India 인도항공.
② air interceptor 공중요격기.
③ Amnesty International 정치범 구제 국제위원회.
④ artificial insemination 인공수정.
⑤ artificial intelligence 인공지능. 인간의 지능에 흡사한 활동을 하는 기계.
⑥ automatic maximum aperture indexing (카메라) 개방 F치 (直) 자동 보정(補正).

AI Avian Influenza 조류(鳥類) 독감 Aves Influenza 조류독감.

AIA ① adventure in attitude 마음의 모험. 미국의 교육전문가 보브 · 콘그린씨가 개발한 연구방법으로 커뮤니케이션의 방법을 그룹으로 연구, 훈련하는 연구방법.
② American Institute of Architects 미국 건축가협회.
③ American Insurance Association 미국보험협회.

AIAA American Institute of Aeronautics and Astronautics 미국 항공우주공학연맹.

AIBA Association International de Boxe Amateur(International Amateur Boxing Association) (프) 국제 아마추어권투연맹.

AIBD ① Asian-Pacific Institute for Broadcasting Development 아시아 태평양 방송개발연구소.
② Association of International Bond Dealers 국제 채권딜러즈 협회.

AIC ① advanced industrial countries 선진공업국.
② aeronautical information circular 항공정보 회람(回覽).
③ American Institute of Chemists 미국 화학자 협회.

AICA Association Internationale de Critique d'Art (프) 국제미술평론가 연맹.

AICD Association for International Cooperation and Development 국제 협력개발협회.

AICHE American Institute of Chemical Engineers 미국 화학 기술자 협회.

AICPA American Institute of Certified Public Accountants 미국 공인 회계사 협회.

AICS Associate of the Institute of Chartered Shipbrokers (영) 공인 선박 중개인 협회 준회원.

AID ① Agency for International Development (미) 국제 개발국. 발전도상국원조기관.
② artificial insemination by donor 남편 이외의 남성의 정자에 의한 인공수정.
③ airborne intelligence display (항공) 기상 정보 표시 장치.
④ American Institute of Decorators 미국 장식가 협회.
⑤ Army Intelligence Department (영) 육군 첩보부.

AIDA attention, interest, desire, action 소비자 심리의 4단계 : 주의, 흥미, 욕망, 구매행위. 소비자의 구매심리의 움직임.

AIDAS attention, interest, desire, action, satisfaction 소비자 심리의 5단계 : 주의, 흥미, 욕망, 구매행위, 만족. 소비자의 구매심리의 움직임.

AIDCA attention, interest, desire, conviction, action 주의, 흥미, 욕망, 확신, 구매행위. 소비자의 구매심리의 움직임.

AIDMA attention, interest, desire, memory, action 주의, 흥미, 욕망, 확신, 구매행위. 광고나 외판원이 판매활동을 효과적으로 실행하기 위한 지침. 소비자의 물건을 사는 심리과정.

AIDP Association Internationale de Droit Penal (International Association of Penal Law) (프) 국제형법협회.

AIDS acquired immune deficiency syndrome 후천성 면역 결핍증. 1981년경 미국에서 발견된 사망률이 매우 높은 병. 주로 동성애 상습자와 마약 상용자가 걸린다.

AIEDP Asian Institute for Economic Development and Planning 아시아 경제개발 계획 연구소.

AIEE ① American Institute of Electrical Engineers 미국 전기 기술자 협회.
② Associate of the Institute of Electrical Engineers (영) 전기 기술자 협회 준회원.

AIETA awareness, interest evaluation, trial, adoption 지명(知名), 관심, 평가, 시용(試用), 수용. * 신제품을 구매 또는 수용하기까지의 소비자 심리의 5단계, 광고계에서는 광고계획과 효과 조사의 기준으로 사용하고 있다.

AIF Atomic Industrial Forum Inc. (미) 원자력 산업 회의.

Al Fatah (反 이스라엘)아랍특공대. (Yasser Arafat가 이끄는 Palestine 해방단체로 1956년

1월 조직)

AIFF audio interchange file format 오디오 인터체인지 파일 포맷 음성 파일의 형식. windows용으로 가장 널리 이용되고 있는 오디오 파일인 wave와 함께 Macintosh에서 음성을 표현하는 표준 오디오 파일 형식의 하나.

AIFT American Institute for Foreign Trade 미국 해외 무역인 양성 학교.

AIFV armored infantry fighting vehicle 장갑 보병 전투차.

AIGA American Institute of Graphic Arts 미국 그래픽 아트 협회.

AIGS Asian Institute of Gemological Sciences 아시아 보석과학 연구소.

AIH artificial insemination by husband 남편 정액에 의한 인공 수정.

AIHA autoimmune hemolytic anemia 자가 면역 용혈성 빈혈 (貧血).

AIHE [F] Association Internationale d'Histoire Economique (=International Economic History Association) 국제 경제사 학회.

AII Air India International 인도 국제공항.

AILA Association International de Linguistique Appliquee (International Association of Applied Linguistics) (프) 국제응용언어학회.

AILAS automatic instrument landing approach system 자동 계기 착륙진입 시스템.

AILC Association Internationale de Litterature Comparee (International Comparative Literature Association) (프) 국제비교문학회.

AILS advanced integrated landing system 개량 종합 착륙 시스템. 전천후 자동 착륙 방식의 하나.

AIM ① air-launched intercept missile 공대공 요격 미사일. ② American Indian Movement 아메리카 인디언 인권 확장 운동 ③ Access for Infants and Mothers 산모보험.

AIME American Institute of Mining Metallurgical and Petroleum Engineers 미국 채광·야금·석유 기술자 협회.

AIMS American Institute of Merchant Shipping 미국 선주 협회.

AIOEC Association of Iron Ore Exporting Countries 철광석 수출국연합.

AIP ① aeronautical information publication 항공정보출판물.

AIPAC

② Afghan Islamic Press 아프간·이슬람통신.
③ American Institute of Physics 미국 물리학회.

AIPAC American Israel Public Affairs Committee 미국·이스라엘 홍보위원회. 미국 외교에서 이스라엘 지지정책을 취하게 하는 정치 압력 단체.

AIPPI Association International pour la protection de la Propriete Industrielle (International Association for Protection of Industrial Property) (프) 국제공업 소유권 보호협회.

AIPS Association International de la Presse Sportive (International Sports Press Association) (프) 국제 스포츠 기자 협회.

AIQ automatic import quota 자동 수입 할당.

AIR All India Radio 인도 국영 방송.

AIREP aircraft inflight report 기상(機上) 실황기상 보고. 민간정기항공기가 관측한 자료를 무선전화로 통보하는 방식.

AIRP Association Internationale de Relations Professionnelles (International Industrial Relations Professional Association) (프) 국제 노사관계 협회.

AIRS automatic image retrieval system 자동 화상검색시스템.

AIS ① accounting information system 회계정보시스템.
② Advanced Information Service (미) ATT의 고도정보서비스.
③ automatic interplanetary station (소련) 자동 행성 간 스테이션.

AISI American Iron and Steel Institute (미국 철강협회, 그의 규격.

AISJ Association Internationale des Sciences Juridiques (International Association of Legal Science) (프) 법학국제협회.

AISP Association of Information System Professionals 정보시스템 전문가 협회 정보시스템 관련 분야에 종사하는 사람들의 모임.

AIT program for Advanced Information Technology (영) 제5세대 컴퓨터 개발계획.

AIU American International Underwriters 미국 국제보험회사.

AIWO Agudath Israel World Organization (이스라엘) 아그다드 이스라엘당.

AJ Al Jihand 알 지하드 이집트 테러단체

AJA Australian Journalists'

Association 호주 신문 협회.

AJC Australian Jockey Club 호주 경마 기수 클럽.

AJL air jet loom 씨실을 공기제트로 투사하는 직조기. 기관은 모두가 국제 민간 항공기구(ICAO)가 정한 표준 ATC方式에 따라 항공사고의 예방, 구조, 항공교통의 질서유지 및 촉진 등에 협력. (약 : ATC)

AJYL Anti-Japanese Youth League 북한 반일청년동맹

AK ① ass kisser 아첨하는 사람.
② Alaska (미) 알래스카 주의 우편 기호.
③ apogee kick 로켓의 타원 궤도 원지점 분사.

a.k.a. also known as 별칭은, 별명은. 인명·지명에 사용한다.

AKA American-Korean Association 한미협회(韓美協會)

AKC American Kennel Club 미국 애견가 클럽.

AKEL (그리스어) Anorthotikon Komma Ergazomenou Laou (=Progressive Party of the Working People) (키프로스) 노동자 진보당.

AKF American Korean Foundation 한미재단(韓美財團)

AKS Academy of Korea Studies 한국정신문화연구원.

ASKWIC author and key word in context (컴퓨터) 자동화된 색인 형식.

Al aluminium 알루미늄. 원자번호 13

AL ① American Legion 미국 재향 군인회.
② Arabian light petroleum 아랍 경질 원유. 중동원유의 수출가격을 결정할 때의 표준원유.
③ Arab League 아랍연맹.
④ Alabama (미) 앨라바마 주의 우편 기호.
⑤ American League (야구) 아메리칸 리그.

Ala. Alabama 알라바마 주.

ALA ① Alliance for Labor Action (美) 노동 행동 동맹.
② American Library Association 미국 도서관 협회. 세계 최고·최대의 국립 도서관 협회. 1876년 설립.
③ Authors League of America 미국 작가 연맹.
④ Automobile Legal Association (美) 자동차 법률 협회.

ALADI Association Lation-Americana de Integracion (Latin American Integration Association) (스) 중남미 통합연합.

ALALC Asociation Lationamericana de Libre Comercio (스) 중남미 자유무역연합.

ALAP

ALAP as low as practicable 실용 가능한 한 얕게.

ALARA ① as low as readily available 용이하게 달성 가능한 한 얕게.
② as low as reasonably achievable 무리가 없는 한 되도록 얕게. 합리적으로 달성 가능한 한 낮게 한다는 뜻으로 원자력발전소 주변의 주민이 가능한 한 피복당하지 않도록 하는 것.

Alas. Alaska 알래스카 주.

ALB ① Air Land Battle (NATO) 적극적 방위전략.
② American Land Bridge 북미태평양 항로와 북미대서양 항로를 미국대륙을 횡단하는 철도로 연결하여 수송하는 극동~유럽간의 복합일관수송루트를 말함.

ALBM airlaunched ballistic missile 공중발사 탄도미사일.

ALC autoclaved lightweight concrete 경량(輕量) 기포콘크리트. 가볍고 방음·단열효과가 크며 강도도 비교적 큰 기포콘크리트.

ALCC airborne launch control center 기상(機上) 미사일 발사 관제 시스템.

ALCM airlaunched cruise missile 공중 발사 순항 미사일.

ALCS airborne launch control system 기상(機上) 미사일 발사 관제 시스템.

ALD Adrenoleukodystrophy 부신 백질이영양증 (염색체열성으로 유전된다는 것으로 밝혀진 휘귀질환)

ALE atomic layer epitaxy 원자층(原子層) 에피택시. 1원자층씩 결정 성장시키는 방법.

ALF Arab Liberation Front 아랍 해방 전선.

ALG antilymphocyte globulin 항림프구 글로불린.(혈구)

ALGOL Algorithmic Language (컴퓨터) 프로그램 언어의 일종. * 수학적 또는 과학적 용도에 적합한 고도프로그램언어.

ALIS ① advanced life information system 생명보험 종합정보시스템.
② automated library information system 자동화 도서관 정보시스템.

ALL air borne laser, laboratory 기상(機上) 레이저 연구실.

ALM assets and liabilities management 자산부채관리.

ALOC air line of communication 항공통상로. 정기 또는 부정기의 민간 항공노선.

ALOTS airborne lightweight optical tracking system (공군) 기상용 경량 광학 추적장치. 제트수송기에 망원카메라를 싣고 고도 1만 미터 이상의 고공으로 올라가 인공위성을 관측하여 위치등을 측정하는 장치.

ALP automatic language processing 자동언어처리.

ALPA Air Line Pilots Association, International 국제여객기 파일럿협회.

ALPS ① advanced linear programming system 고도선형계획시스템.
② automatic linearmotor pneumatic system (일) 자동리니어 모터 공기타이어·시스템. 일본국철(國鐵)의 철도기술연구소가 개발. 추진에는 자석을 사용하고 주행에는 타이어를 사용하는 미래의 고속 통근 수송시스템.

ALRT advanced light rapid transit 도시용혁신적궤도시스템.

a.l.s. autograph letter, signed 자필·자서(自署)의 편지.

ALS ① all weather landing system 전천후 착륙장치.
② autograph letter signed 자필자서의 편지.
③ automatic landing system 자동착륙장치.
④ amyotrophic lateral sclerosis (의학) 근육 위축성 측삭(側索) 경화증.
⑤ antilymphocyte serum 항림프구혈청.

alt. altitude 고도.

ALT ① alternation 교체.
② altitude 고도.
③ approach and landing test (우주공학) 활공착륙실험. 활주로에의 진입, 착륙의 시험·훈련

ALU arithmetic and logical unit (컴퓨터) 산술연산과 논리연산을 실행하는 장치.

ALV autonomous land vehicle 로봇차량.

ALWR advanced light water reactor (원자력) 신형경수로.

ALWT advanced lightweight torpedo (미) 신형경량어뢰. 해군이 개발중인 어뢰로서 속력 약 40km, 도달심도 600m.

a.m. (라) ante meridian (=before noon) 오전.

Am americium 아메리슘. 원자번호 95.

AM ① access method (컴퓨터) 주기억장치의 입출력장치 사이에서 데이타를 전송할 때의 기법. (운영체제에서 입출력을 처리하는 방법.)
② amplitude modulation 진폭변조.
③ associate member 준회원.
④ aviation medicine 항공의학
⑤ Air Medal (미) 항공 훈장.
⑥ airlock module (우주정거장) 에어로크 모듈.
⑦ Albert Medal (영) 앨버트 훈

39

AMA

공 훈장. 인공 구조자에게 수여한다.
⑧ (라) artium magister (= master of art) 문학 석사. 현재는 보통 MA라고 한다.

AMA ① Aerospace Medical Association (미) 우주비행 의학회.
② American Management Association 미국 경영 협회.
③ American Marketing Association 미국 마케팅 협회.
④ American Medical Association 미국 의학 협회.
⑤ American Missionary Association 미국 선교사 협회.
⑥ Australian Medical Association 호주 의사회.
⑦ Automobile Manufacturers Association (미) 자동차 공업회. 현재는 MVMA로 개칭.

amb. ambassador 대사, ambulance 구급차

Amb Ambassador 대사.

AMBO Asian Molecular Biology Organization 아시아 분자 생물 학연구기구.

AMC ① American Motors Corporation 아메리칸 모터즈 회사.
② automatic mixture control 자동 혼합비 조정 장치.

③ aerodynamic mean chord 항공 역학 평균 익현(翼弦).

AMCHAM American Chamber of Commerce in Korea 주한 미 상공회의소

AMD ① absolute mean deviation 절대 평균 편차.
② Advanced Micro Devices, Inc. (미) 반도체 제조회사.

AME astronaut maneuvering eguipment 우주비행사의 우주유영 조종 장치.

AMEDAS automated meteorological date acquisition system (일) 자동기상 관측시스템.

AMES Aeronautical Maritime Engineering Satellite (일) 항공해사 기술 위성.

Amex American Stock Exchange 미국 증권 거래소.

AMEX American Express Co. (미)세계최대의 여행관련서비스회사. 여행자수표와 크레디트카드를 발행하는 국제금융서비스회사.

AMF Arab Monetary Fund 아랍 통화기금.

AMHTS automated multiphase health testing and service system 자동화 종합 건진(建診) 시스템.

AMI airspeed mach indicator 속도 마하계.

AMIC Asian Mass Communication Research and Information Center 아시아 매스컴 연구정보센터.

AMK anti-misting kerosene 증발 억제형 등유.

AML acute myelocytic leukemia 급성 골수 백혈병.

AMM ① anti-missile 공대미사일 · 미사일.
② anti-ballistic missile 미사일 요격미사일.

ammo ammunition 탄약.

AMO Asian Medical Organization 아시아 의료기구.

AMOS automatic meteorological observing station (or system) 자동 기상 관측 스테이션.

AMP Advanced Management Program 상급 경영자 연수 프로그램. * 하버드대학 경영대학원에서 실시하고 있다.

AMPAS Academy of Motion Picture Arts and Science (미) 영화 예술 과학 아카데미. 1927년 창립. 1928년 이래 매년 우수한 영화, 배우에게 Academy Awards 를 수여하고 있다.

AMR ① automatic meter reading 자동검계(檢計).
② average minimum requirement 평균 최소 필요량.
③ American Airlines, Inc. 아메리카 항공. 뉴욕 증권거래서 기호.

AMRAAM advanced medium - range air - to - air missile 신형중거리 공대공미사일.

AMS ① access method service (컴퓨터) 액세스 방식 서비스.
② Agricultural Marketing Service (미) 농무성 농업 시장국.
③ American Mathematical Society 미국 수학 학회.
④ Army Map Service (미) 육군 지도부. * 현재는 DMAHTC 로 개칭.
⑤ Army Medical Service (영) 육군 군의부.
⑥ aeronautical material specification : Aerospace Material Specification 항공 우주 재료 규격.

AMSA advanced manned strategic aircraft (미) 신형유인 전략폭격기.

AMSAM anti - missile surface - to - air missile 미사일 공격 지대공 미사일.

AMSAT amateur satellite 아마추어 무선통신용 위성.

AMSB accelerator molten salt breeder 가속기 용융염(溶融鹽) 증식로.

AMSL above mean sea level 평균 해면상 고도.

AMTB Associated Marine

Transport Bureau 북한 해운 연합총국

AMTICS advanced mobile traffic information & communication system 신자동차 교통정보 통신시스템.

AMTRAK American Track 전미 철도 여객 공사. 정식명은 National Railroad Passenger Corporation

AMU ① Asian Monetary Unit 아시아 통화 단위.
② astronaut maneuvering unit 우주 유영 장치.
③ atomic mass unit 원자 질량 단위.

AMVETS American Veterans of World War II, Korea and Vietnam (미) 제2차 대전 · 한국 전쟁 · 베트남 전쟁퇴역 군인회.

AN ① acrylonitrile 아크릴로니트릴.
② Agencia Nacional Transpress (포르투갈) 브라질 국영 통신.
③ air natural 자연공기냉각.

ANA ① All Nippon Airways (일) 전일공(全日空). 일본의 민간 항공회사의 하나.
② American Newspaper Association 미국신문협회.
③ American Nurse Association 미국 간호사협회.
④ Association of National Advertisers 전미광고주협회.

ANC African National Congress 아프리카 민족회의. 남아프리카 공화국의 인종격리정책철폐를 호소하는 흑인을 중심으로 하는 인종해방조직.

ANCOM Andean Common Market 안데스 공동시장. 콜롬비아, 에콰도르, 페루, 볼리비아, 칠레의 5개국이 1970년에 결성. 1973년에 베네주엘라가 가맹하였고 1976년에 칠레가 탈퇴하였다. 본부 리마.

Andy 남자이름. Andrew의 애칭.

ANF Atlantic nuclear forces 대서양 핵전력.

ANFO Ammonium nitrate fuel oil 질안(窒安) 유제폭약. 다이너마이트에 비하여 취급상 위험성이 적다.

ANG American Newspaper Guild 미국 신문협회. 신문노동자조직.

ANICS Asian newly industrialized countries 아시아 중진국. 한국, 대만, 홍콩, 싱가포르를 지칭.

ANL ① Argonne National Laboratory (미) 아르곤 국립 연구소.
② Australian National Line 호주 국유 해운 회사.

ANLL acute non lymphocytic leukemia 급성 비림프성 백혈병.

ANN Asia-Pacific News Network

아시아・태평양뉴스・네트워크

ANNA ① Army, Navy, NASA, Air Force Geodetic Satellite (미)국방총성・항공 우주국 측지 위성.
② Association of National Numbering Agencies 국제 코드 부여 기관 협의회. (유가증권식별번호체계와 금융상품 분류코드의 보급 관리를 통해 증권분야의 표준화 업무를 주도하는 국제단체로 우리 나라는 증권거래소가 코드부여기관으로 지정되어 있음)

ANOC Association of National Olympic Committee 국가올림픽위원회연합 (ICO에 가맹한 국내 올림픽위원회의 연합체로 1975.5 로마에서 창립)

ANNECS Automated Nikkei Newapaper Editing & Composing System 일본경제신문의 전자편집, 자동조판시스템.

ANOC Association of National Olympic Committee 국가올림픽위원회연합.

ANOP Agencia Noticiosa Portuguesa(Portuguess News Agency) (포) 포르투갈 통신.

ANP ① Aircraft Nuclear - Powered Program (미) 항공기 원자력추진 계획,
② (네덜란드어) Algemeen Netherlands Pres-bureau (=Netherlands News Agency) 네덜란드 통신.

ANPA American Newspaper Publishers Association 미국 신문발행인 협회.

ANRPC Association of National Rubber Producing Countries 천연고무 생산국 연합.

ans. answer 대답 answered 응답

ANS ① American Nuclear Society 미국 원자력 학회.
② Asian News Service 아시아 통신사.
③ Army News Service (미) 육군보도부.
④ Army Nursing Service (영) 육군 간호부대.
⑤ Astronomical Netherlands Satellite 네덜란드의 과학 위성.

ANSA Agenzia Nazionale Stampa Association ANSA통신사. 이탈리아의 대표적인 국제통신사.

ANSC American National Standards Committee 미국 규격위원회.

ANSCII American National Standards Code for Information Interchange (컴퓨터) ANSI가 제정한 8비트의 정보교환용 표준부호.

ANSER automatic answer network system for electronic request (컴퓨터) 음성조화통지시스템. 일본의 NTT가 개발.

ANSI American National Standards Institute 미국 국가 규격 협회. → ASA, USASI

ANSP Agency for National Security and Planning 한국 국가 안전 기획부. 옛명칭 KCIA (Korean Central Intelligence Agency) 중앙 정보부.

ANTA American National Theatre and Academy 미국 연극 아카데미. 1969년 해산.

ANTARA Kantorberita Antara (인도네시아) 안타라통신.

ANTOR Association of National Tourist Office Representatives 외국 정부 관광 대표 협의회.

ANTU alpha-naphthylthioures (상표명) 앤투 : 쥐약.

ANZ Air New Zealand 뉴질랜드 항공.

ANZAC Australia New Zealand Army Corps 오스트레일리아·뉴질랜드 군단(軍團). 제1차, 제2차 세계 대전 때 결성.

ANZAM Australia, New Zealand, Malaysia 오스트레일리아, 뉴질랜드, 말레이시아.

ANZUK Australia, New Zealand, United Kingdom 오스트레일리아, 뉴질랜드, 미국. 태평양 안전 보장조약(Pacific Security Act)의 통칭

ANZUS Australia, New Zealand, United States 오스트레일리아·뉴질랜드·미국. 1951년 이 세 나라는 Pacific Security Act (태평양 안전 보장 조약)을 체결하였다.

a/o account of의 계정.

AO ① analog out put 아날로그 출력.
② automated office 자동화된 사무실.

AOA American Overseas Airlines 미국 해외항공.

AOC ① Association of Olympic Committee 각국 올림픽 위원회 협회.
② aerodrome obstruction chart 비행장 장애물도(圖)

AOD argon oxygen decarbonization (제강) 아르곤과 산소의 혼합가스에 의한 탈탄 (脫炭)

A-OK 만사 오케이.

AOL absent over leave 휴가결근.

AONB Area of Outstanding Natural Beauty (영) 특별히 경치가 좋은 지역.

AOO anode opening odor 양극 개방 악취(陽極開放惡臭)

AOP Aerial Observation Post 대공감시소(對空監視所) (방공관제 레이더의 지리적 장애를 받는 지역에서 육안으로 항공기를 발견, 통신망을 이용하여 방공관제기구에 보고하는 대공 감시 기구)

AOQ average outgoing quality 평균출검(出檢)품질. 선별형 발취(拔取) 검사에서 여러 로트를 검사하였을 때의 수용된 로트의 평균불량율(不良率), 또는 연속 생산형 발취검사에서 수용된 장기간의 평균 불량율.

AOQL average outgoing quality limit 평균 출검 품질한계. 여러 로트를 선별형 발취검사로 검사하였을 때 합격로트의 품질의 평균중 최악의 치(値).

AOR agency of record 지정광고 회사.

AOS ① acquisition of signal 인공위성의 신호를 수신할 수 있는 상태.
② anode opening sound 양극개방음.

AOTS Association for Overseas Technical Scholarship 해외 기술 자 연수 협회

AP ① accounts payable 지불회계
② additional premium (해상보험) 할증보험료.
③ advise and pay 송금환의 통지불.
④ air police (미) 공군헌병대.
⑤ American plan 호텔의 요금제의 하나로서 숙박비에 식사대를 포함시키는 제도.
⑥ application program (컴퓨터) 응용프로그램.
⑦ arithmetic progression 등차수열(等差數列)

⑧ Associated Press 미국의 통신사.
⑨ attached processor 주기억장치를 갖지 않은 CPU.
⑩ authorization to pay 지불승인.

APA ① American Pharmaceutical Association 미국 약학회.
② American Philological Association 미국 언어 학회.
③ American Philosophical Association 미국 철학 협회.
④ American Press Association 미국 신문 협회.
⑤ American Psychiatric Association 미국 정신 의학회.
⑥ American psychological Association 미국 심리학회.
⑦ Australia Press Agentur (독) 오스트리아 통신사.
⑧ American Photographic Association 미국 사진협회.
⑨ American Protestant Association 미국 프로테스탄트 협회.
⑩ Army Procurement Agency (미) 육군 조달 본부.

APAA Asian Patent Attorneys Association 아시아 변리사 협회.

APACHE acute physiology and chronic evaluation 급성기(急性期) 생리학과 장기 건강 평가.

APACL Asian People's Anti-Communist League 아시아 반공연맹.

APACS

APACS adaptive planning and control sequence 판매촉진계획 적합(適合)의 관리수법. 기업이 신제품을 시장에 도입할 때 판매 촉진의 계획, 전개, 실시에 대하여 적합성(適合性), 대체성(代替性)을 고려하는 체계적인 관리수법.

APAR automatic precision approach radar (항공) 자동정측(自動精側) 진입 레이더.

APB ① Accounting Principles Board (미) 회계 원칙 심의회. ② all points bulletin 전국 지명 수배.

APBC Asia Pacific Bankers Club 아시아 태평양 은행가협회(경제 협력체)

APC ① armored personnel carrier 장갑병력수송차. ② Asian Population Conference 아시아 인구회의. ③ Atoms for Peace Conference 원자력 평화 이용 국제회의. ④ automatic phase control (전기) 자동위상제어. ⑤ automatic power control 자동출력제어. ⑥ auto pallet changer 자동가공물 교환장치. ⑦ average propensity to consume 평균소비성향.

APCA Air Pollution Control Association (미) 대기오염 방지 협회.

APCC Asian and Pacific Coconut Community 아시아 · 태평양 코코넛 공동체.

APCWD Asian and Pacific Center for Women and Development (영)아시아 · 태평양 개발행정센터.

APD Avalanche Photo Diode 증폭기능을 가진 고감도(高感度) · 고속응답(高速應答)의 광(光)검출용 다이오드.

APDAC Asian and Pacific Development Administration Center (영) 아시아 · 태평양 개발행전센터.

APDI Asian and Pacific Development Institute (유엔) 아시아 · 태평양 개발연구소.

AP·DJ AP-Dow Jones & Co. Inc. (미) AP · 다우존즈통신.

APEC ① Atlantic Provinces Economic Council (캐나다) 대서양 인접주(州) 경제 평의회. ② Asian Pacific Economic Cooperation 아시아 · 태평양 경제협의체 ③ APEC 에너지실무그룹 ④ APEC 해양자원보존(실무그룹)

A.P.E.C. Atlantic Provinces Economic Council 대서양주 경제평의회.

APEC/EWG APEC Energy Working Group

APECMRC APEC Marine

Resources Conservation APEC 해양자원보호.

APEX advance purchase excursion 선불 저요금 외국여행.

APF authorized program facility (컴퓨터) 허가 프로그램 기능.

APG automatic priority group (컴퓨터) 자동 우선 순위 그룹.

APH anterior pituitary hormone 뇌하수체 전엽 호르몬.

APHA American Public Health Association 미국공중보건협회.

APHIS Animal and Plant Health Inspection Services (미) (농무성) 동식물 위생 검사국.

API American Petroleum Institute 미국 석유협회. API도 (度) 원유의 비중의 단위. 화씨 60℃의 물과 같은 용적의 원유의 비중을 기준으로 계산한다. 작을수록 양질.

APK amplitude phase keying 진폭 위상변조.

APL ① A Programming Language (컴퓨터) 수학적 기호로 수치논리관계를 정확하게 표현하는 프로그램언어.
② average picture level 평균화 상레벨.
③ American President Lines 아메리칸 프레지던트 기선(汽船)회사.
④ Anti-Personnel Landmine 대인지뢰

APN ① Agentsvo Pechati Novosti (러) 노보스티통신사. 소련의 민간통신사.
② Air and Precipitation Monitoring Network (미) 대기 및 강수 감시 관측망.

APO ① Army Post Office (미) 군 사우체국.
② Asian Productivity Organization 아시아 생산성기구.

APOSA Asia, Pacific and Oceania Sports Assembly 아시아, 태평양, 오세아니아 스포츠총회.

app. apparatus ; apparent ; apparently ; appeal ; appended ; appendix ; applied ; appointed ; apprentice ; approval ; approved ; approximate ; approximately.

APP ① Associated Press of Pakistan 파키스탄 국영통신.
② adjusted peak performance, 조정최고성능으로 컴퓨터 성능 표시단위

APPA African Petroleum Producers' Association 아프리카 산유국연합.

APPO Asian-Pacific Postal Union 아시아·태평양 우편연합.

Apr. April 4월.

APR ① alternate path retry (컴퓨터) 대체경로재시행.

② annual percentage rate 연율.

APRA ① (스) Alianza Popular Revolucionaria American (=American Revolution People's Alliance) (페루) 아메리카혁명 인민 동맹.
② Association of Political Risk Analysts 정치적 위기 측정 전문가 협회.
③ Automotive Parts Rebuilders Association (미) 자동차 부품 재조립 협회.

APS ① advertising promise system 광고피해한정(限定)보증시스템.
② Algerie Press Service APS 통신사. 알제리의 국영통신사.
③ American Peace Society 미국 평화 협회.
④ American Philatelic Society 미국 우표 수집 협회.
⑤ American Philosophical Society 미국철학회.
⑥ American Physical Society 미국물리학회.
⑦ auxiliary power supply 보조전원.
⑧ auxiliary propulsion system (우주공학) (속도 · 자세제어용) 보조추진시스템.
⑨ average propensity to save 평균저축성향.

APT ① Advanced Passenger Train 영국의 시속 150km의 초고속열차.
② Asia Pacific Tele- communication Community 아시아 · 태평양 전기통신공동체.
③ Automatically Programmed Tools (컴퓨터) 수치제어공작기계에 사용하는 프로그램언어.
④ automatic picture transmission (기상 · 위성 등의) 자동 영상 송신 장치.

APTA American Public Transportation Association 미국 공공 교통 협회.

APTN Associated Press - Television News 미 통신사

APU ① arithmetic processing unit (컴퓨터) 연산처리장치.
② Asian Parliament Union 아시아 국회의원 연합.
③ Asian Payment Union 아시아 청산동맹.
④ auxiliary power unit 보조동력장치.

APUS auxiliary power unit system 보조동력 시스템.

APV ① adjusted present value 수정현재가치.
② administrative point of view 경영관리적관점.

APWA American Public Work Association 미국 공공 사업 협회.

APWIB American Prisoner of War Information Bureau 미국인 포로 정보국.

APWR advanced pressurized water reactor 신형 가압수(加壓

水)형 원자로.

AQ ① accomplishment quotient 성적지수.
② achievement quotient 학력지수.

AQL acceptable quality level 합격 품질수준. 생산, 출하, 납품시에 사용되는 최저한의 허용 품질 수준.

Ar(or A) argon 아르곤. 원자번호 18.

AR ① account receivable 미수금 회계.
② acknowledgment of receipt 접수통지.
③ advice of receipt 접수통지.
④ aircraft rocket 항공기 탑재 로켓.
⑤ all risks (해상보험)전 위험 담보.
⑥ armed robbery 무장강도.
⑦ average revenue 평균수입.

ARA ① Air Reserve Association (미) 항공 예비역군인회.
② American Railway Association 미국 철도 협회.
③ Associate of the Royal Academy (영) 왕립 미술원 준회원 * Royal Academy의 공식 명은 Royal Academy of Arts.

ARABSAT Arab Satellite Communications Organization 아랍위성통신기구.

ARAD Associate of the Royal Academy of Dancing (영) 왕립 음악원 준회원.

ARAM Associate of the Royal Academy of Music (영) 왕립 음악원 준회원.

ARAMCO Arabian American Oil Company 아랍·아메리카 석유 회사.

ARAS Associate of the Royal Astronomical Society (영) 왕립 천문학원 준회원.

ARB ① Air Registration Board (영) 민간 항공기 등록 협회.
② Asian Reserve Bank 아시아 준비 은행.

ARBA Associate of the Royal Society of British Artists (영) 왕립 화가 협회 준회원.

ARBS Associate of the Royal Society of British Sculptors (영) 왕립 조각가 협회 준회원.

ARC ① anti reflective coating 반사방지도장.
② automatic relay calculator 자동릴레이계산기.
③ automatic resolution control 자동해상도(解像度)제어.
④ Addiction Research Center (영) 마약 중독 연구센터. NIMH (국립 정신 위생 연구소)의 기관, Kentucky주 Lexington에 있다.
⑤ Aeronautical Research Council (영) 농업 연구 협의회.

49

⑥ Agricultural Research Council (영) 농업 연구 협의회.
⑦ AIDS-related complex 에이즈 관련 증후군.
⑧ airborne radio communication (항공) 기상 무선 통신.
⑨ American Red Cross 미국 적십자사.
⑩ Appalachian Regional Commission (미) 애팔래치아 지역 위원회.

ARCA Associate of the Royal College of Art (영) 왕립 미술가 협회 준회원.

Archie 남자이름 Archibald의 애칭.

ARCM Associate of the Royal College of Music (영) 왕립 음악가협회 준회원.

ARCO Associate of the Royal College of Organists (영) 왕립 파이프 협회 준회원.

ARCRU Arab Currency Related Unit 아랍 통화 계산 단위.

ARCS ① Associate of the Royal College of Science (영) 왕립과학 협회 준회원. ② Associate of the Royal College of Surgeons (영) 왕립 외과의 협회 준회원. ③ Australian Red Cross Society 호주 적십자사.

ARD acute respiratory disease 급성 호흡기 질환.

ARDC Air Research and Development Command (미) 항공기술 본부.

ARDE (스) Alianza Revolucionaria Democratica (=Revolutionary Democratic Alliance) (니카라과) 민주 혁명 동맹.

ARDG Army Research and Development Group (미) 육군 연구 개발국.

ARDS adult respiratory distress syndrome 성인형 호흡 곤란증후군.

ARE ① audio response equipment 음성응답제어장치. ② Arab Republic of Egypt 이집트·아랍 공화국.

ARENA (스) Alianza Republicana Nacionalists (=Republican Nationalist Alliance) (에살바도르) 민족주의자 공화동맹.

ARF ① Advertising Research Foundation (미)광고연구재단. ② ASEAN Region Forum 아세안지역포럼. 타이, 필리핀, 말레이시아, 인도네시아, 싱가포르, 브루나이 등 아세안 6개 회원국이 주도하는 아시아 지역 다자안보 협의체.

ARG Atlantic Fleet Amphibious Ready Group 대서양 함대 양륙 즉응군(揚陸卽應郡)

ARH active radar homing (군) 미사일에서 전파 또는 초음파등을 복사(輻射)하여 그의 반사파를 포착하여 목표를 추적·명중시키는 방법.

ARI acid rain index 산성우 지수.

ARIBA Associate of the Royal Institute of British Architects (영) 왕립 건축가 협회 준회원.

ARIC Associate of the Royal Institute of Chemistry (영) 왕립 화학 협회 준회원.

ARICS Associate of the Royal Institute of Chartered Surveyors (영) 왕립 공인 측량사 협회 준회원.

ARIEL Automated Real-Time Investment Exchange Limited (영) 자동증권거래시스템.

Ariz. Arizona 애리조나주.

Ark. Arkansas 아칸소주.

ARL acceptable reliability level 합격신뢰도 수준.

ARM ① Abortion Rights Mobilization (미) 중절권을 위한 동원. 임신중절을 선택할 권리를 주장하는 단체. ② adjustable rate mortgage (미) 변동이자율 주택융자 ③ anti radar missile 대(對) 레이더 미사일. ④ asynchronous response mode (컴퓨터) 비동기 응답 모드.

ARMS atmospheric roving manipulator system (해양공학) 대기압 이동 조정시스템. 대기압이 유지된 구형 실내에 두사람의 승무원을 수용하고 관찰, 및 조정기로 작업을 할 수 있다. 작업심도는 915m.

ARNGUS Army National Guard of the United States 미국 육군 주병(州兵)

ARO Asian Regional Organization-International Confederation of Free Trade Union 국제자유노동조합연합 아시아지역조직.

ARP ① air raid precautions (영) 공습경계경보. ② anti-radar projectile 대(對) 레이더탄. 적의 레이더의 발신원을 탐지하여 목표를 파괴하는 미사일의 총칭.

ARPA Advanced Research Projects Agency (미) 고등연구계획국. 국방성 부속의 군사용 우주계획추진기관.

ARPANET ARPA network (미) ARPA가 제작한 전미국 컴퓨터·네크워크

ARPS Associate of the Royal Photographic Society (영) 왕립 사진가 협회 준회원.

ARQ automatic request for repetition (컴퓨터) 자동 재송(再送) 요구.

ARR accounting rate return 회계적 이익률

51

ARRA

ARRA Rescue Agreement(외기권 조약 제5조 및 제8조를 구체화하기 위한 세부규칙을 담고 있는 협정으로, 1967. 12 UN총회 결의로 채택되어 1968. 12. 발효. 정식명칭은 '우주비행사의 구조, 우주비행사의 귀환 및 외기권에 발사된 물체의 회수에 관한 협정' - Agreement on the Rescue of Astronauts, the Return of Astronautsand the Return of Objects Launched into Outer Space'임) 구조협정(救助協定)

ARRADCOM Armament Research and Development Command (미 육군) 무기 연구 개발 사령부.

ARRC associate, Royal Red Cross (영) 2급 적십자 훈장

ARS ① Advanced Record System 미국에 있어 행정기관 상호를 연결하는 기록통신시스템.
② audio response system (컴퓨터) 음성응답시스템. 음성에 의한 명령으로 기계가 작동하거나 또 컴퓨터가 응답하는 시스템.

ARSA ① Associate of the Royal Scottish Academy (영) 왕립 스코틀랜드 미술원 준회원.
② Associate of the Royal Society of Arts (영) 왕립 예술 협회 준회원.

ARSH Associate of the Royal Society of the Promotion of Health (영) 왕립 건강 증진 협회 준회원.

ARSL Associate of the Royal Society of Literature (영) 왕립 문학 협회 준회원.

ARSR air route surveillance radar 항공로 감시레이다. 항공관제 시스템에 사용되는 장거리·초고도 탐지용 레이다.

art. article (문법) 관사.

Art 남자이름. Arthur의 애칭.

ARTC air route traffic control 항공로 교통관제.

Artic or Arty 남자이름. Arthur의 애칭.

ARTS ① Alpha Repertory Television Servic (미) ABC의 교양프로그램.
② automated radar terminal system 터미널 관제정보 처리 시스템.

ARU audio response unit 음성 응답 장치. 크레디트 카드 신용 확인에 사용되고 있다.

ARV American Reversed Version 미국 개정 번역 성서 = ASV

ARW Air Raid Warning 공습경보

ARWS Associate of the Royal Society of Painters in Water colours (영) 왕립 수채화 협회 준회원.

As arsenic 비소. 원자번호 33.

AS ① account sales 매상계산서.
② acrylonitrile styrene resin AS 수지
③ after service 애프터서비스.
④ age sampling 경년(經年) 발취검사. 소정의 사용시간에 달한 일군(一群)에서 샘플을 발취하여 실시하는 검사.
⑤ alkyl sulfate 세제의 원료.
⑥ American Society of Civil Engineers 미국 토목 협회, 그의 규격.
⑦ Anglo-Saxon 앵글로색슨.
⑧ automatic synchronizer 자동동기장치.

ASA ① American Standards Association 미국규격협회.
② Association of Southesat Asia 동남아시아 연합.

ASAE American Society of Agricultural Engineering 미국 농·공업회.

ASALA American Secret Army for the Liberation of Armenia 아르메니아 해방을 위한 아르메니아 비밀군.

ASALM advanced strategic air-launched missile 신형 전략 공중발사 미사일.

ASAN Association of South Asian Nations 남아시아 제국연합.

ASAP as soon as possible 지급.

ASAT ① anti-satellite weapon 위성공격병기. 통신위성, 조기경계위성 등의 군사위성을 파괴하는 병기.
② attack satellite 공격위성.

ASBC American Society of Biological Chemists 미국 생화학학회.

ASBM air-to-surface ballistic missile 공대지 탄도 미사일.

ASBU Arab States Broadcasting Union 아랍 국가들의 방송 연합.

ASC ① American Security Council (미) 국가안전보장회의.
② advice of schedule change (항공) 정기편 시각 변경 통지.
③ All Savers Certificate (미) 저축자 증권.
④ altered state of consciousness (기도, 단식 등에 의한) 이상한 정신 상태.
⑤ American Society of Cinematographers 미국 영화 카메라맨 협회.
⑥ automatic selectivity control (전기) 자동 선택도 제어.

ASCA ① Asian Students Cultural Association 아시아 학생 문화 협회.
② Association for Science Cooperation in Asia 아시아 과학협력 연합.

ASCAP American Society of Composers, Authors and Publishers 미국작곡가, 저작가, 출판자 협회. 저작권의 보호

53

활동을 하고 있다.

ASCC automatic sequence controlled calculator (컴퓨터) 1944년에 하버드대학의 H.Aiken과 IBM사가 협력하여 완성한 초기의 릴레이 계산기.

ASCE American Society of Civil Engineers 미국 토목 학회.

ASCII American Standard Code for Information Interchange (컴퓨터) 미국정보교환 표준코드.

ASCM anti-ship cruise missile 대함순항미사일.

ASCS Agricultural Stabilization and Conservation Service (미) (농무성) 농업 안정 보전국.

ASCU Association of State Colleges and Universities (미) 주립 대학 협회.

ASD accumulated standardized data 누적 표준화 데이터. INPADOC가 각국과의 교환으로 제공하는 특허문헌의 서지적(書誌的)사항 10데이터(문헌발행국, 문헌의 종류, 문헌번호, 출원번호, 출원일, 문헌발행일, 국제특허분류, 우선국, 주장국, 우선권 주장번호. 우선권 주장일)

ASDE Airport Surface Detecting Equipment 공항면 탐사장치. 공항 지표면의 교통을 감시하는 레이더장치.

ASDF Air Self-Defense Force (일) 항공자위대.

ASE ① American Stock Exchange 미국증권거래소. ② automatic stabilization eqipment (항공) 자동안전장치. 항공기의 타면(舵面)을 자동적으로 조작하여 정안정(靜安定)을 부여하는 장치.

ASEAN Association of Southeast Asian Nations 동남 아시아 제국연합. 태국, 인도네시아, 말레이시아, 필리핀, 싱가포르의 5개국이 1967년에 결성한 지역협력기구. 1984년에 브르나이가 가맹.

ASEF Asia-Europe Foundation (ASEM) 아시아 · 유럽재단.

ASEM Asia-Europe Meeting 아시아 · 유럽 (정상)회의.

ASEM Asia Europe Meeting (한 · 중 · 일 동북아 3개국 및 동남아의 아세안 회원국 7개국 등 아시아 10개국과 EU 15개국 등 모두 25개국이 참여하는 정상회의) 아시아 유럽 정상 회의

ASF advanced streaming format 에이에스에프 새로운 멀티미디어 파일 표준의 확장 판으로 볼 수 있다.

ASET aeronautical service earth terminal 항공업무지구국. ＊항행(航行) 위성시스템의 지상국.

ASFA Aquatic Sciences and Fisheries Abstracts 해수 · 담수 화학 및 어업정보시스템. FAO와

IOC의 정보시스템.

ASG ① acrylonitrile styrene glass fiber 글라스 섬유강화 스티렌수지.
② Association of Student Governments (미) 학생 자치회 협회.

ASGS automatic software generation system 프로그램 자동 생성(生成)시스템.

ASH Action on Smoking and Health 금연 건강 증진 협회.

ASHI American Society of Home Inspectors 미국 가옥 검사관협회.

ASHRAE American Society of Heating Refrigeration and Air - Conditioning Engineers 미국 열·냉동·에어컨디셔닝 공학회.

ASI ① Agenzia Spaziale Italiana 이탈리아 우주공사.
② Asian Statistical Institute 아시아 통계연구소.

Asiad : Asian Games 아시아 경기 대회.

ASIASAT ASIA SATellite communication 아시아 위성통신. 한국, 일본에서 페르시아 연해까지의 지역을 대상으로 한 통신 위성.

Asiatom Asian Atomic Energy Community 아시아 원자 에너지 지역

ASIC application specific integrated circuit 특정 용도 집적회로.

ASID American Society of Interior Designers 미국 실내 장식가 협회.

ASIK American school in Korea 재한 미국인 학교.

ASIO Australian Security Intelligence Organization 호주 보안 첩보 기관.

ASIP application specific integrated processor 특정용도를 위한 마이크로 프로세서.

ASIS American Society for Information Science 미국 정보 과학 학회.

ASL American sign language 미국과 캐나다의 수화법.

ASLA American Society of Landscape Architects 미국 조경가 협회.

ASLB Atomic Safety and Licensing Board (미) 원자로 안전 허인가 회의.

ASM Air-to-Surface Missile 공대지(空對地) 미사일

ASMMT American Society of Mining and Metallurgical Engineers 미국 채광 금속 학회.

ASMS Advanced Strategic Missile System (미) 신형전략미사일시스템.

ASN Agentstvo Sovietskikh Nyus (러) 모스크바 방송의 뉴스를 제공하는 일본의 통신사.

ASNE American Society of Newspaper Editors 미국 신문 편집자 협회.

ASO area of safety operation 안전 작동 영역.

ASOCIO Asia Oceania computing Industry Organization 아시아-오세아니아 컴퓨터 기업 연합. 아시아와 오세아니아 지역의 컴퓨터 서비스, 소프트웨어 기업의 연합체.

ASOSAI Asian Organization of Supreme Audit Institutes 아시아지역 최고회계 감사기구.

ASP ① American Selling Price 미국 판매가격. 미국이 외국 제품을 수입할 때 수입세를 부과하는 기준이 국내도매가격. ② Anglo-Saxon Protestant 앵글로 색슨계 신교도. WASP (White, Anglo-Saxon, Protestant)이지만, White(백인)는 당연한 것이므로 이것을 빼고 ASP라고도 한다. ③ (Association of Software Processors) 소프트웨어 교수연합. 소프트웨어를 개발하는 사람들의 모임.

ASPAC Asian and Pacific Council 아시아·태평양 각료이사회.

ASPCA American Society for the Prevention of Cruelty to Animals 미국 동물 애호협회.

ASPEC ① Asian Pacific Energy Study Conference 아시아·태평양에너지 연구회의. ② Asia Pacific Economic Cooperation 아시아·태평양 경제협의회.

ASPJ airborne self-protection jammer (미) 기상(機上)자위용 전자방해장치.

ASPU Asian Sports Press Union 아시아 스포츠 기자연맹.

ASQC American Society for Quality Control 미국 품질관리 협회.

ASR ① airport surveillance radar 공항감시레이더. ② automatic send receive set (컴퓨터) 자동송수신장치. ③ automatic speed regulator 자동 속도 조정기.

ASRAAM advanced short-range air-to-air missile 신형 단거리 공대공 미사일.

ASROC anti-submarine rocket 대잠수함 로켓.

AS/RS automated storage/retrieval system 자동화된 상품창고.

ass. assistant ; association.

ASSR Autonomous Soviet Socialist Republic 자치 소비에

트 사회주의공화국.

AST Atlantic Standard Time 대서양 표준시.

ASTA American Society of Travel Agents 미국 여행업자 협회.

ASTD American Society for Training and Development 미국 교육 개발 학회.

ASTM American Society for Testing and Materials 미국 재료시험 협회. ASTM Standards ASTM규격.

ASTMS Association of Scientific, Technical and Managerial Staffs (영) 과학 기술 관리자 협회.

ASTP Apollo Soyuz Test Project 아폴로·소유즈 공동우주비행계획.

astro. 우주행사(astronaut의 약어)

ASU Arab Socialist Union 아랍 사회주의자연합. 1962년 결성, 1980년 해산.

ASUW anti-surface ship warfare 대(對)수상 함전.

ASV air-to-surface vessel radar 기상(機上) 대수(對水)레이더.

ASW ① anti-submarine warfare 대잠수함전.
② anti-submarine weapon 대잠수함병기.

ASYNC Asynchronous Communication (컴퓨터) 비동기 통신.

At astatine 아스타틴. 원자번호 85.

AT ① achievement test 학력 성취도 시험
② alternative technology 대체기술. 자연파괴나 에너지 낭비의 재래기술에 대신하는 자원 순환이나 에너지 절약형의 새로운 기술.
③ anaerobic threshold 운동부하가 강해질수록 에너지 공급은 유산소(有酸素)에서 무산소(無酸素)로 이행하게 되는데 그 경계가 되는 운동강도(運動強度).
④ automatic teller = ATM 현금 자동 예금 지불기.
⑤ automatic transmission 자동 변속기.

ATA ① actual time of arrival (항공) 실도착 시각.
② Air Transport Association of America 미국 항공 수송 협회.
③ Albanian Telegraph Agency 알바니아통신.

ATAR anti-tank aircraft rocket 항공기탑재 대전차로켓.

AT&T American Telephone & Telegraph Co. =ATT 아메리칸 전화전신회사.

ATB advanced technology bomber 고등 기술 폭력기. 미국에서 개발중인 신형폭격기.

ATBM Anti-tactical ballistic missile 전술탄도탄 요격미사일.

ATC

ATC ① adaptive transform coding (컴퓨터) 적응변환부호화.
② agro-techno complex 농업·기술복합체. 농업을 공업화하여 다각적·계획적으로 추진하는 것.
③ air traffic control 항공교통관제.
④ American Television & Communications Corp. (미) 케이블·텔레비전회사.
⑤ automatic tool changer 자동도구 제어 장치.
⑥ automatic train control 자동열차제어 장치.

ATCC air traffic control center 항공 관제 센터.

ATCM Antarctic Treaty Consultative Meeting 남극조약협의회의.

ATCS air traffic control system 항공교통관제시스템. 레이더 등으로 수집된 비행데이터를 처리하여 항공교통업무의 안전을 도모하는 시스템.

ATCT Airport Traffic Control Tower 공항관제탑

ATD ① actual time of departure 신출발시작.
② advanced technology development 선진기술개발.

ATDA augmented target docking adapter (NASA)표적용 인공위성.

ATE automatic test equipment 자동 시험 장치. 자동검사장치.

ATF advanced tactical fighter 신형 전술 전투기.

ATG anti-tank gun 대전차포.

ATGM anti-tank guided missile 대전차유도미사일.

ATICS Automobile Traffic Information & Control System (일) 자동차교통정보시스템.

ATIS ① automatic terminal information service 비행장정보방송업무. 공항에 이착륙하는 항공기에 필요한 정보를 송신하는 업무.
② automatic Transmitter identification system 자동식별부호 발사방식.

ATL automated tape library 자동화 테이프 라이브러리.

ATM ① anti-tank missile 대전차미사일.
② automatic (or automated) teller machine AT 자동예금겸 현금지불기.

ATMI American Textile Manufacturers Institute 미국섬유제조업자 협회.

ATO automatic train operation 자동열차운전장치.

ATP ① advanced turbo-prop engine (컴퓨터) 선진 터보 프로프 엔진. 항공기의 다음 세대의 엔진.

② adenosine triphosphate (생화학) 아데노신 삼인산. 생물의 에너지 전달체
③ (프) Agence Tchadienne de Press (=Chad Press Agency) 국영차드 통신.
④ Association of Tennis Professionals (미) 프로테니스 선수 협회.

ATR advanced thermal converter reactor 신형 열전환 원자로.

ATS ① Administrative Terminal System (컴퓨터) 사무관리용 단말시스템.
② application technological satellite 응용기술위성. 통신, 기상, 과학위성 등의 기술을 실험하기 위한 인공위성.
③ automatic train stop 자동열차정지장치.
④ automatic transfer services 자동대체서비스. 은행과의 사전계약에 의하여 예금자의 구좌에서 각종불입을 자동적으로 처리해 주는 제도.

att. attention ; attorney

ATT American Telephone & Telegraph Co. = AT&T 아메리카 전화전신회사.

attn. attention 주의. 편지에는 for the attention of~ (…앞)의 의미로 사용한다.

ATTU Asian Table Tennis Union 아시아 탁구연합.

atty. attorney (미) 변호사.

Atty. Attorney General Gen. (미) 법무 장관.

ATU address transformation unit (컴퓨터) 어드레스변환장치.

ATV all-terrain vehicle 전지형 (全地形) 만능차.

Au aurum(gold) (라)금. 원자번호 79.

AU astronomical unit 천문단위. 태양지구간의 평균거리.

AUA Austrian Airlines 오스트리아 항공.

Aug. August 8월.

AUM air-to-underwater missile 공대수중 미사일.

AUP Australian United Press 오스트레일리아 국내통신.

AUS Army of the United States 미육군. 비상시 미국 육군기구.

Aussie Australian 호주의/ 호주 사람.

auto automobile 자동차

AUTOCAP Automobile Consumer Action Program (미) 자동차 소비자 행동 계획

AUTODIN automatic digital network 자동 디지털 통신망.

A.D.F. automatic direction finder 자동방향탐지기.

AUTONET 부가 가치 통신망

59

(VAN)서비스의 일종. 미국의
APA사가 제공하는 VAN서비스
이다.

AUTOPASS automatic parts
assembly system (컴퓨터) IBM
사가 개발한 로봇언어.

AUW all up weight 총중량.

aux. auxiliary 보조의 : auxiliary
lens (焦點거리를 조절하게 하는)
보조렌즈

Av Avenue = ave., AVE

AV. ① ad valorem 종가(從價)의.
= ad val. 가격에 따른
② audio visual 시청각의.
③ Authorized Version (성서)
흠정역(欽定譯) 성서.

A/V ① audio-visual 시청각의.
② ad valorem (라) 가격에 따라.

AVA Audio Visual Age 국제영상
소프트웨어 추진협의회.

AVC ① audio video computer 오
디오 · 비디오 · 컴퓨터.
② automatic volume control
(라디오) 자동음량조절.
③ American Veterans'
Committee 미 재향군인회.

ave. avenue = Av., AVE길, 길에
붙는 말.

AVE audio-visual education 시청
각 교육.

AVF all-volunteer force 전 지원
병군. 일본의 자위대나 영국군과
같이 병원(兵員) 전부가 지원에
의하여 구성된 군대.

AVI ① automatic vehicle
identification 자동교통정보제
공시스템.
② audio video(visual)
interleaved 음성 · 화상 압축
규격 Microsoft사에서 만든
Windows용 음성, 화상 압축
규격

AVM automatic vehicle
monitoring(system) 자동배차
모니터링. 컴퓨터 연동의 무선택
시 배차시스템.

AVMA American Veterinary
Medical Association 미국 수의
학회.

A.V.O. Avoid Verbal Orders 문서
주의. 미국의 기업내에 침투하고
있는 사고방식이며 구두로 전달
하는 것은 내용이 정확히 전해지
지 않을 위험성이 높고 증거가 남
지 않으므로 가급적 문서 또는 메
모를 하라는 것.

AVR ① automatic voltage
regulator 자동전압조정기. 컴
퓨터의 전원전압 변동에 의한
오(誤) 작동을 방지하는 장치.
② automatic volume
recognition 자동볼륨인지.

AVRDC Asian Vegetable Research
and Development Center 아시
아 소채연구개발센터.

AVSECOM aviation security

command 항공안전보장부대. *
공항의 안전보장을 위한 특수부대.

AVT added value tax 부가가치세.

AVVI altitude vertical velocity indicator 고도·연직(鉛直)속도계. 스페이스셔틀의 탑재계기. 항행중의 고도와 속도의 연직성분을 표시한다.

AW atomic warfare 원자력 전쟁.

AWA American Wrestling Association 미국 레슬링 협회.

AWACS airborne warning and control system (미) 공중 경계 관제 시스템.

AWC ① Association of the Wildlife Conservation 야생생물보존협회.
② Association of World Citizens 세계시민연합 NGO

AWES Association of WEST European Shipbuilders 서유럽 조선업자 협회.

AWI American Watchmakers' Institute 미국 시계 제조업자 협회. 옛명칭은 Horological Institute of America.

AWL absent with leave 유급휴가.

AWLS all weather landing system 전천후 착륙장치.

AWOL ① absentee without leave (미군) 무단외출자(결근자).
② absent without leave (미군) 무단외출(결근).

AWRE Atomic Weapons Research Establishment (영) 원자병기 연구소.

AWS ① automatic weather station 자동기후 관측소.
② automatic weather system 자동기상관측시스템.

AWU atomic weight unit 원자량 단위.

AXAF Advanced X-ray Astrophysics Facility 미국이 아인슈타인 위성에 이어 X-선 천문관측을 위하여 계획하고 있는 대형위성.

AXEL an Extensible Engineers Language (컴퓨터) 회화형 데이터 해석 시스템.

AYC American Youth Congress 미국 청년회의.

AYD American Youth for Democracy 미국 민주주의 청년단.

AYH American Youth Hostels 미국 유스호스텔 연맹.

AZ Arizona (미) 애리조나 주의 우편 기호.

AZAP Agence Zaire Presse(Zaire Press Agency) (프) 자이르 통신.

AZAPO American Azanian People's Organization (남아프리카) 아자니아 인민 기구. 아자

AZLK

니아는 아프리카 민족주의자 용어로 「남아프리카」를 일컬음.

AZLK Avtomobilny Zavod po Imeni Leninsko해 Komsomola (Automobile Factory Named After Lenin's Komsomol)(러) 소련의 자동차공장.

AZT azidothymidine AIDS바이러스의 발전을 방지하는 약.

B 붕소 Boron [硼素元素] (주기율표 제3B족에 속하는 비금속 원소, 원자번호 5, 원자량 10.81)

B3G Beyond 3G : 4세대 무선 통신 시스템이다.

B8ZS Bipolar with an 8 Zero Suppression (Substitution) binary 8-zero substitution (2진수 8제로 대치)의 약어이며, T1 회선과 E1회선에서 사용하는 라인 코드유형으로, 이 경우 링크를 통해 8개의 제로를 연속으로 보내면 특수 코드로 대치된다. 그 다음에 이 코드는 그 연결 상대측에서 해석이 된다. 이 기법은 데이커 스트림에 관계없이 1의 밀도를 보장하는 방법이 된다. 때때로 bipolar 8-zero substitution(바이폴라 8-제로 대치)이라고도 한다.

b. born : (b. 1938 = 1938년 生) 태생

B(-) bomber 爆擊機 : B-1 미국이 제작하려는 최신제트폭격기

Ba barium 바륨. 원자번호 56.

BA ① baccalaureus artium (bachelor of arts) (라) 문학사.
② bank acceptance 은행 인수 어음.
③ bank automation 은행 자동화.
④ Bank of America 아메리카 은행.
⑤ British Academy 영국학사원.
⑥ British Airways 영국항공.

B&A Building & Apartment 빌딩/건물구내 네트워크 공급 서비스이다.

BA Behavior Aggregate 같은 DSCP를 가지고 있는 모든 패킷의 집합을 말함.

BAA bachelor of applied arts 응용 미술 학사.

BAAE bachelor of aeronautical and astronautical engineering 항공 우주 항행 공학사.

B.A.A.S British Association for the Advancement of Science 영국科學振興協會

Baathist Party : Iraq, Syria, Jordan 등에 있는 社會主義政堂의 이름(바트당).

B&B bed and breakfast (영) 민숙. 숙박료에 조식이 포함되어 있는 간이여관.

BABS blind approach beacon system 맹목착륙원조 무선장치.

BAC ① blood alcohol concentration 혈액 중 알코올 농도.
② Business Advisory Council (미) 경제 자문 위원회.

B&C broadcasting and communication 방송과 통신.

BACAT barge aboard catamaran 거룻배 수송용 쌍동선.

BACCUS Basic Calculus (컴퓨터) 일본인이 개발한 후지쯔(富士通) 회화형 언어.

BACIE British Association for Commercial and Industrial Education 영국 상공 교육 협회.

BACIS budget accounting information system 예산회계 정보 시스템.

B.A.C Business Advisory Council 經濟諮問委員會. 경영자 자문 위원회.

BADEA Banque Arabe pour le Developpment Economiqueen Afrique (프) 아랍·아프리카 경제개발은행.

BADGE Base Air Defense Ground Environment (미) 반자동방공경계 관제조직.

BAe British Aerospace PLC 영국의 항공기 제조회사.

BAE bachelor of aeronautical engineering 항공 공학사.

BAEA British Actor's Equity Association 영국 배우 조합.

BAED bachelor of arts in education 교육학사.

BAeE bachelor of aeronautical engineering 항공 공학사. = BAE.

BAEE bachelor of elementary education 초등교육학사.

BAF banker adjustment factor 선박용의 연료 중유의 급등으로 선박회사가 하주에게 부담시키는 연료할증의 과징금.

BAg baccalaureus agriculturae (bachelor of agriculture) (라) 농학사.

BAH Bahrain International Airport 바레인국제공항. (바레인 소재 국제공항)

BAI ① baccalaureus artis ingeniariae(bachelor of engineering) = BEng. 공학사.
② Bio Activation Inducement 순천연물질을 초물리적 메카니즘으로 물성을 융합시킨 특수 에너지를 가진 생체 활성 화 유도체.
③ Board of Audit and Inspection 감사원

BAII Bank of Arab International Investment 아랍 국제 투자은행.

BAJ Basic Abstracts Journal 화학 분야 특허에 관한 영문 초록지 (抄錄誌)

BAK Broadcast Access key (BCMCS) 특별한 BCMCS 프로그램의 하나 이상의 멀티캐스IP 흐름에 접속할 수 있게 한다. 각각의 암호화된 BCMCS 프로그램은 다른 BAK를 가지고 있다.

BAL ① basic assembly language (컴퓨터) 기본 어셈블리언어. ② blood alcohol level 혈액중 알코올 농도.

BALUN BALanced, UNbalanced, balanced, unbalanced (평형, 비평형)의 약자로서 평형회선과 비평형 회선 사이에서 임피던스를 일치시키는 데 사용되는 장치이다. 일반적으로 트위스트드페어 동축 케이블이다.

BALPA British Airline Pilots Association 영국 민간 수송기 조종사 협회.

BAM ① Baikul-Amur Mainline (구소련)바이칼 아무르 철도 (鐵道) ② Basic access method (컴퓨터) 기본 접근 방식. ③ Bell Atlantic Mobile/Build Ahead Margin/Business Activity Monitoring 전화기의 발명가이자 회사 설립자인 'Bell(미국)'의 이름을 딴 단체. digital wireless technology 기술의 상업화에 선도적인 역할을 수행하고 있다.

BAMBI ballistic missile bombardment(or boost) intercepter 대륙간 탄도탄 탐지 파괴 위성.

BANCS Bank Cash Service (일) 13개 도시 은행공통의 자동현금 입출시스템.

BAOC Barring of All Outgoing Calls 신청자에 한하여 기본 그룹내의 모든 사용자에게 전화를 할 수 있는 서비스이다.

BAP Bandwidth Allocation Protocol 시스템 관리자가 멀티링크 PPP번들에 새로운 링크가 들어오는 것을 통제할 수 있는 PPP 보강 프로토콜이다.

BAr bachelor of architecture 건축학사.

BAR Browning automatic rifle 브라우닝 자동소총.

BA rate bank(er's) acceptance rate 은행 인수어음 할인율 인수수수료 연율.

B&B ① bed and breakfast (英) 민박(民泊). 숙박료에 아침 식사가 포함된 간이 여관. ② bread and butter 버터를 바른 빵.

Bar-B-Q barbecue 바베큐.

B&C ① ball and chain 처(妻) ② broadcasting and communication 방송과 통신.

BARRNeT BayArea Regional Research Network 베이 지역 연구용 네트워크의 약자로 샌프란시스코 베이 지역에 서비스를 제공

BART

하는 지역 네크 워크이다. BARRNet 백본은 캘리포니아 주립 대학의 네 개의 캠퍼스 (Berkeley, Davis, Santa Cruz, San Francisco) 스탠포드 대학교, Lawrence Livermore National Laboratory, NASA Ames Research Center 등으로 구성되어 있다. BARRNet은 현재 BBN Planet에 속해 있다.

BART Bay Area Rapid Transit 샌프란시스코 시 고속 통근용 철도.

B&S brandy and soda 소다수를 탄 브랜디.

BASE Brokerage Accounting System Element 증권회계시스템.

BASF Basf AG (독) 서독의 종합학 회사

BASIC Beginner's All-Purpose Symbolic Instruction Code(컴퓨터) 초보자용 프로그램 언어.

BAS ① basic air speed 기준 대기 속도. IAS에 대하여 계기오차를 수정한 것.
② building automation system 빌딩 자동화 시스템.

BASH Bourne Again Shell (대화형 유닉스 쉘) 이 쉘은 Free Software Foundation에서 내어 놓은 일군의 GNU이다. 이 쉘의 최종 목적은 IEEE Posix shell을 대신하는 것이고, 그 쉘에서 작동되는 여러 풀(full) 그림들을 실행할 수 있도록 하는 데 있다.

BASN Broadband Access Serving Node 광대역 접속을 지원해 주는 노드를 말한다.

BASIS Battelle Automated Search Information System (미) 정보서비스의 일종.

BAT : B.A.T Industries 세계최대의 담배회사. Kool, Pall, Mall, Viceroy, Lucky, Strike, Benson & Hedges, Raleigh, Belair 등을 생산.

BATS Broadcast Air-interface Transport Service 에어 인터페이스에서 브로드캐스트를 전송해 주는 서비스이다.

BATT., Battn.,batt. battalion 대대

BAW ① British Airways 영국항공.
② bulk acoustic wave 벌크파 (波) 고체 또는 액체를 전파하는 탄성파 또는 초음파중 고체 또는 액체속을 전파하는 파동.

B&W ① black and white 흑과 백.
② bread and water 조식(祖食)

bay be[stand] at bay 궁지에 빠져 있다.

b.b base(s) on balls (야구) 4구 (출루)

BB brokers' broker 중개증권회사.

BBA ① bachelor of business administration 경영관리학사.
② British Bankers' Association 영국은행협회.

BBB ① bed, breakfast and bath 욕실이 있고 조식을 제공하는 여관.
② Better business Bureau (미) 상사(商事)개선협회. 부정한 영업활동을 규제하기 위하여 업자가 뉴욕에 설립한 자주단체. 광고의 자주규제, 소비자의 불만처리를 맡고 있다.

BBBC British Board of Boxing Control 영국 복싱 관리 위원회.

BBC British Broadcasting Corporation 영국 방송협회.

BBD ① beta binomial distribution (통계)베타 이항분포(二項分包).
② bucket brigade device (컴퓨터) 버킷·릴레이소자. 전기신호의 전파속도를 늦추는 소자.

BBFC British Board of Film Classification 영국 영화 분류국. 옛 명칭은 British Board of Film Censors.

bbl. barrel(s).

BBP butyl benzyl phthalate 부탈산 브틸벤질.

BBS ① bulletin board system 공개 전자 게시판.
② Big Brothers and Sisters 형자회. 연장의 청년남녀가 제매에 해당하는 소년 소녀의 뒷바라지를 하는 것.

BBT basal body temperature 기초체온.

BC ① bachelor of chemistry 화학사.
② bachelor of commerce 상학사.
③ bill for collection 대금징수어음.
④ binary counter (컴퓨터) 2진 카운터.
⑤ birth control 산아제한.
⑥ British Corporation for the Survey and Registry of Ships 영국선급협회.
⑦ buyer's credit 바이어즈구매자 신용크레디트.

B.C. Blue Cross 의료보험회사. (2008년 Anthem으로 바뀌었음)

B.C. before Christ 기원전.

BC biological and chemical weapons 병기 생물병기와 화학병기.

BCAL British Caledonian Airlines 영국 칼레도니아 항공.

BCAR British Civil Airworthiness Requirements 영국 민간 내공성 (耐空性) 기준.

BC-BG Bon Chic, Bon Genre (프) 세련된 취미가 고상한 사람.

BCC ① block check character (컴퓨터) 블록검사문자.
② blind carbon copy 익명 복사본. 전자우편을 보낼 때 각 개인별로 보내는 방법.

BCD ① binary-coded decimal (컴퓨터) 2진화 10진. 10진수의 각 자릿수를 2진법에 의하여 표현한 것.
② Binary-Coded Decimal

BCE

Notation 2진화 10진법 코드.

BCE ① bachelor of chemical engineering 화학공학사.
② bachelor of civil engineering 토목공학사.

BCEC blue-collar, ethnic Catholic (미) 소수 민족의 구교도노동 계급

BCG bacille de Calmette et Guerin(Galmette-Guer-in vaccine) 결핵예방백신.

BCG-CWS BCG cell wall skelton 비특이성 면역활성제의 하나.

BCh (라) baccalaureus chirurgiae (=bachelor of surgery) 외과 의학사. = BS, ChB.

BChE Bachelor of chemical engineering 화학 공학사.

BCI brain computer interface 인간의 생각이나 심리 작용만으로 컴퓨터를 작동시키는 방법.

BCIV Business Council for International Understanding 국제 이해 촉진 경영 협의회.

BCL ① bachelor of civil law 민법학사.
② broadcasting listener 해외방송청취자.
③ broadcast listening 방송청취.

BCM black contemporary music 1970년대 이후의 흑인의 팝뮤직의 총칭.

BCN ① broadband communication network 광대역(廣帶域)통신망. 유선텔레비젼, 텔레비전화, 데이터통신 등의 다양한 통신을 한가닥의 동축(軸) 케이블로 하는 통신망.
② Barcelona Airport 바르셀로나공항. (스페인 바르셀로나 도심에서 13km 떨어진 곳에 있는 공항.)

BCO binary-coded octal 2진화 8진수.

BCom bachelor of commerce 상학사(商學士)

BCP byte control protocol 바이트 제약통신규약.

BCR ① Bell Communication Research (미) 벨연구소.
② bio clean room 무균실.
③ bar code reader 바코드 판독기

BCS ① bachelor of commercial science 상학사.
② business communication system (컴퓨터) 상업용 통신시스템. 상업용을 목적으로 한 컴퓨터에 의한 통신시스템.

BCT ballistic conveyance transistor 탄도수송트랜지스터.

BCTOC Busan Container Terminal Operation Company 부산 콘테이너 부두운영공사.

BCTS broadcasting and communication technology satellite 방

송통신 복합형 위성구상.

BCU ① big closeup (영화·텔레비) 클로즈업.
② bus control unit 버스 제어 유니트.

BCW buffer control word (컴퓨터) 버퍼제어어.

Bd Boulevard 대로(大路). =Blvd., BLVD.

BD ① bachelor of divinity 신학사
② back draft 은행환어음
③ bill discounted 할인어음.
④ brought down 차기이월.
⑤ binomial distribution (통계) 2항분포(二項分包).

BDA bilateral development aid 2국간개발원조.

BDAM basic direct access method (컴퓨터) 기본직접 액세스방식.

BDC Bureau of Domestic Commerce (미) 국내 상업국. Department of Commerce (상무성) 소속.

BDH Bridgehead 교두보

BDI ① Bundesverband der Deutschen Industrie (Federation of German Industry) (독) 서독 공업 연맹.
② Bradley International Airport 브래들리국제공항 [美] 1. 국제 코네티컷주 윈저락스 소재 국제공항 2. L.A. 국제공항.

BDLC basic date link control procedure (컴퓨터) 기본전송제어 프로시저.

BDM bomber defense missile 요격기방어미사일.

BDP Botswana Democratic Party 보츠와나 민주당.

BDOS basic disk operating system (컴퓨터) 기본디스크 운영체제. 개인용 컴퓨터용 OS를 구성하는 3가지 기능(CCP, BDOS, BIOS)의 하나로서 디스크의 관리를 담당한다.

BDR bearer depositary receipts 무기명 예탁증권.

BDS book detection system 도서관의 도서를 무단 지출하는 것을 발견하는 장치.

BDSA Business and Defense Services Administration (미) 방위 산업 협력국. * 1977년 BDC에 통합.

BDSc bachelor of dental science 치과의학사.

BDST British double summer time 영국 이중 서머 타임.

Be beryllium 베릴륨. 원자번호 4.

BE ① bachelor of engineering 공학사.
② bill of entry 입항(入港)신고.
③ bill of exchange 환어음.
④ bio-engineering 생체공학.
⑤ biological engineering 생물

공학. 생체공학.

Bes Beatrice의 애칭. 여자이름.

BEA Bureau of Economic Analysis (미) (상무성) 경제 분석국.

BEAC Banque des Etats de l'Afrique Centrale(Bank of Central African Countries) (프) 중부아프리카 제국은행.

BEAM brain electrical activity mapping 뇌파형도 작성.

BAc bachelor of economics 경제학사.

BECO booster engine cutoff 발사 로켓의 엔진의 연소를 정지시키는 것.

BEd bachelor of education = EdB 교육학사.

BEDD basic engineering design date 기본설계조항.

BEE bachelor of electrical engineering 전기공학사.

Beeb BBC(영국 방송협회)의 별명.

BEF band elimination filter 대역(帶域)저지 필터. * 특정의 주파수대를 제거하는 필터.

BEI Banque Europeenne d'Investissement(European Investment Bank) (프) 유럽투자은행.

Belg. Belgian ; Belgic ; belgium 벨기에.

BELGA (프) Agence Telegraphique Belge de Presse 벨기에 통신.

BEM bug-eyed monster 공상과학소설 등에 나타나는 곤충과 같은 눈을 가진 우주인.

BEn Benjamin의 애칭. 남자이름.

BEMA Business Equipment Manufacturers Association (美) 사무 기기 제조업 협회.

BENELUX Belgium, the Netherlands, Luxemburg 벨기에, 네델란드, 룩셈부르크.

BEng bachelor of engineering = BAI 공학사.

BEP ① back end processor (컴퓨터) 백엔드 프로세서. 비수치적 처리.
② break-even point 손익 분기점.

BEQ Bachelor Enlisted Quarters 독신하사관숙소 (독신하사관들이 거주하는 군 지급 숙소)

BER bit error rate 비트실패율.

Bert Bertram, 남자이름. Albert, Herbert, Robert의 애칭.

Bess Elizabeth의 애칭. 여자이름.

Bessie or Bessy 여자이름. Elizabeth의 애칭.

BEST battery energy storage test (미) 전지에너지 축적시험.

BET Black Entertainment Television (미) 흑인용 오락TV

BETA battlefield exploration and target acquisition(미) 전장탐사 목표포착.

Beth Elizabeth의 애칭. 여자이름.

BETRO British Export Trade Research Organization 영국무역진흥회.

BETS British English Teachers Scheme (일) 영국인 영어 교사 계획.

Betsy Elizabeth의 애칭. 여자이름.

Betty Elizabeth의 애칭. 여자이름.

BeV 10億電子 볼트. (billion electron volt의 약)

BEX broadband exchange 광대역(廣大域) 교환.

b.f. boldface (인쇄) 볼드체.

B/F brought forward 앞 페이지로부터의 이월.

BFA bachelor of fine arts 미술학사.

BFG blast furnace gas 고로가스. 철광석 제련시 고로(高爐)에서 배출되는 가스. 주로 CO, CO_2 N_2 등으로 되어 있으며 저발열량(低發熱量)의 연료가스로 사용된다.

BFI British Film Institute 영국 영화 협회.

BFO best frequency oscillator 맥놀이 주파수 발진기.

B.F.O. British Foreign Office 영국 외무성.

BFP biological false positive (의학) 생물학적 허위 양성.

BFPO British Forces Post Office 영국군 우체국.

BFRM boron fiber reinforced metal 보론 섬유 강화 금속.

BFRP boron fiber reinforced plastics 보론 섬유 강화 플라스틱.

BFS beam-foil spectroscopy 빔 포일 분광(分光).

BFT biofeedback training 생물 피드백 훈련.

BG ① Business Girl 여사무원. 미영에서는 CG가 일반.
② Body Guard 호위.
③ Bowling & Golf 볼링과 골프에 열중하다

BGA Better Government Association (미) 정부 개혁 협회.

BGM background music 배경음악.

BGN Board on Geographic Names (United States) 미국지명위원회

BGO Bismuth Germanium Oxide 4게르만산(酸) 3비스무트. X-선, 감마선등의 방사선을 검출하는데 사용하는 결정재료.

BGV background video 백그라운드 · 비디오. 환경영상, 환경비디오.

BH ① bill of health 건강진단서.
② Blue House 청와대.

BHA butylated hydroxyanisole 산화 방지제의 일종.

BHC benzene hexachloride 살충제.

BHD bulkhead 간막이벽.

BHDF British Hospital Doctors' Federation 영국 병원 의사 연맹.

BHI(SHI) biosynthetic human insulin 반합성 사람 인슐린. (미) Information Dynamics 사의 정보서비스.

BHN basic human needs 의식주와 교육 등 인간으로서 최저한의 필요한 욕구.

BHP brake horsepower 제어마력.

BHS British Home Stores (영) 소매점의 연쇄점.

BHT butyrated hydroxytoluenc 산화방지제의 일종.

Bi bismuth 비스무트. 원자번호 83.

BIAC Business and Industry Advisory Committee 경제 산업 자문 위원회. OECD소속의 민간기관.

BIB Board for International Broadcasting (미)국제방송이사회.

BIBNET Bibliographic and Information Network. (미) Information Dynamics사(社)의 정보서비스

b.i.d. (라) bis in die (=twice a day) (처방) 1일 2회.

BIE Bureau International des Exposition (International Bureau of Expositions) (프) 만국박람회 국제사무국.

BIEM. Bureau International de l'Edition Mecanique (International Bureau of the Mechanic Edition) (프) 국제 레코드 저작권 협회사무국.

BIF banded iron formation 호상(호狀)철광층.

B.I.F. British Industries Fair 영국 산업 박람회.

BIFF 불법사이트 warez 그룹에서 초보자를 나타낼 때 사용하는 용어.

bil. billion. 10억

Bill William의 애칭. 남자이름.

Bill of Rights, the 權利章典(국민의 기본적 인권에 관한 선언. 영국에서는 1689년 제정된 법률을 말하고 미국에서는 1791년헌법에 부가된 10條項의 수정법을 말함).

Billy William의 애칭. 남자이름.

BIM British Institute of Management 미국 경영 관리 협회.

BINAC binary Northrop automatic computer (컴퓨터) 2 진식 프로그램내장식 계산기.

BIND Berkeley Internet Name domain 버클리 인터넷 이름 도메인 버클리에 있는 캘리포니아 주립대학에서 개발한 인터넷 UNIX

서버 프로그램.

BIOS ① basic input output system (컴퓨터) 기본 입출력 시스템. ② biosatellite 생물위성.

BIOSIS Biosciences Information Service (미)생물과학 정보 서비스.

BIP biological index of pollution 생물학적 오염지표.

BIPM Bureau International des Poids et Mesures (International Bureau of Weights and Measures) (프) 국제 도량형국.

BIPS billion instuctions per second (컴퓨터) 1초간에 10억 회의 명령을 실행하는 것.

Bircher John Birch 협회 회원 John Birch Society = 반공극우 단체 이름

BIRD Banque Internationale pour le Reconstruction et le Developpement(International Bank for Reconstruction and Development) (프) 국제부흥개발은행. 통칭 세계은행.

BIRPI Bureaux Internationaux Reunion pour la Protection de Propriete Intellectuelle (프) 지적소유권 보호합동 국제사무국.

BIS ① Bank for International Settlements 국제 결제 은행. ② business information system 서비스, 사무 정보 시스템 사무실에서 필요한 업무를 처리하기 위하여 컴퓨터, 프린터 등의 컴퓨터 시스템을 이용하여 처리하는 시스템.

BIU bus interface unit 프로세서와 버스와의 접속을 제어하는 LSI칩.

biz business 사업, 사무.

BJ bachelor of journalism 신문학사.

BJP Bharatiya Janata Party 인도 인민당.

BJT bipolar junction transistor 양극형 접속 트랜지스터.

Bk berkelium 버클륨. 원자번호 97. (방사성 원소)

Bk. bank 은행.

bkg banking 은행업.

BKP (불가리아어) Bulgarska Komunisticheska Partiya (=Bulgarian Communist Party) 불가리아 공산당.

BL ① bachelor of laws = BLL, LLB 법학사. ② bachelor of letters = BLit, BLitt, LitB, LittB 문학사. ③ bank loan 은행 융자. ④ bill of lading 선하증권. ⑤ British Leyland 영국의 최대 국영의 자동차 제조회사. ⑥ business lady 직업여성.

BLA Bachelor of Liberal Arts 文學史. 문학사

BLAISE British Library Automatic Informations Service 영국국립

BLC

도서관의 정보서비스.

BLC boundary layer control (항공) 경계층 제어.

BLD beam-lead device (컴퓨터) 빔·리드 소자.

bldg. building.

BLEU blind landing experiment unit 항공기 전천후 자동착륙장치.

BLISS Basic Language for Implementing System Software (컴퓨터) 미국의 카네기·멜론대학이 개발한 시스템 작성언어.

BLL (라) baccalaureus legum (=bachelor of laws) 법학사. = BL, LLB

BLLD British Library Lending Division 영국 도서관 대출부.

BLMC British Leyland Motor Corporation 영국의 자동차 제조회사. 1975년 국유화되어 BL로 변경.

BLP butyl lauryl phthalate 가소제의 일종.

BLS ① Bureau of Labor Statistics (미) 노동통계국.
② bus location system 버스의 위치를 센터에 알려 차가 몰려 다니는 것을 방지하는 시스템.

BLT bacon-lettuce-and-tomato sandwich 베이컨·레티스·토마토 샌드위치.

BLvd boulevard = BLVD, Bd. 대로(大路).

BM ① baccalaureus medicinae (bachelor of medicine) (라) 의 학사.
② ballistic missile 탄도미사일.
③ barrels per month 석유정제에 있어 1개월당 통유(通由)능력.
④ basal metabolism 기초대사.
⑤ Battle Management 전투관리. 소형, 대용량화한 컴퓨터를 구사하여 보다 과학적, 합리적인 전투지휘를 하기 위한 조직적 행동.
⑥ bowel movement 변통.
⑦ break-down maintenance 사후보전.

BMA British Medical Association 영국 의사회.

BMC ① British Motor Corporation 영국 자동차회사. 영국의 최대의 자동차회사.
② bulk molding compound 압축성형과 사출성형에 사용하는 복합재료.

BMD ① ballistic missile defense 탄도미사일방어. 탄도미사일에 대한 요격망.
② biomedical computer program (컴퓨터) 의학용 통계해석 프로그램. 캘리포니아대학과 국립위생연구소가 개발.

BME bachelor of mechanical engineering 기계공학사.

BMEP brake mean effective pressure (항공) 정미(正味) 평균

유효 압력.

BMEWS Ballistic Missile Early Warning System (미) 탄도미사일 조기경계조직. 북극을 넘어 공격해온 소련의 ICBM을 조기에 탐지하기 위하여 북극권에 설립한 초대형 레이더 시스템군.

BMF bond management fund 수익증권 저축. 통화 채권 펀드.

BMJ British Medical Journal 영국 의사 저널.

BMOC big man on campus 인기가 있는 유력한 학생. 보통 과외활동의 리더를 말함.

BMP Bitmap Microsoft사에서 규정한 Windowns95 페인트 프로그램에서 비엠피 형식으로 이미지 파일을 저장한다.

BMR basal metabolic rate 기초대사율.

BMT Brooklyn-Manhattan Transit Lines 뉴욕 지하철 3계통의 하나.

BMTE Bundesministerium fur Teknik und Forschung (= Federal Ministry of Technique and Research) [통일 전 서독]의 연방 연구 기술청.

BMus bachelor of music 음악학사.

BMW Bayerische Motoren Werke (=Bavarian Motor Works) (독일) 바바라아 자동차 회사.

BMX bicycle motocross 바이시클 모토크로스. 미국에서 탄생한 새로운 자전거경기.

bn 10억.

BN boron nitride 질소화붕소.

BNA ① Bakhtar News Agency 아프가니스탄 국영통신사. ② (라) Basle Nomina Anatomica (=Basle anatomical nomenclature) 바젤 해부학회 명명법(命名法).

BNDD Bureau of Narcotics and Dangerous Drugs (미) (사법성) 마약 단속국. 현재는 DEA로 개칭.

BNDP Brunei Nationnal Democratic Party 브루네이 국가 민주당.

BNF Botswana National Front 보츠와나 민족 전선.

BNFL British Nuclear Fuels Limited 영국 원자력연료공사.

BNOC ① British National Oil Corporation 영국 군영석유회사. 북해원유의 판매회사. ② British National Opera Company 영국 국립 오페라단.

BNP ① Bangladesh Nationalist party 방글라데시 민족당. ② Basotho National Party (레소토 왕국) 바소토 국민당.

BNSC British National Space Center 영국국립우주센터.

BO ① blackout (연극) 조명을 갑자기 끄는 무대효과.
② box office 매표소.
③ branch office 지점.
④ brought over 이월.

B/O back order 이월주문. (재고품이 떨어져) 납품을 못하고 있는 주문.

BOA Bank of America 아메리카 은행.

BOAC British Overseas Airways Corporation 영국 海外航空會社.

BOC Bell Operating Company (미) 벨 전화 운영회사.

BOD ① biochemical oxygen demand 생물화학적 산소요구량. 하천, 못, 늪, 호수, 공장 배수 등의 유기오염지표의 하나.
② biological oxygen demand 생물학적 산소요구량.

BOE Bank of England (영) 잉글랜드 은행.

BoF Bank of France 프랑스은행

BOJ Bank of Japan 일본은행.

BOL beginning of life (원자력) 수명초기.

BOM business office must 광고관련 신문기사. 광고주와의 관계로 꼭 게재하도록 영업부에서 의뢰하는 기사.

BOOB attack bolt out of the blue attack 핵 미사일에 의한 기습.

BOP Articles ① Balance of Payment Articles (GATT) 국제수지조항. * 국제수지 적자국 특혜조항.
② Business Owners Policy 사업체 보험 증서

BOPI Bulletin Officiel de la Propriete Industrielle(Official Bulletin of the Industrial Property) (프) 공업소유권공보.

BOQ Bachelor Officers' Quarters 독신장교 숙소.

BOS basic operating system (컴퓨터) 기본운영체제.

BOSCOM Boston Computer (미) 보스턴의 상설컴퓨터 전시장.

Bosox Boston Red Sox (야구) 보스턴 레드 삭스. 아메리칸 리그 소속팀

BOSS ① bioastronautics orbiting space station 우주항공 생물학궤도스테이션.
② Bureau of State Security 남아프리카 공화국의 비밀 첩보조직.

BOT ① balance of time 잔여형기.
② balance of trade 무역수지.
③ beginning of tape (컴퓨터) 자기 테이프의 시초.
④ Build Operation Transfer 플랜트수출에 있어 수출기업이 자금조달, 건설, 관리운영을 하여 그의 이익으로 대금을 회수하며 일정한 기간후에 플랜트

를 매도하는 방식.

BOTB British Overseas Trade Board 영국해외무역위원회.

BOW basic operating weight (항공) 기본 운용 중량.

BP ① beautiful people 국제사교계에서 활약하고 있는 사람들, 우아한 생활을 하고 있는 부호들, 현대적 센스를 가지고 있는 사람들.
② below proof (주류) 표준강도 이하.
③ bills payable 지불어음.
④ birthplace 출생지.
⑤ Black Panthers (미) 흑표범당. 흑인의복지향상을 목적으로 하는 전투적 조직.
⑥ bleached pulp 표백펄프.
⑦ blood pressure 혈압.
⑧ blue print 청사진.
⑨ boiling point 비점.
⑩ British Patent 영국특허.
⑪ British Petroleum Co. 영국석유회사.
⑫ Bishop, bishop 주교

B/P Before Permit 수입 허가전 화물 인수보증.

BPA ① Business Publications Audit of Circulations (미) 업계지부수공사기관.
② Black Power Alliance 영국유색. 인종동맹.

BPAM basic partitioned access method (컴퓨터) 기본구분 액세스법.

BPBG butyl phthalyl butyl glycolate 부틸 프탈릴 부틸 글리콜레이트.

BPCD barrel per calender day 1 역일(曆日) 당통유량(석유정제량)

BPD barrels per day 원유의 1일 생산 배럴 수.

BPE bachelor of physical education 체육학사.

BPharm bachelor of pharmacy 약학사.

BPhill baccalaureus philosophiae (bachelor of philosophy) (라) 철학사.

BPI ① bit(s) per inch (컴퓨터) 1 인치당 비트수.
② brainpower index 국민의 종합적 지능지수.
③ byte(s) per inch (컴퓨터) 1 인치당 바이트수.

BPICA Bureau Permanent International des Constructeurs d'Automobiles (International Permanent Bureau of Automobile Manufacturers) (프) 국제자동차회의소.

BPM beats per minute 1분당 비트수. 레코드에 들어 있는 곡(曲)의 속도를 나타내는 기호.

BPO ① Berlin Philharmonic Orchestra 베를린 교향악단.
② British Post Office 영국우편공사.

BPOE Benevolent and Protective Order of Elks (미) 엘크스 자선 보호회. 1867년 창립.

BPP Botswana People's Party 보츠와나 인민당.

BPR (스) Bloque Popular Revolucionario (= Popular Block of Revolution) 엘살바도르 혁명 조직.

BPS ① basic programming system (컴퓨터) 기본프로그래밍 시스템.
② bit(s) per second (컴퓨터) 1초간에 전송되는 비트수.
③ byte(s) per second (컴퓨터) 1초간에 전송되는 바이트수.
④ Bookvalue Per Share 주당순 자산가치 (기업이 보유하고 있는 총 자산에서 부채를 뺀 금액을 다시 발행주수로 나눈 값)

BPSD barrel per stream day 1작업량 일당통유량(석유정제량)

BPSS basic packet-switching service (미) ATT의 패킷 교환 서비스.

Br bromine 브롬. 원자번호 35.

BR ① bills receivable 인수어음.
② breeder reactor 증식로.
③ butadiene rubber 합성고무. 타이어, 신발, 산업용품에 사용.
④ Blue Round 다자간 노동협상.

bra brassiere 브래지어.

BRAIN Bio-oriented Technology Research Advancement Institution 생물계 특정산업 기술 연구추진기구.

Braz. Brazil 브라질.

BRCS British Red Cross Society 영국 적십자사.

BRD (독) Bundes Republik Deutschland (=Federal Republic of Germany) 독일 연방 공화국. = FRC.

BREMA British Radio Equipment Manufacturers' Association 영국 무선 기기 공업회.

Brig. Brigade 여단.

Brig. Gen. Brigadier General 준장.

BRITRAIL British Rail = BR 영국 국유 철도.

Brit. Mus. British Museum 대영박물관.

BRM biological response modifier 생물학적 응답 조절물질.

BRS Bibliographic Retrieval Services (미)정보 서비스의 일종.

BS ① bachelor of science = BSc, SB, Scb 이학사.
② backspace character (컴퓨터) 후퇴문자.
③ balance sheet 대차대조표.
④ bill of sale 매도증서.
⑤ brainstorming 각자가 자유로 의견을 내놓아 해결하는 방법.
⑥ British Standards 영국공업

⑦ broadcasting satellite 방송위성.
⑧ business school 경영대학원.

B/S bit per second = BPS.

BSA ① Boy Scouts of America 미국 보이 스카우트단.
② Business Software Alliance 상업용 소프트웨어 저작권 보호 협회. 불법 복사의 근절을 목표로 하여 1988년에 설립된 상업 패키지 소프트웨어의 국제적인 저작권 보호 단체.

BScA bachelor of science in agriculture 농학사.

BSE ① bachelor of science in engineering 공학사.
② Bovine Spongiform Encephalopathy 광우병(狂牛病).

BSEE bachelor of science in electrical engineering 전기공학사.

BSFF buffer stock financing facility 완충재고 융자제도. * 1차 상품의 국제적 완충재고의 협정에의 출자금의 융자를 원활히 하기 위한 제도.

BSI ① British Standards Institution 영국규격협회.
② British Standard of Industry 영국공업규격.
③ business survey index 경기실사지수.

BSK Boy Scouts of Korea 한국보이 스카우트 연맹.

BSO ① Bismuth Silicon Oxide 광전도효과와 전기광학효과를 가진 단결정. 화상기억·재생 소자로서 주목을 받고 있다.
② blue-stellar object 준준성(準準星) = 청색 항성상 천체.

BSocSc bachelor of social science 사회학사.

BSP ① bank settlement plan 은행 집중 항공권 결제방식.
② business system planning (컴퓨터) IBM사가 개발한 정보시스템.

BSPP Burma Socialist Programme Party 미얀마 사회주의 계획당. 현재 국명은 미얀마.

BSR ① blip-scan ratio 블리프 스캔 비율. 레이더의 스크린상의 발광휘점의 주사속도.
② bulk shielding reactor 대량차폐로. 원자로의 일종.

BSS ① Bangladesh News Agency 방글라데시 통신.
② Broadcasting Satellite Service 방송위성서비스.

BST British Standard Time 영국표준시.

B-52 strategic bomber B52 전략폭격기.

BSU Black Students Union (미) 흑인 학생 조직.

Bt. Baronet 준남작.

BT ① bachelor of teaching 교육

학사.
②bathythermograph 심해 수온 측정기.
③behavior therapist 행동요법사.
④British Telecommunications Corporation 영국 전기통신주식회사.

B.T. bacon-and-tomato sandwich 베이컨 토마토 샌드위치.

BTA ①best time available (광고) 취득가능최적시간대. 텔레비전, 라디오의 광고시간을 주문할 때 사용함.
②border tax adjustment 국경세조사. 수출품에는 수출국의 세의 전부 또는 일부를 면제하고 수입품에는 국산품에의 세의 전부 또는 일부를 과세하는 것.
③British Tourist Authority 영국관광청(英國觀光廳)

BTAM basic telecommunication access method (컴퓨터) 기본 원거리통신 액세스방식.

BTB back to back 서로 등을 맞댄, 연속적.

BTC British Transport Commission 영국 운수 위원회.

BTh (라) baccalaureus theologiae (= bachelor of theology) 신학사.

BTI Balanced Technology Initiative (미) 균형기술구상. 통상 전력의 강화, 개선을 위한 장기적 기술전략을 말한다.

BTL ①behind the lens 렌즈후방.

②Bell Telephone Laboratory, Inc. (미) 벨 전화 연구소.

BTM bedtime music 취침시에 듣는 음악.

BTN Brussel's Tariff Nomenclature 브뤼셀 판세품목 분류표.

BTO ①big time operator 거물, 수완가,
②bounding through overcast 맹목폭격. 전자 조종장치를 사용하여 구름을 통하여 폭격하는 것.

BTR bicycle trial 자전거 시험 경기.

btry battery 포대 건전지

BTS ①block tool system 기계·공구·주변기기를 조합(組合)한 시스템.
②broadcasting technical standard 방송기술규격. * NHK가 정한 방송설비에 관한 규격.

BTU British thermal unit 영국 열량단위. 1파운드의 물의 온도를 화씨 1도를 올리는데 필요한 열량: 대략 252Cal에 해당한다.

B.T.U.C. British Trade Union Congress 영국 무역 노동 조합 회의 (勞動組合 會議).

BTV Business TV 비즈니스 텔레비전. 통신위성을 이용한 기업용의 영상네트워크.

B-2 Bomber-2 미공군이 B-IB의

후계로 개발하고 있는 고도기술 폭격기.

BTWC : Biological and Toxin Weapons Convention (세균 및 독 성무기 금지협약)

BTX benzene toluene xylene 방향족 탄화수소의 벤젠, 톨루엔, 트실렌의 총칭.

BUDPLAN budget and plans generator 예산재무계획 생산 프로그램. IBM사의 컴퓨터의 응용 프로그램.

BUIC Back Up Intercept Control 미국의 예비 요격 관제 시스템. 미국·캐나다 합동의 SAGE를 뒷받침하는 유인(有人)요격 전투기 유도관제 시스템.

BUP British United Press 영국 연합 통신사.

BUPPIES black urban professional 전문직을 가진 성공한 흑인 Yuppies.

BV ① book value 장부가격.
② brightness value 명도의 지수. 사진의 파사체의 명도를 나타내는 지수.
③ Bureau Veritas 프랑스의 선급협회. 여타 선급협회와는 달리 선박 외에도 항공기, 자동차, 빌딩에 대한 검사도 하고 있다.

BVD 각종 남성용 내의류의 상품명. BVD는 이것을 매출한 회사의 3명의 창립자 Bradley, Voorhees, Day의 머리 글자.

BVE butyl vinyl ether 부틸 비닐 에테르.

BVM Blessed Virgin Mary 성모 마리아.

BVR beyond visual range 유시계 외. 목시 범위외 또는 수평선너머 지구의 뒤쪽.

B.V.Sc Bachelor of Veterinary Science 수의학 박사.

BW ① bacteriological warfare 세균 전쟁.
② biological warfare 생물전쟁.
③ black and white 사진 등의 흑백. 컬러에 대하여.
④ bonded house 보세창고.
⑤ bond with warrant 신주 인수권부 사채.

BWC Convention on the Prohibition of the Development, Production and Stockpiling of Bacteriological [Biological] and Toxin Weapons and on their Destruction 생물 무기 금지 협약

BWC Biological Weapons Convention 생물 병기 조약.

BWE Bucket wheel excavator 연속식 굴착 기계.

BWG Birmingham wire gauge 버밍엄 선경(線俓) 게이지.

BWI business warning indicators 경기예고지표.

BWO backward-wave oscillator 후진파발진기.

BWOC big woman on campus (미) 대학 및 고교에서 인기 있는 여학생.

BWR boiling water reactor 비등수형 원자로.

BWS Back Warning System 후방경보장치.

B.W.T Bonded Warehouse Transaction 先輸入.

BWTA British Women's Temperance Association 영국 여성금주 협회.

BX Base exchange 공군(해군)기지의 매점.

BY Budget Year 회계연도.

BYO ① bring your own 먹을 것 마실 것을 각자 지참하는 파티. ② bring your own(grog) (오스트레일리아) 술을 지참해도 좋은 레스토랑.

BYOB ① bring your own beer 각자 맥주지참. ② bring your own booze 각자 술 지참. ③ bring your own bottle 각자 술 지참.

BYOG bring your own girl 각자 여성동반.

BYOL bring your own liquor 각자 술 지참.

BYU Brigham Young University, LDS 교회(예수그리스도 후기성도교회)에서 설립한 학교, 학비가 가장 저렴한 초교파 명문대학 유타주 플로보에 있음.

BZ ① Buffer Zone 완충지역 ② benzene 벤젠

C ① carbon (化學) 탄소. 원자 번호 6.
② catcher (野球) 포수.
③ Centigrade or Celsius (溫度) 섭씨.
④ copyright 저작권을 나타내는 기호. C기호라고도 함.

ca[L] circa (=about) 대략.

Ca calcium (化學) 칼슘. 원자 번호 20.

CA ① California (美) 캘리포니아 주(州)의 우편 기호.
② capacity alignment (컴퓨터) 할당 용량.
③ carbonic anhydrase 탄산 무수화(無水化) 효소.
④ cellulose acetate 아세트산 셀룰로오스.
⑤ Central America 중미(中美)
⑥ certificate of airworthiness 내공(耐空) 증명서.
⑦ change of address 주소 변경.
⑧ chartered accountant 공인 회계사.
⑨ Chemical Abstracts 화학 분야의 초록지(抄錄誌)
⑩ chlormadinone acetate 클로르마디논 아세테이트. 경구 피임약.
⑪ chronological age (心理學)

역년령(曆年齡)
⑫ current account 당좌 계정.

C/A (capital account) 자본계정 (=current account) 당좌계정.

CAA ① carbonic anhydrase 탄산 무수화 효소.
② charged particle activation analysis 하전 입자 방사화 분석(荷電粒子放射化分析)
③ Civil Aviation Authority (英) 민간 항공국.
④ Clean Air Act (美) 대기 정화법.

CAAC Civil Aviation Administration of China 중국 민용 항공 총국, 중국 민항.

CAB ① Central African Bank 중앙 아프리카 은행.
② Citizens' Advice Bureau (英) 시민 상담소.
③ Civil Aeronautics Board = USCAB (美) 민간 항공 위원회. 1985년 2월 해산.

CABEI Central American Bank for Economic Integration 중미 경제 통합 은행.

CACB compressed air circuit breaker 압축 공기 회로 차단기 (遮斷器)

CACCI Confederation of Asian Chambers of Commerce and Industry 아시아 상공 회의소 연합회.

CACM Central American Common Market 중미 공동 시장. 1961년 발족.

CAD computer aided design 컴퓨터를 사용해서 하는 설계.

CADAM computer aided design and manufacturing (美) CAD/CAM 시스템의 일종.

CAD/CAE computer aided design / computer aided engineering 컴퓨터에 의한 설계·엔지니어링.

CAD/CAM computer aided design /computer aided manufacturing 컴퓨터에 의한 설계·제조.

CADD computer aided drug desingn 컴퓨터에 의한 약의 조합(調合).

CADMAT computer aided design, manufacturing and testing 컴퓨터 지원 설계·제조·검사.

CAE ① computer aided education 컴퓨터를 이용한 교육.
② computer aided engineering 컴퓨터를 이용하는 공학 기술. CAD로 작성한 제품 모델을 컴퓨터 내에서 상세하게 검토하여 그 데이터를 토대로 모델을 수정하는 시스템.

CAEC Council of Arab Economic Unity 아랍 경제 통일 이사회(理事會).

CAEE Committee on Aircraft Engine Emissions 항공기 엔진 배출가스위원회.

CAES compressed air energy storage 압축 공기에 의한 에너지 저장.

CAF ① cost and freight 운임 포함 가격.
② currency adjustment factor 통화 시세 변동 할증료.

CAFE corporate average fuel economy standards (美) 회사 평균 연료 절약 기준.

CAFEA Commission on Asian and Far Eastern Affairs, (국제 상업 회의소의) 아시아 극동 문제 위원회. 1953년 CAPA-ICC로 개칭.

CAFISS credit and finance information switching system (일) 가맹한 소매상, 호텔, 백화점, 레스토랑 등과 각 크레디트카드 회사간의 정보교환을 중계하는 NTT가 개발한 시스템.

CAFTA Central American Free Trade Association 중미(中美) 자유 무역 연합.

CAGS certificate of advanced graduate study 고등 대학원 연구 증서.

CAH chronic active hepatitis 만

성 활동성 간염.

CAI computer-aided instruction 컴퓨터를 이용한 교육. 컴퓨터를 이용하여 개인의 능력에 따른 개별 지도를 하는 교육시스템.

Cal. California = Calif (美) 캘리포니아 주(州).

CAL ① China Air Lines (자유 중국) 중화 항공.
② computer-aided learning 컴퓨터를 사용하는 학습.
③ Continental Air Lines = CO (美)콘티넨틸 항공.
④ Conversational Algebraic Language (컴퓨터) 고수준 언어의 일종.

CALC Clergy and Laity Concerned (미) 반전(反戰) 시민 운동 조직.

CALL computer-aided language learning 컴퓨터 이용 언어 학습.

CALS ① (commerce at light speed) 칼스, 고속 상거래 생산성 향상을 위한 종합적 관리 개념.
② computer aided acquisition and logistics support 칼스, 군수 지원 시스템.
③ continuous acquisition and life cycle support 칼스, 경영 지원 통합시스템.

Cal State California State College (미) 캘리포니아 주립(州立) 대학.

Caltech California Institute of Technology = CIT (미) 캘리포니아 공과 대학.

CAM ① computer-aided manufacturing 컴퓨터를 사용해서 하는 제조.
② content addressed memory (컴퓨터) 내용 호출 메모리.

CAMAC computer-aided measurement and control (컴퓨터) 계측 기기와 컴퓨터 사이의 인터페이스의 표준규격.

CAMD computer aided molecular design 컴퓨터지원 분자설계. 컴퓨터에 필요한 데이터를 입력하면 그래픽 디스플레이 상에 분자의 입체화상이 표시되며 이 화상을 보면서 분자설계를 할 수 있다.

CAMP continuous air monitoring program 연속 대기 감시 계획.

CAMS containment atmosphere monitoring system (원자력) 격납용기내 분위기 모니터. 원자로 용계측기.

CAMSEQ-I Conformational Analysis of Molecules in Solution by Empirical and Quantum mechanical Technique System 용액중의 분자의 특성을 분자구조로 추정하는 시스템.

CAN cancel character (컴퓨터) 취소 문자.

C&C ① cash and carry = CC 배달없는 현금 판매의.

② computer and communications 컴퓨터와 통신 기술을 통합한 정보 기술. 대표적인 예는 on-line 시스템임.

C&F cost and freight = CF 수출항 인도 운임 포함 가격.

CANDU Canadian Deuterium Uranium Reactor 캐나다 중수형(重水型) 발전용 원자로.

CANTRAN cancel transmission 전송(傳送)취소.

C&W ① Cable & Wireless (英) 국제 통신 회사.
② country and western (音樂) 컨트리 앤드 웨스턴.

CAP ① Civil Air Patrol 민간 공중 초계 부대.
② clean air package 오염 장지 엔진.
③ climate application program 기후 응용 계획.
④ Code of Advertising Practices (영) 광고 강령 위원회.
⑤ Common Agricultural Policy (EEC) 공통 농업 정책.
⑥ compliance aid for pharmaceuticals 약(藥) 복용시 지시장치.
⑦ computer - aided (or assisted) printing 컴퓨터 도입 인쇄(印刷).
⑧ computer - aided (or assisted) processing 컴퓨터 도입 가공(加工).
⑨ computer - aided (or assisted) production 컴퓨터 도입 생산(生産).

CAPA-ICC Commission on Asian and Pacific Affairs, International Chamber of Commerce 국제 상업 회의소 아시아 태평양 문제 위원회. 구칭 CAFEA.

capcom capsule communicator 지상 기지의 우주선교신 담당자.

CAPD continuous ambulatory peritoneal dialysis 계속식(式) 휴대형 복막 투석법. 신부전(腎不全) 치료법.

CAPM capital asset pricing model 자본 자산 평가 모델.

Cap Sep capsule separation 우주선을 발사 로켓에서 분리(分離)하기.

CAR ① Central African Republic 중앙 아프리카 공화국.
② civil air regulations (美) 민간 항공 규칙.
③ computer-aided retrieval 컴퓨터와 마이크로 사진 기술을 결합한 검색 시스템.

CARA Classification and Ratings Administration (美) 영화 분류· 기준 심사 위원회.

CARD ① Campaing Against Racial Discrimination (英) 인종 차별 철폐 운동.
② computer - aided research and development 컴퓨터 이용 연구 개발.

CARE Cooperative for American Relief Everywhere 미국 해외 원조 협회. 이전 Cooperative for American Remittances to Europe, 다음으로 Cooperative for American Remittances to Everywhere의 약어였음.

CARICOM Caribbean Community 카리브 공동체(共同體).

CARIFTA Caribbean Free Trade Association 카리브 자유 무역 연합.

CARS certificates for automobile receivables 자동차 수취(受取) 계정 증서.

CAS ① calibrated air speed 수정 대기 속도(修正對氣速度).
② Chemical Abstracts Service 화학 정보 검색 서비스기관. 본부 : 미국 오하이오 주(州) 콜럼버스시(市).
③ collision avoidance system 충돌 방지 시스템.
④ control augmentation system 조종성 증강 장치.
⑤ Controlled Atmosphere Storage 냉장고를 밀폐시켜 온도를 섭씨 0도로 내려 냉장고 내부의 산소의 양을 줄이고 탄산가스의 양을 늘려 농산물의 호흡 작용을 위축시켜 변질되지 않게 하는 저장 방법.

CASS computer aided sales and service 컴퓨터를 이용한 세일즈와 서비스 점포.

CASTASLA Conference on the Application of Science and Technology to the Development of Asia (유네스코) 아시아 개발 과학 기술 적용 회의.

CAT ① city air terminal 공항 전용 버스 터미널.
② Civil Air Transport (자유 중국) 민항 공운 공사(民航空運公社).
③ clear air turbulence (航空) 청천 난류(晴天亂流).
④ College Ability Test (美) 대학생 학력 테스트.
⑤ computer aided teaching 컴퓨터에 의한 교육.
⑥ computer aided testing 컴퓨터에 의한 제품 검사.
⑦ computer-aided translation 컴퓨터에 의한 번역.
⑧ computer aided type setting 전산 사식(電算寫植).
⑨ computerized axial tomography 컴퓨터화(化) 체축(體軸) 단층사진. computer assisted tomography 라고도 함.
⑩ credit authorization terminal (컴퓨터) 크레디트 카드의 신용도를 조회하기 위한 단말기.

CATS computer-aided teaching system 컴퓨터에 의한 교육 시스템.

CATSS computer-aided ticket selling system 컴퓨터 이용 티켓 판매 시스템.

CATV ① cable television 유선 텔레비전.

② community antenna television 공동 안테나 텔레비전.

CAV constant angular velocity 광학식(光學式) 비디오 디스크에서 각 트랙에의 1프레임분을 기록하는 방법.

CAVOK ceiling and visibility OK (航空機) 호천후(好天候) 통보.

CAVU ceiling and visibility unlimited (航空) 시계 양호(視界良好).

CB ① center (full) back (축구) 센터 (풀)백.
② citizen's band 시민 라디오. 일반 시민이 근거리 통신에 이용할 수 있는 주파수대, 또는 transceiver(송수신기)등의 무선 통신 장치(裝置).
③ Companion of the Most Honourable Order of the Bath (英) 배스 3등 훈작사.
④ Conference Board (美) 전미 산업 심의회. 구칭 NICB (National Industrial Conference Board)
⑤ Construction Battalion 미군 건설 대대.
⑥ convertible bond 전환 사채.
⑦ corner back (미식 축구)코너 백.

CBA ① Commercial Bank of Australia 오스트레일리아 상업은행.
② Commonwealth Broadcasting Association 영연방 방송협회.
③ Council for British Archaeology 영국 고고학 평의회.

CBBB Council of Better Business Bureau, Inc. (미) 전국 규모의 기업의 광고를 심사하는 기관.

CBC ① Canadian Broadcasting Corporation 캐나다 방송협회 (協會).
② certified business communicator (美) 공인 비즈니스 커뮤니케이터.
③ complete blood count 혈산 (血算).

CBD ① cash before delivery 선금불(先金佛).
② central business district 중심 업무 지구.

CBE ① Commander of the Order of the British Empire (英) 대영 제국 3등 훈작사.
② computer based education 컴퓨터에 의한 교육.

CBEMA Computer and Business Equipment Manufacturers Association (美) 계산기 사무 기기 제조 공업회.

CBF cancer breaking factor 암 파괴 인자.

CBG ① carrier battle group (美) 항공 모함 전투그룹.
② corticosteroid-binding globulin 코르티코스테로이드 결합 글로불린.

CBI ① computer-based

instruction 컴퓨터를 이용하여 독학하기 위한 장치.
② Confederation of British Industry → FBI 영국 산업 연맹. 경영자 단체.
③ cumulative book index 도서 누적 색인.

CBL ① competence based learning 능력에 따른 학습.
② computer based learning 컴퓨터에 의한 학습.

CBM ① [F] Cars et Bus Le Mans 프랑스의 영업용(用) 차 전문 메이커.
② Confidence Building Measures 국가간 신뢰 양성 조치.
③ constant boiling mixture 함께 끓는 혼합물.

CBMS computer based message system 컴퓨터에 의한 메시지 시스템.

CBN ① Christian Broadcasting Network (美) 기독교(敎) 방송망.
② cubic boron nitrite 입방 질화(窒化) 붕소.

CBO ① Congressional Budget Office (美) 연방 의회 예산 사무국(局).
② Collateralized Bond Obligation 채권 담보부 증권.

CBOE Chicago Board Options Exchange 시카고 주식 옵션거래소.

CBRW Warfare chemical, biological and radioactive warfare 화학·생물·방사능전.

CBS ① certified bilingual secretary 공인 2개 국어 비서.
② CBS Inc. 미국 최대의 방송 회사. 구칭 Columbia Broadcasting System.
③ Christian Broadcasting System 기독교 방송. 1954년 12월 설립된 우리 나라 최초의 민간방송으로 하루 평균 21시간의 방송을 실시하여 복음·교양 방송에 중점을 둠.

CBT ① Chicago Board of Trade 시카고 선물(先物) 거래소.
② Computer based training 컴퓨터에 의한 훈련.

CBTV coalition for better television (미) 텔레비전 정화 운동.

CBU ① Caribbean Broadcasting Union 카리브해(海) 방송연합.
② cluster bomb unit 산탄형 폭탄. 강구(鋼球)나 철편(鐵片)을 넣은 폭탄.

CBW ① chemical and biological warfare 생물 화학전.
② chemical and biological weapon 생물 화학 무기.

CBX computerized branch exchange 컴퓨터화한 구내 교환 설비.

cc. cubic centimeter(s) 세제곱 센티미터.

CC

CC ① cash and carry = C & C 배달 없는 현금 판매의.
② chamber of commerce 상공 회의소.
③ charges collect 운임 착지불.
④ civil commotion 폭동.
⑤ computer communications 컴퓨터 통신.

CCA ① car cargo 승용차와 화물을 싣는 자동차 운반선.
② chromate copper arsenate 크롬 코퍼 아르세네이트. 복재 방부재.
③ circuit court of appeals (美) 연방 순회 항소 법원. 1948년 (court of appeal)로 개칭.

CCAMLR Commission for the Conservation of Antarctic Marine Living Resources 남극 해양생물자원 보존 위원회.

CCC ① Capital Cities Communications 미국의 텔레비전·라디오 방송 회사. 1985년 방송을 ABC 매수.
② car and container carrier 자동차 운반선.
③ Civilian Conservation Corps (美) 민간 식림 치수단(民間植林治水團).
④ command, control, communications 지휘·관제·통신.
⑤ Commodity Credit Corporation (美) (농무성) 상품 금융 공사. 농산물의 가격 안정 정책을 함.
⑥ Customs Cooperation Council 관세 협력 이사회.

CCCN Customs Cooperation Council Nomenclature = BTN 관세. 협력 이사회 품목 분류표.

CCCO Central Committee for Conscientious Objectors (美) 양심적 참전거부자 대책 중앙 위원회.

CCCP [R] Soyuz Sovetskikh Sotsialisticheskikh Respublik (Union of Soviet Socialist Republics) = USSR 소비에트 사회주의 공화국 연방. ※ 영어의 S는 러시아어로 C, R은 P로 씀. 구소련을 지칭함.

CCD ① charge-coupled device (컴퓨터) 전하 결합소자(電荷結合素子). ※ 1970년에 미국의 벨 연구소가 발표한 반도체 소자.
② Conference of Committee on Disarmament → ENDC 국제 연합 군축 위원회 회의.

CCDN [F] Center de Compilation de Donnees Neutronique (=Neutron Data Compilation Center) (OECD의) 중성자 데이터 편집 센터.

CCDS Centers for Commercial Development of Space (NASA) 우주 상업 촉진센터.

CCE communication control equipment (컴퓨터) 통신 제어 장치.

CCF ① Chinese Communist

Forces 중국 공산당.
② Combined Cadet Force (英) 연합 장교 양성대(隊).
③ Cooperative Commonwealth Federation (캐나다) 협동공화 연합.
④ [F] Credit Commercial de France 프랑스의 주요은행의 하나.

CCH channel-check handler (컴퓨터) 채널 체크 핸들러.

CCI chamber of commerce and industry 상공 회의소.

CCIA Computer Communication Industry Association (미) 컴퓨터 통신 산업협회.

CCIM Certified Commercial Investment Member 부동산투자분석사[美] (미국 자격증의 하나)

CCIR [F] Comite Consultatif International des Radio communications (=Inter-national Telecommunications Consultative Committee) 국제 무선 통신 자문 위원회. ※ ITU (국제 전기 통신 연합)의 상설 기관의 하나.

CCIS coaxial cable information system 동축(同軸) 케이블 정보 시스템.

CCITT [F] Comite Consultatif International Telegraphiqueet Telephonique (=International Telegraph and Telephone Consultative Committee)전화, 통신 자문 위원회. ※ 국제 연합의 하부 조직 ITU(국제 전기 통신 연합)의 상설 기관의 하나.

CCK cholecystokinin 콜레시스토키닌. ※ 쓸개즙의 분비를 촉진시키는 위장 호르몬.

CCL ① Caribbean Congress of Labor 카리브해(海) 노동 회의(會議).
② critical crack length (原子力) 한계 구열장(限界龜裂長).

CCLAW close-combat laser weapon 근접 전투용 레이저 강습 무기.

CCLF cephalin - cholesterol - lecithin flocculation test 세팔린 콜레스테롤 레시틴 서상[면상] 반응.

CCM ① Caribbean Common Market 카리브 공동 시장.
② counter-clockwise movement 역(逆) 시계 회전 운동.

CCMS ① checkout, control and monitor subsystem (우주工學) 점검(點檢)·초(秒) 읽기·발사 관제 시스템.
② Committee on the Challenges of Modern Society 세계의 자동차 증가에 따르는 영향, 대기 오염 문제, 재해 방지 등의 문제를 토의·검토하는 위원회.

CCND Children's Campaigning for Nuclear Disarmament 어린

91

CCOPE

아이들의 반핵 군축 운동. 1982
년에 미국에서 발족, 제외국(諸外
國)으로 확산.

CCOPE Cooperative Convection
Precipitation Experiment (美)
협동 대류 강우 실험.

CCP ① Chinese Communist
Party 중국 공산당.
② communication control processor 통신 제어 처리 장치.
③ Consolidated Cryptologic
Programme (軍) 통합 암호계획.

CCPEON Commission
Consultative pour la Production
d'Electricite d'Origine Nucleaire
(프) 원자력 발전 자문 위원회.

CCPIT China Council for the
Promotion of International
Trade 중국 국제 무역 촉진 위원회.

CCPS computer-aided
cartographic processing system
컴퓨터 지도처리시스템.

CCR ① Commission on Civil
Rights (美) 공민권 위원회.
② cyclic catalytic reforming
process 재순환 접촉 개질법.

CCRS capital cost recovery
system (美) 자본 상각 시스템.

CCS ① central control station 중
앙 제어국.
② Civil Communications
Section Training Program
최고 경영자 훈련 강좌.

CCTV ① China Central Television
(중국) 중앙 전시대.
② Closed circuit television 유
선 (有線) 텔레비전.

CCU ① cardiac care unit 심장 질
환 집중 치료실.
② circulatory care unit 순환기
질환 집중 치료실.
③ communication control unit
(컴퓨터) 회선(回線) 제어 장치
(裝置).
④ coronary care unit 관상(冠
狀)증 환자 집중 치료 병동, 관
상증 환자실.

CCUS Chamber of Commerce of
the United States 미국 상공 회
의소.

CCV control configured vehicle
운동성 우선 형태 항공기. 조종
장치가 기체의 형상을 정하는 항
공기.

CCW carrying a concealed
weapon 은닉 흉기 소지.

cd. candela 광도(光度) 단위의 하나.

Cd cadmium (化學) 카드뮴.
원자번호 48.

CD ① cash dispenser 현금 자동
지급기.
② certificate of deposit 양도성
정기 예금 증서.
③ civil defense 민간 방위.
④ Committee on Disarmament
군축 위원회.
⑤ compact disc 콤팩트 디스크.

광(光) 신호로 기록한 음을 재생하는 소형 레코드.
⑥ contagious disease 전염병.

CDA [네덜란드語] Christen-Democratisch Appel (=Christian Democratic Appel) (네덜란드) 트리스트교(敎) 민주세력(정당명).

CDB Caribbean Development Bank 카리브 개발 은행.

CDC ① calculated date of confinement 분만 예정일.
② call directing code 수신인 지정 코드.
③ Canada Development Corporation 캐나다 개발 공사.
④ Center for Disease Control (美) 방역 센터.
⑤ China Development Corporation 자유 중국 개발 신탁 공사(公司).
⑥ Commonwealth Development Corporation (英) 연방 개발 공사.
⑦ Control Data Corporation 미국의 컴퓨터 메이커.
⑧ course and distance calculator (航空) 항정(航程) 계산기(機).

CDCS child dominated couples 자기 중심적으로 키웠기 때문에 어버이를 위압하는 행동을 하는 어린이를 가진 어버이. 특히 베이비붐 세대의 어버이.

CDE Conference on Disarmament in Europe 유럽 군축 회의(會議).

CdF [F] Charbonnage de France (=French National Coal Board) 프랑스 국영 석탄 공사.

CDF ① combined distributing frame 결합 배선반(結合配線盤).
② cumulative distribution function (數學) 누적 분포 함수.

CDFC Commonwealth Development Finance Company (英) 연방 개발 금융 회사.

CDI ① conventional defense initiative 비핵 방위 구상.
② course deviation indicator (航空) 코스 편차 지시기.

CD-1 Compact Disk-Interactive 오디오용 CD를 가정이나 교육용의 정보 기록 매체로서 사용하기 쉽게 만든 것.

CDM Clean Development Mechanism 청정개발체제 (교토의 정서에 의거 온실가스 감축목표를 받은 선진국들이 감축 목표가 없는 개도국에 자본과 기술을 투자하여 발생한 온실가스)

CDMA code division multiple access 부호 분할 다중 접근.

CDO Collateral Debt Obligation 담보 보증 채권

CDP ① career development plan 경력 개발 계획.
② certificate in data processing

데이터 처리 면허증.
③ climate data program 기후자료 계획.

CDR Curacao Depositary Receipt 쿠라사우 예탁 증권.

CD-ROM compact disc-read only memory 콤팩트 디스크를 읽는 전용 기억 장치로 직경이 12cm인 원반에 문자수 3억자를 수록.

CDS ① central data system 중앙 데이터 시스템.
② Collateralized Debt Obligations 부채 담보 채권
③ [F] Centre des Democrates Sociaux (=Center of Social Democrats) (프랑스) 민주 사회 중도파. ※ 1976년 프랑스의 민주 중도파와 중도 민주 진보파가 합동하여 결성(結成)한 정당.
④ [S] Centro Democratico y Social (=Democratic and Social Center) (스페인) 민주 사회 중도파.
⑤ [P] Partido do Centro Democratico Social (=Central Social Democratic Party) (포르투갈) 사회 민주 중앙당.

CDT Central Daylight Time (美) 중앙 여름 시간.

CDU [G] Christlich Demokratische Union (=Christian Democratic Union)(독일) 크리스트교(敎) 민주 동맹.

CDV Compact Disc video CD의 응용기술의 하나로서 음성과 영상을 수록한 것.

CDW collision damage waiver 자동차 차량 추돌 파손 책임 면제.

Ce cerium (化學) 세륨. 원자번호 58.

CE ① Church of England = C of E 영국 국교회.
② cost engineering 코스트 공학(工學).
③ Council of Europe 유럽 이사회. 1949년 발족. 본부 : 스트라스부르(프랑스).
④ Capital Expenditure 자본적 지출.
⑤ Continuing Education 연장교육 갱신교육

CEA ① Canadian Export Association 캐나다 수출 협회.
② carcioembryonic antigen 아마 태아성 항원(胎兒性抗原). ※ 악성 종양 검사의 하나.
③ [F] Commissariat a l'Energie Atomique (=Atomic Energy Commission) (프) 원자력청.
④ Council of Economic Advisers (to the President) (美) (대통령의) 경제 자문 위원회.
⑤ Consumer Electronics Association 가전협회[家電協會, 美] (미국 가전분야 650여 업체 회원사 단체로 가전제품 전문전시회를 개최함.
⑥ California Earthquake Authorization 가주 지진 보험(미국)

CEAO [F] Communaute Economique de l'Afrique de l'Ouest (=West African Economic Community) 서아프리카 경제 공동체.

CEB can eating bird 빈 깡통을 찌부러뜨려서 재생 이용을 위해 저장하는 기계.

CEC ① Commission of European Community 유럽 공동체 위원회(委員會).
② Commonwealth Economic Committee 영연방 경제 위원회(委員會).

CED ① cohesive energy density 응집 에너지 밀도.
② Collins English Dictionary (英) 콜린스 영어 사전.
③ Committee for Economic Development (美) 경제 개발 위원회.

CEDEAO [F] Communaute Economique des Etats de l'Afrique de l'Ouest (=Economic Community of West African States) 서아프리카 제국 경제 공동체.

C.E.B. Combined Economic Board 한미합동경제 위원회

CEDEL Centrale de Livraison de Valeurs Mobilieres S.A. (프) 유로채(債)의 집중예탁·집중결제 기관.

CEE [F] Commission Internationale de Reglementation enveu de l'Approbation de l'Equipment Electrique (= International Commission on Rules for the Approval of Electrical Equipment) 국제 전기 기기 승인 규정 위원회.

CEEB College Entrance Examination Board (美) 대학 입시 위원회.

C.E.E.C. Council for European Economic Cooperation 유럽 經濟協調委員會.

CEGB Central Electricity Generating (英) 중앙(中央) 전력청.

CEI Council of Engineering Institutions (美) 기술 학회(學會) 협의회.

CEIP Carnegie Endowment for International Peace (美) 카네기 국제 평화 기금.

celeb celebrity 명사(名士).

CELSS Closed Ecological Life Support System (우주공학) 폐쇄생태계 생명 유지 시스템.

CEMF Counter electromotive force 역기전력(逆起電力).

CEN [F] Comite Europeen de Normalisation (=European Committee for Standardization) 유럽 규격 조정 위원회.

CENEL [F] Comite Europeen de Coordination des Normes Electrotechniques (=European Committee for the Coordination of Electrotechnical Standards) 유럽 전기 기술 규격 조정 위원회.

CEng chartered engineer (英) 공인 기사.

CENTO Central Treaty Organization 중앙 조약 기구

CEO chief executive officer 최고 경영 책임자.

CEP circular error probable 원형 공산(圓形公算) 오차. 미사일이나 폭탄이 50%의 확률로 낙하하는 원의 반경.

CEPES [F] Comite Europeen pour le Progres Economiquet Social (= European Committee for Economic and Social Progress) 유럽 경제 사회 개발 위원회.

CEPS Center for European Policy Studies 유럽 정책 연구센터.

CEPT [F] Conference Europeenne des Administrationsdes Postes et des Telecommunications (= European Conference of Postal and Telecommunications 유럽 우편 전기 통신 주관청 회의.

CEQ Council on Environmental Quality (美) 환경 문제 위원회 (委員會).

CER ① cation exchange resin 양이온 교환 수지(樹脂).
② conditioned emotional response (心理)조건부에 따라 생기는 정동반응(情動反應).

CERBP Committee of Experts on Restrictive Business Practices 제한적상관행(商慣行) 전문가위원회. DECD의 조직.

CERDS charter of Economic Rights and Duties among States 국가 간 경제 권리 의무 헌장.

CERI Centre for Educational Research and Innovation (OECD의) 교육 연구 혁신 센터.

CERN [F] Conseil Europeen pour la recherche Nucleaire (= European Council for Naclear Research) 유럽 원자핵 공동 연구소. 1953년 발족. 현재는 OERN으로 개칭.

CES centralized extension system or central extension system 사업소 집단 전화.

CET ① common external tariff 대외 공통 관세. 역내 관세(및 수량 제한)의 철폐와 함께 EC의 관세 동맹의 핵심 사항. 1957년 1월 1일 시점에서 초기 가맹 6개국의 관세율의 산술 평균을 대외 공통 세율로 하여 1968년 7월 1일에 완성. 그후 신규 가맹국과의 사이에서도 실현되고 있음.
② Central European Time 중앙 유럽 표준시.

CETA Comprehensive Employment and Training Act (美) 정부 자금을 받아 주정부나 지방 자치제가 실업자의 직업 훈련, 공공 사업

등을 행하는 계획.

CETI communication with extraterrestrial intelligence 외계의 지적 생물과의 교신.

CETV communication & entertainment television 정보의 교류나 오락을 위한 텔레비전.

cf. [L] confer (=compare) 참조.

Cf californium (化學) 칼리포르늄. 원자번호 98.

CF ① carbon fiber 탄소 섬유.
② carried forward 이월.
③ center fielder (野球) 센터, 중견수.
④ center forward (축구) 센터 포워드.
⑤ centrifugal force 원심력.
⑥ commercial film 광고 선전용 텔레비전 필름.
⑦ cost and freight = C & F 운임 포함 가격.
⑧ cross fade (放送) 하나의 음(音)을 점차 작게 하면서 다른 음을 크게 해가는 수법.
⑨ cash flow 현금흐름.

CFA ① certified financial analyst 공인 재무 분석가.
② Citizens for America (美) 보수적 대중 압력 단체.
③ Commission of Fine Arts (美) 미술 위원회.
④ [F] Communaute Financiere Africaine (=African Financial Community) 아프리카 금융 공동체.
⑤ Chartered Financial Analyst 재무 분석사 [美] (미국 Association for Investment Management and Research에서 주관하는 자격시험 자격증)
⑥ Consumer's Federation of America 미국소비자연맹 (미국의 소비자단체 2백여 개가 모인 소비자운동조직. 1968년 설립, 본부 워싱톤 소재.)

CFC ① chloro fluoro carbon 프레온가스. 분무기의 분사제. 냉매(冷媒)로 사용함.
② ROK-US Combined Forces Command 한미연합군사령부.

CF&C cost, freight and commission 운임 수수료 포함 가격(價格).

CF&I cost, freight and interest 운임 이자 포함 가격.

CFDT [F] Confederation Francaise Democratique des Travailleurs (=French Confederation of Democratic Workers) 프랑스 민주 노동 총연합.

CFE controlled flash evaporation 제어 플래시 증발.

CFF compensatory financing facility (IMF의) 보상 융자 제도 (制度).

CFF Critical Fusion Frequency 임계융합주파수.

CFI consumption forecasting indicator (일) 소비예측지수.

97

CFIT controlled flight into terrain 정상으로 조종되고 있는 공기가 지물(地物)이나 해면에 격돌하는 사고.

CFL ① Cease Fire Line 휴전선 ② Coordinated Fire Line 사격 협조

CFM ① chloro fluoro methane 클로로 플루오로 메탄. 스프레이의 분사제·냉매(冷媒). ② cubic feet per minute 매분세제곱 피트.

CFO Chief of Financial Officer 최고재무 책임자.

CFP ①Certified Financial Planner 공인 재정 설계사 ② [F] Comoagnic Francaise des Petroles (= French Petroleum Company) 프랑스의 반관 반민 석유 회사.

CFR ① Code of Federal Regulations (英) 연방법. 연방부에서 제정·고시된 규칙을 항목별로 편집한 것. ② commercial fast reactor (英) 상업용 고속 원자로.

CFRC carbon fiber reinforced concrete 탄소 섬유 강화콘크리트.

CFRM carbon fiber reinforced metal 탄소 섬유 강화 금속.

CFRP carbon fiber reinforced plastics 탄소 섬유 강화플라스틱.

CFS ① container freight station 컨테이너 화물 센터. ② cubic feet per second 매초 세제곱 피트.

CFT complement fixations test (免疫學) 보체 결합시험(結合試驗).

CFTC Commodity Futures Trading Commission 상품 선물 거래 위원회. [F] Confederation Francaise de Travailleurs Chr (=French Confederation of Christian Workers) 프랑스 크리스트교 (敎) 노동자 연합.

CFV cavalry fighting vehicle (美) 기병 전투차.

CG ① career girl 직업 여성. ② center of gravity 중심(重心). ③ character generator 문자 신호 발생기. ④ Coast Guard 연안 경비대. ⑤ computer graphics 컴퓨터 그래픽스. 벡터 그래픽스 (vector graphics)와 래스터 그래픽스(raster graphics)등 두 가지 방식이 있음. ⑥ consul general 총영사. ⑦ consultative group 자문 위원회. ⑧ guided missile cruiser 유도 미사일 순양함. ⑨ Consignment Goods 위탁상품.

CG 18 Consultative Group (유엔) 18개국협의 그룹.

CGA command guidance system (미사일)유도 사령(司令)방식.

CGBR central government borrowing requirement 중앙 정부 차입 수요.

CGC[F] Confederation Generale des Cadres(General Confedera-tion of Cadres) (프랑스) 간부 총동맹. 노동자 전국 조직.

CGE[F] Compagnie Generale d'Electricite (=Electric Company) 프랑스의 대중전(大重電) 메이커

CG 18 Consultative Group (國聯) 18개국 협의 그룹.

CGFPI Consultative Group on Food Production investment in Developing Countries (國聯) 개발 도상 국가 생산 투자 협의회.

CGH Cape of Good Hope 희망봉.

CGI computer-generated image (航空) 컴퓨터 작상(作傷).

CGIL[I] Confederazione Generale Italiana del Lavoration (Italian General Confederation of Labor) 이탈리아 노동 총동맹(總同盟).

CGM ① coffin ground-attack missile 은폐 진지에서 지상 혹은 수상의 목표를 공격하는 미사일.
② Conspicuous Gallantry Medal (英) 수훈장(殊勳章).

CGN nuclear-powered guided missile cruiser 원자력 유도 미사일 순양함.

CGP chemical ground pulp 약품 처리를 한 쇄목(碎木)펄프.

CGRT compensated gross registered tonnage 표준 화물선 환산 톤. 선박의 크기를 조선 공사량으로 나타내는 지표.

CGS ① centimeter, gram, second system 센티미터 · 그램 · 초(秒)를 길이 · 질량 · 시간의 기본 단위로 하는 시스템.
② Chief of the General Staff (英) 참모총장.

CGT ① capital gains tax 자본 이득세.
② [F] Confederation Generale du Travail (= General Confederation of Labor) (프랑스) 노동 총동맹.

CGT-FO[F] Confederation Generale du Travail-Force Ouvriere (=General Confederation of Labor - Worker's Force) = FO (프랑스) 노동 총동맹 [노동자의 힘] 파(派).

CGTU[F] Confederation Generale du Travail Unitaire (=General Confederation of United Labor) (프랑스) 통일 노동 총동맹.

CH ① center half(back) (축구) 센터 하프(백).
② clearing house 어음 교환소.
③ custom house 세관.

④ Order of the Companions of Honour (英) 명예훈위(名譽勳位). 1917년 제정. 국가에 공로가 있던 남녀 65명에게 수여됨.

CHAMPUS Civilian Health and Medical Program of the Uniformed Services (英) 군속 건강 의료 계획.

ChB ① bachelor of chemistry 화학사.
② [L] chirurgiae baccalaureus (=bachelor of surgery) = Bch, BS 외과의학사.

ChD ① [L] chirurg doctor(=doctor of surgery) 외과 의학 박사.
② doctor of chemistry 화학 박사.

CHD congenital heart disease 선천성 심장 질환.

CHDL computer hardware description languages 컴퓨터 하드웨어 기술 언어.

CHESS Community Health and Environment Surveillance System (美) 대기 오염 역학적 감시 시스템.

CHF ① congestive heart failure 울혈성 심부전.
② critical heat flux (原子力) 임계 열 유속(流束).

CHINCOM China Committee for Export Control 중공 무역 통제 위원회.

CHIPS Clearing House Interbank Payments System (美) 은행간 온라인 자금 결제 시스템.

Chisox Chicago White Sox(野球) 시카고 화이트 삭스. 아메리칸 리그 소속 팀.

ChM ① [L] chirurgiae magister (=master of surgery) 외과 의학 석사.
② master of chemistry 화학 석사.

CHMOS complementary high performance MOS 고성능 금속 산화막 반도체.

CHN Cable Health Network (美) 건강문제 전문 텔레비전 네트워크.

CHQ Corps Headquarters 軍團 司令官.

CHR contemporary hits radio 히트곡(曲) 라디오 프로그램.

CHS ① Centre on Human Settlement, United Nations 유엔 인간거주센터.
② Commission on Human Settlement, United Nations 유엔인간거주위원회.

CHT cylinder head temperature (航空) 실린더 헤드 온도.

CHU centigrade heat unit 열(熱) 에너지 단위.

CI ① cast iron 주철, 무쇠.
② Channel Islands 영국 해협제도.
③ color index 색지수(色指數).
④ corporate identity ; corporate identification 기업 인식.

기업의 이미지를 대중에게 알리기.
⑤ cut in (영화) 삽입 자막, (방송) 음이나 소리가 별안간 들어가기.
⑥ Imperial Order of the Crown of India (英) 인도 왕관 훈장 (勳章).
⑦ Consumers International 국제 소비자 연맹.
⑧ Cirrus 권운(卷雲) (5~13km의 고도에서 생기는 희고 섬세하나 느낌을 주는 줄무늬 또는 명주실 모양의 구름으로 상층운에 속하는 10종 기본 雲形의 하나)
⑨ Curie 퀴리 (방사능 또는 방사성 물질의 방사량을 표시하는 단위).
⑩ Composite Index 경기종합지수

CIA Central Intelligence Agency (美) 중앙 정보국. 1947년 국가 안전 보장법에 따라 만들어진 기관으로 미국 정책의 최고 결정 기관인 국가 안전 보장 회의에 필요한 정보를 제공하기 위해 설립.

CIAB Coal Industry Advisory Board 석탄 산업 자문 위원회. 국제 에너지 기관.

CIAM [F] Congres International de l'Architecture Moderne (= International Congress of Modern Architecture) 근대 건축 국제 회의.

CIAP ① climatic impact assessment program 고도 비행의 대기 · 기후에 대한 영향 조사.
② [S] Comite Interamericano de la Aliance para el Progreso (= Inter American Committee of the Alliance for Progress) = ICAP 진보를 위한 동맹 · 미주(美洲) 회의.

CIB continuously issuable bonds 연속발행채. 표면이율, 이자지불일, 상환기일이 같은 채권을 연속하여 발행하는 것.

CIC ① combat information center 전투 정보 지휘소.
② commander in chief = C in C, CINC 최고 사령관.
③ compensated ionization chamber (原子力) 보상형(補償形) 이온화 상자.
④ Consumer Information Center (美) 소비자 정보 센터.

CICCP Committee for Information, Computer and Communication Policy OECD의 정보, 전산기 및 통신정책위원회.

CICS customer information control system 고객 정보 관리 시스템.

CICT ① Commission on International Commodity Trade 국제 상품 무역 위원회.
② [F] Conseil Internation du Cinema et de la Television (=International Film and Television Council) 국제 영

101

화 텔레비전 협의회.

CID ① Committee for Imperial Defence (英) 국방 위원회.
② Criminal Investigation Department (英) 런던 경시청 수사과.
③ Criminal Investigation Division (美육군) 범죄 수사부.
④ cubic inch displacement (자동차 엔진의 세제곱인치 배기량(量).

CIDA Canadian International Development Agency 캐나다 국제 개발국.

Cie[F] Compagnie (=Company) 회사.

CIE ① [F] Commission Internationale de l'Eclairage (=International Commission on Illumination) 국제 조명 위원회.
② Commission on Invisible Exports (OECD의) 무역외 거래 위원회.
③ Companion of the Order of the Indian Empire (英) 인도 제국 3등 훈작사.

CIEC Conference on International Economic Cooperation 국제 경제 협력 회의. 1975년 선진국 8개국과 발전 도상국 19개국에 의해 결성.

CIECC[S] Consejo Interamericano para la Educacion, la Ciencia, y la Cultura (=Inter-American Council for Education, Science, and Culture) (美洲기구) 미주 교육 과학 문화 이사회.

CIEE Council on International Education Exchange 국제 교육 교환 협의회.

CIEP Council on International Economic Policy (美) 국제 경제 정책 위원회.

CIEPS[F] Conseil Internationale de l'Education Physiqueet Sportive (=International Council of Sport and Physical Education) 국제 스포츠 체육 협의회.

CIES ① [F] Comite International des Entreprises a Succursales (=International Association of Chain Stores) 국제 체인 스토어 협회.
② Council for International Exchange of Scholars 국제 학자 교환 협의회.

CIF ① cartilage-inducing factor 뼈를 만드는 연골의 생성을 촉진하는 호르몬상(狀) 단백질.
② cost, insurance and freight 보험료 운임 포함 가격. 매도자가 상품의 선적에서 목적지까지의 원가격과 운임·보험료 일체를 부담할 것을 조건으로 하는 무역 계약.
③ customer information file 고객 정보 파일.

CIF&C cost, insurance, freight and commission 보험료 운임 수

수료 포함 가격.

CIF&CI or CIFC&I cost, insurance, freight, commission, and interest 보험료 운임 수수료 이자 포함 가격.

CIFEN [F] Compagnie Internationale pour le Financement de l'Energie Nucleaire (=International Company for Financing Nuclear Energy) 국제 원자력 개발 회사.

CIFM computer input from microfilm 마이크로필름에 기록되어 있는 정보를 직접 컴퓨터에 입력하는 장치.

ciggie or ciggy cigarette 궐련.

CIIA Canadian Institute of International Affairs 캐나다 국제 문제 연구소.

CIM ① coffin intercept missile 은폐 진지에서 공중 목표를 향해서 발사되는 미사일. ② computer input from microfilm (컴퓨터) 마이크로필름에 기록되어 있는 정보를 직접 계산기에 입력하는 장치. ③ computer integrated manufacturing 컴퓨터 적분 생산. 제품의 모양 결정에서 설계·생산·검사·반출에 이르기까지의 정보를 컴퓨터로 통합·처리하는 방식.

CIMA cross impact matrix analysis 상호 영향 관련 분석법. 어느 특정분야의 장래의 발전이 다른 분야의 미래에 대하여 어떠한 영향을 주는가를 평가·측정하는 것.

CIMS Council for International Military Sports 국제 군인 체육회.

C-in-C commander in chief = CIC, CINC 최고 사령관.

CINC commander in chief = CIC, C-in-C 최고 사령관(司令官).

CINC · EUR Commander in Chief, European Command 유럽 주재 미군최고 사령관.

CINC · LANT Commander in Chief, Atlantic 대서양 미군 최고 사령관.

CINC PAC Commander in Chief, U. S. United Command, Pacific Area 미태평양지구 통합군 최고 사령관.

CINC SAC Commander in Chief, Strategic Air Command 전략 공군 최고 사령관.

CINDA computer index of neutron data (國際原子力機關) 중성자 데이터의 컴퓨터화 문헌 색인.

CINS child(ren) in need of supervision → JINS, MINS 요(要) 감시 소년 소녀.

CIO ① chief information officer 정보 주임. ② [F] Comite International Olympique (=International Olympic Committee) = IOC

국제 올림픽 위원회.

CIOCS communications input / output control system 통신입출력 제어 시스템.

CIOMS Council for International Organizations of Medical Sciences 국제 의학 단체 협의회.

CIOS [F] Conseil International pour l'Organisation Scientiique (=International Council for Scientific Management) 국제 과학적 경영 관리 협의회. 1975년 World Council of Management(세계 경영 협의회)로 개칭했으나 약칭은 CIOS가 그대로 사용되고 있음.

CIP ① catalog information provider 카탈로그 정보 제공업자(提供業者).
② cataloging in publication 출판물 목록 작업.
③ climate investigation program 기후 영향 조사 계획.
④ cold isostatic pressing 냉간 정수압(冷間靜水壓) 프레스.

CIP-Test company image profile test 이미지 조사의 한 방법으로서 기업에 필요하다고 판단되는 이미지 항목을 설정하고 연상되는 것을 체크시켜 연상률을 그래프화하여 기업 이미지를 도시하여 비교하는 방법.

CIPEC [F] Conseil Intergouvernemental des Pays Exportateurs Cuivre (=Intergovernmental Council of Copper Exporting Countries) 구리 수출국 정부간 협의회. 참가국 : 칠레 · 페루 · 자이르 · 잠비아 · 인도네시아.

CIPSH [F] Conseil International de la Philosophie et des Sciences Humaines (=Council for Philosophy and Humanistic Studies) 국제 철학 인문 과학 협의회.

CIQ custom, immigration, quarantine 세관 · 출입국 관리 · 검역.

CIR circle 서클.

CIRRIS cold infrared ray inspection system 극저온(極低溫) 적외선 센서. 미사일 감시장치.

CIS ① Center for Integrated System (美) 스탠퍼드 대학의 직접 회로 연구 센터.
② [F] Centre International d'Informations de Securite etd'Hygiene du Travail (=International Occupational Safety and Health Information Centre) 국제 노동 안전 위생 정보센터.
③ Chemical Information System (美) 화학 물질에 관한 데이터 뱅크.
④ communication interface system (美) 대(對) 오비터 교신 시스템.
⑤ community information

system 지역 정보 시스템.
⑥ Congressional Information Service (美) 의회 정보(情報) 서비스.
⑦ corporate identification system 기업 선전용 디자인 통일(統一).
⑧ Criminal Investigation Service (필리핀) 국가 경찰 군범죄 수사국.

CISA certified Information system Auditor 국제 공인 정보 시스템 감리사.

CISAC[sisak] [F] Confederation Internationale des societes d'Auteurs et Compositeurs (=International Confederation of Societies of Authors and Composers) 작가·작곡가 협회 국제 연합.

CISC complex instruction set computer 복합명령컴퓨터.

CISH[F] Comite International des Sciences Historiques (=International Committee for Historical Science) 국제 역사학 위원회.

CISL[I] Confederazione Italiana Sindacati Lavoration (=Italian Confederation of Trade Unions) 이탈리아 노동 조합 연맹.

CISNAL[I] Confederazione Italiana Sindacati Nazionali (=Italian Confederation of National Workers' Unions) 이탈리아 민족 노동 조합 연맹.

CISPR Conmite International Special des Perturbations Radioelectriques (프) 국제 무선 장해 특별위원회.

CISS Conmite International des Sport des Sourds (프) 청각장애자 경기연맹.

CISTI Canadian Institute of Scientific and Technical Information 캐나다의 정보 서비스.

CISV Children's International Summer Villages 국제 하기(夏期) 소년 소녀촌.

CIT ① California Institute of Technology = Caltech (美) 캘리포니아 공과 대학.
② Committee for Invisible Transactions = CIE 무역외 거래 위원회.

CITE cargo integration test equipment (宇宙工學) 실장(實裝) 테스트 장치.

CITES Convention on International Trade in Endangered Species 멸종 지경에 이른 종(種)의 관한 무역에 관한 조약.

CITIC China International Trust and Investment Corporation 중국 국제 신탁 투자 공사.

CITO Charter of International Trade Organization 국제 무역 헌장.

CITS Chinese International Travel Service 중국 국제 여행사(社).

CIWS close in weapon system 근접 방공을 위한 함재기관포(砲).

CK ① central kitchen 중앙 집중 조리장.
② corner kick (축구) 코너 킥.

CKD complete knock down 완전 현지 조립.

CKDC car and KD set carrier 녹다운(knockdown) 차(車)도 싣는 자동차 운반선.

CKO Chief Knowledge Officer 최고 지식 경영자.

Cl chlorine (化學) 염소. 원자번호 17.

CL ① center line 중심선.
② center linkman (축구) 센터 링크맨.
③ computer lady 컴퓨터 관계의 일을 하는 여성.
④ container load 컨테이너 하나에 만재한 화물.

CLASS Chrysler Laser Atlas Satellite System (美) 위성 이용 자동차 도로 정보 시스템.

CLB center left (full) back (축구) 센터 레프트 (풀)백.

CLC course line computer (航空) 코스 계산기.

CLD chemical luminescence detector 화학 발광 검출기. 연소배출가스중의 대기오염물질의 농도를 측정하는 장치.

CLDAS clinical laboratory data acquisition system 임상검사 데이터 수집 시스템.

CLE Continuing Legal Education (美) 변호사 계속 교육 계획. 변호사에게 정기적으로 새 법률 또는 법 개정에 대하여 연수시키는 교육 제도.

CLGP cannon launched guided projectile (美) 포(砲)발사형유도 포탄.

CLI computer led instruction 각종 교육 기기에 의한 일제 수업 시스템.

CLMS clinical laboratory management system 임상 검사 실관리시스템.

CLU Chartered Life Underwriter 공인생명보험사.

CLV constant linear velocity (전자공학) 선속도일정. 비디오 디스크의 기록방식의 일종이며 디스크의 외측과 내측의 정보량 밀도가 같게 기록한다. 재생시간은 양면으로 2시간.

clx climax 클라이맥스.

Cm curium (化學) 퀴륨. 원자번호 96.

CM ① command module (달 여행 우주선의) 사령선.

② commercial message (라디오·텔레비전의) 상업 광고 방송. CM에 나오는 성우를 CM 탤런트, CM의 내용을 노래로 만든 것을 CM송이라 함.
③ common memory 공통 메모리.
④ corrective maintenance 사후 보전.
⑤ court martial 군법 회의.
⑥ cruise missile 순항 미사일.

CMA ① Cash Management Accounts (美) 투자 신탁에 융자 기능이나 카드나 수표 결제 기능을 첨부한 종합 금융 서비스 상품. 미국 최대의 증권 Merrill Lynch회사 사(社)가 개발(開發).
② certified medical assistant 공인 의사보.
③ Chemical Manufacturers Association (美·日) 화학 공업 협회.
④ Continental Marketing Association (美) 회원 조직의 염가 판매 센터.
⑤ Country Music Association (美) 컨트리 뮤직 협회.

CMC ① Cable Music Channel (美) 음악 비디오 전문의 케이블 텔레비전 방송.
② carboxy methyl cellulose 카르복시 메틸 셀룰로오스.
③ Commission on Money and Credit (美) 통화 신용 위원회 (委員會).
④ cruise missile carrier 순항 미사일 모함(母艦).

CME Chicago Mercantile Exchange 시카고 상업거래소.

CMEA Council for Mutual Economic Assistance = COMECON 공산권 경제 상호 원조 회의. 구소련·동유럽의 경제 협력 기구.

CMEP Critical Mass Energy Project (美) 원자력 비판 단체.

CMF ① chloroflumethane 냉각제 또는 에어로졸의 분사제로 사용된다.
② customer management file 고객 관리 파일.

CMG Companion of the Order of St. Michael and St. George (英) 성미카엘·성조지 3등 훈작사.

CMH Congressional Medal of Honor (美) 명예 훈장. 수훈 전투원에 대하여 의회의 이름으로 대통령이 수여함. 정식명은 Medal of Honor.

CMI ① Central Monetary Institutions (英) 공적 금융 기관.
② computer managed instruction 컴퓨터에 의한 교육 관리 시스템.
③ Cornell Medical Index (美) 코넬 대학 의학부 고안의 건강 조사용 심리 테스트.

CML chronic myelocytic leukemia 만성 골수성 백혈병.

CMM coordinate measuring

107

C.M.M.F.

machine 좌표 측정 기계.

C.M.M.F. Committee on Merchant Marine Fisheries 상선어업 위원회.

CMO Collateralized Mortgage Obligations 미국의 대부·채권 담보증권의 일종.

CMOS complementary metal-oxide semiconductor = NMOS, PMOS (컴퓨터) 상보성(相補性) 금속 산화막 반도체(半導體).

CMP ① Controlled Material Plan (美) 할당 통제 물자 계획. ② counter-military potential 대(對) 군사 목표 파괴 능력.

CMR construction manager 발주자로부터 CM업무를 위임받은 사람. 발주자의 입장에서 종합적인 건설관리를 하여 경비의 절감·공기의 단축등을 실현한다.

CMS cash management service 자금 관리 서비스. 기업이 자사(自社)의 자금 상황을 파악하고 자금을 효율적으로 관리할수 있도록 하는 은행 서비스.

CMT cassette magnetic tape 카세트자기테이프.

CMU chlorophenyl dimethyl urea 클로로페닐 디메틸 요소(尿素).

CMV cucumber mosaic virus 오이 모자이크 바이러스. 토마토의 질병.

CN chloroacetophenone gas 최루 가스의 일종.

CNA ① Canadian Nuclear Association 캐나다 원자력 협회. ② Central News Agency (자유 중국) 중앙 통신사.

CNAA Council for National Academic Awards (英) 학사원상(常) 평의회.

CNAC Conference of the None Aligned Countries 비동맹제국 회의.

CNC computerized numerical control 컴퓨터 수치 제어. 마이크로 컴퓨터를 내장한 NC(수치 제어) 장치를 말하며 신뢰성이 높고 사용이 용이함.

CND Campaign for Nuclear Disarmament 핵무장 반대운동.

CNEA [S] Comision Nacional de Energia Atomica (=National Commission for Atomic Energy) (아르헨티나) 원자력 위원회.

CNEN ① [P] Comisao Nacional de Energia Nuclear (=National Commission Nuclear Energy) (브라질) 원자력 위원회. ② [S] Comision Nacional de Energia Nuclear (=National Commission for Nuclear Energy)(멕시코)원자력 위원회. ③ [I] Comitato Nazionale per l'Energia Nucleare (=National Commission for Nuclear

Energy) (이탈리아) 원자력 위원회.

CNES [F] Centre National d'Etudes Spatiales (=National Center for Space Studies) (프랑스) 국립 우주 개발 센터.

CNEXO [F] Centre National pour Exploitation des Oceans (=National Center for Ocean Exploitation) (프랑스) 국립해양 개발 센터.

CNG compressed natural gas 압축 천연 가스.

CNIEC China National Import and Export Corporation 중국수출입공사.

CNN Cable News Network (美) 뉴스 전문의 유선 텔레비전.

CNO ① Chief of Naval Operations 해군 작전 부장. 해군 참모 총장에 해당.
② [F] Comite National Olympique (=National Olympic Committee) = NOC 각국 올림픽 위원회.

CNOJSC China Nankai Oil Joint Service Corp 중국 남해 석유합판공사.

CNOOC China National Offshore Oil Corp. 중국 해안 석유회사.

CNP credit note payable 지불 어음.

CNPF [F] Conseil National du Patronat Francais (=National Council of French Employers) 프랑스 경제 단체 연합회.

CNT ① [S] Comando Nacional de Tradajadores (=National Command of Workers) (칠레) 전국 노동자 본부.
② [F] Confederation Nationale de Travail (=National Confederation of Labor) (프랑스) 전국 노동 연맹.

CNTP Committee for National Trade Policy (美) 국가 무역 정책 위원회.

c/o (in) care of ~씨 댁[방(方)].

Co cobalt (化學) 코발트, 원자번호 27.

CO ① carbon monoxide 일산화탄소(一酸化炭素).
② Colorado (美) 콜로라도 주(州)의 우편 기호.
③ commanding officer 사령관.
④ conscientious objector 양심적 병역 기피자.
⑤ Continental Air Lines = CAL (美) 콘티넨털 항공.
⑥ cut out 방송 소리나 음이 갑자기 꺼지기.

COAS crewmen optical alignment sight (宇宙工學) 광학 관찰용 기기.

COAX coaxial cable 동축케이블.

COBOL common business oriented language (컴퓨터) 사무 처리용 고급 프로그램 언어.

1959년 개발.

COC ① Combat Operations Center (美) (공군의) 전투 지휘소.
② Cost Capital 기회비용.

COCOM Coordinating Committee for Export to Communist Areas 대(對)공산권 수출 통제 위원회. 1949년 설립.

COCORP Consortium for Continental Reflection Profiling 대륙지각 반사법협의회(大陸地殼反射法協議會).

COD ① carrier on board delivery (美) 항공모함 탑재 수송기(機).
② cash on delivery 대금 상환(相換) 인도.
③ chemical oxygen demand 화학적 산소 요구량.
④ collect on delivery 대금 상환 인도.
⑤ Concise Oxford Dictionary 콘사이스 옥스퍼드 사전.
⑥ crack opening displacement (原子力) 개구 변위(開口變位).

CODASYL Conference on Data System Language (美) 데이터 시스템 언어 협의회. 미국 정부, 컴퓨터 메이커, 사용자 회의 단체로 구성된 조직. 1959년 발족.

CODATA Committee on Data for Science and Technology 과학기술 데이터 위원회.

CODE Cable Online Data Exchange (美) 온라인 데이터 베이스.

CODEC coder and decoder (컴퓨터) 부호 해독기(符號解讀器).

CODECO computer departure control 항공기 출발전 승객·화물 중량·기체 밸런스 체크 시스템.

CODENE [F] Comite pour le Desarmement Nucleaire en Europe (=Committee for Nuclear Disarmament in Europe) 유럽 핵 폐기 위원회.

C of E Church of England = CE 영국 국교회.

COE Center of Excellence (일) 고등과학연구소. 세계최고 수준의 기초과학연구소로 설립계획.

COG coke oven gas 코크스로(爐) 가스.

COGEMA [F] Compagnie Generale des Materes Nucleaires (= General Company of Nuclear Materials) (프랑스)핵 연료 공사.

COGO coordinate geometry (컴퓨터) 토목 공학에서 측량 결과의 면적 계산을 하는 언어.

COGP Commission on Government Procurement (美) 정부조달 위원회.

COI Central Office of Information (英) 중앙 정보국.

COID Council of Industrial Design (英)공업 디자인 협의회.

COINS computerized information system 컴퓨터 정보 시스템.

Coke Coca-Cola 코카 콜라.

col. colonel 육군 대령.

Col. Colorado = Colo. (美) 콜로라도 주(州).

COL ① computer oriented language 컴퓨터용 언어. ② cost of living 생계비.

COLA ① cost of living adjustment 생계비 연동 조항. 소비자 물가의 변화에 따라 자동적으로 임금을 증감시켜 노사 협약 기간 중의 구매력을 유지시키는 것이 그 목적임. ② cost of living allowance 생활비 수당.

Colo. Colorado = Col. (美) 콜로라도 주(州).

COM ① coal oil mixture 석탄 석유 혼합 연료. ② computer output on microfilm 컴퓨터의 출력 정보를 마이크로필름에 기록한 것, 그 방식, 또는 장치.

COMECON Council for Mutual Econonic Assistance = CMEA 공산권 경제 상호 원조 회의. 구소련·동유럽의 경제 협력 기구.

COMEX commodity exchange 상품 거래소.

COMINFORM Communist Information Bureau 1947년 서방(西方)진영과 공산 진영간의 알력이 심해지자 9개국의 공산당이 정보교환 및 상호활동 조정을 위하여 Belgrade에 설립한 기구이름.

COMINT communications intelligence 통신 도청에 의한 정보 수집 (활동).

COMINTERN Communist International 공산주의 인터내셔널.

COMISCO Committee of International Socialist Conference 국제 사회주의자 회의 위원회.

COMPACT Committee to Preserve American Color Television 미국 텔레비전 산업 보호 위원회.

COMSAT Communications Satellite Corporation (美) 통신 위성 회사. 미국의 국책 회사로 세계 통신 위성망을 만드는 것이 목적임.

COMSEC communications security 통신 보전.

COMTRAC computer-aided traffic control 컴퓨터에 의한 운전 제어 시스템.

CONAD Continental Air Defense Command (美) 본토 방공군(防空軍). 육·해·공 3군(軍)의 통합군. 1975년 폐지.

condo condominium 분양 맨션.

CONEFO Conference of Newly

confab

Emerging Forces 신흥국 세력 회의.

confab confabulation 회의.

conj. conjunction (文法) 접속사.

con-man confidence man 사기꾼.

Conn. Connecticut (美) 코네티컷 주(州).

Contra[S] contrarevolucinario (=counterrevlutionist), contrarevolucion (counterrevolution) 반혁명. 분자 혹은 반혁명. 온두라스 혹은 코스타리카에서 니카라과의 산디니스타 민족 해방 전선에 반기를 들고 이의 타도를 위해 활동하는 세력을 이르는 말.

CONTU National Commission on New Technological Users of Copyrighted Works (미) 저작권을 가진 저작자의 신기술사용에 관한 위원회.

CONUS Continental United States 미국 본토.

COO chief operation officer (기업의) 최고 업무 집행 책임자.

co-op ① cooperative dwelling 공동 주택.
② cooperative society 생활 협동 조합.
③ cooperative store 생활 협동 조합 매점.

CO·OP cooperative advertisement 협동 광고.

COPE Committee on Political Education (미) 정치교육위원회. AFLCIO의 정책이나 정치적 선전 조합원에 대한 정치적인 호소 등의 입안이나 결정을 한다.

COPEI[S] Comite de Organizacion Politica Electoral Independiente-Partido Social Cristiano (=Social Christian Party) (베네수엘라) 크리스트교 (敎) 사회당.

COPUOS U.N. Committee on the Peaceful Uses of Outer Space 국제 연합 우주 공간 평화 이용 위원회.

COPWE Commission for Organizing the Party of the Working People of Ethiopia 에티오피아 노동 인민당 조직 위원회.

COR country oriented rock (音樂) 현대 미국을 대표하는 대중 음악의 하나.

CORE Congress of Racial Equality (美)인종 평등 회의. 1942년 결성.

CORMES communication oriented message system 온라인 메시지 처리시스템.

corp. corporation 협회.

CORSA Cosmic Radiation Satellite 코르사위성. 일본이 발사한 우주방사선연구위성.

COS ① cash on shipment 선적불 (船積拂).

② chief of staff 참모장.

COSATU Congress of South African Trade Unions 남아프리카 노동 조합 회의.

COSMETS Computer System Meteorological Services (일) 기상 자료 종합 처리 시스템.

COSPAR Committee on Space Research 국제 우주 공간 연구위원회. 1958년 설립. 우주 관측 정보의 교환을 촉진시키는 기관.

COSTI Committee on Scientific and Technical Information (美) 연방 과학 기술 정보 위원회.

CO_2 carbon dioxide 이산화탄소.

COW crude oil washing (유조선 내부의) 원유 세정.

COZI communications zone indicator 통신 지역 표시기.

CP ① Canadian Press 캐나다 통신.
② card punch (컴퓨터) 카드 펀치.
③ cerebral paralysis 뇌성마비 (腦性痲痺)
④ charter party 용선 계약.
⑤ chemical pulp 화학 펄프.
⑥ command post 지휘소.
⑦ commercial paper 단기 약속 어음. 기업어음의 일종으로 지난 1981년 기업의 단기 운영 자금 조달을 쉽게 하기 위해 새로 도입한 어음 형식으로 기업과 투자자 사이의 금리를 자유로이 결정할 수 있음.
⑧ Conservative Party 보수당.
⑨ Continental Plan 아침 식사만을 포함한 호텔 요금. 유럽에서 가장 일반적.
⑩ counter purchase 보증 수입.

CPA ① Canadian Pacific Airlines = CP Air, CPAL 캐나다 태평양 항공.
② Cathay Pacific Airways 캐세이 태평양 항공.
③ certified public accountant (美) 공인 회계사.
④ critical path analysis → CPM, CPS (컴퓨터) 대형 계획의 최적 스케줄 분석.

CP Air Canadian Pacific Airlines = CPA, CPAL 캐나다 태평양 항공.

CPAL Canadian Pacific Airlines = CPA, CP Air 캐나다 태평양 항공.

CPB Corporation for Public Broadcasting (美) 공공 방송 협회(協會).

CPBW charged particle beam weapon 하전 입자(荷電粒子)빔 무기.

CPC ① card programming control (컴퓨터) 자동 제어 시스템의 일종.
② Community Patent Convention 유럽 공동체 특허 조약.
③ concrete plastic composite 콘크리트·플라스틱 복합체.
④ concrete polymer composite 수지 강화(樹脂强化) 콘크리트
⑤ continuous path control 연

속 궤적(軌跡) 제어.

CPCC Communist Party Central Committee (구소련) 공산당 중앙 위원회.

CPCU chartered property and casualty underwriter 공인 손해 보험사(士).

CPD comprehensive program on disarmament 포괄적 군축계획. 핵무기도 일반 무기도 폐기하려는 국제 연합의 계획.

CPDA Council for Periodical Distributors Associations (美) 정기 간행물 판매자 협회.

CPER computed price earnings ratio 예상 주가 수익률.

CPF ① chemical processing facility 고레벨 방사성 물질 연구시설.
② coated-particle fuel 피복입자(被覆粒子)연료. 고온가스로 용핵연료.

CPG ① Center for Public Integrity 미 정부, 공직자 감시단체
② Contingency Planning Guidance 비상계획지침

CPGRP cost per gross rating point(광고방송) 연(延) 시청률당 경비.

CPI ① Central Patent Index (英) 특허 정보 서비스.
② character(s) per inch (컴퓨터) 자기(磁氣) 테이프 1인치당 자수(字數).
③ Communist Party of India (인도) 우파 공산당.
④ Conference Papers Index (美)과학 기술 논문 데이터베이스.
⑤ consumer price index 소비자 물가 지수.
⑥ corruption Perceptions Index 부패지수. TI에서 발표하는 국가별 청렴도 순위

CPI-M Communist Party of India-Marxism (인도) 좌파 공산당.

CPISRA Cerebral palsy International Sports and Recreation Association 뇌성마비자 경기연맹.

CPI-U consumer price index urban consumers 도시 소비자 물가 지수.

CPI-W consumer price index wageearners 노동자 소비자 물가 지수.

CPK creatine phosphokinase 크레아틴 포스포키나아제. 인산의 결합·해당(解糖)을 촉매하는 효소에 의한 허혈성 심장질환 검사.

CPL ① Canadian Pacific Limited 캐나다 종합 운수 회사.
② Combined Program Language (컴퓨터) 비수치(非數値) 문제에 대하여 ALGOL형 언어의 적용 범위를 확대하려 한 언어. 영국의 케임브리지 대학과 런던 대학이 개발.

CPM ① counts per minute (放射能) 매분의 카운트 수(數).
② critical path method → CPA, CPS (컴퓨터) 대형 계획 유효 순서 결정 방법.

CP/M control program for micro computer 8비트 마이크로 컴퓨터용의 오퍼레이팅 시스템.

CPO ① Central Post Office 중앙 우체국.
② concurrent peripheral operation (컴퓨터) 동시 주변 기기 조작.

CPP ① career path program 종업원에게 갖가지 일을 시켜서 능력을 높이는 계획.
② Communist Party of the Philippines 필리핀 공산당.

CPR ① Canadian Pacific Railway 캐나다 태평양 철도.
② cardiopulmonary resuscitation 심폐 기능 회복 [소생]법.
③ cost per response 효과에 대응하는 광고 경비.

CPS ① Canadian Pacific Steamship Line 캐나다 태평양 기선회사.
② certified professional secretary 공인 비서.
③ consumer price survey 소비자 물가 조사.
④ critical path scheduling → CAP, CPM (컴퓨터) 계획 전체를 소정의 목표에 적합한 형태로 조정하도록 한 관리 수법.
⑤ cut and put-on system 잘라서 붙이는 전표 회계 제도.

CPSA Consumer Product Safety Act (美) 소비자 제품 안전법(法).

CPSC Consumer Product Safety Commission (美) 소비자 제품 안전 위원회.

CPSU Communist Party of the Soviet Union 구소련 공산당(黨).

CPT ① colored people's time (美) 흑인 시간.
② cost per thousand (광고) 독자, 시청자 1,000명당 경비.

CPU central processing unit (컴퓨터) 중앙 처리 장치.

CPX command post exercise (軍) 지휘소 훈련.

CQ ① call to quarters 아마추어 무선의 교신희망 신호.
② conditionally qualified 조건부 합격.

CQD ① come quick danger SOS 전(前)에 사용된 해난 통지 신호.
② customary quick dispatch (용선 계약에서) 정박 기간을 한정치 않고 가능한 빨리 하역한다고 하는 조건.

Cr chromium (化學) 크롬, 크로뮴.
※ 원자번호 24.

CR ① card reader (컴퓨터) 카드 판독기.
② carriage return character

(컴퓨터) 복귀문자(復歸文字)
③ chloroprene rubber 클로로프렌 고무.
④ clean room 클린 룸.
⑤ consumers' research 소비자 조사.
⑥ control rod (原子力) 제어봉(制御棒)
⑦ conversion ratio (原子力) 전환율.

CRA ① Community Reinvestment Act 지역사회 재조성법
② Civil Rights Association (북아일랜드) 인권 협회.

CRAF Civil Reserve Air Fleet (美) 민간 예비 항공 수송 부대(部隊).

CRAM card random access memory (컴퓨터) 자기(磁氣) 카드식(式) 기억 장치.

CRB ① center right (full)back (축구) 센터 라이트 (풀)백.
② Central Reserve Bank (美) 중앙 준비 은행.

CRC ① cyclic redundancy check (컴퓨터) 주기(周期)여유도 검사(檢査).
② Corporate Restructuring Company 기업 구조 조정 전문 회사. (시장 기능을 통한 구조조정 촉진을 위한 1999 2. 제정된 산업발전 법에 의거 설립된 회사)

CRD ① chronic respiratory disease 만성 호흡기 질환.
② control rod drive (原子爐) 제어봉 구동(驅動).

CRDM control rod drive mechanism (原子爐) 제어봉 구동(驅動) 기구.

CREEP Committee to Re-elect the President (美) 대통령 재선 위원회. 1972년 닉슨 대통령 재선 운동을 위해 설립.

CREST Committee on Reactor Safety Technology (OECD)의 원자력 안전 기술 위원회.

CRF ① chronic renal failure 만성 신부전.
② corticotropin releasing factor 부신 피지 자극 호르몬 방출 인자.

CRI Committee for Reciprocity Information (美) 호혜(互惠) 정보 위원회.

CRJE conversational remote job entry (컴퓨터) 회화식 원격 작업 입력.

CRM ① Customer Relationship Management 고객관계관리 (기존 고객의 정보를 종합적으로 분석해 선별된 고객으로부터 수익을 창출하고 장기적인 고객 관계를 가능케 하는 솔루션)
② Certified Reference Material 인증표준물질 (인증서가 붙어 있는 표준물질로 하나 이상의 특성값을 나타내는 단위의 정확한 표시에 대한 소급성을 확립하는 절차에 따라 인증되고,

각 인증값에는 표기된 신뢰수준에서의 불확도가 주어진 것)

CRP ① climate research program 기후 연구 계획.
② C-reaction protein C 반응성 단백. 류머티즘성(性) 질환 검사의 하나.

CRS ① congenital rubella syndrome 선천성 풍진(風疹) 증후군.
② Congressional Research Service (美) 국회 조사부.

CRT cathode ray tube 음극선관 [브라운관].

CRU collective reserve unit (經濟) 복합 준비 단위.

Cs cesium (化學) 세슘. 원자번호 55.

CS ① center striker (축구) 센터 스트라이커.
② communication satellite 통신 위성.
③ container ship 컨테이너선(船).
④ core spray system (원자로(原子爐)의) 노심(爐心) 스프레이 시스템.
⑤ [F] Credit Suisse 스위스 은행. 본사 - 취리히.

CSA Canadian Standards Association 캐나다 규격 협회.

CSAS command stability augmentation system (航空) 조종 및 안정성 증대 장치.

CSC ① Civil Service Commission (美) 문관 인사 위원회.
② Conspicuous Service Cross (英) 수훈 십자장.

CSCE Conference on Security and Cooperation in Europe 유럽 안전 보장 협력 회의. 제1회는 1975년 헬싱키에서 개최(開催).

CSD constant speed drive 정속 구동 장치(定速驅動裝置).

CSDC circuit switched digital capability (美) 회선 교환(回線交換) 디지털 기능. AT&T Communications 사(社)의 디지털 전송 서비스.

CSE Certificate of Secondary Education (英) 중등 교육 검정증. 중등학교 제5학년 학생 가운데서 평균 이하의 능력자를 대상으로 하는 과목별 학력 시험. 취직 희망자도 고용주도 이것을 이용함.

CSF colony stimulating factor 콜로니 자극 인자. 조혈 촉진 인자의 하나.

CSI ① Companion of the Most Exalted Order of the Star of India (英) 인도의 별 3등 훈작사.
② Consumer Survey Index 소비자 동향 지수.
③ Consumer Sentiment Index 소비자 심리 지수.

CSIN Chemical Substances Information Network (美) 정보

CSIRO

서비스의 일종.

CSIRO Commonwealth Scientific and Industrial Research Organization (오스트레일리아) 연방 과학 산업 연구 기구.

CSIS Center for Strategic and International Studies (美) 전략(戰略) 국제 연구 센터. 워싱턴의 Georgetown University 소속.

CSISRS Cross section information and storage retrieval system (原子力) 단면적 정보 격납 검색 시스템.

CSM ① corn, soya, milk 옥수수가루·콩가루가루·우유(牛乳)를 혼합(混合)한 식품(食品).
② command and service modules 달 여행 우주선의 사령선과 기계선.

CSDC circuit switched digital capability (미) 회선교환디지털 송신. 아날로그 교환기를 사용하여 대량의 디지털데이터를 송신하는 방법.

CSNI Committee on the Safety of Nuclear Installations (OECD의) 원자력 시설 안전 위원회.

CSO Central Services Organization (美) 중앙 서비스 조직. 해체로 생긴 일곱 개의 전화 회사가 설립한 회사.

CSOC Consolidated Space Operations Center 통합 우주 작전 센터.

CSP control switching point (電話) 통제 교환국.

CSR ① CSR Limited 오스트레일리아 정당 회사(精糖會社). 구 칭 Colonial Sugar Refining Company.
② Customer Service Representative 고객 관리자

CSRC China Securities Regulatory Commission 중국 증권 감독 관리 위원회

CSRS Cooperative State Research Service (美) (농무성) 농업 연구 조성국.

CSSL continuous system simulation language (컴퓨터) 연속 시스템 시뮬레이션 언어.

CST ① Central Standard Time (美) 중앙 표준시.
② condensate storage tank (原子力) 복수 저장 탱크.
③ critical solution temperature 임계 용해 온도(臨界溶解溫度).

CSU ① [G] Christlich Soziale Union (=Christian Social Union) (독일) 크리스트교(敎) 사회 동맹.
② constant speed unit 정속 장치(定速裝置).
③ California State University 캘리포니아 주립 대학

CT ① cable transfer 전신·전보 환(換).
② cell therapy 세포 요법.

③ computerized tomography 컴퓨터 처리 X선 단층 촬영 장치.
④ Connecticut (美) 코네티컷 주(州)의 우편 기호.

CTA ① Committee for Technical Assistance (발전 도상국을 위한) 기술 원조 위원회.
② control area (航空)관제구(區).

CTB Comprehensive Test Ban 포괄적 핵실험 금지.

CTBT Comprehensive Test Ban Treaty 포괄적 핵실험 금지 조약.

CTC ① centralized traffic control 열차 집중 제어 장치.
② Cotton Textile Committee (GATT의) 면제품 위원회.

CTCA channel to channel adapter (컴퓨터) 채널간 결합 장치(裝置).

CTCD Chamber's 20th Century Dictionary (英) 체임버 20세기 사전.

CTD ① charge transfer device 전하 이송 소자(電荷移送素子).
② Committee on Trade and Development (GATT의) 무역 개발 위원회.

CTF coal-tar fuel 콜타르 연료.

CTK [체코語] Cestoslovenska Tiskova Kancelar (=Czechoslovak National Press) 체코슬로바키아 국영 통신.

CTM continuous transit by magnets 자석식(式) 연속 수송 시스템.

CTMC communications terminal module controller (컴퓨터) 통신 제어 장치.

CTNC Commission on Transnational Corporations 다국적 기업위원회. 유엔의 기관.

CTO combined transport operator 복합 수송업자.

CTOL conventional take off and landing 통상 이착륙(기).

CTPT Continuing time Preliminary tremor 초기이동 계속시간.

CTR ① center 센터.
② controlled thermonuclear reactor 제어 열핵 융합로.

CTS ① cold type system 사진 식자.
② computerized type setting 컴퓨터 조판.
③ crude oil terminal station 원유 비축 기지.
④ crude oil transshipment station 원유 중계 기지.
⑤ Computer Type System 전산 신문 제작 시스템. 컴퓨터에 의한 신문 편집·제작 시스템.

CTSS Compatible Time Sharing System (美) 매사추세츠 공과대학에서 1964년에 개시된 타임 셰어링 시스템.

CTT capital transfer tax (英) 자

본 이동세.

CTV Canadian Television Network, Ltd. 캐나다 텔레비전 네트워크.

CTW Children's Television Workshop (美) 어린 아이용 텔레비전 제작소.

CTZ control zone (航空) 관제권(圈).

Cu[L] cuprum (=copper) (化學) 구리. 원자번호 29.

CU ① close up 클로즈업.
② Consumers Union (美) 소비자 동맹.

CUF Catholics United for the Faith (美)보수적 카톨릭 신자단체.

CUFT Center for the Utilization of Federal Technology (美) 연방 기술 이용 센터.

C.U.N. Charter of the United Nations. 유엔헌장.

CUP Cambridge University Press (英) 케임브리지 대학 출판국(局).

CURV cable controlled undersea recovery vehicle 원격 조종 해저탐사기.

CV ① containment vessel (原子力) 격납 용기.
② [L] curriculum vitae (= personal history) 이력서.
③ cylinder volume 기통 용적.

CVA ① cerebro vascular accident 뇌졸중.
② Columbia Valley Authority (美) 콜럼비아 강(江) 유역 개발 공사.

CVCF constant voltage and constant frequency power supply 정전압·정주파 전원 장치.

CVCS chemical and volume control system (原子力) 화학 및 체적 제어 계통.

CVD chemical vapor deposition 화학 기상 퇴적(化學氣相堆積).

CVDP compact video Disc player 콤팩트 비디오 디스크 플레이어.

CVI common variable immunodeficiency 항체수(數) 감소.

CVN carrier vehicle nuclear 원자력 추진 항공모함.

CVO Commander of the Royal Victorian Order (英) 빅토리아 상급훈작사.

CVP ① [네덜라드語] Christelijke Volkspartij (= Christian Socialist Party) (벨기에) 크리스트교(敎) 사회당.
② cockpit, volume, profit 비용·매상·이익.

CVR ① carrier vessel reactor 항공 모함용 원자로.
② cockpit voice recorder 조종실 음성 녹음 장치.

CVS ① computer controlled vehicle system 컴퓨터 제어 자동 운전 수송 시스템.

② convenience store 소형 슈퍼마켓.

CVT continuous variable transmission (자동차) 자동 변속장치.

CW ① chemical warfare 화학전(戰).
② continuous wave 연속파(派). 진동으로 변화하지 않는 전파.

CWA ① Civil Works Administration (美) 토목 사업국.
② Clean Water Act 물 청정법.
③ Communication Workers of America 아메리카 통신 노동조합.

CWAC Canadian Women's Army Corps 캐나다육군 여군부대(部隊).

CWB Central Wages Board (英) 중앙 임금 위원회.

CWC Ceylon Workers' Congress (스리랑카)실론 노동자 회의(會議).

CWF coal water fuel 석탄·물 혼합 연료.

Cwlth Commonwealth = C'wealth 영연방.

CWM coal water mixture 석탄과 물의 혼합물.

CWO cash with order 현금불 주문.

CWPS Council on Wage and Price Stability (英) 임금 물가 안정 위원회.

CWQC company wide quality control 전사적 품질관리.

CWS Chemical Warfare Service (美) 화학전 부대.

CX Cathay Pacific Airways 캐세이 태평양 항공.

CY ① city 도시.
② container yard 컨테이너 두는 곳.

CYK consider yourself kissed 애정을 표현하는 메시지.

CYM coefficient yawing moment 편요(偏搖) 모멘트 계수. 편요 모멘트는 차가 옆으로 받았을 때 중심이 수직으로 통과하는 축을 중심으로 회전시키는 움직임을 말한다.

CYN canyon 협곡.

CYO Catholic Youth Organization (美) 카톨릭 청년회.

CZ Canal Zone 파나마 운하의 미국령 지대.

D ① Decimal Day 영국의 통화제도의 십진법 변환의 실시되는 1971년 2월 15일
② D-Day [군] 노르만디 진공의 날. 공격개시 예정일.

D Democrat = Dem. (美) 민주 당원.

DA ① Department of the Army (美) 육군성.
② design automation (컴퓨터) 디자인 자동화.
③ digital to analog (컴퓨터) 디지털에서 아날로그로.
④ district attorney (美)지방 검사.
⑤ doctor of archaeology 고고학 박사.
⑥ doctor of arts 문학 박사.
⑦ Detective Agent 형사.

D/A documents against acceptance 인수 인도. 매출자나 수출상이 발행하는 화환(貨換) 어음의 인수만으로 선적 서류를 내주는 것.

DAA diacetone alcohol 디아세톤 알코올.

DAAD [G] Deutsche Akademische Austauschdienst (=German Academic Exchange) (독일) 독일 학술 교류처.

DAB ① diaminobutyric acid 디아미노 부티르산(酸).
② Dictionary of American Biograpy 미국 인명 사전.
③ Digital Audio Broadcasting 디지털 오디오 방송 (CD와 상응하는 뛰어난 음질의 방송)

DABCO diaza bicyclo octane 디아자 바이시클로 옥탄.

DAC ① Department of the Army Civilian (美) 육군 민간부(民間部).
② Development Assistance Committee (OECD의) 개발 원조 위원회.
③ digital analog converter (컴퓨터) DA 변환기. 디지털 양(量)을 아날로그 양으로 변환하는 장치.

DAChem doctor of applied chemistry 응용 화학 박사.

DAD digital audio disc 디지털화(化)한 신호로 음악 등을 기록한 레코드. 대표적인 예로 일본 소니와 네덜란드의 필립스사(社)가 공동 개발한 CD(Compact Disc).

DADC Digital Audio Disc Corporation (美) 컴팩트 디스크 제조 회사.

DAe doctor of aeronautics 항공

학 박사.

DAE Dictionary of American English 아메리카 영어 사전.

DAeE doctor of aeronautical engineering 항공 공학 박사.

DAF Department of the Air Force (美) 공군성.

DAFCS digital automatic flight control system 디지털 자동항공 비행 제어시스템.

DAg doctor of agriculture 농학 박사.

DAG ① Development Assistance Group 개발원조 그룹. 저개발국 원조 문제 검토를 위한 선진국 회의.
② [G] Deutsche Angestellten-Gewerkschaft (=German Salaried Workers' Union) (독일)독일 회사원 노조.

DAGMAR drift and ground speed measuring airborne radar 편류 및 대지 속도 측정용 기상 레이더.

DAH Dictionary of American History 미국 역사 사전.

DAI distributed artificial intelligence 분산(分散)인공지능.

DAM direct access method (컴퓨터) 직접 접근법.

D&C data processing and communication 데이터 처리와 통신(通信).

D&D ① deaf and dumb 보복(報復)이 두려워 경찰에 알리지 않음.
② death and dying 죽음과 임종.
③ drunk and disorderly 음주 문란.

DANIDA Danish International Development Agency 덴마크 국제 개발 사업단.

DAP ① Democratic Action Party (말레이시아) 민주 행동당(行動黨).
② digital autopilot 디지털 자동 조종.

DAPS direct access programming system (컴퓨터) 직접 접근 프로그래밍 방식.

DAR ① Daughters of the American Revolution 미국 애국여성 단체. 선조가 독립 전쟁 참가자인 여성 단체.
② Defense Acquisition Regulation (美) 병기 조달 규정.

DARA Deutsche Agentur fur Raumfahrtangelegenheit = GSA (German Space Agency) (독) 독일 우주공사.

DArch doctor of architecture 건축학 박사.

DArchE doctor of architectural engineering 건축 공학 박사.

DARCOM Development and Readiness Command (美) 개발 즉응군(卽應軍).

DARPA

DARPA Defense Advanced Research Projects Agency (美) (국방성) 방위 고급 연구 계획국.

DAs doctor of astronomy 천문학 박사.

DAS ① data acquisition system 데이터수집시스템.
② design automation system 설계 자동화시스템.
③ direct acting system 직접 가동시스템.

DASD direct access storage device (컴퓨터) 직접 기억 장치. 대용량(大容量), 고속도의 보조 기억 장치.

DASH drone anti submarine helicopter (美) 대(對) 잠수함 무인 헬리콥터.

DASM delayed action space missile 연기(延期) 우주 미사일

DAT ① differential aptitude test 적성 판별 테스트.
② digital audio tape-recorder 디지털 녹음 재생이 가능한 카세트 리코더. 몇 번이고 복사해도 전혀 잡음이 없는 것이 특징.
③ dynamic address translation 동적(動的) 어드레스 변환.
④ Dental Admission Test 치과대학 입학시험.
⑤ Digital Audio Tape Recorder 디지털 테이프 레코더.

DA-TDMA demand assignment-time division multiple access 위성통신에 있어 각국(各國)의 사용회선을 기준국에서 결정하는 네트워크제어방식.

DAuE doctor of automobile engineering 자동차 공학 박사.

DAV disabled American veterans 미국 상이 군인회.

DAVA Defense Audio Visual Agency (美) (국방성) 국방 시청각 자료국.

DAVAR dealer authorized value added reseller (美) 부가가치 소매업자.

db, dB decibel 데시벨. 음(音)의 강도 단위.

DB ① data bank 데이터 뱅크.
② data base 데이터베이스. 컴퓨터에 의해 처리되는 데이터 파일군. 정보를 체계적으로 정리 축적하여 그 조직내의 이용자에게 필요한 정보를 제공하는 정보 서비스의 심장부.
③ defensive back (미식 축구) 디펜시브 백.
④ [G] Deutsche Bundesbahn (= German Federal Railways) (독일) 독일연방 철도.
⑤ dry basis 건량(乾量) 기준.
⑥ dry bulb temperature 건구(乾球) 온도.
⑦ Death Bomb 수중폭탄.
⑧ Dry Battery 건전지

DBA ① doctor of business administration 경영학 박사.

② Doing Business as 사업경영중.

DB/DC data base / data communication 데이터베이스/데이터 통신.

DBAP data base access protocol 데이터 베이스관리, 데이터베이스제어 등 네트워크의 데이터베이스를 통일적으로 조작하기 위한 기능을 정하는 프로토콜.

DBE Dame Commander of the Order of the British Empire (英) 대영 제국 2등 훈공장 여성 수훈자.

DBH diameter at breast height (林業) 흉고직경(胸高直經).

DBiCh doctor of biochemistry 생화학 박사.

DBiE doctor of biological engineering 생물 공학 박사.

DBiPhy doctor of biophysics 생물 이학 박사.

DBiS doctor of biological sciences 생물학 박사.

DBMS data base management system (컴퓨터) 데이터 베이스 관리 시스템.

DBS ① dibutyl sebacate 세바스산(酸) 디부틸.
② direct-broadcast satellite 직접 방송 통신 위성. 각 가정에 설치한 포물면(面) 안테나 (parabolic antenna)를 향해 직접 TV전파를 송신하는 인공위성.

DC ① [I] Partito Democrazia Cristiana (=Christian Democratic Party) (이탈리아) 크리스트교(敎) 민주당.
② decimal classification (圖書館) 십진 분류법(十進分類法).
③ data communication 데이터 통신.
④ device control character (컴퓨터) 장치 제어 문자.
⑤ Dewey classification = DDC (圖書館) 듀이 분류법.
⑥ direct current (電氣) 직류.
⑦ District of Columbia (美) 컬럼비아 특별구. 수도 워싱턴의 행정상의 정식 명칭.
⑧ doctor of chiropractic 척추 지압 요법 박사.
⑨ draft card (美) 징병 카드.
⑩ dead cross 데드 크로스. 단기 주가 이동 평균선이 장기 주가 이동 평균선을 위로부터 아래로 급속히 돌파하는 현상을 나타내는 주식 용어. 이 현상은 약세 시장의 강력한 전환 신호를 의미함.
⑪ declining balance 가속상각법.

DCA ① Defense Communications Agency (美) (국방성) 국방 통신국.
② dicarboxylic acid 디카르복시산(酸).
③ doctor of commercial arts 상업 미술 박사.

DCAA Defense Contract Audit

Agency (美) (국방성) 국방계약 감사국.

DCAT digital circuit access and terminating equipment (컴퓨터) 회선 종단 장치(回線終端裝置).

DCB ① Dame Commander of the Most Honourable Order of the Bath (英) 배스 2등 훈공장 여성 수훈자.
② data control block (컴퓨터) 데이터 제어 블록.

DCC dark curtain closed (연극) 조명(照明)이 꺼진 채로 막을 닫기.

DCCP data communication control procedure (컴퓨터) 데이터 통신 제어 순서.

DC/DC Converter direct current / direct current converter 직류 전압을 승압, 강압하는 콘버터. 컴퓨터 내에 이용된다.

DCE ① data circuit terminating equipment (컴퓨터) 데이터 회선 종단 장치.
② doctor of civil engineering 토목 공학 박사.
③ domestic credit expansion 국내 신용 확대.

DCF discounted cash flow 자금 계획의 재정 분석의 한 방법.

DCGG [G] Deutsche Continental Gas Gesellschaft 연료를 주축으로 하는 독일의 지주 회사(指株會社). Conti gas라고도 약칭함.

DCh [L] doctor chirurgiae (=doctor of surgery) 외과학 박사(博士).

DChE doctor of chemical engineering 화학 공학 박사.

DCL ① doctor of canon law 교회법 박사.
② doctor of civil law 민법학 박사.
③ doctor of classical literature 고전 문학 박사.
④ doctor of commercial law 상법 박사.
⑤ doctor of comparative law 비교 법학 박사.

DCM ① displays and controls module (宇宙工學) 표시(標示)·제어 장치.
② Distinguished Conduct Medal (英) 공로장. 하사관 이하에게 수여됨.
③ doctor of comparative medicine 비교 의학 박사.

DCMG Dame Commander of the (Most Distinguished) Order of St. Michael and St. George (=DMG) (英) 성(聖)미카엘·성(聖)조지 2등 훈공장 여성 수훈자.

DCMU dichlorophenyl dimethyl urea 제초제로 사용되는 화합물.

DCNA data communication network architecture (일) 데이터 통신망아키텍쳐.

DCP ① data communication processor 데이터 통신기.

NASA가 개발한 발신 장치.
② doctor of city planning 도시 계획 박사.

DCr doctor of criminology 범죄학 박사.

DCR doctor of comparative religion 비교 종교학 박사.

DCRK Democratic Confederal Republic of Koryo 고려민주연방공화국 (1980. 10 북한 제6차 당대회의[고려민주연방 공화국 창립방안]에 의거 제시된 형태로 [연방통일정부] 수립 후 그 밑에 남북이 지역자치제를 실시하는 연방국가를 창립하여 1민족 1국가, 2제도 2정부로 통일하는 형태의 국가)

DCS ① data collection system (컴퓨터) 데이터 수집(收集) 시스템.
② data control system (컴퓨터) 데이터 제어 시스템.
③ Defense Communications System (美) 방위 통신(通信) 시스템.
④ doctor of commercial science 상학 박사.
⑤ dorsal column stimulator 척주 자극 장치. 척주 신경을 자극하여 아픔을 완화하는 장치.

DCs developing countries 발전도상국.

DCT digital communications terminal 디지털 통신 단말기.

DCTL direct coupled transistor logic (컴퓨터) 직결형(直結形) 트랜지스터 논리 회로(論理回路).

DCVO Dame Commander of the Royal Victorian Order (英) 빅토리아 2등 훈위 여성 수훈자.

DD ① demand draft 요구불 어음.
② destroyer 구축함.
③ direct deal 직접 거래.
④ dishonorable discharge 불명예 제대.
⑤ display design 쇼 윈도우 등의 진열 디자인.
⑥ doctor of divinity 신학 박사.
⑦ documentary draft 화환(貨換) 어음.
⑧ drunken driver 음주 운전자.
⑨ drunken driving 음주 운전.

DDA ① digital differential analyzer (컴퓨터) 계수 미분 해석기
② Doha Development Agenda 도하 개발 아젠다.

D-Day ① 행동 개시 예정일.
② 1944년 6월 6일. 제2차 세계대전 중, 연합군이 군함・수송선・상륙용 주정 4천척으로 프랑스의 노르망디에 상륙(上陸)한 날.
③ Decimal Day (英) 화폐 제도를 십진법으로 바꾼 날. 1971년 2월 15일.

DDB double declining balance method 잔고 저감법(殘高低減法).

DDC ① Dewey decimal classification = DC (圖書館)

DDD

듀이 십진 분류법.
② direct digital control 컴퓨터로 플랜트를 직접 제어하기.

DDD ① deadline delivery date 인도(引渡) 마감일.
② direct distant dialing (전화) 구역외 직통 다이얼통화.

DDE dichloro diphenyl ethylenc (化學) 무색 결정성 살충제.

DDEP defense development exchange program 방위 기술 교환 계획.

DDG guided missile destroyer → DD (美) 유도 미사일 구축함(驅逐艦).

DDM doctor of dental medicine = DMD 치과 의학 박사.

DDN Defense Data Network 방위 데이터 통신망 미국 국방성의 시스템.

DDP distributed data processing (컴퓨터)분산형 데이터 처리(處理).

DDPS direct data processing system (컴퓨터) 직접 데이터처리 시스템.

DDR dynamic device reconfiguration (컴퓨터) 동적(動的) 장치 재편성.

DDS ① deep diving system 심해 잠수 시스템.
② doctor of dental science 치과학 박사.
③ doctor of dental surgery 구강 외과 박사.
④ drug delivery system 약제 수송 시스템. 약물 송달 체계를 뜻하는 말. 필요로 하는 기관이나 조직에 요구되는 만큼 의약을 보내 다른 부위로 퍼져 나가는 것을 막아 약으로 인한 부작용을 가능한 한 줄인 새로운 약제 투여 시스템.
⑤ decision support system 의사 결정 지원 시스템 비즈니스에서의 비정형 적인 의사 결정을 지원하는 시스템.

DDT ① dichloro diphenyl trichloroethane 디디티. 방역 살충제의 일종.
② Don't do that (속) 중지해라.
③ Drop dead twice! (속) 딱 질색이다.
④ dynamic debugging tool (컴퓨터) 디버깅[오류 수정] 작업에 쓰는 프로그램.

DDVP dimethyl dichlorovinyl phosphate 유기 인제(有機燐劑) 살충제.

DDX Digital Data Exchange (컴퓨터) 디지털 · 데이터 교환장치.

DE ① defensive end (미식 축구) 수비측 포지션의 하나.
② Delawre (美) 델라웨어 주(州)의 우편 기호.
③ destroyer escort vessel 호위 구축함.
④ doctor of engineering = DEng, DIng, EngD 공학 박사.
⑤ doctor of entomology =

DEnt 곤충학 박사.

DEA Drug Enforcement Administration (美) (법무성) 마약 단속국. 구칭 BNDD.

DEAE diethylaminoethyl 디에틸아미노에틸.

Dec. December 12월.

DEc doctor of economics 경제학 박사.

DEC Digital Equipment Corporation 미국 제2위의 컴퓨터 메이커.

DECB data event control block (컴퓨터) 데이터 사상(事象) 제어 블록.

DECON defense readiness condition 방공 준비 태세(態勢).

DEd doctor of education = EdD 교육학 박사.

DEE doctor of electrical engineering 전기 공학 박사.

deejey DJ (속) 디스크 자키(disk jockey).

DEF·CON defense condition (美) 방위 준비 태세(態勢).

DEG diethylene glycol 디에틸렌글리콜.

Del. Delaware (美) 델라웨어 주(州).

DEL ① delete character (컴퓨터) 말소 문자.
② doctor of English literature 영문학 박사.
③ deli delicatessen 조제 식품. 조제 식품판매점.

DELP ① Development of Earth's Lithosphere Project 국제 지각 탐사 개발 계획.
② Democratic Front for the Liberation of Palestine 팔레스타인 해방민주전선.

DEMA Defense Media Agency 국방 홍보원

Dem. ① Democrat = D (美) 민주당원.
② Democratic Party (美) 민주당.

demo demonstration 데모, 시위 운동.

demob ① demobilization 동원 해제.
② demobilize 동원 해제하다.

DEMS digital electronic message service 디지털 전자 메시지 서비스. 디지털 종단 시스템(DTS)을 통하여 제공되는 모든 서비스.

DEng doctor of engineering = DE, DIng, EngD 공학 박사.

DEnt doctor of entomology = DE 곤충학 박사.

DES ① Data Encryption Standard (美) 데이터 암호화 규격.
② Department of Education and Science (英) 교육(敎育) 과학성.
③ diethylstilbestrol 디에틸 스

DESC

틸베스트롤. 합성 여성 호르몬의 일종.

DESC Defense Electronics Supply Center (美) (국방성) 방위 전자 기기 공급 센터.

DET diethyltryptamine 디에틸트립트아민. 환각제의 일종.

DETAB Decision Table Language (컴퓨터) COBOL에 의거한 프로그램 언어.

DEW ① directed-energy weapon 에너지 지향형 병기. SDI (전략 방위 구상) 계획에서 유력시되는 주력 무기, 레이저 무기, 입자 빔 무기 등의 우주 무기.
② distant early warning 원거리 조기 경보. 미국의 북부국경, 알래스카와 그린랜드를 잇는 선에는 DEW line 이라고 하는 방공 레이더망이 설치되어 있음.

DEWK double employed with kids 어린이를 가진 맞벌이 부부.

DEWS Distant Early Warning System 원거리 조기 경보망.

DEX Denden K.K. electronic exchange 전신전화 주식회사형 전자 교환기.

DF ① Defender of the Faith = FD 신앙의 옹호자. 영국왕의 전통적 칭호.
② defense (축구) 디펜스.
③ direction finder 방향 탐지기.
④ direction finding 방향 탐지.

DFA distributed virtual file access 분산(分散) 파일 접근.

DFC Distinguished Flying Cross (英・美) 공군 수훈 십자장.

DFDR digital flight data recorder → FDR 디지털식(式) 비행데이터 기록 장치.

DFG diode function generator (컴퓨터) 다이오드 함수(函數) 발생기.

DFLP Democratic Front for the Liberation of Palestine 팔레스타인 해방민주 전선.

DFM Distinguished Flying Medal (英) 공군 수훈장. 하사관에게 수여됨

DFMD distributed virtual file management domain 분산(分散) 파일 관리 영역.

DFT diagnostic function test (컴퓨터) 기능 진단 테스트.

DFVLR [G]Deutschc Forschungsund Versuchsanstalt fur Luftund Raumfahrt (=German Research and Experiment Institution for Air and Space Travel) 독일 항공 우주 연구소.

DG ① defensive guard (미식 축구) 디펜시브 가드.
② drop goal (럭비) 드롭 골.

DGB [G] Deutscher Gewerkschaftsbund (=German Labor Federation) (독일) 독일

노동 총동맹.

DGSE [F] Direction Generale de la Securite Exterieure (=General Directorate for External Security)(프랑스) 대외(對外) 치안 총국.

DGT [F] Direction Generale des Telecommunications (=National Telecommunications Authority) (프랑스) 전기 통신 총국.

DH ① decision height 비행기가 착륙하기 위한 강하를 중지하고 상승으로 전환할 때의 고도.
② defense half (미식축구) 디펜스 하프.
③ designated hitter (野球) 지명 타자.
④ doctor of humanities = DHu, HHD 인문 과학 박사.

DHA dehydroacetic acid 디히드로아세트산. 살균제.

DHC district heating and cooling 지역 열공급, 1개소 또는 수개소의 열공급프랜트에서 지역내에 있는 주택과 빌딩에 증기, 온수, 냉수 등으로 열을 공급하는 시스템.

DHEA Dehydroepiandrosterone (인체 내 부신에서 생성되는 생식 호르몬)

DHEc doctor of home economics 가정학 박사.

DHHS Department of Health and Human Services (美) 후생성.

DHL ① Dalsey Hillbom Linn 항공속달편.
② diesel hydraulic locomotive 액압(液壓)디젤기관차.

DHP delivered horse power 전달마력(傳達魔力).

DHS Department of Homeland Security 미 국토 안보부.

DHSC DaiHan Shipbuilding Corporation 대한조선공사.

DHu doctor of humanities = DH, HHD 인문 과학 박사.

DHUD Department of Housing and Urban Development = HUD (美) 주택 도시 개발성.

DHy doctor of hygiene 위생학 박사.

DI ① Department of the Interior (美) 내무성.
② diffusion index 경기 동향 지수.
③ digital interface (컴퓨터) 디지털 인터페이스. (디지털 접속장치)
④ discomfort index 불쾌 지수.
⑤ drug information 의약품 정보.
⑥ disposable income 가처분소득(可處分所得). 개인 소득에서 세금·이자·지출 등 비소비 지출을 뺀 잔액으로 개인이 소비나 저축으로 자유롭게 처분할 수 있는 소득.

DIA ① Defense Intelligence Agency (美)(국방성) 국방정보국.
② doctor of industrial arts 공

DIALINDEX

예 기술 박사.
③ document interchange architecture 문서교환 구조 문서의 교환을 하기 위해 필요한 프로토콜과 데이터 포맷의 규정.
④ document information accessing 문서 정보 검색문서 정보를 검색하는 정보 검색 시스템의 일종.

DIALINDEX (美) DIALOG Information Services, Inc. 가 제공한 모든 데이터 베이스 파일 색인을 하나로 정리한 것.

DIALOG (美) Dialogue 세계 최대의 데이터베이스 제공 회사 DIALOG Information Service 및 동사(同社)가 제공한 데이터베이스 시스템의 명령.

DIANE Direct Information Access Network for Europe EC 가맹국이 창설한 데이터베이스· 접근용 국제 정보 교환망.

DIC dielectric isolation circuit 절연체 분리 회로.

DID densely inhabited district 인구 밀집 지구.

DIDC Depository Institudions Deregulation Committee (美의회) 예금금리 규제 폐지 위원회.

DIET 다이어트 파일을 압축하는 프로그램.

DIKO [그리스語] Demokratiko Komma (=Democratic Party) (키프로스) 민주당.

DIL doctor of international law 국제법 박사.

DIM nonthermal decimetric emission 비열(非熱) 데시미터 방사(放射).

DIMDI [G] Deutsches Institut fur Medizinische Doku-mentation und Information (= German Institute for Medical Documentation and Information) 독일 의학 다큐멘테이션 정보 협회.

DIN [G] Deutsche Industrie Norm (=German Industrial Standard) 독일 공업 규격.

DINA ① [S] Direccion de Inteligencia Nacional (=Directorate of National Intelligence) 칠레의 비밀 경찰.
② direct internal noise amplification 직접 소음 증폭.

DIng [L] doctor ingeniariae (=doctor of engineering) = DE, DEng, EngD 공학 박사.

DINK double income no kids 여피에 이은 최근 미국 베이비붐 세대의 생활 양식·가치관을 대변하는 말. 딩크족은 의도적으로 자녀를 두지 않는 맞벌이 부부로 대신 사회적 관심을 확대하고 개인의 자유와 자립을 존중하며 일에서 보람을 찾으려 함. 딩크족을 남녀 자립의 완벽한 실현이라고 보는 견해와 과도한 물질성 때문에 문명병으로 보는 견해 등 여러 가지로 평가됨.

DINKS double income no kids 어린이가 없는 맞벌이 부부.

DINS digital inertial navigation system 디지털식(式) 관성 항법 장치.

DIP ① de-inking pulp 탈묵(脫墨) 펄프.
② drip infusion pyelography 점적 신우 촬영(點滴腎盂撮影).
③ dual inline package (電子工學) 듀얼 인라인 패키지.

DIPS Dendenkosha Information Processing System 일본전신전화주식회사의 정보처리시스템.

DIS ① Defense Investigative Service (美) (국방성) 국방조사국.
② Draft International Standard 데이터 통신에 관한 국제 규격안.
③ drive information system 드라이브 정보 시스템.
④ Deposit Insurance System 예금보험제도.

DISAM Defense Institute of Security Assistance Management (美) (국방성) 국방 안전 보장 원조 관리 연구소.

DISC Domestic International Sales Corporation (美) 국제 판매 회사.

disco discotheque 디스코(텍).

DISOSS Distributed Office Support System 분산형 사무 지원 시스템 IBM의 오피스 시스템.

DISY [그리스語] Demokratikos Synagermos (=Democratic Rally)(키프로스) 민주 연합.

DITI Department of International Trade and Industry (美) 통상 산업성.

DIVAD division(al) air defense (美) Ford Aerospace and Communications Corp. 가 제작한 방공 무기.

DIY do it yourself 자신이 하기. 제1차 세계 대전 후 영국에서 물자 부족·인력 부족의 상황 속에서 자신의 일은 자신이 해야 된다는 사회 운동.

DJ ① disk(or disc) jockey = deejay 디스크 자키.
② Dow Jones & Co., Inc. (美) 다우 존스. 다우평균 주가를 발표하는 경제 보도 회사.

DJIA Dow-Jones Industrial Average (美) 다우 공업주 평균 주가 지수.

DK ① dining room-kitchen 식당 겸 부엌.
② don't know (여론 조사에서) 잘 모르겠다고 답하는 사람.

DKNY Donna Karan New York (도나 카라이 디자인한 브랜드 의류)

DKP [G] Deutsche Hommunistische Partei (=German Communist Party) (독일) 독일 공산당.

133

dl. deciliter 데시리터.

DL ① dead load 사하중(死荷重).
② diesel locomotive 디젤 기관차.
③ diesel locomotive difference of latitude 위도차(緯度差).
④ doctor of laws = LLD 법학 박사.
⑤ doctor of literature / letters = DLit, DLitt, LitD, LittD 문학 박사.

DLA Defense Logistics Agency (美) 방위 병참국.

DLBS development loan through the banking system 개발 금융 차관.

DLC ① data link control (컴퓨터) 전송 제어.
② direct lift control (비행기) 직접 양력(揚力) 제어.

DLE data link escape character (컴퓨터)전송 제어 확장 문자(文字).

DLF Development Loan Fund (美) 개발 차관 기금.

DLH [G] Deutsche Lufthansa AG (독일) 루프트한자 항공회사.

DLit, Dlitt [L] doctor of literature / letters = DL, LD, LitD, LittD 문학 박사.

DLM [L] dosis letalis minima (=minimum lethal dose) 최소 치사량.

DLO ① dead letter office 배달 불능 우편 취급소. 영국에서는 현재 RLO로 개칭.
② difference of longitude 경도차(經度差).

DLP Defense Language Program 미 국방성 어학프로그램.

DLR Deutsche Forschungsanstalt fur Luft und Raumfahrt (독) 독일 항공우주연구소.

DLS ① Defense Legal Services Agency (美) (국방성) 국방법무국.
② digital local switching system 디지털 가입자 교환기.
③ doctor of library science 도서관학 박사.

DM ① [G] Deutsche Mark (= German mark) 독일 마르크.
② diabetes mellitus 진성 당뇨병.
③ direct mail 다이렉트 메일. 직접 개인이나 가정으로 보내는 광고 우편물.
④ doctor of mathematics 수학 박사.
⑤ doctor of medicine = MD 의학 박사.
⑥ Domain Name 인터넷 접속이름.

DMA ① Dance Masters of America 미국 무용 교사 협회.
② Defense Mapping Agency (美) (국방성) 국방 지도 제작국(局).
③ direct memory access (컴퓨터) 직접 기억 장치 접근.

DMAHTC Defense Mapping Agency Hydrographic

Topographic Center → AMS (美) 국방 해도(海圖) 지도부(部).

DMB dual mode bus 수동(手動)과 자동 운전의 양용버스.

DMC ① Democratic National Committee (美) 민주당 전국 위원회.
② direct numerical control 직접 수치 제어.

DMD [L] dentariae medicinae doctor (=doctor of dental medicine)= DDM 치과 의학 박사.

DME ① dimethoxy ethane 디메톡시 에탄.
② distance measuring equipment 거리 측정기.
③ doctor of mechanical engineering 기계 공학 박사.
④ dropping mercury electrode 적하(滴下) 수은 전극.

DMG Dame Commander of the Order of St. Michael and St. George = DCMG (英) 성(聖) 미카엘·성(聖)조지 2등 훈공장 여성 수훈자.

DMI ① direct manipulation interface 디스플레이의 화면상에서 손작업을 시뮬레이트할 수 있는 것과 같이 직접 조작이 가능한 인터페이스를 가진 시스템.
② desktop management interface 데스크탑 매니지먼트 인터페이스 데스크탑 관리용의 표준 API(Application)

DMIX digital multimedia information multiplexer 디지털 회선(回線) 각종 미디어 다중(多重) 장치.

DMK Dravida Munnetra Kazgham (인도) 드라비다 진보 동맹(同盟).

DMKP Dalit Mazdoor Kisan Party (인도) 피압박 노동자 농민당.

DML data manipulation language (컴퓨터)데이터베이스 조작 언어.

DMM digital multimeter 다기능 디지털 전압계.

DMNA dimethylnitrosamine 디메틸니트로사민. 강력한 발암 물질.

DMOS double diffused metal oxide semiconductor → MOS (컴퓨터) 이중 확산 금속 산화물 반도체.

DMP ① dimethyl phthalate 프탈산(酸) 디메틸.
② Mine Sweeping Destroyer 기뢰 제거 구축함.

DMS doctor of medical science(s) 의학 박사.

DMSO dimethyl sulfoxide 디메틸술폭시드. 용제(溶劑), 진통 항염증제.

DMSP Defense Meteorological Satellite Program (美) 방위기상위성 계획.

DMT dimethyltryptamine 디메틸트립트아민. 환각제의 일종(一種).

135

DMU decision-making unit 의지 (意志) 결정자.

DMus doctor of music 음악학 박사.

DMV Department of Motor Vehicle 교통국.

DMZ demilitarized zone 비무장지대. 한국전(戰)과 인도차이나전(戰)의 휴전 협정에서 휴전선 양쪽에 설치키로 한 비무장 완충 지대.

DN ① dinitrocyclohexyl phenol 디니트로 시클로헥실 페놀. 농약의 일종.
② Drawing Number 도면번호.

DNA ① Defense Nuclear Agency (美)(국방성) 국방 핵무기국(局).
② deoxyriboncleic acid → RNA 디옥시리보핵산(核酸). 일부의 바이러스를 제외한 모든 생물의 유전자의 본체가 되는 고분자 물질.

DNB ① [G] Deutsches Nachrichtenburo (=German News Agency) 독일 통신사.
② Dictionary of National Biography 영국 인명 사전.

DNBP dinitrobutyl phenol 디니트로 부틸 페놀. 농약의 일종.

DNC ① Democratic National Committee (美) 민주당 전국 위원회.
② direct numerical control (컴퓨터) 직접 수치 제어. 오토메이션의 가장 발달된 방식인 NC를 더욱 발전시킨 것. NC가 작업순서를 종이 테이프에 타자하여 이것을 기계에 끼워 넣어 작동시키는데 비해 DNC는 종이 테이프를 쓰지 않고 직접 자동적으로 기계가 이를 조작함.

DNF did not finish 미완성.

DNI Director of National Intelligence 미 국가정보장.

DNIC data network identification code 데이터망 식별 부호.

DNL dynamic noise limiter 재생 때만의 처리로 테이프의 잡음을 줄이는 방식.

DNN dinitro naphthalene 디니트로 나프탈렌.

DNS Dacom net service 한국 데이터 통신이 국제공중 데이터 통신망을 이용하여 세계 각국의 정보를 서비스해 주는 통신서버.

DNT dinitro toluene 디니트로 톨루엔.

DNV Det Norsk Veritas 노르웨이 선급협회.

DNZ denuclearized zone 비핵무장지대.

do. ditto 동상(同上).

DO ① dark open (연극) 조명을 끈 채 막을 올리기.
② delivery order 화물 인도 지시서.
③ designated office 지정 관청.

④ dissolved oxygen 용존 산소(溶存酸素).

DOA ① dead on arrival 도착전 사망. ② Department of the Army (美) 육군성.

DOB date of birth 생년월일.

DOBIS [G] Dortmunder Bibliotheks System 독일의 정보 시스템.

DOC direct operating cost 직접 운항비.

DOD Department of Defense (美) 국방성.

DODCI Department of Defense Computer Institute (美) 국방성 컴퓨터 연구소.

DOE ① Department of Education → HEW (美) 교육성. ② Department of Energy (美) 에너지성. ③ Department of Environment (英) 환경성.

DOF delivery on field 원산지 인도.

DOHC double overhead camshaft 2두상(頭上) 캠축(軸). 자동차 엔진의 마력을 증폭시키는 장치.

DOI Department of Insurance 보험국(미국).

DOM ① dimethoxy methylamphetamine 디메톡시 메틸암페타민. 환각제의 일종. ② dirty old man 어린 아이에게 음란한 짓을 하는 성적 변질가.

DOMA Deep Ocean Minerals Association (일) 심해저 광물자원 개발 협회.

DOMP disease of medical practice 의료 행위에 의해서 생기는 질병.

DON ① Department of the Navy (美) 해군성. ② distribution octane number 디스트리뷰션법(法)에 의한 옥탄가(價).

DOP dioctyl phthalate 프탈산(酸) 디옥틸. 합성 수지 가소제(可塑劑).

DOR digital optical record 디지털 광학기록. 레이저광(光)을 사용하여 디지털식으로 음이나 화상을 기록하는 것.

DORAN Doppler range and navigation 도플러 효과를 이용한 거리 측정 장치.

DOS ① dioctyl sebacate 세바스산(酸) 디옥틸. ② disc operating system (컴퓨터) 자기(磁氣) 디스크 이용 시스템.

DOT ① Department of Transportation (美·캐나다) 운수성(運輸省). ② Department of the Treasury (美) 재무성.

DOV data over voice 데이터를 음성과 함께 송신하는 것.

DOVAP Doppler velocity and

position (NASA) 우주선, 미사일의 위치와 속도를 도플러 효과를 이용하여 계산하는 시스템.

DOZ dioctyl azelate 아젤라인산(酸) 디옥틸.

DP ① data processing (컴퓨터) 데이터 처리.
② data processor (컴퓨터) 데이터 처리 장치.
③ deferred payment 연불(延拂).
④ degree of polymerization 중합도(重合度).
⑤ Democratic Party (우간다) 민주당.
⑥ [S] Demoracia Popular (= People's Democratic Party) (에콰도르) 인민 민주당.
⑦ depositary receipt 예탁 증권.
⑧ dew point 이슬점, 노점(露店).
⑨ displaced person(s) 난민(難民). 전쟁으로 고국을 잃은 사람.
⑩ dissolving pulp 용해 펄프.
⑪ doctor of pharmacy 약학 박사.
⑫ documents against payment 어음 대금 지불에 대한 선적 서류 인도.
⑬ double play (野球) 더블 플레이.
⑭ dynamic programming 동적(動的) 계획법.

DPA ① [G] Deutsche Presse-Agentur (= German Press Agency) (독일) 통신.
② dichloropropionic acid 디클로로프로피온산(酸).

DPB deposit pass book 예금 통장.

DPC ① data processing center (컴퓨터) 정보 처리 센터.
② data processing consultant (컴퓨터) 정보 처리(處理) 콘설턴트.
③ Data Processing Crime 컴퓨터 범죄의 다른 이름. ※ 컴퓨터와 관련하여 발생하는 범죄로 프로그램을 바꾸어 쓴다거나 부정한 데이터를 입력하여 돈을 사취하는 것을 그 예로 들 수 있음.
④ Defense Planning Committee (NATO) 방위 계획 위원회.

DPCM differential pulse code modulation (컴퓨터) 차분(差分) 펄스 부호 변조(變調).

DPE ① Defense Production Administration (美) 국방 생산국(局).
② developing, printing, enlarging (寫眞) 현상·인화·확대(擴大).
③ doctor of physical education 체육학 박사.

DPG ① diphenyl guanidine 디페닐 구아니딘.
② diphosphoglyceric acid 글리세르산(酸공)이인산.

DPH ① doctor of public health 보건학 박사.
② doctor of public hygiene 공중 위생학 박사.

DPhC doctor of pharmaceutical chemistry 약화학 박사.

DPhil [L] doctor philosophiae (=doctor of philosophy) = PhD (철학) 박사.

DPI ① Disabled Persons International 장애자 인터내셔널.
② dot per inch 단위 인치당 점의 개수 프린터, 스캐너 등에서 1인치에 출력되는 도트(점)의 수로 나타내는 단위(해상도).

DPM ① disintegration per minute (방사성 원소의) 1분간당 붕괴율.
② doctor of preventive medicine 예방 의학 박사.

DPMA Data Processing Management Association (美) 정보처리 관리 협회.

DPN diphosphopyridine nucleotide 디포스포피리딘 뉴클레오티드. 수소 원자를 전달하는 보효소(補酵素).

DPNH reduced diphosphopyridine nucleotide 환원형 디포스포피리딘 뉴클레오티드.

DPP Direct product Profit 직접 제품 이익 시스템. 신종상품 관리 기법으로 미국 소매업계에 급속히 보급되고 있음.

DPPH diphenyl picryl hydrazyl 디페닐 피크릴 하이드라질. (결핵 치료약)

DPR digital pulse receiver (전화) 다이얼 펄스 수신기.

DPRK Democratic People's Republic of Korea 조선민주주의 인민공화국.

DPS ① data processing system 데이터 처리 시스템.
② disintegration per second (방사성 원소의) 매초 붕괴율.
③ doctor of political science 정치학 박사.

DPSK differential phase-shift keying 차동 위상 편이 변조(差動位相偏移變調).

DPT ① dinitroso pentanethylene tetramine 다니트로소 펜타메틸렌 테트라민.
② dipropylphyptamine 디프로필펍트아민. 환각성 마약.

Dr. Doctor 박사. 의사.

DR ① dead reckoning (航空) 추측 항법.
② design review 설계 심사.
③ digital radiography 디지털 뢴트겐 장치.
④ direct reduction steelmaking 직접 환원 제철법.
⑤ dispatch rider (美) (해병대) 전령.
⑥ dock receipt 부두 화물 수취증.
⑦ Dominican Republic 도미니카 공화국.

DRA Development Restriction Area 개발제한구역.

DRAM dynamic random access memory (컴퓨터) 기억 보지(記

DRAW

憶保持) 동작이 필요한 수시 읽기 기록 기억 장치.

DRAW direct read after write 녹화 가능 비디오 디스크 방식(方式).

DRC data recording control (컴퓨터) 데이터 기록 제어 기구.

DRD data recording device (컴퓨터) 데이터 기록 장치.

DRG Defense Research Group (美) 방위 연구 그룹.

DRO ① destructive read out (컴퓨터) 파괴성 읽기.
② digital read out (컴퓨터) 수치 표시 장치.

D.R.P. Democratic Republican Party 民主共和黨.

DRX drachma 그리스의 화폐 단위.

DS ① data set 데이터 세트.
② depositary shares 예탁 주식.
③ doctor of science = DSc, ScD, SD 이학 박사.
④ Doppler sonar 도플러 수중 음파 탐지기.
⑤ Discount Store 할인점.

DSA digital subtraction angiography 동맥 협소화나 폐색 등을 발견하는 혈관 조영법.

DSAA Defense Security Assistance Agency (美) (국방성) 국방 안전 보장 원조국.

DSARC Defense Systems Acquisition Review Council (美) 방위 시스템 조달 평가 회의.

DSB ① Defense Science Board (美) 방위 과학국.
② double side-band modulation 양측 파대 변조(兩側波帶變調).

DSc doctor of science = DS, ScD, SD 이학 박사.

DSC ① direct sideforce control 직접 횡력 제어(直接橫力制御).
② Distinguished Service Cross (英·美) 수훈 십자장.

D.S.C. Distinguished Service Cross 십자 무공훈장.

DSCB data set control block 데이터 세트 제어 블록.

DSCS Defense Satellite Communications System (美) 국방위성 통신망.

DSD Deep Submergence Device 심해 잠수장비.

DSE German Foundation for International Development 독일국제개발재단

DSDL data storage description language (컴퓨터) 데이터 기억 기술 언어.

DSDP Deep Sea Drilling Project (美) 심해 굴삭 계획.

DSI ① digital speech interpolation 디지털 음성 삽입.
② Declared Site Inspection 공개 장소검사.

DSL deep scattering layer 심해 음파 산란층.

DSM Distinguished Service Medal (英·美) 수훈장. 미국에서는 군인 일반에게, 영국에서는 하사관 이하의 해군 병사에게 수여됨.

DSM Deputy Section Manager 대리

DSMAC digital scene matching area correlator 디지털 지형도 상관 장치.

DSN deep space network 심우주 (深宇宙) 통신망.

DSo doctor of sociology 사회학 박사.

DSO Distinguished Service Order (英) 수훈장.

DSP ① Defense Support Program (美) 방위 지원 계획. ② digital signal processor 디지털 신호 처리기 디지털 신호처리 전용의 원칩 마이크로프로세서.

DSR ① debt service ratio 할부 상환 금액 비율. ② dynamic spatial reconstructor (의學) 동적(動的) 공간적 재구성 장치. 체내의 심장·폐 등의 장기를 이체 표시하는 장치.

DSRV deep submergence rescue vehicle 심해 구조 잠수정.

DSS decision support system (컴퓨터) 의사결정 지원(支援) 시스템.

DSSP Deep Submergence System Project (아메리카 해군의) 침몰선 수색·구조 계획.

DSSV deep submergence search vehicle 심해 수색 잠수정.

DST daylight saving time 여름 시간.

DSTN dual scan super twisted nematic 휴대용 컴퓨터인 노트북에서 사용하는 액정 디스플레이 표시 장치.

DSU digital service unit (컴퓨터) 회선 종단 장치.

DSW direct step on the wafer 고해상도 노광장치(高解像度 露光裝置).

DT ① defensive tackle (미식 축구) 수비 라인 엔드의 안쪽에 있는 선수. ② delirium tremens (알코올 중독에 의한) 진전 섬망증.

DTA differential thermal analysis 시차열(示差熱) 분석.

DTAX domestic telecommunication automatic exchange 국내 통신 자동 중계 시스템.

DTB draft tube bulb crystallizer 드래프트 튜브형(型) 정석기(晶析器).

DTE ① data terminal equipment (컴퓨터) 데이터 단말 장치. ② Dial Telephone Exchange 자동 전화 교환대.

DTEL digital telephone 디지털 전화기.

DTh doctor of theology 신학 박사.

DTIC Defense Technical Information Center (美) 국방 기술 정보 센터.

DTL diode transistor logic (컴퓨터) 다이오드 트랜지스터 논리 회로.

DTN diphtheria toxin normal 디프테리아 표준 혈청.

DTP ① data transfer protocol (컴퓨터) 데이터 전송 시스템. ② desktop publishing 탁상 출판, 전자 출판 컴퓨터를 이용하여 각종 서적이나 보고서, 유인물 등의 편집과 출력을 하는것.

DTPA diethylene triamine pentacetic acid 디에틸렌 트리아민 펜타 아세트산.

DTR diffusion transfer reversal process 신속 사진법.

DTV desktop video 탁상용 비디오 개인용 컴퓨터에 의한 비디오 제작 시스템.

3-D TV three dimensional 입체 텔레비젼.

DVX digital voice exchange 디지털 음성교환.

DTY draw textured yarn 연신(延伸) 가공사(加功絲).

DU depleted uranium 감손(減損) 우라늄.

DUC data unit control layer 데이터 유닛 제어층.

DUI ① data unit control information 데이터 유닛 제어 정보. ② driving under the influence (of alcohol and / or drugs) 음주 운전 또는 마약의 영향하에서의 운전.

DUMBO Down Under the Manhattan Bridge Overpass (미) 뉴욕의 브루클린 방향 맨하탄 다리 옆.

DV Distinguished Visitor 중요 방문자 내빈, 귀빈

DVB divinyl benzene 디비닐 벤젠.

DVD Digital Versatile Disk 디지털 다기능 디스크.

DVE digital video effect 디지털 비디오 효과.

DVI Digital Video Interactive 화상압축(저장) = 디지털 비디오 저장 기술.

DVM digital volt meter 디지털 전압계.

DVM(S) doctor of veterinary medicine (and surgery) 수의학 박사.

DVR Digital Video Recorder 디지털 비디오 녹화기.

DVS doctor of veterinary surgery 수의 외과학 박사.

DW ① deadweight 중량 톤.

② dock warrant (英) 항만 창고 증권.

DWBA distorted wave Born approximation (電子物理) 왜곡파(歪曲波) 보른 근사(近似).

DWI driving while intoxicated 음주 운전.

DWIA distorted wave impulse approximation 왜곡파(歪曲波) 임펄스 근사(近似).

DWIM Do what I mean 속 이용자의 실수를 자동적으로 보충하는 컴퓨터 명령.

DWL designed waterline 계획 흘수선. (배의 수선)

DWM deadweight machine 실하중 표준기.

dwt. deadweight ton 재화(載貨) 톤, 중량 톤.

DX long distance reception 장거리 수신.

DXT deep X-ray therapy 심부(深部) X광선 치료.

Dy dysprosium (化學) 디스프로슘. 원자번호 66.

dyn Dyne [단위] (힘의 크기 계량단위)

DYNAMO Dynamic Models (컴퓨터)1961년에 Massachusetts Institute of Technology (MIT)가 제작한 프로그램 언어.

dz. dozen(s) 12개 1묶음.

DZ dizygotic twins 이란성 쌍생아.

E einsteinium [화] 아인슈타늄의 화학기호.

E erg [이] ① 에너지 작업량 단위. ② 모래 사막

e. electron 전자.

E. east(ern) 동쪽(의).

E-3 Electric Entertainment Expo 세계최대의 게임전시회.

E-3A Early Warning 공중 조기 경보 통제기.

EA ① Eighth (us) Army 미 8군.
② Electronic Attack 전자공격.
③ Electronic Arrays (美) 반도체 메이커.
④ Enemy Aircraft 적 항공기.
⑤ Engagement Area 교전지역.
⑥ European Accreditation 유럽인정기구. (유럽지역내 국가간 인정에 대한 통일된 접근방식을 제공하고, 지정 인증서 및 시험/검사/교정 성적서에 대한 전세계적인 통용, 측정의 소급성 달성, 인정기관간의 신뢰구축 등을 통한 역내 무역장벽의 해소를 목적으로 European Accreditation of Certification 와 European Cooperation for Accreditation of Laboratories 두 기관이 EA로 통합되면서 현재 유럽의 모든 적합성평가 활동을 수행하는 기관으로 2000. 6 네덜란드 법에 의거 법인으로 설립.

EAA Export Administration Act (美) 수출 관리법.

EAB Ethics Advisory Board (美) 윤리 권고 위원회.

EAC East African Community 동아프리카 공동체. 케냐·우간다·탄자니아 3국으로 결성. 1977년 폐지.

EACM East African Common Market 동아프리카 공동 시장(市場).

EADB East African Development Bank 동아프리카 개발 은행.

EAEC ① East African Economic Community 동아프리카 경제 공동체.
② European Atomic Energy Community 유럽 원자력 공동체. 보통 EURATOM으로 알려짐.
③ East Asian Economic Caucus 동아시아 경제협력체.

EAES European Atomic Energy Society 유럽 원자력 학회.

EAFA East Asian Fraternity Association (일) 동아 친선협회.

EAL Eastern Air Lines (美) 이스턴 항공.

EAM electrical accounting machine 전기식 회계기.

EAMA [F] Etats Africains et Malgache Associes (=Associated African and Malaggasy States) 아프리카·마다가스카르제국 연합.

EAN European article number 유럽 상품 코드 넘버.

EANDC European American Nuclear Data Committee 구미(歐美) 핵 데이터 위원회.

E.&O.E. errors and omissions excepted 오기(誤記)와 탈락은 제외함.

E. and P. Extraordinary and Plenipotentiary 특명전권의.

EAP Enlarged Access Policy = EAR 증액융자제도.

EAR ① Enlarged Access to Fund Resources 증액융자제도.
② 미국 수출 관리규정. 테러지원국가로 지정된 국가에 인도적 지원을 제외한 무기, 무기로 사용되거난 개발될 수 있는 제품의 수출을 통제하고 수입에도 막대한 제재관세를 부과하여 통제하는 제도이다.

EA-ROM electrically alterable read only memory (컴퓨터) 소거(消去) 재기입 롬(ROM). 기억시킨 데이터를 전기적(電氣的)으로 개서(改書)할 수 있는 ROM.

EAS equivalent air speed (航空) 등가 대기 속도(等價對氣速度).

EASCOM Eighth U.S. Army Support Command 미8군 사령부.

EASSS engine automatic stop and start system 엔진 자동정지 시동장치.

EATA East Asia Travel Association 동아시아 관광 협회.

EAX electronic automatic exchange 전자(電子) 자동 교환.

EB ① electron beam lithography equipment 전자 빔 묘화(描畵) 장치. 반도체 제조 장치.
② electronic banking 전자 기기를 이용한 금융서비스.
③ emergency brake 긴급 자동열차 정지 장치.
④ Encyclopedia Britannica 대영 백과 사전.

EB electronic book 전자 북. 지름 8cm의 CD-ROM에 문자나 음성, 그래픽 등의 데이터를 넣어 전용의 플레이어로 재생되는 것.

EB electronic book G 전자 북 지. 전자북의 확장된 규격. 텍스트 데이터와 화상 데이터를 지원한다.

EB electronic book XA 전자북

엑스에이. 음성, 그래픽스 등의 데이터를 수록한 전자책의 명세.

EB Encyclopedia Britannica film 브리태니커 백과사전영화. 사전에 취재한 교육영화.

EBCDIC extended binary coded decimal interchange code (컴퓨터) 확장 2진화(進化) 10진(進) 코드.

EBDC Ethylene Bisdithyo Carbamate 농약 성분의 하나. 살균제 등 각종 농약의 원료로 광범위하게 사용되었지만 1986년부터 발암성 문제가 제기되어 미국 환경 보호청의 특별조사를 받고 있는 중임.

EBIC European Banks' International Corporation 유럽 국제 은행. 1970년 브뤼셀에 설립한 은행.

EBM ① electron beam machining 전자 빔 가공.
② electron beam melting 전자 빔 용해법.

EBR ① electron beam recorder 전자 빔 기록 장치.
② electron beam recording 전자 빔 기록.
③ experimental breeder reactor 실험용 증식 원자로.

EBRD European Bank of Reconstruction & Development 유럽부흥개발은행.

EBRI Employee Benefit Research Institute 고용자 이익 연구소.

EBS ① emergency broadcast system 긴급 방송 시스템.
② Educational Broadcasting System 교육방송.

EBU European Broadcasting Union = UER 유럽 방송 연합.

EBW electron beam welding 전자 빔 용접.

EC ① electronic combat 전자 전투.
② end of curve (토목) 곡선 종점(曲線終點).
③ European Community 유럽 공동체. European Coal and Steel Community (유럽 석탄 철강 공동체), European Economic Community (유럽 경제 공동체), European Atomic Energy Community (유럽 원자력 공동체) 세 기관의 통괄 조직으로 1967년 7월 1일 설립.

ECA Economic Commission for Africa 아프리카 경제 위원회. 국제 연합 경제 사회 이사회의 하부 조직. 1958년 설립. 본부 : 아디스아바바(에디오피아).

ECAC European Civil Aviation Conference 유럽 민간 항공회의.

ECAD electronic computer aided design 컴퓨터 원용 전자설계.

ECAFE Economic Commission for Asia and the Far East 아시

아 극동 경제 위원회. 국제 연합 경제 사회이사회의 하부 조직. 1947년 설립, 1974년 ESCAP으로 개칭.

ECAT Emergency Committee for American Trade 아메리카 무역 긴급 위원회. 1969년 결성.

ECB European Central Bank 유럽 중앙은행.

ECC ① end of circular curve (토목) 원곡선 종점.
② error correcting code (컴퓨터) 착오 교종 코드.
③ European Cultural Center 유럽 문화 센터. 본부 : 제네바.

ECCA [S] Empresa Consolidada Cubana de Aviacion 쿠바항공.

ECCM electronic counter countermeasure 대전자 무기 대책. ECM에 대항하는 수단.

ECCS emergency core cooling system (원자로) 긴급 노심(爐心) 냉각 장치. 원자로 안의 물이 감소하거나 파이프류가 파손되어 급속히 냉각수가 없어지게 되는 돌발 사고를 대비하여 설치한 긴급시의 안정 장치.

ECD economic cooperation among developing countries 발전 도상국간 경제 협력.

ECE Economic Commission for Europe 유럽 경제 위원회. 국제 연합 경제 사회 이사회의 하부 조직, 1947년 설립. 본부 : 제네바.

ECFI electronic controlled fuel injection 전자제어연료분사.

ECG ① electrocardiogram = EKG 심전도(心電圖).
② electrocardiograph 심전계 (心電計).

ECGD Export Credits Guarantee Department (英)수출 신용 보증국.

ECGF export credit guarantees facility 수출신용보증제도.

ECGI electronic controlled gasoline injection 전자제어가솔린분사.

ECIP Energy Conservation Investment Program 에너지 보존 투자 계획.

ECJ European Court of Justice 유럽 사법재판소.

ECL ① English Comprehension Level Test 미군 영어능력 측정시험.
② emitter coupled logic (컴퓨터) 이미터 결합형 논리(論理) 회로.

ECLAC Economic Commission for Latin America and Caribbean 라틴 아메리카·카리브 경제 위원회. 국제 연합 경제 사회 이사회의 하부 조직. 1948년 설립. 본부 : 샌디에이고.

ECLSS environmental control and life support system 환경제어 생명 유지 시스템.

ECM

ECM ① electrochemical machining 전기 화학적 연마.
② electronic countermeasure → ECCM 전자 무기 대책. 적의 레이더를 방해하거나 교란시키는 방법. 적의 탐지 기능을 저하시키는 대(對)레이더 방해 전파 발사 장치 외에 적레이더 특성을 분석하여 그릇된 정보를 주는 기능도 있음.
③ European Common Market → EEC 유럽 공동 시장.
④ external cardiac massage 체외(體外) 심장 마사지.

ECMA European Computer Manufacturers Association 유럽 컴퓨터 제조 공업회.

ECNR European Council of Nuclear Research 유럽 공동원자핵연구소.

ECO ① Economic Cooperation Organization 이란·파키스탄·터키 경제 협력 기구.
② electro-coupled oscillator 전자 결합 발진기.

ECOA Equal Credit Opportunity Act (美) 크레디트 차별 철폐법. 은행 융자나 크레디트 카드 발행 시에 남녀 차별을 금지하는 법률.

ECOCEN Economic cooperation Center 경제협력센터. ASPAC 의 기관.

ECOF eccentric core optical fiber 편심(偏心) 코어광(光) 섬유.

E-COM electronic computer originated mail (美) 컴퓨터 이용 속달우편 제도.

ECOP Economic Cooperation 대일(對日) 청구권자금 중 유상자금 (재정차관).

ECOR International Engineering committee on Oceanic Resources (미) 해양자원 국제공업위원회.

ECOSOC Economic and Social Council 경제 사회 이사회. ※ 국제 연합의 주요 기관의 하나, 경제·사회·문화·교육·보건 문제를 연구하고 총회에 보고 또는 권고함.

ECOWAS Economic Community of West African States = ECWAS 서아프리카 제국 경제 공동체. ※ 1975년 설립, 가맹국 16개국.

ECP Euro Commercial Paper 유로 기업어음.

ECPNL equivalent continuous perceived noise Level 등가(等價) 평균소음 레벨.

ECR ① electronic cash register 전자식 금전 등록기.
② electronic cyclotron resonance 전자 사이클로트론 공명(共鳴).
③ Export Control Regime 수출통제체제.

ECRH electron cyclotron resonance heating 전자 사이클

로트론 공명 가열(共鳴加熱).

ECS ① environmental control system 환경 제어 시스템.
② experimental communications satellite 실무용(用) 통신위성.

ECSC European Coal and Steel Community 유럽 석탄 철강 공동체. ※ 유럽에 석탄과 철강의 단일 시장을 설정하고 생산, 가격 경쟁, 노동 조건 등을 가맹국이 공동 관리하기 위한 목적에서 1952년 8월에 발족.

ECSOC Economic and Social Council 경제 사회 이사회.

ECSW extended channel status word (컴퓨터) 확장 채널 상태어(狀態語).

ECT ① eddy current test 와전류 탐상 검사(過電流探傷檢査).
② electro convulsive therapy 전기 충격 요법.
③ emission computed tomography 이미션 단층 촬영.
④ environment control table (컴퓨터) 환경 제어 테이블.

ECTL emitter coupled transistor logic (컴퓨터) 이미터 트랜지스터 논리 회로.

ECU ① electronic control unit 전자 제어 장치.
② English Church Union 영국 교회·동맹.
③ European Clearing Union 유럽 결제 동맹.
④ European Currency Unit 유럽 통화 단위. EUA(유럽 계산 단위)와 함께 EC(유럽 공동체) 통화의 바스켓 방식으로 되어 있으며 그 구성 비율은 각국의 경제력에 의해 정해져 있음.
⑤ European Currency Unit 유럽 통화 단위.

ECVT electronic controlled variable transmission 전자제어 무단(無段)변속기. * 자동차용으로 발진에서 고속까지 변속쇼크가 적으며 수동, 자동에 이은 제3의 변속기라고 불린다.

ECWA Economic Commission for Western Asia 서아시아 경제위원회. 1974년 설립. *본부 : 베이루트.

ECWAS Economic Community of West African States = ECOWAS 서아프리카 제국 경제 공동체.

ECZ equatorial convergence zone (氣象) 적도 수속대(赤道收束帶).

ED ① effective dose (약의) 유효량.
② Efficiency Decoration (英) 능률 훈장.
③ electronic dummy 전자 의장 인형.
④ elemental diet 성분 영양식.
⑤ environmental disruption 환경 파괴.
⑥ ex dividend 배당락.

149

⑦ export declaration 수출 신고.
⑧ extra duty 할증세.
⑨ [edition] 인쇄물의 판.
⑩ Electronic Deception 전자기만.

E/D card embarkation and disembarkation card 출입국카드.

EDA ① Economic Development Administration (美) (상무성) 경제 개발국.
② Education Development Association (英) 교육 진흥회.
③ ethylene diamine 에틸렌 디아민.

E-Day Entry Day 영국이 유럽 공동 시장에 가맹한 날, 즉 1973년 1월 1일.

EdB bachelor of education = BEd 교육학사.

EDB ethylene dibromide 2브롬화 에틸렌. 발암성의 우려가 있는 살충제, 가솔린 첨가물.

EDC ① electronic digital computer 계수형 컴퓨터.
② ethylene dichloride 이염화(二鹽化) 에틸렌.
③ European Defense Community 유럽 방위 공동체.

EDCF Economic Development Cooperation Fund 대외 경제 협력 기금. 우리나라가 대(對)개발 도상국 자본 협력을 통하여 개발 도상국의 경제 발전을 지원하는 동시에 개발도상국과의 경제 교류(交流)를 증진할 목적으로 설치한 기금. 1987년 7월 설치.

EdD doctor of education = DEd 교육학 박사.

EDD ① English Dialect Dictionary 영국 방언 사전(辭典). Joseph Wright가 혼자서 편집. 전6권, 1896-1905년 출판.
② expected date of delivery 분만 예정일.

EDDS Electronic Data Processing System 전자정보처리방식.

EDEK [그리스語] Eniea Demokratiki Enosi Kyprou (=Unified Democratic Union of Cyprus) (키프로스) 민주 중앙(中央) 연합.

EDF ① emergency decontamination facility 긴급 쟁화 시설(施設).
② Environmental Defense Fund (美) 환경 방위 단체.
③ European Development Fund 유럽 개발 기금.

EDI ① Electronic Data Interchange 전자 데이터 교환. 전표 등 서류에 의해 이루어지던 기업간 거래정보의 교환을 네트워크를 통해 전기통신을 이용하여 수행하는 데이터 유통 수단.
② Estimated Daily Intake 추정 일일섭취량.

EDL electric discharge laser 전

기 방전 레이저.

EdM master of education = MEd 교육학 석사.

EDM electric discharge machining 방전 가공.

EDMS Electronic Document Management System 전자 문서 관리 시스템.

EDNA ethylene dinitramine 에틸렌 디니트라민.

EDP ① electronic data processing (컴퓨터) 전자 데이터 처리(處理).
② executive leadership development program 경영 능력개발 프로그램.

EDPM electronic data processing machine (컴퓨터) 전자 데이터 처리 기계.

EDPS electronic data processing system (컴퓨터) 전자 데이터 처리 시스템. 모든 데이터를 컴퓨터에 입력시키면 다음은 사람의 손을 비릴지 않더라고 컴퓨터가 종합적으로 일을 처리하는 방식.

EDR European Depositary Receipt 유럽 예탁 증권.

EDRAW erasable direct read after write (컴퓨터) 소거(消去)·재기입형 기억장치.

EDRC Economic and Development Review Committee 경제개발 검토 위원회. OECD의 하부 기관.

EDRTS Experimental Data Relay Tracking Satellite 실험용 데이터중계·추적위성.

EDS ① English Dialect Society 영어 방언 학회.
② exchangeable disk store (컴퓨터) 교환 가능 디스크 장치 (裝置).
③ Exxon Donor Solvent Process 미국·일본·독일·이탈리아의 민간협력에 의한 Exxon 그룹 중심의 석탄 액화 계획.

EDSAC electronic delay storage automatic calculator 사상초(史上初)의 프로그램내 내장 계산기. 1949년에 케임브리지 대학의 Milkes가 중심이 되어 개발.

EDT ① Eastern Daylight Time (美) 동부 여름 시간.
② electrical discharge tube 방전관(放電管).
③ ethylene diamine tartarate 타르타르산 에틸렌 디아민.

EDTA ethylenc diamine tetra acetic acid 에틸렌 디아민 사(四)아세트산. 혈액 응고 저지제.

EDTV Extended Definition Television 화질 향상을 목표로 개발 진행 중인 텔레비전의 하나.

EDU European Democratic Union 유럽 민주 동맹.

EDVAC electronic discrete

variable automatic computer 프로그램 내부 기억 컴퓨터. 1951년 완성.

EDXS energy dispersive x-ray spectroscopy 에너지 분산형 x-선 분광법.

EE ① electric engineer 전기 기사.
② electronic engineer 전자 기사.
③ electronic eye (카메라) 자동 전자 노출 기구.
④ environmental engineering 환경 공학.

EEA European Economic Area 유럽 경제 지역.

EEC ① electronic engine control 자동차 엔진 전자 제어.
② electronic eye camera 자동 전자 노출 카메라.
③ European Economic Community 유럽 경제 공동체. 가맹국간의 지역 관세의 철폐, 무역확대, 지역내 사회보장제도와 노동조건의통일, 자본과 노동력이동의 자유화 등을 목적으로 1958년에 설립되었고 1973년에 EEC로 발족.

EECA European Electronic Component Manufacturers Association 유럽 전자 부품 제조자협회

EECO European Economic Cooperation Organization 유럽 경제 협력 기구.

EEG ① electroencephalogram 뇌파도(腦波圖).
② electroencephalograph 뇌파계(計).
③ electroencephalography 뇌파 기록법.

EEI Edison Electric Institute (美) 에디슨 전기 협회.

EENT eyes, ears, nose, throat 눈·귀·코·목구멍.

EEO equal employment opportunity 고용 기회 균등.

EEOC Equal Employment Opportunity Commission (美) 고용 기회 균등 위원회.

EEP Register of Experts / Eminent Persons 전문가 저명 인사 등록.

EEPROM electrically erasable, programmable read only memory → EPROM (컴퓨터) 전기적(電氣的) 소거(消去) 기입 가능한 읽기 전용 기억 장치.

EER energy efficiency ratio 에너지 효율화.

EERI Earthquake Engineering Research Institute 지진 공학 연구소.

EES European Economic Space 유럽 경제 영역.

EETS Early English Text Society (英) 초기 영어 텍스트 협회(協會).

EETU/PTU Electrical, Electronic,

Telecommunication Union/Plumbing Trades Union (英) 전기・전자・통신・배관 노조(勞組).

EEZ exclusive economic zone 전관 경제 수역(專管經濟水域).

EF elector fax 직접식(式) 정전 전사 방식(靜電轉寫方式) 복사기.

EFA ① European fighter aircraft 유럽 전투기. 영국・프랑스・독일이 공동 개발을 계획 중.
② Essential Fatty Acid 필수 지방산(必需脂肪酸).

EFAS electronic flash approach system (航空)섬광 등화 진입 방식.

EFC emergency fuel control (航空) 비상 연료 관제 장치.

EFCC Export Finance Corporation of Canada 캐나다 수출 금융 공사.

EFD electro fluid dynamics 전기 유체 역학.

EFE [S] Agencia EFE (=EFE Agency) 스페인 국영 통신.

EFF Extended Fund Facility (IMF) 확대 신용 공여 제도. 1974년 창설.

EFI ① electronic fuel injection 전자식 연료 분사.
② Economic Freedom Index 경제 자유 지수.

EFL ① effective focal length 유효 초점 거리.
② English as a foreign language 외국어로서의 영어.

EFO error, freak, oddity 우표 제조 과정에서 생긴 실수.

EFS electronic filing system 도면 및 문서를 image data로 읽어 광디스크에 등록, 문서를 검색, 편집, 출력하는 시스템이다.

EFT electronic funds transfer 전자식 자금 이동.

EFTA ① European Free Trade Area 유럽 자유 무역 지역.
② European Free Trade Association 유럽 자유 무역 연합. 영국・스웨덴・노르웨이・덴마크・스위스・오스트리아・포르투갈 등 7개국간에 1960년 5월에 결성되 자유 무역 지역. 핀란드는 준가맹국.

EFTPOS electronic funds transfer at point of sales 판매시 전자식 자금 이동.

EFTS electronic funds transfer system 전자식 자금 이행 결제 시스템. 기업 금융서비스인 펌뱅킹(firm banking), 가정 금융서비스인 홈뱅킹, 은행간 서비스인 인터뱅킹 등에 이용.

EFV equilibrium flash vaporization 평형 플래시 증발.

e.g. [L] exempli gratia (= for example) 예를 들면.

EG ethylene glycol콜.   폴리에스

테르 섬유의 원료(原料).

EGC enamelled glass costing 글라스질(質) 코팅.

EGD electro gas dynamics 전기유체 역학.

EGF epidermal growth factor 상피(上皮) 성장 인자.

EGI electronic gasoline injection (자동차) 전자 제어 가솔린 분사 방식.

EGL Electric Galvanizing Line 전기 아연 도금 라인. 강재(鋼材)의 표면에 피복처리를 하여 방청 기능을 강화하기 위한 생산설비.

EGO eccentric orbiting geophysical observatory 편심궤도(偏心軌道) 지구권 관측 위성.

EGR exhaust gas recirculation 배기 가스 재순환 장치.

EGT exhaust gas temperature 배기 가스 온도.

EHC electric hydraulic control system (原子力) 전기 유압식 제어 장치.

EHF extremely high frequency → VHF 초고주파(超高周波). 파장 1센티에서 1밀리까지.

EHL effective half life 유효 반감기(半減期).

EHM engine heavy maintenance 엔진의 각 부품의 정기검사.

EHP ① effective horsepower 유효 마력.
② equivalent horsepower 상당 마력.

EHV extra high voltage 최고전압.

EI ① emission index 배출지수. 배기 중의 대기오염성분의 질량(質量) 통도를 단위연료량에 대하여 나타낸 것.
② Engineering Index (미) 엔지니어링 · 인덱스. 데이터베이스 기술 문헌 색인.
③ exposure index 노출지수.
④ external information 외부정보. 컴퓨터 · 프로그램을 사용하기 위하여 사용자에게 제공된 자료에 기록되어 있는 정보.

EIA ① Electronic Industries Association (美) 전자 공업회.
② Energy Information Administration (美) (에너지성) 에너지 정보국.
③ environmental impact analysis 환경 영향 해석.

EIB ① European Investment Bank 유럽 투자 은행.
② Export-Import Bank 수출입 은행.

EIBK Export-Import Bank of Korea 한국 수출입 은행.

EICAS engine indication and crew alerting system 엔진 등의 감시경보장치.

EID electron impact desorption 전자 충격 이탈법.

EIES electronic information exchange system 전자 정보 교환 시스템.

EIL The Experiment in International Living 국제생활체험. 가정체재를 통하여 국제친선의 촉진을 도모하는 세계적인 조직.

EIS educational information system 교육 정보 시스템.

EITC earned income tax credit 근로 소득 세금 공제.

EIU Economic Intelligence Unit (영) 민간경제조사기관.

EJ electronic journalism 전파 저널리즘.

EJC Engineers Joint Council (美) 공학자 합동 위원회. 현재는 AAES로 개칭.

EKG [G] Electro Kadiogramm (=electrocardiogram) = ECG 심전도(心電圖).

EL ① electric locomotive 전기 기관차.
② electro luminescence 전계 발광(電界發光).
③ electronic learning 전자 학습.
④ export license 수출 승인.

ELD economic load dispatching 경제 부하 배분(經濟負荷配分).

ELDO European Launcher Development Organization 유럽 로켓 개발 기관.

ELF ① Eritrean Liberation Front 에리트레아 해방 전선.
② extremely low frequency 극저주파(極低周波).
③ Equity Linked Fund 주가지수 연계펀드.

ELINT Electronic Intelligence (美) 군사 통신 탐지 위성. 전파의 강약·방향·파장(波長) 등을 조사하여 경계 레이더의 전파인지 미사일에 직결된 전파인지 등을 판독하거나 통신 정보라 불리는 통신 내용을 포착하기도 함.

ELR emergency locking retractor (자동차) 긴급 로크식(式) 감는 장치. 평상시에는 느슨하게 하고 긴급시에는 시트 벨트를 꼭 죄는 장치.

ELS Equity Linked Securities 주가 연계 증권.

ELSEC electronic security (컴퓨터) 전자 보전(電子保全). 정보가 새지 않도록 보호하기.

ELSS extravehicular life support system 우주선외(外) 생명유지 장치.

ELT ① emergency landing transmitter (航空) 불시착 발신장치.
② English language teaching 영어 교육.

ELV expendable launch vehicle 소모형(型) 발사 로켓.

EM ① electronic mail 전자 우편.

② electron microscope 전자 현미경.
③ end of medium character (컴퓨터) 매체 종단 문자.
④ enlisted man 하사관.
⑤ effective micro - organism 유효 미생물군 : 광합성 세균 효모균, 유산균, 누룩균등 호기성 형기성 미생물들의 복합체.

EMA European Monetary Agreement 유럽 통화 협정.

E-mail electronic mail 전자우편. 컴퓨터와 컴퓨터, 개인과 개인들 간의 전자 편지나 메시지를 전달하는 하나의 방법.

EMC ① electromagnetic compatibility 전자 환경 정합성(電磁環境整合性).
② encephalo myocarditis 뇌심근염(腦心筋炎).
③ [F] Entreprise Miniere et Chimiqe (= Mineral and Chemistry Enterprise) (프랑스) 국영 광업 회사.

emcee MC 사회자. master of ceremonies의 약자.

EMCF European Monetary Cooperation Fund 유럽 통화 협력 기금.

EMDI Estimated Maximum Daily Intake 추정일일최대섭취량.

EMF ① electromagnetic flowmeter (原子力) 전자 유량계(電磁流量計).
② electro motive force 기전력(起電力).
③ European Monetary Fund 유럽 통화 기금.

EMG ① electro myogram 근전도(筋電圖).
② electro myograph 근전 기록장치.

EMGP ethyl methyl glycol phthalate 프탈산(酸) 에틸메틸글리콜. 가소제(可塑劑).

EMI ① electromagnetic interference 전자(電磁) 방해. 전자 기기가 다른 기기를 방해하는 잡음.
② Economic Misery Index 경제고통지수.
③ Efficiency of Management 경영효율지표.
④ European Monetary Institute 유럽통화기구.

EMIF emerging markets investment funds 도상국 시장 기금.

EMIP equivalent mean investment period 등가평균 회수기간.

EMIS ① electronic marketing and information system 특정한 이용자끼리 상품의 매매정보를 교류시켜 조건을 의논하여 거래를 성립시키는 시스템. 소위전자거래소.
② electronic materials information service 전자재료 정보서비스. 기본적인 전자재료의 성질(性質) 데이터와 공급정

보를 모은 온라인정보 서비스.

EMK ① emergency medical kit 긴급용 의약품 키트.
② ethyl-methyl ketone 에틸 메틸 케튼.

EML electromagnetic launcher 전자(電磁) 사출 장치.

EMM Economic Ministers Meeting (ASEM) 경제장관회의.

E-MOS enhancement MOS → MOS (컴퓨터) 엔핸스먼트형(型) MOS.

EMP ① electromagnetic pulse 전자(電磁) 펄스.
② electromagnetic pump 전자(電磁) 펌프.

EMR educable mentally retarded 교육이 가능한 지진아.

EMS ① engine modification system 엔진 개량 방식.
② European Monetary System 유럽 통화 제도. EC(유럽공동체) 역내 통화의 변동폭에 한도를 정한 고정 환율 제도로 통화 안정을 위해 1979년 3월 13일 발족.
③ Extended Memory Specification EMS 메모리. 퍼스널 컴퓨터의 OS의 일종인 MS-DOS는 용량이 640 킬로바이트까지의 램(RAM : Random Access Memory)만을 취급하므로 그 대책으로서 확장 메모리를 응용 소프트의 데이터 영역을 위해 확보하는 메모리가 EMS 메모리.

EMT emergency medical technician 긴급 의료 기사.

EMU ① electromagnetic unit 전자 단위(電磁單位).
② European Monetary Unit 유럽 통화 단위.
③ extravehicular mobility unit 우주선외(宇宙船外) 활동용 우주복.

EMV expected monetary value 기대 화폐치(期待貨幣値).

ENA Ethiopian News Agency 에티오피아 통신.

END European Nuclear Disarmament 유럽 핵군축 운동.

ENDC Eighteen-Nation Disarmament Committee (國聯) 18개국 군축 위원회. 1961년 설립. 1969년 참가국 증가에 따라 CCD로 개칭.

ENDF evaluated nuclear data file 평가필 핵 데이터 파일.

ENDOR electron nuclear double resonance 전자핵 이중 공명(電子核二重共鳴).

ENEA European Nuclear Energy Agency 유럽원자력기관.

ENEL [I] Ente Nazionale per Elettrica l'Energia (=National Corporation of Electric Energy) (이탈리아) 전력 공사.

157

ENG ① electronic news gathering 소형 포터블 VTR과 텔레비전 카메라를 사용한 뉴스 취재.
② England, English 영국의

EngD doctor of engineering = DE, DIng, DEng 공학박사.

ENI [I] Ente Nazionale Idrocarburi (=Natinal Corporation of Hydrocarbon) (이탈리아)탄화 수소 공사.

ENIAC electronic numerical integrator and calcula-for 진공관을 사용한 세계 최초의 전자계산기. 미국 펜실베이니아 대학의 J.P. Eckert, J.W. Mauchly 등이 1946년에 완성(完成).

ENL English as a native language 모국어로서의 영어.

ENMOD Environmental Modification (美) 환경 파괴 무기 금지 조례.

ENPLA engineering plastic 엔지니어링 플라스틱. 소위 플라스틱과 다른 점은 비약적으로 내열성이 높다. 또 강성(剛性)이 높고 취약하지 않으며 전기절연성이 있다.

ENG enquiry character (컴퓨터) 문의용 문자.

ENRC Energy and Natural Resources Committee 에너지 천연 자원 위원회.

ENS European Nuclear Society 유럽 원자력 학회.

ENSA Entertainment National Service Association 영국군 위안 봉사회.

ENT ears, nose, throat 이비인후(과).

EO ① elected office 선택 관청.
② ethylene oxide 산화(酸化) 에틸렌.
③ [L] ex officio (=from office) 직권상의

E.O.B. Executive office Building 미국의 행정부빌딩. 화이트하우스의 별관.

e.o.d. every other day 격일.

EOD ① end of data (컴퓨터) 데이터 끝.
② explosive ordnance disposal 폭발물 처리.

EOE end of extent (컴퓨터) 익스텐트 끝.

EOF end of file (컴퓨터) 파일 끝.

EOG ethylenc oxide glycol 에틸렌 옥시드 글리콜.

EOI economic order interval 최적 발주간격. 발주와 발주사이의 가장 경제적인 간격.

EOKA [그리스어語] Ethniki Organosis Hypriakou Agonos (=National Organization of Cypriot Combatants) (키프로스) 그리스계 주민 투쟁 조직.

EOL end of life (原子力) 수명 말기.

e.o.m. end of month 월말.

EONR European Organization for Nuclear Research 유럽합동원자핵연구기관.

EOP Executive Office of the President (미) 대통령부.

EOQ economic order quantity 경제적 발주량.

EOR explosive ordnance reconnaissance 폭발물 수색.

EORSAT electronic intelligence ocean reconnaissance satellite 전자 정보 해양 정찰 위성.

EOS electronic ordering system 컴퓨터에 의한 발주 처리 시스템.

EOT ① end of tape (컴퓨터) 테이프 끝.
② end of transmission (컴퓨터) 전송 종료(傳送終了).

EOV end of volume (컴퓨터) 볼륨 끝.

EOY end of year 년(도)말.

EP ① elliptically polarized light 타원 편광(楕圓偏光).
② European Plan 호텔 요금에 식사를 포함하지 않는 제도.
③ extended playing 1분간 45회전 레코드.

EPA ① Educational Paperback Association (美) 교육 페이퍼백 협회.
② eicosapentaenoic acid 아이코사펜타엔산(酸).
③ Environmental Protection Agency (美) 환경 보호국.

EPB Economic Planning Board 경제 기획원. 국민 경제의 종합적 개발 계획 수립과 발전, 국내외 경제 협력을 담당하는 국무총리 소속하의 중앙 행정 기관.

EPBX electronic private branch exchange 전자식 구내 교환기.

EPC ① Economic Policy Committee 경제 정책 위원회. OECD위원회의 하나.
② ethylene propylene copolymer 에틸렌 프로필렌 공중 합체(共重合體).
③ European Patent Convention 유럽 특허 조약.
④ European Political Community 유럽 정치 공동체.

EPCM engineering, procurement, construction, maintenance 설계 · 조달 · 건설 · 보전.

EPCOT Experimental Prototype Community of Tomorrow 실험 미래 도시. 미국의 Walt Disney Productions의 1982년에 Florida 주(州) 에 만든 컴퓨터화(化) 유원지.

EPD excess profits duty 초과 이득세.

EPDM ① Ethiopian People's Democratic Movement 에티오피아 인민 민주 운동.
② ethylene propylene diene methylenc rubber 에틸렌 프로

159

필렌 공중합체(共重合體) 고무.

EPI ① Economic Policy Institute 미 경제정책연구소.
③ Earth Policy Institute 미 지구 정책연구소.

EPIE Educational Products Information Exchange Institute (美) 교육용 상품 정보 교환 협회.

EPL excess profits levy → EPT (英) 초과 이득세.

EPLF Eritrean People's Liberation Front (에디오피아) 에리트레아 인민 해방 전선.

EPLI Employee Practice Liability Insurance 종업원 실무 책임 보험.

EPMA electron probe micro analysis 전자 프로브 미량 분석. 물질에 전자선을 쬐어 원자를 들뜨게 하여 발생하는 특성 X선을 분석함으로써 물질의 정량 원소 분석을 행하는 방법.

EPN ethyl para nitrophenyl 유기 인제(有機燐制). 살충제의 일종.

EPNdB effective perceived noise decibels (航空) 실효 감각 소음 데시벨.

EPNL effective perceived noise level (航空) 감각 소음 효과 레벨.

EPNS electro plated nickel silver 전기 도금 양은.

EPO ① emergency power off (컴퓨터) 긴급 전원 절단.
② erythropoietin 에리트로포이에틴. 신장에서 만들어지는 당단백질 중혈 호르몬.
③ European Patent Office 유럽 특허청.

EPPI expected profit with perfect information 완벽 정보에 의한 기대 이익.

EPR ① ecological planning region 생태 지역 계획.
② electron para magnetic resonance 전자 상자성 공명 (電子常磁性공명).
③ engine pressure ratio 발동기 압력비(比).
④ ethylene-propylene rubber 에틸렌 프로필렌 고무.
⑤ extended power relay 외부 전원 계전기.

EPRI Electric Power Research Institute (美) 전력 연구소.

EPROM erasable and programmable read-only memory → EEPROM (컴퓨터) 자외선으로 소거(消去)하고 새로이 프로그램 가능한 읽기 전용 기억 장치.

EPS ① electrical power system (電子工學) 전력 시스템.
② electronic post service 전자 통신 서비스.
③ Emergency Procurement Service (美) 군수품 독점 매입 기관.
④ expanded polystyrene 확장

폴리스티렌.

EPT ① early pregnancy test 조기 임신 테스트.
② excess profits tax → EPL 초과 이득세.

EPTA Expanded Program of Technical Assistance (국연) 확대 기술 원조 계획.

EPU European Payments Union 유럽 결제 동맹.

EPWR emergency power 비상 지휘권.

EPZ export processing zone 수출 촉진 특별 지구.

EQ ① educational quotient 교육 지수.
② encephalization quotient 체중과 뇌중량과의 관계 지수.
③ environmental guality 환경의 질.
④ Emotional Quotient 감성지수.

EQUAPAC Equatorial Pacific 적도 부근 태평양 국제 공동(共同) 관측.

Er erbium (化學) 에르븀. 원자번호 68.

ER ① earned run (野球) 투수의 자책점.
② electronic reconnaissance 전자 정찰.
③ [L] Elizabetha Regins (= Queen Elizabeth) 엘리자베스 여왕.

④ emergency room 응급 치료실.
⑤ enhanced radiation 방사능 강화.
⑥ Expected Returns 기대수익률.

ERA ① earned run average (野球) 투수의 방어율.
② Economic Regulatory Administration (美) 경제 규제국.
③ electron ring accelerator 전자 링 가속기.
④ Equal Rights Amendment (美) 남녀 평등 헌법 수정 조항. 1972년 연방 의회가 수정을 승인했으나 성립에 필요한 4분의 3주(州)의 비준을 얻지 못하여 성립되지 못함.

ERAM extend range antitank mine 원거리 대전차 지뢰.

ERB enhanced radiation bomb = ER/RB, ERW 방사능 강화 폭탄. 통칭 중성자 폭탄

ERC Energy Resources Council (美) 에너지 자원 심의회.

ERCS Emergency Rocket Communication System (美) 긴급 로켓 통신 시스템.

ERD Emergency Reserve Decoration (英) 긴급(緊急) 예비군 훈장.

ERDA Energy Research and Development Administration → AEC (美) 에너지 연구 개발국. 1977년 Department of Energy 에 통합.

ERG electro retinogram 망막 전위도(網膜電位圖).

ERIC Educational Resources Information Center (美) 교육자원 정보 센터.

ERIS exoatmospheric reentry vehicle interceptor system 대기권외(外) 재돌입체 요격 시스템.

ERISA Employee Retirement Income Security Act (美) 퇴직자 수입 보증법.

ERM Exchange Rate Mechanism 유럽통화제도의 환율구조.

EROA Economic Rehabilitation Account for Occupation Area → GARIOA 점령 지역 경제 부흥 원조비.

EROPA Eastern Regional Organization on Public Administration 극동 지역 공공 행정 기구.

EROS earth resources observation satellite 지구 자원 관측 위성.

ERP ① error recovery procedures (컴퓨터) 에러 회복(回復) 순서.
② European Recovery Program (美) 유럽 부흥(復興) 계획 (1948~51). 통칭 Marshall Plan.

ER/RB enhanced radiation/reduced blast bomb = ER, ERW 중성자 폭탄.

ERS ① earth resources satellite 지구 자원 위성.
② Economic Research Service (美) (농무성) 경제 조사국.
③ emergency radio service 긴급 무선.

ERTA Economic Recovery Tax Act (美) 경제 재건 세법.

ERTS ① earth resources technology satellite 지구 자원 탐사 위성. LANDSAT의 구칭.
② European Rapid Train System 유럽 쾌속 열차 조직.

ERW enhanced radiation weapon = ER, ER/RB 방사능 강화 무기. 중성자 폭탄의 정식 명칭.

Es einsteinium (化學) 아인시타이늄. 원자번호 99. (우라늄 원소의 하나)

ES electron synchrotron 전자(電子) 싱크로트론.

ESA ① easy and speedy accounting 전표만으로 회계를 처리하는 방식.
② Employment Standards Administration (美) (노동성) 노동 기준국.
③ European Space Agency 유럽 우주 기관.

ESAF Enhanced Structural Adjustment Facilities 확대구조 조정 기관.

ESANET European Space Agency Network 유럽 우주기구

네크워트.

ESB electrical stimulation of the brain 뇌전기 자극.

ESC ① Economic and Social Council (국연) 경제 사회 이사회(理事會).
② escape character (컴퓨터) 확장 문자.
③ European Security Conference 유럽 안전 보장 회의. 구소련 주최.
④ European Space Conference 유럽 우주 회의.

ESCA electron spectroscopy for chemical analysis 광전자 분광법(光電子分光法).

ESCAP Economic and Social Commission for Asia and the Pacific 아시아·태평양 경제 사회 위원회. 국제 연구함의 지역 경제 위원회의 하나. 1947년 설립. 본부 : 방콕. 구칭 ECAFE.

ESCB European System of Central Banks 유럽 중앙 은행 제도.

ESD extra super duralumin 초초(超超)두랄루민.

ESF erythropoietin stimulating factor 적혈구 생성 촉진 자극 요인.

ESI ① Economic Strategy Institute 미 경제전략연구소.
② Environmental Sustainability Index 환경지속지수.

ESL English as a second language 제2 언어로서의 영어.

ESM electronic support measure 적의 통신방식이나 레이더주파수 등의 전자정보의 수집활동.

ESN ① educationally subnormal 교육적으로 표준 이하의.
② Enterprise Science News (美) 의학·과학 통신사.

ESO electrical spinal orthosis 전기 척추 교정.

ESOC European Space Operation Center 유럽 위성 운영 센터 유럽 우주 기관(ESA)에서 발사하는 위성의 운영 관리 센터.

ESOL English for the speakers of other languages 다른 언어를 쓰는 사람을 위한 영어.

ESOP Employees Stock Ownership Plan (美) 종업원 주식 소유계획.

ESP ① English for Specific Purposes 특수 목적을 위한 영어(英語).
② extrasensory perception 초감각적 지각.

ESPN Entertainment and Sports Programming Network (美) 오락 스포츠 텔레비전 방송망.

ESPRIT European Strategic Program for Research and Development in Information Technology 유럽 정보 기술 연

ESPT

구 개발 전략 계획.

ESPT English Speaking Proficiency Test 영어능력 평가 시험.

Esq. Esquire 편지 등에 쓰는 남성의 경칭.

ESR ① electron spin resonance 전자 스핀 공명(共鳴).
② erythrocytes sedimentation rate 적혈구 침강 속도.

ESRANGE European Sounding Rocket Launching Range 유럽 관측 로켓 발사장.

ESRIN European Space Research Institute 유럽 우주(宇宙) 연구소.

ESRO European Space Research Organization 유럽 우주 연구 기구.

ESS ① electronic switching system 전자 교환 시스템.
② English speaking society 영어 회화 클럽.

ESSA ① Environmental Science Services Administration (美) 환경 과학 업무국. NOTT의 구칭.
② Environmental Survey Satellite 미국 환경 과학 업무국이 발사한 기상 위성.

EST ① Eastern Standard Time (美) 동부 표준시.
② electro shock therapy(or treatment) 전기 쇼크 요법.

③ Erhardt Seminar Training 에르하르트식(式) 세미나 훈련 (訓練).

ESTA Electronic System for T ravel Authorization 전자 여행 허가제 http://esta.cbp.dhs.gov

ESU electrostatic unit 정전(靜電) 단위.

ESV ① earth satellite vehicle 지구 궤도 위성.
② experimental safety vehicle (美) 실험 안전차. 현재 RSV 로 개칭.

ESWL extracorporeal shock wave lithotripte (의학) 체외 충격파에 의한 신장 결석 분쇄기.

ET ① effective temperature 유효 온도.
② elapsed time 경과 시간.
③ Employment and Training Administration (美) (노동성) 고용 훈련국.
④ engineering test 기술 시험.
⑤ enhanced telecommunication 고도 통신.
⑥ external tank (宇宙) 외부 연료 탱크.
⑦ extra terrestrial 지구외 생물, 우주인. 1982년 개봉. Steven Spielberg 감독의 미국 영화의 주인공.

ETA ① estimated time of arrival 도착 예정 시각.
② ethanoltoluene azeotrope 에

타놀틀루엔계(系) 공비 혼합물 (共沸混合物).

ETACCS European Theater Air Command and Control Study 유럽 전역(戰域) 항공 지휘 관제 연구.

ETAP Expanded Technical Assistance Program (국연) 확대 기술 원조 계획.

ETAT English Translation Approval Test 영어번역 자격시험.

ETB end of transmission block character (컴퓨터) 전송(傳送) 블록 종결 문자.

etc. [L] ET CETRA (=and so forth) 등등.

ETC ① European Travel Commission 유럽 여행 위원회. ② export trading company 수출 무역 회사.

ETD estimated time of departure 출발 예정 시각.

ETF ① Enhanced Tactical Fighter 고성능 전술전투기. ② Exchange Traded Fund 상장지수펀드.

ETI European Transuranium Institute (독일) 유럽 초(超)우라늄 원소 연구소.

ETNF Euro-Theater Nuclear Forces 유럽 전역(戰域) 핵(核)전력.

ETO European Theater of Operations 유럽 작전 지역. 제2차 세계 대전 당시의 용어.

ETR engineering test reactor 공학 시험 원자로.

ETRI Electronic & Telecommunication research Institute (한) 전자 통신 연구소.

ETS ① Educational Testing Service → NET (美) 교육 테스트 기구.
② engineering test satellite 기술 시험 위성.
③ estimated time of separation 군속 제대 예정일.

ETT English Teaching of Theatre separation (英) 영어 교육 극단(劇團).

ETU Electrical trades Union (英) 전기 노동자 조합.

ETUC European Trade Union Confederation 유럽 노동 조합 연합.

ETV educational television 교육 텔레비전.

ETX end of text character (컴퓨터) 텍스트 종결 문자.

Eu europium (化學) 유로퓸. 원자번호 63.

EU ① enriched uranium 농축 우라늄.
② Evangelical Union 복음주의 연맹.

③ Europe Union 유럽연합.
EUA European Unit of Account 유럽 계산 단위.

EUL end user language (컴퓨터) 최종 사용자 언어.

EUNC Eritrean United National Council 에리트레아 통일 민족 평의회.

EURAIL PASS European Railway Pass 유럽횡단국제 특급 열차전선(全線)에 승차할 수 있는 패스.

EURATOM European Atomic Energy Community → EAEC 유럽 원자력 공동체.

EURCO European composite unit 유럽 복합 단위. 1973년에 유럽 투자 은행이 발행한 유로채(債).

EUREKA European Research Coordinating Agency 유럽 첨단 기술 공동 연구 기구. 미국의 전략 방위 계획에 도전하여 유럽 스타워즈 기술 개발을 위한 프랑스의 계획.

EURIT European Investment Trust 유럽 투자 신탁 기관.

EUROCEAN European Oceanographic Association 유럽 해양 학회.

EUROCHEMIC European Company for the Chemical Reprocessing of Irradiated Fuels 유럽 핵연료 재처리회사. OECD·NEA의 기관.

EURONET European Information Network EC제국을 연결하는 정보망.

EUROSAT European Satellite Corporation 유럽 통신 위성회사. 1972년 발족. 본사 : 제네바.

EUROSPACE Committee for European Space Research 유럽 우주 산업 연합회. 1961년 발족.

EUROTRA European Translation 유럽 다언어간(多言語間) 컴퓨터 번역.

Eurovision European Television 유럽 국제 텔레비전 교환 방송.

EUSA Eighth U.S. Army 美八軍

EUT equivalent unijunction transistor 등가 단접합(等價單接合) 트랜지스터.

EUV extreme ultraviolet rays 극(極) 자외선.

eV electron volt 전자 볼트.

EV ① electric vehicle 전기 자동차. ② evaporator (原子力) 증발기. ③ expected value 기대값. ④ exposure value (사진) 노광지수.

EVA ① ethylene vinylacetate copolymers 에틸렌 아세트산 비닐 공중합체.
② extravehicular activity 우주선의 활동.
③ Economic Value Added 경제적 부가가치.

EVCS extravehicular communications system 우주선 외 통신장치.

EVOP evolutionary operation 진화 운전.

EVP executive vice president 전무.

EVPI expected value of perfect information 완전 정보의 기대값.

EVR ① electronic video recorder 전자식 녹화 재생기. ② electronic video recording 전자식 녹화 재생.

EW ① electronic warfare 전자전(電子戰). ② enlisted woman (or women) 여자 하사관.

EWC electric water cooler 전기 냉수기.

EWO Essential Work Order (英) 주요 관무령(管務令).

EWR early warning radar 조기 경보 레이더.

EWS ① engineering work station 고도화(高度化)한 CAD/CAM 시스템. ② Emergency Warning System 긴급경보방송.

EWSM electronic warfare support measures 전자전(戰) 지원 대책.

exam examination 시험.

EXC external character code specification (컴퓨터) 외자 부호 지정.

EXEC executive control program (컴퓨터) 전체를 제어하는 주(主) 프로그램.

EXIM Export Import 수출입.

EXIMBANK Export Import Bank 수출입 은행(銀行).

EXPO exposition 박람회.

EXPRESS Experimental Press Information Processing System 실험용 신문 정보 처리 시스템.

ext. extension 내선 번호(內線番號).

EXW exercise walking 보행운동. 건강증진 및 지구력을 높이는 것을 목적으로 하는 보행운동.

EYP Electronic Yellow Pages (美) 전자식 직업 전화부.

e-zine electronic magazine 전자 잡지. 인터넷상에서 읽을 수 있도록 전자 형태로 구성된 잡지.

f. ① female 여자.
② feminine 여자의.

F ① Fahrenheit (溫度) 화씨.
② fluorine (化學) 플루오르. 원자번호 9.
③ focal length (카메라)초점 거리.

F-86 Fighter-86 = F-86 戰鬪機

FA ① factory automation 공장 자동화.
② fielding average (野球)수비율.
③ focus aid (카메라) 초점 조정 보조 기구.
④ Football Association (英) 축구 협회.
⑤ foreign exchange allocation 수입 외화 자금 할당.
⑥ Front Aviation (구소련) 전선 (前線) 공군.

f.a. free alongside 선측인도(船側引渡).

FAA ① Federal Aviation Aministration (美) (운수성) 연방항공국.
② Fellow of the Australian Academy of Science 오스트레일리아 학사원 특별 회원.
③ Fleet Air Army → RNAF (英) 해군 항공대.
④ free of all average (해상 보험) 전손 부담(全損負擔).

FAAAS ① Fellow of the American Academy of Arts and Sciences 미국 학사원 특별 회원.
② Fellow the American Association for the Advancement of Science 미국 과학진흥협회 특별 회원.

FAADS Forward Area Air Defense System (美) 전선 방공시스템. 전장의 전차와 병사를 공습에서 지키기 위한 미 육군 조직.

FAB ① fast attack boat 고속 공격정.
② first aid box 구급 상자.

FABMDS field army ballistic missile defense system 야전군 탄도 미사일 방어용 미사일.

FAC forward air controller 전방 정찰기.

FACCA Fellow of the Association of Certified and Corporate Accountants (英) 공인 법인 경리사협회 특별 회원.

FACP Fellow of the American College of Physicians 미국 내과 의사회 특별 회원.

FACS ① Fellow of the American

College of Surgeons 미국 외과 의사회 특별 회원.
② fluorescent - activated cell sorter 형광 이용 세포 분리 장치(裝置)

FAD flavin adenine denucleotide 플라빈 효소군의 보(補) 효소의 하나.

F. & D. freight and demurrage 운임체선료(滯船料).

FAE fuel air explosive 기화(氣化) 폭탄.

FAGS Fellow of the American Geographical Society 미국 지리학회 특별 회원.

FAI ① [F] Federation Aeronautique Internationale (=International Aeronautic Federation) 국제 항공 연맹.
② Italian Assistance Fund for Emergency Aid Department of Cooperation for Development 이탈리아 긴급 개발 협력 원조 기금.

FAIA ① Fellow of the American Institute of Architects 미국 건축가협회 특별 회원.
② Fellow of the Association of International Accountants (英) 국제 회계사협회 특별 회원.

FAIAA Fellow of the American Institute of Aeronautics and Astronautics 미국 항공 우주 공학 연맹 특별 회원.

FAKR freight all kinds rate 품목 무차별 운임.

FALN [S] Fuerzas Armadas de Liberacion Nacional (=Armed Forces of National Liberation) 푸에르토리코 국민해방군.

FAM ① foreign air mail 외국 항공 우편.
② frequency modulation amplitude modulation 하나의 방송 전파에 FM과 AM을 동시에 방송하는 방식.

FAME forecasts and appraisals for management evaluation 경영 평가 예측 사정 시스템.

FAMS Forecasting and Modeling System 예측 모델 작성 시스템.

FANY First Aid Nursing Yeomanry (英) 응급 간호사 부대.

FAO Food and Agriculture Organization (國聯) 식량 농업 기구(機構).

FANUC Foreign Affairs and National Unification Committee (한) (국회의) 외무통일위원회.

FAPIG First Atomic Power Industry Group (일) 제1원자력 산업그룹.

FAQ ① fair average quality 중등품.
② free alongside quay 부두 인도 가격.
③ frequently asked question 빈번하게 묻는 질문.

169

FAR ① Federal Aviation Regulations (美) 연방 항공 규칙.
② Federation of Arab Republics 아랍 공화국 연합.

FARC [S] Fuerzas Armadas Revolucionarias Colombianas (=Armed Forces of Colombian Revolution) 콜롬비아 혁명군(革命軍).

FARN [S] Fuerzas Armadas de Resistencia Nacional (=Armed Forces of National Resistance) (엘살바도르) 민족저항군.

FAS ① Federation of American Scientists 미국 과학자 연맹 (聯盟).
② fetal alcohol syndrome 태아성 알코올 증후군.
③ fixed airlock shroud (우주 스테이션) 고정 에어로크 슈라우드.
④ flexible assembly system (컴퓨터) 플렉시블 조립 시스템. 소량 다품종의 생산에 적합한 융통성 있는 자동 조립 시스템.
⑤ Foreign Agricultural Service (美) (농무성) 대외 농업국(局).
⑥ free alongside (the) ship 선측(船側) 인도 가격.
⑦ factory automation system 공장 자동화 시스템.

FASB Financial Accounting Standards Board (美) 재무 회계 기준 심의회.

FASCAM family of scatterable mines (美) (육군) 항공기를 이용하여 살포, 부설하는 지뢰.

FASCOM field army support command 야전군 지원 사령부.

FASE fundamentally analyzable simplified English (컴퓨터) (데이터 처리를 위한) 간이 영어.

FAX facsimile 팩시밀리.

FB ① feed back 피드 백.
② fullback (스포츠) 풀백.
③ Fighter Bomber 전폭기.
④ Floating Bridge 부교.
⑤ Forward Boundary 전방 전투지경선.

FBA Fellow of the British Academy 영국학사원 특별 회원.

FBC ① feed back carburetor control (자동차) 피드백·카뷰레터 제어장치.
② fluidized bed combustor 유동층 연소보일러.
③ fluidized-bed combustion 유동층 연소.

FBCS Fellow of the British Computer Society 영국 컴퓨터 학회 특별 회원.

FBE foreign bill of exchange 외국환 어음.

FBI ① Federal Bureau of Investigation (美) 연방 수사국. 1909년 미법무성내에 검찰국이 설치되었다가 1935년 FBI로 개

칭. 여러 주(州)에 걸친 범죄의 수사와 공안 정보의 수집을 임무로 하며 직접 범죄 수사를 담당하는 요원을 G맨(Government man)이라고 함.
② Federation of British Industries 영국 산업 연합회. 현재는 CBI(Confederation of British Industry)로 개칭.

FBIM Fellow of the British Institute of Management 영국 경영학회 특별 회원.

FBM fleet ballistic missile 함대 탄도 미사일.

FBR fast breeder reactor 고속 증식 원자로.

FBS ① fasting blood sugar 공복시 혈당(血糖).
② forward base system 전진 기지 시스템.

FBY Future Budget Year 내년도 예산.

f.c. fielder's choice (野球) 야수 선택.

FC ① fine ceramics 파인 세라믹스.
② forward center (배구) 포워드 센터.
③ franchise chain 프랜차이즈 체인. 상품을 제조·판매하는 메이커 또는 판매업자가 프랜차이저(franchiser : 체인 본부)가 되어 독립 소매점을 프랜차이지(franchisee : 가맹점)로 하여 소매 영업을 하는 형태.

FCA ① Farm Credit Administration (美)농업 금융국.
② fast critical assembly (原子力) 고속 증식로 입해 실험 장치(裝置).
③ Fellow of the Institute of Chartered Accountants (英) 공인 회계사협회 특별 회원.
④ Foreign Currency Authorization 외화(外貨)승인.

FCAP facsimile signal conversion and procedure control equipment 팩시밀리 신호 변환 제어 장치.

FCB file control block (컴퓨터) 파일 제어 블록.

FCBP foreign currency bills payable 외화 지불 어음.

FCC ① Federal Communications Commission (美) 연방 통신 위원회.
② fleet command center 함대 지휘 센터.
③ fluid catalytic cracking 유동식 접촉 분해.
④ Federal Communication Commission 미연방통신위원회.

FCCA Fellow of the Association of Certified Accountants (英) 공인 회계사협회 특별 회원.

FCFS first come, first served 빠른 자가 승리.

FCI ① flux change per inch (컴퓨

터) 1인치당 자속(磁束) 변화 (變化).
② fuel coolant interaction (原子力) 연료 냉각재(材) 상호작용.

FCIA Foreign Credit Insurance Association (美) 외국 신용보험 협회.

FCIC Federal Crop Insurance Corporation (美) (농무성) 연방 농산물 보험 공사.

FCM Futures Commission Merchant 선물중개회사.

FCN Treaty Friendship, Commerce and Navigation Treaty 우호통상 항해조약.

FCO Foreign and Commonwealth Office (英) 외무 연방성.

FCP female chauvinist pig (美俗) 여성 우월론자.

FCP Forward Command Post 전방 지휘소.

FCS ① Fellow of the Chemical Society (英) 화학회 특별 회원(會員).
② fire control system 화기 관제 장치.
③ flight control system 비행 조종 컴퓨터 시스템.
④ Future Combat System 미래형 전투체제.

FCT function cost table 기능 코스트 테이블.

FCU fuel control unit 연료 관제 장치.

FD ① [L] Fidei Defensor (=Defender of the Faith) = DF (英) 신앙의 옹호자. 영국 왕에 대한 칭호.
② floor director (방송) 조연출.
③ floppy disk (컴퓨터) 플로피 디스크.
④ freezed dry 순간 동결(凍結) 건조.
⑤ full duplex 전이중 통신 방식 (全二重通信方式).
⑥ Forceps Delivery 겸자분만 (인공분만).

F.D. Fire Department 소방서.

FDA Food and Drug Administration (美) (보건 복지성) 식품의약품국.

FDC ① floppy disk controller 플로피 디스크 제어 장치.
② food distribution center (美) 식품 유통 센터.
③ Fire Direction Center 사격 지휘소.

FDD floppy disk (driving) device (컴퓨터) 플로피 디스크를 구동시키는 장치.

FDDI fiber distributed data interface 광섬유분산 데이터 인터페이스 100M비트/초의 링형 LAN의 명칭.

FDDP floppy disk drive processor 플로피 디스크 드라이브 프로세서.

FDF flight data file 비행 데이터 파일.

FDGB Ferier Deutscher Gewerks Band 자유 독일 노동 연맹.

FDIC ① facsimile data conversion and interface control equipment 팩시밀리 데이터 변환 접속 장치.
② Federal Deposit Insurance Corporation (美) 연방 예금 보험 공사.

FDJ (독) Freie Deutsche Jugend (=Free German Youth) (통일 전 동독) 자유 독일 청년단.

FDL ① fast deployment logistics ship (美) (해군) 도속 수송선.
② final defense line (軍事) 최종 방어선.

FDM ① finite difference method 유한 차분법(有限差分法).
② frequency division multiplex (컴퓨터) 주파수 분할 다중 전송 방식.

FDMA frequency division multiple access 주파수 분할 다원접속.

FDN ① [S] Frents Democratico Nicaraguense (=Democratic Front of Nicaragua) 니카라구아 민주 전선.
② [S] Fuerza Democratica Nicaraguense (=Nicaraguan Democratic Force) 니카라구아 민주 세력.

FDOI first day of issue (우표 등의) 발매 첫날.

FDOS floppy disk operating system (컴퓨터) 보조 기억 장치로 플로피 디스크를 사용한 오퍼레이팅 시스템.

FDP ① fibrin degradation product 피브린 분해 산물. 혈액 응고 기능 검사.
② flight data processing system 비행 계획 정보 처리(處理) 시스템.
③ [G] Freie Demokratische Partei (=Free Democratic Party) (독일) 자유 민주당.

FDR ① flight data recorder → DFDR 비행 기록 장치.
② formal design review 공식 설계 심사.
③ Franklin Delano Roosevelt 미국 제32대 대통령 (1882-1945).
④ [S] Frente Democratico Revolucionario (=Democratic Revolutionary Front) (엘살바도르) 민주 혁명 전선.

FDS flight director system (航空) 플라이트 디렉터 시스템.

FDX full duplex (通信) 전이중(全二重).

Fe [L] ferrum (=iron) 철. ※ 원자 번호 26.

FE formal effector (컴퓨터) 서식 제어.

FEA ① Federal Energy Administration (美) 연방 에너지국. 1977년 Department of Energy 에 통합.
② Foreign Economic Administration (美) 해외 경제 감리국(局).

FEAF Far East Air Force (美) 극동 공군.

Feb. February 2월.

FEBA forward edge of the battle area (軍事) 최전선(最前線).

FEC ① Federal Election Commission (美) 연방 선거 위원회(委員會).
② freestanding emergency clinic (美) 독립 단기 치료소. 예약 없이 빨리 치료하는 진료소.

FECB Foreign Exchange Control Board 외환관리위원회.

FECL Foreign Exchange Control Law 외환관리법.

Fed ① Federal Government (美) 연방 정부.
② Federal Reserve Board (美) 연방 준비 제도 이사회. 미국 금융 기관을 총괄.
③ Federal Reserve System (美) 연방 준비 제도.

FEDREG 미국 연방 정부 관보 (Federal Register)의 온라인 데이터 베이스.

FEER fundamental equilibrium exchange rate 기초적 균형환율.

FEI [F] Federation Equestre Internationale (=International Equestrian Federation) 국제 승마 연맹.

FEL free electron laser 자유 전자 레이저.

FELLX Fusion Electromagnetic Induction Experiment (미) 아르곤 국립연구소에 건설중인 핵융합실험장치.

FELV feline leukemia virus 고양이 백혈병 바이러스.

FEM finite element method 유한 요소법(有限要素法).

FEMA Federal Emergency Management Agency (美) 연방 긴급시 관리국.

FEN [fen] Far East Network (美) 극동 주둔군 방송.

FEOGA [F] Fond Europeen d'Orientation et de Garantic Agricole (European Agriculture Orientation and Guarantee Fund) 유럽 농업 지도 보증 기금.

FEP front end processor (컴퓨터) 전치 처리 장치(前置處理裝置).

FEPA Fair Employment Practices Act (美) 공정 고용 관행법(慣行法).

FEPC Fair Employment Practices Committee (美) 공정

고용 관행 위원회.

FER ① forward engine room 전 부기관실.
② function execution rate 기능 실행속도. 컴퓨터의 기능을 평가·비교하는 지표.

FERC Federal Energy Regulatory Commission (美) (에너지성) 연방 에너지 감리 위원회.

FES [G] Friedrich Ebert Stiftung (=Friedrich Ebert Foundation) (독일) 프리드리히 에베르트 재단.

FESCO Far Eastern Shipping Co (소련) 극동 해운공사.

FESEM Field emission scanning electron microscope 주사형(走査型) 전자 현미경.

FESPIC Far Eastern and South Pacific Paralympics 극동 남태평양 신체 장애자 스포츠 대회.

FET ① federal excise tax (美) 연방 물품세.
② field effect transistor 전기장 효과(效果) 트랜지스터.

FEU forty foot equivalent unit 40 피트짜리 컨테이너 한 개의 분량을 나타낸 단위.

FFF ① forced flute (석유 스토브) 강제급 배기식(强制給排氣式).
② front engine, front drive (자동차)전기관(前機關) 전륜구동.
③ Fast Forward 테이프를 고속으로 전진시키는 과정.

FFA ① free from alongside 선측(船側) 인도.
② Future Farmers of American 미국 농업 교육 진흥회.
③ Free Fire Area 화력자유지역.

FFAR folding fin aircraft rocket 접는 날개식(式) 항공기용(用) 로켓탄.

FFB Federal Financing Bank (美) 연방 금융 은행.

FFC first flight cover 신설 항공우편 노선의 제1편에 탑재된 봉서(封書) 및 엽서.

FFCB Federal Farm Credit Bank (美) 연방 농업 금융 은행.

FFD ① failed fuel detection (原子力) 파손 연료 검출.
② forward floating depot 전선 해양상 병참함(艦).

FFF field-assisted fine finishing 전장(電場) 자장(磁場)원용연마.

FFG guided missile frigate 미사일 탑재 프리깃.

FFH Freedom from Hunger 기아로부터의 자유. FAO가 행하는 기아 구제 운동.

FFHC Freedom from Hunger Committee 기아해방운동위원회.

FFR ① Federation Fund Ratio 미 연방자금 금리.
② Radar Picket Frigate 레이더 초계함.

175

FG ① field goal (미식축구) 필드골.
② frequency generator 주파수 발전기.

FGA free of general average (해상 보험) 공동 해손(海損)부담보.

FGCS fifth generation computer system 제5세대 컴퓨터.

FGDS [F] federation de la Gauche Democrate et Socialiste (=Federation of the Democratic and Socialist Left) (프랑스) 좌익 연합.

FGGE First GAPR Global Experiment 최초의 전지구 실험.

FGIS Federal Grain Inspection Service (美) 연방 곡물 검사소 (檢査所).

FGM field guided missile 야전 유도 미사일.

FGMDSS Future Global Maritime Distress and Safety System 장래의 전세계적인 해난 안전 제도.

FGP Foster Grand parents Program (美) 양조부모 계획.

FGS Fellow of the Geological Society (英) 지질학회 특별 회원 (會員).

f.g.t. freight 화물, 운송료.

FH ① fire hydrant 소화전(消火栓).
② frequency hopping 주파수 호핑.

FHA ① Federal Highway Administration = FHWA (美) (운수성) 연방 도로국.
② Federal Housing Administration (美) (주택 도시 개발성) 연방 주택국.

FHC Financial Holding Company 금융지주회사.

FHI [F] Federation Halterophile Internationale (=International Weight lifting Federation) = IWF 국제 웨이트 리프팅 연맹.

FHLBs Federal Home Loan Banks (미) 연방주택대부 은행.

FHLBB Federal Home Loan Bank Board (美) 연방 주택 금융 은행 이사회.

FHM fuel handling machine (原子力) 연료 교환기.

FHWA Federal Highway Administration = FHA (美) (운수성) 연방 도로국.

FI ① Fighter Interceptor 전투요격기.
② Foreign Intelligence 해외정보.
③ fade in → FO (영화·텔레비전) 화면이 차츰 밝아지기 (라디오) 음성이 차츰 커지기.
④ family identity 가족의 독자성 추구.
⑤ [F] Federations Internationales de Sport Amateur (=International Amateur Sport Federations) = FIS, IF, ISF국제 경기 연맹.

FIA ① [F] Federation Internatinale de l'Automobile (=International Automobile Federation) 국제 자동차 연맹. 국제 자동차 레이스 통괄 기관.
② [F] Federation Internatinale des Acteurs (=International Federation of Actors) 국제 배우 연맹.
③ Fellow of the Institute of Actuaries (英) 보험 계리사협회 특별 회원.
④ Free Investment Area 투자 자유 지역.

FIAC [F] Federation Internatinale Acteur de Cyclisme (=International Amateur Cycling Federation) 국제 아마추어 사이클 경기 연맹. ※ 1965년 설립.

FIAC Foire International Art Comtemporary 세계 3대 현대미술제의 하나.

FIAT [I] Fabbrica Italiana Automobili, Torion (=Italian Automobile Factory in Turin) 이탈리아의 자동차 회사.

FIATA [F] Federation Internatinale des Associations de Transitaires et Assimiles (=International Federation of Forwarding Agents Associations) 운송업 협회 국제 연맹.

FIB ① [F] Federation Internatinale de Baseball (=International Baseball Federation) 국제 야구 연맹.
② [F] Federation Internatinale de Boules (=International Bowling Federation) 국제 볼링 연맹.
③ Fellow of the Institute of Bankers (英) 은행협회 특별 회원.
④ International Basketball Federation 국제농구연맹.

FIBA [F] Federation Internatinale de Basketball Amateur (International Amateur Basketball Federation) 국제 아마추어 농구 연맹.

FIBT [F] Federation Internatinale de Bobsleigh et de Tobogganing (=International Bobsledding and Tobogganing Federation) 국제 봅슬레이 및 터보건 연맹.

FIBV 세계증권거래소 연맹 International Federation of Stock Exchanges 세계증권거래소 연맹으로 개칭.

FIC ① [F] Federation Internatinale de Canoe (=International Canoe Federation) ICF 국제 카누 연맹.
② film integrated circuit (컴퓨터) 막집적 회로(膜集積回路).
③ Flight Information Center 비행 정보 센터.
④ French Immersion Course (캐나다) 프랑스 어(語) 특훈코

스. 영어를 사용하는 학교에 개설.

FICPI [F] Federation Internatinale des Conseile Propriete Industrielle 국제 변리사 연맹.

FICS Fast Industrializing Countries 급성장 공업국군(急成長工業國郡). 한국·자유 중국·홍콩을 일컬음.

FID ① [F] Federation Internatinale de Documentation (=International Federation for Documentation) 국제 다큐멘테이션 연맹. 1938년 창설.
② film integrated design 전자 회로를 필름에 인쇄하는 기술 (技術).
③ flame ionization detector 수소염 이온화(化) 검출기.
④ free indirect discoures 간접 자유 화법.

FIDE Federation Internatinale des Echecs (=International Chess Federation) 국제 체스 연맹.

FIDES [F] Fonds D'Investissement pour le Developpement Economique et Social (=Investment Funds for Economic and Social Development) 경제 사회 개발 투자 기금.

FIDO ① flight dynamics officer 우주선 조종 기사.
② fog investigation and dispersal operations 파이도. 비행장의 안개 소산 장치.

FIE [F] Federation Internatinale d'Escrime (=International Fencing Federation)국제 펜싱 연맹.

FIEE Fellow of the Institution of Electrical Engineers (英) 전기 기술자협회 특별 회원.

FIEJ [F] Federation Internatinale des Editeurs de Journaux et Publications (=International Federation of Newspaper Publishers) 국제 신문 발행인 협회. 1948년 설립. 본부 : 파리.

FIEP [F] Federation Internatinale d'Education Physique (=International Federation for Physical Education) 국제 체육 학회.

FIFA [F] Federation Internatinale de Football Association (=International Federation of Association Football) 국제 축구 연맹. 1904년 설립.

FIFO first-in first-out (컴퓨터) 선입 선출.

fig. figure 숫자, 도표, 삽화.

FIG [F] Federation Internatinale de Gymnastique (=International Gymnastic Federation) 국제 체조 연맹. 1881년에 설립. 본부 : 스위스.

FIH ① Federation Internatinale de Handball (=International Handball Federation)= IHF 국제 핸드볼 연맹.
② [F] Federation Internatinale

de Hockey (=International Hockey Federation) 국제 하키 연맹.

FIJ ① [F] Federation Internatinale des Journalistes (=International Federation of Journalists) = IFJ 국제 기자 연맹(聯盟).
② [F] Federation Internatinale de Judo (=International Judo Federation) = IJF 국제 유도 연맹.
③ Fellow of the Institute of Journalists (英) 신문 기자협회 특별 회원.

FIL [F] Federation Internatinale de Luge de Course (=International Luge Federation) 국제 루지 연맹.

FILA [F] Federation Internatinale de Lutte Amateur (=International Amateur Wrestling Federation) 국제 아마추어 레슬링 연맹.

FILO first in last out (컴퓨터) 선입 후출.

FIM ① field intercepter missile 야전용 대공 미사일.
② flight interruption manifest (항공편의 운항이 불가능하게 되었을 때의) 일괄 운송 위탁 서류.

FIMS [F] Federation Internatinale de Medicine SDportive (=International Federation of Sports Medicine) 국제스포츠 의학 연맹.

FINA [F] Federation Internatinale de Natation Amateur (=International Federation of Amateur Swimming) 국제 아마추어 수영 연맹.

FINET Financial Information Network (美) 금융 정보망.

FINNIDA Finnish International Development Agency 핀란드 국제 개발 사업단.

FIN Stat. financial statements 재무제표.

FIO free in and out 하역비(荷役費) 선주 무부담.

FIPP [F] Federation Internatinale de la Presse Periodique (=International Federation of the Periodical Press) 국제 정기 보도 간행물 연맹.

FIPS Federal Information Processing Standard 연방정보 처리표준.

FIQ [F] Federation Internatinale des Quilleurs (=International Bowlers' Federation) 국제 볼링 연맹.

FIR ① far infrared rays 원적외선 (遠赤外線).
② flight information region 비행 정보 구역.

FIRA [F] Federation Internatinale de Rugby Amateur (=Inter-

179

national Amateur Rugby Federation) 국제 럭비 연맹.

FIRS [F] Federation Internatinale de Roller Skating (=International Roller Skating Federation) 국제 롤러 스케이팅 연맹.

FIS ① family income supplement (英) 저소득 세대 보조금.
② [F] Federation Internatinale de Ski (=International Ski Federation) 국제 스키연맹.
③ [F] Federation Internatinale de Sport Amateur (=International Amateur Sport Federation) = FI, IF, ISF 국제 경기 연맹.
④ foreign Industrial Standard 해외 공업 규격.

FISA ① [F] Federation Internatinale des Societes d'Aviron (=International Rowing Federation) 국제 조정 연맹(聯盟).
② [F] Federation Internatinale des Sports Automobiles (=International Auto Sports Federation) 국제 자동차 경기 연맹.

FISB [F] Federation Internatinale de Softball (=International Softball Federation) 국제 소프트볼 연맹.

FISE [F] Federation Internatinale Syndicale de i'En-seignement (=International Federation of Teachers' Unions) 세계 교원 조합 연맹.

FISP [F] Federation Internatinale des Societes de Philo- sophie (=International Fede- ration of Philosophical Societies) 국제 철학회 연맹.

FISU [F] Federation Internatinale du Sport Universitaire (=International University Sports Federation) 국제 대학 스포츠 연맹.

FIT ① Fashion Institute of Technoiogy (美) 뉴욕에 있는 패션 대학.
② free in truck 화차(貨車)인도.

FITA [F] Federation Internatinale de Tir a l'Arc (=International Archery Federation) 국제 궁도 연맹.

FITASC [F] Federation Internatinale de Tir aux Armes Sportives de Chasse (=International Federation of Sport Shooting) 국제 엽총 사격 연맹.

FITT [F] Federation Internatinale de Tennis de Table (=International Table Tennis Federation) = ITTF 국제 탁구 연맹.

FIVB [F] Federation Internatinale de Volleyball (=International Volleyball Federation) 국제 배구 연맹.

FK free kick (축구) 프리 킥.

FKI Federation of Korean Industries (한국) 전국경제인연합회.

FL ① flanker (미식 축구·럭비) 플랭커.
② Florida (美) 플로리다 주(州)의 우편 기호.
③ fluorescent luminescence 형광 표시관.
④ forward left (배구) 포워드 레프트.
⑤ Flight Level 비행고도.
⑥ Focus Lenz 포커스렌즈연습.

FLAD fluorescence activated liquid crystal display 형광 집광판식(式) 디스플레이.

FLAG Federation of Parents and Friends of Lesbians and Gays (美)동성애자의 부모와 친구 연맹.

FLBM fleet launching ballistic missile 수상 함정 탑재 탄도 미사일.

FLEA flux logic element array (컴퓨터) 집속 논리 회로 소자군(集束論理回路素子群).

FLETC Federal Law Enforcement Training Center (美) (재무성) 연방법 집행 훈련 센터.

FLIP floating instrument platform 해양 조사선.

FLIR forward-looking infrared radar 적외선 전방 감시장치.

FLN [F] Front de Liberation Nationale (=National Liberation Front) (알제리) 민족해방 전선.

FLOP floating-point operation (컴퓨터) 부동소수점 연산. 소수점의 위치를 자동적으로 계산하는 연산방법. 수의 단위가 일정치 않은 과학기술의 계산에 편리하다.

FLOPS floating operations per second (컴퓨터) 1초당 유동소수 연산수(流動小數演算數).

FLOT [flat] forward line of own troops 아군 부대 최전선.

FLQ [F] Front de Liberation du Quebec (=Quebec Liberation Front) (캐나다) 퀘벡 해방 전선.

FLRA Federal Labor Relations Authority (美) 연방 노사 관계국.

FLSA Fair Labor Standards Act (美) 공정 노동 기준법.

FLT failure location technics (컴퓨터) 고장 발견 기법(技法).

FLTSATCOM Fleet Satellite Communications System (美) 함대 위성 통신 시스템.

flu influenza 인플루엔자.

Fm fermium (化學) 페르뮴. 원자번호 100.

FM ① facilities management 요원 파견. 기업의 컴퓨터실 관리 운영을 위한 요원 파견.
② Finance Minister 재무 장관.
③ Foreign Minister 외무 장관.

④ frequency modulation 주파수 변조(變調).

FMB Federal Maritime Board (미) 연방해사위원회. * 상무성의 외국(外局).

FMC ① Federal Maritime Commission (美) 연방 해사 위원회(委員會).
② flexible manufacturing cell 플렉시블 가공 셀. NC 공작기계와 로봇을 짜맞춘 것.

FMCS Federal Mediation and Conciliation Service (美) 연방 조정 화해 기관.

FMCT Fissile Material Cut-off Treaty 무기용 핵분열물질 생산 금지 조약.

FMEA failure mode effect analysis 고장 모드 영향 해석.

FMF ① Fleet Marine Force (美) 함대 해병 부대.
② flexible manufacturing factory → FMS 플렉시블 생산 공장(工場).

FM-FDMA frequency modulation -frequency division multiple

FmHA Farmers Home Administration (美) 농민 주택국.

FML flexible manufacturing line 플렉시블 생산라인.

FMLN [S] Frente Farabundo Marti de Liberacion Nacional (=National Liberation Front of Farabunde Marti) (엘살바도르) 바라분도 마르티 민족 해방 전선.

FMM flexible manufacturing machine 플렉시블 생산기계.

FMMS flexible manufacturing management system 플렉시블 생산매니지먼트 시스템.

FMPS flexible mass production system 플렉시블 대량생산시스템. 다품종대량생산시스템.

FMPT first material processing test 제1차 재료실험. 1991년 7월 예정으로 되어있는 미·일공동의 스페이스 셔틀을 이용하는 무중량(無重量) 재료실험.

FMN flavin mononucleotide 플라빈 모노뉴클레오티드. 플라빈 효소의 보효소 분자.

FMS ① file management system 파일 관리 시스템.
② flexible manufacturing system 플렉시블[융통성] 생산 시스템. ※ 소량 다품종의 생산에 적합한 자동화 생산 시스템.
③ foreign military sales (美) 대외 군사 판매. ※ 미국 무기 수출 방식의 하나.
④ factory management system 공장 관리 시스템. 경영 의사 결정과 생산 정보에 관한 계획, 창출.

FMVSS Federal Motor Vehicle Safety Standard (美) 연방 자동차 안전 기준.

FN [F] Front National (=National Frint) (프랑스) 국민 전선(戰線).

FNF Families Need Fathers (美) 부권(父權) 옹호 단체.

FNMA Federal National Mortgage Association (美) 연방 저당권 협회.

FNN Financial News Network (美) 경제 뉴스 전문의 케이블 텔레비전.

FNS Food and Nutrition Service (美) (농무성) 식량 영양구.

FO ① [F] Confederation Generale du Travail-Force Ouvriere (=General Confederation of Labor-Workers' Force) = CGT-FO (프랑스)노동 총동맹(總同盟) [자동자의 힘] 파(派).
② fade-out → FI (영화·텔레비전)화면이 차츰 어두워지기 (라디오) 음성이 차츰 약해지기.
③ Foreign Office 외무성.
④ fuel oil 연료유.

F/O Firm Offer 매도확약서.

FOA Foreign Operations Administration (美) 대외 활동 본부(本部).

FOB free on board 본선 인도 가격.

FOB&C free on board and commission 수수료본선인도.

FOBS fractional orbital bombardment system 부분 궤도 폭격 시스템. 지상 공격용 핵 위성.

FOC free of charge 무료.

FOCAL formulating on line calculations in algebraic language (컴퓨터) 고급 프로그램 언어의 일종.

FOD free of damage 손해 면제.

FOE ① Fraternal Order of Eagles 이글 공제 조합.
② Friends of the Earth 지구의 친구. 반(反) 원자력 단체(團體).

FOET Foundation on Economic Trends 경제 동향 연구 재단

FOFA Follow on Forces Attack 후속 전력 공격. NATO가 1983년 11월에 채택 결정한 통상 전력 강화 계획.

FOG-M Fiber Optic Guided Missile 광파이버유도미사일.

FOI ① freedom of information 정보의 자유.
② free of interest 무이자.

FOIA Freedom of Information Act (美) 정보의 자유법.

FOM fosfomycin 포스포마이신. 항생 물질의 일종.

FOMC Federal Open Market Committee (美) 연방 공개 시장 위원회.

FOQ free on quay 부두 인도 가격.

FOR ① Fellowship of Reconciliation 화목회(會). 크리스트 교도의 평화 단체.

FORATOM

② free on rail 철도 화차 적화 (積貨) 인도 가격.

FORATOM [F] Forum Atomique Europeen (=European Atomic Forum) 유럽 원자력 산업회의.

FOREST Freedom Organization for the Right to Enjoy Smoking Tobacco (英) 흡연권협회.

FOREX ① foreign exchange 외국환. ② foreign exchange rate 환율.

FORMAC Formula Manipulation Compiler (컴퓨터) 1964년에 IBM 사가 개발한 수식(數式) 처리 언어.

FORTRAN Formula Translation (컴퓨터) 1956년 IBM사가 개발한 과학 기술 계산용 프로그램 언어.

FOS free on steamer 기선 적화 (汽船積貨) 인도 가격.

FOSS fiber optics sonar system 광파이버소나시스템.

FOT ① free on truck 트럭 적화 (積貨) 인도가격.
② fuel oil tank 연료 탱크.

4-H 4-H Club (美) 농무성에 본부를 둔 농촌 청년 교육 기관의 한 단위. ※ 네 개의H는 head, heart, hands, health를 뜻함.

FOV field of view (航空) 시야(視野).

FOW free on wagon 화차인도.

FP fission product 핵분열 생성물.

FPA ① Family Planning Association 가족 계획 협회.
② Federation of Motion Picture Producers in Asia 아시아 영화 프로듀서 연맹. 1954년 결성.
③ Foreign Press Association (美) 외국 기자 협회.
④ free of particular average (보험)단독 해손 부담보(不擔保).

FPB fast patrol bost 고속 초계정.

FPC ① Federal Power Commission (美) 연방 전력 위원회.
② fish protein concentrate 어류(魚類) 농축 단백.
③ fuel pool cooling and filtering system (原子力) 연료 풀냉각 정화 시스템.

FPCC Fusion Power Coordination Committee (美) 핵융합 조정 위원회.

FPD flame photometric detector 염광(炎光) 광도 검출기.

FPDI flight path deviation indicator 비행 경로 편차 지시기.

FPF Final Protective Fire 최후방 어사격.

FPL Popular Forces of Liberation (엘살바도르 등의) 인민해방군.

FPLA Fair Packaging and Labeling Act (美) 적정 포장 표시법(法).

FPLMTS future public land mobile telecommunication system 미래 공중 이동 통신 시스템 미래의

공중 이동 통신 방식 이동체 ISDN이라고도 한다.

FPO ① field post office 야전 우체국.
② fleet post office 함대 우체국.

FPO [G] Freiheitliche Partei Osterreichs (=Freedom Party of Austria) 오스트리아 자유당.

f.p.s. feet per second 매초 ~피트.

FPS ① Fellow of the Pharmaceutical Society (英) 약학회 특별 회원.
② flexible path system 융통성 물류(物流) 관리 시스템.
③ Fire Power Score 화력지수.

FPU ① field pickup 야외 중계.
② field pickup unit 텔레비전 탑송 수신 안테나.

FQDN fully qualified domain name 에프큐디엔 인터넷상의 특정 주컴퓨터를 지시하는 풀 어드레스.

Fr francium (化學) 프랑슘. 원자번호 87.

FR ① forward right (배구) 포워드 라이트.
② front engine, rear wheel drive (자동차) 전기관(前機關) 후륜 구동.
③ Fusion Reactor 핵융합로.

FRA Federal Railroad Administration (美)(운수성) 연방 철도국.

FRAD Fellow of the Royal Academy of Dancing (英) 왕립 무용원 특별 회원.

FRAG fragmentation 파편.

FRAI Fellow of the Royal Anthropological Institute (英) 왕립 인류학회특별 회원.

FRAM Fellow of the Royal Academy of Music (英) 왕립 음악원 특별 회원.

FRAS ① Fellow of the Royal Asiatic Society (英) 왕립 아시아협회 특별 회원.
② Fellow of the Royal Astronomical Society (英) 왕립 천문학회 특별 회원.

FRB ① Federal Reserve Bank (英) 연방 준비 은행.
② Federal Reserve Board (美) 연방 준비 제도 이사회. 대통령이 임명한 7명의 위원으로 구성되며 연방 준비 은행을 통할하고 공정 보합(步合)의 변경 등을 행함.
③ Federal Reserve Board 미 연방 준비제도이사회.

FRC ① Federal Radiation Council (美)연방 방사선 심의회.
② Federal Radio Commission (美) 연방 라디오 위원회.
③ fiber reinforced cement 섬유 강화 시멘트.
④ fiber reinforced ceramics 섬유 강화 세라믹스.
⑤ Foreign Relations Committee (美) 상원 외교 위원회.

FRCD floating rate certificate of deposit 변동 이식부(利息付) 양도 가능 정기 예금 증서.

FRCM ① Fellow of the Royal College of Music (英) 왕립 음악협회 특별 회원.
② fiber reinforced composite material 섬유 강화 복합 재료 (材料).

FRCP Fellow of the Royal College of Physicians (英) 왕립 내과의협회 특별 회원.

FRCS ① Fellow of the Royal College of Surgeons (英) 왕립 외과의협회 특별 회원.
② forward reaction control system (電子工學) 전부(前部) 반동 자세 제어 장치.

FREEDOM free form design oriented manufacturing system 자유 형식 설계 지향 제조 시스템.

FRELIMO [P] Frente de Libertacao de Mocambique (=Mozambique Liberation Front) 모잠비크 해방 전선.

FRF flight readiness firing (宇宙工學) 예비 연소.

FRG Federal Republic of Germany = BRD 독일 연방 공화국(共和國).

FRGS Fellow of the Royal Geographical Society (英) 왕립 지리학회 특별 회원.

Fri. Friday 금요일.

FRIBA Fellow of the Royal Institute of British Architects (英) 왕립 건축사협회 특별 회원.

FRIC Fellow of the Royal Institute of Chemistry (英) 왕립 화학회 특별 회원.

FRICS Fellow of the Royal Institute of Chartered Surveyors (英) 왕립 공인 측량사협회 특별 회원.

fridge refrigerator 냉장고.

FRITALUX France, Italy, Belgium, Netherlands & Luxemburg 프랑스 · 이탈리아 · 벨기에 · 네덜란드 · 룩셈부르크 5개국 경제동맹.

FRM fiber reinforced metal 섬유 강화 금속.

FRN floating rate note 변동 이자부 채권. ※ 일정기간 마다 이율이 시장 실세 금리와 연동하여 변화하는 채권.

FRP fiber reinforced plastics 섬유 강화 플라스틱. 수명이 길고 가볍고 강하며 부패하지 않는 특징을 가진 수지로 욕조 · 요트 · 공업용 절연 자재 등에 폭넓게 쓰임.

FRPP fiber reinforced polypropylene 섬유강화폴리프로필렌.

FRPS Fellow of the Royal Photographic Society (英) 왕립 사진가협회 특별 회원.

FRR flight readiness review 비행 준비 점검.

FRS ① Federal Reserve System (美) 연방 준비 제도.
② Fellow of the Royal Society (英) 왕립협회 특별 회원.
③ fleet readiness squadron 함대 즉응 부대.

FRSA Fellow of the Royal Society of Arts (英) 왕립 예술 협회 특별 회원.

FRSC Fellow of the Royal Society of Canada 왕립 캐나다 학사원 특별 회원.

FRSE Fellow of the Royal Society of Edinburgh (英) 왕립 에든버러 학사원 특별 회원.

FRSGS Fellow of the Royal Scottish Geographical Society (英) 왕립 스코틀랜드 지리학회 특별 회원.

FRSH Fellow of the Royal Society for the Promotion of Health (英) 왕립 건강 증진협회 특별 회원.

FRSI flexible reusable surface insulation (宇宙工學) 굴곡성 재사용 가능 표면 열재(熱材).

FRSL Fellow of the Royal Society of Literature (英) 왕립 문학협회 특별 회원.

FRSS Fellow of the Royal Statistical Society (英) 왕립 통계학회 특별 회원.

FRTP fiberglass reinforced thermoplastics 열가소성 수지(熱可塑性樹脂)를 사용한 섬유 강화 플라스틱.

FRUS Foreign Relations of United States 미국 외교 기밀 문서(文書).

FS ① Fabian Society (英) 페이비언 협회. 1884년 Sidney Wedd, Bernard Shaw 등이 설립한 점진적 사회주의 단체.
② feasibility study 가능성 조사.

FSA ① Fellow of the Society of Actuaries (美) 보험 계리사협회 특별 회원.
② Fellow of the Society of Antiquaries (英) 골동품 연구가 협회 특별 회원.
③ Fellow of the Royal Society of Art (英)예술협회 특별 회원.
④ [F] Fonds de Soliddarite Africanne (=Fund of African Solidarity) 아프리카 연대 기금. ※ 1975년(年) 설립. 1976년 로 개칭.
⑤ Food Security Act 식량안전보장법.

FSA, F.S.A. Federal Security Agency 미국 연방 안보국.

FSAR Final Safety Analysis Report (原子力) 최종 안전 해석 보고서.

FSC ① Financial Supervisory

FSCC

Commission 금융감독위원회.
② Federal Safety Council 연방 보안위원회.
③ Federal Supreme Court 연방고등법원.

FSCC, F.S.C.C. Federal Surplus Commodities Corporation (미) 연방잉여 물가 배상배급공사.

FSDE full scale engineering development 전면적 기술 개발.

FSE Fellow of the Society of Engineers (英) 기술가협회 특별 회원.

FSF ① Fellow of the Institute of Shipping and Forwarding Agents (英)수송협회 특별 회원.
② Flight Safety Foundation (美) 비행 안전 재단.

FSH follicle stimulating hormone 난포(卵胞) 자극 호르몬.

FSI fuel sodium interaction (原子力) 연료 나트륨 상호 작용.

FSK frequency shift keying 주파수 변위(變位) 방식.

FSLIC Federal Savings and Loan Insurance Corporation (美) 연방 저축 금융 공사.

FSLN [S] Frente Sandinista de Liberacion Nacional (=Sandinist National Liberation Front) (니카라과) 산디니스타 민족 해방 전선.

FSM ① Fabryka Samochodow Malolitrazowych 폴란드의 국영 자동차 메이커.
② finite state machine 유한 상태 기계.
③ Free Speech Movement (美) 언론의 자유 운동.

FSO ① Fabryka Samochodow Osobwych 폴란드의 국영 자동차 메이커.
② foreign service officer (美) 국무성의 해외 근무 직원.

FSP Food Stamp Program (美) 식량 구입표 제도. 생활 곤궁자나 실업자가 식량을 싸게 구입할 수 있게 정부가 구입표를 발행하는 제도.

FSQS Food Safety and Quality Service (美)식품 안전 품질 공사.

FSS ① fixed service structure (宇宙工學) 고정식 정비탑.
② 연방 보급국(美) Federal Supply Service(미국 조달청의 부서명).

FSSG Force Service Support Group (美) 해병역무 지원군(群).

FSSU Federated Superannuation Scheme for Universities (英) 대학 교원 공통 퇴직 계획.

FSTOC facsimile storage and conversion system 팩시밀리 축적 변환 장치.

FSX fighter support (일) 차세대 주력 지원 전투기.

ft. foot, feet 피트.

FT ① Financial Times 파이낸셜

타임스. 영국의 경제지.
② floor technician (방송) 플로어에서 일하는 기사.
③ Flying Tiger Line = FTL 플라잉 타이거 항공. 미국의 항공 회사.
④ functional test 기능 시험.

FTA ① Fluorescent Treponemal Antibody Test [의]형광항체법.
② Free Trade Agreement 자유무역협정.

FTAA Free Trade Area of Americas 미주자유무역지대.

FTAT fluorescent treponemal antibody test 형광항체법(螢光抗體法). 매독 검사법의 하나.

FTC ① Federal Trade Commission (美) 연방 거래 위원회.
② Fair Trade Commission 공정거래위원회.
③ Free the Children 아이들을 구하라 ; NGO
④ Free Trade Commission 미연방통상위원회.

FTI Financial Times Index 파이낸셜 타임즈 주가지수.

FTL Flying Tiger Line, Inc. = FT (美) 플라잉 타이거 항공. 국제선으로 화물만을 취급함.

FTP ① falling to pieces (美俗) 피로 곤비(疲勞困憊).
② file transfer protocol (통신 네트워크) 파일 전송 규약.

FTS Federal Telecommunications System (美) 연방 전기 통신 시스템.

FTSE Financial Times Stock Exchange 영국의 세계주가지수.

FTX field training exercise 기동훈련.

FUBAR fouled up beyond all recognition (미군 속어) 모두 끝장이다.

FUO fever of undetermined origin 원인 불명의 발열.

FUV far ultraviolet rays 원자외선 (遠姿外線).

FW forward (스포츠) 포워드, 전위 (前衛).

FWD ① front-wheel drive (자동차) 전륜 구동.
② four wheel drive (자동차) 4륜 구동.

FWE foreign weapons evaluation 외국 무기 평가.

FWH flexible working hours 융통성 극무 시간.

EWPCA ① Federal Water Pollution Control Act (美) 연방수질 오염 방지법.
② Federal Water Pollution Control Administration (美) 연방 수질 오염 방지국.

FWS Fish and Wildlife Service (美)(내무성)어류 야생 생물국(局).

189

FWT fresh water tank 민물 탱크.

FWY freeway (美) 고속 도로.

FX ① Foreign Exchange 외화, 외환
② fighter X 차세대 주력 전투기

FY fiscal year 회계 연도.

FYDP Five-Year Defense Program (美) 방위력 정비 5개년 계획.

FYI for your information 참고하는 정도로. 미국의 ABC방송은 이 명칭의 건강 상담 프로그램을 방송하고 있음.

F.Y.O. for your eyes only 친전 (親展).

FZ fishery zone 어업전관수역.

FZS Fellow of the Zoological Society (英) 동물학회 특별 회원 (會員).

g. gram(s) 그램.

G ① G-rated film (미) 모든 연령층의 관람이 허용된 영화. G는 general을 뜻함.
② giga 10^9
③ Government 정부.
④ grid 문자판, 방송망.
⑤ (사단급 이상) 處, 參謀(部).
⑥ 가우스 Gauss(자기유도의 단위)
⑦ 기가 Giga-(계량 보조단위 접두어).

G. gravity, gravitation 중력(重力). G-1 = 인사처, G-2 = 정보처, G-3 = 작전처, G-4 = 군수처.

3G good material, good design, good price 상가활성화방안.

G-3 Group-3 중남미 3개국 경제협력체. 베네수엘라, 멕시코, 콜롬비아.

G-6 Group-6 아-태 6개국 시장협의회. 미, 일, 중, 홍콩, 싱가폴, 호주.

G-7 Group of Seven 서방선진 7개국(미국, 일본, 영국, 프랑스, 서독, 이탈리아, 캐나다)의 재무장관, 중앙은행 총재회의.

G-8 Group-8 G-7 + 러시아.

G-10 Group of Ten GAB 협정가맹의 선진 10개국(미국, 영국, 서독, 프랑스, 이탈리아, 일본, 캐나다, 네덜란드, 벨기에, 스웨덴).

G24 The Conference of Ministers of the Group of Twenty four 중진국 개발도상국 24개국 재무장관회의.

G30 Group of thirty 국제금융 문제에 관하여 상호이해를 깊이하며 정책내용을 검토하는 것을 목적으로 설립된 민간단체.

G4 팩시밀리 G4 facsimile 화상정보를 전화회선으로 전송하는 장치.

Ga gallium 갈륨. 원자번호 31.

Ga. Georgia 조지아 주.

GA ① general agency 총대리점.
② general agent 총대리인, 총대리점.
③ General Assembly 유엔총회.
④ general average (해상보험) 공동해손(海損).

GAAP generally accepted accounting principles 일반으로 인정된 회계원칙.

GaAs gallium arsenide 적외발광 다이오드, 레이저다이오드, 적색 발광다이오드 등에 사용된다.

GAASF General Association of Asia Sports Federations 아시아 경기 연맹총연합회.

GAB General Arrangements to Borrow 국제통화기금의 일반차입협정.

GABA 서남 Africa에 있는 France 공동체 내의 자치 공화국 이름.

GAC granular active carbon 입상 활성탄.

GAF general merchandise, apparel, furniture and appliance market 일반백화시장.

GAFES Geoson Advertising Forecast and Evaluation System 광고 전략 모델.

GAISF General Association of International Sports Federations 국제 스포츠 연맹 기구.

GAIU Graphic Arts International Union 인쇄예술국제연합.

gal/hr gallon per hour 갤런 매시.

GAL Green Alternative Lists (독) 녹색당 반핵, 환경보호를 표방하는 독일의 정당.

Gallup poll[survey] 갤럽 여론(與論)조사.

gals. gallons

GALVI galvanized iron 아연도금 철판, 함석판.

GALVNM galvanometer 검류계.

GAM ① graphics access method 도형액세스방식.
② guided aircraft missile 유도 항공기미사일.

GAMA General Aviation Manufacturer's Association (美) 일반 항공기 제조업자협회.

GAMC General Agreement on Multinational Corporations 다국적 기업에 관한 일반 협정.

GAN global area network (컴퓨터) 원격지의 컴퓨터를 연결하는 네트워크.

GANEFO Games of New Emerging Forces 신흥국 스포츠대회.

GAO General Accounting Office (미) 회계감사원.

GAP Good Agricultural Practice 표준영농규범. (효과적이고 신뢰할수 있는 해충의 관리를 위해 필요한 현실적 조건하에서 국가가 공인한 농약의 안전 사용규범)

GAPA ground to air pilotless aircraft 지대공 무인 비행기.

GAPP Good Analytical Practice for Pesticides (농약에 대한 모범분석규범으로 잔류농약을 분석하는 경우 신뢰성 있는 결과를 얻기 위해 분석자, 시설 및 방법 등에 대하 적절한 실시기준을 지칭).

GAR Grand Army of the Republic (美) (남북 전쟁에 참가한) 북군 육해군 군인회.

GARIOA Government (Appropriation for) Relief in Occupied Areas 가리오아 기금(基金). 미국의 피 점령지에 대한 구제 예산.

GARP Global Atmospheric Research Program (미) 지구대기 개발계획. 장기적인 기상예보의 과학적 기초의 확립을 목적으로 세계 기상기관과 국제 과학연합의 공동기획.

GAS get away special NASA의 스페이스 셔틀이용 실험 서비스의 하나.

GASP Group Against Smoker's Pollution (미) 금연운동그룹.

G&T gin and tonic 진토닉.

GATD graphic analysis of three-dimensional data 3차원 데이터 도형 해석 프로그램.

GATS General Agreement on Trade in Service 서비스 교역에 관한 일반 협정.

GATT General Agreement on Tariffs and Trade 관세무역에 관한 일반 협정.

GAW guaranteed annual wage 연간 보증 임금.

GAZ [R] Gorkovski Avtomobilny Zavod (=Gorkovski Automobile Factory)
구.소련의 국영 자동차 공장.

GB ① games behind (野球) 게임차(差).
② giga byte (컴퓨터) 10억 바이트.
③ goofball 수면제, 정신 안정제, 바르비탈제(劑) ; 마리화나, 마약.

GBC ① Global Bearer Certificate 포괄무기명증서.
② German Berarer Certificate 독일무기명증서.

GBE Knight (or D') Grand Cross of the Order of the British Empire (영) 대영 제국 1등 훈작사.

GBG garbage 쓰레기.

GBH grievous bodily harm 중상.

GBI General Business Index 경기종합지수.

GBMD global ballistic missile defense 전지구탄도 미사일방위.

GBS George Bernard Shaw 영국 극작가, 비평가(1856~1950).

GBY God bless you 행운을 빈다.

GC ① garbage collection 쓰레기수집.
② gas chromatography 가스 크로마토그래피.

G.C. ① general cargo 일반화물.
② general catalog 총카탈로그.

GCA ground controlled approach system 지상유도 레이더착륙장치.

GCB ① global corruption barometer 세계 부패 척도
② Knight(or Dame) Grand Cross

of the Most Honourable Order of the Bath = KGCB (英) 배스 1등 훈작사.

GCC ① Gulf Cooperation Council 페르시아만안협력회의. ② gasification combined cycle 가스화 혼합 사이클. ③ ground control center 지상관제센터.

G.C.D., g.c.d. greatest common divisor 최대공약수(最大公約數)

GCE General Certificate of Education (영)일반교육검정증. 학력증명을 위한 국가 시험 합격증서.

GCEP gas centrifuge enrichment plant 기체원심분리농축플랜트. 우라늄 농축공장.

G.C.F., g.c.f. greatest common factor 최대공약수

GCFBR gas cooled fast breeder reactor GFR가스 냉각고속증식원자로.

GCHQ Government Communications Head quarters (영) 정부통신본부. 전파방수해독기관.

GCI ground controlled interception 지상유도요격.

GCIE Knight Grand Commander of the Most Exalted Order of the Indian Empire (영) 인도 제국 1등 훈작사.

GCM ① general courtmartial 고등 군법 회의.

② Greatest Common Measure 최대공약수.

GCMG Knight (or Dame) Grand Cross of the Most Distinguished Order of St. Michael and St. George (영) 성 미카엘, 성 조지 1등 훈작사. 1818년 제정.

GCOS Global Climate Observing System 지구기후 관측시스템. (1990년 개최된 제2차 세계기후회의에서 제창된 대기, 해양, 설빙, 생물권 등 기후계 전체에 미치는 종합적인 관측 시스템으로 ① 기후계의 감시 및 기후변화 검출과 생태계 등의 기후변화 영향감시 ② 각국의 경제 발전을 위한 자료 이용 ③ 기후계의 이해촉진과 모델에 의한 예측능력의 향상을 목적으로 함.

GCP ① gas centrifuge plant (원자력) 가스원심분리플랜트. ② good clinical practice 신약의 임상시험의 실시에 관한 기준.

GCR ① gas cooled reactor 가스 냉각원자로. ② ground controlled radar 지상관제레이더. ③ ground coded recording (컴퓨터) 고밀도화가가능한 자기 테이프 기록방식.

GCSI Knight Grand Commander of the Most Exalted Order of the Star of India 인도의 성 1등 훈작사.

GCT Greenwich Cicil Time 그리니치상용시(常用時).

GCVO Knight (or Dame) Grand Cross of the Royal Victorian Order (영) 빅토리아 1등 훈작사.

g.d. good delivery 有效引渡.

Gd gadolinium 가돌리늄. 원자번호 64.

GD ① Geneva Conference on Disarmament 제네바 군축회의.
② good design 우수디자인.
③ grand diffusion 염가 대량판매 서적.

GDCF gross domestic capital formation 국내총자본 형성.

GDCH glycerol dichlirohydrin 글리세롤 디클로로하이드린.

GDE gross domestic expenditure 국내총지출.

GDI ① god damned independent (미 속어) 학생 우호회(fraternity 또는 sorority)에 속하지 않는 학생.
② Gender Development Index 여성개발지수 (각국별 여성의 소득, 교육수준, 평균 수명 등을 근거로 여성개발정도를 산출하는 지수).

GDL gas dynamic laser 가스동력 레이저.

GDM graded direct method 계단적 직접교수법.

GDP ① gaseous diffusion plant 기체확산 플랜트.
② geodynamic project 지구역학탐사계획.
③ gross domestic product 국내총생산.
④ guanosine diphosphate 구아노신 이(二) 인산.

GDR German Democratic Republic 독일민주공화국(동독).

GDSS group decision support system 집단의사결정 지원시스템.

Ge germanium 게르마늄. 원자번호 32.

GE ① General Electric Company 미국의 전기기기회사.
② grant element 증여상당부분. 정부차관의 대부조건이 상업베이스의 융자와 비교하여 발전도상국에 어느 정도 유리한가를 나타내는 지수.

GEC ① = GE.
② General Electric Company 제너럴 일렉트릭사(社). 영국 최대의 전기 메이커. 미국의 동명(同名) 회사와는 관계없음.

GECQ Group of Experts on Custom Questions Affecting Transport 수송에 관한 관세문제 전문가 위원회.

GED ① general educational development 종합교육개발.

195

② general adaptation syndrome 일반 환경 적응 증후군(症候群).

GEM ① ground effect machine 지면효과기(機). 수상, 빙상 지면을 공기쿠션의 이용에 의하여 이동하는 탈것. (호바크라프트)
② guidance evaluation missile 유도 정도 측정 미사일.
③ Gender Empowerment Index 여성권한지수. (각국여성의 소득 분포, 전문직 종사율, 의회내 여성의원 수 등을 기준으로 하여 경제적 의사결정에 대한 여성의 참여도를 나타내는 지수).

GEMMAC general manufacturing management automated control 록키드사와 GM사가 공동개발한 종합관리시스템.

GEMS Global Environmental Monitoring System 지구환경모니터링시스템. 기상변화, 대기오염에 의한 인간의 건강 변화, 해양오염등의 정보를 수집한다.

Gen. General 장군.

GEN Oslo Gardermoen Airport 오슬로공항 (노르웨이의 수도 오슬로 근교에 있는 공항)

GEO ① Genetically Engineered Organisms (생명공학 기술을 이용한 생물체에 대한 용어의 하나).
② geosynchronous earth orbit 정지궤도. 지표상 36,000km.

GEODSS ground based electro optical deep space surveillance 지상설치전자광학식심(深) 우주탐사. 전자 광학식 망원경으로 인공위성이 어떠한 용도의 위성인가 무엇을 탑재하고 있는가 활동중인가 아닌가를 식별한다.

GEOMIPS geographic data management and image processing system (미) 지질데이터관리·화상 처리시스템.

GEOS geodetic satellite 미국의 측지위성.

GES Gilt-Edged Securities 길트에지드증권 (영국 중앙정부 발행 채권).

GESAMP Group of Experts on the Scientific Aspects of Marine Pollution 해양오염과학전문그룹. IAEA의 조직.

GESP general extra sensory perception 일반 초감각 지각.

GETU General Federation of Trade Unions (英) 노동 조합 동맹.

GeV giga electron volt 10억전자볼트.

GF ① General Foods Corporation 미국의 식품 회사.
② girl friend 여자친구.
③ glass fiber 글라스 파이버, 유리 섬유.

GFCP general function checkout program (컴퓨터) 시스템 확인테

스트 · 프로그램.

G·FLOPS giga floating operations per second (컴퓨터) 매초 10억회의 부동소수점연산을 하는 속도.

GFP government furnished property 관급품.

GFR gas cooled fast breeder reactor = GCFBR 가스 냉각고속 증식원자로.

GFRC glass fiber reinforced concrete 글라스 섬유강화 콘크리트.

GFRP glass fiber reinforced plastics = GRP 유리 섬유 강화 플라스틱.

GFS Girls' Friendly Society (미) 소녀 우호회.

GFTU General Federation of Trade Unions (영) 노동조합연맹.

GFWC General Federation of Women's Clubs (미) 부인클럽 총연합.

GG ① government to government 정부간 거래. 원유매매의 경우 등.
② graduate gemmologist 보석 감정기능자격자.

GG government to government oil dealing 정부간 거래원유.

GGG gadolinium gallium garnet 실리콘 다음의 메모리의 소재로서 기대되는 신소재.

GGO Greater Greensboro Open 그린즈보로 오픈 골프 토너먼트. 미국 노스캐롤라이나 주.

GGPA graduate grade point average (미) 졸업시 학과 성적 총평균.

GH growth hormone 성장 호르몬.

GHA Greenwich hour angle 그리니치시각(時角).

ghetto 한 도시에서 소수 민족들이 모여 살고 있는 지구.

GHOST Global Horizontal Sounding Technique 정점(定點) 고공기상관측법.

GHQ ① general headquarters 총사령부.
② general health question index 영국에서 발견된 정신 안정 조사 수법.

GHSV gas hourly space velocity 기체시공간속도.

GHV gross heating value (연료의) 총발열량.

GI ① galvanized iron 아연 도금 철판.
② government issue 미병, 정부 발행의, 관급의.

GIA ① Grauda Indonesian Airways 가루다 인도네시아 항공. = GA.
② Gemological Institute of America 아메리카 보석학회.

GI

GI bill 제대 美兵 수호법.

GIC guaranteed interest contract 이율보증보험계약.

GIF Global Infrastructure Fund (일) 세계 공공투자기금.

GIFS Generalized Interrelated Flow Simulation (컴퓨터) 화학공업에 있어서의 프로세스의 분석을 수학적 모델을 사용하여 시뮬레이트하는 프로그램.

GIGO garbage in, garbage out (컴퓨터) 불완전한 데이터를 입력하면 불완전한 답만이 출력된다는 것.

GILSP good industrial large scale practice 우량공업제조규범.

GIONS Games Information On-Line Network System 경기운영시스템.

GIPS giga instruction per second 컴퓨터가 1초간에 10억의 명령을 실행하는 지표.

GIRO 지로 (그리스어로 회전이란 뜻) 일정한 금액을 온라인을 통하여 받을 사람과 보낼 사람의 계좌번호를 이용하여 송금하는 것.

GIS ① gas insulated substation 가스절연변전장치.
② generalized information system 범용정보시스템.
③ global information system 전지구적 정보시스템.

GIT ① group inclusive tour 항공권외에 숙박, 지상수송, 관광 등을 포함한 단체여행.
② Goods in transit 미학상품 운송중 매입상품.

GK. ① Greek 희랍의.
② goal keeper (스포츠) 골키퍼.

GKS graphical kernel system ISO에 채용된 그래픽・소프트웨어 범용화(汎用化)를 위한 2차원・3차원용 표준규격.

GL ① grand luxury 스케일이 크고 사치한.
② Guideline Level 지침기준(指針基準) (중금속, 농약 등 오염물질의 허용기준으로 일반적으로 산업체 등에 권고하는 기준의 의미가 강하며 Action Level에 비하여 법적인 구속력이 적음).

GLC ① gas liquid chromatography 기체액체 크로마토그래피.
② Greater London Council (英) 대런던 시의회.

GLCM ground launched cruise missile 지상발사순항미사일.

GLLD ground laser locator designator 지상레이저 목표표시장치.

GLM graduated length method 스키의 지도법의 하나. 초보자에게는 최초 짧은 스키를 신고 기술의 진보에 따라 차차 긴 것으로 가는 것.

GLO ground liaison officer 地上

連結將來.

G-LOC G-induced loss of consciousness G(중력의 가속도)부하에 의하여 일어나는 파일럿의 의식상실.

GLP Good Laboratory Practice 의약품 안전성 시험 실시기준.

Gm giga meter 10억 미터.

GM ① general manager 총지배인. ② General Motors Corporation (미) 자동차 제조회사. ③ guided missile 유도미사일.

GMAT Graduate Management Admission Test 경영학 전공 지망자를 위한 대학원 입시.

GMAW gas metal arc welding (원자력) 마그용접.

GmbH Gesellschaft mit beschrankter Haftung (Company limited) (독) 주식회사, 유한책임회사.

GMC (프) Groupe Mode Creat (=Mode Creation Group) 파리의 6개 디자이너 하우스 단체.

G-M counter Geiger Muller counter 가이거·뮐러 계수관.

GMDA ground miles and drift angle computer (항공) 대지(對地) 속도 및 편류 각도 산정기.

GMDSS global maritime distress and safety system 전세계적 해상조난안전시스템. IMO가 추진.

Gmen government men (미) FBI 소속의 수사관.

GMF ground mobile forces 지상 기동 부대.

GMO Genetical Modified Organism 유전자 재조작 생물체. (일반적으로 생산량 증대 또는 유통·가공상의 편의를 위하여 유전공학기술을 이용, 기존의 번식방법으로는 나타날 수 없는 형질이나 유전자를 지니도록 개발된 생물체)

GMP Good Manufacturing Practice 의약품의 제조 및 품질 관리에 관한 기준.

GMQ good merchantable quality 판매적성품질. 무역계약의 품질 조건의 하나, 해당 상품의 품질이 시장에서 상품으로서의 품질을 가지고 있는 것을 매도인이 보증하는 것.

GMS ① general merchandise store 대중 잡화점. 백화점과 달리 중간층의 수용에 맞는 상품을 대량 판매하는 대형점. ② geostationary meteorological satellite (일) 정지 기상 위성. ③ Global Messaging Service 전자우편, 팩시밀리, 전자사서함, 전자 데이터 교환, 음성 DB 등이 복합된 기본 및 부가통신 서비스를 말한다.

GMT Greenwich Mean Time 그리니치표준시.

GMWU National Union of

GN

General and Municipal Workers (영) 일반 도시 노조.

GN global negotiations 포괄적 교섭.

GNA Ghana News Agency 가나통신사.

GND gross national demand 국민총수요.

GNE gross national expenditure 국민총지출.

GNH gross national happiness 국민 총행복.

GNI gross national income 국민총소득.

GNMA Government National Mortgage Association (미) 정부 주택저당금고.

GNP gross national product 국민총생산.

GNR Great Northern Railway (미) 그레이트 노던 철도.

GNS ① Gross National Supply 국민 총공급.
② Group of Negotiations on Services (GATT) 서비스 협상그룹.
③ GEOnet name server 지도명,지면 서버

GNU GNN is not UNIX 미국의 Free Software Foundation (FSF)시가 무상으로 배포하고 있는 소프트웨어의 총칭 또는 개발 프로젝트 이름.

GNW ① gross national wealth 국민 총자산.
② gross national welfare 국민 총복지.

G.O. Grunerts operation 그루네트 수술법.

GOAL ground operations aerospace language 스페이스셔틀 비행용 컴퓨터 언어.

g.o.b. good ordinary brand 중(中)의 상(上) 물건.

GODP good out door practice 우량옥외 취급규범. 유전자 조작한 식물의 안전성을 확보하기 위한 환경을 규정한 것.

GOES geostationary operational environment satellite (미) 정지 실용환경위성. 미국의 정지 기상위성.

GOFS global ocean flux study 대양 중에서의 물질, 에너지의 흐름을 이해하기 위한 연구.

GOLKAR [인도네시아語] Sekber Golongan Karya (= Joint Secretariat of Functional Groups) (인도네시아) 골카르. 공무원조직, 노조 연합, 전국 청년 위원회 등 관민 여러 분야의 단체를 집결한 정치 조직.

GOM grand old man 원로, 고로.

G.O.P., GOP ① Grand Old Party (미국)共和당. Republican Party.
② general outpost 일반 전초

(前哨). 주력 부대를 방호하기 위한 목적으로 운용되는 부대.

GOST Gosudarstvennij Obshchesoyuznij Standart (러) (소련) 공업제품의 국정규격.

GOT glutamic oxaloacetic transaminase 글루타민산(산) 옥살로아세트산 전이 효소. 이 효소가 혈액 속에 과다하면 허혈성 심장 질환의 우려가 있음.

Gov. Governor 知事, 총독.

GOVT government = Gov'T 정부.

GP ① gallup poll (미) 갤럽 여론 조사.
② grand prix 대상.

GPA grade point average 성적 평균치. 미국대학의 성적 평가법.

G.P.A. General Procurement Agency[Agent] 물자조달청.

GPCP Global Precipitation Climate Program 지구 강수 기후 계획.

GPI ground position indicator (항공) 지상위치지시기.

GP-IB general purpose interface bus 범용인터페이스버스. *계측 시스템에 있어서 컴퓨터와 측정기를 포함한 기기간의 데이터전송을 규정하는 버스.

GPL general public license 지피엘. 일반 공용 라이센스 FSF의 소프트웨어 라이센스 요건의 하나.

GPM graduated payment mortgage 누진적 할부 상환 저당물건.

GPO Government printing Office (미) 정부인쇄소.

GPPS general purpose polystylene 일반용 폴리스틸렌 수지

GPR Global Defense Posture Review 해외주둔미군재배치전략.

GPS global positioning system (미) 전 지구 위치파악시스템. 지구주위에 24개의 NAVSTAR위성을 쏘아 올려 각기 위성에서 발신하고 있는 고유의 펄스 전파를 수신하여 상대관계로 자기의 현재위치를 파악할 수 있다.

GPSG generalized phrase structure grammar 일반화 구(句) 구조 문법.

GPSP good postmarketing surveillance practice (일) 의약품의 시판후 조사의 실시에 관한 기준.

GPSS General Purpose System Stimulations (컴퓨터) IBM사가 개발한 모의실험용 언어.

GPT glutamic pyruvic transaminase 글루타민산 피루빈산 전이 효소. 혈액 속에 이 효소가 과다하면 간장 질환의 우려가 있다.

GPU groud power unit (항공) 지상전원차. 항공기가 지상에 있을 때 엔진을 작동시켜 발전 · 공조를 하는 것은 비경제적이므로 전기나 냉각공기 · 난방공기를 공급

GPU

하기 위한 기외동력장치.

G.P.U., GPU (소련의) 國家政治保衛部.

GPWS ground proximity warning system (항공)지상접근경보장치.

GQ good quality 양품질(良品質).

GR Green Round 그린라운드 (환경과 무역의 연계에 관한 다자간 협상이란 뜻으로 사용됨. 환경보호를 목적으로 하는 환경정책 수단의 효율성을 높이기 위해 무역규제조치를 시행하는 환경정책과 무역의 연계를 의미하는 용어).

GRACE graphic arts composing equipment 컴퓨터 · 시스템에 의한 인쇄기.

GRAS general recognized as safe (미) 식품의약품국 합격증.

GRAS list generally recognized as safe list (미) 식품의약품국에서 안전성을 인정받은 식품의 리스트.

GRB gamma-ray burst 감마선방출. 1년에 약5회의 율로 인공위성에 의하여 검출된 급격하고 짧고 강대한 감마선의 방출을 말한다.

Gr. Br(it). Great Britain 대영제국.

GRC ① glass fiber reinforced cement 유리섬유강화시멘트.
② glass fiber reinforced concrete 유리섬유강화콘크리트.

GRCM Graduate of the Royal College of Music (英) 왕립음악대학 졸업생.

GRDP Gross Regional Domestic Product 지역내총생산.

GRDTN graduation 눈금, 농축.

GRE Graduate Record Examination (미) 대학원에의 진학희망자를 대상으로 하는 시험.

GRF growth hormone releasing factor 성장 호르몬 촉진인자(因子).

GRFI Group Radio frequency Interference 전자파 장해 전문 그룹 IEEE가 1985년에 전자파 장해를 전문으로 다루는 것을 목적으로 만든 그룹.

GRID gay related immuno-deficiency disease 동성애와 관련된 면역 부전증, 후천성 면역 결핍증, ※ AIDS의 구칭.

GROM graphic read only memory 컴퓨터 · 그래픽용 롬.

GSA General Services Administration 조달청. 미국 독립행정기관

GSDF Ground Self Defense Force 日本의 육군 자위대.

GRP ① glass fiber reinforced plastics GFRP 유리 섬유강화 플라스틱.
② gross rating point 종합시청률. 특정광고 · 방송프로 및 광고 캠페인에 대한 시청자, 청취자, 독자의 수의 측정치.

GRT ① gross registered tonnage (선박) 총등록톤수.
② group rapid transit (자동운전) 중량궤도 교통기관.

GRTS group rapid transit system 중량(中量) 궤도 고속수송시스템.

GS ① ground speed 대지속도.
② group separator 그룹분리문자.

GSA General Services Administration (미) 조달청.

GSC Global Standards Collaboration * 세계 표준화 협의체 ITU의 국제 표준화 활동을 주도하는 핵심 국가 및 지역 표준화 기관들의 협의체인

GSDF Ground Self-Defense Force (일) 육상자위대.

GSE ground support equipment (항공) 지상지원기기, 트랩, 정비·테스트장치, 보급장치 등 항공기의 활동을 지원하는 지상기기의 총칭.

G-7 Group of Seven → G-5, g-10 서방 7대국(미국 · 영국 · 프랑스 · 독일 · 일본 · 캐나다 · 이탈리아)의 재무장관 · 중앙은행 총재 회의. 1986년 발족.

GSFC Goddard Space Flight Center (미) 고다드 우주비행센터.

GSI giant scale integration (컴퓨터) 거대규모집적회로.

GSK Girl Scouts of Korea 한국 걸스카우트 연맹.

GSL guaranteed student loan (미) 정부원조학비대부금.

GSM general sales manager 판매부장.

GSMD Guildhall School of Music and Drama (영) 길드홀 음악 연극 학교.

GSO geostationary orbit 정지 궤도.

GSP ① Generalized System of (Trarff) Preferences (미) 개발 도상국으로 부터의 공업제품에 대한 특혜관세.
② good supplying practice 의약품의 유통과정에 있어서의 품질확보를 위한 기준.
③ Government Selling Price 정부공식판매가격. 산유국 정부가 설정하는 원유의 공식판매가격.

GSR Galvanic Skin Reponses 피부 전기반사기. 거짓말탐지기.

GSS project Globe Surveillance Station 전 지구 감시용 우주기 계획.

GST Greenwich Sidereal Time 그리니치 항성시(恒星時).

GSTDN ground space tracking and data network 우주추적데이터 통신망지상국.

GSTP Global System of Trade Preferences among Developing Countries 개발도상국간 특혜무역제도.

203

G-suit 전투비행복.

GSV guided space vehicle 비행 경로(徑路)를 제어하는 수단을 내장하고 있는 우주비행체.

GSW gross salary man welfare 월급장이 총복지.

Gt Gigaton ①중량의 단위(10억톤) ② 핵폭탄의 폭발력의 단위. TNT10억톤에 상당한 폭발력.

GT ① Greenwich time 그리니치시 ② gross tonnage (선박) 총톤수. ③ group technology 유사부품 가공법. * 모양, 크기, 가공공정들이 비슷한 공작물을 일정한 그룹으로 모아 집약(集約) 가공하는 방법.

GTAW gas tungsten arc welding (원자력) 디그용접.

GTC good till canceled 취소될 때까지 유효.

GTE General Telephone and Electronics Corp (미) 제너럴 전화 전자 회사.

GTF glucose tolerance factor 내당인자(耐糖因子).

GTH gonado tropic hormone 성선(性腺) 자극 호르몬.

GTM good this month 금월중 유효.

GTOL ground effect take-off and landing airplane 강착장치(降着裝置)로서 에어쿠션을 사용하는 비행기.

GTP ① group transfer polymerization (화학) 관능기(基)이행중합. ② guanosine triphosphate 구아노신 삼인산염.

GTR Government Transportation Requirement 공무출장.

GTS gas turbine ship 가스 터빈선 (船).

GTW good this week 금주중 유효.

GU Guam 괌도(島)의 우편 기호.

GUI graphical user interface 그래픽 사용자 인터페이스 컴퓨터의 운영 체제나 소프트웨어 등에서 문자를 중심으로 하는 것이 아니라 그림 등의 그래픽 데이터를 이용하여 시각적 처리를 할 수 있도록 하는 사용자 인터페이스 형식.

GULP Grenada United Labor Party 그레나다 통일 노동당.

GUM Gosudarstvenny : Uninersal'nyi magazin 러시아 연방 모스크바의 붉은 광장에 있는 국립 백화점.

GUPS 캄보디아 문제에 관한 4대 현안. Genocide(학살), United Nations(국제 연합), Power sharing(권력 배분), Settlers(정착자)의 머리 글자를 따서 만든 신조어.

GUT grand unified theory 대통일 이론.

GVT gravity vacuum transit 중력

진공열차. 미국에서 연구중인 미래의 교통기관.

GW ① giga watt 10억 와트.
② Gateway 출입구 출입문.
③ Guerrilla Warfare 게릴라전 유격전.
④ Guided Weapon 유도무기

GWS growing without school 자택 교육.

GYM gymnasium 체육관.

GYRO gyroscope 자이로스코프.

GZ ground zero 폭심지.

H ① heroin 헤로인.
② hydrogen (化學) 수소. 원자번호 1.

4-H 4-H Club (미) 농무성에 본부를 두고 있는 농촌 청년교육기관의 한 단위. 4개의 H는 head, heart, hands, health를 뜻한다.

ha. hectare 헥타르.

h.a. hoc anno(in the year) (라) 금년 중에.

Ha hahnium 하늄. 원자번호 105.

Ha. Hawaii (미) 하와이 주.

HA ① Hawaiian Airlines 하와이 항공.
② home automation 가정 자동화.

HAA ① height above airport 공항 상공 고도.
② hepatitis associated antigen 간염 관련 항원.

HAB high altitude bombing 고고도(高高度) 폭격.

HABITAT U.N. Commission on Human Settlements UN 인간 거주 위원회.

HAC high altitude compensator 고도보상장치. 공기밀도는 고도가 높을수록 낮아지므로 가솔린 엔진의 공연화(空燃化)는 낮아진다. 이러한 변화를 자동적으로 조정하는 연료조정 기화기(氣化器).

HAI ① Health Action International 건강을 위한 국제 운동.
② hot air intake 자동난기도입 (暖氣導入) 장치. 에어클리너에 일정한 온도의 공기를 도입하는 장치.

H&I harassment and interdiction 야간적차(敵車)의 침입을 방지하기 위하여 행해지는 무차별포격.

HAIR Highway Advisory Information Radio (일) 노측(路側) 통신 시스템. 도로상의 교통량 측정 장치나 패트롤카 등에서 수집한 도로 정보를 연선에 설치한 안테나로 카라디오를 통하여 운전자에게 제공하는 신 교통 정보 시스템.

HALO high altitude large optics 고고도 대형광학장치.

h. and c. hot and cold 연간 및 냉각.

HALW High Active Liquid Waste 고준위 폐기용액.

HAPP high altitude pollution program (미) 고고도 대기오염 조사계획.

HAR hemo agglutination reaction 적혈구 응집 반응.

HARM high speed antiradiation missile 고속대레이더미사일.

HATS high altitude test stand 고공 연소 시험장치. 지상에서 고공의 압력환경을 만들어 연소시험을 실시하는 설비.

HAW high activity waste 고방사성 폐기물.

HAZ heat affected zone 열 영향부, 변질부.

Hb hemoglobin.

HB ① halfback (스포츠) 하프백.
② hard and black 연필의 경도 표시.
③ home banking 가정에서의 은행업무 취급.
④ Hepatitis B B형 간염.

HBD hydroxybutyrate dehyrogenate 히드록시 낙산 탈수소 효소. * 허혈성 심장 질환 검사의 하나.

HBM His (or Her) Britannic Majesty (영) 국왕(여왕) 폐하.

HBN hazard beacon 위험 항공 등대.

HBO Home Box Office 미국 최대의 유료 유선 TV. * Time Inc. 의 자회사가 운영하며 영화, 스포츠, 오락 프로그램을 방송하고 있다.

H-bomb hydrogen bomb 수소 폭탄.

HBS Harvard Business School (미) 하버드 대학 대학원 경영학 연구과.

HC ① hard copy 종이 등에 인쇄한 컴퓨터 출력.
② hard cover 두꺼운 표지의 책.
③ House of Commons (영) 하원.
④ hydrocarbon 탄화 수소.
⑤ Hemisphere Country 중남미 국기.

HCB hexachlorobenzene 헥사틀로로벤젠. 간장 장애를 일으키는 유해 물질.

h.c.f. highest common factor 최대 공약수.

HCF high cycle fatigue 고사이클 피로.

HCFA Health Care Financing Administration (미) (보건복지성) 의료 융자국.

HCG human chorionic gonadotropin 임산부의 소변에서 검출되는 호르몬.

HCL high cost of living 물가고.

HCMOS high-density complementary metal oxide semiconductor 고밀도 상호 보충형 금속 산화막 반도체.

HCN Hydrogen Cyanide 시안화수소(一化水素).

HCPWR high conversion pressurized water reactor 고전환가압수로.

HCS high carbon steel 고탄소 강철.

HCSI Holt Children's Services Inc. (한) 홀트 아동 복지회.

HD ① honorable discharge (군사) 명예 제대. 무사고 제대.
② Huntington's disease 헌팅턴병. 근육의 불수의(不隨意) 운동이 정신 장애 증상으로 진행하여 마침내 죽음에 이르는 유전성 병.

HDBMS hierarchical database management system 계층적 데이터 베이스 관리 시스템 계층적 데이터 모델을 따라 데이터 베이스내의 데이터를 조작하는 데이터 베이스 관리 체계(DBMS)

HDC hydrodynamic chromatography 하이드로 다이내믹크로마토그래피.

HDD hard disk drive 고정 자기 디스크 장치.

HDEP high definition electronic production 전송이나 출력 장치에 대한 고려 없이 최대의 해상도를 지니도록 만든 표준 영상.

HDG heading (항공) 기수 방위.

HDI Human Development Index 인간개발지수.

hdkf. handkerchief.

HDL high density lipoprotein 고비중 리포단백.

HDLC high-level data like control (컴퓨터) 데이터 통신의 전송 제어 순서의 하나.

HDPE high density polyethylene 고밀도 폴리에틸렌.

HDR hot direct rolling 직접 압연.

HDS Office of Human Development Services (미) (보건복지성) 복지 사업국.

HDTV high definition TV 고선명도·고품위 텔레비전.

HDV heavy duty vehicle (자동차) 중량차.

HDW hardware 하드웨어.

HDX half duplex (통신) 반이중. 동시에 한 방향밖에 통신할 수 없는 양방향 통신.

He helium (화학) 헬륨. 원자 번호 2.

HE ① high explosive 고성능 폭약.
② His (or Her) Excellency 각하.
③ home electronics 가정전자제품.
④ human engineering 인간 공학.

H.E. His(Her) Excellency 각하. 대신, 대사 등에 사용하는 존칭.

HE Heavy Equipment 중장비.

HEAO high energy astronomy observatory 고 에너지 천체관측 위성.

HEAT [hi:t] high explosive anti-tank 고성능 유탄.

HEATS housing heating total system 온수순환의 난방시스템.

HEB home economist in business = HEIB 기업내 가정학사(家政學

土). 기업에 고용되어 불평처리 등의 소비자 대책뿐 아니라 소비자의 소리를 기업활동에 반영시키는 임무를 가지고 있다.

HEED high energy electron diffraction 고속전자선 회절법(回折法).

HEF high energy fuel 고에너지연료. * 로켓의 연료.

HEHC High Explosive High Capacity 고성능 고폭탄.

HEIB home economist in business 기업내 가정학사(家政學士). 기업 안에서 소비자 창구나 상품개발부분 등 소비자와 관련이 있는 부문에서 일하면서 소비자의 불만을 해결해 주며 소비자의 의견을 제품에 반영시키는 일을 담당함.

HEF high energy fuel 고에너지 연료.

HEL [hel] ① helicopter 헬리콥터. ② high energy laser 고에너지 레이저.

Hel Amb helicopter ambulance 구급용 헬리콥터.

HELW high energy laser weapon 고에너지 레이저 병기.

Hemisphere country 중남미 국가.

HEMT high electron mobility transistor 고전자 이동도 트랜지스터.

HENDEL helium engineering demo-nstration loop 대형 구조 기기 실증시험 루프.

HEOS highly eccentric orbit satellite 고이심 궤도위성(高離心軌道衛星). 유럽 우주 연구 기구(ESRO)가 개발한 우주공간 조사용 인공위성.

HEPA high-efficiency particulate air filter 클린룸용 초고성능 필터.

HERALD harbor entrance ranging and listening device 항만의 입구의 해면하에 설치하는 측거청음장지(測距聽音裝持).

HERP Harvard Economic Research Project 하버드 경제 연구소.

HESH high explosive, squash head 점착유탄.

HESP high energy solar physical observatory (일) 1990년대에 발사예정인 태양관측위성.

HETP hexaethyl tetraphosphate (화학) 헥사에틸 테트라 포스페이트. 살충제용.

HEU High Enriched Uranium 고농축 우라늄.

HEW Department of Health, Education and Welfare (미) 보건교육 복지성. 개조(改組) 결과, 현재는 DOE와 HHS로 분리되어 있다.

HEWD Hamlyn Encyclopedic World Dictionary (영) 햄린 세계 백과 사전.

HEX

HEX heat exchangers 열교환장치.

Hf hafnium (화학) 하프튬. 원자 번호 72.

HF high frequency 단파, 고주파.

HFBR high flux beam reactor 고중성자 속(束) 빔 원자로.

HFF high pressure fuel filter 고압 연료 여과기.

HFRA Honorary Fellow of the Royal Academy (영) 왕립 미술원 명예특별 회원.

HFS High Frontier Study (미) 탄도 미사일 요격 시스템.

HFSP Human Frontier Science Program 최첨단 과학을 사용하여 인간생체의 메커니즘을 해명하는 계획. 1987년 베네치아·수뇌 회담에서 일본이 제창함.

Hg (라) hydrargyrum (=mercury) (화학) 수은. 원자번호 80.

HG ① High German 고지(高地) 독일어.
② Holy Ghost 성령.
③ Home Guards (영)국토 방위군.
④ Horse Guards (영)근위 기병대.

HGC Hercules Graphics Card 허큘레스 그래픽 카드 미국의 Hercules사에서 제작한 IBM-PC용 그래픽 카드.

HGH human growth hormone 인간 성장 호르몬.

HGMF high gradient magnetic filter 고구배(高勾配) 자기 분리.

HGMS high gradient magnetic separation 고구배(高勾配) 자기 분리.

HGV heavy goods vehicle (영) 중량 적재물 차량.

HH ① Her Highness 비(妃)전하.
② His Highness 전하.
③ His Holiness 로마 교황의 존칭.

HHA Hamburger Hochbahn AG (독일) 함부르크 시영교통 회사.

HHC hand-held computer 손으로 쥘 수 있는 크기의 컴퓨터.

HHD ① (라) humanitatum doctor (=doctor of humanities) 인문과학 박사 = DH, DHu
② hypertensive heart disease 고혈압성 심장 질환.

HHFA Housing and Home Finance Agency (미) 주택금융공사.

HHHH Head, Heart, Hand, and Health = 4 · H클럽.

H-hour 공격 개시시간. D-day 공격개시 예정일.

HHS Department of Health and Human Services (미) 보건복지(후생)성. → HEW.

HHT ① hand held terminal 휴대용 단말장치.
② high-high tensile steel 고고장력강. Cr-Mn-Si 합금강.

HI ① Hawaii (미) 하와이 주의 우

편 기호.
② home improvement 가정 개선.
③ Hydraulic Lift 유압 승강기.

HIAA Health Insurance Association of America 미국 생명보험협회.

HIC hybrid integrated circuit 혼성 집적 회로.

HID ① headache, insomnia, depression 두통, 불면증, 우울증.
② high intensity discharge lamp 고광도·고출력 램프.

HIDAM hierarchical indexed direct access method (컴퓨터) 계층 색인 직접 액세스 정보처리 방식.

hi-fi high fidelity 고충실도음재생장치. 원음을 충실하게 재생하는 것 또는 장치.

HIH ① Her Imperial Highness 비(妃)전하.
② His Imperial Highness 전하.

HII Health Insurance Institute (미) 건강 보험 협회.

HILAC heavy ion linear accelerator 중이온 선형 가속기.

HIM His (or Her) Imperial Majesty 폐하.

HiMAT highly maneuverable aircraft technology 고운동성 항공기 기술.

HIMES highly maneuverable experimental space vehicle 고운동성 관측용 우주 비행체.

HIP ① higher intermediate point (항공)고액 운임적용 중간 지점.
② hot isoelastic pressing 열간 정수압소결법(熱間靜水壓燒結法).

HIPO hierarchy plus input-process-output 하이포, 계층적 입력-처리-출력 기술 방법. 시스템을 설계하는 경우, 그것을 계층 구조화하여 생각하고, 각 모듈을 입력, 처리, 출력의 부분으로 나누어 기술하는 방식.

HIPPO Hippopotanus 하마.

HIPS high impact polystyrene 내충격성 폴리스티렌 수지. 고무물질에 의하여 보강된 폴리스티렌.

HIS hospital information system 병원정보시스템.

HISAM hierarchical indexed sequential access method (컴퓨터) 계층 색인 순차 액세스 정보처리 방식.

HIT ① hemagglutination inhibition test (적) 혈구 응집 억제 테스트.
② home information terminal 가정 정보 단말기.

HIV human immunodeficiency virus 인간 면역결핍증 바이러스.

HJ (라) hic jacet = HJS

HJS (라) hic jacet sepultus (=here lies buried) 여기에 묻혀 잠들다. 묘비명의 첫 문구.

HK Hongkong 홍콩.

HKA

HKA Hongkong Airways 홍콩 항공.

HKDR Hong Kong depository receipt 홍콩예탁증권.

hl hectoliter 100리터.

HL ① hill 언덕.
② House of Lords (영) 상원.

HLA ① human leukocyle antigen 인간 백혈구 항원.
② Human Life Amendment (미) 인간의 생명에 관한 헌법 수정안. 인간의 생명은 수태의 시점부터 시작된다고 규정하는 헌법 수정안. 1982년 9월 15일 하원에서 1표차로 부결되었다.

HLB hydrophile lipophile balance 계면활성제의 친유성과 친수성의 조화.

HLC high speed liquid chromatography 고속 액체 크로마토그래피.

HLD half lethal dose 50% 치사량.

HLL high level language 고급언어.

HLLV heavy lift launch vehicle 중량물 발사 로켓.

HLLW high level liquid waste 고레벨 방사성폐액.

HLW high level waste 고 레벨 방사성폐기물.

HLZ helicopter landing zone 헬레콥터 착륙 지역.

HM His (or Her) Majesty 폐하.

HMAS His (or Her) Majesty's Australian Ship 호주 군함.

HMC His (or Her) Majesty's customs 영국 세관.

HMCF hypergol maintenance and checkout facility 자연성 연료 보수 점검 시설.

HMCS His (or Her) Majesty's Canadian Ship 캐나다 군함.

HMD hyaline membrane disease (신생아의) 히알린 막증.

HMDA hexamethylene diamine 헥사메틸렌디아민.

HMG ① His (or Her) Majesty's Government (영) 정부.
② human menopausal gonadotropin 폐경후 여성의 소변으로 나오는 성선 자극 호르몬.

HMMWV high-mobility multipurpose wheeled vehicle 고기동성 다목적 유륜(有輪) 차량.

HMNZS His (or Her) Majesty's New Zealand Ship 뉴질랜드 군함.

HMO health maintenance organization 보건 기관.

HMOS high-performance MOS 고성능 MOS.

HMP (라) hoc monumentum posuit (=erected this monument) 기념비 건립자의 이름에 붙이는 문구.

HMS ① His (or Her) Majesty's Service (영) 관용 우편물에 인쇄하는 문구.

② His (or Her) Majesty's Ship 영국 군함.

HMSO His (or Her) Majesty's Stationery Office (영) 용도국 (用度局).

HMW-HDPE high molecular weight high density polyethylene 고분자량 고밀도 폴리에틸렌.

HNC Higher National Certificate (영) 고등 2급 기술 검정합격증.

HND Higher National Diploma (영) 고등 1급 기술 검정 합격증.

HNP Herstigte National Party (남아프리카) 재생 국민당.

Ho holmium (화합) 홀뮴. 원자번호 67.

HO ① head office 본사.
② Home Office (영) 내무성.

HOCM hypertrophied obstructive cardiomyopathy 비대성 폐색성 심근 장애.

HOE homing overlay experiment 신형 ABM. ICBM이 나오는 열을 추적하는 적외선 센서와 컴퓨터 탑재.

HOLC Home Owners' Loan Corporation (미) 주택 소유자 자금 대부 회사.

HOLLAND Hope our love lasts and never dise. 우리의 사랑이 영원하여 결코 소멸하지 않기를 바라며.

Hon. Honorable 각하.

HOPE Health Opportunity for People Everywhere 병원선(船) 운영 계획.

HOTOL horizontal take off and landing 수평이착륙형 스페이스 플레인. 활주로를 이용하여 수평으로 쏘아 올리는 로켓.

HOW[hau] howitzer 유탄포.

HP ① Hewlett Packard Co. 휴리 팩카드 사. 미국 최대의 전자 계측기 메이커.
② Horsepower 마력.
③ hot press (기계) 가열 프레스.
④ Houses of Parliament (영) 상하 양원.

hpa hectopascal 기압의 단위. 1 hpa = 1 mb.

HPD hematoporphyrin derivative 헤마토포르피린 유도체. 암 등의 질병을 치료하는 방법

HPGC heading per gyrocompass (항해) 전륜(轉輪) 나침반에 의한 전진.

HPI history of present illness 현재의 병 이력.

HPLC high performance liquid chromatography 고성능 액체 크로마토그래피.

HPO Highway Post Office 고속도로 우체국.

HPP Hydroelectric Power Plant

HPPE

수력발전소.

HPPE high pressure polyethylene 고압법(高壓法) 폴리에틸렌.

HPTE high precision tracking experiment 고정밀도 추적실험. 저에너지 레이저 광선을 스페이스셔틀에 도달시키는 실험.

HPU hydraulic power unit 수력발전장치.

HPV human powered vehicle 인력거.

HQ headquarters 본부.

HQ-VHS high quality video home system VHS방식의 고화질화 기술로 개발된.

hr. hour 시간.

HR ① home run (야구) 홈런.
② House of Representatives (미) 하원, (일) 중의원.
③ human relations 인간 관계.
④ House Resolution 하원결의안.
⑤ H. R. House of Representatives 하원.

HR도 Hertzsprung-Russel diagram 금세기초에 고안된 항성(恒星)의 특성을 나타낸 도표.

HRAF human relations area files 지역별 인간 관계 자료.

HRC Human Rights Commission 인권 옹호 위원회.

HRH ① Her Royal Highness 비(妃)전하.
② His Royal Highness 전하.

HRIP (라) hic requiescit in pace (=here rests in peace) 여기에 편히 잠들다.

HROI Honorary Member of the Royal Institute of Oil Painters (영) 왕립 유화 화가 협회 명예 회원.

hrs. hours 시간.

HRSA Health Resources and Services Administration (미) (보건 복지성) 보건 자원 업무국.

HRSI high temperature reusable surface insulation 내고열 타일.

HRV high resolution visible imaging system 고분해능(高分解能) 화상시스템.

HS ① high school 고등학교.
② Harmonized Commodity Description and Coding System 통일상품분류제도.

HSAC Health and Social Affairs Committee (한) (국회의) 보건 사회위원회.

HSC House Steering Committee (한) 국회 운영위원회.

HSCC high stable cabin craft 흔들리지 않는 배.

HSE high speed signal control equipment 고속 신호 제어 장치.

HSGT high speed ground transportation 초고속 육상 수송기관.

HSH ① Her Serene Highness 비(妃)전하.
② His Serene Highness 전하.

HSI ① horizontal situation indicator 수평 상태 지시기. 종합계기 표시 방식에 의한 항법용 계기.
② High Speed Internet.

HSLN high speed local network 고속 지역 통신망 고가격의 고속 입·출력 장치를 연결하여 높은 처리율을 얻기 위하여 설계된 고속의 지역 통신망.

HSP high speed printer (컴퓨터) 고속 인자(印字) 장치.

HSRI Highway Safety Research Institute (미) 고속 도로 안전연구소. 미시간 대학내.

HSS (라) Historicae Societatis Socius (= Fellow of the Historical Society) (영) 역사 학회 특별 회원.

HSSI high speed serial interface 고속 시리얼 인터페이스 WAN (wide area network)상에서 고속 시리얼 통신 (최대 52 까지)을 하기 위한 네트워크표준.

HSST High Speed Surface Transport (일) 고속지표 수송기. 일본항공이 개발하고 있는 신형고속수송기술.

HST ① Harry S Truman 미국 제33대 대통령(1884-1972).
② Hawaiian Standard Time 하와이 표준시.
③ hypersonic transport 극초음속(極超音速) 여객기.
④ Hubble Space Telescope 허블우주망원경 (대기권 밖에서 우주관측을 정밀히 행하기 위하여 고안된 반사망원경).

HSUS Humane Society of the United States 미국 동물 애호협회.

HSYNC horizontal synchronization signal (TV) 수평 동기(同期) 신호.

HT ① high tension 고압.
② horizontal tabulation character (컴퓨터) 수평 태브 문자.

HTA heavier than air craft 중(重)항공기. 중량이 부력보다 큰 항공기의 총칭.

HTGCR high temperature gas-cooled reactor = HTGR 고온가스 냉각원자로.

HTGR High Temperature Gas Reactor 고온 가스로 내의 온도가 높은 원자로.

HTML Hyper Text Markup Language 하이퍼텍스트 기술 언어. 하이퍼텍스트 또는 하이퍼미디어를 생성하는 프로그램 언어.

HTML Extension HTML 확장 규약.

HTN Home Theater Network (미) 극 영화를 중심으로한 유료 CATV.

HTR high temperature reactor 고온 원자로.

HTS ① heights 하이츠.
② high tensile steel 고장력 강철.

HTTP Hyper Text Transfer Protocol 하이퍼텍스트 전송 규약. 인터넷을 통하여 하이퍼텍스트 문서를 송·수신하기 위한 웹 서버에서 사용되는 프로토콜.

HTV hypersonic test vehicle 극초음속(極超音速) 실험기.

HUD ① Department of Housing and Urban Development (미) 주택 도시 개발청. = DHUD.
② head-up display 투과성 반사경에 의해 파일럿의 시야내에 계기 등의 정보를 표시하는 장치.

HUDC Housing and Urban Development Corporation (일) 주택, 도시 정비 공단.

HUGO Human Genome Organization 인간 유전자 해석 기구. 인간 유전자를 해석하기 위한 기술 개발 및 정보 처리를 국제 협력을 통해 달성하기 위해 발족된 국제 기구. 1988년 가을에 결성. 본부: 제네바.

HUMINT human intelligence 스파이에 의한 정보수집.

HUK hunter killer 대잠 소해(對潛掃海) 부대.

HUS Hemolytic Uranic Syndrome 용혈성 요독 증후군 (신장과 신경학적 쇠퇴가 특징인 질병으로 특히 체력이 약한 노인이나 5세 이하의 어린이 등은 치명적인 상태가 되며 결국에는 사망에 이르기도 함).

HUT households using television 총세대시청률.

HVAC heating, ventilating and air conditioning 난방, 환기, 냉방.

HVAR high velocity aircraft rocket 항공기 탑재고속로켓.

HVD hypertensive vascular disease 고혈압성 혈관 질환.

HVJ월스 Hemagglutinating Virus of Japan[의] 인플젼저를 일으키는 월스의 일종.

HVN ① Home Video Network (미) 자동 VTR 녹화 방식 방송. 1982년에 ABC가 발표하였다.
② (미) ABC방송이 에 발표한 공중파를 이용한 유료 텔레비전 서비스.

HVO hydrothermal vent ores 열수광상(熱水鑛床). 해저하의 금속을 용해한 300~400도의 열수가 해저에서 분출하여 해수로 냉각되어 이상(泥狀) 또는 괴상의 황화물로 되어 해저에 침전된 것, 철, 동, 아연, 유황, 코발트, 은, 셀렌 등을 함유하고 있다.

HW ① hardware (컴퓨터) 하드웨어.
② highway 주요도로.

HWGCR heavy water gas-cooled reactor 중수감속 가스냉각 원자로.

HWL high water level 만조면.

HWM high-water mark 고수표.

HWR heavy water reactor 중수 원자로.

HWY Highway 고속도로.

hypo hyposulfite 하이포 아황산염.

Hz hertz 주파수 · 진동수의 단위.

I iodine (화학) 옥소, 요오드. 원자번호 53.

Ia. Iowa (미) 아이오와 주.

IA ① Institute of Actuaries (영) 보험 계리사 협회.
② Iowa (미) 아이오와주의 우편 기호.
③ Implement Arrangement 이행약정.
④ Intelligence Agency 정보기관.
⑤ Invisible assets 무형자산.

IAA ① indoleacetic acid 인돌아세트산. 식물 생장 촉진제.
② Industrial Advancement Administration (한) 공업진흥청.
③ International Academy of Astronautics 국제 우주 항행 학회.
④ International Advertising Association 국제 광고 협회.

IAAF International Amateur Athletic Federation 국제 육상 경기 연맹.

IAAP International Association of Applied Psychology 국제 응용 심리 학회.

IAATM International Association for Accident and Traffic Medicine 국제 사고 교통 의학회.

IAB International Association of Broadcasting 국제 방송 협회.

IABA International Amateur Boxing Association 국제 아마추어 복싱 협회.

IABSE International Association for Bridge and Structural Engineering 국제 구조 공학 협회.

IAC ① International Aerobatic Club 국제 곡예비행 클럽.
② International Analysis Code 국제 해석 통보 방식.
③ International Apprentices Competition 국제 직업 훈련 경기 대회. 통칭 기능 올림픽.
④ International Association for Cybernetics 국제 사이버네틱스 협회.
⑤ International Athletes' Club 국제경기자 클럽.

IACB Inter Agency Consultative Board (UN)관련 기관 자문위원회.

IACD International Association of Clothing Designers 국제 의류 디자인협회.

IACP ① International Association of Chiefs of Police 국제 경찰 장관 협회.
② International Association of

Computer Programmers 국제 컴퓨터 프로그래머 협회.

IACS International Association of Classification Societies 국제 선급 연합회. (1968년 7개 선급으로 설립되었으며 선박의 해상안전과 해양오염 방지를 위한 기술문제의 연구 및 관련정보 교환, IMO관련 기술자문과 관련 국제단체와의 협력추진을 목적으로 하고 있는 기관).

IACU International Association of Catholic Universities 국제 카톨릭교(敎) 대학 협회.

IAD ① International Astrophysical Decade 국제 우주 물리학 10년. ② International Authority Depository 특허 미생물 국제 기탁 기관.

IADA International Atomic Development Authority 국제 원자력 개발 기관. 1946년에 Bernard Baruch가 제창.

IADB ① Inter America Defense Board 미주 방위 위원회. ② Inter-America Development Bank 미주 개발 은행. ＊1966년 설립. 본부 워싱턴. ＝IDB

IADS integrated air defense system 통합 방공 조직.

IAEA International Atomic Energy Agency 국제 원자력 기관. 1957년 설립. 본부 비엔나.

IACOSOC Inter American Economic and Social Council (UN) 미주 경제 사회 이사회.

IAEE International Association for Earthquake Engineering 국제 지진 공학회.

IAESTE International Association for the Exchange of Students for Technical Experience 국제 학교 기술 연수 협회.

IAF ① International Aeronautical Federation 국제 항공 연맹. ② International Astronautical Federation 국제 우주 비행연맹.

IAFF International Association of Fire Fighters 국제 소방사 연합.

IAGC ① instantaneous automatic gain control 순간 자동 이익 조절. ② International Association of Geochemistry and Cosmochemistry 국제 지구 화학 · 우주 화학 협회.

IAHE International Association for Hydrogen Energy 국제 수소 에너지 협회.

IAHR International Association for Hydraulic Research 국제 수리학 협회.

IAI Institute of International Affairs 이탈리아 국제 문제연구소.

LAL international algebraic language (컴퓨터) 국제 대수 언어.

IALA

IALA International Association of Lighthouse Authorities 국제항로표지협회.

IALC ① instrument approach and landing chart (항공) 계기 진입착륙도.
② International Association of Lions Club 국제라이온스클럽.

IAM International Association of Machinists and Aerospace Workers 국제 기계공·우주 항공 노동자 조합.

IANEC Inter American Nuclear Energy Commission 미주기구 원자력위원회.

IAP International airport 국제 공항.

IAPA ① Inter American Press Association 미주 신문 협회. IPA라고도 한다.
② International Airline Passengers Association 국제 여객기 승객 협회.

IAPF Inter American Peace-keeping Force 미주 평화유지군.

IAPH International Association for Ports and Harbors 국제 항만 협회.

IAPIP International Association for the Protection of Industrial Property 국제 공업 소유권 보호 협회.

IAQ International Academy for Quality 국제 품질 아카데미.

IAQC International Association of Quality Circles 국제 품질 관리 협회.

IARC International Agency for Research on Cancer 국제 암연구 기구.

IARF International Association for Religious Freedom 국제 종교의 자유협회.

IARU International Amateur Radio Union 국제 아마추어 무선연맹. 1925년 창립.

IAS indicated airspeed (항공) 지시 대기 속도.

IASC International Accounting Standards Committee 국제 회계 기준 위원회.

IASP International Association for Suicide Prevention 국제 자살 방지 협회.

IASPEI International Association of Seismology and Physics of the Earth's Interior 국제 지구 내부 지진 물리 학회.

IASY International Active Sun Years 태양 활동기 국제 관측의 해. =IYAS.

IATA International Air Transport Association 국제 항공 운송 협회.

IAU ① International Association of Universities 국제 대학 협회.
② International Astronomical Union 국제 천문학 연합.

IAUP International Association of University Presidents 국제 대학 총장 협회.

IAUPE International Association of University Professors of English 국제 대학 영어 교수 협회.

IAUPL International Association of University Professors and Lecturers 국제대학 교수 협회.

IAWE International Association for Wind Engineering 국제 풍력 공학회.

IB ① Institute of Bankers (영) 은행 협회.
② International Baccalaureate 대학 입학 국제 자격 제도.
③ international broking 해외 중계 업무.

IBA ① Independent Broadcasting Authority (영)독립 방송 공사. 1972년 ITA(Independent Television Authority)대신 발족.
② indolebutyric acid 인돌부티르산.
③ International Bar Association 국제 법조 학회.
④ International Bauxite Association 국제 보크사이트 연합.
⑤ Insurance Brokers Association 보험 중계사 협회.

IBE International Bureau of Education 국제 교육국. 1925년 발족.

IBEC International Bank for Economic Cooperation 국제 경제 협력 은행. 1963년 설립. 본점 모스크바.

IBEW International Brotherhood of Electrical Workers 국제 전기공 조합.

IBF ① International Badminton Federation 국제 배드민턴 연맹.
② international banking facilities 국제 은행 업무.
③ International Boxing Federation 국제 복싱 연맹.

IBFAN International Baby Food Action Network 국제 유아용 식품 네트워크.

IBG inter block gap (컴퓨터) 블록 간의 갭.

IBI ① International Bank for Investment 국제 투자 은행. 1971년 설립.
② International Broadcasting Institute 국제방송협회.

ibid., IB. (라) ibidem (=in the same place) 같은 장소에, 같은 책에, 같은 장에.

IBK Industrial Bank of Korea (한) 기업은행

IBM ① International Brotherhood of Magicians 국제 마술사 연맹.
② International Business Machines Corporation (미) 아이 비 엠 사. 세계 최대의 사무기, 컴퓨터 메이커.

221

IBN identification beacon 신호 항공 등대.

IBP International Biological Programme 국제 자연 보호 연합(IUCN)의 국제적인 협력 활동.

IBRD International Bank for Reconstruction and Development 국제 부흥 개발 은행. 통칭 World Bank (세계은행). = BIRD

IBS International Broadcasting System 국제 방송인 협회.

IBSFC International Baltic Sea Fishery Commission 국제발틱해 어업 위원회 (발틱해 수역의 과학적 조사, 어업 조정, 어획 쿼타 및 집행계획 등을 수립 운영하기 위해 1973년 설립. 회원국은 EEC 핀란드, 독일, 폴란드, 스웨덴, 러시아 6개국임).

IBSS international business satellite service 국제 비즈니스 위성 서비스 북미-우주 사이에 콤샛(COMSAT)의 통신 위성이 전송하는 데이터에 지상국을 통하지 않고 사용자가 직접 접근할 수 있는 서비스.

IBSA International Blind Sports Association 시각장애자 경기 연맹.

IBST International Bureau of Software Test 미국의 소프트웨어 테스트 회사.

IBWM International Bureau of Weights and Measures 국제도량형국.

IBY International Biological Year 국제 생물의 해.

IC ① inspected and condemned 검사 불합격.
② integrated circuit (컴퓨터) 집적 회로.
③ interchange 고속 도로 출입구.
④ ionization chamber 전리함 (電離函).
⑤ Image Center 방사선검사실 (X선 판독실).

ICA ① Institute of Contemporary Arts (영) 현대 예술 협회.
② International Cartographic Association 국제 지도학 협회.
③ International Coffee Agreement 국제 커피 협정.
④ International Communication Agency (미) (국무성) 국제 교류국.
⑤ International Communication Association 국제 통신 협회.
⑥ International Cooperation Administration (미) (국무성) 국제 협력국. 1961년 AID로 개칭.
⑦ International Cooperative Alliance 국제 협동 조합 동맹.

ICAAAA Intercollegiate Association of Amateur Athletes of America 미국 대학 스포츠 연맹. = IC4A

ICAC International Cotton Advisory Committee 국제 면화 자문 위원회.

ICAD integrated computer aided

design and manufacturing system 통합된 컴퓨터 지원 설계 생산시스템.

ICAF Industrial College of the Armed Forces (미)군수 산업대학.

ICAN International Commission for Air Navigation 국제 항공위원회.

ICANN Internet Corporation for Assigned Names and Numbers 인터넷주소기구(인터넷 관련 기업, 기술 및 학술기관, 사용자 단체 등으로 구성되니 인터넷 주소 관리 기구로 1998년 설립).

ICAO International Civil Aviation Organization 국제 민간 항공 기구. UN전문 기관의 하나. 1947년 발족. 본부 몬트리올.

ICAP Inter American Committee of the Alliance for Progress 진보를 위한 동맹·미주 회의. = CIAP

ICAS International Computer Access Service 국제 컴퓨터 액세스 서비스. 외국 컴퓨터와 국내의 단말기를 접속하는 국제 전신 전화 주식 회사의 서비스.

ICB International Credit Bank Geneva 제네바 국제 신용은행.

ICBL International Campaign to Ban Landmines 국제지뢰금지운동(1992년 미국에서 창립된 단체, 대인 지뢰 사용 금지 및 제거를 위한 노력으로 1997 노벨 평화상 수상).

ICBM inter continental ballistic missile 대륙간 탄도 미사일.

ICBP International Council for Bird Preservation 국제 조류 보호 협의회.

ICC ① Indian Claims Commission (미) 인디언 요구 위원회.
② integrated communication controller (컴퓨터) 통신 제어 기구.
③ International Chamber of Commerce 국제 상공 회의소.
④ International Computation Center 국제 계산 센터.
⑤ International Control Commission 국제 휴전 감시 위원회.
⑥ International Corrosion Council 국제 금속 부식 협의회.
⑦ Interstate Commerce Commission (미) 주간(州間) 통상 위원회.

ICCA International Cocoa Agreement 국제 코코아 협정.

ICCAT International Commission for the Conservation of Atlantic Tunas 대서양참치보존위원회.

ICCC International Council for Computer Communication 국제 컴퓨터 통신 회의.

ICCE International council for computers in Education 국제 교육용 컴퓨터 협의회 컴퓨터 전문 과정 이전의 과정을 교육하는

ICCF

사람들의 국제적인 조직.

ICCF International Correspondence chess Federation 국제 통신 체스 연맹.

ICCH International Commodities Clearing House 국제 상품 청산 회사.

ICD International Classification of Diseases 국제 질병 분류.

ICDC ① Industrial and Commercial Development Corporation (케냐) 상공업 개발 공사.
② Iran Chemical Development Co 이란 화학 개발 주식회사.

ICE ① Institution of Chemical Engineers (영) 화학 기술협회.
② Institution of Civil Engineers (영) 토목 기술 협회.
③ internal combustion engine 내연 기관.
④ International Cometary Explorer (미) 핼리 혜성 탐사기.
⑤ International Cultural Exchange 국제 문화 교류.

ICEM ① Intergovernmental Committee for European Migration 유럽 이주 정부간 위원회. 1952년 성립.
② International Congress on Electron Microscopy 전자 현미경 검사 국제 회의.

ICES Integrated Civil Engineering System (컴퓨터) 토목관계의 계산에 사용되는 언어.

ICF ① International Canoe Federation 국제 카누 연맹. = FIC
② International Casting Federation 국제 캐스팅 연맹.
③ International Congress on Fracture 국제 파괴 학회.

ICFC Industrial and Commercial Finance Corporation (영) 상공 금융 공사.

ICFTU International Confederation of Free Trade Unions 국제 자유 노조 연합. 1949년 결성. 본부 브뤼셀.

ICG ① indocyanine green 인도시아닌 그린. 간 기능 검사용 주사제로 사용되는 색소.
② International Commission of Glass Status 국제 유리 위원회.

ICGNE International Consultative Group on Nuclear Energy 국제 원자력 협의 그룹.

ICH International Conference on Harmonization on Technical Requirement for Registration of Pharmaceuticals for Human Use 국제조화회의. (신약의 연구 개발 과정에서 수행되는 실험에 대한 중복 투자의 감소를 위하여 제품허가에 관한 기술적인 지침과 요건의 해석 및 적용에 있어서의 합의에 도달하기 위한 권고안 작성을 목적으로 유럽, 미국, 일본의 정부 관계자 및 제약협회로 구성된 국제회의)

ICI ① Imperial Chemical Industries Ltd. (영) 임페리얼 화학회사. 영국 최대의 화학 메이커.
② International Commission on Illumination 국제 조명 위원회.

ICID International Commission on Irrigation and Drainage 국제 관계 배수 위원회.

ICIPE International Center of Insect Physiology and Ecology 국제 곤충 생리 생태 센터. 1970년 케냐에 설립.

ICIREPAT Paris Union Committee for International Cooperation in Information Retrieval Among Patent Offices 특허청간의 정보 검색에 관한 국제 협력을 위한 파리 동맹 위원회.

ICITO Interim Commission for International Trade Organization 국제 무역기구 잠정위원회.

ICJ International Court of Justice 국제 사법 재판소. 소재지 네덜란드의 헤이그.

ICL International Computers Ltd. 아이 시 엘 사. 영국 최대의 컴퓨터 메이커.

ICM Intergovernmental Committee for Migration 정부간 이민위원회.

ICMSF International Commission on Microbiological Specifications for Foods 국제 식품미생물규격위원회.

ICMP Internet Control Message Protocol 인터넷 제어 메시지 프로토콜 네트워크층의 인터넷 프로토콜.

ICN (라) in Christi nomine (=in Christ's name) 예수 그리스도의 이름.

ICNAF International Commission for the Northwest Atlantic Fisheries 북서대서양 어업국제 위원회.

ICO ① International Coffee Organization 국제 커피 기구.
② International Commission for Optics 국제 광학 위원회.
③ Islamic Conference Organization 이슬람 국가회의 기구.

ICOGRADA International Council of Graphic Design Associations 국제 그래픽 디자인 협회 협의회.

ICOLD International Commission on Large Dams 국제 대규모 댐 위원회.

ICOM International Council of Museums 국제 박물관 회의.

ICOMOS International Council of Monuments and Sites 국제 기념물 유적 회의.

ICOO Iraq Company of Oil Operation 이라크 석유사업회사.

ICOT Institute for the New Generation Computer Technology (일) 신세대 컴퓨터 기술개발기

ICP

구. 제5세대 컴퓨터의 연구 개발을 목적으로 하고 있다.

ICP ① integrated communication control processor (컴퓨터) 통신 제어 처리 기구.
② International Council of Psychologists 국제 심리학자 회의.

ICPO International Criminal Police Organization 국제 형사 경찰 기구. 통칭 Interpol.

ICPOAE International Conference on the Peaceful Use for Atomic Energy 원자력평화이용국제회의.

ICPP Idaho Chemical Processing Plant 아이다호 화학처리공장. 사용한 핵연료 재처리 공장.

ICPR International Committee on Prostitutes' Right 매춘부의 권리를 위한 국제 위원회.

ICPTD International Committee for Prevention and Treatment of Depression 우울증 예방과 치료를 위한 국제 위원회.

ICPUAE International Conference on the Peaceful Uses of Atomic Energy 원자력 평화 이용 국제 회의.

ICR ① Institute for Cancer Research (미) 암 연구 학회.
② International Congress of Radiology 국제 방사선의학회.

ICRC International Committee of the Red Cross 적십자 국제 위원회. 1863년 설립. 본부 제네바.

ICRP International Commission on Radiological Protection 국제 방사선 방호 위원회.

ICRU International Commission on Radiation Units and Measurements 국제 방사선 단위 측정 위원회.

ICS ① inter communication system (항공) 기내 통화 장치.
② International Correspondence School (미) 국제 통신 학교.
③ International Copyright Society 국제저작권협회.

ICSA International Computer Security Association 국제컴퓨터보안협회.

ICSB International Council for Small Business 중소기업국제협의회.

ICSC Interim Communications Satellite Committee 잠정 통신 위성 위원회.

ICSEI International Cooperation System on Examination of Invention 발명품 심사에 관한 국제 협력 시스템.

ICSH ① International Committee for Standardization of Hematology 국제 혈액 표준화 위원회.
② interstitial-cell-stimulating hormone 간세포 자극 호르몬.

ICSID ① International Centre for

Settlement of Investment Disputes 투자분쟁해결 국제 센터.
② International Council of Societies of Industrial Design 국제 공업 디자인 단체협의회.

ICSPE International Council of Sport and Physical Education 국제 스포츠 체육 협의회.

ICSPRCP International Center for the Study of the Preservation and the Restoration of Cultural Property 국제 문화재 보호 연구 센터.

ICSSW International Congress of School of Social Work 국제 사회사업 교육 회의.

ICSU International Council of Scientific Unions 국제 학술 연합.

ICSW ① International Conference of Social Work 국제 사회 사업 회의.
② International Council on Social Welfare 국제사회 복지 협의회. * 본부 비엔나.

ICT ① inclusive conducted tour 모든 비용을 포함하고 수행원을 동반하는 여행.
② inter coast transport 해로 운송.

ICTP International Center for Theoretical Physics 국제 이론 물리학 센터.

ICTS intermediate capacity transit system 리니어 모터 구동 신교통 시스템.

ICU ① intensive care unit (병원의) 집중 치료부. → ITU
② interface control unit (컴퓨터) 인터페이스 제어 장치.

ICV infantry combat vehicle = IFV 보병전투차.

ICW interrupted continuous wave 단속 지속파(斷續持續波).

ICWU International Chemical Workers Union 국제 화학 노동 조합.

ICY ① International Communications Year 국제 커뮤니케이션의 해(1983년)
② International Cooperation Year 국제 협력의 해(1965년).

id. (라) IDEM (=the same) 동상 (同上).

Id. Idaho = Ida., ID 아이다호 주.

ID ① Idaho (미) 아이다호 주의 우편 기호.
② identification 신분 증명.
③ industrial design 공업 디자인.
④ industrial dynamics 기업 활동에 영향을 주는 여러 요인의 해석.
⑤ infantry division 보병 사단.
⑥ inside diameter 안지름.
⑦ intelligence department 정보부.
⑧ (스) Izquierda Democratica (=Leftist Democratic Party) (에콰도르) 민주 좌익당.

IDA ① International Development Association 국제 개발 협회. 1960년 설립. 세계 은행의 자매 기관.
② iron deficiency anemia 철분 결핍 빈혈.

IDACA Institute for the Development of Agricultural Cooperations in Asia (일) 아시아 농업 협동조합 진흥기구.

IDB ① illicit diamond buyer 불법 다이아몬드 바이어.
② illicit diamond buying 불법 다이아몬드 구입.
③ in daddy's business (영) 아버지의 사업 계승자.
④ Industrial Development Board (UN) 공업 개발 이사회.
⑤ Inter american Development Bank 미주 개발 은행. 1966년 설립. 본부 워싱턴. 이슬람 개발 은행.

IDB 6 Islamic Development Bank 이슬람 개발 은행.

IDBI Industrial Development Bank of India 인도 산업 개발 은행.

IDBP Industrial Development Bank of Pakistan 파키스탄 산업 개발 은행.

IDCA International Development Cooperation Agency (미) 국제 개발 협력국.

IDCSP initial defense communications satellite program 초기 방위 통신 위성 계획.

IDD international direct dialing 국제 직접 다이얼 통화. = IDDD

IDDM insulin dependent diabetes mellitus 인슐린 의존성 당뇨병.

IDDN Integrated Defence Digital Network (일) 방위통합 디지털 통신망.

IDE Institute of Developing Economics(일)아시아 경제연구소.

IDDRG International Deep Drawing Research Group 국제 디프 드로잉 가공 연구회.

IDEP Institut Africain de Development Economique et de Planification Nation Unies (프) 유엔 아프리카 경제개발계획연구소.

IDF ① intermediate distributing frame (컴퓨터) 중간 배선판.
② International Dairy Federation 국제 낙농 연맹.

IDI ① Institut de Developpement Industriel (=Industrial Development Institute) (프) 산업 개발 협회. 1970년 설립.
② Institut de Droit International (=Institute of International Law) (프)국제법 협회.

IDL international date line 국제 날짜 변경선.

IDMS integrated database management system 통합 데이터 베이스 관리 시스템 분산된 데이터

베이스들 간의 데이터 교환이나 데이터 조작 언어 변환 등의 작업을 하나의 시스템으로 통합하여 관리하는 데이터베이스 관리 시스템.

IDN ① (라) in Dei nomine (=in the name of God) 신의 이름으로. ② integrated digital network 통합 디지털 망.

IDNDR International Decade for Natural Disaster Reduction 국제 방재(防災) 10년. 1990~2000년까지의 국제통일행동계획. 지진, 태풍, 홍수 등의 자연재해에 의한 피해를 감소시키는 것이 목적이다.

IDO International Disarmament Organization 국제 군축기구.

IDP ① inosine diphosphate 이인산 이노신. ② integrated data processing (컴퓨터) 집중 데이터 처리. ③ international driving permit 국제 운전 면허증.

IDPR Inter Domain Policy Routing 자유 시스템(system) 사이의 폴리시를 동적(dynamic)으로 교환하는 도메인간 라우팅 프로토콜.

IDR ① Individual Retirement Account (미)개인 퇴직 적립금. ② international depositary receipt 국제 예탁 증권.

IDS International Development Strategy (UN) 국제 개발 전략.

IDTS international document transmission service 국제 문서 전송 서비스 국제 간 문서의 전송을 주로 위성 회선을 이용하여 송수신하는 서비스.

IDTV Improved Definition Television 화면 개량형 텔레비전. 주사선의 수동 현재의 텔레비전 방식을 변경하지 않고 수상기의 개량만으로 화질을 높이는 방식.

IDU International Democratic Union 국제 민주 동맹.

IDV (독) Der International Deutschlehrerverband (=International Association of Teachers of German) 국제 독일어 교사 연맹.

i.e. (라) id est (=that is) 즉.

IE industrial engineering 산업 공학.

IEA ① International Economic Association 국제 경제학 협회. ② International Education Association 국제 교육 협회. ③ International Energy Agency 국제 에너지 기관. * OECD의 하부 기관. 1974년 설립.

IEC ① integrated electrotechnical component 대규모 집적 회로. ② International Electrotechnical Commission 국제 전기표준 회의. 1908년 발족.

IECOK International Economic Consultation Organization for Korea 대한민국 제 경제 협의체.

IECQ IEC quality assessment system for electronic components 국제 전기 표준회의(IEC)의 전자 부품 품질 인정제도.

IEE Institution of Electrical Engineers (영) 전기 기술자 협회.

IEEE Institute of Electrical and Electronics Engineers (미) 전기 전자 기술자 협회.

IEF ① International Equestrian Federation 국제 곡마 연합. ② Index of Economic Freedom 경제자유지수.

IEFC International Emergency Food Commission 국제 비상시 식량위원회.

IEP ① International Energy Program 국제 에너지 계획. ② isoelectric point 전기적으로 같은 포인트. 등전점(等電點).

IEPA Intra European Payments Agreement 유럽 지역 지불협정.

IEPC International Economic Policy Council 국제 경제정책회의.

IER ion exchange resin 이온 교환 수지.

IERE Institution of Electronic and Radio Engineers 전자 라디오 기술자 협회.

IES Illuminating Engineering Society 조명 공학 협회.

IET interest equalization tax (미) 이자 평형설. 1963년 창설. 1974년 폐지.

IETF Internet Engineering Task Force 인터넷 기술 특별 조사 위원회 인터넷의 기술적인 문제들에 대한 관심을 가지고 있는 인터넷 구조 위원회(IAB)의 조사 위원회.

IEX ion excited X-ray spectroscopy 이온 여기(勵起) X선 분광법.

IF ① interferon 인터페론. 바이러스 증식 억제 물질. ② intermediate frequency 중간 주파. ③ International Amateur Sport Federations 국제 경기 연맹. = FI, FIS, ISF

IFA Instrumented Fuel Assembly 계기 연료 집합체.

IFABC International Federation of Audit Bureau of Circulation 국제 판매 부수 조사 연맹.

IFAC International Federation of Automatic Control 국제 자동제어 연맹.

IFAD International Fund for Agricultural Development 국제 농업 개발 기금. 1977년 설립. 본부 로마.

IFALPA = International Federation of Air Line Pilots' Associations = IFAPA

IFANS Institute of Foreign Affairs

and National Security (한) 외교 안보 연구원.

IFAP International Federation of Agricultural Producers 국제 농업 생산자 연맹.

IFAPA International Federation of Airline Pilots' Associations 국제 민간 항공 조종사 협회 연합회. = IFALPA

IFATCA International Federation of Air Traffic Control Association 국제 항공 교통 관제 협회.

IFAW International Fund for Animal Welfare 국제 동물 애호기금.

IFB ① International Fuel Bank 국제 핵 연료 은행.
② invitation for bid 입찰공고.

IFC International Finance Corporation 국제 금융 공사. 개발 도상국의 사기업에 투자를 목적으로 1956년 설립한 국제 투자 기관.

IFCTU International Federation of Christian Trade Unions 국제 기독교 노동 조합 연맹. * 1920년 결성. 1968년 WCL로 개칭.

IFF ① Identification, Friend or Foe (군사) 적·아군 식별 장치.
② Institute for the Future (미) 미래 연구소.

IFFPCS Integrated Flight, Fire and Propulsion Control System 파일럿 지원시스템. 탑재무기의 제어뿐 아니라 비행이나 추력의 제어도 파일럿에 대신하여 할 수 있는 시스템. 다음 세대의 전투기에 도입하기 위하여 연구중.

IFHP International Federation for Housing and Planning 국제 주택 계획 연합.

IFI International Federation of Industrial Designers 국제 공업 디자이너연맹.

IFIA International Federation of Inventors' Associations 발명가 협회국제연맹.

IFIAS International Federation of Institutes for Advanced Study 국제 고급 연구소 연합.

IFIP International Federation for Information Processing 국제 정보 처리 학회 연합.

IFIS Instrument Flight Instructors School (미 해군) 계기 비행교원 학교.

IFJ International Federation of Journalists 국제 저널리스트 연맹. * 1952년 설립. 본부 브뤼셀.= FIJ

IFLA ① International Federation of Landscape Architects 국제 조경가 협회.
② International Federation of Library Associations 도서관 협회 국제 연맹.

IFNP International Federation of Newspaper Publishers 국제 신

문 발행자 협회.
IFO identified flying object 확인 비행 물체. → UFO
IFORS International Federation of Operational Research Societies 국제 오퍼레이션 리서치 학회.
IFP (프)Institut Francais du Petrole (=French Petroleum Institute) 프랑스 국립 석유연구소. * 1945년 설립.
IFPI International Federation of Phonograph and Videogram Producers 국제 레코드 비디오 제작자 연맹.
IFPMM International Federation of Purchasing and Material Management 국제 자재구매 관리연맹.
IFRRI International Food Policy Research Institute 국제식품정책연구소.
IFPTE International Federation of Professional and Technical Engineers 국제 전문 기사 연맹.
IFR ① in flight refueling 공중 급유. ② instrument flight rules 계기 비행 규칙.
IFRB International Frequency Registration Board 국제 주파수 등록 위원회.
IFRC ① International Fusion Research Council 국제 핵융합 연구회의.
② International Future Research Conference 국제미래학회의.
③ International Federation of Red Cross 국제 적십자사 연맹.
IFRI International Francais des Relations Internationales (프) 프랑스 국제관계 연구소.
IFS ① integrated flight system (항공) 종합 계기 장치.
② International Foundation for Science 국제 과학 재단.
IFSDR inflight engine shutdown rate 비행중 엔진 정지율.
IFTA ① International Federation of Teachers' Associations 국제 교육 단체 연맹.
② International Federation of Travel Agencies 국제 여행업자 연맹.
IFTR International Federation of Theatre Research 국제 연극 연구 연맹.
IFTU International Federation of Tarde Unions 국제 노동 조합 연맹. WFTU의 전신.
IFTW International Federation of Transport Workers 국제 운수 노조 연합회.
IFUW International Federation of University Women 국제 대학 여성 연맹.
IFV infantry fighting vehicle 보병 전투차.

IFWTO International Federation of Woman's Travel Organizations 국제 여성관광인 연맹.

IG immunoglobulin 면역 글로불린.

IGA International Grains Arrangement 국제 곡물 협정.

IGAS International Graphic Arts Show 국제 그래픽 아트 종합 기재전. 인쇄 기재 단체 협의회의 주최로 2년마다 일본의 도쿄에서 열리는 아시아 지역에서 최대의 그래픽 아트 종합 전시회.

IGBP International Geosphere Biosphere Project 국제 지권(支圈) 생물권(生物圈) 공동 연구 계획.

IGC intellectually gifted children 지적 우수아.

IGCC Intergovernmental Copyright Committee 정부간 저작권 위원회.

IGD International Games for Deaf & Mutes 국제 농아 경기 대회.

IGDA International Group Developers Association 국제게임개발자협회.

IGDS Intercontinental Group of Department Stores 대륙간 백화점 그룹.

IGE inside ground effect 지면 효과내(內).

IGES initial graphics exchange specification 다른 CAD/CAM시스템 사이에서 도형이나 기하형상(形狀) 데이터의 변환을 가능케 하는 표준.

IGF International Genetics Federation 국제 유전학 연합.

IGFA ① Interessen Gemeinschaft der Farbenindustrie Aktiengesellschaft (독) 독일 염료 트러스트.
② International Game Fish Association 국제 낚시 연맹.

IGFET insulated gate field effect transistor 절연 게이트 전계 효과 트랜지스터.

IGGI Inter-Governmental Group for Indonesia 인도네시아 채권국 회의.

IGM International Grand Master 국제 체스 명인.

IGMPC International Group for Mercury Producing Countries 국제 수은 생산국 그룹.

IGO inter governmental organization 정부간조직.

IGOSS Integrated Global Ocean Service System (유네스코) 전세계 해양 정보 서비스 시스템.

IGT ① impaired glucose tolerance 내당 장해(耐糖障害).
② Institute of Gas Technology 가스 기술 협회.
③ insulated gate transistor 절연 게이트형 트랜지스터.

IGTA International Gay Travel

Association 국제 동성애 여행협회.

IGU ① International Gas Union 국제 가스 연합.
② International Geographical Union 국제 지리학 연합.

IGY International Geophysical Year 국제 지구 관측의 해. 1957년 7월부터 1958년 12월까지.

IHD International Hydrological Decade 국제 수문학(水文學) 10년 계획. 유네스코가 수자원 조사 연구와 그 사업 계획을 위하여 지정한 1965~74년의 10년간.

IHEU International Humanist and Ethical Union 국제 인문 윤리학 연합.

IHF ① Institute of High Fidelity (미) HiFi 기기 제조 업자 협회.
② International Handball Federation 국제 핸드볼 연맹. = FIH
③ International Hospital Federation 국제 병원 연맹.

IHO International Hydrographic Organization 국제 수로 기관.

IHRIM International Association for Human Resource Information Management 국제 인적자원정보관리협회.

IHP indicated horsepower 지시 마력.

IHT Institute of High Technology (일) 첨단 기술 대학.

IHVE Institution of Heating and Ventilation Engineers (영) 난방 환기 기술자 협회.

IHW International Halley Watch 국제 헬리혜성 관측.

IHX intermediate heat exchange (원자력) 중간 열교환기.

IIA integrated ignition assembly 집적형 점화장치.

IIAS International Institute of Administrative Sciences 국제 행정 학회.

IIASA International Institute for Applied System Analysis 국제 응용 시스템 분석 연구소.

IIB ① (프) Institut International des Brevets (=International Patent Institute)국제특허위원회.
② International Investment Bank 국제 투자 은행.

IIC ① International Institute for Conservation of Historic and Artistic Works 문화재 보존 국제 연구소.
② International Institute of Communications 세계 통신 방송 기구.

IICA Instituto Interamericano de Ciencias Agricolas (스) 미주 농업과학 협회.

IIE ① Institute for International Economics 국제 경제 연구소.
② Institute of Industrial Engineers (미) 공업 기술자 협회.

③ Institute of International Education (미) 국제 교육 협회.

IIEC Inter-Industry Emission Control (미) 산업간 배기 오염 제어 계획.

IIED International Institute for Environmental Development 국제 환경 개발 협회.

IIEP International Institute for Educational Planning 국제 교육 계획 연구소.

IIF Institute of International Finance 국제 금융 협회. 1983년 설립. 본부 워싱턴.

IIHF International Ice Hockey Federation 국제 아이스하키 연맹.

IIIA International Investment Insurance Agency 국제투자보험공사.

IIL integrated injection logic (컴퓨터) 집적 주입 논리회로.

IILS International Institute for Labour Studies 국제 노동과학 연구소.

IINA International Islamic News Agency 국제 회교 통신사.

IINS integrated information network system 고도 정보 네트워크 시스템.

IIP ① index of industrial production 광공업 생산 지수.
② instantaneous impact prediction (항공) 순간 낙하 예측.
③ International Institute of Philosophy 국제 철학회.

IIR ① imaging infrared (군사) 적외선 영상 방식.
② International Institute of Refrigeration 국제 냉동 협회.
③ isobute-neisoprene rubber 부틸 고무.

IIRA International Industrial Relations Association 국제 노사관계 연구 협회.

IIS ① integrated instrument system (항공) 종합 계기 장치.
② International Institute of Sociology 국제 사회학 협회.

IISEE International Institute of Seismology and Earthquake Engineering 국제 지진 공학 연구소.

IISI International Iron and Steel Institute 국제 철강 협회. 1967년 설립, 본부 브뤼셀.

IISS International Institute for Strategic Studies 국제 전략 연구소.

IIT International Investment Trust 국제 투자 신탁 회사.

IITA International Institute of Tropical Agriculture 국제 열대 농업 연구소.

IIW International Institute of Welding 국제 용접 학회.

IJC International Journalists' Congress 국제 저널리스트 회의.

IJCAI International Joint Conference on Artificial Intelligence 인공지능 국제회의.

IJF International Judo Federation 국제 유도 연맹. = FJJ.

IJPC Iran-Japan Petrochemical Company 이란 일본석유화학. 이란국영석유 회사와 미쓰이그룹 5사가 공동출자한 합병회사.

IKBS Intelligent Knowledge Base System(영) 고급지식 베이스시스템. 인공지능 연구 국가프로젝트.

Ike ① Dwight David Eisenhower 미국 제34대 대통령(1890~1969). ② 남자이름. Isaac의 애칭.

IKF International Kendo Federation 국제 검도 연맹.

IL ① Illinois (미) 일리노이 주의 우편 기호. ② import license 수입 승인증. ③ inside left (축구) 인사이드 레프트.

ILA ① International Law Association 국제법 협회. ② International Longshoremen's Association 국제 항만 노동자 협회.

ILAB International League of Antiquarian Booksellers 국제 고서적상 연맹.

ILAS instrument low approach system 계기 착륙 유도방식.

ILC International Language Center 국제 어학 센터. 본부 런던.

ILF infra low frequency 초저주파 (超低周波).

ILGWU International ladies' Garment Workers' Union 국제 여성복 생산 노동 조합.

ILHR International League for Human Rights 국제 인권연맹.

ILI index of linguistic insecurity 언어 불안정도 지수.

Ⅲ. Illinoois (미) 일리노이 주.

ILO International Labor Organization (UN) 국제 노동 기관.

ILP Independent Labour Party (영) 독립노동당.

ILPES Instituto Latinoamericano de Planificacion Economicay Social (Nation Unidas) (스) (유엔) 미주경제사회계획협회.

ILRAD International Laboratory for Research on Animal Disease (케냐) 국제 동물 질병 연구소.

ILS instrument landing system (항공) 계기 착륙 방식.

ILSI International Life Sciences Institute 국제생명과학협회.

ILTE International Lawn Tennis Federation 국제정구연맹.

ILEF International Lawn Tennis Federation 국제 정구연맹. 현재는 ITF로 개칭.

ILU Institute of London Underwriters 영국 보험업자 협회.

ILWU International Longshoremen's and Warehousemen's Union 국제 항만 창고 노동자 조합. 1937년 설립. 본부 샌프란시스코.

ILY International Literacy Year 국제 식자년(識字年). 1990년.

ILZSG International Lead and Zinc Study Group 국제 납 아연 연구회.

IM ① individual medley (스포츠) 개인 메들리.
② intensity modulation 강도 변조.
③ intercept missile 요격 미사일.
④ inter modulation (전기) 상호 변조.

IMA International Mineralogical Association 국제 광물학 연합.

IMADR The International Movement Against all forms of Discrimination and acism 반차별 국제운동.

IMAID Integrated Image Analysis System (미)통합화상 해석 시스템.

IMAX Eye Max 일반 35mm 영화 화면의 10배인 가로 25m, 세로 18m인 초대형 스크린과 6본(本) 트랙에 의한 웅장한 음향이 특징인 영화 형태.

IMBA International Mountain Bicycling Association 국제산악자전거협회.

IMC ① instrument meteorological conditions 계기 비행을 필요로 하는 기상 상태.
② International Material Conference 국제 원료 회의.
③ International Music Council 국제 음악 평의회.

IMCO Inter-Governmental Maritime Consultative Organization 정부간 해사(海事) 협의 기관. 1959년 설립. 1982년 IMO로 개칭.

IMEC International Movements for Environment Conservation 국제 환경보존 운동.

IMEDE (프) Institut pour l'Etude des Methodes de Direction de l'Entreprise (=Institute for the Study of Methods for Directing the Enterprise) 기업 경영 연구소. 본부 스위스 로잔느.

IMEKO (독) International Messtichnische Konfo deration (=International Measurement Confederation) 국제 계측 협회.

IMF ① International Meeting on Ferroelectricity 강전도성 국제 회의.
② International Metalworkers Federation 국제 금융 노동 조합.
③ International Monetary Fund 국제 통화 기금. 1944년 설립.

IMI International Management Institute 국제 매니지먼트 연구소.

IMIC International Medical Infor-

237

IMIS

mation Center 국제 의학 정보 센터.

IMIS ① integrated management information system (컴퓨터) 집중 경영 정보 시스템.
② integrated motorist information system (미) 종합 운전자 정보 시스템.

IML 계획 International Microgravity Laboratory Program 국제 미소 중력 실험계획.

IMM ① Institution of Mining and Metallurgy (영)채광 야금협회.
② International Money Market 국제 통화 시장.

IMO International Maritime Organization (UN) 국제 해사(海事)기관. 원래 IMCO(1959년 설립)였는데 1982년에 개칭.

imp ① import 수입.
② imported 수입된.
③ importer 수입상.

IMP ① inosine monophosphate 이노신인산.
② interface message processor (컴퓨터) 인터페이스 메시지 프로세서.
③ interplanetary monitoring platform 혹성간 공간 관측 위성.

IMPACT inventory management program and control techniques (컴퓨터) IBM사가 개발한 재고 관리 이론과 그것을 실시하는 프로그램.

IMPAT impact avalanche transit time diode 초고주파(超高周波)의 발진·증폭용 소자.

IMR infant mortality rate 유아 사망률.

IMS ① Indian Medical Service (영) 인도 의료 봉사단.
② Information Management System (컴퓨터) IBM사가 제공하는 데이터베이스 관리 시스템.
③ International Magnetic System 자기권(磁氣圈) 관측 사업 계획.
④ International Metallographic Society 국제 금속 조직 학회.
⑤ International Musicological Society 국제 음악 학회.
⑥ inventory management simulator 재고 관리 시뮬레이터.
⑦ inventory management system 재고 관리 시스템.

IMSA International Monetary Stabilization Accounts 국제 통화 안정계정.

IMT International Military Tribunal 국제 군사 재판.

IMT International Mobile Telecommunication 2000 국제 이동 전화 통신 2000 10MAz 대역폭의 광대역 코드 분할 다중접속 (WCDMA)방식, 기지국 제어기, 무선 ATM교환기 및 사용자 정보 관리 시스템 등으로 구성된 차세대 전환 통신 시스템.

IMTS International Machine Toll

Show 국제공작 기계 견본시. 시카고에서 격년에 개최.

IMU ① inertial measurement unit (우주공학) 관성 측정 장치. ② International Mathematical Union 국제 수학 연합.

IN ① Indiana (미) 인디애나 주의 우편기호. ② Information Network 고도 정보 통신 서비스. IBM사 제공.

INA ① Institution of Naval Architects (영) 조선(造船)학회. ② Integrated Industrialization in Non-Metropolitan Area 비도시 지역 통합 공업화 계획. ESCAP (UN 아시아 태평양 경제사회 이사회) 프로젝트의 하나. ③ Iraqi News Agency 이라크 통신.

INAH isonicotinic acid hydrazide 이소니코틴산 히드라지드.

INAS integrated navigation attack system (항공) 통합형 항법공격 시스템.

INAS-MH International Association Sports for Persons with Mental Handicap 정신박약자 경기연맹.

INB international brand 해외시장에도 진출하고 있는 국제적 상표.

inc. including ; inclusive ; income ; incorporated ; increase

INC ① Indian National Congress (인도) 간디파 국민 회의파. ② (라) in nomine Christi (=in Christ's name) 그리스도의 이름으로.

INCB International Narcotic Control Board 국제 마약통제 위원회.

INCC International Nuclear Credit 국제 원자력 금융.

INC-S Indian National Congress-S (인도) 파와르파 국민회의파 총재. Sharad Pawar.

ind. independence ; independent ; index ; indicated ; indicative ; industrial ; industry.

Ind. Indiana (미) 인디애나 주.

IND. ① Independent Lines 뉴욕 지하철의 3계통 중 하나. ② (라) in nomine Dei (=in the name of God) 신의 이름으로. ③ investigational new drug 연구용 신약.

INDC International Nuclear Data Committee 국제 핵 데이터 위원회.

inf. information 정보, 통지, 뉴스.

INF intermediate-range nuclear forces 중거리 핵전력. 옛 명칭은 TNF.

INFA International Nuclear Fuel Authority 국제 핵 연료공사.

INFB International Nuclear Fuel Bank 국제 핵연료 은행.

INFCE

INFCE International Nuclear Fuel Cycle Evaluation 국제 핵연료 사이클 평가. 핵의 군사이용을 막으면서 원자력의 평화 이용을 촉진하는 방법의 검토·평가.

INFOMART Information Market (미) 텍사스 주에 있는 정보산업 전시물.

INFORMEX Informex S.A. 멕시코 통신.

INFOSTA Information Science and Technology Association 정보과학기술협회.

INFOTERRA International Referral System for Sources of Environmental Information 국제 환경 정보 시스템. UNET에 의하여 설립, 운영되고 있으며 세계 각지의 환경정보를 제공하는 정보시스템.

INGO International Non-Government Organization 비(非) 정부 간 국제기구.

INGRES interactive graphics and retrieval system (미) 도형 데이터베이스관리시스템.

INH isonicotinic acid hydrazide 이소니코틴산 히드라지드. 결핵 예방 치료약.

INID Internationally Agreed Numbers for Identification of Data 서적 데이터 식별을 위한 국제 합의 번호.

INIS International Nuclear Information System 국제 원자력 정보 시스템.

INLA Irish National Liberation Army 아일랜드 민족해방군.

INMARSAT International Marine Satellite Organization 국제해사 위성기구. 해사통신위성을 중계로 하여 전 세계적으로 선박과 지상 사이의 전화·팩시밀리 등에 의한 교신을 위하여 설립된 기구.

INMM Institute of Nuclear Materials Management (미) 핵 물질 관리연구소.

INN Independent Network News (미) 독립 방송국 뉴스 공급 기관.

INOC Iraqi National Oil Company 이라크 국영 석유 회사.

INP ① index number of prices 물가 지수.
② International News Photo 국제 뉴스 사진 통신.

INPADOC International Patent Documentation Center 국제 특허 다큐멘터이션 센터.

INPFC International North Pacific Fisheries Commission 국제 북태평양 수산위원회 (북태평양의 어종에 관한 과학적 연구 검토 및 어족자원에 관한 연구협력을 위해, 1952. 5 설립. 회원국은 캐나다, 일본, 미국 3개국임).

INPO Institute of Nuclear Power Operation (미) 원자력 발전운명

연구 협회.

INRA International Natural Rubber Agreement 국제 천연고무협정.

INREU international noise reference unit (항공) 만국소음 측정단위.

INRIA Institut National de Recherche en Informatique et en Automatique (프) 국립 정보 처리 자동화 연구소.

INRO International Natural Rubber Organization 국제 천연고무 기구.

INS ① Immigration and Naturalization Service 이민국.
② inertial navigation system 관성 항법 장치.
③ international News Service 아이 엔 에스. 미국의 통신사. 1958년 UP와 합병하여 UPI가 되었다.

INSEE (프) Institut National de la Statistics des Etudes Economiques (= National Institute of Statistics and Economic Research) 프랑스 국립 통계 경제 연구소.

INSPEC Information Services in Physics, Electrotechnology, Computers and Control of the Institution of Electronic Engineers (영) 물리학, 전자 공학, 컴퓨터, 제어 공학의 세계 최대의 데이터 베이스.

INSTAC Information Technology Research & Standardization Center 정보 기술 연구 표준원 (일본의 정보기술 표준화추진 전담기관으로서, 1985. 7 민간회사들로 구성된 민간기구).

INSTRAW International Research and Training Institute for the Advancement of Women (UN) 여성의 향상을 위한 국제 훈련 연수소.

INTAL Instituto para la Integracion de America Latina (스) 라틴아메리카 통합연구소.

INTELPOST International Electric Post (mail) 국제 전자 우편 서비스 미국의 우편 공사(USPS)와 콤샛(COM-SAT) 공동에 의한 국제 전자 우편 서비스.

INTECOL International Association for Ecology 국제 생태학회.

INTELSAT International Telecommunications Satellite 국제통신 위성 기구.

INTERALIS International Advanced Life Information System 국제 생명보험 종합정보시스템.

Interpol International Criminal Police Organization 국제 형사 경찰 기구. = ICPO.

INTIB Industrial and Technological Information Bank 공업기술 정보뱅크.

int'l international 국제적.

241

INTOR International Tokamak Reactor 인톨 계획. IAE에서 핵융합의 실험로의 국제 공동설계가 실시되고 있으며 이 계획을 말한다.

INTOSAI International Organization of Supreme Audit Institution 최고 회계검사기관 국제조직.

INTUC Indian National Trade Union Congress 인도노동 조합 회의.

inv. invoice 송장.

INVESTEXT Investment TEXT 미국 기업 2,500사와 외국기업 1,000사에 관한 투자리포트를 온라인으로 제공하는 데이터베이스 (Business Research Corp. 제공).

invt. inventory 재산목록. 재고품 목록.

INVITE integrated visual telecommunication system 종합화상 통신 시스템. 종합 정보 통신망 (ISDN)의 전송 용량으로서 음성, 컬러 동화상, 컬러 정지화상, G4 팩시밀리(FAX), 외부 데이터를 동시 전송할 수 있는 종합 화상 통신 시스템.

I/O input-output unit (컴퓨터) 컴퓨터의 입출력장치.

IOA International Olympic Academy 국제 올림픽 아카데미. 매년 7월 그리스의 올림피아에서 개최.

IOAS integrated office automation system 종합 사무 자동화 체계. 여러 가지 사무 자동화 기기 들을 묶어 하나의 총괄 시스템 (total system)화하여 사용함으로써, 개별적으로 사용했을 경우 보다 더 큰 효과를 거둘 수 있게 하기 위한 것.

IOC ① input-output controller (컴퓨터) 입출력 제어 장치. ② International Olympic Committee 국제 올림픽위원회. ③ Inter-governmental Oceanographic Commission (유네스코) 정부간 해양학 위원회.

IOCS input-output control system (컴퓨터) 입출력 제어시스템.

IOCU International Organization of Consumers' Unions 소비자연합 국제기구.

IOE International Organization of Employers 국제 경영자단체연맹.

IOEC integrated opto electronic circuits 광집적회로.

IOF International Orienteering Federation 국제 오리엔티어링연맹.

IOFC Indian Ocean Fishery Commission 인도양 수산 위원회. (1967. 6 설립. 회원국은 호주, 바레인 등 45개국으로 우리 나라는 1967. 12 가입함. 인도양 및 인접 해역 - 남극해 제외-의 수산자원 개발과 보존을 위한 활동을 수행).

IOJ International Organization of Journalists 국제 저널리스트기구.

IOM International Organization for Migration 국제이민기구.

IOMTR International Organization for Motor Trades and Repair 국제 자동차 판매 수리 협회.

IONDS Integrated Operational Nuclear Detection System 통합 운용 핵 탐지 시스템.

IOOC International Olive Oil Council 국제 올리브유 이사회.

IOP input-output processor 입출력 프로세서.

IOPC International Oil Pollution Compensation 국제유류오염보상기금.

IORM Improved Order of Red Men (미) 1843년 Baltimore에 인디언의 생활향상을 목적으로 설립된 자선 단체.

IOS ① intelligent office system 자동화된 사무실.
② International Organization for Standardization = ISO 국제 표준화기구.
③ Investors Overseas Services, Ltd. 국제 투자신탁회사.

IOSCO International Organization of Securities Commissions 국제증권위원회기구. (각국 정부의 금융시장 및 증권관련 관리 감독 기관 협의기구).

IOSD International Organizations Sports Disabled 국제 장애자 스포츠 연맹.

IOU ① input-output control unit (컴퓨터)단말을 제어하는 유닛.
② I owe you 약식 차용 증서.

IP ① industrial policy 산업 정책.
② information provider 정보 제공자.
③ innings pitched (야구) 투구 횟수.
④ installment plan 분할 지불 방식.
⑤ Internet Protocol 인터넷 접속장치.

IPA ① information process analysis 정보 처리 분석.
② Inter - American Press Association 미주 신문 협회. = IAPA.
③ Intergovernmental Personnel Act (미) 관청 인사 교류법. 1970년 제정.
④ International Palaeontology Association 국제 고생물학 협회.
⑤ International Pharmaceutical Abstracts 국제 약학 초록.
⑥ International Phonetic Alphabet 국제 음표 문자.
⑦ International Phonetic Association 국제 음성 학회.
⑧ International Publishers Association 국제 출판사 협회.
⑨ isopropyl alcohol 이소프로필 알코올.
⑩ Internet Protocol Address 인터넷 접속주소.

IPAI International Primary Aluminum Institute 국제 알루미

뉴제런 협회. 1972년 설립.

IPAP Investment Promotion Action Plan (ASEM) 투자촉진 행동계획.

IPB International Peace Bureau 국제 평화 사무국. * 1982년 설립. 본부 제네바.

IPC ① International Patents Classification 국제 특허 분류.
② International Petroleum Co. 인터내셔널 석유 회사.
③ International Players Championships 국제 테니스 선수권 대회. = IPT.
④ Iraq Petrolem Co. 이라크 석유 회사.
⑤ Internal Policy Commission 북한 대내정책위원회.
⑥ International Peace Conference 국제평화회의.

IPCC Intergovernmental Panel on Climate Change 기후 변동에 관한 정부간 협의체.

IPCS Institution of Professional Civil Servants (영) 공무원 협회.

IPDC International Program for the Development of Communications 국제 통신 개발 계획.

IPE isopropyl ether 이소프로필 에테르.

IPEA International Preliminary Examining Authority 국제 특허 예비 심사 기관.

IPECK International Private Economic Council of Korea (한) 국제 인간 경제 협의회.

IPF Intergovernmental Panel on Forests 정부간 산림패널.

IPI International Press Institute 국제 신문 편집인 협회. * 1950년 설립. 본부 취리히.

IPI Service Interior Point Intermodal Service 한국, 일본 등을 비롯한 극동지역의 주요 항만으로부터 미국의 서안(西岸)이나 동안(東岸)을 경유하여 미대륙의 주요 도시까지 선사(船社)가 일관적으로 수송해 주는 서비스.

IPL initial program loader (컴퓨터) 프로그램을 주기억 장치에 기억시키기 위한 프로그램.

IPL-V information processing language-V (컴퓨터) 리스트 처리용 언어. 1959년 RAND사가 발표.

IPM International Plutonium Management 국제 플루토늄 관리체제.

IPMA International Personnel Management Association 국제 인사 관리 협회.

IPN inter penetrating polymer network 상호침입 고분자 그물코. 다성분계(多成分系) 고분자 재료.

IPOD International Project of Ocean Drilling 국제 심해 저굴착

계획.

IPOP International Polar Orbiting Platform 국제 극궤도 플랫폼 계획.

IPOT inductive potential divider (컴퓨터) 유도형 퍼텐셜 분할기.

IPPF International Planned Parenthood Federation 국제 가족계획 연맹.

IPPNW International Physicians for the Prevention of Nuclear Wars 핵전쟁 방지 국제 의사 의회.

IPR ① initial pressure regulator (원자력) 인구 압력 조정 장치. ② Institute of Pacific Relations 태평양 문제 조사회. ③ Intellectual Property Rights 지적재산권.

IPRA International Peace Research Association 국제 평화 연구협회.

IPS ① Institute for Policy Studies (미) 정책연구소. ② International Plutonium Storage 국제 플루토늄 저장. 잉여 플루토늄을 국제 관리하에 저장하는 제도.

IPSA International Political Science Association 세계 정치학회.

IPT ① Improved Programming Technique 개량 프로그래밍 기술. IBM사가 개발한 프로그램 생산성·신뢰성 향상 기법. ② International Players Tennis Championship = IPC 국제 테니스 선수권 대회.

IPTC International Press Telecommunications Committee 국제 신문통신 위원회. 뉴스의 교환에 우주통신을 사용하기 위하여 설립된 국제조직.

IPTS International Practical Temperature Scale 국제 실용 온도눈금.

IPU Inter Parliamentary Union 국제 의회 연맹.

IQ ① import quota 수입할당. ② improved quality 품질향상. 노사가 협조하여 생산물의 품질향상에 관하여 의논하여 서로 협력하는 것. ③ intelligence quotient 지능지수.

IQC Internal Quality Control 내부 품질관리.

IQSY International Quiet Sun Year 국제정온(靜穩) 태양관측년. 1964~65년.

Ir iridium (화학) 이리듐. 원자번호 77.

IR ① information retrieval (컴퓨터) 정보 검색. ② interrogator responsor (항공) 질문 송수신기. ③ isoprene rubber 이소프렌 고무. ④ Investor Relations 투자설명회.

IRA ① individual retirement annuity (미) 개인 적립 퇴직 연금. ② Irish Republican Army (영)

IRAN

아일랜드 공화국군. 북 아일랜드의 독립을 지향하는 카톨릭 교도의 반정부 지하조직. → UDA.

IRAN inspect and repair as necessary (항공기) 필요에 따라 실시하는 점검 수리.

IRANAIR Iran National Airlines 이란 항공.

IRAS infrared astronomical satellite 적외선 천문 위성.

IRB International Resources Bank 국제 자원 은행.

IRBM intermediate range ballistic missile 중거리 탄도 미사일.

IRC ① Industrial Reorganization Corporation(영)산업 재편성 공사.
② international record carrier (미) 국제 기록 통신 업자.
③ International Red Cross 국제 적십자사.
④ International Rescue Committee 국제 구제 위원회.
⑤ International Rice Commission (FAO) 국제 미곡 위원회.

IRCAM Institut de Recherche et de Coordination Acoustique Masique (프) 음향·음악의 탐구와 조정 센터. 조르쥐퐁피두 국립 문화 예술 센터의 음악 연구 기관.

IRCCD infra-red charge coupled device 적외선 전하 결합소자.

IRF International Road Federation 국제 도로 연맹.

IRFB International Rugby Football Board 국제 럭비 풋볼 보드.

IRG inter-record gap (컴퓨터) 레코드 사이에 아무것도 기록되어 있지 않은 부분.

IRH infrared homing 적외선 추적.

IRI (이) Istituto per la Ricostruzione Industriale (= Institute for Industrial Reconstruction) (이탈리아) 산업 부흥 공사.

IRIS infrared intruder system 적외선 잠입 탐지 장치.

IRLS ① infrared line scan 적외선 라인 스캔 장치.
② interrogation recording location system (기상) 원격 자료 수집 시스템.

IRM ① Information Resource Management 정보자원관리.
② intermediate range monitoring 중간 영역(領域) 모니터.

IRNA Islamic Republic News Agency (이란) 국영 이슬람 공화국 통신.

IRO International Refugee Organization (유엔) 국제 난민구제기구.

IRP indefinite repeat (컴퓨터) 거의 같은 처리 과정을 반복하여 실행하는 것.

IRPA International Radiation Protection Association 국제 방사선 보호학회.

IRPP Institute for Research on Public Policy (캐나다) 공공 정책연구소.

IRPTC International Register of Potentially Toxic Chemicals 국제 유해 화학 물질 등록 시스템.

IRQ intervention required (컴퓨터) 개입요구.

IRR internal rates of return 내부 수익률.

IRRI International Rice Research Institute (필리핀) 국제 벼농사(稻作)연구소.

IRS ① Incident Reporting System (원자력) 원자로 사고 통보시스템.
② information retrieval system 정보검색시스템.
③ Institut fur Reactor sicherheit (Institute for Reactor Safety) (서독) 원자로안전협회.
④ Internal Revenue Service (미) 국세청.
⑤ Information and Records Section 정보기록부.

IRSG International Rubber Study Group 국제 고무 연구회. * 1944년 설립.

IRT Interborough Rapid Transit Lines 뉴욕 지하철의 3계통 중 하나.

is island.

IS ① information separator (컴퓨터) 정보 분리 문자.
② information system 정보 시스템.
③ insertion sequence (생화학) 삽입 배열.
④ Installment Sales 할부판매.

ISA ① International Searching Authority 국제 특허 출원조사 기관.
② International Shakespeare Association 국제 셰익스피어 협회.
③ International Sociological Association 국제 사회학회.
④ international standard atmosphere (항공) 국제 표준대기.
⑤ International Sugar Agreement 국제 설탕 협정.

ISACA Information Systems Audit and Control Association 정보 시스템 감사 및 제어 협회 EDP(electronic data processing) 시스템 감사인의 기술과 사회적 지위의 확립을 목적으로 하여 1969년에 설립된 국제 조직인 EDPAA(EDP auditors association ; EDP 감사인 협회)가 1994년 6월에 개칭하였다.

ISBD International Standard Bibliographic Description 국제표준서지기술(서지 기술을 위한 국제표준으로서, 1970년대에 IFLA에 의해서 제정됨. 서지 정보를 구

ISAM

제적으로 표준화하고 호환성을 확립하기 위해 각국의 목록 규칙은 이 ISBD에 따라 제정되거나 개정되며 5년마다 수정되고 있음).

ISAM indexed sequential access method (컴퓨터) 색인 순차 액세스 방식.

ISAS International Stained Glass Art Society 국제 스테인 글라스 예술 협회.

ISBN International Standard Book Number 국제 표준 도서 번호.

ISC ① idle speed control 무가치 회전수 제어.
② International Sericultural Commission 국제 양잠 위원회.
③ International Society of Cardiology 국제 심장 학회.
④ International Society of Chemotherapy 국제 화학 요법 협회.
⑤ International Sugar Council 국제 설탕 이사회.
⑥ interstate commerce (미) 주간(州間) 통상.

ISCCP International Satellite Cloud Climatology Project 국제위성운 기후계획. 적도상에 있는 각국의 정지 기상위성의 구름의 화상을 자료로 전지구적인 구름의 분포도를 작성하여 기후의 연구를 하는 계획.

ISCED International Standard Classification of Education 국제교육 표준 분류.

ISCM International Society for Contemporary Music 국제 현대 음악 협회.

ISCO International Standard Classification of Occupation 국제 표준 직업 분류.

ISCSC International Society for the Comparative Study of Civilizations 국제 비교문화 연구학회.

ISD International subscriber dialing 국제전화 가입자 다이얼통화. 국제자동전화.

ISDB integrated services digital broadcasting 통합 서비스·디지털방송.

ISDN integrated services digital network 종합 정보 통신망. 위성통신, 광섬유 등 대용량 동신기술과 디지털전송기술을 이용한 통신망이며 전화, 전신, 데이터, 화상, 음성 등의 정보의 교환과 전송을 디지털 통신망으로 가능하게 한 종합 정보 통신망이다. INS의 국제적 호칭.

ISEAS Institute of Southeast Asian Studies 동남 아시아 연구소.

ISES International Solar Energy Society 국제 태양 에너지 학회.

ISF ① industrial space facility 민간 우주 공장. 미국 스페이스·인다스트리즈사와 웨스팅하우스사가 공동 개발한 우주 시설로서 우주공장을 쏘아 올려 기업에게 임대하여 신약, 신

소재의 개발·제조 등에 제공하는 것.
② International Amateur Sport Federation = FI, FIS, IF 국제 경기 연맹.
③ International Shipping Federation 국제 해운 연맹.
④ International softball Federation 국제 소프트볼 연맹.
⑤ International Sports Federation 국제 경기단체 연맹. 국제 스포츠 연맹.

ISFC International Society and Federation of Cardiology 국제 심장재단.

ISFET ion selected field effect transistor 이온선택 전계효과 트렌지스터.

ISFM International Spent Fuel Management 국제 사용 후의 핵연료관리.

ISFMS indexed sequential file management system 색인순차 파일 관리 시스템.

ISG International Silk Guild 국제 생사 조합.

ISHM International Society for Hybrid Microelectronics 국제 하이브리드·마이크로 일렉트로닉스협회.

ISI International Statistical Institute 국제 통계 협회.

ISIC International Standard Industry Classification 국제 표준 산업 분류.

ISIM International Society of Internal Medicine 국제 내과 학회.

ISIN International Securities Identification Numbering System 국제 증권 식별 번호체계. (유가증권의 매매와 결제, 예탁 및 보관 등 유가증권의 관리에 있어 특정 유가증권을 식별하는데 이용되는 국제적으로 표준화된 식별 번호체계로 국제표준화기구가 제정한 기준).

ISIS International Satellite for Ionospheric studies (캐나다) 국제 전리층 연구 위성.

ISL International Sports Culture and Leisure Marketing 국제적 규모의 스포츠 대회를 이용한 광고 선전, 스폰서 계약 등을 대리하는 회사.

ISM ① in store marketing 매장(賣場)에서 어떻게 하면 매상을 올릴 수 있는가 하는 연구.
② interpretive structural modeling 구조해석수법.

ISMA International Securities Market Association 국제 증권 시장협회.

ISMGF International Stroke Mandeviile Games Federation 국제 척수장애자 경기 연맹.

ISN internal statement number (컴퓨터) 내부 문(文) 번호.

ISO ① International Standardization Organization 국제표준화기구.

ISOC

② International Sugar Organization 국제 설탕 기구.

ISOC Internet Society 인터넷 학회, 인터넷 소사이어티 인터넷의 이용이나 기술에 관한 국제적인 협조와 협력을 추진하고, 자원 봉사자를 주축으로 한 비영리 단체.

ISOD International Sports Organization for the Disabled 국제 장애자 경기 연맹.

ISODE ISO Development Environment 국제 표준화 기구 개발 환경 OSI(open systems interconnection)의 트랜스포트층 레벨의 프로토콜 인터페이스를 TCP/IP 프로토톨 스택으로 제공하는 소프트웨어.

ISO-IS International Standardization Organization International Standard 국제 표준화기구의 국제규격.

ISONET ISO International Standardization Organization Network 국제 표준화 기구의 정보 네트워크

ISOTYPE international system of typographic picture education 국제 도형 교육 시스템.

ISP Imperial Smelting Process 임페리얼 정련법.

ISPA International Society for the Protection of Animals 국제 동물 애호 협회.

ISPM international solar polar mission 태양극궤도 관측 계획.

ISPN ① integrated service packet network 종합패킷 교환네트워크.
② International Standard Program Number 국제 표준 프로그램 번호.

ISR information storage and retrieval 정보의 축적과 검색.

ISRD International Society for Rehabilitation of the Disabled 신체장애자 갱생 국제협회.

ISRO International Securities Regulatory Organization 국제 증권규제기구.

ISS ① International Social Service (유엔) 국제 사회 사업단.
② International Space Station Program 국제 우주 정류장 계획.
③ ionosphere sounding satellite (일) 전리층 관측위성.

ISSA International Social Security Association 국제 사회보장 협회.

ISSC International Social Science Council 국제 사회과학 협의회.

ISSCC International Solid State Circuits Conference 국제 고체 회로 회의.

ISSF International School Sports Federation 국제 학교 스포츠 연맹.

ISSMFE International Society for Soil Mechanics and Foundation Engineering 국제 토질 기초공학회.

ISSN International Standard Serial Number (미) 국제 표준축차(逐次) 간행물 번호. 미국에서 간행되는 정기간행물에 미국의 의회도서관에서 부여하는 번호.

ISSO International Space Sciences Organization 국제우주과학기구.

IST information science technology 정보과학의 기술.

ISTC International Science and Technology Center 국제과학기술센터.

ISTEC International Superconductivity Technology Center (일) 국제 초전도 산업기술 연구센터.

ISTP International Solar Terrestrial Project (우주) 태양·지구계 물리 관측 계획. 지구의 자기권을 국제협력으로 종합적으로 탐사하는 계획.

ISU ① International Shooting Union 국제 사격 연맹.
② International Skating Union 국제 스케이트 연맹.

ISV ① independent software vendor 컴퓨터 제조 회사가 관계가 없는 소프트웨어 판매업자.
② international scientific vocabulary 국제 과학 용어.

ISY International Space Year 국제 우주년. 1992년.

IT ① inclusive terms 호텔의 식사대 포함 숙박료.
② inclusive tour 항공권, 숙박, 지상수송, 관광 등이 포함된 관광여행.
③ income tax 소득세.
④ information technology 정보기술.

ITA ① International Tin Agreement 국제 주석 협정.
② International Trade Administration (미) 상무성 국제통상국.
③ Independent Television Authority (英) 독립 텔레비전 공사. 1945년 설립, 1972년 IBA로 개칭.
④ initial teaching alphabet 초기 교육용 알파벳.

ITAA Information Technology Association of America 미국 정보 기술 협회. 미국의 컴퓨터 소프트웨어, 서비스 기업 및 컴퓨터 메이커의 연합체.

ital. italic(s) 이탤릭 체

IT&T ITT

ITAR International Traffic in Arms Regulation 국제 무기 거래규정.

ITC ① inclusive tour charter 포괄 여행 차터. 불특정 여객을 모아 비행기를 전세 내는 것.
② integrated traffic control system 적체교통 제어 시스템.
③ intelligent terminal controller 지능 단말기.
④ International Tin Council 국제 주석 이사회.

ITCC

⑤ International Toastmistress Club 국제 여성 사회자 클럽.
⑥ International Trade Charter 국제 무역 헌장.
⑦ International Trade Commission (미) 국제 무역 위원회.
⑧ International Translations Centre 국제 번역 센터.
⑨ investment tax credit 세액 공제 투자.

ITCC International Telephone Consultative Committee 국제 전화 자문위원회.

ITCZ Inter tropical Convergence Zone (기상) 열대수속대(收束帶).

ITEA International Test and Evaluation Association 국제 시험평가 협회.

ITEP Korea Institute of Industrial Technology Evaluation and Planning 한국 산업기술 평가원.

ITER International Thermal nuclear Experimental Reactor Project 국제 열핵 융합실험로 프로젝트.

ITF ① International Tennis Federation 국제 테니스 연맹.
② International Trade Fair 국제 견본시.
③ International Transport Worker's Federation 국제 운수노동자 연합.

ITI International Theatre Institute 국제 연극 협회. UNESCO의 외곽단체.

ITLOS International Tribunal for the Law of the Sea 국제해양법 재판소. (1994. 11 발효된 'The United Nations Convention on the Law of the Sea에 의거 설립된 국제기구로 독일 함부르크市에 소재).

ITIRC Technical Information Retrieval Center IBM 기술정보 센터.

ITIT Institute for Transfer of Industrial Technology (일) 공업기술 이전 연구소.

ITO ① instrument take off 계기 이륙.
② International Trade Organization (유엔) 국제무역기구.

ITOS improved TIROS Operation Satellite (미) 개량형 타이로스 실용위성. 주야를 통하여 지상을 촬영한다.

ITP ① idenosine triphosphate 아데노신 삼인산.
② intelligent terminal test program (컴퓨터) 인텔리전트 단말 테스트 프로그램.

ITRA International Tire and Rubber Association 국제 타이어고무 협회.

ITS ① international telecommunications services 국제 전기통신 서비스.
② International Trade Secretariat 국제 산업별 조직. ICFTU 계의 산업별 조직의 모임.

252

ITSC ① Institute for Technological and Scientific Cooperation (미) 기술 과학 협력원.
② International Thermal Spraying Conference 국제 용사 회의. 용사(溶射) (세라믹, 금속, 플라스틱)에 관한 연구, 기술의 발전을 촉진하는 단체.

ITT International Telephone and Telegraph Corporation (미) 국제 전화 전신회사.

ITTA International Tropical Timber Agreement 국제 열대 목재 협정.

ITTCS International Telephone and Telegraph Communication System 국제 전화 전신 통신 시스템.

ITTF International Table Tennis Federation 국제 탁구 연맹.

ITTO International Tropical Timber Organization 국제 열대목재 기구.

ITU ① International Telecommunications Union (유엔) 국제 전기 통신 연합.
② International Typographical Union 국제 활판 인쇄 노동조합.

ITU-T International Telecommunications Union Telecommunication recommendation 국제 전신 전화 유니온.

ITV ① Independent Television (영) 독립방송텔레비전. IBA의 텔레비전방송.
② instructional television 공업용 텔레비전. CCTV라고도 함.
③ instructional television 교육 텔레비전.

IU international unit 국제단위.

IUAI International Union of Aviation Insurers 국제 항공 보험 연합.

IUB International Union of Biochemistry 국제 생화학 연합.

IUCD intrauterine contraceptive device = IUD 자궁내 피임기구.

IUCN International Union for Conservation of Nature and Natural Resources 국제 자연 보호 연합.

IUCW International Union for Child Welfare 국제 아동복지 연합.

IUD intrauterine device = IUCD 자궁내 피임기구.

IUDZG International Union of Directors of Zoological Gardens 국제 동물원장 연맹.

IUE International Union of Electrical Radio and Machine Workers 국제 전기 기계공 노동조합.

IUGG International Union of Geodesy and Geophysics 국제 측지학·지구물리학연합.

IUGS International Union of Geological Sciences 국제 지질 과학 연합.

IULA International Union of

IULLA

Local Authorities 국제 지방 자치제 연합.

IULLA International Union of Language Laboratory 국제 어학 실습실 연합.

IUMI International Union of Marine Insurance 국제 해상 보험 연합.

IUOE International Union of Operating Engineers 국제 기계 운전자 노동 조합.

IUOTO International Union of Official Travel Organizations 관설(官設) 관광기관 국제 동맹. 1946년 설립. 본부 제네바.

IUPAB International Union of Pure and Applied Biophysics 국제 순수 응용 생물 물리학 연합.

IUPAC International Union of Pure and Applied Chemistry 국제순수 응용 화학 연합. 1919년 설립.

IUPAP International Union Pure and Applied Physics 국제 순수 응용 물리학 연합.

IUPHAR International Union of Pharmacology 국제 약리학 연합.

IUPS International Union of Physiological Science 국제 생리학 연합.

IUREP International Uranium Resources Evaluation Project 국제 우라늄 자원 평가계획.

IUS inertial upper stage (로켓) 스페이스 셔틀의 상단 로켓.

IUSSP International Union for the Scientific Study of Population 국제 인구문제 연구연합.

IVA intravehicular activity 우주선 내 활동. 우주선내에서 실행되는 실험·식사 등 모든 활동.

IVB invalidity benefit (영) 상병수당(傷病手當). 국민보건제도에서 6개월 이상 병으로 취로하지 못하는 자에 지급된다.

IVBF International Volleyball Federation 국제 배구 연맹.

IVD interactive video disk 대화형 비디오 디스크 개인용 컴퓨터에서 레이저 디스크(LD)와 같은 동화상이 들어간 비디오 디스크를 대화형(interactive)으로 조작하도록 하는 것.

IVD-LAN integrated voice and data local area network 음성 데이터 통합 랜. 이미 설치된 전화선을 써서 음성과 데이터의 양방 통신을 가능하게 하는 것.

IVE isobutyl vinyl ether 이소부틸 에테르.

IVF invitro fertilization 시험관내 수정.

IVPN international virtual private network 국제 가상 사설망 공중 전화 회선을 회사 내 전용선으로 사용하여, 통신 비용을 절감할 수 있는 방법.

IVS International Voluntary Service 국제 의용봉사단.

IVT integrated video terminal 종합 비디오 터미널.

IWA ① International Whaling Agreement 국제 포경 협정. ② International Wheat Agreement 국제 소맥 협정.

IWC ① International Whaling Commission 국제 포경 위원회. ② International Whaling Convention 국제 포경 회의. ③ International Wheat Convention 국제 소맥 위원회. ④ International Wheat Council 국제 소맥 이사회.

IWF ① International Weightlifting Federation = FHI 국제 역도 연맹. ② Inter Working Function 이동통신시스템과 인터넷을 연결하기 위한 무선 데이터 장치.

IWG Inter-Governmental Working Group 정부간 작업부회.

IWGP International Wrestling Grand Prix 국제 레슬링 그랑프리.

IWRA International water Resources Association 국제 수자원 협회.

IWRAW International Women's Rights Action Watch 국제 여성의 지위 감시운동.

IWS International Wool Secretariat 국제 양모 사무국.

IWSA International Water Supply Association 국제 수도 협회.

IWSG International Wool Study Group 국제 양모 연구회.

IWTC International Women's Tribune Center 국제 여성 운동센터. 여성 운동의 정보 수집과 활동을 원조하는 민간 기관.

IWTD Inland Water Transport Department (영) 내륙 수운(水運) 관리국.

IWTO International Wool Textile Organization 국제 양모 기구. 본부 런던.

IWW Industrial Workers of the World 세계 산업 노동자 조합.

IWY International Women's Year 국제 여성의 해(1975년).

I.X., IX Jesus Christ.

IYAS International Years of the Active Sun = IASY 태양 활동기 국제관측년.

IYC International Year of the Child 국제 아동년. 1979년.

IYDP International Year of the Disabled Persons 국제 장애자년. 1981년

IYF International Year of the Family 국제가족년. 1994년.

IYHF International Youth Hostel Federation 국제 유스호스텔 연맹.

IYP International Year of Peace 국제 평화의 해. 1986년.

IYQS International Year of the Quiet Sun = IQSY 국제 적인태양관측년. 1946년-65년.

IYRU International Yacht Racing Union 국제 요트 경기 연맹.

IYSA International Youth Service Agency (미) 국제 청년 봉사 기관. 발전도상국 원조를 목적으로 설립, 평화부대의 정부내의 정식 명칭.

IYSH International Year of Shelter for the Homeless 국제 노숙자. 1987년.

IYSM(UN) International Youth and Student Movement for the United Nations 유엔을 위한 국제청년·학생운동.

IYY International Youth Year 국제 젊은이의 해. 1985년.

Ja. Jauary (Jan) 1월.

JA ① joint account 공동예금계좌. ② jewish Agency 유태인 기관.

JAA Japan Asia Airways 일본 아시아 항공.

JAAA Japan Amateur Athletic Association 일본체육협회.

JAAS Japanese Association for American Studies (일) 아메리카학회.

Jackie Jacqueline의 애칭.

JADACS Japanese Self Defense Force Automatic Data Communication System (컴퓨터) 일본 육상 자위대 데이터 통신 시스템.

JAEC Atomic Energy Commission of Japan (일) 원자력위원회.

JAF Japan Automobile Federation 일본 자동차연맹.

JAFRI Japan Atomic Energy Research Institute 일본 원자력연구소.

JAFS Japan Friendship Society, Japan 일본 아시아 우호 협회.

JAIDO Japan International Development Organization 일본국제협력 기구.

JAIF Japan Atomic Industrial Forum 일본 원자력 산업 회의.

JAIMS Japan America Institute of Management Science 일미 경영과학 연구소.

JAL Japan Air Lines 일본항공.

Jan. January 1월.

JAMSTEC Japan Marine Science and Technology Center 일본 해양과학 기술센터.

JAN Japanese article number code 일본 상품 코드.

JANA Janahiriya News Agency 리비아 국영통신사.

JANET joint academic network 자네트 영연방 국가간의 네트워크.

JAP Jewish American Princess (미) 과보호의 환경에서 자라고 혼자서는 아무 것도 할 줄 모르는 미국 태생의 유태계의 젊은 여성. 남성인 경우에는 Prince가 됨.

JAPATIC Japan Patent Information Center 일본 특허 정보 센터.

JAPIC Japan Pharmaceutical Information Center 일본 의약정보 센터.

JAPIO

JAPIO Japan Patent Information Organization 일본 특허정보기구.

JARE Japanese Antarctic Research Expedition 일본 남극탐험.

JARL Japan Amateur Radio League 일본 아마추어 무선연맹.

JARO Japan Advertising Review Organization 일본 광고 심사 기구.

JAS ① Japan American Society 일미협회.
② Japanese Agricultural Standards 일본 농업 규격.

JASA Japan Amateur Sports Association 일본 체육 협회.

JASC Japan America Student Conference 일미 학생 회의.

JASDF Japan Air Self-Defence Force 일본 항공 자위대.

JAT Jugoslovenski Aerotransport (=Yugoslavian Air Transport) 유고슬라비아 항공.

JATEC Japan Technology & Economics Center 일본 기술 경제 센터.

JATO jet-assisted takeoff 분사 식이륙.

JBS John Birch Society 존 버치 협회. 반공극우단체.

JC ① junior chamber = jaycee, JCC 청년 회의소.
② Jesus Christ 예수 그리스도.

JCAB Japan Civil Aviation Bureau (일) (운수성) 항공국.

JCAE Joint Committee on Atomic Energy (미) 상하양원 원자력합동위원회.

JCAH Joint Committee on Accreditation of Hospitals (미) 병원인정합동기구.

J-car 제너럴 모터즈의 소형차. 1956년 발매.

JCB job control block (컴퓨터) 실행 조절 차단.

JCC Junior Chamber of Commerce 청년 회의소.

JCCI Japan Chamber of Commerce and Industry 일본 상공 회의소.

JCI Junior Chamber International 국제 청년 회의소.

JCIF Japan Center for International Finance (일) 국제 금융 정보 센터.

JCL job control language (컴퓨터) 실행 조절 언어.

JCP ① job control program 실행 관리 프로그램.
② Japan Communist Party 일본 공산당.

JCR ① junior combination room (영) (Cambridge 대학의) 저학년생 사교실.
② junior common room (영) (Oxford 대학등의) 저학년생

사교실.

JCS Joint Chiefs of Staff (미) 통합 참모 본부.

JCST Japan Central Standard Time 일본 중앙 표준시.

JD ① juvenile delinquency 소년 소녀 비행.
② juvenile delinquent 비행소년 또는 소녀.
③ (라) juris doctor (=doctor of jurisprudence) 법학 박사.
④ (라) jurum doctor (=doctor of laws) 법학 박사.

JDCA Japan Data Communications Association 일본 데이터 통신 협회.

JDL Jewish Defence League 유태인 방위 연맹.

JDR Japan Depositary Receipt 일본 예탁 증권.

JEI Japan Economic Institute (미) 워싱턴에 있는 일본정부 출자의 조사홍보기관.

JEM Japanese Experiment Module 유인 우주 기지 계획의 일본 실험 모듈.

JEN Junctor Equipment Number 접속기기 번호.

JEPS job entry peripheral services (컴퓨터) 실행입력 주변 서비스.

JES Japanese Engineering Standards 일본 기술표준규격.

JESSI 프로젝트 Joint European Submicron Silicon Project 유럽 기업연합에 의한 차세대 반도체 개발계획.

JET Joint European TOKAMAK (or Torus) (영) 유럽공동체의 토 거맥형 핵융합실험장치.

JETRO Japan External Trade Organization 일본 무역 진흥회.

JEV Japanese encephalitis virus 일본 뇌염 바이러스.

JFC Joint Force Commander 합동군사령관

JFCE Japan Federation of Commodity Exchanges (일) 전국 상품 거래소 연합회.

JFET junction field effect transistor 접합형 전계효과 트랜지스터.

JFK John Fitzgerald Kennedy 케네디 미국 제35대 대통령.

JFI Japan Fund Inc. (미) 대일투자 신탁회사.

JGSDF Japan Ground Self Defence Force (일) 육상 자위대.

JHQ Joint Headquarters 합동 사령부.

JHS junior high school 중학교.

JI job instruction 업무의 교육법. 감독자 훈련의 기본과정의 하나.

JIBICO Japan International Bank

JICA

and Investment 일본 국제 투자 은행.

JICA Japan International Cooperation Agency (일) 국제 협력 사업단. 발전도상국에 대한 기술원조를 담당하는 기관.

JICST Japan Information Center of Science and Technology 일본 과학 기술 정보 센터.

JIIA Japan Institute of International Affairs 일본 국제문제 연구소.

JIMC Joint Industrial Mobilization Committee 공동 산업 동원 위원회.

JNF Jewish National Fund 유태인 민족기금.

JINS juvenile(s) in need of supervision 요감시 미성년자.

JIS Japanese Industrial Standards 일본 공업 규격.

JIT ① job instruction training 직업 훈련.
② just-in-time 일본의 도요다 자동차가 개발한 무재고 생산방식.

JKCA Japan Korea Cultural Association (일) 한일문화협회.

JM job method 업무 개선법. 감독자 훈련의 기본과정의 하나.

JMP joint manpower program 통합 인적 자원 계획.

JMSDF Japan Maritime Self-Defence Force (일) 해상 자위대.

JMTC Joint Military Technology Commission 무기 기술 공동 위원회. 미일간의 무기기술의 공여에 관하여 협의·결정하는 기관.

JNA Jordan News Agency 요르단 통신.

JNC Japan Nuclear Cycle Development Institute 일본 핵연료 주기 개발 기구.

JND just noticeable difference (심리) 최소 인지 차이.

JNOC Japan National Oil Corporation (일) 석유 공단.

JNR Japanese National Railways 일본 국유 철도. 1987년 민간기업으로 이행.

JNTA Japan National Tourist Association 일본 관광협회.

JNTO Japan National Tourist Organization (일) 국제 관광 진흥회.

J.O.C. Japan Olympic Committee 올림픽위원회.

JOM Japan Offshore Market 일본 오프쇼어시장.

JOP Joint Operations 합동작전.

JOPAL Journal of Patent Associated Literature 특허 관련 문헌 저널.

JOSS Johnniac Open Shop System (컴퓨터) Rand사가 개발한 과학 기술 계산 언어.

JOT Joint Observer Team 共同

감시소조.

JOVLAL Jules Own Version of IAL (컴퓨터) 수식해석(數式解析)용 언어.

JP ① jet propulsion 제트추진.
② justice of the peace 치안판사.
③ judiciary Proceedings 재판 절차.

JPC ① Japan Patent Classification 일본 특허 분류.
② Japan Productivity Center 일본 생산성 본부.

JPG job performance guide (미) 직무수행기준.

JPIC Justice, Peace and the Integrity of Creation 창조의 정의, 평화, 완전.

JPL Jet Propulsion Laboratory (미) 제트 추진 연구소.

JPN ① Japan 일본.
② Japanese 일본인.

JPO Junior Professional Officer (국제기구)초급전문가.

JPS Jewish Publication Society of American (미) 유태인 출판 협회.

JR job relations 사람을 다루는 방법. 감독자 훈련의 기본 과정의 하나.

JRC Junior Red Cross 청소년 적십자.

JRDB Joint Research and Development Board (미) 종합 연구개발 심의회.

JRDC Research Development Corporation of Japan (일) 신기술 개발 사업단.

JSA ① Japan Standards Association 일본 규격 협회.
② Joint Security Area 공동경비구역.

JSB Japan Satellite Broadcasting Inc. 일본 위성방송. 민간의 위성 방송회사.

JSC Johnson Space Centre (미) 존슨우주센터.

JSD Japanese Standard of Dietetic Information 일본 영양성분 기준.

JSD [L] jurum scientiae doctor (=doctor of juristic science) 법학 박사.

JSDA Japan Securities Dealers' Association 일본 증권업 협회.

JSDF Japan Self Defense Force 일본 자위대.

JSF ① Japan Science Foundation 일본 과학기술 진흥재단.
② Japan Special Fund 일본 특별기금.

JSIA Justice System Improvement Act (미) 사법 제도 개선법.

JSIC Japan Standard Industry Classification 일본 표준 산업 분류.

JSNP Japan Satellite News Pool 일본 위성중계 협력기구.

JSP Josephson signal processor (컴퓨터)조지프슨 신호 처리 장치.

JST Japan Standard Time 일본 표준시.

JSTARS Joint Surveillance Target Attack Radar System 통합 감시·목표공격 레이더 시스템. 미 육·공군이 NATO전선에서 사용하고 있는 신형전자 정찰기에 장비하고 있는 미사일 발사 지휘 장치.

JTB ① Japan Traffic Bureau 일본 교통 공사.
② Japan Travel Bureau 일본 여행 공사.

JTBI JTB International 국제 일본 교통 공사.

JTIDS joint tactical information distribution system 통합전술정보배분센터.

Jul. July 7월.

Jun. June 6월.

JUNET Japan University Network (일) 대학간 과학기술정보 네트워크. 일본의 대학간을 연결할 뿐아니라 국제적인 네크워트의 일부로도 되어 있다.

JUP Jamiatul Ulamae Pakistan 파키스탄 장로당(長老黨).

JUSB Japanese University Sports Board 일본유니버시아드 위원회.

JUST Japanese Unified Standards for Telecommunications 일본 통신규격.

JV joint venture 공동 기업.

JVP [신할리즈語] Janatha Vimukti Peramuna (=People's Liberation Front) (스리랑카) 인민 해방 전선.

K ① Kalium(potassium) (라) 칼륨, 포타슘. 원자번호 19.
② Kelvin 절대온도의 단위. 절대온도 = -273℃. (예) 90K = -183℃.

K., k. karat (Kt. 라고도 약함). carat = 보석의 중량단위. karat = 금의 순도를 나타내는 단위.

K critical point (스키) 극한점을 말하며 점프대의 착륙면이 끝나고 권외부가 시작하는 점. 이 이상 뛰면 위험하다는 지점이며 적색 라인으로 표시한다.

K-QA Korean Quality Control Engineers Association 한국품질관리기사협회 (QC기사 및 품질관련 전문인의 단체로서 교육훈련, 품질경영 진단 및 지도, 국내외 품질관련 제반 인증에 관한 지도기관으로 1988. 10 설립).

KA Korean Army 한국 육군.

KAA Korea Advertisers Association 한국 광고주 협회.

KAAA Korea Amateur Athletic Association 대한체육회.

KAB Korea Appraisal Board 한국감정원.

KABC Korea Audit Bureau of Circulations 한국 ABC협회. 신문잡지발행부수심사협회.

KAC Kwajalein Atoll Cooperation 크와제린 환초(環礁)조합.

KADIZ Korea Air Defense Identification Zone 한국방공식별구역.

KADU Kenya African Democratic Union 케냐·아프리카 민주주의 동맹.

KAEB Korean Atomic Energy Bureau 한국 원자력국.

KAEC Korean Atomic Energy Commission 한국 원자력위원회.

KAERI Korean Atomic Energy Research Institute 한국 원자력 연구소.

KAETCH Korea Automotive Technology Institute 자동차부품연구원.

KAF ① Korean Air Force 한국 공군.
② Kinase activating factor (生化學) 키나아제 활성 인자.

KAFA Korean Air Force Academy 韓國 空軍士官學校(한국 공군 사관학교)

KAIF Korean Atomic Industrial Forum 한국 원자력 산업회의.

KAISER Knowledge Acquisition Oriented Information Supplier 대규모의 지식 베이스를 대상으로 한 지식 베이스 관리 소프트 웨어.

KAIST Korean Advanced Institute of Science & Technology 한국 과학기술원.

KAL Korean Air Lines=KE 대한항공.

KAMA Korea Automobile Manufacturers Association 한국자동차 제조 협회.

KAN ① Korean article number 한국 상품코드.
② Korean Association Newspapers 한국 신문 협회.

Kans. Kansas = Kan. 캔사스주.

KANU Kenya Africa National Union 케냐·아프리카 민족 동맹.

KAO Korea Astronomy Observatory 천문대.

KAPH Korean Artist Proletarian Federation 북한 조선 프롤레타리아 예술 동맹.

KAPL Knolls Atomic Power Laboratory (미) 놀즈 원자력 연구소.

K&R Kiss and ride system 출근하는 남편을 부인이 자가용으로 역이나 버스정거장까지 데려다 주는 이동방식.

KARI Korean Aerospace Research Institute 한국 항공 우주 연구소.

KARICO Korea Agricultural Rural Infrastructure Corporation 농업기반공사. (2000. 1 농지개량조합, 농지개량조합연합회, 농어촌진흥공사를 통합 발족한 기관).

KAST Korean Academy of Science and Technology 한국과학기술한림원(과학기술에 전문적인 식견을 가진 석학들을 회원으로 하여 각 부문별 전문성을 활용함으로써 국가 과학기술의 진흥과 창달에 기여를 목적으로 1994. 11조직.

KATA Korea Association of Travel Agents 한국 일반 여행업협회.

Kate 여자이름. Catherine, Katherine, Katherine의 애칭.

KATUSA Korean Augmentation Troops to U.S. Army (주한) 미군파견 한국군인.

KAVA Korean Association of Voluntary Agencies 한국 외원(外援) 단체 협회.

Kay 여자이름. Catherine, Katharine Katherine의 애칭.

KB ① Key board 키보드.
② Kilo byte (컴퓨터) 킬로바이트.

KBA ① Korean Businessmen's Association 한국 경영자 협회.
② Korea Broadcasters Association 한국방송협회.

KBC Korean Broadcasting Commission 한국 방송 위원회. 방송법에 의해 설치된 법적 기관.

KBE Knight Commander of the

Order of the British Empire (영) 대영 제국 2등 훈작사.

KBI Korean Broadcasting Institute 한국 방송 개발원. 1989년 4월 설립된 재단 법인.

KBL [Pilipino語] Kilusang Bagong Lipunan (=New Society Movement) (필리핀) 신사회 운동. 정당명. 마르코스 전 필리핀 대통령의 강권 정치 체재를 지탱시켰던 여당.

KBMS knowledge base management system 지식 베이스 관리 시스템. 저장된 지식을 자동적으로 구성하고, 제어하며, 전달하고, 갱신함으로써 지식 베이스를 관리하는 시스템.

KBO Korea Baseball Organization 한국 야구 위원회.

KBPS kilo bits per second 단위 시간당 킬로 비트수. 데이터의 전송 속도. 1초당 1024 bit (1024 bit/s)의 배수.

kbps kilo bit(s) per second 초당 킬로비트. 정보의 전달속도의 단위.

KBS Korean Broadcasting System 한국 방송공사.

KBSI Korea Basic Science Institute 한국기초과학지원연구원. 기초과학연구에 필수적인 연구 장비를 통한 연구지원 및 공동연구 수행을 목적으로 지난 1988 설립.

KC ① kilo character 킬로 자(字). 1000자.
② KC Ling's Counsel (英) 칙선 변호사.

KCK Korean Customs Administration 한국 관세청.

K-car (미) 크라이슬러 소형차.

KCAF Korean Culture & Arts Foundation 한국 문화예술 진흥원.

KCB Knight Commander of the Most Honourable Order of the Bath (영) 바스 2등 훈작사.

KCC Korea Chamber & Commerce 대한 상공 회의소.

KCCI The Korea Chamber of Commerce & Industry 대한상공회의소.

KCF Korean Christian Federation 한국 기독교 연맹.

KCG Korea Coast Guard 해양 경찰청.

KCIA Korean Central Intelligence Agency 한국 중앙정보부. 1980년 ANSP로 개칭.

KCID Korean Cosmetic Ingredient Dictionary 한국 화장품 원료집.

KCl Potassium Chloride 염화칼륨.

KCIE Knight Commander of the Most Eminent Order of the Indian Empire (영) 인도 제국 2등 훈작사.

KCMG Knight Commander of the Most Distinguished Order of St. Michael and St. George (영) 성

KCN

미카엘 성조지 2등 훈작사.

KCN Potassium Cyanide 청산가리(靑酸)

KCNA Korean Central News Agency 한국 중앙통신.

KCPB Korea Consumer Protection Board 한국 소비자 호보원. (소비자의 기본 권익을 보호하고 소비생활의 합리화를 도모하며 나아가 국민경제의 건전한 발전에 기여를 목적으로 소비자 보호법에 의해 1987. 7. 설립).

KCR Korean Cataloging Rules 한국목록규칙.

KCS ① Kansas City Standard 캔사스시 규격. 오디오 카세트 테이프에의 표준녹음 · 재생규격. ② thousand characters per second 1초당 1,000자. ③ Korea Customs Service 관세청.

KCSC The Korea Cadastral Survey Corporation 대한 지적 공사.

KCSI Knight Commander of the Most Exalted Order of the Star of India (영) 인도 성 2등 훈작사.

KCTU Korean Confederation of Trade Union 민주노총.

KCVO Knight Commander of the Royal Victorian Order (영) 빅토리아 2등 훈작사. → DCVO.

KCWS Korea Church World Service 한국 기독교 세계 봉사회.

KD ① Knockdown 때려 눕히기 ② Knocked down 낙찰.

KDC Korean Decimal Classification 한국십진분류법.

KDB Korea Development Bank 한국 개발은행.

KDD Kokusai Denshin Denwa Co., Ltd. (일) 국제 전신 전화 주식 회사.

KDF Knocked-down furniture 조립식 가구.

KDFC Korea Development Finance Corporation 한국개발금융공사.

KDI Korea Development Institute 한국 개발원.

KDIC Korea Deposit Insurance Corporation 예금보험공사. (1995년 제정된 예금자보호법에 따라 1996. 4 설립).

KDPC Korea Design & Packing Center 한국 디자인 포장센터.

KDS Korea Securities Depository 증권예탁원(證券預託院). (1974. 12 한국 증권 대체 결제 주식회사로 출범하여 1994. 4 현 재명의 개원한 기관).

KE ① Knowledge Engineer 지식 공학 기술자. ② Knowledge Engineering 지식 공학. ③ Korea Air = KAL 대한 항공.

KEC Korea Electric Company 한

국 전력 회사.

KECF Korea-ESCAP Cooperation Fund 한국 협력기금

KECO Korea Electric Company 한국 전력.

KEDI Korean Educational Development Institute 한국 교육 개발원. 1972년 설립.

KEDO Korean Peninsula Energy Development Organization 한반도 에너지 개발기구.

KEE knowledge engineering environment system 지식 공학 환경 시스템 방법(tool) 표현을 기반으로 하는 지식공학 이외에도 규칙 기반, 절차 지향적・객체 지향적 표현방법을 제공하는 시스템.

KEIC Korea Export Industrial Corporation 한국 수출 산업 공단.

KEF ① Korea Euro Fund 코리아 유로펀드.
② Korean Employer federation 한국 경영자 총연합회.

KEIDANREN Federation of Economic Organizations (일) 경제 단체 연합회.

KEMCO Korea Energy Management Corporation 한국 에너지 관리 공단.

Ken 남자이름. Kenneth의 애칭.

KEPAD Korea Employment Promotion Agency for the Disabled 한국 장애인 고용 촉진 공단. (장애인 고용 촉진등에 관한 법률에 의거 1990. 9 설립된 기관).

KEPCO Korean Electric Power Corporation 한국 전력 공사.

KERI Korea Electric Technology Research Institute 한국 전기 연구소.

KERIS Korea Education and Research Information Service 한국교육학술정보원. (1999. 4 한국교육학술원법에 따라 종전의 멀티미디어 교육지원센터와 첨단학술정보센터를 통합하여, 교육학술 정보화를 추진하는 정부출연기관으로 발족).

KESCO Korea Electrical Safety Corporation 한국 전기 안전공사.

KET Korea Equity Trust 외국인 전용수익증권의 일종.

KETEL Korea Economic Daily Telepress (한) 매일 경제데이터뱅크 * 국내외의 경제뉴스, 산업, 경제, 증권, 문화 등에 관한 데이터뱅크.

KeV kilo electron volt 킬로 전자 볼트.

KEW Kinetic energy weapon 운동 에너지 병기. 고속으로 가속되 물체가 가진 운동에너지에 의하여 목표를 파괴하는 병기.

KF ① Korea Fund 코리아펀드.
② Kooperativa Forbundet 스웨덴의 생활 공동 조합.

KFC Kentucky Fried Chicken Corporation (미) 캔터키 프라이드 치킨사(社).

KFP Korean Fighter Program (한국) 차세대전투기 구매 및 공동생산계획.

KFSB Korea Federation of Small Business 중소기업 협동조합 중앙회.

KFF Korea Football Federation 대한축구협회.

KFQ Korea Foundation for Quality 한국품질재단.

KFS Korea Forest Service 산림청.

KFTA Korea Foreign Trade Association 한국 무역협회.

KFU Korean Farmers Union 대한농민회.

KFX Korean Foreign Exchange 한국 정부 보유외환.

kg. kilogram(s) 킬로그램.

KG Knight of the Order of the Garter (영) 가터 훈작사.

KGB Komitet Gosudarstvennoi Bezopasnosti (Committee of State Security) (러) 국가보안위원회.

KGC Korea Gas Corporation 한국 가스 공사.

KGCB Knight Grand Cross of the Most Honourable Order of the Bath (영)바스 1등 훈작사. = GCB

KGF Knight of the Order of the Golden Fleece (스페인, 오스트리아) 금양모 훈작사.

KGLP Korea Good Laboratory Practice 한국 의약품 안전성 시험관리 기준(개발된 신물질의 유효성 평가를 위한 임상시험에 앞서 동물을 사용하여 일반 및 특수 독성 등을 실시해야 하는 바, 이에 필요한 시험기준과 시험실시기관에 대한 관리 기준으로서 조직, 시설장비, 인력구성, 실험동물 사육에 관한 사항을 정한 기준).

KGMP Korea Good Manufacturing Practice 한국 우수 의약품 제조 기준.

KGSC Korea Gas Safety Corporation 한국 가스 안전 공사.

KGSP Korea Good Supplying Practice 한국 우수 의약품 유통 관리 기준(의약품 유통과정에서 안전성·유효성이 보장될 수 있도록 하기 위해 의약품 도매상의 시설 및 취급에 관한 사항을 정한 기준).

KGTRI Korea Ginseng and Tobacco Research Institute 한국 인삼 연초 연구소.

kgw kilogram weight 중량 킬로그램.

kgwm kilogram weight meter 중량 킬로그램미터. 일의 단위.

kggwm/s kilogram weight meter per second 초당 중량 킬로그램미터. 공율(工率)의 단위.

KH Korea Herald (한국) 영자 일간지.

KHC Korea Highway Corporation 한국 도로 공사.

KHD Klockner Humboldt Deutz 독일의 엔진, 터빈, 트랙터 등의 제조 회사.

KHIC Korea Heavy Industry Co. 대한 중공업 회사.

KHz kilohertz 킬로헤르츠.

Kia Kia Industrial Company Ltd. (한) 기아산업.

KIA Killed in action 전사자(戰死者).

KIAA Korea Industrial Advancement Administration 한국 공업 진흥청 국제 표준화 기구(ISO), 국제 전기 표준회의(IEC) 등 국제 표준화 기구에 등록 사용하여 온 우리나라의 대표 기관의 공식 명칭.

KIC Korea Institute of Criminology 한국형사정책연구원 (1988. 8 제정 한국형사정책연구원법에 의거국가의 형사정책수립과 범죄방지를 통한 국민의 삶의 질 향상을 목적으로 설립된 연구기관).

KICOX Korea Industrial Complex Corporation 한국 산업 단지 공단 (산업단지 조성과 공장용지를 분양하고, 국가산업단지의 효율적인 관리와 입주기업체의 경쟁력 강화를 위한 지원 업무를 수행기관으로 1997. 1 5개 권역별 국가산업단지 관리공단 통폐합하여 발족).

KICS Korea Information and Communication Standards 한국 정보 통신 표준

KICT Korea Institute of Construction Technology 한국건설기술연구원 (건설기술의 연구개발, 정책개발, 건설 기자재의 조사·시험 및 품질관리, 시설물 유지관리 기법에 대한 여구개발 및 기술보급을 위해 1983. 6 설립된 기관)

KID key industry duty 기초산업 보호관세.

KIDA Korea Institute for Defense Analyses 한국 국방 연구원

KIDP Korea Institute of Design Promotion 한국 디자인 진흥원 (산업디자인의 개발촉진 및 진흥을 위한 사업을 효율적이고 체계적으로 추진하기 위하여 1970 설립된 한국디자인 포장센터를 2001. 4 현재 명칭으로 개편.)

KIEE Korea Institute of Electrical Engineers 대한 전기 학회.

KIEF Korea Institute for Industrial Economics and Technology 한국 산업 연구원.

KIEP Korea Institute for International Economic Policy 대외경제정책연구원. (우리 나라 경제의 국제적 능력과 능동적인 대외경제외교의 추구를 뒷받침할 정책연구 수행을 목적으로 1989. 12발족된 정부출연 연구기관).

KIET

KIET Korea Institute for Economics and Technology 한국 산업 경제기술 연구원.

KIF Korea Institute of Finance 한국 금융 연구원. (금융 산업·정책 발전을 위한 연구를 수행할 목적으로 1991 설립)

KIGAM Korea Institute of Geoscience and Mineral Resources 한국지질자원연구원 (1918 설립된 지질 조사소를 모태로 지질조사 및 광물자원탐사에 대한 연구기관. 2001. 1 한국자원연구소에서 현재명칭으로 변경).

KIHASA Korea Institute for Health and Social Affairs 한국 보건사회연구원 (1971 설립된 보건, 의료, 사회복지 및 이와 관련된 모든 분야의 정책과제를 연구 분석하는 기관).

KII Korean Information Infrastructure 한국 초고속 정보 통신망 구상 계획. 1994년 4월에 정부가 책정한 초고속 정보.

KIKO Knock-in, Knock-Out 기업과 은행이 환율 상하단을 정해 놓고 그 범위 내에서 지정환율로 외화를 거래하는 상품

KIMC Korea Iron Mining Co. 대한 철강 협회.

KIMM Korea Institute of Machinery & Metals 한국 기계 연구소.

KINU Korea Institute for National Unification 통일연구원.

KIPI Korea Interior Point Intermodal 한국 내륙지 복합 운송.

KIPO Korea Intellectual Property Office 특허청.

KIPA Korea IT Industry Promotion Agency 한국 소프트웨어 진흥원 (1998. 9 설립된 소프트웨어산업진흥법 제17조에 의한 특수법인).

KIPS ① Knowledge Information Processing System 지식 정보 처리 시스템. 방대한 지식을 처리 하기 위하여 제5세대 컴퓨터로 1990년대의 실현을 목표로 연구개발중이다.
② Korean Information Processing System 한국 정보 처리 시스템.

KISA Korea Information Security Agency 한국정보보호진흥원 (정보화촉진기본법에 의거 1996. 4 한국정보보호센터로 설립, 2001. 7 현재 명칭으로 변경).

KISDI Korea Information Society Development Institute 정보통신정책연구원 (1988 통신개발연구원법을 모태로 설립후 1997 현재 명칭으로 개칭된 연구기관).

KIST Korean Institute for Science and Technology 한국 과학 기술 연구소.

KISTEP Korea Institute of Science & Technology Evaluation and Planning 한국과학기술기획

평가원 (1987. 1 설립된 한국과학기술원 부설 과학시루정책연구평가센터를 모체로 2001. 7 현재 조직으로 개편).

KIT Korea International Trust 외국인 전용수익증권(外國人受益證券)의 일종.

Kitty 여자이름. Catherine, Katherine의 애칭.

KITA Korea International Trade Association 한국무역협회.

KITECH Korea Institute of Industrial Technology 한국생산기술연구원 (중소기업의 경영 안정 및 구조조정 촉진에 관한 특별 조치법에 의거 1989. 10 산업계 생산기술의 종합적 연구개발을 수행을 위해 설립된 기관).

KJCA Korea Japan Cultural Association 한일 문화 협회.

KJV King James Version 흠정(欽定) 영역 성서.

KK Kabushiki Kaisha 주식회사의 약칭.

KKK Ku Klux Klan (미) KKK단. 흑인 박해를 위한 백인 비밀 결사.

KLA Korean Leprosy Association 한국 나병 협회.

KLAC Korea Legal Aid Corporation 대한 법률 구조 공단.

KLAFIR Korea Local Authorities Foundation for International Relations 지방자치단체국제화재단 (1994. 7 지방자치단체들이 국제 경쟁력을 갖고 선진지방 행정으로 나아가도록 지원하기 위해 설립).

KLI Korea Labor Institute 한국 노동연구원 (1988 개원된 노동문제 전문 공공연구기관).

KLM Koninkijkr Luchtvaart Maatschappij (Royal Dutch Airlines) (네) 네덜란드 항공.

KLRI Korea Legislation Research Institute 한국법제연구원 (법령 정보를 체계적으로 수집·관리하고 법제에 관하여 전문적으로 조사·연구함으로써 국가입법정책의 지원, 법령정보의 신속·정확한 보급, 법률문화의 향상을 목적으로 1990. 7 설립된 정부출연 연구기관).

KLWC Korea Labor Welfare Corporation 한국 근로 복지공사.

Km. kilometer(s) 킬로미터.

KM ① kanamycin 카나마이신. ② Korea Military 한국군.

KMA ①Korean Military Academy 한국 육군 사관 학교 (韓國陸軍士官學校)
② Korea Medical Association 대한 의사 협회.
③ Korea Management Association 한국 능률협회.

KMAG Korea Military Advisory Group (미) 대한군사고문단.

271

KMC Korea Marine Corps 한국 해병대.

KMG Knight Commander of Order of St. Michael and St. George (영) 성 미카엘 성 조지 2등 훈작사.

KMI Korea Maritime Institute 한국 해양 수산 개발원 (한국 해양 수산 개발원법에 의해 1997. 4 설립된 기관).

KMIC Korea Medical Insurance Corporation 한국 의료보험 관리공단.

KMP key measurement point (원자력) 기간 측정점.

KMP ① Korean Peninsula Marshall Plan 한반도 마샬 플랜 ② Korean Maritime Police 해양경찰.

KMPA Korea Maritime and Port Administration 한국해운항만청.

KMPC Korea Mining Promotion Corporation 대한 광업 진흥공사.

KMRWC Korea Merit Reward Welfare Corporation 한국 보훈복지 공단.

KMS Knowledge Management System 지식관리시스템.

KMTATIS Korea Mobile Telecommunications Advanced Traffic Information System 지능형 교통 정보 시스템. 개발한 교통 정보에 관한 서비스 시스템.

KNA Kenya News Agency ① 케냐 통신사. 국영 통신사. ② Korea Naval Academy 해군사관학교.

KNCC Korean National Council of Churches 한국 기독교 교회협의회.

KNDU Korean National Defense University 국방대학교.

KNHC Korea National Housing Corporation 대한 주택공사.

KNOC Korea National Oil Corporation 한국석유공사 (석유자원의 탐사 및 개발, 석유의 비축과 유통으로 안정적인 수급을 보장하기 위하여 1979 설립).

KNP Koran National Police 한국 국립 경찰.

KNR Korean National Railroad 철도청.

KNRC Koran National Red Cross 대한적십자사.

KNT Korea Nineteen Ninety Trust 외국인 전용수익증권의 일종.

KNTC Korea National Tourism Corporation 한국 관광 공사.

KNTO Korea National Tourist Organization 한국관광공사.

KO knockout 넉아웃.

KOAMI Korea Association of Machinery Industry 한국 기계 산업 진흥회.

KOBACO Korea Broadcasting Advertising Corporation 한국방송 광고 공사. 1981년 1월에 설립된 특수 법인.

KOC ① Korean Olympic Committee 한국 올림픽 위원회. ② Kuwait Oil Company 쿠웨이트 석유회사.

KOCHAM Korea Chamber of Commerce and Industry 대한상공회의소.

KOCOAL Korea Coal Corporation 대한 석탄 공사 (석탄광산의 개발촉진과 석탄의 생산·가공·판매 및 그 부대 사업을 운영하는 기관으로 1950 설립).

KOEX Korea Exhibition Center 한국 종합전시장.

KOFEX Korea Futures Exchange 한국선물거래소. (1995. 12 제정된 선물거래법에 의거 1999. 1 설립된 기관).

KOICA Korea International Cooperation Agency 한국국제협력단. (정부차원의 대외무상협력사업을 전담 실시하는 기관으로 1991. 4 설립)

KOIS Korean Overseas Information Service (한국) 공보처 해외공보관.

KOLAND Korea Land Corporation 한국토지공사. (토지자원의 효율적인 이용을 촉진하고 국토의 종합적인 이용 및 개발을 도모하기 위하여 1979 설립)

KOMSEP Korea Security Printing & Minting Corporation 한국조폐공사.

KOR Komitet Obrony Robotnilkow (폴란드)사회 자위 위원회.

KORDI Korea Ocean Research & Development Institute 한국해양연구원. (1973.10 한국과학기술연구소 부설 해양개발연구소로 설립되어 2001. 1. 현재 명칭으로 변경된 연구기관).

KORECO Korea Resources Recovery and Reutilization Corporation 한국 자원 재생 공사.

KORES Korea Mining Promotion Corporation 대한광업진흥공사. (1967 민영광산의 합리적 개발과 해외광물자원 확보를 위한 광업종합 조성 기관으로 설립된 기관).

KORMARC Korean Machine Readable Cataloging 한국문헌자동화목록

KORSTIC Korea Scientific & Technological Information Center 한국 과학기술정보센터.

KOSOC Korea Oil Storage Company 대한 석유 저장 주식 회사.

KOSDAQ Korea Securities Dealers Automated Quotation 코스닥.

KOSEF Korea Science and Engineering Foundation 한국 과학재단. (1976 제정된 한국과학재단

273

법에 의거 1977. 5 설립된 기관).

KOSHA Korea Occupational Safety & Health Agency 한국산업 안전공단. (산업재해예방에 관한 사업을 효율적으로 수행함으로써 근로자의 안전과 보건을 유지 증진하고 사업주의 재해예방활동을 촉진하기 위해 한국산업안전공단법에 의거 1987. 12. 설립).

KOTI Korea Transport Institute 교통개발연구원. (1985. 11 설립된 기관).

KOTRA Korea Trade Promotion Corporation 대한 무역진흥공사.

KOVA Korea Venture Business Association 벤처기업협회. (벤처 회원기업 활성화와 기술혁신을 통한 국제 경쟁력 강화로 국가 경제에 공헌을 목적으로 1995. 12 설립).

KOWACO Korea Water Resources Corporation 한국수자원공사. (수자원을 종합적으로 개발, 관리하여 생활용수 등의 공급을 원활하게 하고 수질을 개선함으로서 국민 생활의 향상과 공공복리의 증진에 이바지함을 목적으로 1967. 11 설립된 기관).

KOWOC Korean World Cup Committee 월드컵 한국 조직 위원회 Korean Organizing Committee for the 2002 FIFA World Cup Korea / Japan (공식명칭 2002 FIFA 월드컵 한국 조직위원회).

KP ① kitchen police (군사) 취사근무.
② Knight of the Order of St. Patrick (영) 성 패트릭 훈작사.
③ (러) Kommunis-ticheskaya Partiys (=Communist Party) (소련) 공산당.

KPA Korean Procurement Agency (of the U.S. Army) 주한미군 구매처.

KPC Korea Productivity Center 한국 생산성본부.

KPEC Korea Press Ethics Commission 한국 신문 윤리 위원회 (韓國新聞倫理委員會).

KPM King's Police Medal (영) 경찰 공로 훈장.

KPNLF Khmer People's National Liberation Front (캄보디아) 크메르 인민 민족 해방 전선.

KPO (독) Kommunistische Partei Osterreichs (=Communist Party of Austria) 오스트리아 공산당.

Kr krypton 크립톤. 원자번호 36.

KR ① Kennedy Round 케네디 라운드. 가트의 관세 일괄 인하 교섭(1964-67)
② Korean Register of Shipping 한국 선급협회.

KRC Korean Red Cross 대한 적십자사.

KREEP potassium, rare earth element and phosphate 크리프. 우주비행사가 달에서 채취한 황

갈색의 유리모양의 광물.

KREI Korea Rural Economic Institute 한국농촌경제연구원. (농축산물의 생산 및 유통, 농업구조 농지제도 및 농촌지역 종합 개발 등에 대한 연구를 위해 1978. 4 설립된 기관).

KRET Korean Rural Economy Institute 한국 농촌 경제 연구원.

KRF Korea Research Foundation 한국 학술 진흥 재단.

KRIHS Korea Research Institute for Human Settlements (한) 국토 개발 연구원.

KRL Knowledge representation language 지식 표현 언어 지식 베이스 시스템. (knowledge based system)에 입력하는 지식을 일정한 규칙으로 표현하기 위한 언어.

KS ① Kansas (美) 캔자스 주(州)의 우편 기호.
② King's Scholar (英) 왕실 장학 기금 급비생.
③ Korean(Industrial) Standards 한국 공업 규격.

KSA ① Korea Shipping Association 한국 해운 조합.
② Korea Standard Association 한국 공업 표준 협회.

KSC ① Kennedy Space Center 케네디 우주센터.
② Korea Software Center 소프트웨어 지원센터.
③ Korea Sports Council 대한체육회.

KSCI Korea Standard of Cosmetic Ingredients 한국화장품원료기준. (약칭 장원기, 화장품의 원료로 쓰이는 물질에 대하여 그 성상 및 규격에 관한 기준).

KSE Korea Stock Exchange 한국증권거래소.

KSEA Korean-American Scientists and Engineers Association 재미 한인 과학 기술자 협회.

KSFC Korea Software Financial Cooperative 소프트웨어 공제조합. (S/W 산업의 진흥을 위하여 사업자에게 자금대여, 채무보증, 이행보증, 자금투자 및 고유 목적사업을 하기 위하여 설립된 특수법인).

KSIC Korean Standard Industrial Classification 한국표준산업분류.

KSME Korean Society of Mechanical Engineers 대한기계학회.

KST Korean Standard Time 한국표준시.

KSWVH Korean Society for the Welfare of the Visually Handicap 한국 시각 장애자 복지회.

KT ① Korea Times (한국) 영자 일간지.
② Korea Trust 회국인 전용 수익 증권의 일종.

KTA ① Korea Traders Association 韓國貿易人協會(한국무역인협회).

② Korea Tuberculosis Association 大韓結核協會(한국 결핵 협회).

KTB Korea Tourist Bureau 대한여행사.

KTCR Korean Peninsula Cooperative Threat Reduction (한반도 협력위협감소).

KTMC Korea Tungsten Mining 大韓重石會社.

KTS Koea Tourist Service 한국국제관광공사.

KTX Korea Train Express 한국고속철도.

KUB Kidneys, ureter, bladder 신장, 요관, 방광.

Ku KLUX(Klan) 3Ks (남북전쟁 후 흑인과 북부인을 위압하기 위하여 남부지방에서 결성된 비밀단체).

KUNA Kuwait News Agency 쿠웨이트 통신.

KUT Korea University of Technology and Education 한국기술교육대학교 (지식근로자를 교육훈련하는 능력개발전문가와 현장기술자를 양성하기 위하여 정부출연으로 1992. 2 설립된 대학).

KUTV (러) Kommunisticheskii Universitet Trudyashchikhasy Vostoka (=Communist University for Eastern Workers) (소련) 동양 근로자 대학. 1921년 모스크바에 설립.

KVA kilo volt ampere 전기 단위

KVTMA Korea Vocational Training & Management Agency 한국 직업 훈련 관리 공단.

kw kilowatt 킬로와트.

KW Kilo Word (컴퓨터) 1000기계 워드. 컴퓨터 분야에서는 1024 워드. 워드라는 것은 컴퓨터가 1회의 명령을 처리하는 비트열(列)을 말한다.

KWDI Korea Women's Development Institute 한국 여성 개발원.

kWh kilowatt(s) hour 킬로와트시. 작업·열량의 단위. 1킬로와트의 공율로 1시간에 할 수 있는 작업의 량 또는 그에 상당한 열량.

KWIC keyword in context (컴퓨터) 표제어가 문맥에 포함된 채 인쇄된 색인.

KWL Kuwait Airways 쿠웨이트항공.

KWOC keyword out of context (컴퓨터) 표제어가 문맥 첫머리에 놓여서 인쇄된 색인.

KWP Korean Worker's Party 조선노동당.

Ky Kentucky = Ken. 켄터키 주.

KY Kentucky (미) 켄터키 주의 우편 기호.

KYA Korea Youth Association 한국 청소년 연맹.

l. liter(s) 리터.

L 로마숫자의 50.

L. pound(영국의 화폐 단위).

L-19 Liaison Aircraft 19 L-19 連結機(군용경비행기).

La lanthanum 란타늄. 원자번호 57.

La. Louisiana 루이지애나 주.

L.a. letter of advice (어음발행) 통지장, 송하 통지장, 적하통지서.

LA ① laboratory automation 연구소 자동화.
② Latin America 중남미.
③ Legislative Assembly 입법부. 2원제 입법부의 하원.
④ Library Association (영) 도서관협회.
⑤ Loan Agreement 차관협정
⑥ local authority 지방자치제.
⑦ Los Angeles 로스앤젤레스.
⑧ low alochol 저알코올 맥주 (low alcohol beer)의 호칭. 저알코올맥주 알코올 함유량은 2~3%.

L/A letter of Authority 어음 매입 매수 권자.

LAB Lliys Aereo Boliviano 볼리비아 항공.

lab laboratory 연구소.

LABAN Lakas ng Bayan (=People's Power Movement) (필리핀) 인민의 힘. 정당명.

Labor Management Relations Act 노사 관계법 (Taft Hartley Low)

LABS low altitude bombing system 저공 폭격시스템. 저공에서 목표 직전에서 급상승으로 이행, 상승하면서 폭탄을 투하하는 공격법을 자동적으로 하는 시스템.

LACA Latin America Coffee Agreement 중남미 커피협정.

LACE lysergic acid diethlamide 환각제의 일종.

LACIE Large Area Crop Inventory Experiment (미) 광역곡물 수량조사실험. NASA, USDA, NOAA를 중심으로 하여 실시된 인공위성에 의한 곡물수량(收量) 예측 프로젝트.

LACM Latin America Common Market 중남미 공동시장.

L&D loss and damage 손실과 손해.

LADB laboratory animal data bank (미) 실험동물에 관한 데이터뱅크.

LAFTA

LAFTA Latin American Free Trade Association 중남미 자유무역연합.

LAGB Linguistics Association of Great Britain 영어 언어학회.

LAGEOS Laser Geodynamic satellite (미) 레이저 지구 역학 위성.

LAIA Latin American Integration Association 중남미통합연합.

LAM (포) Linhas Aereas de Mocambique (=mozambique Airline) 모잠비크 항공.

LAMDA London Academy of Music and Dramatic Art (영) 런던 음악 연극 학원.

LAN local area network 기업내 정보통신망, 근거리 정보통신망.

LAN Card 랜 카드 랜 환경을 만들어 주는 하드웨어 장치. 사운드 카드 형태로서, NIC(Network Interface Card)라고도 한다.

LANDSAT land satellite 지상관측 위성.

LAN/MAP local area network/manufacturing automation protocol 공장용 LAN의 통신규약.

LANWAIR land, water, air의 혼성어. 육해공항. 육해공 터미널. 철도와 버스의 역, 항구, 공항 등을 유기적으로 결합한 거대시설 또는 그의 연락시설.

LARC low altitude ride control 저공비행제어.

LAS ① League of Arab States 아랍 제국 연맹.
② linear alkyl benzenesulfonic acid 세제의 성분으로 사용됨.

LASA large aperture seismic array 지하 핵실험 탐지용 초원거리 지진검출장치.

LASER light amplification by stimulated emission of radiation 레이저 유도방출에 의한 광의증폭.

LASH lighter aboard ship 화물을 실은 거룻배를 그대로 싣고 수송하는 배. 신속히 화물을 처리할 수 있다.

LASL Los Alamos Scientific Laboratory (미) 로스 알라모스 과학 연구소.

LASO Latin America Solidarity Organization 중남미 단결 기구. 공산주의 단체 1996년 결성.

LAT local apparent time 진태양 (眞太陽) 지방시. 해시계로 표시되는 시간.

LATA Local Access and Transport Area 미국에서 한 지역 전화회사가 서비스를 담당하는 구역.

LAUK Library Association of the United Kingdom 영국 도서관 협회.

LAW ① light antitank weapon 경대전차병기. 보병 한 사람이 운반·사용할 수 있는 경량의 대전차 로켓 병기의 총칭.
② low active waste (원자력) 저

레벨 방사성폐기물.

LAX Los Angeles International Airport 로스앤젤레스 국제공항.

lb. [L] libra (=pound) 파운드. 중량 단위.

LB ① Labrador (캐나다) 래브라도 주(州).
② left (full)back (축구) 레프트 (풀)백.
③ linebacker (미식축구)라인백커.

LB Langmuir Blodgett film 랑그뮤어 블로제트 막(膜). 기능성의 유기초박막으로 바이오센서, 절연성초박막 등 분자기 능소자로서의 응용이 주목되고 있다.

LBC London Broadcasting Company (영) 런던 방송국.

LBG liquefied butane gas 액화 부탄가스. 가스라이터 등에 사용.

LBJ Lyndon Baines Johnson 미국 제36대 대통령.

LBO leveraged buyout 주로 차입금에 의한 회사매수. ＊매수대상이 되어 있는 회사의 자산, cash flow를 담보로 한 차입금을 매수자금에 충당한다.

LBP laser beam printer 레이저 · 빔 · 인자기.

l.c. lower case (인쇄) 소문자.

LC ① landing craft 상륙용 주정.
② letter of credit 신용장.
③ light change 극장 등에서 무대를 밝게 한 채로 다음 장면으로 옮기는 것.
④ liquid crystal 액정.
⑤ Lord Chancellor (英) 대법관.

L.C. Library of Congress미국 國會圖書館.

LCAC landing craft air cushion 에어쿠션 상륙용 주정.

LCC ① launch control center (케네디 우주센터의) 스페이스셔틀 발사용 발사 관제 센터.
② Library of Congress Classification (미)의회도서관분류표.
③ light curtain closed 극장의 무대에서 조명을 킨 채로 막을 내리는 것.

LCCN Library Congress Card Number (미) 의회도서관 목록카드번호.

LCD ① liquid crystal digital 액정 디지털.
② liquid crystal diode 액정소자.
③ liquid crystal display 액정표시장치.

LCF ① liquid chemical fuel 액상 화학 연료.
② low cycle fatigue 저사이클 피로. 비행시 마다 하중(荷重)에 의하여 생기는 기체의 피로 현상.

LCI landing craft, infantry 보병 상륙용 주정(舟艇).

LCJ Lord Chief Justice (영) 고등법원의 수석 재판관.

LCL ① less than carload lot 한 화차미만의 화물.
② less than container load 컨테이너 한 개미만의 화물.

LCM ① (라) legis comparative magister (=master of comparative law) 비교 석학 석사
② lincomycin 린코마이신.
③ lowest (or least) common multiple 최소 공배수.

LCMARC Library of Congress Machine Readable Cataloging (미) 국회 도서관 기계 가독(可讀) 목록.

LCMP loosely coupled multi processing system (컴퓨터) 소결합 다중처리 시스템.

LCN local classification number (항공) 하중(荷重) 분류넘버.

LCP liquid crystal printer 액정 프린터.

LCR landing craft rubber 상륙용 주정(舟艇) 고무.

LCRM logarithmic counting rate meter (원자력)대수계수율 계(計)

LCROV low cost remotely operated vehicle 저가격 원격 작업기.

LCP landing craft personnel 병원(兵員) 상륙용 주정(舟艇).

LCS large capacity storage (컴퓨터) 대용량기억장치.

LCT landing craft tank 전차 상륙용 주정.

LCU ① line circuit unit (컴퓨터) 가입자(加入者)회로유닛.
② line control unit (컴퓨터) 회선제어유닛.
③ logical control unit (컴퓨터) 논리제어유닛.

LCVD liquid crystal video isplay 액정화상디스플레이.

LCVG liquid cooling and entilation garment 액체 냉각식통기복.

LCVP landing craft, vehicle, ersonnel 차량병원(兵員) 상륙주정.

Ld. Limited(Ltd.라고도 함) 유한인 회사.

LD ① laser diode 레이저 다이오드, 반도체다이오드.
② Laser Disk 레이저 디스크.
③ learning disability 학습장애.
④ lethal dose 치사량.
⑤ light director (방송)조명담당자.

LD Doctor of Letters 문학박사.

LDAE Longman Dictionary of American English 롱맨 영어사전.

LDB logical database 논리적 데이터베이스.

LD-BLC low drag boundary layer control (항공) 저항 감소 경계(境界) 제어.

LDC less developed country 후발 개발도상국.

LDCE Longman Dictionary of

Contemporary English 롱 맨 현대 영어 사전. = LDOCE

LDDC least developed among developing countries 최후발(最後發)발전도상국.

LDEF ① long duration experimental facility 장기 우주실험 시설. 신재료, 우주물리, 생물학 등의 연구를 위하여 스페이스 셔틀에서 방출되는 장치.
② long duration exposure facility 장시간 노출위성. 스페이스셔틀이 소정의 궤도에 오른 후 본체에서 떨어져 장시간 우주공간에서 실험을 실시하는 위성.

LDH lactate dehydrogenase 젖산 탈수소 효소.

LDI landing direction indicator (항공) 착륙방향지시기.

LDL low density lipoprotein 저밀도 단백질.

LDMS library data management system 도서관 데이터관리시스템.

LDOCE Longman Dictionary of Contemporary English = LDCE 롱맨 현대 영어 사전.

LDP Liberal Democratic Party 일본자민당(日本自民黨)

LDPE low density polyethylene 합성수지. 필름, 전선피막에 이용.

LDR ① linear decision rule (컴퓨터) 선형의사결정규칙.
② London Depositary Receipts 런던예탁증권.

LD-ROM laser disk read only memory 레이저 디스크 롬 LD에 CD-ROM의 기능을 추가한 것. 1989년 12월에 일본의 Pioneer사가 규격을 발표, 1993년 8월에 레이저 액티브와 소프트웨어를 발표하였다.

L-driver learner driver 가면허의 운전사.

LDS ① Latter day Saint=Mormon 교도. (예수그리스도 후기성도 교회 유타주 솔트레이크에 본부가 있음.)
② licenser in dental surgery 치과의 개업 면허 소지자.

LDT light duty truck 경량트럭.

LDV ① liquid crystal video display 액정 화상 디스플레이.
② light duty vehicle (자동차) 경량차.

LE ① left end (미식 축구) 레프트 엔드.
② lupus erythematosus 홍반성 낭창(狼瘡).

LEA local education authority (영) 지방 교육 당국.

LEAA Law Enforcement Assistance Administration (미) (사법성) 법집행 원조국.

LEASAT Leased Satellite 미해군의 통신위성.

LED light emitting diode 발광 다

LEED

이오드(전극).

LEED low energy electron diffraction 저에너지 전자 회석(回析).

LEET Legal Education Eligibility Test 법학 적성 시험.

LEL lower explosion limit 폭발하한계(下限界). 가스폭발이 시작되는 가스농도의 하한계.

LEM lunar excursion module 달 착륙선.

LEMRAS Law Enforcement Manpower Resources Allocation 경찰력 적정 배치 시스템.

LEMS linear econometrics modeling system 선형 계량 경제모델 작성 시스템.

LEMUF limits of error on material unaccounted for (원자력) 불명물질의 오차한계.

LEO low earth orbit 저주회(周回)궤도.

LEP large electron positron collider 대형 전자양전자 충돌형가속기.

LEPRA Leprosy Relief Association (영) 나병 구제 협회.

LER licence event reports (미) 원자력 발전소 운전기록.

LES Launch Escape System 탈출로켓.

LET linear energy transfer (원자력) 선 에너지부여.

LETF launch equipment test facility 로켓발사장치 시험시설.

LEU Low Enriched Uranium 저농축 우라늄.

lez [lez] lesbian 동성애의 여자.

LF ① line feed character (컴퓨터) 개행(改行)문자.
② long frequency 장파.
③ low fat 저지방.
④ low frequency 저주파.

LFC laminar flow control (항공) 층류(層流)제어.

LFD ① least fatal dose 최소치사량.
② low fat diet 저지방식.

LFF low pressure fuel filter (항공) 저압연료여과기.

LG ① left guard (미식 축구) 레프트 가드.
② letter of guarantee 지불 보증장.

LGB Laser Guided Bomb 레이저 유도폭탄.

LGEOS laser geodynamic satellite 레이저 지구역학 위성.

LGFM London Gold Futures Market (영) 런던 금 선물 거래시장.

LGM ① little green man 지적(知的)우주인.
② silo launched guided missile (미) 사일로 발사 유도미사일.

LGU Ladies Golf Union 여자 골프 연합.

LH ① low-noise high-output 저

잡음 고출력.
② Lufthansa German Airlines 루프트한자 독일항공.
③ Luteinizing Hormone 뇌하수체 전엽에서 분비되는 생식선 자극호르몬.

LHC Lord High Chancellor (영) 대법관.

LHD (라) litteraum humaniorum doctor (=doctor of humanities) 인문 과학 박사.

LHRF luteinizing hormonereleasing factor 황체 형성 호르몬 방출 인자.

LHRH luteinizing hormonereleasing hormone 황체 형성 호르몬 방출 호르몬.

Li lithium 리튬. 원자번호 3.

LI left inner (축구) 레프트 인너.

lib liberation 해방. 권리확장운동 또는 운동가. 여성 해방운동.

LIBID London Interbank Bid Rate 유럽시장의 거래의 기준이 되어 있는 런던의 은행간 거래에 있어서의 거래선의 레이트. LIBOR와의 차는 보통 0.125%.

LIBOR London Interbank Offered Rate 런던은행간 거래금리.

LIC ① low income country 저소득국.
② Low Intensity Conflict 저강도분쟁. 전후 빈발한 자유진영 제국에 대한 테러, 파괴동작, 폭등, 내란 등을 총칭한 것.

LICS low income countries 저소득군. 1인당 GNP가 410달러 이하(1980년)의 나라들.

LIF leukocyte inhibitory factor 백혈구 유동 저지 인자.

LIFFE London International Financial Futures Exchange 런던 국제금융선물거래소.

LIFO last in, first out 나중에 넣은 것을 먼저 빼는 처리방식.

LIM ① linear induction motor 리니어 모터.
② liquid injection molding 열경화성(硬化性) 수지의 성형.

LIMRA Life Insurance Management and Research Association 생명보험 경영 연구 협회.

LIONS Liberty(자유), Intelligence (지성) of our nation's safety (우리 국민의 안전)의 의미 로써 1917년 미국 텍사스, 달라스 에서 출범한 실업가 봉사 단체.

L.I.P. Life Insurance Policy 생명 보험 증권.

LIPS logical inference per second 매초 추론(推論)회수. 삼단논법을 1초간에 몇 번 실행할 수 있는가의 단위, 제5세대 컴퓨터 또는 인공지능의 논리사고 속도.

liq liquidator 청산인.

LIQ Liquor store (미) 술집. 주로 미국의 흑인이 쓰는 말.

LISP

LISP List Processor (컴퓨터) MIT 가 개발한 고급프로그램언어.

Lit(t). B. Lit(t)erarum Baccalaureus 문학사(文學士).

Lit(t). D. Lit(t)eratum Doctor 문학박사(文學博士).

LIW low intensity warfare 핵전쟁도 통상전쟁도 아닌 신형의 강도가 얕은 전쟁.

liz lesbian 여자의 동성애자.

LJ lord justice (미) 재판관.

LJC Legislation And Judiciary Committee (한) (국회의) 법제사법 위원회.

LK ① lake 호수.
② living room kitchen 거실겸 부엌.

l.l. loco laudato (in the place quoted) (라) 인용문 중에.

LL ① language laboratory 어학실습실.
② left linkman (축구) 레프트 링크맨.
③ Little League (美) 소년 야구리그.
④ long life 장기 보존. 초(超)고온에서 살균한 우유를 LL Milk 라고 함.

LLA Lesortho Liberation Army (레소토왕국) 레소토 해방군.

LL.B. Legum Baccalaureus 법학사(法學士).

LLBA Language and Language Behavior Abstracts (미) 언어와 언어 활동에 관한 문헌의 데이터 베이스.

LLC ① land locked country 내륙국(內陸國)
② Laparoscopic Laser Cholecystectomy 레이저 복강경 담낭 절제술.

LL.D. Legum Doctor 法學博士.

LLDC least less developed countries 후발개발도상국.

L-LDPE linear low density polyethylene 합성수지. 농업용 폴리에틸렌필름이나 폴리봉지등의 원재료로 사용된다.

LLLTV low light level TV = LLTV 저광량(低光量) 텔레비전.

LLLW low level liquid wastes 저레벨(방사성)액체폐기물.

LLM (라)legum magister (=master of laws) 법학 석사.

LLN lower limits of normal 정상하한(下限).

LLTV low light TV = LLTV 저광량 텔레비전.

LLW low level wastes 저레벨(방사성)폐기물.

LM ① light music 경음악.
② linar motor car 리니어모터카.
③ lunar module 달착륙선.
④ Legion of Merit (美軍)훈공장.
⑤ licenser in medicine 의사 개

업 유자격자.
⑥ licenser in midwifery 조산원 개업 유자격자.

LMA laser emission microanalysis 레이저마이크로 분석법.

LME ① liquid metal embitterment 액체 금속 취화(脆化).
② London metal Exchange 런던금속거래소.

LMED Longman Modern English Dictionary 롱 맨 현대 영어사전.

LMFBR liquid metal fast breeder reactor 액체 금속층 고속증식로.

LMFR liquid metal fueled reactor 액체 금속 연소 원자로.

LMG liquefied methane gas 액화 메탄가스.

LMRA Labor Management Relations Act (미) 노동관계법. 통칭 Taft Hartly Act.

LMSA Labor Management Services Administration (미) 노동청 노사 관계국.

LMT local mean time 지방 평균시.

LMTD log mean temperature difference 대수(對數)평균온도차.

LN ① local national 현지 고용인.
② luminometer number 연휘(煙輝)지수. 제트연료의 발연성(發煙性)을 나타내기 위한 규격치(規格置).

LNA low noise amplifier 저잡음 증폭기.

LNG liquefied natural gas 액화 천연 가스.

LNS local network system 로컬 정보망

LO ① light open 무대에서 조명이 켜진 채로 막을 여는 것.
② light operator (방송) 조명장치 조작자.

LOA ① length over all 배의 전장.
② Letter of Agreement 협정서.

LOB left on bases (야구) 잔루.

LOC line of communication 통신선.

LOCA loss of coolant accident (원자력) 냉각재 상실사고.

loc. cit loco citato (in the place cited) (라) 상기인용문 중.

LOD The Little Oxford Dictionary 옥스퍼드 소사전.

LODE large optics demonstration experiment (미) 위성에 장치한 반사경으로 입자 빔을 목표에 지향(指向)시키는 계획.

lo-fi low fidelity 라디오·스테레오의 하이파이가 아닌 재생장치.

LOFT ① loss of fluid test (원자력) 유체상실시험. 냉각 재장치 상실 시험.
② low frequency radio telescope 저주파 무선 망원경.

LOGCOMD logistical command

LOGO

병참부.

LOGO언어 LOGO language 로고언어. *MIT에서 개발한 도형묘화(猫畵)를 목적으로 한 언어로서 유아나 초등교육과정의 아동에게 컴퓨터의 구조를 이해시키는 데 최적(最適)의 언어.

LOH light observation helicopter 경관측 헬리콥터.

LOI ① Letter Instruction 훈령 ② Letter of Intend 의향서.

Lo-Lo lift on, lift off 수직형 하역방식. 크레인 또는 데릭 기중기를 사용하여 매어달아 하역을 하는 컨테이너선의 하역방식.

LOP line of position (항공) 위치선.

LORAN long range electronic navigation 로란항법. 비행기나 선박이 2개 이상의 무선국에서 발신한 전파의 도착 시간차로 위치를 측정하며 항해하는 방식.

LORCS League of Red Cross and Red Crescent Societies = LRCS 적십자 및 적신월사(赤新月社)연맹. 회교국에서는 십자(十字)마크를 싫어하며 초승달을 사용하므로 적십자 대신에 적신월사라고도 한다.

LOS ① land observation satellite 육지 관측 위성. ② Law of the Sea 해양법. ③ line of scrimmage (미식 축구) 스크리미지 라인. ④ line of sight 조준선. ⑤ loss of signal 신호 두절.

LOW launch on warning 경보와 동시발사. ICBM 조기 경보시스템이 ICBM의 미래를 감지하는 동시에 보복조치로서 ICBM를 발사한다는 미국의 핵전략.

LOX liquid oxygen 액체산소.

LP ① laser printer 레이저프린터. ② linear programming (컴퓨터) 선형계획법. ③ line printer 고속 인쇄 장치. 컴퓨터로부터의 출력을 한줄씩 모아 인쇄하는 인자기. ④ lipoprotein 리포단백. ⑤ liquefied petroleum 액화 석유. ⑥ long playing record LP판 레코드. 1분간 $33\frac{1}{3}$회전의 레코드.

LPC ① leaf protein concentrate 녹엽(綠業)단백. ② linear predictive coding 선형 예측법.

LPCI low pressure core injection system (원자력) 저압주입시스템.

LPCVD low pressure chemical vapor deposition 감압 화학적 기상(氣相) 성장법.

LPD landing platform dock 도크 (dock)형 강습함.

LPDR Laos People's Democratic Republic 라오스 인민공화국.

LPF leukocytosis promoting factor 백혈구 촉진 인자.

LPG liquefied petroleum gas 액화 석유 가스.

LPGA Ladies Professional Golfers Association 여자 프로 골프 협회.

LPH landing platform helicopter 헬리콥터 탑재 대형 양륙함(揚陸艦).

LPID logical page identifier 논리 페이지 식별자(識別子).

LPM ① line(s) per minute 1분당 인자행수(行數). line printer 의 출력속도를 나타낸다.
② line printer machine = LP라인 프린터.

LPN ① licensed practical nurse (美)면허 견습 간호사. 간호학교를 졸업하지 않았으나 병원 등에서 훈련을 받고 자격을 얻은 간호사.
② logical page number 논리 페이지 번호.

LPO London Philharmonic Orchestra 런던 교향 악단.

LPPE low pressure polyethylene 저압법 폴리에틸렌.

LPRM local power range monitoring system (원자력) 국소 출력영역 모니터·시스템.

LPRP Laos People's Revolutionary Party 라오스 인민 혁명당.

LPS ① launch processing system (宇宙工學) 발사 준비 작업 시스템.
② Lord Privy Seal (英)옥새 상서

LPTV low power television 저출력 텔레비전. 시청지역 작은 저출력 텔레비전 방송, 시청지역은 반경 20~25km정도.

LPV landing platform vehicle 차량 양륙용(揚陸用)주정.

Lr lawrencium 로렌슘. 원자번호 103.

LR ① laser range finder 레이저 조준기.
② Lloyd's Register (영) 로이드 선급협회.

LRA long range aviation (소련) 장거리 공군.

LRAL long run average cost 장기 평균 비용.

LRBM long range ballistic missile 장거리 탄도미사일.

LRC ① linguistics research center 언어학 연구 센터.
② longitudinal redundancy check (컴퓨터) 수평 용장(冗長) 검사.

LRCS League of Red Cross Societies 적십자 연맹.

LRF laser range finder 레이저 준기.

LRINF Long Range INF 사정거리 1000km이상의 INF.

LRL Lunar Receiving Laboratory (미) 달 자료 연구소.

LRMC longrun marginal cost 장기 한계 비용.

LRP long range planning 장기계획

LRSI low temperature reusable

surface insulation (우주공학) 저온용 내열타일. 스페이스 셔틀 오비터의 표면의 최고온도 371~649℃에 달하는 부분에 사용되는 내열재.

LRT light rail transit 경량 궤도 운행 시스템. 경량노면전차를 사용하는 교통시스템.

LRTNF long range theater nuclear forces 장거리전역(戰域)핵전력.

LRU line replaceable unit (군사) 라인 교환식 장치.

LRV ① light rail vehicle 경량노면전차. 도로상에 부설한 선로를 달리게 하는 전차.
② lunar roving vehicle 월면 작업차.

LS ① last shipment 최종선적.
② long shot (사진) 멀리 찍기.
③ low sulphur 저유황.
④ Listing Securities 상장증권.

LSA Linguistic Society of America 미국 언어 학회.

LSAT Law School Admission Test (미) 법률 전공 지망자를 위한 대학원 입시.

LSB ① least significant bit (컴퓨터) 최하위의 문자.
② lower side band 하측파대(下側波帶).

LSD ① landing ship dock 도크형 양륙주정(揚陸舟艇).
② least significant digit 컴퓨터의 1용어로서 10진법으로 나타낼 수 있는 수치의 최하위의 자릿수.
③ lysergic diethylamide 환각제의 일종.

LSE ① local system environment 로컬 시스템 환경. OSIE가 개방 시스템간의 범위인 것에 대하여 시스템 내부의 범위를 말한다.
② London Stock Exchange 런던 증권 거래소.

LSI large scale integrated circuit (컴퓨터) 대규모 집적회로.

LSM ① letter sorting machine 봉서분류기.
② linear synchronous motor (전기) 리니어동기기(同期機).
③ lunar shuttle module 월 왕복 착륙선.

LSMFT Lucky Strike means fine tobacco (미) 럭키 스트라이크는 좋은 담배. 광고 선전 문구.

LSO London Symphony Orchestra 런던 교향악단.

LSP linear programming system 선형 계획 시스템.

LSS life support system 생명유지장치. 우주 공간에서 비행사의 생명을 유지하기 위한 호흡용 산소·온도 조절 용수(水) 순환장치·전원 등을 비축한 장치.

LSSD level sensitive scan design (컴퓨터) IBM사의 논리설계수법.

LSSM local scientific survey module NASA의 단거리과학탐사선. 월면 과학조사용.

LSSP Lanka Sama Samaja Party (스리랑카) 평등 사회당.

LST ① landing ship tank 전차 양륙 주정.
② large space telescope project (미) 대형우주망원경위성.
③ local standard time 지방표준시.

LSU landing ship utility 다용 상륙용 주정(舟艇).

LSV liquid space velocity 액공간 속도.

Lt. Lieutenant 중위.

LT ① left tackle (미식 축구) 레프트 태클.
② letter telegram 서신 전보.
③ living together 동서(同棲).
④ local time 지방시(時).

L/T long ton 영(英)톤. 대(大)톤. 1016, 047kg에 상당함.

LTA ① Lawn Tennis Association (영) 정구협회.
② lighter than air aircraft 공기보다 가벼운 항공기. 비행선이나 기구 등. 일반 비행기는 HTA라고함.
③ Long Term Agreement 국제면제품 장기협정.

LTBT The Limited Test Ban Treaty 부분적 핵 실험금지조약.

Ltb. Limited Liability 유한회사.

LTD laser target designator 레이저 목표 조준기.

LTER lot tolerance failure rate 로트 허용 고장율.

LTL less than truck load 트럭 한 대 분보다 적은화물.

LTLT low temperature long time pasteurization 저온장시간살균. 62~26℃, 30분간 살균한 우유.

LTP low temperature passivation 저온도처리 반도체의 박막(薄膜)을 만드는 기술의 하나.

LTPD lot tolerance percent defective 로트 허용 불량품.

LTR living together relationship 동서, 내연관계.

LTS long distance inter toll switching system (전화) 장거리교환장치.

LTV Loan to Value 현싯가 까지의 융자 한도액

Lu lutetium 루테튬. 원자번호 71.

LU ① letter of the undertaking 보증서.
② loudness unit 음량의 단위.
③ Labor Union 노동조합.

LUA ① launch under attack 공격하에서의 발사.
② letter of undertaking and authorization 보증 수권서(保證 授權書).

LUB logical unit block (컴퓨터)

289

LUF

논리장치 제어블록.

LUF lowest useful high frequency (무선) 최저사용 주파수.

LULAC League of United Latin American Citizens (미) 중남미계 미국인 연맹.

LUT line unit 회선접속장치.

LV ① laser vision 비디오 디스크의 한 방식.
② light value 필름의 감도와 셔터의 속도, 조리개의 값을 조합한 수치.
③ linear velocity 선속도.

LVM Luna, Venus and Mars Program 달, 금성, 화성탐사계획.

LVIP landing vehicle, tracked, personnel (미) 수륙 양용 장갑 병원(兵員) 수송차.

Lw lawrencium 로렌슘. 원자번호 103.

LWIR long wave infrared 장파장(長波長) 적외선.

LWL low-water level 간조면(干潮面) 저수위.

LWM low water mark 저수계, 저조표(低潮標).

LWR light water reactor 경수 원자로.

LWV League of Women Voters (미) 여성 유권자 동맹.

lx lux 럭스. 조도(照度)의 단위.

LYON Liquid Yield Option Notes (미) 유동성 자산 취득권에 따른 채권. Meril Lynch사 발행의 제로 쿠폰.

LZ landing zone 상륙(착륙)지역.

LZT Local Zone Time 지방시간.

m. maiden ; male ; married ; masculine ; medium ; meter(s) ; million(s) ; minute(s) ; month ; moon ; mountain

M ① Mach number 고속비행체의 속도를 나타내는 단위.
② magnitude 매그니튜드. 지진의 강도를 나타내는 단위.
③ medium 중위(中位).
④ mega 메가.
⑤ metro 지하철.
⑥ money supply 통화 공급량.
⑦ multidivisional 다각적, 다원적.
⑧ nautical mile 해리. 1M = 1852m
⑨ Project Mercury 머큐리계획.
⑩ 로마 숫자로서 1,000.

M. Monsieur(Mr. Sir) (프) 씨. 남성에 대한 존칭.

M-16 미국의신형 小총. 한국군의 주 소화기임.

MA ① Maritime Administration (미) 운수성 해운국.
② master of arts 문학석사.
③ mechological assessment 기계생태학적 사전평가. 로봇 등의 신기술을 도입할 때 그의 영향을 사전에 평가하는 것.
④ mental age 정신연령.
⑤ Military Academy 육군사관학교.

M.A. mental age 정신연령.

MAA ① medium Anti Aircraft Artillery 중고사포
② Military Armistice Agreement 군사정전협정.

M&A merger and acquisition 합병과 매수.

MAAG military assistance advisory group (미) 군사 원조 고문단.

MAB ① Man and the Biospace Program (유네스코) 인간과 생물권계획.
② Marine Amphibious Brigade (미) 해병대 수륙 양용전(兩用戰)여단.

MABE master of agricultural business and economics 농업경영 경제학 석사.

MAC ① maximum allowable concentration 최대 허용농도.
② mean aerodynamic chord 공력평균익현(翼弦).
③ Military Armistice Commission 군사정전위원회.
④ multi-access computer 다중액세스·컴퓨터
⑤ multiple analogue component

MAC

차세대 텔레비전 방식. 송신방식을 변경하지 않고 수상기 측에 화상 메모리를 가지게 하는 등 개선을 하는 차세대(次世代) 텔레비전 방식.

MAC시스템 multi access computer system 다접속 컴퓨터시스템. 미국 각지의 대학이 매사추세츠 공과대학의 컴퓨터를 텔레파 타이프에 의하여 이용하는 시스템.

MACS multiple access computer system 다중병행(竝行) 처리 방식.

MAD ① magnetic abnormal detector 자기 이상 탐지기. 대잠(對潛) 작전용 항공기가 장비하고 있는 잠수함 탐지장치의 하나.
② Mutual Assured Destruction 상호 확실파괴. 미국과 소련은 상대방으로부터 선제 핵공격을 받더라도 이에 보복하여 상대에게 큰 피해를 줄 수 있을 만큼의 핵전력을 보유하고 있는 상태를 말한다.

MADD Mothers Against Drunk Driving (미) 음주 운전 방지 어머니회.

MADI maximum acceptable daily intake 1일 섭취 허용량.

MADM medium atomic demolition munition 비교적 간단히 운반할 수 있는 원자폭탄.

MADT micro alloy diffused transistor 마이크로합금 확산 트랜지스터.

MAERP Mutual Atomic Energy Reinsurance Pool (미) 원자력 보상 재보험 풀.

MAESA Multichannel Acoustic Emission Source Analyzer 다채널 음향 방출원 분석 장치.

MAF ① minimum audible field 최소 청역(聽域)
② Marine Amphibious Force 미해병대 상륙 작전부대.

MAFF ① Ministry of Agriculture, Fisheries and Food (영) 농어업 식량청.
② Ministry of Agriculture, Forestry & Fisheries (한) 농림수산부.

MAG Maximum available gain 최대 유능 이득

MAGTF Marine Air Ground Task Force (미) 해병대 공륙(空陸) 임무 부대.

MAI Multilateral Agreement on Investment 다자간 투자협정.

MALEV Magyar Legckozlekedesi Vallalat 헝가리 국영 항공.

MALS master of arts in library science 도서관학 문학 석사.

MALT master of arts in language teaching 어학 교육 석사.

MAN metropolitan area network 대도시 통신망 대도시 근교에 부설된 데이터 통신망.

MANA Malawi News Agency 말라위 통신.

M&A merger and acquisition 합병과 매수. 경제의 성숙화, 여유 자금의 증가, 주가의 약세 등을 배경으로 미국에서 1982년부터 1986년까지 붐을 일으킨 기업의 매수·합병.

MAO monoamine oxidase 모노아민 산화 효소. 간기능 검사에 사용.

MAOI monoamine oxidase inhibitors 모노아민 산화 효소 억제제. 혈압 강하 의약품.

MAP ① management assesment program 관리비용 제도 ② manifold air pressure (항공) 흡기압력. ③ manufacturing automation protocol 생산자동화를 위한 통신 프로토콜. 공장내의 자동화 기기 상호간의 통신이나 정보교환의 표준화를 위한 것이다. ④ Middle Atmospheric Program 중층대기관측계획. ⑤ Military Assistance Program 상호방위원조계획. ⑥ Modified American Plan 1박 2식의 호텔 요금제.

MAPA Manila Action Plan for Apec 마닐라 실행계획.

MAPI Machinery and Allied Product Institute (미) 기계공업협회.

MAPU (스) Movimento de Acction Popular Unitaria (=Unired Popular Action Movement) (칠레) 통일인민 행동 운동.

Mar. March 3월.

MAR ① memory address register 메모리·어드레스·레지스터. (주소 인식 장치) ② multifunctional array radar 다용도 군별(群別) 레이더. 미사일의 형을 식별할 수 있다.

MARC machine readable catalog 컴퓨터 판독가능 목록. 출판물의 서적명, 저자, 출판자, 분류 등을 수록한 자기테이프.

MARC II Machine Readable Catalog II 미국의회 도서관에서 수록한 단행본의 카탈로그 정보의 데이터베이스.

March master of architecture 건축학 석사.

Marisat maritime satellite (미) 해상 통신 위성. 해군함정, 민간상선, 해양개발 양상기지(洋上基地) 등의 통신 중계에 사용하기 위한 정지위성(靜止衛星).

MARMAP Marine Resources Monitoring Assessment and Prediction (미) 해양 생물 자원 조사.

MARPOL International Convention for the Prevention of Marine Pollution from Ship 선박에 의한 해양 오염방지를 위한 국제협약.

MARS ① magnetic electronic automatic reservation system

MARV

전자 자기 자동예약시스템.
② manned astronautical research station 유인 우주 비행 연구소. 통칭 space laboratory
③ Multiple Access Reservation System (일) 철도의 좌석예약 시스템.

MARV maneuverable reentry vehicle 기동핵탄두. 적의 미사일 공격을 피하거나 정확히 목표에 명중하도록 유도할 수 있는 미사일 탄두.

MAS ① Malaysia Airline System 말레이시아 항공.
② Minerals Availability System (미) 광물 가채성(可採性)시스템.
③ Ministry of Aerospace Industries 중국 항공 우주성.
④ Mutual Assured Security 상호 확증 안전 보장.

M&S maintenance and support 整備 및 支援.

MASER microwave amplification by the stimulated emission of radiation 분자증폭기. 레이더 등에 사용한다.

MASH ① manned anti submarine helicopter 유인대잠(大潛) 헬리콥터
② mobile army surgical hospital (미) 육군 이동 외과병원.

Mass. Massachusetts 매사추세츠주.

MAT ① machine aided translation 기계원용(援用) 번역.
② master of arts in reaching 교육학석사.
③ missile anti tank 대전차 미사일.

MATCH Mothers Apart From Their Children (미) 일 때문에 아이들과 떨어져 있는 어머니회.

MATIF Marche a Terme des Instruments Financiers (프) 프랑스의 금융선물시장.

MATS Military Air Transport Service (美) 군용 항공 수송 본부. MAC (Military Airlift Command)의 구칭.

MATSYS Matrix System 행렬(行列)계산시스템 IBM의 소프트웨어.

MATV master antenna televeision 공동 시청 텔레비전.

MATVS master antenna televeision system 텔레비전 공동시청 방식.

MAUV multiple autonomous undersea vehicle 해중작업로봇.

MAV Magyar Allamvasutak 헝가리의 국유 철도.

MAVICA Magnetic Video Camera 전 전자식 정지(靜止) 카메라. 소니가 개발.

MAVR modulating amplifier by variable reactance 마이크로파 증폭장치.

max. maximum 최대량, 최대한.

mb millibar(s) 기압의 단위.

Mb megabit 메가비트. 100만 비

트, 정보량의 단위.

MB ① maternity benefit (영) 출산급부금.
② medicinae baccalaureus (bachelor of medicine) (라) 의학 석사.
③ mega byte (컴퓨터) 메가바이트. 100만 바이트. 정보량의 단위.
④ minimum bid 최소입찰치(最小入札値).
⑤ musicae baccalaureus (bachelor of music) (라) 음악학 석사.

MBA ① master of business administration 경영관리학석사.
② material balance area (원자력) 물질수지(收支)구역.
③ Mortgage Bankers Association of America 미국 저당 대부 은행협회.

MBAS methylene blue active substance 메틸렌블루 활성물질. 폐수 중의 세제량의 지표.

MBB magnetic blow out circuit breaker 자기차단기.

MBC Munhwa Broadcasting Company 문화방송국(文化放送局)

MBCS member of the British Computer Society 영국 컴퓨터 협회 회원.

MBD millions of barrels of oil per day 석유 100만 배럴/일.

MBDA Minority Business Development Agency (미) 상무성 소수 민족 기업 진흥국.

MBE Molecular beam epitaxy 분자선 에피택시.

MBFR Mutual and Balanced (Armed) Force Reduction 중부 유럽 상호 균형 병력 삭감 교섭.

MBGO management by group objective 집단목표관리.

MBIM member of the British Institute of Management 영국 경영학회 회원.

MBK Medications and Bandage Kit 의약품, 붕대세트. SOMS의 A형.

MBL Marine Biological Laboratory (미) 해양 생물학 연구소.

MBMD maximum bending moment diagram 최대 휨 모멘트 다이어그램.

MBMO Management by Multiple Objectives 다수 목표관리.

MBO management by objectives 목표관리. 작업의 자주성을 중시하는 관리의 이념·방식. 작업원에 업무목표를 제시하고 그의 달성방법은 작업원 자신에게 일임한다.

MBOU member of the British Ornithologists' Union 영국 조류학자 연합 회원.

MBP marine biotelemetry project 해양생물원격계측계획.

mbps megabits per second 초당 메가비트. 정보처리의 속도 단위.

MBR ① material balance report (원자력) 물질수지(收支)보고. ② memory buffer register 메모리·버퍼·레지스터. ③ methacrylate butadiene rubber 합성고무의 일종.

MBS ① methyl methacrylate butadiene styrene ② mortgage backed securities 담보부 증권. 주택용·상업용 부동산을 담보로한 대부증권을 유가증권화 한 것. ③ Mutual Broad Casting System (미) 라디오만의 전국네트워크를 가진 방송회사.

MBT main battle tank 주력 전투전차.

MBWA ① management by walking around 상사가 직장내를 돌아다니며 하는 경영·관리. ② management by walking away 현장책임경영. 현장에 책임을 가지게 하는 관리.

MBX management by exception 예외에 의한 관리.

Mc megacycle 주파수의 단위.

MC ① machining center 복합자동공작기계. 공구를 자주적으로 교환하며 여러 가지 가공을 할 수 있는 공작기계. ② marginal cost 한계비용. ③ Marine Commission 해사위원회. ④ Marine Corps (미) 해병대. ⑤ master of ceremonies 사회자. ⑥ Member of Congress (미) 국회의원. ⑦ memory card 메모리카드. 자기카드 또는 IC카드. ⑧ ROK-US Military Committee 한미 군사위원회.

MCA ① manufacturers' consumer advertising 생산자의 소비자에 대한 광고. ② maximum credible accident (원자력) 최대상정(想定)사고. ③ Monetary Compensatory Amount 국경 조정금. EC의 공통농산물 가격을 유지하는 제도. ④ multichannel access system 복수채널을 복수의 가입자가 공용하는 통신시스템.

MCAT Medical College Admission Test (미) 의과대학 입학 테스트.

MCC ① Microelectronics and Computer Technology Corp (미) 컴퓨터관리기술 연구 개발 회사. ② mission control center (우주) 우주 관제센터.

MCCA Mercado Comun Centroamericano (Central America Common Market) (스) 중미 공동시장.

MCD magnetic card 자기카드.

MCE master of civil engineering 토목공학석사.

MCH machine check handler 컴퓨터로 기계의 에러를 분석하여 회복을 시도하는 프로그램.

MCHFR minimum critical heat flux ratio (원자력) 최소한계 열류속비(熱流束比).

mCi milicurie 1000분의 1퀴리.

MCi megacurie(s) 100만 퀴리.

MCI ① machine check interruption (컴퓨터) 기계검사인터럽션.
② Microwave Communications of American, Incorporated (미) 마이크로웨이브 통신회사
③ Meal Combat Individual 전투식량.

MCIC machine check interrupt code 기계검사 인터럽트 코드.

MCIS multicurrency intervention system 복수통화 개입제도.

MCLS mucus lymph node syndrome 점막·피부·림프절 증후군.

MCM Multi Country Model (미) 다국모델. 연방 준비제도가 개발한 세계경제모델.

MCNC Microelectronics Center of North Carolina (미) 노스캐롤라이나 주와 주내(州內) 6개 대학과의 공동출자에 의해 최대규모 집적회로와 컴퓨터 교육연구시설.

MCO miscellaneous charges order 해외여행 유가증표(證票). 항공회사, 여행 대리점이 발행하며 여객의 제 지불에 사용한다.

MCom master of commerce 상학 석사.

MCP ① master control processor 주제어처리장치.
② master of city planning 도시계획 석사.

MCR ① magnetic character reader (컴퓨터) 자기문자판독기.
② mark card reader (컴퓨터) 마크카드판독기.

MCS ① maritime communication subsystem 해상통상서브시스템.
② master of commercial 상학 석사.
③ master of computer science 컴퓨터학 석사.
④ merchandising cycle system 상품의 계획에서 판매·평가까지의 사이클을 각 단계에 따라 컴퓨터로 추적 분석하는 상품관리시스템.
⑤ missile control system 미사일제어시스템. 아메리카·마이크로파 통신회사.

MCU ① machine control unit. NC 공작기계시스템의 제어장치.
② magnetic card unit 자기카드장치.

MCVD modified chemical vapor deposition 개량화학기상(氣相)성장법. 광섬유모재(母材) 제조기술의 일종.

Md mendelevium 멘델레븀, 원자번호 101.

Md. Maryland 매릴랜드주.

MD ① magnetic disk (컴퓨터) 자

MD

기 디스크.
② major descriptor 가장 중요한 검색어.
③ merchandising 상품유통의 합리적인 관리방법.
④ mean deviation 평균편차.
⑤ mechanical design 기구설계.
⑥ medicinae doctor(doctor of medicine) = DM (라)의학박사.
⑦ micro disc 연주시간 10분의 DAD
⑧ mini disc 연주시간 60분의 DAD
⑨ module design 모듈설계.

MD Missile Defense 미사일방어체제.

MDA ① methyl di-amphetamine 흥분제의 일종.
② multiple docking adapter (우주스테이션) 다량(多量) 도킹·어댑터
③ mutual defense assistance 상호방위원조.

MDAP Mutual Defense Assistance Program (미) 상호방위원조계획.

M-day mobilization day (군대) 동원(개시)일.

MDB (포) Movimento Democratico Brasileiro (=Brazilian Democratic Movement)브라질 민주주의 운동.

MDC more developed country 중진국.

MDF ① main distribution frame 주배선반.
② master distribution frame 본배선반.
③ medium density fiber board 중질섬유판.

MDI ① manual data input 수동 입력.
② Magnetic Direction Indicator 자기 방향 지시기.

MDINC manual data input numerical control MDI NC.

MDiv master of divinity 신학석사.

MDL military demarcation line 군사경계선.

Mdlle., Mlle. Mademoiselle(Miss) (프) 양, 영양. 소녀 또는 미혼여성에 대한 존칭.

Mdme., Mme. Madame(Mrs.) (프) 부인. 기혼부인에 대한 존칭.

MDN (스) Movimiento Democration Nicaraguense (=Nicaraguan Democratic Movement) 나카라과 민주 동맹.

MDR minimum daily requirement 최소 1일 필요량.

MDS ① management decision system 경영의사결정시스템.
② microcomputer development software 마이크로컴퓨터 개발용 소프트웨어.
③ microcomputer development system 마이크로컴퓨터 개발 시스템.
④ Multipoint Distribution Service (미) 소출력의 유선 텔레비전

mdse merchandise 상품.

MDSS management decision support system 경영의사 결정 지원시스템.

MDT ① mean down time (컴퓨터) 평균고장시간.
② Mutual Defense Treaty 상호방위조약.

MDU mobile diving unit 이동식 잠수장치.

Me. Maine 메인 주.

ME ① macro engineering 거대공학.
② managing editor 편집장.
③ master of engineering = MEng 공학석사.
④ mechanical engineering 기계공학.
⑤ medical electronics 의용전자공학.
⑥ medical engineering 의용공학.
⑦ micro electronics 미소전자학.
⑧ Middle East 중동.

M.E. ① military engineer 공병.
② mining engineer 광산엔지니어.

ME metal evaporated tape 테이프 금속을 증착한 자기테이프.

MEA minimum enroute instrument altitude 최저계기 비행고도.

MEc master of economics 경제학석사.

med medicine 의사, 의학생 medics = medical soldier 위생병.

Med Mediterranean Sea 지중해

MEd master of education 교육학석사.

MED ① minimal effective dose 최소유효량.
② molecular electronic device (전자공학) 분자전자디바이스.

MEDC Middle East Defense Community 중동방위공동체.

MEDI Marine Environment Data Information Referral System UNESCO 국제해양학위원회의 해양환경 데이터베이스.

MEDLAS medical information analysis system 의료 정보 분석 시스템.

MEDISDC Medical Information System Development Center 의료정보시스템 개발센터.

Medit. Mediterranean (Sea), the 지중해.

MEDLARS medical literature analysis and retrieval system (미) 의학문헌 검색시스템.

MEDILINE Medlars on line (미) 의학정보 온라인 서비스.

MEDO Middle East Defense Organization 중동반공군사동맹.

MEECN Minimum Essential Emergency Communications Network 필요 최소한도 긴급통신망.

MEED medium energy electron

diffraction 중속(中速) 전자석 회석법(回析法).

MEES Middle East Economic Survey 중동의 석유 경제전문지.

MEET Maekyung Economic Electronic Telepress (한) 매경경제 전자신문.

MEF Minerals and Energy Forum 광산물 · 에너지 포럼. PECC의 하부조직.

MEI marginal efficiency of investment 투자의 한계 효율.

MEK methyl ethyl ketone 도료용제.

MEL master of English literature 영문학석사.

MELR minimum effective liquid rate 최소 유효 액류량(液流量).

memo memorandum 메모.

MENA Middle East and North Africa Economic Summit 중동·북아프리카 경제 정상회의.

M. Eng. Master of Engineering 공학석사(工學碩士).

MEOW moral equivalent of war (美) 전쟁에 임할 때와 같은 정도의 정신적 노력. 1977년 4월 카터 대통령의 연설 속의 문구.

MEP ① macro engineering project 대형기술계획. ② Member of the European Parliament 유럽의회의원.

MER Mortgage Electronic Registration Systems 채권자가 집의 지불상환금을 인터넷으로 추적하는 기관

MERM multilateral exchange rate model 다(多) 통화간 환율 · 모델.

Met. ① Metropolitan Museum of Art 메트로폴리탄 미술관. ② Metropolitan Opera House 메트로폴리탄가 극장.

METADEX Metals Abstracts Index (미) 금속관계 초록색인.

METO ① maximum except take off 최대출력. ② Middle East Treaty Organization 중동조약기구.

Met. R. Metropolitan Railway 지하철도 (런던) 이름.

Metro Metropolitan Railway 파리의 지하철.

MEU A dictionary of Modern English Usage 현대 영어 용법사전. H. W. Fowler저.

Mev mega electron volt 메가 전자볼트.

MEW ① measure of economic welfare 경제복지수준. ② microwave early warning radar (항공) 마이크로파 조기경계 레이더.

MEY maximum economic yield 최대경제생산량.

MEZ (독) Mitteleuropaische Zeit

(=Central European Time) 중앙 유럽 표준시.

MF ① medium frequency 증파.
② microfilm 마이크로필름.
③ microfiches 마이크로피시.
④ mini floppy disk 미니플로피 디스크.

M/F manifest 적하(積荷)목록.

MFA ① master of fine arts 미술학 석사.
② Mobilization for Animal Coalition 국제적인 민간동물 보호단체.
③ multi fiber agreement 국제섬유협정.
④ Multinational Fiber Agreement 다국간섬유협정.

MFB motion feedback 소형스피커의 저음(低音) 재생기술의 하나.

MFC main fuel control (항공) 주 연료관제장치.

MFCM multi function card machine 다능(多能) 카드 처리 장치.

mfd. manufactured 제조된.

mfg. manufacturing 제조하는.

MFG magneto Fluidgraphy 자성유체기록. 극자성 초미입자를 유성액체에 분산시킨 잉크에 의한 기록방식.

MFLOPS million floating point operations per second 1초간~100만회의 부동(浮動) 소수점연산.

MFN most favored nation 최혜국.

M.F.N.C. most favored nation clause 최혜국 약관.

MFO Multinational Force and Observers 다국적 감시군.

MFP Multi Function Polis 21세기형 다기능 미래도시.

M.F.R. Multi Function Array Rader 多自的 레이더.

MFS Mobilization for Survival (미) 생존을 위한 동원. 핵폐기절, 군축 등을 슬로건으로 하는 운동의연합체.

Mg magnesium 마그네슘. 원자번호 12.

MG ① machine gun 기관총.
② micrographic 마이크로 필름에 대한 대량의 화상정보의 보관, 검색, 전달에 관련한 기술.
③ motor generator 전동발전기.

mGal milligal 가속도의 단위.

MGB (러) Ministeratvo Gosudarstvennoi Bezopasnosti (=Ministry of National Security) (소련) 국가 보안성. KGB의 전신.

MGE movable genetic element 이성 유전 요소.

MGM Metro Goldwyn Mayer 미국의 영화제작회사. 현재는 호텔. 향락지 등도 경영하며 MGM/ UA Entertainment Co.라고 한다.

MgO Magnesium Oxide 산화마그

네슘.

MGR ① manager 매니저.
② mobile guided rocket 이동식 유도 로켓.

MH ① marital history 결혼력.
② mental health 정신위생.
③ medal of Honor 명예훈장 미 최고훈장.

MHBM Modern heavy ballistic missile 근대중장비 탄도미사일.

MHD magneto hydro dynamics 전자유체역학.

MHF master history file 주이력 (主履歷)파일.

M.H.R. Member of the House of Representatives 하원의원.

MHS message handling system 정보단말장치에 의한 상포통신시스템.

MHT manned hypersonic transport 유인극초음속기.

MHV ① manned hypersonic vehicle = MHT.
② miniature homing vehicle 위성 파괴용탄두부(彈頭部).

MHW mean high water 평균고수위.

mi. mile(s)

MI ① machine intelligence AI(인공지능)의 별칭.
② marine insurance 해상보험.
③ Military Intelligence (영) 군사 첩보부.
④ misery index 궁핍지수.
⑤ Management Index 경영지표.

M.I. Marine Insurance 해상보험.

MIA missing in action 전투중의 행방불명자.

MIB Market Information Bank 시장 정보은행.

MIC ① management of indirect cost 간접부문 효율화계획.
② mature industrial country 성숙공업국.
③ methyl isocyanate 농업용 살충제.
④ military industrial complex 군산복합체.
⑤ minimum inhibitory concentration 최소발육저지농도.
⑥ Microfloppy Industry Committee 마이크로 플로피 산업 위원회.

MICA Multi National Investment Company for Africa 아프리카 민간 투자회사.

MICE member of the Institution of Civil Engineers (영) 토목 기술자 협회 회원.

Mich. Michigan 미시간 주.

MICOS meteorological information confidential on-line system 기상정보제공시스템.

MICR ① magnetic ink character reader (컴퓨터) 자기 잉크 문자 판독기.

② magnetic ink character recognition (컴퓨터) 자기 잉크 문자 인식.

MICRO microelectronics Innovation and Computer Research Organization (미) 마이크로 전자공학 기술혁신 및 컴퓨터 개발기구.

MICS middle income countries 중소득군. NICS와 LICS와의 중간에 위치하며 1인당 GNP가 달러 (1980년)의 사이의 나라들.

MICV mechanized infantrycombat vehicle 기계화 보병 전투차.

MIDAS ① missile defense alarm system 미사일방위경보시스템.
② Modified Integration Digital Analog Simulation (컴퓨터) 디지털·시뮬레이션언어.

MIDI musical instrument digital interface 디지털방식의 전자 악기를 상호 연동시키기 위한 통일규격.

MIDIST Mission Interministerielle de I' Information Scientifique et Technique (프) 과학기술정보위원회.

MIEE Member of the Institution of Electrical Engineers (英) 전기 기술자 협회 회원.

MIF migration inhibitory factor 유주 저지 인자(遊走沮止因子).

MIG Mikoyan i Gurevich (러) (소련) 미그전투기.

MIGA Multilateral Investment Guarantee Agency 국제투자보증기구. 세계은행의 하부기관.

MIL ① magnetic indicator loop 자기탐지환상선.
② Military Specifications and Standards 미군용 규격.

MILSATCOM Military Satellite Communications System (미) 군사위성통신시스템.

MILSTAR military strategic, tactical and relay satellite communications program (미) 전략전술중계용 군사 통신 위성계획.

MILSTD Military Standard 미국 군용규격(납품계수검사용).

MIM mobile interceptor missile 지상 이동시기 대공미사일.

MIMD multiple instruction multiple data stream 다중명령 다중데이터처리.

MIME multipurpose internet mail extensions 다목적인터넷 전자우편 확장 인터넷상의 전자 우편으로 화상이나 음성을 포함한 멀티미디어정보를 보낼때의 표준규격.

MINET Medical Information Network (미) 의학정보 네크워크.

MIMM member of the Institution of Mining and Metallurgy (영) 채광 야금 협회 회원.

Minn. Minnesota 미네소타 주.

303

MINS

MINS Minor(s) In Need of Supervision (미) 후견을 필요로 하는 미성년자.

MINURSO Mission Des Nations Unies pour L'rganization d'un Referendum au Sahara Occidental 유엔 서부 사하라 평화 유지단.

MIOS metal insulator oxide semiconductor 금속 절연물 산화막 반도체.

MIP ① marine insurance policy 해상보험증권.
② marketing intelligence processing 마케팅전략정보처리.
③ monthly investment plan 매월 일정금액 투자계획.
④ music, information, personality 음악, 정보, 개성. 텔레비전시대에 라디오를 부흥시키는 3가지 요소.

MIPA member of the Institute of Practitioners in Advertising (영) 광고업자 협회 회원.

MIPS million instructions per second (컴퓨터) 1초간에 몇 100만회의 명령을 실행할 수 있는가를 나타내는 지수.

MIPTC Men's International Professional Tennis Council 남자 국제 프로 테니스 협의회.

MIR minimum irrigation rate 최소 관액(灌液) 유량(流量).

MIRACL mid infrard advanced chemical laser 중적외선 신형 (新型) 화학레이저.

MIRV multiple independently targeted reentry vehicle 복수 개별목표유도탄두(彈頭). 1기의 탄도 미사일에 복수의 탄두(핵)을 적재시켜 각기 목표를 공격할 수 있게 한 탄두시스템.

Mis. Missouri 미조리 주.

MIS ① management information system 경영정보시스템.
② marketing information system 마케팅정보시스템.
③ medical information system 의료정보시스템.
④ metal insulator semi conductor 금속절연체반도체.

MISD multiple instruction single data stream 다중 명령 단일 데이터처리.

MISL Major Indoor Soccer League (미) 실내 축구 리그.

Miss. Mississippi 미시시피 주.

MIT ① Massachusetts Institute of Technology 매사추세츠공과대학.
② master instruction tape (컴퓨터) 특정의 한조의 프로그램을 실행하는 데 필요한 것을 모두 기억하고 있는 자기 테이프.

MITI Ministry of International Trade and Industry (일) 통산성.

MIZEX Marginal Ice Zone Experiments (미) 연빙(緣氷)연구계획. 북극해, 남극해의 해빙(海氷)의 면적은 계절에 따라 변화하며 이 해빙은 해양학, 기상학, 생물학에 중요한 의의를 가지고 있을 뿐 아니라 해저자원. 수산자원의 개발, 해운, 군사 작전에도 깊은 관계가 있다. 특히 얼음과 해수와 대기 사이의 작용을 이해하기 위한 연구를 말한다.

MJB Max, Joseph, Bransten MJB 제품의 커피. MJB는 회사를 설립한 3명의 이름의 머리글자다. Mocha, Java, Brazil(모카, 자바, 브라질)의 커피를 혼합했다는 것은 속설.

MJI member of the Institute of Journalists (영) 신문인 협회 회원.

MKS system meter kilogram second system 미터, 킬로그램, 초계.

MKSA system meter, kilogram, second, ampere system 미터, 킬로그램. 초, 암페어를 기본단위로 하는 전자(電磁) 단위시스템.

mkt market 시황, 시장.

ML ① magnetic levitation 자기부상. ② master of laws = LLM 법학석사.

MLA Modern Language Association of America 미국 근대어 협회.

MLB Service ① Mini Land Bridge Service 극동에서 선적된 화물이 미국의 태평양 서안(西岸) 항구에서 하양되어 철도나 트럭에 의해 북미대륙을 횡단, 미국 대서양안의 동부 및 걸프지역 항구의 터미널까지 운반되는 서비스. 극동에서 미국서안 - 대륙횡단 - 미국동안 - 구주대륙으로 연결되는 land bridge의 축소판이라는 의미에서 MLB라고 불리워지고 있다.
② Major League Baseball(미국 야구 리그)

MLC ① multilayer ceramic 다층(多層) 세라믹.
② Martial Law Command 계엄사령부.

MLD ① median lethal dose 반수치사량.
② minimum lethal dose 최소치사량.

MLE molecular layer epitaxy 분자층 에피택시법. 두 종류의 원료가스를 사용하여 한쪽의 가스분자를 기판위에 1분자층만 흡착시킨 후 또 하나의 가스를 공급하여 쌍방의 가스분자가 기판표면에서 분해, 반응하여 결정이 퇴적하는 성장법.

MLF multi lateral nuclear force 다각적 핵전력.

MLGW maximum landing gross weight 최대착륙중량.

MLit., Mlitt master of literature or master of letters 문학 석사.

MLM Mars Landing Module 화성

착륙선.

MLN (스) Movimiento de Liberacion Nacional (=National Liberation Movement) (과테말라) 국민 해방 운동당.

MLP ① mobile launcher platform 이동로켓발사대.
② multi-link procedures 멀티링크처리.

MLPC [F] Mouvement pour la Liberation du Peuple Centrafricain (=Movement for the Liberation of Central African People) 중앙 아프리카 인민 해방 운동.

MLR minimum lending rate (영) (잉글랜드 은행의) 공정보합.

MLRS multiple launch rocket system (미육군) 다연장(多連裝) 로켓탄 발사 시스템.

MLS ① microwave landing system 마이크로파 착륙유도장치.
② multimedia learning system 멀티미디어 학습 시스템 학교용 멀티미디어 교육 시스템.

MLSS mixed liquor suspended solids 혼합액 부유물질농도.

NLT median lethal time (원자력) 50% 치사시간.

MLTA multiple line terminal adapter 다중회선 어댑터.

MLVSS mixed liquor volatile suspended 혼합액휘발성 부유물질 농도.

MLW ① maximum landing weight (항공기) 최대착륙중량.
② medium level wastes 중레벨(방사성) 폐기물.

MM ① main memory 주기억장치.
② material management 물질관리.
③ moving magnet 가동자석.

MMA ① methyl methacrylate 합성수지의 원료.
② Metropolitan Museum of Art 메트로폴리탄 미술관.
③ Modern Management Association 근대경영협회.
④ Money Market Account = MMDA 금융시장예금구좌.

MMC Money Market Certificate 금융시장금리 연동형 정기예금.

MMD maximum mixing depth 최대혼합층(混合層) 고도. 혼합층 고도는 하루 중에서도 시각에 따라 다르며 그의 최대치를 MMD 라고 하고 하루 중 오염물질이 가장 희박하다.

MMDA Money Market Deposit Account (미) 금융시장예금구좌. 증권회사의 MMF에 대항하여 은행이 제공하고 있는 고금리예금.

MME master of mechanical engineering 기계공학석사.

MMF ① magnetomotive force 기자력(起磁力).
② Money Market Fund = MMF

(미) 증권회사가 매출하고 있는 고금리의 투자신탁.

MMI man machine interface 인간과 기계의 접촉면. 기계를 다루기 쉽게 하려는 인간공학의 문제의 하나.

MMIC monolithic microwave integrated circuit 모노리스·마이크로파 집적회로.

MML micro to mainframe link (컴퓨터) 개인용 컴퓨터와 호스트터 머신을 온라인으로 연결하여 데이터를 공유화(共有化)하거나 처리의 분산화(分散化)를 도모한 시스템.

MMM multi media multiplexer 매체 다중화 장치.

MMMF Money Market Mutual Fund = MMF 단기금융자산투자신탁.

MMN Money Market Note (미) 변동 금리부 중기채권.

MMO music minus one 보컬 또는 제 악기의 솔로부분 (독창·독주)을 빼고 녹음한 레코드.

MMPI Minnesota Multiphasic Personality Index (미) 미네소타 다중 인격 목록.

MMR man made rock (원자력) 인조 암초.

MMRBM mobile medium range ballistic missile (미) 기동성 중거리탄두탄.

MMS multimission modular spacecraft 다목적 모듈실 우주선.

MMSE multiuse mission support equipment 발사용 미션 지원 설비.

MMT ① methylcyclopentadienyl manganese tricarbonyl 옥탄가를 높이기 위하여 가솔린에 가입하는 유기금속화합물.
② multiple mirror telescope 다면 반사망원경.

MMU ① manned maneuvering unit 우주선의 활동용 조종장치. 우주비행사의 선외활동 지원장치.
② manned maneuvering unit 부착식 유영장치.

MMus master of music 음악학 석사.

MMW millimeter wave radar 밀리파 레이더.

Mn manganese 망간. 원자번호 25.

MN ① merchant navy 상선(商船).
② Minnesota (미) 미네소타 주의 우편 기호.

MNC multinational corporation 다국적 기업.

MND Ministry of National Defense 國防部(국방부).

MNE multinational enterprises 다국적 기업.

MNF ① multilateral nuclear force 다각적핵전력.
② Multinational Forces 국제 감시군.

MNLF

MNLF Moro National Liberation Front (필리핀) 모로 민족 해방 전선.

MNP microcom networking protocol 마이크로컴퓨터 통신망 규약 Microcom사가 설계한 통신 프로토콜의 일종.

MNR (스) Movimento Nacionalista Revolucionario (=National Revolutionary Movement) (볼리비아) 민족 혁명 운동.

MNRM Mozambique National Resistance Movement 모잠비크 민족 저항 운동.

Mo molybdenum 몰리브덴. 원자번호 42.

Mo. Missouri = Mis 미주리 주.

MO ① machinery space zero people 기관실 무인화.
② mail order 통신판매. 우편에 의한 수주와 발주.
③ manually operated 수동(의).
④ mineral oil 광유.
⑤ money order 우편환.

MO disc magnetic optical disc 광자기디스크.

MOB management by objective 목표에 의한 관리.

MOBS multiple orbit bombardment system 다궤도 폭탄.

MOC ① Ministry of Communications (한) 체신부.
② Ministry of Construction (한) 건설부.
③ Ministry of Culture (한)문화부.

MOCVD metal organic chemical vapor deposition 유기금속기상성장법(氣相成長法). 화학반응을 이용하여 기체의 상태(기상)에서 결정을 성장시키는 방법을 기상성장법이라 한다.

MOD Ministry of Defence (영) 국방성.

Mod E Modern English 근대영어.

MODEM modulator demodulator (컴퓨터) 변복 조정 장치. 컴퓨터와 통신회선 사이를 통하게 하는 장치.

MODM Multiple Objective Decision Making 다목표 의사 결정.

MOF ① manned orbital facility 우주공장. NASA의 시설.
② mixed oxide fuel (원자력) 혼합 산화물 연료.

MOHS Ministry of Health and Social Affairs (한) 보건 사회부.

MOI Ministry of Information (한) 공보처.

MOJ Ministry of Justice (한) 법무부.

MOL ① maintenance oriented language (컴퓨터) 회화형 보수용(會話型保守用) 언어.
② manned orbital laboratory 유인궤도실험실. 우주관측이 목적.

MOLAB Mobile Lunar Laboratory 이동월면실험실.

MOMA Museum of Modern Art in New York (미) 뉴욕근대미술관.

Mont. Montana 몬태나 주.

Montsame Mongolian News Agency 몽고 인민공화국 국영통신.

MONUA United Nations Observer Mission in Angola 앙골라 평화유지 감시단.

MOP managing office productivity 사무소의 생산성 관리.

MOR middle of the road 마음 편히 들을 수 있는 음악.

MOS ① management operating system   표준경영관리방식. 컴퓨터에 의하여 경영 각 부문의 업무를 종합적으로 관리하는 시스템.
② marine observation satellite 해양관측위성.
③ Mars Orbit Station 화성궤도 스테이션.
④ Metal oxide semiconductor (컴퓨터) 금속 산화막 반도체.

MOSFET metal oxide semiconductor field effect transistor 모스소자, 모스전계효과(電界效果)트랜지스터.

MOSIC metal oxide semiconductor integrated circuit 금속 산화막 반도체 집적회로.

MOSS ① market oriented sector selective (미·일) 시장분야 별 개별 회의 국제 경쟁력이 있으면서 일본시장에 참여할 수 없는 제품의 무역장해요인을 분야별로 토의하는 방식.
② middle aged over stressed semiaffluent suburbanite 교외에 거주하고 있는 스트레스 과잉인 비교적 부유한 중년.

MOT Ministry of Transportation 교통부.

MOU memorandum of understanding 양해각서.

MOUSE minimum orbital unmanned satellite of the earth 소형 정보수집 위성.

MOX mixed oxide fuel (원자력) 혼합산화물연료. 천연우라늄이나 재처리로 회수한 산화우라늄을 혼합하여 만든 연료.

MP ① mechanical pulp 쇄목(碎木)펄프.
② medium playing record Mp반. 33회전 ⅓의 Lp반과 회전수는 같지만 홈의 폭을 넓게하여 큰 음량의 녹음을 가능하게 한 음반.
③ melting point 융점.
④ Member of Parliament (영) 런던 경찰청.
⑤ Metropolitan Police (영) 런던 경찰청.
⑥ Military police 헌병.
⑦ multiprocessor 다중프로세서.
⑧ Member of Parliament (영, 캐, 호주 등) 하원의원.

309

MPA ① maritime patrol aircraft 해양초계항공기.
② master of public administration 행정학석사.
③ multiple processor architecture 다중처리구조.
④ multi-purpose additive 만능 첨가제.
⑤ Magazine Publishers Association (미) 잡지 발행자 협회.

MPAA Motion Picture Association of America 미국 영화 협회.

MPC ① marginal propensity to consume 한계소비성향.
② maximum permissible concentration 방사성강하물(放射性降下物)의 최대허용량.
③ military policy currency 군표.
④ mathematics, physics, chemistry 수학·물리·화학.
⑤ Multi Party Conference (나미네아) 다당 회의.

MPCS manufacturing planning and control system 생산계획 관리 시스템.

MPD maximum permissible dose 방사선의 최대허용량. 방사선을 받고 신체에 장해를 일으키지 않는 범위의 최대치.

MPEAA Motion Picture Export Association of America 미국 영화 수출협회.

MPEG motion pictures experts group 엠펙, 동영상 표준화 그룹.

MPES multinational production enterprises(among developing countries) (발전도상국간) 다국간생산기업.

m.p.g. mile per gallon 1갤런당 주행 마일수.

m.p.h. mile per hour 1시간당 주행 마일수.

MPH master of public health 공중 보건학 석사.

MPI marginal propensity to import 한계수입성향.

MPL maximum permissible level (원자력) 최대허용레벨.

MPLA (포) Movimento Popular de Libertacao de Angola (=Popular Movement for the Liberation of Angola) 앙골라 해방 인민 운동.

MPN most probable number 최확수(崔確數)

MPOS Moon Polar Orbit Satellite 월극 궤도 위성.

MPR (인도네시아) Majelis Permusyawaratan Rakyat (= People's Consultative Assembly) (인도네시아) 국민 협의회.

MPS ① marginal propensity to save 한계저축성향.
② material production in space 우주에서의 물질제조.
③ Material Product System 물적 생산물 방식. 사회주의 제국의 통일국민 경제통계지표체계.

MPSR multipurpose support room (우주공학)다목적 지원실. MPST가 대기하고 있는 방.

MPST multipurpose support team (우주공학) 다목적 지원팀. MCC 내의 팀의 하나. 비행전의 계획, 작업스케줄, 인원배치 등의 책임을 가지고 있는 팀.

MPT multi purpose terminal 다목적 단말기.

MPU microprocessor unit (컴퓨터) 초소형 중앙연산처리장치.

MPV multipurpose passenger vehicle 다목적 승용차.

MPX multiplex 다중(多重) 송신 전자 시스템.

MQ Moral Quotient 도덕지수.

MQF mobile quarantine facility NASA의 이동식 격리장치. 달에서 귀환한 비행사를 달자료 연구소까지 운송하기 위한 버스 모양의 격리실.

MR ① marginal revenue 한계수입. ② mate's receipt 본선(本船) 화물 수취증.

M.R. motivational research 구매동기 조사.

MRA ① Moral Rearmament 도덕재무장운동. ② Market research Association 무역이나 부동산 거래및 교역 정보를 공유하는 연합회

MRASM medium range air to surface missile 중거리공대함(空對艦)미사일.

MRBM medium range ballistic missile 중거리탄도 미사일. 사정거리 800~2400km.

MRC Medical Research Council 의학연구회[英]

MRCA multiple role combat aircraft 다목적 전투기.

MRD Movement for the Restoration of Democracy (파키스탄) 민주 회복 운동.

MRE Microbiological Research Establishment (영) 미생물 연구소.

MRFA Mutual Reduction of Forces and Armaments (In the Conference on Associated Measures in Central Europe) 중부 유럽 상호 병력 군비 삭감 교섭.

MRG (프)Mouvement des Radicaux de Gauche (=Leftwing Radicals Movement) (프랑스) 좌파 급진 운동.

MRGS member of the Royal Geographical Society (영) 왕립 지리학회 회원.

MRH member of the Royal Household 왕족.

MRI magnetic resonance imaging 자기공명 영상법.

MRL Maximum Residue Limits 최대

311

잔류허용기준. (식품 또는 동물사료 표면 및 내부에 법적으로 잔류가 허용된 잔류 농약등의 최대농도).

MRMIP The California Major Risk Medical Insurance Program 가주중병의료보험제도.

MRND (프) Mouvement Revolutionnaire National Pour le Developpement (=National Revolutionary Movement for Development) (루안다) 국가 개발 혁명 운동. 1975년에 결성된 정당.

MRP ① machine readable passport 기계 판독식 여권.
② manufacturing resources planning 자재소요량관리.
③ materials requirements planning 자재소요량계획. 다품종 소량생산에 유효한 생산재고관리방식.
④ (프) Mouvement, Revolutionnaire Populaire (=People'a Republican Movement) 인민공화파. 카톨릭교 좌의 정당.

MRT mass rapid transit 대량수송교통기관.

MRV ① moon roving vehicle 월면차.
② multiple reentry vehicle 다탄두재돌입미사일.

MRW maximum ramp weight (항공기) 최대 램프중량.

MS ① maiden surname 여성의결혼전의 성.
② management science 경영과학.
③ manuscript 원고.
④ master of science = MSc, ScM, SM 이하석사.
⑤ medium shot 파사체의 인물의 무릎 위를 찍는것.
⑥ mild steel 연강.
⑦ mission specialist 우주비행사 중에서 특별 임무를 가진 과학자.
⑧ motor ship 발동기선.
⑨ Mississippi 미국 중남부에 있는 미시시피 주(州).
⑩ Microsoft 회사

MSA ① Mutual Security Act (미) 상호안전보장법.
② Mutual Security Agency (미) 상호안전보장본부.

MSAC most seriously affected countries 석유 위기때 가장 심각한 타격을 받았던 나라들.

MSB most significant bit 최상위의 비트. 컴퓨터의 1워드를 구성하는 비트 중 가장 왼쪽에 있는 비트.

MSBLS microwave scanning beam landing system 마이크로파 주사(走査) 착륙시스템.

MSBR molten salt breeder reactor 용융염(熔融鹽) 증식원자로.

MSC ① Manned Spacecraft Center (미) 유인우주비행센터.
② Mass storage control (컴퓨터) 대용량 기억제어기구.

MSCR molten-salt converter reactor 용융염전환원자로.

MSD most significant digit (컴퓨터) 최상위의 숫자. 수의자리 표시에서 수값의 크기에 가장 큰 영향을 미치는 유효숫자로서 가장 왼쪽 자리의 수. 10진법의 수 389에서 최상의 숫자는 3이다.

MSDF Maritime Self-Defense Force (일) 해상자위대.

MSDOS microsoft disk operating system (컴퓨터) 16비트 개인용 컴퓨터용 DOS

MSF ① mass storage facility (컴퓨터) 대용량기억장치.
② message stock file (컴퓨터) 메시지 축적파일.

MSFC Marshall Space Flight Center (미) 마셜 우주비행센터.

MSG Mono sodium glutamate 화학 조미료.

MSH melanocyte stimulating hormone 멜라닌 자극 호르몬.

MSHA Mine Safety and Health Administration (미) 노동성 광산 안전보건국.

MSI medium scale integrated circuit (컴퓨터) 중규모집적회로.

MSL mean sea level (항공) 평균조위(潮位), 평균해면.

MSLS master of science in library science 도서관학 이학 석사.

MSM ① Meritorious Service Medal (미 육군) 공훈장.
② (프) Mouvement Socialiste Militant (=Militant Socialist Movement) (모리셔스) 사회주의 투쟁 운동. 정당명.

MSN Microsoft network 마이크로 소프트 네트워크.

MSocSc master of social science 사회학 석사.

MSPB Merit Systems Protection Board (미) 메리트 시스템 보호 위원회.

MSQG Madison Square Garden (미) 뉴욕의 세계 최대 실내 경기장.

MSR ① missile site radar 미사일 기지레이더. 교전중의 미사일의 비행을 감시하는 레이더.
② molten salt reactor 용융염(熔融鹽). 원자로.

MSS ① manned space station 유인 우주 스테이션.
② mass storage system (컴퓨터) 대용량 기억 시스템.
③ multi spectral scanner (or sensor) system 다중 파장 동시촬영기.
④ manuscripts 원고.

MSSP message send service procedure (컴퓨터) 메시지송출(送出) 서비스처리.

MST ① moisture proof cellophane 방습 셀롤판.
② Mountain Standard Time (미) 중서부 기준시간.

MSTS Military Sea Transportation Service 미군 군사 해상수출부.

MSV mass storage volume (컴퓨터) 대량 기억 볼륨.

MSW ① master of social work 사회 사업 석사.
② medical social worker (영) 의료 사회 복지사.
③ municipal solid waste 도시의 고체폐기물.

MSX Microsoft Extended Basic (컴퓨터) 마이크로 소프트사가 제작한 프로그램언어.

MSY maximum sustainable yield 최대 지속 생산량. 매년 재생산되는 자원의 증가분만 어획(漁獲)하면 근원이 되는 자원량은 온존되어 지속적으로 어획을 할 수 있다. 또 생물의 특성으로 증가분이 최대가 되는 적도의 자원량이 있으며 그리하여 지속 가능한 어획량도 최대로 된다는 것이다. 이것을 말한다.

Mt. Mount(ain) 산.

MT ① machine translation 기계 번역.
② magnetic tape 자기 테이프.
③ mail transfer 우편환.
④ manual transmission AT차에 대하여 클러치페달이 있는 보통 차를 말한다. (수동 변속기)
⑤ medical technologist 위생 검사기사. 혈액검사 등을 하는 기사.
⑥ megaton 메가톤. 핵병기의 폭발에너지의 단위. TNT 100만톤에서 방출되는 에너지와 같다.
⑦ miniature tube 소형진공관.
⑧ mission timer (로켓) 미션·타이머.
⑨ Montana (미) 몬태나 주의 우편기호.

M/T Measurement Ton 용적톤. 1입방미터 또는 40입방피트를 1톤으로 한다.

MTA ① medical technical assistant (미) 의료 조수.
② Metropolitan Transportation Authority (미) 뉴욕시와 주변의 7개 counties의 공공 교통기관을 경영하는 조직.

MTB ① Materials Transportation Bureau (미) 운수성 물자수송국.
② motor torpedo boat 어뢰정.

MTBF mean time between failures (컴퓨터) 평균무고장시간. 시스템의 고장이 발생하는 평균적인 시간폭.

MTC ① Metropolitan Transportation Commission (미) 도시 교통위원회.
② Maritime Transport Committee 해운위원회. (경제 협력개발기구 산하 기구).

MTCR Missile Technology Control Regime 미사일 기술통제체제.

MTEFL master in the teaching of English as a foreign language 외국어로써의 영어 교육학 석사.

MTF must touch flesh (영 속어)

성적 매력이 있는 남자.

MTGW maximum takeoff gross weight = MTOGW (항공) 최대이륙총중량.

mth. month 달.

MTh master of theology 신학 석사.

MTI moving target indicator (항공) 이동 목표 지시 장치.

MTM methods time measurement 동작평균시간측정법. 한가지 작업을 마치는데 필요한 평균시간을 측정하는 방법.

MTN multilateral trade negotiations GATT의 다각적 무역교섭.

MTO ① Multilateral Trade Organization 다각적 무역기구.
② multi modal transport operator = CTO 복합운송운영자.

MTOGW maximum takeoff gross weight = MTGW (항공) 최대이륙총중량.

MTP management training program 관리자 훈련계획.

MTR ① material testing reactor 재료 시험 원자로. 원자로에 사용하는 재료를 시험하기 위한 원자로.
② missile tracking radar 미사일 추적(追跡) 레이더.

Mt. Rev. Most Reverend 대사교. 대주교.

MTS ① meter ton second 길이에 미터, 질량에 톤, 시간에 초를 사용하는 단위계.
② multichannel television sound 음성다중텔레비전음성.

MTSNTI International Center for Scientific and Technical Information (소) 과학 기술 정보 국제 센터.

MTT minimum time track 항공기의 최단시간 항로.

MTTA Machine Tool Trades' Association (영) 공작 기계 공업회.

MTTF mean time to failure 평균 고장시간. 고장의 수리·재생을 하지 않은 부품. 기기의 평균 사용기간.

MTTFF mean time to first failure 시스템, 기기, 부품 등의 최고의 고장까지의 동작시간의 평균치.

MTTR mean time to repair (컴퓨터) 평균 수리 시간.

MTU magnetic tape unit 자기 테이프 장치.

MTV Music Television (미) 음악 방송 텔레비전. 록음악을 24시간 계속 방송하는 유선텔레비전.

MTX middle trainer X 차기 중간 제트 연습기.

MUD Multi User Dungeon Game 머드 게임. 롤 플레잉의 일종인 던전 게임(감옥에서 빠져 나오는 게임)에서 여러 명이 다함께 참가하는 것.

MUF ① material unaccounted for 핵물질 불명량(不明量). 핵연료공장에서는 보유량, 수불, 폐기 등을 기재한 장부를 비치하고 정기적으로 실제의 양과 대조하고 있다. 이렇게 하여도 원인불명의 손실이 생기는 경우를 말한다.
② maximum usable frequency 최고 사용 주파수.

MULDEM multiplexer demultiplexer 다중화장치/다중분리장치.

MULTICS multiplex of information and computing service 대형컴퓨터 공동이용 방식.

MUMPS Massachusetts General Hospital utility multiprogramming system 매사추세츠 종합병원에서 개발한 의학용 프로그램언어.

MUN Model United Nations 모의 유엔 회의.

MUSICAL Music Score Assignment Language 악보의 내용을 표현하기 위한 컴퓨터언어.

MUST manned undersea station 유인해중 스테이션.

MUT mean up time 평균동작가능 시간.

mV millivolt 1000분의 1볼트.

MV ① market value 시장가격.
② megavolt 100만 볼트.
③ merchant vessel 상선.
④ motor vessel 발동기선.

MVC more volatile component 경질(輕質)성분.

MVD, M.V.D. Ministerstvo Vnutrennikh Del 소련 내무성 (비밀경찰이며, 1946년, NKVD를 바꾼 것).

MVE methyl vinyl ether 메틸 비닐 절연체.

MVMA Motor Vehicle Manufacturers Association of the United States 미국 자동차 공업회.

MVO Member of the Royal Victorian Order (영) 빅토리아 4등 또는 5등 훈작사.

MVP ① mehtyl vinyl pyridine 메틸 비닐 피리딘. 메틸 비닐 합성수지.
② most valuable player 최우수 선수.

MVR ① Market Value Ratios 시장 가치 비율.
② Moter Vehicle Record 운전기록.

MVS multiple virtual storage (미) IBM사의 대형컴퓨터용 운영체제.

MVT multiprogramming with a variable number of tasks IBM사의 다중프로그래밍 기능제어용 프로그램.

mW milliwatt 1000분의 1와트.

MW ① megawatt 메가와트.

② molecular weight 분자량.

MWA ① Modern Woodmen of America 우애 클럽의 명칭.
② Mystery Writers of America 미국 추리 작가 협회.

MWD megawatt day 메가와트 일 (日). 핵연료의 연소율을 나타내는 단위.

MWIA Medical Women's International Association 국제 여의 사회.

MWL Muslim World League 이슬람 세계 연맹.

MWS management work station (컴퓨터) 관리자용 조작탁(操作卓).

MX ① missile, experimental 차기 ICBM.
② 핵미사일의 이름(미국).

MYOB Mind your own business 쓸데없는 참견이다.

n noun (문법) 명사.

N ① November 11월.
② nitrogen [화]질소의 화학기호.

n/a ① no account 거래 없음. 구좌 없음.
② not applicable 관련 사항 없음.

Na natrium(sodium) (라) 나트륨. 원자번호 11.

NA ① Narcotics Anonymous 마약 환자 구제회.
② not available 입수불능.
③ numerical aperture 개구수 (開口數). 현미경의 대물 렌즈의 해상력의 척도.

N.A. ① no answer 회답 없음. 앙케이트의 회답란에 기입되는 약어로 회답이 없음을 나타냄.
② not available 입수불능.
③ Naval Academy 미국 해군 사관 학교(海軍士軍官學校).

N/A new account 신규구좌.

NAA ① National Aeronautics Association 전미(全美) 비행가협회.
② National Association of Accountants (美) 전국 회계사 협회.
③ neutron activation analysis 중성자 방사화 분석.
④ North Atlantic Assembly 북대서양 의회.
⑤ Newspapers Association of America 미 신문협회.

NAACP National Association for the Advancement of Colored People (미) 전미 흑인 지위 향상 협회. (주의 : AA를 double A로 읽을 수 있음).

NAAFI Navy, Army and Air Force Institute (영) 육해공군 후생 기관.

NAAU National Amateur Athletic Union 전 미국 아마추어 체육연맹.

NAB National Association of Broadcasters (미) 전국 방송회사 협회.

NABA North American Broadcasters Association 북미방송협회.

NABE National Association of Business Economists (미) 전국 기업 이코노미스트 협회. = 전국 기업 경제인 협회.

NAC National Advisory Council on International Monetary and Financial Problems (미) 국제 통화 금융문제 국가자문위원회.

NACA National Advisory Committee for Aeronautics (미) 항

공 자문위원회.

NACF National Agricultural Cooperative Federation 農業協同組合 = (노동협동조합)

NACHA National Automated Clearing House Association 전미 자동결제 협회.

NACS ① National Association of College Stores (미) 전국 대학 서점 협회.
② National Association of Computer Stores (미) 전국 컴퓨터 매장 협회.

NACU National Association of Colleges and Universities (미) 전국 대학 협회.

NAD ① nicotinamide adenine dinucleotide 니코틴아미드 아데닌 디누클레오티드.
② Not on Active Duty 예비역

NADA National Automobile Dealers Association (미) 자동차 딜러 협회.

NADGE Nato Air Defence Ground Environment 북대서양 조약기구 자동 방공경계 관제조직.

NAEB National Association of Educational Broadcasters (미) 전국 교육방송자 협회.

NAEC National Association of Electric Companies 전미 전기 사업 연합회.

NAFO North Atlantic Fisheries Organization 북대서양 어업기구.

NAFSA National Association for Foreign Student Affairs (미) 외국인 학생원조 협회.

NAFTA North Atlantic Free Trade Area 북대서양 자유무역지역.

NAHB National Association of Home Builders of the United States 미국 가옥 건축자 협회.

NAIA National Association of Intercollegiate Athletes (미) 전국 대학 운동 경기자 협회.

NAICS North American Industry Classification System 북미산업 분류체계 (1997 개편된 미국, 캐나다, 멕시코 3국의 공통 산업분류체계)

NAIRU Non Accelerating Inflation Rate of Unemployment 인플레이션을 가속(加速)하지 않는 실업률.

NAK ① negative acknowledge (컴퓨터) 부정응답문자.
② negative acknowledge (컴퓨터) 부정응답. 전송기 기간에 있어서 접선상태에서 이상이 있거나 송신중에 오류가 있을 때 수신측이 보내는 응답.

NAL National Aerospace Laboratory (일) 항공 우주 기술 연구소.

NALC National Association of Letter Carriers (미) 전국 우편 배달부 조합.

NALEAO National Association of

NALGO

Latin Elected and Appointed Officials (미) 전국 라틴계 공직자 연맹.

NALGO National and Local Government Officers' Association (영) 국가·지방 공무원 조합.

NAM ① National Association of Manufacturers 전국 제조업자협회
② Non aligned Movement 비동맹 운동
③ new age music 뉴에이지 뮤직. 재즈와 클래식 음악을 기본으로 일본·인도·브라질 등의 요소를 가미한 일종의 퓨전.

NAMM National Association of Music Merchants 미국 악기상 (商) 협회.

NAMUCAR (스) Naviera Multinacional del Caribe (=Caribbean Multinational Navigation) 카리브 공동 해운 회사.

NANA North American Newspaper Alliance 북미 신문 연합.

NANBA North American National Broadcasters' Association 북아메리카 방송 연맹.

NAND not and (컴퓨터) 부정논리적(積).

NAP negative adjustment policy 소극적 조정 정책.

NAPA ① National Association of Performing Artists (미) 전국 공연 예술가 협회.
② National Automotive Parts Association (미) 전국 자동차 부품 협회.

NAPALM naphthene palmitate 네이팜탄의 재료 팔미트산염

napalm bomb 네이팜탄, 네이팜 탄.

NAPAN National Association to Prevent Addiction to Narcotics 전미 마약중독 방지협회.

NAPCA National Air Pollution Control Administration (미) 국가 대기오염 규제국.

NAPLPS North American Presentation Level Protocol Syntax (컴퓨터) 화상표시 절차 표준화 규약. 비디오텍스의 북미표준방식.

NAR National Association of Real Estate 전미 부동산 협회.

NARA National Addict Rehabilitation Act (미) 마약 중독자 갱생법.

NATAL National Abortion Rights Action League (미) 임신 중절권리 옹호 전국연맹.

NARAS National Association of Recording Arts and Science (미) 전국 녹음 예술 기술 협회.

NARB National Advertising Review Board (미) 전국광고심사위원회. CBBB의 부속기관.

NARC NARCOTIC (미) (연방) 마약 취제관.

NARC National Advertising Review Council (미) 전국광고심사협의회. NARB와 전국 광고부를 감독한다.

NAREB National Association of Real Estate Boards (미) 전국부동산 조합협회.

NARMIC National Action/Research on the Military Industrial Complex 국방(방위) 산업체 전국 실천 연구.

NAPF National Association of Pension Funds 전국 연금 협회[英]

NAPM National Association of Purchasing Management 전국 구매 관리협회 [美]

NARO National Agricultural Research Organization 농업 기술 연구 기구 [日] (일본 獨立行政法人)

NAS ① National Academy of Sciences 전미(全美) 과학 아카데미.
② National Aerospace Standard 미국 항공 우주 규격.
③ National Association of Schoolmasters (英) 전국 교장 협회.
④ Naval air station (美) 해군 항공 기지.
⑤ Noise Abatement Society (英) 소음 방지 협회.

NASA National Aeronautics and Space Administration (미) 항공우주국.

NASACOM National Aeronautics and Space Administration Communication's Network NASA의 우주여행을 위한 세계적인 지상통신망.

NASAP Nonproliferation Alternative System Assessment Program (미) 핵불확산대체 시스템평가계획.

NASARR north american searching and ranging radar 북미 탐색 측거(測距) 레이더.

NASBIC National Association of Small Business Investment Companies 전국중소기업투자회사협회.

NASCAR National Association of Stock Car Auto Racing (미) 전국 자동차 경주 협회.

NASCO North Atlantic Salmon Conservation Organization 북대서양연어보존기구. (1982 설립, 회원국은 캐나다, 덴마크, EEC 등 9개국으로 북위36° 이북의 대서양 수역 연어자원 관련 과학자료 분석 및 보급, 국제협력을 통한 북대서양 수역 연어보호 등의 업무 수행기관).

NASD National Association of Securities Dealers (미) 전국 증권업 협회.

NASDA National Space Development Agency of Japan (일) 우주개발사업단.

NASDAQ National Association of Securities Dealers' Automated Quotation (미) 전국 증권거래협회 시세 자동전달시스템.

NASE National Association for the Self-Employed 전국 자영업 협회[美]

NASL North American Soccer League 북미 축구 연맹.

NASP U.S. National Aerospace Plane 미국우주항공기. 보통 활주로에서 이·착륙하며 대기권내에서는 초고속램제트(ramjet)권외에서는 액체수소 로켓을 이용하고 최고마하 25의 속도를 목표로 개발 연구중이다.

NAT ① National Arbitration Tribunal (영) 전국 중재 재판소. ② North Atlantic Treaty 북대서양 조약.

NATA North American Telecommunications Association 북미 전기 통신 업회.

NATCA National Air Traffic Controllers' Association (미) 전국 항공 관제관 조합.

Nat. Gal. National Gallery 런던의 國立美術館 (국립 미술관).

NATIS National Information System 전국 정보시스템. UNESCO의 제안에 의한다.

NATIV North American Test Instrument Vehicle (미공군) 공기 역학 연구용 유도미사일.

NATM new Austrian tunnelling method 오스트리아식 신터널 굴착공법.

NATO North Atlantic Treaty Organization 북대서양 조약기구.

NATOICS NATO Integrated Communications System 북대서양 조약 기구 통합 통신 시스템.

NAV net asset value 순 자산가치.

NAVI new advanced vehicle with intelligence 전자 제어 자동 변속기.

NAVLAS noise and vibration laboratory automation system 진동, 소음의 실험해석의 전산시스템.

NAVSPASUR Naval Space Surveillance System (미) 해군 우주 감시 시스템.

NAVSTAR navigation satellite (우주) 항행위성, 항해위성. 이 인공위성에서 발사되는 전파를 비행기나 선박이 수신하여 자기의 위치를 알 수 있다.

NAWBO National Association of Women Business 전국 여성 경영자 협회[美]

NAWC Naval War College (미) 해군 대학.

NAWCH National Association for the Welfare of Children in Hospital (영) 전국 입원 아동 복지 협회.

NAZI Nationalsozialistische Deutsche Arbeiterpartei (National Socialist German Workers' Party) (독) 국가사회주의 독일노동자당.

Nazism National Socialism 민족사회주의.

Nb niobium 나오븀, 원자번호 41.

NB ① national brand 일류제조업체의 상표.
② new bonds 신발행 채권.
③ nota bene(note well) (라) 주의하시오.

NBA ① National Bankers Association (美) 전국 은행 협회.
② National Bar Association (美) 전국 변호사 협회.
③ National Basketball Association (美) 전국 농구 협회.
④ National Boxing Association (美) 전국 프로 복싱 협회. ※ 현재는 해체됨.
⑤ National Braille Association (美) 전국 점자 협회.

NBAA National Business Aircraft Association (미) 전국 비즈니스 항공기 협회.

NBC ① National Broadcasting Company (미) NBC 방송.
② nuclear, biological, chemical 핵·생물·화학.

NBCC National Book Critics Circle (미) 전국 서적평가 연맹.

NBED New Bantam English Dictionary 신밴텀 영어사전.

NBER National Bureau of Economic Research (미) 전미 경제 연구소.

NBFM narrow band frequency modulation 협대역(狹帶域) 주파수 변조.

NBG no bloody good (영 속어) 전혀 안돼.

NBI neutral beam injection 중성입자 가열장치.

N-bomb nuclear bomb 핵폭탄.

NBP Name Binding Protocol 엔비피, 네임 바인딩 프로토콜 Apple Talk의 네임 서비스를 정의하는 프로토콜.

NBPI National Board for Prices and Incomes (영)물가소득 위원회.

NBR acrylonitrile butadiene rubber 합성고무.

NBS National Bureau of Standards (미) 상무성 표준국.

NBSDES National Bureau of Standards Data Encryption Standard 표준국 데이터 암호화 기준.

NC ① net capital 순 자본.
② no change 변경 없음.
③ Nordic Council 북유럽 이사회(아이랜드, 놀웨이, 덴마크, 스웨덴, 핀랜드)
④ numerical control (컴퓨터) 수치제어.

N.C. North Carolina NC 노스 캐롤라이나 주.

N/C new charter 신 용선계약.

NCA ① National Coal Association (미) 전미 석탄협회. ② National Communications Association (미) 전미 통신협회.

NCAA National Collegiate Athletic Association 전미 대학 체육협회.

NCADV National Coalition Against Domestic Violence (미) 전국 가정내 폭력 반대 연합.

NCAES The National Center for the Analysis of Energy System (미) 국립 에너지 시스템 분석 센터.

NCAR National Center for Atmospheric Research (미) 국립 대기연구센터.

NCASA National Coalition Against Sexual Assault (미) 전국 성폭력 반대 연합.

NCB ① National Central Bureau 국가 중앙 사무국. ICPO 가맹국에 설치. ② National Coal Board (영) 석탄 공사.

NCC ① National Climatic Center 전미 기상 센터. 세계 최대의 기상 데이터 센터. ② National Computer Conference (미) 전국 컴퓨터 회의. ③ National Council of Churches of Christ (미) 전국 그리스도 교회협의회. ④ network control center 네트워크 제어 센터. ⑤ New Common Carrier (일) 제1종 전기 통신 사업자의 총칭.

NCCB National Council of Civil Liberties (영) 전국 시민 자유 협의회.

NCCD National Council on Crime and Delinquency 전미 범죄 비행 협의회.

NCCDE National Coordinating Council on Drug Education (미) 전국 마약 교육 정보 연락 협의회.

NCCJ National Conference of Christians and Jews (미) 전국 그리스도교도 유태인 회의.

NCCK The National Council of Churches in Korea 한국 기독교 교회 협의회

NCCL National Council for Civil Liberties (영) 전국 시민의 자유 협의회.

NCCM National Council of Catholic Men (미) 전국 남성 카톨릭교도 협의회.

NCCW National Council of Career Women (미) 전국 여성 경력 사원인 협의회.

NCD negotiable certificate of deposit 양도성 정기예금증서.

NCDC ① New Community Deve-

lopment Corporation (미) 신지역 사회 개발 공사.
② The National Climatic Data Center 국립 기후 자료센터.

NCES National Center for Educational Statistics (미) 전국 교육 통계 센터.

NCGA National computer Graphics Association 미국 컴퓨터 그래픽스 협회. 미국의 컴퓨터 그래픽스 전문가들로 이루어진 단체.

NCHS National Center for Health Statistics (미)전국 건강 통계 센터.

NCHW nickel chromium heating wire 니켈 크롬 전열선(電熱線).

NCI National Cancer Institute (미) 국립 암 연구소.

NCIC National Criminal Information Center (미) 전국 범죄 정보 센터.

NCL ① National Consumers League 전미 소비자 연맹.
② numerically controlled lathe NC 선반.

NCLIS National Commission on Libraries and Information Sciences (미) 도서관 및 정보 과학에 관한 전국 위원회.

NCLK network clock 디지털 교환기.

NCMI National Classical Music Institute (한) 국립 국악원.

NCMT numerical controlled machine tool 수치제어공작기.

NCNA new china News Agency (중국) 신화통신사.

NCND Neither Confirm Nor Deny 해외에 있는 핵무기의 존재를 시인도 부인도 하지 않는 미국의 핵정책.

NCO non-commissioned officer 하사관. = noncom

NCP National Convention Party (갬비아) 민족 회의당.

NCPAC National Conservative Political Action Committee (미) 전국 보수 정치 행동 위원회.

NCPC National Capital Planning Commission (미)수도계획위원회.

NCPDM National Conference of Physical Distribution Management (미) 전국 물적 유통관리 협의회.

NCR ① NCR Corp. National Cash Register 금전 등록기 회사.
② nitrile chloroprene rubber
③ no carbon required 카본지 불필요.

NCRP National Council on Radiation Protection and Measurement (미) 방사능 방호측정 위원회.

NCS ① National Commission on Space (미) 국가 우주위원회.
② network coordination station 통신망 관리국.

NCSC National Council of Senior Citizens (미) 전국 노인 협의회.

NCSD National Council on Sustainable Development 국가지속가능발전위원회. (1992 지속가능한 개발을 새로운 패러다임으로 하는 국가정책을 시행해 나가기로 약속한 리우 세계 환경정상회의의 결의에 따라 UN이 각국에 동 위원회의 설치 권고하여 세계 100여국에서 설치, 운영중이며 우리 나라도 2000년, 9 대통령자문 지속가능 발전위원회가 설립 운영되고 있음).

NCSI National Consumer Satisfaction Index 국가 고객 만족 지수

NCSNP National Committee for a Sane Nuclear Policy (미) 건전 핵 정책 추진 위원회.

NCTA National Cable Television Association (미) 전국 유선 텔레비전 사업자 연맹.

NCTE National Council of Teachers of English (미) 전국 영어 교사 협의회.

NCTR National Center for Toxicological Research 국립 독성 물질 연구센터[美] (식품의 약국 산하기관).

NCTV National Coalition on Television Violence (미) 전국 텔레비전 폭력 반대 연합.

NCU ① network control unit (컴퓨터) 통신망 제어장치.

② National Cyclists' Union (英) 전국 사이클리스트 연합(聯合).
③ nervous care unit 신경병 집중 치료실.
④ network control unit 컴퓨터 망 제어 장치.

NCV no commercial value 상품 가치 없음.

NCW not complied with 미실시.

Nd neodymium 네오디뮴. 원자번호 60.

ND ① National debt 국채.
② neutral density 중성농도.,
③ ND filter 중성농도 필터. 각 파장의 빛을 균등하게 흡수하여 광량(光量)을 제한한다.

N/D non destructive 비파괴의.

NDA ① National Defense Agency (일) 방위청.
② new drug application 신약 신청. 새로 개발한 약물 또는 처음으로 의료에 사용하는 약품을 의약품으로 제조하는 허가를 보사부에 신청하는 것.
③ non destructive assay 비파괴 측정.

NDAC ① National Defense Advisory Commission (미) 국가 방위 자문 위원회.
② Nuclear Defense Affairs Committee NATO의 핵방위 문제위원회.

N.Dak. North Dakota = N,D., ND 노스 다코타 주.

NDB non directional radio beacon 무지향성 무선표식. 무지향성의 전파를 발사하여 방향을 알림.

NDBMS network database management system 네크워크 데이터베이스 관리 시스템 네트워크 데이터베이스와 이것을 관리하는 프로그램들로 이루어진 시스템.

NDC National Defence Committee (한) (국회의) 국방위원회.

NDD Nuclear Detection Device 핵 탐지 장치.

NDDS Nuclear Detonation Detection System 핵폭발 탐지체제.

NDE non destructive evaluation 비파괴 평가.

NDEA National Defense Education Act (미) 국방 교육법. 1958년 성립.

NDEX Newspaper Index 신문색인. 미국 10대 신문 기사의 데이터베이스.

NDL (독) Norddeutscher Lloyd 독일의 선박 회사.

NDP net domestic product 국내 순 생산.

NDP National Democratic Party 독일국가민주당.

NDPS National Data Processing Service (영) 전국 데이터 처리 기관.

NDR ① National Driver Register (미) 전국운전자 등록부.
② nondestructive read (컴퓨터) 비파괴 판독(判讀).

NDS ① nuclear explosion detection satellite 핵 폭발 탐지위성.
② National Defense Strategy 국방전략.

NDSL National Direct Student Loan (미) 대학생 학비원조 연방정부 대부금.

NDT non destructive test (원자력) 비파괴 시험. 감마선, X선, 중성자선으로 투시하여 밖에서 기기의 내부를 검사하는 방법.

NDU National Defence University (미) 국방대학.

Ne neon 네온. 원자번호 10.

NE Nebraska (미) 네브래스카 주의 우편 기호.

NEA ① National Editorial Association (미) 전미 편집자 협회.
② National Education Association (미) 전미 교육협회.
③ National Endowment for the Arts 전미 예술기금.
④ Newspaper Enterprise Association (미) 신문사업조합.
⑤ Nuclear Energy Agency 원자력기관. OECD의 하부기관.

NEACD Northeast Asia Cooperation Dialogue 동북아 협력 대화.

NEACP National Emergency Airborne Command Post (미) 전국

NEACRP

긴급 공중 지휘기.

NEACRP Nuclear Energy Agency Committee for Reactor Physics 원자력기관 로(爐) 물리 위원회. OECD-NEA의 기관.

NEACSNI NEA-Committee on Safety of Nuclear Installation NEA 원자력시설 안전위원회.

NEANDC Nuclear Energy Agency Nuclear Data Committee 원자력 기관 핵데이터 위원회 OECDNEA의 기관.

NEASED Northeast Asia Security Dialogue 동북아 다자 안보 대화

NEASPEC North East Asian Subregional Program for Environmental Cooperation 동북아 환경 협력 계획.

NEATO Northeast Asia Treaty Organization 동북아 조약기구.

NEB ① National Enterprise Board (영) 국영 기업청. ② New English Bible 신 영역 성서.

Nebr. Nebraska 네브래스카 주.

NEC ① National Electrical Code 미국 전신코드. ② National Emergency Council (미) 국가 비상 대책 심의회. ③ Nippon Electric Corporation 일본 전기 주식 회사. ④ Nuclear Energy Commission (미) 핵 에너지 위원회.

NECC National Educational Computing Conference 미국 교육 컴퓨터 협회. 컴퓨터를 교육 분야에 이용하는데 관심을 가진 교육자들의 모임.

NECD National Economic Development Council 영국 국민경제 개발 심의회.

N.E.D. New English Dictionary 옥스퍼드 영어 대사전.

NECS newly exportoriented countries 신흥 수출 지향국. 말레이시아, 태국, 인도네시아 등의 동남아시아 제국.

NEDC National Economic Development Council (영) 국민경제 개발 심의회.

NEDO New Energy and Industrial Technology Development Organization 신 에너지·산업 기술 종합 개발 기구.

NEEDS Nikkei Economic Electronic Data Bank System (일) 일본 경제 신문사의 경제 데이터 뱅크.

NEFA nonestified fatty acid 비에스테르형 지방산.

NEI non est inventus(it has not been found) (라) 소재 불명 보고.

NEISS National Electronic Injury Surveillance System (미) 전미 전산기 위해 감시 시스템. 생활용품의 안전에 관련한 안전사고

및 그의 위험이 있는 것을 위해 정보로서 수집하고 사고의 방지와 신속한 처리를 실시하는 시스템을 위해 정보시스템이라고 한다. 1972년 미국 소비자 제품 안전위원회가 전국 119의 병원에서 상품사고의 정보를 온라인으로 수집하고 있는 시스템.

NEJM New England Journal of Medicine (미) 뉴잉글랜드 의학 잡지.

NELSON new editing and layout system of newspapers (일) 대형 컴퓨터에 의한 신문 편집 시스템.

NEMA National Electrical Manufacturers Association (미) 전국 전기 기기 제조 업자 협회.

NEMP nuclear electromagnetic pulse 핵전자 펄스.

NEMS ① National Environmental Monitoring System 전국 환경 감시 시스템.
② National Emergency Management System 국가 위기 관리 체계

NEO near earth orbit 지구 근방 궤도. 150~40,000km의 인공위성의 궤도.

NEP New Economic Policy (소련) 신경제 정책.

NEPA National Environmental Policy Act (미) 국내 환경 정책법.

NERC National Environment Research Council (영) 자연 환경조사회.

NERVA nuclear engine for rocketvehicle application 로켓선용 (船用) 원자력 엔진.

n.e.s. not elsewhere specified (or stated) 별다른 특별 기재가 없는 경우.

NES News Election Service (미) 개표 속보 서비스.

NESDA National Electronic Service Dealers Association (미) 미국 전자 서비스업자 연맹.

NESDIS National Environmental Satellite, Data and Information Service (미) 국립 환경 위성자료 정보서비스.

NEST Nuclear Emergency Search Team (미) 핵긴급수사대.

NESTOR Neutron Data Storage and Retrieval System (일) 중성자 데이터 격납 검색 시스템.

NETM new electronic technology television media 텔레비전을 통한 새로운 정보시스템. 예컨대 CATV, 고품위 텔레비전 등을 사용한 정보시스템.

net pr. net proceeds 순 수령액, 순·매상고.

NETR nuclear engineering test reactor (미) 핵 공학 시험로.

NEUDADA neutron data direct

Nev.

access (프)중성자 격납 검색 시스템.

Nev. Nevada 네바다 주.

NEW net economic welfare 순 경제 복지.

NEWRAD new generation weather radar (미) 차기 기상 레이더.

n/f N/F no funds 예금액 없음.

NF ① National Front 국민 전선, 민족전선.
② noise figure, noise factor 잡음지수.
③ nonfiction 논픽션.
④ Norme Francaise (French Standards)(프)프랑스국가규격.
⑤ Nuclear Fission (Fusion) 핵분열(융합).

NFA net foreign assets 순 외화자산.

NFAA Nuclear Fuel Assurance Act (미) (1976년) 핵 연료 보증법.

NFC nuclear fuel cycle (원자력) 핵 연료 사이클. 핵연료가 제조되어 사용되고 재처리, 재가공 등의 과정을 밟는 일련의 순환.

NFCS nuclear forces communications satellite 핵전력통신위성.

NFIP Nuclear Free Independent Pacific 비핵독립태평양.

NFL National Football League (미) 전국 축구 연맹. 미국프로 미식 축구의 통제 기관. 여기에 소속된 내셔널(NFC)과 아메리칸(AFC)의 두 conferences의 승자가 전국 우승을 다툰다.

NFLPA National Football League Players' Association (미) 전국 축구 리그 선수 협회.

NFPA ① National Fire Protection Association (미)전국 방화 협회.
② National Food Processors Association 전국식품가공협회[美]

NFRW National Federation of Republican Women (미) 전국 공화당 여성 연맹.

NFS not for sale 비매품.

NFSL National Front Salvage Libya 리비아 구제 민족전선.

NFTC National Foreign Trade Council (미) 전국무역진흥회.

NFU National Farmers Union (영) 전국 농민 조합.

N-fuel unclear fuel 핵연료. 토륨, 플루토늄, 천연 우라늄 등을 지칭한다.

NFWI National Federation of Women's Institutes (英) 전국 여성 협회 연맹.

NG ① National Guard (미) 민병.
② net gain 순 수익.
③ no good 실패. 영화촬영이나 배우의 연기의 실패를 말한다.
④ National Gallery (英) 국립 미술관.

⑤ nose guard (미식 축구) 노즈 가드. 코 보호대.

NGA ① National Geographical Association (영) 전국 지리학 협회.
② National Graphical Association (영) 전국 인쇄 제도공 조합.

NGC New Gatalogue of Nebulae and Clusters of Stars 성운목록, 성운, 성단의 위치표.

NGF nerve growth factor 신경 발육 인자.

NGL natural gas liquid 천연 가솔린.

NGO nongovernmental organization 민간 단체.

NGPA Natural Gas Policy Act (미) 천연 가스 대책법.

NGSDC National Geophysical & Solar Terrestrial Data Center (미) 국립 지구물리 및 태양·지구 데이터 센터.

NGTF National Gay Task Force (미) 전국 동성연애자 특별위원회.

NH New Hampshire (미) 뉴햄프셔 주(州)의 우편 기호.

N.H. New Hampshire 뉴햄프셔 주.

NHC National Health Center (한) 국립 보건원.

NHGRI National Human Genome Research Institute 국립 인간 게놈 연구소[美]

NHI National Health Insurance (일·영) 국민 건강 보험.

NHIC National Health Insurance Corporation 국민건강 보험공단.

NHK Nippon Hoso Kyokai 일본 방송 협회.

NHL National Hockey League (미) 전국 하키 연맹.

NHLBI National Heart, Lung and Blood Institute (미) 전국 심장, 폐, 혈액 학회.

NHP nominal horsepower 공칭 (公稱) 마력.

NHR National Hunt Rules (영) 전국 수렵 규칙.

NHRA National Hot Rod Association (미)전국 고속 자동차 협회.

NHRD National Human Resource Development 국가 인적자원 개발

NHS National Health Service (영) 국민 건강보험 제도.

NHTSA National Highway Traffic Safety Administration (미) 국가 도로교통 안전국.

Ni nickel 니켈. 원자번호 28.

NI ① National income 국민소득
② National Insurance (영) 국민 보험.

NIA ① National Insurance Act (미) 국민보험법.
② Newspaper Institute of America 미국 신문연구소.

NIAE National Institute of Agricultural Engineering (미) 전국 농공학 학회.

NIAS National Institute of Agrobiological Sciences 농업 생물 자원 연구소[日] (일본 獨立行政法人).

NIC ① National Incomes Commission (영) 국민 소득 위원회.
② National Industrial Conference 전국 산업 회의.
③ negative impedance converter 부성(負性)임피던스 변환기.
④ newly industrializing country 신흥공업국.
⑤ National Intelligence Council 미 국가 정보 위원회.

NIB ① National Information Bureau 미국정보국.
② Noninterference Basis 불간섭주의

NICAP National Investigations Committee on Aerial Phenomena (미) 전국 대기 현상 조사 위원회.

NICB National Industrial Conference Board (미) 전국 산업심의회. CB(Conference Board)의 옛명칭.

NICE National Institute of Ceramic Engineers (미) 전국 세라믹 기술자 협회.

NICS newly industrializing countries 신흥공업제국.

NICU neonatal intensive care unit 신생아 집중치료실.

NID Naval Intelligence Division (영) 해군 정보부.

NIDA National Institute of Drug Abuse (미) 국립약해연구소.

NIDDM non insulin dependent diabetes mellitus 인슐린 비의존성 당뇨병.

NIDL New International Division of Labour 신 국제 분업.

NIDS New International Development Strategy 신 국제 개발 전략.

NIE ① National Institute of Education (미) 국립교육연구소.
② newspaper in education 교육에 신문을. 초등학교에서 대학에 이르기까지의 교육에 신문을 교재로 사용하기 위한 신문사와 학교와의 공동활동.

NIEHS National Institute for Environmental Health Science (미) 국립 환경보건 과학 연구소.

NIEO new international economic order 신 국제 경제 질서.

NIES Newly Industrialized Economics 신흥 공업 경제 지역. 신흥 공업 경제군.

NIF Note Issuance Facility 중장기 인수(中長期引受) 단기 증권 발행 방식. 팔다 남은 증권은 은행에서 매수한다.

NIFO next in first out 차입선출 (次入先出).

NIH National Institute of Health (미) 국립 보건연구소.

NIIO new international information order 신 국제 정보 질서.

NIM National Institute for Metallurgy 남아프리카 국립 제련연구소.

NIMH National Institute of Mental Health (미)국립 정신 위생 연구소.

NIMO new international military order 신 국제 군사 질서.

NIO National Institute of Oceanography (영)국립 해양 학연구소.

NIOC National Iranian Oil Company 국영 이란 석유공사.

NIOSH National Institute for Occupational Safety and Health (미) 국립 직업 안전 건강 연구소.

NIRA ① National Industrial Recovery Act (미)전국 산업 부흥법. ② National Institute for Research Advancement (일) 종합 연구 개발 기구.

NIRC National Industrial Relations Court (英) 산업 관계 재판소. 부정 산업 행위를 다루는 재판소.

NIRS (미) Nuclear Information and Research Service 핵에 관한 정보와 조사 서비스.

NIS ① national information system (컴퓨터) 국가 정보 시스템. ② not in stock 재고 없음. ③ National Innovation System 국가혁신체계. ④ National Intelligence Service 국가 정보원. ⑤ National Intelligence System 국가 정보 체계. ⑥ Newly Independent States 신생 독립국.

NIS National information system (일) 전국 정보망. 전국의 정보처리조직을 통신망으로 연결하려는 구상.

NISE National Institute of Special Education 국립 특수 교육종합 연구소.

NIST ① National Information System for Science and Technology (일) 전국 과학기술 정보 시스템. ② National Institute of Standards and Technology (미) 국립 표준 기술 연구소.

NIT ① National Intelligence Test (미) 전국 지능 테스트. ② negative income tax 역소득세. 저소득자에게 지급되는 생활보조금 직접교부. ③ National Invitational Tournament (美) 전국 농구 선발대회(大會).

NIV Net Investment Value 순수투자 가치.

NJ New Jersey (미) 뉴저지 주(州)의 우편 기호.

N.J. New Jersey 뉴저지 주(州).

NJT National Jewish Television (미) 전국 유태인 TV.

NKGB (러) Narodny Komissariat Gosudarstvennoi Bezopasnosti (=People's Commissariat of State Security) (소련) 국가 안전 인민 위원회. 비밀 경찰. 1943년부터 1946년까지 있었다.

NKVD (러) Narodny Komissariat Vnutrennikh Del (= People's Commissariat for Internal Affairs) (소련) 내무 인민 위원부. 1946년 MVD로 개칭.

NL ① new line (컴퓨터) 복귀개행 (復歸改行).
② 미국 직업 야구 연맹 이름. AL = American League = 미국 직업 야구 연맹 이름.

NLETS National Law Enforcement Teletype System 미국법 집행 텔레타이프 시스템.

NLF National Liberation Front 민족 해방 전선.

NLL Northern Limit Line 북방 한계선.

NLLST National Lending Library for Science and Technology (영)과학 기술 대본(貸本) 도서관.

NLM National Library of Medicine (미) 국립 의학 도서관.

NIP ① neighborhood loan program (미) 소액 융자 제도. 주에 의한 금융제도로서 은행의 대부를 받을 수 없는 저소득층을 대상으로 소액의 담보로 융자한다.
② night flight landing practice 야간 이착륙 훈련.

NLRA National Labor Relations Act (美) 전국 노동 관계법. 통칭 Wagner Act.

NLRB National Labor Relations Board (미) 전국 노동 관계국

nm ① nautical mile 해리(海里).
② nonmetallic 비금속(의).
③ nuclear magneton 핵자자.

Nm normal m³ 온도 0℃, 1기압에서의 1m³중의기체의 양. 배출가스의 농도 규제에 사용한다.

NM New Mexico (미) 뉴멕시코 주의 우편 기호.

N.M. New Mexico (미) 뉴멕시코 주.

NMA National Micrographics Association (미) 전국 마이크로 사진 협회.

NMC ① National Meteorological Center 각국의 국내기상중추
② nuclear material control 핵 물질 관리.

NMCC National Military Command Center (미) 국가 군사지휘 센터. 전군을 일원적으로 지휘하는 기관.

NMCS National Military Command System (미) 국가 군사지휘 시스템.

NMD National Missile Defense 국가 미사일 방어망.

NME New Musical Express (영) 주간 음악 정보지.

N.Mex. New Mexico = N.M. 뉴멕시코 주.

NMF natural moisturizing factor 자연 보습 인자. 각질층에 있으며 피부의 보습기능에 중요한 작용을 하고 있는 수용성의 물질.

NMIS nuclear materials information system 핵물질 정보 시스템.

NMM nuclear materials management 핵물질 관리.

NMOS N-channel metal oxide semiconductor (컴퓨터) 형금속 산화막 반도체.

NMP net material product 순 물적 생산. 사회주의 경제 성장지표.

NMR nuclear magnetic resonance 핵자기 공명.

NMR-CT nuclear magnetic resonance computerized tomography 핵자기 공명(共鳴) 컴퓨터 처리 단층 촬영장치.

NMS ① National Market System for Securities (증권) 전국 증권 시장 제도. 모든 증권의 사는 사람이나 파는 사람이 전국 동일조건으로 참가할 수 있는 증권시장.
② nuclear materials safeguards 핵물질의 보장조치.

NMSS Office of Nuclear Materials Safety and Safeguards (미) 핵물질안전·보장조치실. NRC의 기관.

NMU National Maritime Union (미) 전국 해운 노동 조합.

NNA ① National News Agency 레바논 국영통신.
② National Newspaper Association (미) 전국 신문협회.
③ neutral and non-aligned 중립국과 비동맹국.

NNASC Neutral National Armistice Supervisory Commission 한국 정전 위원회 중립국 휴전 감시 위원단.

NND new and non official drugs 국방외신약.

NNE net national expenditure 국민 순 지출.

NNI net national income 국민 순 소득.

NNK non nuclear kill 비 핵 요격 시스템. 비래(飛來)하는 탄도미사일을 핵병기를 사용하지 않고 파괴하는 수단의 총칭.

NNP net national product 국민 순 생산.

NNPA Nuclear Non Proliferation

Act (미) 핵 확산방지법.

NNPT Nuclear Non Proliferation Treaty 핵 확산 방지조약.

NNS net national satisfaction 실질 국민 만족도.

NNSS Navy Navigation Satellite System (미) 해군 항행 위성 시스템.

NNSW non-nuclear strategic war 비 핵전략 전쟁.

NNW net national welfare 순 국민 복지.

NNWC non nuclear weapon country 핵병기 비보유국

n/o not(yet) out 미간(未刊) 미발표(未發表).

No nobelium 노벨륨. 원자번호 102.

No., no numero 제…번, 제…호.

N.O. no order 지시 없음.

NOA Not, Or, Ane (컴퓨터) 논리 회로 Not와 Or와 And.

NOAA ① National Oceanic and Atmospheric Administration (미) 상무성 해양 대기권국. 해양조사, 기상서비스 환경데이터 서비스, 이업서비스 해양광물, 해양계측 등을 취급. ② 해양대 기권국에 소속하는 기상위성/ TOS의 애칭(愛稱).

NOAA Satellite National Oceanic and Atmospheric Administration Satellite (미) 해양 대기청의 기상 관측 위성.

Nobel laureate 노벨賞 수상자.

NOC ① National Olympic Committee 국내 올림픽 위원회. ② Network Operations Center 네트워크 운영 센터. 통신망을 유지하고 관리하는 조직이나 사이트(site).

NOCC Network Operations Control Center (미) 네트워크 오퍼레이션즈 관제센터.

NODC national Oceanographic Data Center (미) 국립 해양 과학 데이터센터.

NOIC Non operated Invested Capital 비사업용 투하 자본.

NOK next of kin 최근친자.

NOMA National Office Management Association (미) 전미 사무 관리 협회.

non-U not upper class → U (英) 상류 계급답지 않음.

n.o.p not otherwise provided 별도의 규정이 없으면.

NOP ① National Opinion Polls (英) 전국 여론 조사 회사. ② Not our publication 당사(當社)의 출판물이 아님.

NOPEC Non OPEC Petroleum Exporting Countries 비 OPEC 석유수출국.

NOR not or (컴퓨터) 부정논리화 (否定論理和).

NORAD ① North American Aerospace Defence Command 북미 대륙 항공 우주 방위군(사령부).
② North American Air Defence Command 북미 대륙 방공군.

NORC Nippon Ocean Racing Club 일본 외양범주 협회.

NORIANE Normes et Reglements Informations Automatisee Accessible en Ligne (프) 공업 규격 문헌 정보 데이터베이스.

Norinco China North Industries Corporation 중국 북방 공업 공사.

NORS National Organization for Rivers 전국 하천 기구[美]

NOS network operating system 네트워크내 일괄관리 소프트웨어.

NOSS Naval Ocean Surveillance Satellite (미) 해군 해양감시 위성.

NOTAM notice to airman 항공정보

Nov. November 11월

NOW ① National Organization for Women 전미 여성연맹.
② negotiable order of withdrawal (미) 수표발행이 가능한 저축예금.

NOWPAP Northwest Pacific Action Plan 북 서태평양 보전 실천계획.

NOx nitrogen oxide(s) 질소산화물. 광화학 스모그의 발생원(發生源).

NOYS National Organizations for Youth Safety 전국 청소년 안전 기구[美]

Np reptunium 넵투늄. 원자번호 93.

NP ① Nacionalista Party (필리핀) 국민당.
② notary public 공증인.
③ nurse practitioner (美) 견습 간호사.

NPA ① National Planning Association (美) 국민 계획 협회.
② New People's Army (필리핀) 신인민군. 공산당의 게릴라 군사 조직.

NPAC National Peace Action Coalition 전미 평화 행동 연합.

NPA Colour National Petroleum Association Colour NPA색 * 석유 색상(色相)의 표식 방법.

NPB Nippon Professional Baseball 일본프로야구.

NPBW neutral particle beam weapon 중성자 빔 병기.

NPC ① National Patent Council (미) 전국 특허협의회.
② National Petrochemical Company (이란)국영 석유화학회사.

NPCA National Parks and Conservation Association (미) 국립공원보존협회.

337

NPCC National Pollution Control Council (미) 국립 공해 대책 심의회.

NPIC National Photographs Interpretation Center 국가 사진판독 센터[美]

NPD Nationaldemokratische Partei Deutschlands (=German National Democratic Party) (통일 전 서독) 독일 국가 민주당.

NPG Nuclear Planning Group NATO의 핵계획그룹.

NPH neutral protamine Hagedorn 신 인슐린.

NPL National Physical Laboratory (영) 국립 물리학 연구소.

N-plant nuclear power plant 원자력발전소.

NPN ① negarive positive negative N형 반도체와 P형 반도체 및 N형 반도체의 접속 상태로 된 트랜지스터.
② National Party of Nigeria 나이지리아 국민당.
③ nonprotein nitrogen 비(非)단백 질소.

NPO Non Profit Organization 비영리단체(非營利團體) (경제성장과 소득수준의 향상에 따라 사회 구성원의 가치관이 다양해지는데 이러한 수요를 정부가 아닌 민간차원에서 실현하기 위해 조직되는 단체)

NPP ① National People's Party (남아프리카) 민족 인민당.
② neighborhood police post (싱가포르) 파출소.

NPS ① new production system (일) 초 합리화 경영. 도요다 자동차가 개발한 신 생산 방식.
② nuclear power station 원자력발전소.

NPSH net positive suction head 유효 흡인두(有效吸引頭).

npt normal pressure and temperature 상온상압.

NPT ① non-packet mode terminal (컴퓨터) 패킷처리 기능을 갖지 않은 일반단말장치.
② Nuclear Non Proliferation Treaty = NNPT 핵확산방지조약.

NPV net present value 순 현재가치.

NQL National Quarantine Laboratory 중앙 방역 연구소.

NQOS not quite our sort 우리의 동료가 아님.

NQR nuclear quadruple resonance 핵4극(極)공명.

NR ① natural rubber 천연고무.
② New International Round 신 국제 라운드.
③ noise rating 소음평가.
④ noise reduction 자기녹음테이프의 잡음을 적게 하는 회로.
⑤ non resident 비거주자.
⑥ normal range 정상범위.

NRA ① National Resistance

Army (우간다) 국민 저항군.
② National Rifle Association (美·英) 전국 라이플협회.
③ National Recovery Administration 미국 부흥국.

NRBC nuclear red blood cell 유핵 적혈구.

NRC ① National Research Council (미) 학술연구회의.
② Nuclear Regulatory Commission (미) 원자력 규제 위원회.

NRCC National Research Council of Canada 캐나다 국가 연구회의.

NRDC ① National Research Development Corporation (英) 국립 연구 개발 공사.
② National Resources Defence Council (美) 자연 자원 보호 협의회.

NRM normal response mode (컴퓨터) 정규 응답 모드.

NREN National Research and Education Network 전미국 교육 연구 네트워크 프로젝트.

NRF La Nouvelle Revue Francaise 신 프랑스 평론, 프랑스의 문예잡지.

NRMA National Retail Merchants Association (美) 전국 소매상 협회.

NRP New Republican Party (남아프리카) 신공화당.

NRTS National Reactor Test Station (美) 국립 원자로 시험장

NRZ non return to zero (컴퓨터) 비(非)제로 복귀. 자기 기록 방식의 일종.

NS ① nano second 10억분의 1초.
② Nova Scotia (캐나다) 노바 스코샤 주(州).
③ nuclear ship 원자력선(船).

NSA ① National Security Agency (美) 국가 안전 보장국.
② National Shipping Authority (美) (상무성) 전국 선박국.
③ National Skating Association (美) 전국 스케이트 협회.
④ National Standards Association (美) 전국 규격 협회.
⑤ National Student Association (美) 전국 학생 협회.
⑥ Nuclear Science Abstracts 원자핵과학 초록(抄錄).

NSACS National Society for the Abolition of Cruel Sports (英) 전국 잔혹 스포츠 폐지 협회.

NSC ① National Security Council (美) 국가안전 보장 회의.
② noise suppression control 잡음 억제.

NSCI National Customer Satisfaction Index 국가 고객 만족지수 (국내외에서 생산, 국내 최종 소비자에게 판매되고 있는 제품 및 서비스 품질에 대해 해당 제품을 직접 사용해 보고 이 제품과 관련된 서비스를 받아 본 고객이 직접 평가한 만족수준의 정도를 모델링에 근거하여 측정 계량화

NSCR

한 지표).

NSCR National Society for Cancer Relief (英) 전국 암 구제 협회.

NSEI National Software Engineering Institute (미) 산, 관, 학 합동에 의한 소프트웨어 기술센터.

NSF ① National Science Foundation (미) 미국과학재단.
② not sufficient funds 예금부족, 자금부족.

NSG Nuclear Suppliers Group 원자력 공급(국가)그룹.

NSI New Social Indicatior (일) 국민 생활 지표. 생활수준을 수입뿐 아니라 생활환경, 건강유지 등의 다방면에서 포착한 것.

NSIDC National Snow and Ice Center (미) 국립 설(雪) 및 빙(氷) 센터.

NSL ① normal system load 통상 하중(荷重). 구조설계에 있어서의 통상의 하중.
② nuclear safety line 핵 안전선.

NSM New Smoking Material (영) 담배 대용품. 상표명.

NSP (the Agency for) National Security Planning 국가 안전 기획부.

N.S.P.C.A. National Society for the Prevention of Cruelty to Animals 동물애호협회(미국).

NSPCC National Society for the Prevention of Cruelty to Children (영) 전국 아동학대 방지 협회.

NSPC National Security Planning Council 국가 안보 기획 위원회.

NSR neutron source reactor 중성자원(源)로.

NSRB National Security Resources Board (미) 국가 안전 보장 자원 위원회.

NSRT North South Round Table 남북 원탁 회의. 제3세계의 개발 문제를 중심으로 남북관계의 여러 문제에 관하여 의논하는 비정부 조직.

NSSL National Seed Storage Laboratory (미) 농무성 종자 저장 연구소.

NSSS nuclear steam supply system 원자력 증기 공급 설비.

NST National Subscription Television (미) 전국 시청 계약.

NSTA National Science Teachers Association (미) 전국 과학 교육 협회.

NSTL National Space Technology Laboratories (미) 국립 우주 기술 연구소.

N-sub nuclear powered submarine 원자력 잠수함.

NSW New Sounth Wales (호주) 뉴 사우스 웨일스 주(州).

NSWP non-Soviet Warsaw Pact

소련을 제외한 바르샤바 조약 가맹국.

NT ① National Trust 명승사적 보존 단체.
② New Testament 신약성서.
③ nose tackle (미식 축구) 노즈 태클.
④ Nano Technology 나노(100억 문의) 초정밀 제어기술.

N/T Net Tonnage 순 톤수. 직접 영업행위에 사용되는 장소, 즉 화물·여객의 수용에 제공되는 용적을 뜻한다. 총 톤수와 같이 100입방피트 = 1톤으로 계산한다.

NTA Nei til Atomvapen (No to Nuclear Weapon) (덴마크어) 반핵 그룹 연합체.

NTB ① non tariff trade barriers 비 관세 장벽.
② Norsk Telegrambyra 노르웨이 통신사.

NTC non trade concerns (UR) 비교역(非交易) 요소. 농업은 생산성, 효율성이라는 개념이외에 그 자체를 유지함으로써 식량의 안정적 공급, 환경보존, 전통문화의 유지, 균형적 지역 개발 기능 등에서 공업부문과 동일하게 취급될 수 없다는 것이 한국, 일본·스위스 등을 포함한 여러 나라의 국제교역의 일반적인 인식이다. 이와 같이 농업이 지니고 있는 고유의 비교역적 요소를 총칭하여 NTC라고 한다.

NTD National Theater of the Deaf (미) 전국 농아자 극단.

NTE National Trade Estimate 무역 장벽 보고서.

NTFA National Track and Field Association 전미 육상 경기 연맹.

NTFS Nano Technology File System 윈도우 파일 시스템.

NTIA National Telecommunications and Information Administration (미) 상무성 전기통신 정보국.

NTIS National Technical Information Service (미) 상무성 기술정보국.

NTM National Technical Means 자국의 기술수단. 국비관리협정의 준수를 검증하는 자국(自國)의 관리하에 있는 기술 수단을 말하며 현대의 군비 관리협정의 주요한 검증수단이다.

NRP Network Time Protocol 네트워크 타임 프로토콜 인터넷상에서의 통신을 위해 각각의 컴퓨터 사이에 시간을 동기시키는 데 사용하는 프로토콜.

NTP normal temperature and pressure 상온상압.

NTS Nevada Test Site (미) 네바다 시험장. 네바다 주에 있는 핵병기 시험장.

NTS National Television System Committee 미국, 캐나다, 일본에서 채용된 칼라 텔레비전 장식.

NTSC National Transportation Safety Board (미) 전국 교통안전 위원회.

NTCS National Television System Committee 미국 텔레비전 방송 위원회.

NTT Nippon Telegraph and Telephone Corporation 일본 전신전화 주식회사.

NTU number of transfer units 이동 단위수.

NUAAW National Union of Agricultural and Allied Workers (영) 전국 농업 노동 조합.

NUAC National Unification Advisory Council 민주 평화 통일 자문회의.

NUB National Unification Board (한) 국토 통일원.

NUBE National Union of Bank Employees (영) 전국 은행 노동조합.

NUCLEBRAS (포) Empresa Nucleares Brasileiras S.A. (=Nuclear Corporation of Brazil) 브라질 원자력 개발 공사.

NUCS Newly Underdeveloped Countries 신저개발국.

NUDETS nuclear detonation detection and reporting system 핵폭발 경보조직.

NUGMW National Union of General and Municipal Workers (영) 전국 일반 시청 노동 조합.

NUJ National Union of Journalists (영) 전국 신문 기자 조합.

NUL ① national Urban League (미) 전국 도시동맹. 흑인의 지위향상을 지향하는 단체.
② null character (컴퓨터) 공문자(空文字).

NUM National Union of Mineworkers (영) 전국 광산 노동조합.

NUMMI New United Motor Manufacturing Inc. (美) 도요다 · GM 합병 자동차 회사. 1984년 설립. 본사 공장 : 캘리포니아 주(州) Fremont

NUPE National Union of Public Employees (영) 전국 공무원 조합.

NUR National Union of Railwaymen (영) 전국 철도 종업원 조합.

NURE National Uranium Resource Evaluation Program (미) 국가 우라늄 자원평가계획.

NUS ① National Union of Seamen (영) 전국 선원 조합.
② National Union of Students (영) 전국 학생 연맹.

NUSEC National Union of Societies for Equal Citizenship (영) 전국 시민 평등 단체 연맹.

NUSS nuclear safety standards 원자력 안전 기준.

NUT National Union of Teachers (영) 전국 교원 조합.

NUTS Nuclear Utilization Strategy 핵사용 전략.

NUWW National Union of Women Workers (영) 전국 여성 노동자 연맹.

NV Nevada (미) 네바다 주의 우편 기호.

NVCA National Venture Capital Association 전국 벤처 캐피탈 협회[美]

NVG night vision goggles 야간 투시 보안경.

NVM nonvolatile memory 비휘발성 메모리, 영구 기억 장치 전원을 차단하고 에너지의 공급을 중단하여도 그 기억 내용에 변화가 없는 기억 장치.

NVOCC non vessel operating common carrier 수송수단을 가지고 있지 않은 해상 화물 운송업자. 비선박 운항업자.

NV RAM nonvolatile RAM 비휘발성 램. 갑작스런 정전에도 기억이 지워지지 않는 램.

NW ① Nuclear Warfare 핵전 ② Nuclear Warhead 핵탄두. ③ North West 북서쪽.

N.V.S. no voting stock 무의결권주.

NWA Northwest Airlines 서북 항공.

NWC National War College (미) 국방전략대학.

NWFZ nuclear weapon free zone 핵병기 금지지역.

NWG national welfare growth 국민 복지 성장률.

NWHN National Women's Health Network (미) 전국 여성보건 네크워크.

NWICO new world information & communication order 신세계 정보 통신 질서. 세계 정보 격차의 시정을 목적으로 하여 유네스코 (UNESCO)에서 제창하는 것.

NWP net material product GNP에서 서비스산업부문을 뺀 것을 말한다.

NWPC National Women's Political Caucus (미) 전미 부인 정치 연맹. 여성운동의 영향하에 연방의회여성의원이 초당파조직으로서 형성된 위원회.

NWR Nuclear Weapon Report 핵무기 보고.

NWS ① North Warning System (미) 북방경보시스템. ② Nuclear Weapon State 핵 보유국.

NWSA National Women's Studies Association 전미 여성학 협회.

NWSF Nuclear Weapon Storage Facility 핵무기 저장 시설.

NWTI Nuclear Weapon Technical

Inspection 핵무기 기술검사.

NY New York (미) 뉴욕 주(州)의 우편 기호.

N.Y. New York 뉴욕 주, 뉴욕 시.

NYA National Youth Administration (미) 청소년국.

NYAS New York Academy of Sciences (미) 뉴욕 과학 아카데미.

NYC New York City 뉴욕 시.

NYCC New York Convention Center (미) 뉴욕 회의장 센터.

NYMEX New York Mercantile Exchange 뉴욕상업 거래소.

NYNEX (미) 1984년 ATT의 해체로 탄생한 New York라 New England 지역 전신 전화 → see RBOC 회사의 하나.

NYP not yet published 미발행.

NYPD New York Police Department 뉴욕 시경 본부.

NYSE New York Stock Exchange 뉴욕증권거래소.

NYT New York Times 뉴욕타임즈지(紙).

NZ New Zealand 뉴질랜드.

NZBC New Zealand Broadcasting Corporation 뉴질랜드 방송회사.

NZPA New Zealand Press Association NZPA통신사. *뉴질랜드 통신.

O oxygen 산소. 원자번호 8.

O. Ohio 오하이오 주.

OA ① office automation 사무자동화.
② on account 외상판매.
③ on the air 방송중.
④ outstanding account 외상계정

OAA orbiter access arm (로켓) 오비터 연락 통로.

O&C operations and checkout (우주공학) 작업과 점검.

OAEC Organization for Asian Economic Cooperation 아시아 경제 협력 기구.

OAG Official Airline Guide 공식 항공 시각표.

OALD Oxford Advanced Learner's Dictionary of Current English 옥스퍼드 고급 최신영어 사전.

O&M organization and methods 사무소, 공장의, 조직 효율화.

OANA Organization of Asian News Agencies 아시아 통신 연맹.

OAO ① one and only 애인.
② orbiting astronomical observatory 천체 관측 위성.

O&O owned and operated 직영 방송국.

OAP ① old age pension 노령 연금.
② old age pensioner 노령연금 수급자.

OAPEC Organization of the Arab Petroleum Exporting Counties 아랍 석유수출국 기구.

O&R ocean and rail 해륙운송.

OAS ① old age security 노령자 생활보장.
② on active service 현역의
③ Organization of American States = OEA 미주기구.

OASDHI Old Age, Survivor, Disability and Hospital Insurance (미) 노령, 유족. 불구병원보험.

OASDI Old Age, Survivor, and Disability Insurance (미) 노령, 유족, 불구보험.

OASI Old Age and Survivors Insurance(미) 노령자 유족보험.

OASIS Oceanic and Atmospheric Scientific Information System (미) 해양, 대기 과학 정보 시스템.

OAT outside air temperature (항공) 외기온도.

345

OAU Organization of African Unity = OUA 아프리카 통일기구.

OB ① off Broadway 뉴욕시 브로드웨이 주변의 소극장에서 공연되는 전위연극.
② old boy 졸업생, 선배.
③ out of bounds (골프) 코스 외로 볼이 벗어나는 것.

OBA octave band analyzer 옥타브 밴드분석기.

OBE ① Office Business Procedure by Example IBM사가 개발한 OA용 커뮤니케이션언어.
② Office of Business Economics (미) 기업 경제국.
③ operating basis earthquake (원자력) 운전기준지진.

OBF Oriental Boxing Federation 동양 권투연맹.

OBI omni bearing indicator (항공) 음니 방향 지시기.

obit obituary 사망광고, 사망기사.

obj. object ; objection ; objective

OBO Carrier Ore Bulk Oil Carrier 광석과 벌크 화물, 석유등을 다 실을 수 있도록 고안된 선박.

OBOY over privileged baby of yuppies 풍족하며 특권을 가진 부부의 아기.

OBR out bordered recorder 외부 기록 기능.

obs. observation ; observatory ; obsolete ; obstetrical ; obstetrics.

OBS operational bioinstrumentation system 생체계측 시스템. 우주선내의 동물, 인간에 부착한 기기를 사용하여 호흡수, 맥박, 체온 등의 생체정보를 기록하는 시스템.

OBU offshore banking unit 오프쇼어 금융창구.

OBV on balance volume (증권) 일정기준일 이후 상승 주식의 거래량은 가산하고 하락주식의 거래량은 공제하여 산출된 누계를 말한다. 이것을 그래프화하여 시장의 장세를 판단하려고 하는 방법이다.

OC ① Office of Censorship 검열국.
② on condition 고장전에 교환하거나 점검 정비하는 것.
③ open charter 보통용선계약,.
④ oral contraceptive 경구피임약.
⑤ organizational climate 조직환경. 기업의 종업원, 관리자의 사기·행동에 영향을 주는 사내의 분위기를 경영학의 입장에서 연구하는 개념.

OCA ① Office of Consumer Affairs (미) 소비자문제 사무국.
② Olympic Council of Asia 아시아 올림픽 회의.

OCAP The Organization of Consumer Affairs Professionals in Business 한국 기업 소비자 전문가 회의.

OCAS Organization of Central American States = ODECA 중

미 기구.

OCC Office of the Comptroller of the Currency 통화감독청(美) (재무부 소속기관으로 은행의 관리감독수행기관).

OCD Office of Civil Defence (미) 민간 방위국.

O.C.D.M. Office of Civil and Defense Mobilization 민간국방동원총본부(미국).

OCI Overseas Consultants Incorporated (미) 해외 기술 고문단.

OCIAA Office of the Coordinator of Inter American Affairs (미) 남북 조정국.

OCL obstacle clearance limit (항공) 장해물 클리어런스 한계.

OCLC Online Computer Library Center (미) 온라인·컴퓨터 도서관센터.

OCO Office of Civilian Operations (미) 민간 작전 본부.

OCOG Organizing Committee of the Olympic Games 올림픽 조직 위원회.

OCP ① Organizing Committee of Paralympics 장애자 올림픽 대회 조직 위원회.
② overland common point 대륙횡단 공통 지점(地點).

OCR ① optical character reader (컴퓨터) 광학적 문자 판독기.
② optical character recognition (컴퓨터) 광학적 문자 인식.

OCR tag optical character reader tag 광학식 문자 판독기용정가표.

OCS operation control system (컴퓨터) 종합적 공장관리.

OCSE Office of Child Support Enforcement (미) 보건 복지성 아동 원호국.

OCSEP Outer Continental Shelf Environmental Assessment Program 대륙붕 환경 아세스먼트계획.

Oct. October 10월.

OCTG oil country tubular goods 유정용 강관(油井用 鋼管).

OCTV open circuit television 개회로텔레비전. 일반 수신용의 텔레비전을 말함.

OCU office channel unit 회선종단 (回線終端)장치.

OD ① doctor of optometry 시력 측정학 박사.
② observable difference 외형적 변화.
③ officer of the day (육군) 당직 장교.
④ officer of the deck (해군) 당직 장교.
⑤ on demand 일람불 어음.
⑥ on demand publishing 응수출판(應需出版).
⑦ optical density 광학 농도.
⑧ organizational development

347

ODA

　조직 개발.
⑨ outside diameter 바깥 지름.
⑩ Over Doctor 취직을 못하고 있는 박사 실업자.
⑪ overdose 약의 적량 초과.
⑫ overdraft 당좌 대월.
⑬ overdue 기한 초과.
⑭ oxygen demand 산소 요구량.

ODA ① Object Definition Alliance 객체 정의 연합 Oracle, XEROX사 등이 멀티미디어 대응의 제품 서비스의 개발을 원활하게 하기 위해 관련 기술의 표준화에 관하여 협의하는 기관의 명칭.
② Open Document Architecture 오디에이, 개방형 문서 구조 서로 다른 기종의 컴퓨터 사이에서 문서를 교환하기 위한 국제 표준 규약(ISO 8613/CCITTT. 400시리즈).

ODECA Organizational de Estrados Centro americanos (Organization of Central American Stares) = OCAS (스) 중미 기구.

ODF Overseas Development Fund (일) 해외개발기금.

ODIF Office Document Interchange Format 사무 문서 교환 방식 ITU-TISO내에서 표준화를 하고 있는 권고 국제 규격의 하나.

ODMG Object Database Management Group 객체 데이터베이스 관리 그룹. 유럽과 미국의 유력 객체 지향 데이터베이스(OODE) 벤더가 조직한 표준화 단체.

ODMR optically detected magnetic resonance 광검출자기공명. 마이크로파를 이용하여 분자의 전자구조를 해석하는 방법.

ODP Ocean Drilling Program 대양저(大洋底) 굴착계획.

ODR omni directional radio range (항공) 전방향식 무선표식.

ODS oxide dispersion strengthened alloy 산화물 분산 강화 합금.

OE opto electronics 광전자공학.

OEA Organizacion de los Estados Americanos (Organization of American States) = OAS (스) 미주 기구.

OEC Office of Economic Coordinator 경제조정관실.

OECD Organization for Economic Cooperation and Development 경제 협력 개발 기구.

OECD EPOC OECD Environmental Policy Committee OECD 환경정책위원회.

OECD-IEA OECD-International Energy Agency OECD 국제에너지기관. 국제적 석유긴급 융통계획을 효과적으로 운영하기 위한 준비를 하는 OECD의 기관.

OECD-NEA OECD-Nuclear Energy Agency OECD 원자력기관.

OECF Overseas Economic Cooperation Fund (일) 해외경제협력기금.

OECS Organization of Eastern Caribbean States 동카리브해 제국기구.

OED Oxford English Dictionary 옥스퍼드 대사전.

OEEC Organization for European Economic Cooperation 유럽경제협력기구.

OEIC opto electronic integrated circuit 광전자 집적 회로.

OEM ① open end marriage 기한 조건이 없는 결혼.
② optical electron microscope 광학전자현미경.
③ original equipment manufacturer 주문자 상표 부착 제조업자.
④ original equipment manufacturing 주문자 상표 부착생산.

OEO Office of Economic Opportunity (미) 경제기획청.

OEOA Office for Emergency Operation in Africa 유엔 아프리카 긴급활동본부.

OEP ① Office of Emergency Planning (미) 긴급계획국. 대통령 직속기관.
② Office of Energy Programs NASA의 에너지 계획국.

OERN Organisation Europeenne pour la Recherche Nucleaire (European Organization for Nuclear Research) (프) 유럽 원자 핵 연구 기구.

OFC oxygen free copper 무산소동.

OFFJT off the job training 직장외 훈련.

off. R official rate 공정금리.

OFHC oxygen free high conductivity copper 산소함유량이 극히 적은 고전도율 동(高電導率銅).

OFT orbital flight test 궤도 비행 테스트.

OFTEL Office of Telecommunications (영) 무역산업성내에 있는 전기통신사업을 감독하는 행정기관.

OG ① old girl 여자의 졸업생, 선배.
② organic glass 유기글라스. 글라스(무기글라스)의 대용으로 사용되는 투명 또는 반투명의 합성수지.

OGL open general licence system 포괄수입허가제.

OGO orbiting geophysical observatory 지구물리관측위성.

OGPS Office of Grants and Program System (미) 농무성 연구조성 프로그램·시스템국.

Oh. Ohio (미) 오하이오주. = OH

OH Ohio (미) 오하이오 주(州)의 우편기호.

OHC (엔진) Over Head Camshaft engine 자동차용 가솔린엔진의 한가지.

OHMS On His(or Her) Majesty's Service (영) 공용. 공문서 등의 무료 배달의 지시.

OHP overhead projector 오버헤드 프로젝터.

OIC ① Office of International Culture (미) 국제 문화국. ② Organization of Islamic Countries 이슬람 국제 회의. ③ operating Invested capital 사업용 투자 자본.

OIE (프) Offoce International des Epizooties (=International Office of Epizootics)국제 수역국(獸疫局).

OIH ovulation-inducing hormone 배란 촉진 호르몬.

OIIG Overseas Investment Insurance Group (미) 해외투자 보험 그룹.

OIML Organisation Internationale de Metrologle Legale (International Organization of Legal Metrology) (프) 국제 법정 계량기구.

OIRG Overseas Investment Reinsurance Group (미) 해외 투자 재보험 그룹.

OIRT Organisation Internationale de Radio Diffusion et Television (International Radio and Television Organization) (프) 국제 방송기구.

OIS office information system 사무 정보 시스템.

OISCA Organization for Industrial Spirit and Cultural Advancement International (일) 산업 특히 농업을 통하여 세계의 우호와 평화를 쌓아올리려는 국제단체. 산업 개발 협력단을 만들어 주로 개발도상국의 기술지도 등을 하고 있다.

OIT Office of International Trade (미) 상무성통상국.

OIT 물자 Office of International Trade Goods (미) 수출통제법으로 규제된 물자.

OJ orange juice 오렌지주스.

OJCS Office of Joint Chiefs of Staff (미) 통합 참모 본부사무국.

OJT on the job training 직장내 훈련.

OK all correct

o.k.a. otherwise known as 별명.

OKF Overseas Koreans Foundation 재외동포재단. (1997. 10 특별법인 재외동포재단법에 의거, 외무부 산하기관으로 설립된 비영리 공공법인).

Okla. Oklahoma 오클라호마 주.

OL ① offer list (UR) 오퍼 리스트. 농업보조금 삭감 및 수입 규제 철폐 계획. ② Orientierungslauf (orien-

teering) (독) 오리엔티어링.
③ overlap 일정한 시간 두 가지 화면이 겹치는 상태.
④ operating leverage 영업 고정비용.

OLAS Organization for Latin America Solidarity 중남미 인민 연대 기구.

OLB outside linebacker (미식축구) 아웃사이드 라인백커.

OLC ordinary living conditions 보통생활조건.

OLE object linking and embedding 객체 연결 및 포함 Windows 환경의 각종 응용 프로그램간에 데이터 교환을 위하여 서로의 데이터를 공유하는 것.

OLCR on line character recognition 온라인 문자인식.

OLR Over Load Relay 과부하계전기.

OLRT on line real time operation (컴퓨터) 온라인·실시간(實時間) 연산.

OLaT Owner Landlord and tenant 건물주와 세입자.

OLT over land transport 육로 수송.

OLTP On Line Transaction Processing 컴퓨터의 온라인처리 시스템.

OLTS on line test system 온라인 검사 시스템 사용자가 프로그램 실행 중에 입·출력 장치의 테스트를 수행할 수 있는 시스템.

OM Organization and methods 조직과 운영.

OMA orderly marketing agreement (미) 시장 질서 유지 협정. 수입을 제한하기 위한 협정.

OMB Office of Management and Budget (미) 행정 관리 예산국.

OMD optical memory disc 광(光) 디스크.

OMPI Organisation Mondiale de la propriete Intellectuelle (World Office of Intellectual Property Organization) = WIPO (프) 세계 지적 소유권 기구.

OMR ① optical mark reader (컴퓨터) 광학적 마크판독기.
② optical mark recognition (컴퓨터) 광학적 마크인식.
③ organic moderated reactor 유기재(有機材) 감속원자로.

OMS orbital maneuvering system (우주공학) 오비터 궤도 조종 시스템.

OMSF Office of Manned Space Flight NASA의 유인 우주 비행국.

ON octane number 옥탄가.

ONC Office of National Construction 국토건설청.

ONO Organization of News Ombudsman 뉴스 옴버즈만 협회.

ONR ① octane number require-

351

O/o

ment 옥탄가 요구치.
② Office of Naval Research (미) 해군 연구국.

O/o order of …의 지시.

OOB off off Broadway 뉴욕시 브로드웨이 주변의 작은 홀, 교회, 카페 등에서 상연되는 초전위 연극.

OOC Olympic Organizing Committee 올림픽 조직 위원회.

OODB object oriented database 객체 지향 데이터베이스 데이터와 절차(procedure)를 일체화한 단위로 다루는 객체지향의 사고방식을 응용한 데이터베이스.

OOF other official flow (일) ODA를 제외한 개발 원조를 위한 정부 자금.

OOP out of print 절판.

OOPL object oriented programming language 객체 지향 프로그래밍 언어 객체 중심 프로그래밍을 위하여 사용되는 언어.

OOS out of stock 품절.

op ① operative 탐정, 형사, 첩보원.
② optical 광학적, 광학식.

op. opus (라) 작품번호.

OP ① observation post 감시소.
② off price 할인.
③ old price 구가격.
④ out of print 절판.

OP 앰프 operational amplifier 연산 증폭기.

OPA Overall Payments Agreement 일본과 파운드 지역 제국과 사이의 포괄적 무역 결제 협정.

OPA, O.P.A. Office of Price Administration 物價管理局.

OPAL older person's active lifestyle 고령자의 활동적인 라이프 스타일.

OPC organic photoconductive conductor 유기광전도체. 빛을 쬐면 전기적 성질이 변하는 유기재료.

OPCODE operations code 작전 통신 용암호.

OP-CON operational control 작전 통제, 병참 보급 지령, 컴퓨터에 의한 작업 통제.

OPCW Organization for the Prohibition of Chemical Weapons 화학 무기 금지 기구.

OPEC ① Organization of Pacific Economic Cooperation 태평양 지역 경제협력기구.
② Organization of Petroleum Exporting Countries 석유 수출국 기구.

OPECNA OPEC News Agency OPEC통신.

op ed, Op Ed opposite editorial 사설란의 맞은편 페이지. 외부의 칼럼니스트를 기용한 특집 페이지인 것이 보통.

OPERA opening, proposal, explain, results, action 관심환기, 제안,

설명, 결과, 행동(주문). 제약회사 브리스톨 마이어사의 해머 국제 훈련 부장이 주창한 판매 전술.

OPF orbiter processing facility (우주공학) 인공위성 정비시설.

OPIC Overseas Private Investment Corporation (미) 해외 민간 투자 회사.

OPM ① Offer of Personnel Management (미) 인사 관리국.
② Offer of Production Management (미) 생산관리국.
③ other people's money 투자용으로 모은 타인의 돈.
④ output per man 1인당 생산량.

opp. opportunity, opposed, opposite.

OPP ① biaxial oriented polypropylene 이축연신(二軸延伸) 폴리프로필렌.
② out of print at present 목하 절판.

OPRC International Convention on Oil Pollution Preparedness, Response and Cooperation 유류오염 대응·대비 및 협력에 관한 국제협력.

OPS ① off price store 할인판매점.
② 이축연신(二軸延伸) 폴리스티렌시트.
③ out placement service 재취직원 조합. 불필요하게 된 사원을 전직시키는 서비스업.
④ oriented polystyrene sheet 재취직원조업. 불필요하게 된 사원을 전직시키는 서비스업.

OPTAT off premise transitional auto mated ticket 컴퓨터로 발권하는 여행 대리점용 항공권.

OPTF optical fiber 광섬유

OPTMS Optimum Money Supply 적정 통화량.

OR ① operating room 수술실.
② operating research (컴퓨터) 운영연구.
③ owner's risk 위험 하주 부담.

ORB owner's risk Breakage 파손 위험 하주 부담.

ORBIT On Line Retrieval of Bibliographic Information Time Shared (미) 온라인 정보 서비스.

ord ordained ; order ; orderly ; ordinal ; ordinance ; ordinary ; ordnance.

ORD owner's risk of damage 손해 위험 하주 부담.

ORDLIX organized design for line and crew system (일) 작업장의 정원을 대폭으로 삭감하는 방법의 하나.

ORDP Office of Rural Development Policy (미) 농무성 농림개발 정책국.

Oreg. Ore = Oregon 오리건 주(州).

ORF owner's risk of fire 화재 하주 부담.

353

ORGANIC

ORGANIC organic structure retrieval and display system 유기 화합물 구조 검색 표시 시스템.

ORP oxidation and reduction potential 산화환원전위.

ORSA Operations Research Society of America 미국 운영 연구 학회.

O.R.T.F. Office de Radiodiffusion Television Francaise (프) 프랑스 국영 방송협회.

Os osmium 오스뮴. 원자번호 76.

OS(ROK) Office of Supply (한국) 조달청.

OS ① on sale 판매품.
② on spot 현장인도.
③ operating system (컴퓨터) 운영체제.
④ out of stock 절품.

OS/2 operating system/2 IBM사와 마이크로 소프트사가 공동으로 개발한 개인용 컴퓨터용 OS.

OSAHRC Occupational Safety and Health Review Commission (미) 직업 안전·보건 심사 위원회.

OSART Operational Safety Review Team 세계의 원자력 발전소의 안전성, 신뢰성 향상을 지향하여 IAEA가 가맹국의 요청에 의하여 원자력 발전소의 운전 관리 상황을 조사하여 국제적으로 경험교류를 하는 전문가팀.

OSCAR Orbiting Satellite Caring Amateur Radio 아마추어 무선가를 위한 전파전파(電波傳播) 실험위성.

OSCE Organization for Security and Cooperation in Europe 유럽안보 협력 기구.

OSCE-ACG Organization for Security and Cooperation in Europe Asian Contact Group OSCE 아시아협력동자국간 접촉그룹.

OSHA Occupational Safety and Health Administration (미) 노동성 직업 안전 보건국.

OSI ① open system interconnection (컴퓨터) 개방형 시스템 간 접속.
② out of stock, indefinitely 무기한 품절.
③ Office of Special Investigation 특별 수사대.

OSO orbiting solar observatory 태양 관측 위성.

OSP official selling prices = GSP 정부 공시 가격.

OSPAAL (스) Organizacion Solidaridad Popular de Afro Asiano y America Latino (=Organization for the Solidarity of Afro Asian and Latin American people) 아시아 아프리카·중남미 인민 연대 기구.

OSPER ocean space explorer 미래의 해중 로봇.

OSRD Office for Scientific Research and Development (미) 과학 연구 개발부.

OSS ocean surveillance satellite 해양 감시 위성.

OST ① Office of Science and Technology (미) 과학기술국.
② Outer Space Treaty 우주 조약

OSTP Office of Science and Technology Policy (미) 과학 기술 정책국. 대통령 직속 기관.

OT ① occupational therapist 직업 요법사.
② occupational therapy 작업요법.

O.T. ① Old Testament 구약성서.
② on truck 화차인도.

OTA Office of Technology assessment (미) 기술사정국. 새로 개발한 과학기술의 의미·중요성을 심리하고 어떠한 조치를 취할 것인가에 관하여 연방의회에 조언하는 정부기관.

OTAC Organization of Technically Advanced Countries 고도 기술국 기구.

OTB off track betting 장외 마권에 의한 도박.

OTC ① Offshore Technology Conference 해양기술회의. 매년 개최되는 해양석유 개발 관련의 국제회의.
② one stop inclusive tour charter 유일목적지 포괄 여행 차터제. 여행사가 항공기를 차터하고 목적지를 1개소로 한정하므로 싼비용으로 관광 여행을 즐길 수 있다.
③ Organization for Trade Cooperation 국제무역협력기구.
④ over the counter drug 일반용약품. 의사의 처방전 없이 약국에서 구입할 수 있는 의약품.

OTEC ocean thermal energy conversion 해양 에너지 변환, 해양온도차 발전.

OTF optical transfer function 광전달 함수.

OTH Over The Horizon 수평선 너머. 종전의 상륙작전과 달리 해안에서 40km가량 떨어진 [수평선 너머] 바다에 함정을 정박시키고 호보크래프트로 시속 74km의 빠른 속도로 병력을 실어 나르는 것이다. 따라서 적에게는 상륙모함이 보이지 않고 상륙 지점을 쉽게 예측할 수 없어 상륙부대의 피해를 국소화시킬 수 있다.

OTH-B 레이더 Over the Horizon Back Scatter Radar 단파가 전리층에 반사·도약하는 특성을 이용하여 그의 미약한 후방 산란파(散亂波)의 반응을 수신하여 지평선의 저쪽에서 접근하는 목표를 탐지하는 원거리 레이더.

OTHR over the horizon radar 초지평선 레이더. 수평선보다 먼 곳에 있는 물체를 포착하는 레이더.

OTI Organizacion de la Television Iberoamericana (= Latin

355

American Television Organization) (스) 중남미 방송 연합.

OTL output transless 출력 트랜스가 없는 증폭 회로.

OTM on line teller machine (컴퓨터) 온라인 예금 지불기.

OTO Office of Trade Ombudsman (일) 시장개방문제에 관한 민원처리본부.

OTP one time programmable EPROM 한 번만 가입 가능한 EPROM.

OTP-EPROM one time programmable-erasable programmable ROM 1회만 읽기가 가능한 EPROM.

OTP-ROM one time programmable ROM 1회만 프로그램이 가능한 ROM.

OTS ① Office of Technical Service (미) 상무성 기술 서비스국.
② open territory system 지역을 특히 정하지 않는 판매방식.
③ orbit test satellite 궤도 실험 위성.
④ avionic threshold switch 글라스 스위치.

OTV orbital transfer vehicle 궤도간 운반선. 우주기지와 정지궤도 사이의 운반선.

OU ① Open University (영) 공개 (방송)대학.
② Oxford University (영) 옥스퍼드 대학.

OUA Organisation de I'Unite Africaine(Organization of African Unity) = OAU (프) 아프리카 통일기구.

OUP Oxford University Press (영) 옥스퍼드 대학 출판국.

OUTLTM output limitation facility (컴퓨터) 출력제한기능.

OV Orbiter vehicle (우주공학) 궤도선, 우주선.

OVA ① overhead value analysis 기업의 간접업무분석.
② Office of Veterans Administration (한국) 수호청.

OVP (독) Osterreichische Volkspsrtei (= Austrian People's Party) 오스트리아 국민당.

O/W oil in water emulsion 수중유형(水中油型)의 유탁액.

OWC one way communication 한방향통신. 한 방향밖에 전송되지 않는 통신방식.

OWF optimum working frequency 최적 사용 주파수.

OWI Office of War Information (미) 전시(戰時) 정보국.

OWL ordinary water level 평수위. 연간을 통하여 185일간은 그 이상 낮아지지 않는 수위.

OWS ① ocean weather ship 정점(定點)관측선.

② office work station 사무실내의 단말로서 개인용 컴퓨터나 워드프로세서 등을 말한다.
③ orbital workshop (우주) 궤도 작업실.

Oxbridge Oxford and Cambridge Universities 옥스퍼드와 캠브리지 대학.

Oxfam Oxford Committee for Famine Relief (영) 옥스퍼드 기아 구제 위원회.

Oxon. ① Oxfordshire (영) 옥스퍼드셔.
② Oxford University 옥스퍼드 대학.

OY optimum yield 최적 생산량.

oz. ounce(s) 온스. 무게 단위.

P phosphorus 인. 원자번호 15.

P-Star Price-Star 신 인플레 지표. FRB가 개발한 통화공급량, 잠재성장력 등을 기초로 적정한 물가수준의 동향을 나타내는 것으로 인플레션행지표의 역할을 함.

P-point (스키) 표준점을 말하며 우수한 점퍼가 그 점프대에서 뛸수 있는 최대거리를 상정(想定)하여 청색라인으로 표시한다.

P=wave primary wave (지진) 종파(縱波).

Pa proto actinium 프로토 악티늄. 원자번호 91.

Pa. Pennsylvania = Penn., Penna. 펜실베이니아 주(州).

PA ① Pan American World Airways 팬 아메리칸 항공.
② particular average (해상보험) 단독해손.
③ pay on application 청구불.
④ performance analysis 작업분석.
⑤ personal assistant 개인비서.
⑥ phthalic anhydride 화공약품. 가소제, 도료에 이용.
⑦ power amplifier 전력증폭기.
⑧ power of attorney 위임권, 위임장.
⑨ press agent 홍보계, 선전계.
⑩ public address system 확성장치.
⑪ public affairs 공공 문제 활동. 기업을 둘러싼 제반환경 즉 공공문제를 기업의 존속을 걸고 개선, 강화하는 기업홍보 업무.
⑫ Prosecuting attorney 검사.

PAA ① Pan American World Airways 팬 아메리칸 항공.
② Polyacrylamide.

PABA para aminobenzoic acid 비타민B 복합제의 일종.

PABX private automatic branch exchange 자동식 구내교환설비.

Pac. Pacific 태평양.

PAC ① Pan Africanist Congress 범아프리카주의자 회의.
② Pan American Congress 범미회의.
③ political action committee (미) 정치활동위원회. 기업, 노동조합, 시민단체, 정치가가 선거자금을 모아 대통령, 연방 상하의원, 주지사 등의 선거에 입후보한 인물에게 정치헌금을 하기 위하여 설립하는 조직.

④ powdered active carbon 입상활성탄.

PACAF Pacific Air Force (미) 태평양공군.

PACE Professional and Administrative Career Examination (미) 전문직, 정부직원채용시험.

PACEX 89 Pacific exercise 89 1989년에 9월에 미국태평양군이 실시한 육·해·공·해병대 4군의 통합연습. 일본, 캐나다, 필리핀, 인도네시아 등이 참가함.

PACIFIC planning, accounting and control information system 건설업 공사 원가 관리 정보 시스템.

PACP package 일괄안 ;
a package deal = 일괄거래. ;
a package proposal = 일괄제의.

PACS Picture Archiving and Communication System 의학 영상의 보관 및 전송시스템.

PACS Pacific Area Standards Congress 태평양 지역 표준 회의 (태평양 연안 국가들의 ISO/IEC의 국제표준화 활동에 효과적으로 참여 할 수 있는 능력을 배양하기 위한 목적으로 1973 설립된 지역 표준 협력 기구, 2001 현재 태평양 지역 국가 21개국이 회원으로 가입).

PAD ① packet assembler/disassembler 패킷 조립 분해 장치.
② problem analysis diagram 문제 분석도.

PADS publication of the American Dialect society 미국 방언 학회 기요(紀要). → ADS

PAE phthalic acid ester 프탈산 에스테르.

PAET planetary atmospheric entry test (혹성) 대기 돌입 실험.

PAFTAD Pacific Trade and Development 태평양 무역 개발 회의.

PAG Pan American Games 범 아메리칸 경기 대회.

PAGEOS passive geodetic satellite 측지용 위성.

PAHs polycyclic aromatic hydrocarbons 다환 방향족 탄화수소 발암물질

PAI personal accident insurance 인신 사고 보험.

PAIGC [P] Partido Africano da Independencia ga Guinee Cabo Verde (=African Party for the Independence of Guinea and Cape Verde) (카보베르데 공화국) 카보베르데 독립 아프리카당 (黨).

PAL ① patent associated literature 특허 관련 문헌.
② phase alternation by line (텔레비전) 팰 방식.
③ Philippine Air Lines 필리핀 항공.

P&L

P&L profit and loss 손익.

PALC precast autoclaved lightweight concrete 틀에 넣어 표면에 무늬를 박은 ALC판.

PAM pulse amplitude modulation 펄스 진폭 변조.

PAN ① peroxy acetyl nirtate 대기 오염물질.
② Pesticide Action Network International 국제 농약 행동 네트워크.
③ polyacrylonitrile 합성 섬유의 원료.

PANA Pan Asia Newspaper Alliance ; Pan Asia News Agency 범아사(凡亞社), 파나 통신. 아시아인이 쓴 아시아의 뉴스를 세계 각국의 신문에 보내는 통신사.

P&F chart point and figure chart (증권) 점수도표. 주가동향을 파악하는 비시계열(非時系列) 차트의 일종.

Pan Am Pan American Airways = PA, PAA 팬 아메리칸 항공.

PANE People Against Nuclear Energy 핵에너지 반대자 동맹.

P&O Peninsular & Oriental Steam Navigation Co. P & O 기선회사.

PAP ① Polska Agencja Prasowa 폴란드 통신.
② Positive Adjustment Policies (OECD) (후진국산업의) 적극적 조정정책. 무역시장에 적극적으로 관여하여 노동, 자본의 유동성을 높여 경쟁력을 붙이려는 정책.

PAPI precision approach path indicator 정밀 진입 경로 지시기.

PAR ① perimeter acquisition radar 주변 포착 레이더. 탄도 미사일에 대한 원거리 탐지 유도레이더.
② precision approach radar (항공) 정측(精測)진입 레이더. 착륙·진입에서 활주로까지의 사이, 항공기를 유도하는 공항의 레이더 장치.

P&R park and ride system 철도역이나 버스정거장까지는 자가용 차를 타고 주차장에 차를 두고 전차나 버스에 갈아타는 이동방식.

paralympics paraplegic olympics 장애자 올림픽 대회.

PARC Palo Alto Research Center (美) 캘리포니아 주(州) 팰로앨토 시(市)에 있는 Xerox Corp.의 중앙 연구소.

PARCOR partial correlation (컴퓨터) 음성 합성 방식의 일종.

PARCS perimeter acquisition radar characterization system 주변 보충 레이더 특성화 시스템.

PARM (스) Partido Autentico de la Revolucion Mexicana (=Mexican Authentic Revolution Party) 멕시코 혁명 정통당.

360

PARS Pars News Agency （이란） 파르스 통신.

PAS photo acoustic spectroscopy 광음향 분광법.

PASC Pacific Area Standards Congress 태평양 지역 표준회의.

PASCAL Philips Automatic Sequence Calculator 고급 프로그램 언어.

PASOK Panhellenic Socialist Union 범 그리스 사회주의 운동당.

Pat ① 남자이름. Patrick의 애칭. ② 여자이름. Patricia의 애칭.

PAT point after touchdown （미식축구） 터치다운 후의 득점.

PATA ① Pacific American Tankship Association 태평양 아메리카 유송(油送)협회. ② Pacific Area Travel Association 태평양 관광 협회.

PATCO Professional Air Traffic Controllers Organization （미） 항공 관제관 조합.

PATH Port Authority Trans Hudson Corp. （미） 뉴저지주와 맨해턴 사이의 통근 열차선.

PATO Pacific Asian Treaty Organization 아시아·태평양 조약 기구.

PATOLIS patent on-line information system （일） 특허 정보 온라인·시스템.

PATTERN planning assistance through technical evaluation of relevance numbers 상대적 중요도수치(重要度數値)의 기술 평가에 의한 기획보조. 관련 수목법(樹木法)에 의한 미래 예측수법. 처음 미국의 기업이 기술 개발 등의 목적으로 채용한 사고법.

PAU Pan American Union 전미주 연합. 1980년 남북아메리카 21 개의 공화국이 친선과 평화를 촉진하기 위하여 설립.

PAVEPAWS precision acquisition of vehicle entry and phased array warning system 바다에서 발사된 미사일을 탐지하는 레이더 시스템.

P&W Pratt & Whitney Co. 세계 최대의 민간기용 제트엔진 제조회사.

PAX private automatic exchange 구내전용(전화)교환기. 구내에 있는 전화기간만전용으로 연결하는 교환기.

P.A.Y.E. pay as you earn 원천과세.

PAYE ① pay as you earn （영） 원천 과세 방식. ② pay as you enter 입장시 지불제, 승차시지불제.

Pb plumbum (=lead) （라） 납. 원자번호 82.

PB ① paperback 종이표지의 보관관의 책. ② particle beam 입자 빔.

PBA

③ Pharmacopoeia Britannica 영국 양국방.
④ police box 파출소.
⑤ private brand 자가상표.

PBA Professional Bowlers' Association (미) 프로 볼링 협회.

PBAA polybutadiene acrylic acid 아크릴산 합성고무수지.

PBAL polybutadiene acrylic acid acrylonitrite 폴리부타디엔 아크릴산 아크릴로니트릴.

PBAN polybutadiene acrylic acid acrylonitrite terpolymer 스페이스셔틀의 고체연료. 로켓부스터의 연료.

PB&J peanut butter & jelly (sandwich) 피넛버터, 젤리의 샌드위치. 어린이들이 즐겨 먹는 점심메뉴.

PBB polybrominated biphenyl 환경 오염물질의 하나.

PBC Pyongwha Broadcasting Corporation 평화(平和) 방송. 1990년 4월 15일 개국한 카톨릭 재단의 종합 방송.

PBEC Pacific Basin Economic Council 태평양 경제 위원회.

PBF power burst facility (원자력) 반응도 사고 연구시설.

PBGC Pension Benefit Guaranty Corporation (미) 연금지급 보증 공사.

PBI ① protein-bound iodine 단백질 결합 요오드.
② poor bloody infantry (영 속어) 보병.

PBN pyrolytic boron nitride 파이럴리틱 질화 붕소.

PBR ① polybutadiene rubber 폴리부타디엔 고무.
② price book value ratio 주가 순 자산 비율.

PBS Public Broadcasting Service (미) 공공 텔레비전 방송시스템.

PBT polybutyrene terephthalate 기계부품 등에 금속 대신 사용되는 특수수지.

PBV post boots vehicle 추진용 부스터를 떼어낸 후의 미사일.

PBW particle beam weapon 입자 빔병기. 하전(荷電) 입자 · 중성 입자 빔을 사용한 초신병기.

PBX private branch exchange 구내(전화) 교환설비. 기업내 및 기업과 외부와의 사이를 연결하는 교환설비.

PC ① patrol car 패트롤카.
② personal computer 개인용 컴퓨터.
③ physical communication 물적 교류.
④ pocket calculator 포켓계산기.
⑤ polycarbonate 열가소성수지.
⑥ precast concrete 공장에서 콘크리트판을 만들어 현장에서 조립하는 건축공법.

⑦ prestressed concrete 인장(引張) 피아노선이 들어 있는 콘크리트.
⑧ prime cost 원가.
⑨ printed circuit 프린트 배선.
⑩ Privy Council (영) 추밀원.
⑪ programmable controller 사전 조절 장치.
⑫ provost court 군사 재판소.

PCB ① polychlorinated biphenyl 환경 오염물질의 하나.
② printed circuit board 프린트 배선 회로용 기관.

PCBA pentachloro benzyl alcohol 염소계 비 수은 농약.

PCC pure car carrier 자동차전용 운반선.

PCCV prestressed concrete containment vessel 콘크리트제 원자로 격납용기.

PCDF polychlorinated dibenzofuran PCB보다 독성이 강한 오염물질.

PCE ① personal consumption expenditure 개인 소비지출.
② [S] Partido Comunista de Espana (=Spanish Communist Party) 스페인 공산당.

PCER price cash-earning ratio 주가 현금수익비율.

PCF (프) Parti Communiste Francais (=French Communist Party) 프랑스 공산당.

PCHIS Population Clearing House and Information System 인구정보시스템. ESCAP의 인구와 가족계획에 관한 정보 서비스 시스템.

PCI ① (이) Partito Comunista Italiano (=Italian Communist Party) 이탈리아 공산당.
② pellet clad interaction (원자력) 펠리트 피복 상호 작용.

PCM ① plug compatible machine (컴퓨터) IBM 컴퓨터에 대한 호환성을 가진 컴퓨터를 말한다.
② pulse code modulation 펄스 부호변조.
③ punched card machine 천공 카드처리기.

PCMI photo chromic micro image 화상처리장치.

PCN personal communication net-work 개인통신망.

PCNB pentachloro nitrobenzene 펜타클로로·니트로벤젠.

PCP ① pentachlorophenol 재목의 방부제, 종이·가죽의 곰팡이 방지제, 제초제, 살충제로서 사용한다.
② phenylcyclohexy piperidine 진정제. 동물을 생포할 때에 사용한다.
③ Pirmary Control Program 기본제어프로그램.
④ process control program 프로세스 제어 프로그램.

PCPI Permanent Committee on Patent Information (WIPO의) 특허정보에 관한 상설 위원회.

PCPV prestressed concrete pressure vessel (원자력) PS콘크리트 압력 용기.

PCQ productivity criteria quotient 생산성 측정기준. 기계 구조에 의하여 생산효율에 차가 생기는 요인을 지수화한 것.

PCR Polymerase Chain Reaction 중합효소연쇄반응. (시험관내에서 DNA를 증폭하는 방법으로 수 시간 내에 특정 부위를 DNA를 10의 5승~10의 8승 배까지 증폭할 수 있어 극미량의 DNA만 있으며 이 반응을 통하여 다량의 DNA를 확보할 수 있게 하는 화학반응. 유전자 염기 서열 분석, 유전자 지문 등에 널리 이용).

PCR Price Cash flow Ratio 주가 현금 흐름 비율.

PCS ① Patent Classification Service (INPADOS의) 국제 특허 분류 정보서비스.
② punched card system 천공 카드 방식.

PCT ① Patent Cooperation Treaty 특허협력조약.
② polychlorinated triphenyl 살충제·환경오염물질의 하나.
③ Parti Communiste Tunisien (=Tunisian Communist Party) (프) 튀니지 공산당.
④ Parti Congolais du Travail (=Congo lese Labor Party) (프) 콩고 노동당.
⑤ peak clad temperature (원자력) 연료 피복 최고 온도.

PCTC pure car and truck carrier 승용차·트럭 운반선.

PCTR pad connection terminal room 로켓 발사 설치실.

PCU power control unit 출력 제어 장치.

PCV ① Peace Corps Volunteers 평화부대.
② pressure containment vessel (원자력) 압력 격납 용기.

pd. paid 지불필.

p.d. per diem(per day) (라) 1일당.

Pd palladium 팔라듐. 원자번호 46.

PD ① physical distribution 물적 유통, 물류.
② producer 프로듀서.
③ program director (방송) 프로그램 디렉터.
④ protective device (컴퓨터) 회선 보호 장치.

P.D. Police Department 경찰국.

PDA ① post deflection acceleration 후단 전자 가속.
② public display of affection (속어) 공공연한 애정 표현.

PDB President's daily briefing (미) 대통령이 매일 아침 실시하는 지시를 위한 모임.

PDC poorer developing countries 빈곤 발전 도상국.

PDCA plan, do, check, action 품질 관리의 실천 순서.

PDD past due date 지불기일(만기일)초과.

PDDM picture data description and management 화상데이터 기술, 관리.

PDE Present Day English 현대 영어.

PDF point detonating fuze 탄두신관(도화관).

PDFLP Popular Democratic Front for the Liberation of Palestine 팔레스타인 해방민주 인민전선.

PDG ① (프) Parti Democratique de Guinee (=Guinea Democratic Party) 기니 민주당.
② (프) Parti Democratique Gabonais (=Gabonese Democratic Party) 가본 민주당.

PDI (인도네시아) Partai Demokrasi Indonesia (=Indonesian Democratic Party) 인도네시아 민주당.

PDL poverty datum line 빈곤선. 생활할 수 있는 최저 소득의 기준선.

PDM ① physical distribution management 물류관리(物流管理)
② pulse duration modulation 펄스 폭 변조.

PDMC Program Deliberation and Mediation Committee 프로그램심의 조정위원회 (프로그램 저작권관련 정책사항 및 기술적 사항을 심의하는 법정 심의기관으로 컴퓨터 프로그램 보호법에 의거 1987. 12. 설립)

PDP ① plasma display panel 방전에 의한 발광을 이용하여 문자·화상을 표시하는 표시장치.
② programmable display pushbutton 필요에 따라 디스플레이를 변경할 수 있는 푸시버튼.

PDPA People's Democratic Party of Afghanistan 아프가니스탄 인민 민주당.

PDQ pretty damn quick (속어) 즉시. 1867년경 보스턴의 코메디언 Dan Maginnis가 만들어 보급시킨 문구.

PDR ① precision depth recorder 정밀심도 기록계. 수중음파 탐지기에 의하여 수심을 측정하여 기록지에 기록하는 기계.
② process data rate 프로세스 데이터 레이트. 정보처리 능력의 단위. 1 PDR은 1초간에 100만 비트를 처리하는 능력.

PDRY People's Democratic Republic of Yemen 예멘 인민 민주 공화국.

PDS public domain software 무료 공개의 소프트웨어.

PDT ① portable data terminal 데이터 엔트리용 휴대용 컴퓨터.
② Pacific Daylight Time 태평양 여름 시간.
③ [포] Partido Democratico Trabalhista (=Democratic Labor Party) 브라질 민주노동당

PDU Pacific Democrat Union 태평양 민주동맹.

PDVAN physical distribution value added network (일) 물류(物流) 합리화를 위한 정보처리 통신망.

PE ① phase encoded 위상 변조 방식. 자기 기록매체에 정보를 기록하는 방법의 하나.
② pentaerythritol 합성 수지도료·고성능 폭약 등의 원료.
③ physical examination 신체검사.
④ polyethylene 합성수지.
⑤ port of embarkation 승선(선적)항.
⑥ price-earning = PER 주가수익률.
⑦ printer's error 오식.
⑧ probable error 확률오차.
⑨ production engineering 생산공학.

PEACE Pacific Economic and Cultural Enclave 태평양 경제 문화권.

PEAP personal egress air pack (스페이스 셔틀의) 1인용 탈출 에어팩.

PEC ① Pacific Economic Community 태평양 경제공동체.
② photoelectrochemical cell 광전기 화학전지.

PECC pacific Economic Cooperation Council 태평양 경제 협력 회의.

PED Penguin English Dictionary 펭귄 영어 사전.

PEEK poly ether ether ketone 내열성 특수 수지.

PEF private equity fund 사모(私募)투자전문회사

PEFCO Private Export Funding Corporation (미) 민간 수출 금융회사.

PEI polyether imide 고내열 특수 수지의 하나.

PEKEMAS Parti Keadilan Masyrkat (=Social Justice Party) (말레이시아) 사회 정의당.

PEL ① permissible exposure limit 건강에 관하여 안전한 허용량.
② picture element (컴퓨터) 회화요소.

PEMEX Petroleos Mexicanos (스) 멕시코 석유 공단.

PEN International Association of Poets, Playwrights, Editors, Essayists and Novelists 국제 펜클럽.

PENAID penetration aid 방어망 돌파 능력.

Penn. Pennsylvania (미) 펜실베

이니아 주(州).

Penny 여자이름. Penelope의 애칭.

PEP precipitation enhancement project 인공강우 프로젝트.

PER price earnings ratio = PE (증권) 주가 수익률.

PERA Production Engineering Research Association (영) 생산기술 연구 협회.

PERT program evaluation and review technique 퍼트법. 복잡한 작업계획을 공정마다 도표를 만들어 작업순서나 작업의 진행 상태를 한눈에 알 수 있게 함으로서 업적의 평가·검토를 실증적으로 실시하는 방법.

PERTAMINA Perusaham bangan Minyak dan Gas Bumi Nasional (인도네시아) 국영석유회사.

PES polyethersulphone 고내열성 특수 수지의 하나.

PET ① parent effectiveness training 어버이가 되기 위한 훈련. ② polyethylene terephthalate resin 식료품의 병, 테이프, 전기 절연재료 등에 사용한다. ③ positron emission tomography 양전자 방사단층 촬영법.

PETN pentaerythritol tetranitrate 4질산 펜타에르트리톨, 작약(炸藥), 협심증 치료약.

PETT positron emission tomograrhy 양전자 방출에 의한 신진대사 단층 촬영.

PF ① panchromatic film 팬크로 필름. ② performance factor 작업율. ③ political fiction 정치공상소설. ④ pro forma invoice 견적 송장.

PFA ① plus for advertisement 구매자 비율. 광고를 보고 산 사람의 비율에서 광고를 보지 않고 산 사람의 비율을 뺀 수치. ② Press Foundation of Asia 아시아 신문재단.

PFC ① Priority Foreign Countries 우선 협상 대상국. ② protein, fat, carbohydrate 단백질, 지방, 탄수화물.

PFD personal flotation device 수중 구명 동의(救命胴衣).

PFLP Popular Front for the Liberation of Palestine 팔레스타인 인민 해방 전선.

PFLP-GC Popular Front for the Liberation of Palestine General Command 팔레스타인 인민 해방 전선 총사령부.

PFM pulse frequency modulation 펄스 주파수 변조.

PFP Progressive Federal Party (남아프리카) 진보 연방당.

PG ① parental guidance suggested (미) 성인대상 영화, 부모동반 지정영화. ② paying guest 하숙인.

③ post graduate 대학원 학생.
④ propylene glycol 부동액, 살균제 등으로 사용.
⑤ prostaglandin 생체내의 생리 활성물질.

PG-13 parental guidance-13 (미) 13세 이하의 어린이는 부모 또는 성인 동반이 필요한 영화.

PGA Professional Golfers' Association of America 미국 프로골퍼 협회.

PGD prostaglandin D 프로스타글랜딘 D. 뇌에서 발견된 생리 활성 물질.

PGI Programme Generale d' Information (프) 종합 정보 프로그램.

PGM precision guided munitions 정밀유도병기. 레이저, 밀리파 레이더 등을 사용한 높은 명중 정도를 가진 병기의 총칭.

PGR psycho galvanic response 정신 전기 반응.

PH ① pinch hit (야구) 대타.
② public health 공중보건.
③ Hydrogen Exponent 폐하수소이온(hydrogenion)과 수식의 P(비)를 합친 말. 수소이온 농도지수.

PHA pulse height analyzer (원자력) 파고(波高)분석기.

PhB (라)philosophiae baccalaureus (=bachelor of philosophy)철학자.

PHB photo chemical hole burning 흑종의 물질에 있어 분자수준의 에너지 상태가 광(光) 작용에 의하여 변화하는 현상.

PHC primary health care 초기 진료.

PhD philosophiae doctor (doctor of philosophy) (라) 박사.

PHIGS Programmer's Hierarchical Interactive Graphics Standard ANSI가 GKS와 같은 수준이면서 보도 고도의 아프리케이션을 목표로한 도형 데이터 처리 표준.

PHM hydrofoil patrol craft 수중익초계선(水中翼哨戒船).

PHO Pan American Health Organization 범미 보건 기구.

PHOTINT photographic inteligelnce 사진정보.

PHP propeller horse power 프로펠러 마력.

PHS Public Health Service (미) 공중보건국.

PI ① Pasteur Institute 파스퇴르 연구소.
② performance index 성능지수.
③ polyimide 내열합성수지.
④ price index 물가지수.
⑤ principal investigator 주임 연구원.
⑥ profitability index 수익성 지표.

PIA ① Pakistan International Airlines 파키스탄 국제항공.

② peripheral interface adapter 8비트 병렬 입출력용 접속장치.

PIANC Permanent International Association of Navigation Congresses (유엔) 상설 국제 항로회의 협회.

PIARC Permanent International Association of Road Congresses (유엔) 상설 국제 도로회의 협회.

PIB polyisobutylene 합성고무의 원료.

PICA Private Investment Company for Asia 아시아 민간 투자 회사.

PICS productivity improvement and control system (컴퓨터) 생산성 향상 관리시스템.

PICU perinatal intensive care unit 주산기(周産期) 집중 치료실.

PID pelvic inflammatory disease 골반 내염증 질환.

PIE Pacific Islands Ecosystem 태평양제국 생태계 문헌정보데이터 베이스.

PII Petroleum Information International (미) 국제 석유 정보기관.

PIK payment in kind (미) 현물지급. 미국에서 농산물과잉으로 농민에게 휴경을 명하였을 경우, 정부가 농민에게 농산물을 현물 지급한다.

PIM ① Parallel Inference Machine (컴퓨터) 병렬추론머신.
② products information management 제품정보관리.

PIMS profit impact of marketing strategy 다른 상황하에 있는 다양한 비즈니스의 경험을 집적하여 실증적으로 이윤(利潤)성과의 영향요인을 분석하여 전략적 시장 계획의 참고로 하기 위한 조사 연구.

PIN ① Patent Information Network (WIPO의) 특허정보 네트워크.
② personal identification number 현금카드의 비밀번호.

PINS person(s) in need of supervision 요감시자.

PIO ① parallel input output 병렬 입출력.
② process input output 프로세스 입출력.

PIO-NET practical living information on line network system (일) 소비 생활정보네트워크 시스템.

PIP ① packet interface processor 패킷 인터페이스 제어장치.
② preparatory investment protection 선행투자보호. *심해 저개발문제, IPT의 구칭.

PIPA Pacific Industrial Property Association 태평양 공업 소유권협회.

PIR property irregularity report

369

(항공) 사고수하물 신고서.

PIS personal inventory system 개별인사관리.

PIU process input unit 프로세스 입력장치.

PIUS process inherent ultimately safe 스웨덴의 원자로 안전 시스템.

PIV peak inverse voltage 피크 역전압.

PIXE particle induced X-ray emission 입자선 여기(勵起) 선방사분석법. 초소형 사이클로트론을 사용하여 원소를 분석하는 방법.

PIXEL picture element (컴퓨터) 회화(繪畵)요소.

PK ① park 공원
② penalty kick (축구, 럭비) 페널티 킥.
③ psychokinesis 염력(念力)행사. 정신력에 의해 물체를 움직이는 일.

PKF Peace Keeping Forces 평화유지군.

pkg package 포장.

PKI Partai Komunis Indonesia (= Indonesian Communist Party) 인도네시아 공산당.

PKO peace-keeping operation (유엔) 평화유지활동.

PKU phenylketonuria 페닐케톤뇨증(尿症). 선천성 지능장애.

PL ① packing list 패킹리스트.
② partial loss (해상보험) 분손.
③ photoluminescence 광자(光子)에 의하여 여기(勵起)되어 일어나는 형광.
④ product liability 제조물책임. 상품결함에 의한 피해에 대한 기업의 책임.
⑤ profit and loss 손익.
⑥ Agencia Informativa Latinoamericana (스) 쿠바의 국영 통신사.

PL-480 Public Law 480 美公法 480號(미국의 농산물을 외국에 증여 또는 차관형식으로 제공하기 위한 법).

P/L profit and loss statement 손익 계산서.

PLA ① Palestine Liberation Army 팔레스타인 해방군. PLO의 군사조직.
② People's Liberation Army 중국의 인민해방군.
③ programmable logic array (컴퓨터) 프로그래머블 논리 아레이(배열).

PLAN problem language analyzer 문제언어 분석프로그램.

PLANCODE planning control and decision evaluation system 경영 계획 작성 평가 시스템.

PLATO programmed logic for automatic teaching operations

(컴퓨터) 자동교육시스템. 컴퓨터와 연결된 단말기 앞에서 학습하는 시스템. 일리노이대학이 개발.

PLBD payload bay door 스페이스 셔틀의 도어.

PLC ① product life cycle 제품 라이프 사이클.
② programmable logic controller 자동 공정 제어장치.
③ Public Limited Company (영) 주식공개주식회사.

PLCC plastic leadless chip carrier (반도체의) 플라스틱 리드레스 칩커리어 납 성분이 없는 플라스틱 칩 전용선.

PLF Palestine Liberation Front 팔레스타인 해방 전선.

PLH (스) Partido Liberal de Honduras (=Liberal Party of Honduras) 온두라스 자유당.

PLI (이) Partito Liberale Italiano (=Italian Liberal Party) 이탈리아 자유당.

PL/I Programming Language I (컴퓨터) IBM사가 개발한 프로그램언어, 과학기술분야에 적합하다.

PLL phase lock loop (전자공학) 위상 록·루프.

PL/M programming language for microcomputer 마이크로 컴퓨터의 고급프로그램언어.

PLN (스) Partido de Liberacion Nacional (=National Liberation Party) (코스타리카) 국민 해방당.

PLO Palestine Liberation Organization 팔레스타인 해방기구.

PLP pay later plan 항공운임 후불제도. 항공회사와 금융기관 사이에 체결된 여행비용 할부제도.

PLR primary loop recirculation system 원자로 재순환시스템.

PLRS Position Location Reporting System (군사) 위치 장소 보고 시스템.

PLSS ① portable life support system 우주비행사가 선외활동을 할 때 짊어지는 생명유지장치.
② precision location strike system 정밀위치표정(標定) 시스템. 적의 레이더기지를 탐지·공격한다.

PLUS parent loan for undergraduate students 대학생을 가진 부모에 대한 학비원조를 위한 대부금.

p.m. ① per mensem 1개월당.
② post meridian 오후.

Pm ① premium 할증금, 프리미엄.
② promethium 프로메튬. 원자번호 61.

PM ① patent map 특허 정보 관리도.
② phase modulation (컴퓨터) 위상변조.
③ plant maintenance 공장의 조직적 관리.

④ preventive maintenance 예방조건.
⑤ preventive medicine 예방의학.
⑥ Prime Minister 수상.
⑦ productive maintenance 생산보전.
⑧ project management 프로젝트관리.
⑨ push money 특별조장금. 소매점이나 외판원에 지불되는 판매촉진보장금.

PMA ① para methoxy amphetamine 환각제의 일종.
② personal management analysis 인사관리분석.

PMAC Provisional Military Administrative Council (에티오피아) 임시 군사 평의회.

P.M.C. Postmaster General (미) 우정장관.

PMD premenstrual disorder syndrome 월경전 긴장 증후군.

PMDB (포) Partido do Movimento Democratico Brasileiro (=Brazilian Democratic Movement Party) 브라질 민주 운동당.

PMG ① Paymaster General (영) 재무성 경리장관.
② Post-master General (미, 영) 우정(郵政) 공사 총재.
③ Provost Marshal General 헌병 사령관.

PMH production per man hour 1인 1시간당 생산고.

PMIG programmer's minimum interface to graphics (컴퓨터) ANSI가 개발중인 도형데이터처리표준.

pmk postmark 우편물의 소인.

PML Pakistan Moslem League 파키스탄 이슬람교도 연맹.

PMMA poly methyl methacrylate 투명합성수지.

PMO postal money order 우편환.

PMOS P-channel metal oxide semiconductor (컴퓨터) P형금속 산화막 반도체.

PMP participative management program 자주 참가 경영계획.

PMS ① performance management system (미) 성능관리시스템. 항공기용.
② Picturephone Meeting Service (미) ATT의 텔레비전회의 서비스.
③ project management system 프로젝트관리시스템.

PMT photomultiplier 광전자 증배관(增倍管).

PMX packet multiplexer 패킷 다중화장치.

PN ① performance number 가솔린의 앤티노크(antiknock)성을 나타내는 지수.
② promissory note 약속어음.

PNA Philippines News Agency 필리핀 국영통신.

PNC ① Palestine National Council 팔레스타인 민족평의회.
② Power Reactor and Nuclear Fuel Development Corporation (일) 동력로·핵연료 개발 사업단.

PND People for Nuclear Disarmament (오스트레일리아) 대중 반핵 그룹의 연합체.

PNdB perceived noise decibel 감각 소음 데시벨.

PNE Peaceful use of nuclear explosion 핵폭발 평화이용.

PNEU Parents' National Educational Union (영) 전국 학부모 교육 연맹.

PNF Palestine National Front 팔레스타인 민족전선.

PNG ① (라) persona non grata (=unacceptable person) 바람직하지 않는 인물.
② Papua New Guinea 파푸아뉴기니. 뉴기니 동반부와 부근 섬들로 이루어진 나라.

PNI produced national income 생산 국민 소득. 사회주의국의 성장지표.

PNL perceived noise level 항공기 지각소음수준.

PNM pulse number modulation 펄스밀도변조.

PNO point of no return 뒤로 물러날 수 없는 상태.

PNP packet network processor 패킷교환기.

PNR passenger name record (항공) 여객예약기록.

Po polonium 폴로늄. 원자번호 84.

PO ① postal order 우편환.
② post office 우체국.
③ private offering 거래소외에서 행하는 증권거래.
④ probation officer 보호관찰관.
⑤ propylene oxide PPG의 원료.
⑥ purchase order 구입주문.

POA palmitoleic acid 팔미톨레산 (酸). 회사(懷死)해 가는 혈관을 활성화 함.

POB post office box 우체국사서함.

POC ① Pacific Ocean Community 태평양 개방공동체.
② Planning Organizing Controlling 계획, 조직, 통제.
③ port of call 기항지.

POCC payload operations control center 페이로드 오퍼레이션 관리 센터.

POD ① payable on death 사후지불.
② pay on delivery 현물상환지불.
③ The Pocket Oxford Dictionary 포켓 옥스퍼드 사전.
④ port oh debarkation 양륙(揚

POE

陸)항.

POE ① port of embarkation 선적항.
② port of entry 통관항.

POGO polar orbiting geophysical observatory 극궤도관측위성.

POL ① Patent Office Library 특허국 도서관.
② problem oriented language (컴퓨터) 문제용 프로그램 언어.

POLEPX Polar Experiment 극기상 관측계획.

Politburo 공산당의 정치국.

POM ① polyacetal resin 합성수지.
② Program Objective Memorandum (미)육군 장기 예산안.
③ purchase order management 발주관리.

POMCUS prepositions overseas material configured in unit sets (미) 육군의 해외사전 배치 군수물자.

POO post office order 우편환.

POP ① point of purchase 점두, 점두광고, 구매시점.
② printing out paper 일광으로 인화되는 인화지.
③ publish or perish 논문 등을 쓰지 않는 사람은 소멸한다는 뜻. 학자·연구자의 평가의 하나로 발표 논문량을 지표로 할 때에 사용되는 말.

POPs Persistent Organic Pollutants 잔류성 유기 오염물질 (분해되기 어렵고 반감기가 긴 오염물질로서 먹이사슬을 통해 생물체에 축적되므로 환경 및 인체에 위해하여 사용에 대한 국제적 규제를 하고 있는 오염물질).

POPLINE population information online 인구문제 문헌 정보 데이터 베이스.

PORSHE plan of Ocean Raft System for Hydrogen Economy 포르세계획. 적도직하의 남태평양에 태양 에너지를 모으는 거대한 뗏목을 띄우고 모은 태양 에너지로 해수에서 수소를 만들어 내는 계획.

POS point of sales (컴퓨터) 판매시점 정보관리.

POSCO Pohang Iron And Steel Co. (한) 포항제철.

POSEIDON Pacific Orient Seismic Digital Observation Network 아시아 태평양 초고성능 지진 관측망.

POSH port outbound, starboard homebound (속어) 부자. 영국과 인도간의 항로에서, 영국에서 인도로 갈 때는 왼쪽, 올 때는 오른쪽 뱃전의 선실이 서늘하여 운임이 비싼데, 그러한 선실을 택할 수 있는 사람이라는 것이 원래의 의미.

POSSLQ persons of opposite sexes sharing living quarters 이성과 함께 생활공간을 같이 하

는 사람들. 동거자.

POST Polymer Science & Technology 고분자화학 공업관계 정보데이터 베이스.

POT plain old telephone 재래식의 검은 전화기.

POTS plain old telephone service 아날로그 음성신호를 전달하는 재래식의 전화 서비스.

POVA productivity of value added 부가가치 생산성.

POW prisoner of war 포로.

POY partially oriented yarn 반연신사(半延伸絲).

p.p. parcel post 소포우편.

PP ① permanent press (의료품의) 수지가공후의 고온·고압 프레스.
② physical productivity 물적 생산성.
③ physical protection 핵물질 보호.
④ point of purchase 구입시점.
⑤ polypropylene 합성섬유·필름의 원료.
⑥ producer's price 생산자가격.
⑦ Purchasing Power 구매력.

PPA point of purchase advertising 구매시 광고. 소매점의 점두에 제시하는 광고·간판.

PPA ① phenyl propanolamine 페닐 프로파놀라민. 체중감량약.
② Progressinve Parties' Alliance (나이지리아) 진보인민동맹.

PPB ① part(s) per billion 10억분의.
② planning programming budgeting 기획계획 예산방식.

PPBS planning, programming, budgeting system 계획기획예산 시스템. 대형·컴퓨터를 사용하여 기업의 계획, 기획, 예산, 편성을 종합적으로 실시하는 것.

PPC plain paper copier 보통지 복사기.

P.P.C. pour prendre conge 작별인사차 왔음을 나타내는 말. (명함의 아래쪽 귀퉁이에 씀). (=to take leave)

PP card prepaid card 선지불 카드.

PPD prepaid 선불한, 발송인 지불.

PPE poly phenylene ether 고기능수지의 일종.

PPFA Planned Parenthood Federation of America 미국 산아 제한 연맹.

PPG polypropylene glycol 합성 수지의 원료.

pph. pamphlet 팜플렛.

pphm. part(s) per hundred million 1억분의.

PPI ① plane position indicator 공항 감시 레이더.
② present position indication 현재위치표시. 로켓 등의 현재

위치를 시시각각 표시하는 것.

PPL polar plasma laboratory 극 플라즈마 실험위성.

P-plane pilotless plane 무인비행기(폭탄을 실은).

PPLO pleuropneumonialike organism (생물) 늑막폐렴 유사세균.

ppm part(s) per million 백만분의.

PPM ① product portfolio management 제품 포트폴리오전략. 많은 제품계열이나 사업간에 어떻게 자금을 배분해야 할 것인가를 결정하여 경영의 효율화를 도모하는 것.
② pulse phase modulation 펄스위상변조. 통신에서 펄스의 위상을 변화시키는 방식.
③ pulse position modulation 펄스위치변조. 통신에서 펄스의 위치를 변화시키는 방식.

PPO ① polyphenylene oxide 고기능수지.
② polypropylene oxide 합성고무. 전기절연재료.
③ preferred Provider Organization 의료보험 : 계약 의사 및 병원 우선 의료 서비스 제도로써 계약 의사 및 병원외에도 의료 서비스를 받을 수 있는 의료 제도.

PPP ① phosphor prepared paper 인광(燐光)처리용지. 발광(發光) 우표용의 종이.
② polluter pays principle 오염자 부담의 원칙.
③ purchasing power parity 구매력평가설(評價說). 두 나라의 환율은 국내 구매력이 같을 때 균형을 이룬다는 설.

pps pulse(s) per second 매초~펄스.

PPS ① polyphenylene sulfide 고내열성 특수수지의 일종.
② post postscriptum (= post postscript) (라) 추추신(追追伸).

PPSEAWA Pan Pacific and South East Asia Women's Association of Japan 일본 범태평양동남아시아 여성협회.

ppt ① part(s) per thousand 천분의.
② part(s) per trillion 1조분의.

PPU Pan Pacific Union 범태평양협회.

PPV pay per view (CATV) 시청한 프로단위로 요금을 징수하는 방식.

PQ Parti Quebecois (프) 캐나다의 퀘벡당(黨). 퀘벡주의 분리·독립을 주장하는 당.

PQQ pyrrolo quinoline quinone 피롤로 퀴놀린 퀴논.

PQR pure nuclear quadruple resonance 핵4극 공명.

PQS percentage quota system 비례할당제. 무역업자들에 수출

량을 할당함으로써 수출총량을 구제하여 수입국과의 마찰을 피하는 것.

pr. preferred(stock) 우선주.

Pr praseodymium 프라세오디뮴. 원자번호 59.

PR ① ply rating 플라이수. 자동차의 타이어의 층(層).
② press release 신문발표.
③ populational representation 비례대표제.
④ public relations 법인 또는 개인의 생존, 번영을 위하여 자기를 둘러싼 환경과의 사이에 양호한 관계를 수립, 유지하는 것. 광고, 선전 활동과 동일시하는 경우가 많다.

PRA ① political risk assessment 정치적 위험도 평가. 미국의 기업 특히 다국적 기업이 실시하는 국제 정세전반 또는 특정한 지역의 정치정세의 조사를 기초로 한 각국의 정치적 위험성의 측정.
② Probabilistic risk assessment 확률적 위험성 평가. 시스템의 위험 발생 확률을 평가하여 이것을 종합하여 전체의 위험성의 확률을 도출하는 것.
③ Public Roads Administration (미) 도로공단.

Pravda 소련 공산당의 기관지.

PRC ① People's Republic of China 중화인민 공화국.
② programmed route control 자동 열차 진로제어.

pre-med pre-medical course 의예과.

PREP pre retirement education program 퇴직전 준비교육.

PRF pulse repetition (or recurrence) frequency (컴퓨터) 펄스 반복 주파수.

PRI ① (스) Partido Revolucionario Institucional (=Institutional Revolution Party) (멕시코) 제도적 혁명당.
② (이) Partito Repubblicano Italiano (=Italian Republican Party) 이탈리아 공화당.

PRIDE National Parents Resource Institute for Drug Education 마약 교육에 관한 미국 학부형 정보 협회.

PRIO International Peace Research Institute, Oslo 오슬로국제 평화연구소.

PRIS power reactor information system 동력로 정보시스템. IAEA가 작성하는 세계의 원자력 발전소에 관한 통계 예측 정보.

PRL (프) Parti Reformateur Liberal (=Freedom and Progress Party) (벨기에) 자유 진보당.

PRM ① power range monitoring system (원자력) 출력 영역모니터 시스템.
② process radiation monitor

377

(원자력) 프로세스 방사선 모니터.

PRN pro re nata (whenever necessary) (라) 임기응변으로.

PRO ① Public Record Office (영) 공립기록보관소. ② public relations officer 홍보 담당자.

Prof., prof. professor 교수.

PROLOG Programming in Logic (컴퓨터) 인공두뇌용 프로그램언어.

PROM programmable read-only memory (컴퓨터) 가변성 읽기 전용 기억 장치.

PROMETHEUS Program of European Transport System with Highest Efficiency and Unprecedented Safety 지구의 온난화 방지 등 환경 개선에 도움이 되고 안전하고 경제적이며 운전하기 쉬운 도로 교통시스템을 유럽 전역에 만들기 위한 기본적인 계획.

PROMIS problem oriented medical information (미) 의료 정보시스템.

PRON [폴란드語] Patriotyczny Ruch Odrodzenia Narodowego (폴란드)국민 부흥 애국 운동.

promo promotion 판매촉진, 광고 선전, 판매촉진활동.

prop property (연극) 소도구(小道具).

propensity to consume 소비성향.

PROPFAD Regional Project for Public Finance and Administration 공공재정 행정지역 프로젝트.

PRPB [F] Parti de la Revolution Populaire de Benin (=Benin People's Revolutionary Party) (베냉 인민 공화국) 베냉 인민 혁명당.

Pros. Atty. Prosecuting Attorney 검찰관.

pro tem pro tempore (=for the time being) (라) 당분간.

prox proximo (= next month) (라) 내월.

PRP Personnel Reliability Program 요원 신뢰도 프로그램.

PRR pulse repetition rate 펄스 반복수.

PRSA Public Relations Society of America 미국 PR협회.

PRSD power reactant storage and distribution (우주공학) 축전배전 시스템.

PRT ① personal rapid transit 개인용 고속 수송시스템. 그물 코와 같이 복잡하게 깔린 궤도를 컴퓨터로 제어된 차량이 도중에 정차하는 일없이 승객을 목적지까지 수송하는 미래의 수송시스템. ② photo-radiation therapy 광자(光子) 방사선요법.
③ preretirement training 퇴직전 준비교육.

PRTS personal rapid transit system 개인용 고속수송시스템.

ps pico second 피코초. 조분의 1초.

4p's product, price, place, promotion 마케팅의 대표적인 4가지 활동영역. 제품정책, 가격정책, 유통정책, 판촉정책.

PS ① passenger ship 여객선.
② payload specialist 스페이스 셔틀의 우주비행사로서 실험장치를 조작하는 과학기술사.
③ pferdestarke 엔진의 마력.
④ point of sales 판매시점 정보관리.
⑤ polystyrene 합성수지.
⑥ post scriptum (=postscript) (라) 추신.
⑦ production sharing 생산물분여. 개발수입의 한 방법으로 발전도상국 등의 미개발지역을 개발하기 위하여 개발에 필요한 자금, 자재, 기술 등을 공여하고 그대신 생산품의 일정한 비율로 인수하는 것.
⑧ purser 상선·비행기의 사무장.

P.S. Parlimentary Secretary 정무차관.

PS방식 production sharing method 투자한 선진국 자본의 상환을 개발도상국의 생산물로 상환하는 방식.

PSA ① Pacific Science Association 태평양 학술 협회.
② public service announcement 공고서비스정보. 자선 목적·비영리 단체의 활동 및 이밖에 시민적인 목적에 적합한 홍보활동.

PSAC President's Science Advisory Committee (미) 대통령 직속 과학 자문위원회.

PSAR preliminary safety analysis report (원자력) 예비 안전 해석 보고서.

PSAT preliminary scholastic aptitude test (미) 진학 적성 예비시험. SAT수험을 위한 예비시험.

PSB photosynthesis bacteria 광합성 세균.

PSBR public sector borrowing requirement 공공부문 차입 수요.

PSC (프) Parti Social Chretien (=Christian Socialist Party) (벨기에) 기독 사회당.

PSD ① position sensor diode 광반도체 위치 검출기.
② programmable signal processor 프로그램 변경식 신호 처리장치.

PSDI (이) Partito Socialista Democratioc Italiano (=Italian Socialist Democratic Party) 이탈리아 시회 민주당.

PSE Producer Subsidy Equivalent 생산자 보조금 상당량. *농업보호수준 지표로서 농업 생산자의 수입에 대한 직접·간접의 정부 보조금 및 내외 가격차의 비율.

PSF polysulfone 고내열성 특수수지의 일종.

PSG Planning Systems Generation 계획제표(諸表) 작성프로그램.

PSI ① weapons of mass destruction proliferation security initative 대량살상무기 확산 방지구상
② personalized system of instruction 개인교수.
③ Policy Studies Institute (영) 정책 문제 연구소.
④ Pollutant Standard Index 대기 오염 지수.
⑤ Principal Supplying Interest(GATT) 주요공급국.

PSK phase shift keying 위상편위 변조(位相偏位變造).

PSO polysulfone 고내열성 특수수지의 일종.

PSOE [S] Partido Socialista de Oberos Espanoles (=Spanish Socialist Labor Party) 스페인 사회 노동당.

PSP Pacific Security Pact 태평양 안전보장조약.

PSPC position sensitive proportional counter (원자력) 비례 계수관(計數管).

PSPDN packet switched public data network (컴퓨터) 패킷 교환망.

PSR Physicians for Social Responsibility (미) 사회적 책임을 다하기 위한 의사 단체.

PSRO professional standards review organization 의료기준조사위원회. 제3자 의사에 의한 의료내용 조사위원회.

PSS professional selling skill 영업부 사원에게 상담(商談)기술을 가르치는 교육 프로그램.

PSSC Physical Science Study Committee (미) 물리 교육 연구 위원회.

PSSI Peace Science Society International (미) 국제평화 과학협회.

PST ① Pacific Standard Time (미) 태평양표준시.
② presenile training 노령전 준비 교육.

PSTM Product Safety Technology Management 제품안전 기술관리.

PSTN public switched telephone network 공중전화망.

PSU [F] Parti Socialiste Unifie (=United Socialist Party) (프랑스) 통일 사회당.

PSUM [S] Partido Socialista Unificado de Mexico (멕시코) 통일 사회당.

PSW ① programmable switch (컴퓨터)프로그래머블·스위치.

② programmable status word (컴퓨터) 프로그램 상태어.

Pt platinum 백금. 원자번호 78.

PT ① participation program (방송) 복수광고주참가 프로그램.
② physical therapist 물리요법사.
③ potential transformer 계기용 변압기.
④ Protection Tariff (duties) 보복관세.

PTA ① parent-teacher association 사친회.
② preferential trading agreement 특혜무역협정.
③ purified terephthalic acid 폴리에스터계 합성섬유, 필름의 원료.

PTAR Prime Time Access Rule (미) ECC에 의한 텔레비전의 프라임타임(골든아워) (오후6-7시)에 대한 상업 프로그램과 규칙.

PTB (포) Partido Trabalhista Brasileiro (=Brazilian Labor Party) 브라질 노동당.

PT boat patrol torpedo boat 초계어뢰정.

PTC positive temperature coefficient thermistor (전자공학) 정(正) 특성 전열 조절기.

PTCA percutaneous transluminal coronary angioplasty 경피(經皮)적 관동맥 혈관 재건법.

PTDC Pacific Trade and Development Conference 태평양 무역개발회의.

PTFE poly tetra fluorothylene 고내열 내화학약품성 합성수지.

PTH para thyroid hormone 부갑상선 호르몬.

PTI Press Trust of India PTI통신사. 인도의 최대의 통신사.

PTM pulse time modulation (컴퓨터) 펄스시 변조.

PTO ① please turn over 다음면에 계속.
② power take off 동력이륙장치. 항공기를 이륙시키기 위한 장치.

PTOC percutaneous transluminal coronary recanalization 경피(經皮)적 관동맥 재소통.

PTP ① paper tape punch 종이 테이프 천공기.
② point to point 점교시(點敎示). 로봇의 동작.
③ press through pack 포장위에서 손가락으로 누르면 정제가 뒷쪽에서 나오는 방식.

PTR ① paper tape reader 종이 테이프 판독기.
② photoelectric tape reader 광전식 테이프판독기.

PTS predetermined time system 예측동작시간법. 작업의 표준시간을 개관적으로 결정하는 방법.

PTSD post traumatic stress disorder 강한 스트레스를 경험한 뒤에 생기는 정신 질환.

PTSPROMT Predicasts Overview of Markets and Technology (미) Predicasts 회사의 정보 데이터베이스.

PTT postal, telephone and telegraph administration 우편 · 전화 · 전신 관리기관.

PTV public television 비영리적 공공 텔레비전.

Pu plutonium 플루토늄. 원자번호 94.

PU polyurethane = PUR 합성수지. 발포형태의 것은 단열재, 쿠션, 매트리스에 사용된다.

PUO pyrexia of unknown origin 원인 불명의 열.

PUPPIES pampered up and coming pubescent 애지중지 자라나 청춘기를 맞게 된 어린이들.

PUREX plutonium reduction extraction (원자력) 플루토늄 환원 추출법.

PUSH People United to Save Humanity (미) 흑인 운동조직. 1971년 설립.

PV present value 현재 가치

PVA ① poly vinyl acetate = PVAC 합성수지의 원료.
② poly vinyl alcohol = PVAL 합성섬유의 원료, 도료, 접착제 등에 사용한다.

PVAC poly vinyl acetate 수용성 비닐계 중합물(重合物).

PVB poly vinyl butyral 투명한 접착제.

PVC poly vinyl chloride 합성수지 염화물 파이프. 필름, 레더에 이용.

PVD physical vapor deposition 물리증착법.

PVDA Partij van de Arbeid (= Labor Party) (네덜란드) 노동당.

PVDC poly vinylidene chloride 합성수지.

PVDF poly vinylidene fluoride 합성수지 불화물.

PVF poly vinyl formal

PVI poly vinyl isobutyl ether

PVO private voluntary organization 민간 비영리단체.

PVP polyvinyl pyrrolidone 약제, 화장품, 세제, 식품, 합성혈장등에 사용한다.

PVS Post Vietnam syndrome 베트남 전쟁후 증후군. 베트남에서 복원한 병사에서 발병한 정신장해.

pvt. private 병졸.

PVT pressure vessel technology (원자력) 압력 용기 공학.

PVV (네덜란드어) Partij voor Virjheid en Vooruitgang (=

Freedom and Progress Party) (벨기에) 자유 진보당.

PW ① police woman 부인경관. ② prisoner of war 전쟁포로 (POW, P.O.W.)

PWA ① people with AIDS 에이즈 환자. 의사가 환자의 프라이버시 보호를 위하여 사용하는 직업용어.
② Public Works Administration 공공사업국.

PWB printed wiring board 인쇄 배선보드.

PWC physical working capacity 신체적 작업능력.

PWF Pacific Wrestling Federation 태평양 레슬링 연맹.

PWM pulse width modulation (컴퓨터) 펄스폭 변조.

PWR pressurized water reactor 가압 수형 원자로.

PX ① para xylene 합성섬유의 원료 ② patrol x (일) 차리대잠초계기 ③ post exchange (미 육군의) 매점. ④ private exchange 사설교환.

PXL patrol X landbase (일) 차기 대잠초계기.

PZ pancreozymin 판크레오지민. 담낭수축・담액 분비촉진 작용을 하는 위장 호르몬.

PZI protamine zinc insulin 프로타민 아연 인슐린. 당뇨병 치료약.

PZPR (폴 語) Polsks Zjednoczona Partia Robotnicza (=Polish United Workers' Party) 폴란드 통일 노동자당. 영어 약어 PUWP.

QA ① qualitative & quantitative analysis 정질량 분석. ② quality assurance 품질보증. ③ question and answer 질의 응답.

Q&A question and answer 문답.

QAB Queen Anne's Bounty （영） 앤 여왕 기금(보조금).

QAC quality assurance control 품질보증관리.

QA furniture quick assembly furniture 속성조립식 가구.

QAM quadrature amplitude modulation 직교(直交) 진폭변조.

QANTAS Queensland and Northern Territory Aerial Services 콴타스항공. 오스트레일리아 국영 항공회사.

QARANC Queen Alexandra's Royal Army Nursing Corps （영） 알렉산드라 여왕 육군 간호 부대.

QARNNS Queen Alexandra's Royal Navy Nursing Service （영） 알렉산드라 여왕 해군 간호 부대.

QB quarterback （축구） 쿼터백.

QBE Query By Example 예시(例示) 조회언어.

QC quality control 품질관리.

QCB queue control block 큐제어 블록.

QC circle quality control circle （일） 큐·시 서클. 직장에서 QC를 실시하기 위하여 자발적으로 조직된 소(小)그룹.

QCD quality, cost, delivery 품질·가격·납기. 수요의 3요소.

QDC quick die change 금형(金型) 신속 교환 시스템.

QE Quick Estimates (of National Income) 국민소득의 4반기 속보. GNP속보치.

QEA Qantas Empire Airways （호주） 콴타스 항공 회사.

QED quantum electrodynamics 양자(量子)전자역학.

QEF （라） quod erat faciendum (= which was to be made or done) 그 일은 해야 할 것이었다.

QEI （라） quod erat inveniendum (=which was to be found out) 이 일은 찾아야 할 것이었다.

QE II Queen Elizabeth II 호화 객선 퀸 엘리자베스 2세호.

q'finals quarter finals 준준결승.

QGM Queen's Gallantry Medal (영) 용감한 행위에 대한 훈장.

QGPC Qatar General Petroleum Corporation 카타르 제너럴 석유회사.

QHM quartz horizontal magnetometer 수정수평자력계.

QID (라) quarter in die(=four times a day) (처방) 하루에 4회.

QIP ① quality improvement program 품질 개선 계획. ② quality inspection point 품질 검사소.

QISAM queued indexed sequential access method 대기(待機) 색인 순차액세스방식.

QL quick loading 급속장전(急速裝塡).

QM quality management (미) 품질관리.

Q.M. quartermaster 兵站장교.

QMC Quartermaster Corps 병참단.

QMG quartermaster general (軍) 병참감.

QMS ① quartermaster sergeant (군) 병참부 하사관. ② Quality Management System 품질경영체제

QNA Qatar News Agency 카타르 국영통신.

QNS quantity not sufficient 분량 부족.

QOL quality of life 여생(餘生)의 질.

QP (라) quantum placet (=as much as you please) (처방) 원하는 만큼.

QPC Qatar Petroleum Company 카타르 석유회사.

QPL qualified products list (미) 인정(認定)제품리스트. 군용(軍用) 제품으로 신뢰성을 유지하기 위한 리스트.

QPM Queen's Police Medal (영) 경찰 공로 훈장.

QRC Quick Reaction Capability 신속대응능력.

QRF Quick Reaction Force 신속대응군 ; 기동타격대

QRP Quick Reaction Program 신속 대응 계획

QS quantity surveyor 건설 적산사(積算士)

QSAM queued sequential access method 대기순 액세스방식.

QSAR quantitative structure activity relationship(s) 정량적 구조 활성상관(해석). 다변량(多變量) 해석 등에 의하여 생물과 약품의 관계를 정량적으로 분석하여 약품설계에 도움을 주려는 것.

QSBO quasi stellar blue object

QSE

항성상(恒星狀) 청색천체.

QSE qualified scientist and engineer (영) 유자격 과학 기술자.

QSG quasi stellar galaxy 항성상(恒星狀) 소우주.

QSO quasi stellar object 항성상 천체.

QSRA Quiet Short Haul Research Aircraft NASA 개발 저소음항공기.

QSRS quasi stellar radio source 준성(準星) 전파원.

QSS quasi stellar radio source 준성(準星) 전파원.

QSTOL quiet short takeoff and landing 무소음 단거리 이착륙(기).

qt. quart 1/4갤런.

QT qualification test 인정시험.

QTAM queued telecommunications access method (컴퓨터) 대기통신액세스방식.

QTAT quick turn around time (美) IBM사(社)의 전자동 반도체 제조시스템.

QUANGO quasi autonomous non governmental organization 반관반민기구. 영국문화 진흥회와 같이 정부가 설립한 단체이지만 민간인이 지도·운영하는 것.

QTAT quick turn around time (美) IBM사(社)의 전자동 반도체 제조시스템.

QTTV Quick Time TV Apple사가 차세대 Quick Time으로 발표한 동화상용의 엔진.

Que. Quebec 캐나다 동부의 주 및 주수도 (프랑스계 시민이 지배적인 위치를 차지하고 있음).

QUICKTRAN quick translation (컴퓨터) FORTRAN 서브세트의 일종으로 다중액세스시스템용으로 설계된 프로그램언어.

QTOL quick take off and landing airplane 무소음 이 착륙기.

QUOTA quantitative trade restriction 수입수량제한.

QWL quality of working life 노동생활의 질적 향상 운동. 일의 보람을 느끼게 하는 운동.

Qz quartz 석영.

R Restricted (미) 부모 또는 성인 동반이 아니면 17세 이하 입장금지의 영화.

® registered trademark 등록 상표.

Ra radium 라듐. 원자번호 88.

RA ① repurchase agreement 되사기 약정.
② response analyzer 반응 분석장치. 교육기기의 하나.
③ Royal Academy (영) 왕립 미술원.
④ Regular Army 정규군.
⑤ Retiring Age 정년.

RAA Royal Academy of Arts (영) 왕립 미술원. = RA.

r&a rail and air 철도편 및 공수.

R&A Royal and Ancient Golf Club of St. Andrews 영국 골프협회의 의미로 사용됨. 영국에는 전국적인 협회조직이 없으므로 세인트 앤드류스가 영국의 전 클럽의 정점으로서 골프협회의 역할을 하고 있다.

RAAF Royal Australian Air Force 호주 공군.

RAAMS remote anti armor mine system 원격 대(對) 장갑 지진 시스템.

R&B rhytnm and blues 리듬 앤드 블루스. 흑인음악의 일종.

RAC ① Royal Aero Club (영) 왕립 비행 그룹.
② Royal Agricultural College (영) 왕립 농업 전문학교.
③ Royal Armoured Corps 영국 기갑 부대.
④ Royal Automobile Club (영) 왕립 자동차 클럽.

RACON radar beacon 레이더비콘.

RAD Royal Academy of Dancing (영) 왕립 무용원.

R&D ① research and development ratio 1주당 연구개발비를 주가(株價)로 나눈 비율을 말한다.
② research and development 연구와 개발.

RADA random-access discrete address 무선의 사용자가 각기 좁은 대역(帶域)을 가지는 대신 전체가 하나의 넓은 대역을 공유하는 통신의 방식.

RADAG Radar Area Correlation Guidance 레이더 지형상관유도장치.

RADAR radio detecting and ranging 레이더, 전파탐지기.

RADOM radar dome 레이더 돔.

RAE Royal Aircraft Establishment (영) 왕립 항공 연구소.

RAEC Royal Army Educational Corps 영국 육군 교육 부대.

R.A.F. Royal Air 영국 공군.

RAFAR radio automated facsimile and reproduction 인스턴트 라디오. 新聞, 電波自動 복사 재생방식.

RAF Royal Air Force 영국 공군.

RAFVR Royal Air Force Volunteer Reserve 영국 공군 지원 예비군.

RAGC Royal and Ancient Golf Club = R & A 스코틀랜드의 St Andrews 골프클럽. 골프의 발상지라고 한다.

RAH Royal Albert Hall (영) (런던의) 로열 앨버트 홀.

RAI (이) Radio Televisions Italiano 이탈리아 방송 협회.

RAKAH Communist Pary of Israel 이스라엘 공산당.

RAM ① radio attenuation measurement 전파감쇠측정.
② random access memory (컴퓨터) 임의 접근기억장치. 수시로 기억을 추가하거나 끄집어낼 수 있고 읽기와 쓰기 양쪽이 가능한 메모리이다. 그러나 전원이 끊어지면 기억내용이 지워져 버린다.
③ Revolutionary Action Movement (미) 혁명행동운동. 인종차별 반대운동단체.

R.A.M. Royal Academy of Music 영국 王立音樂院.

RAMC Royal Army Medical Corps 영국 육군 군의단.

RAMD reliability, availability, maintainability and durability 신뢰성·가동성·정비성·내구성. 병기개발에 있어 중요시되는 4 조건.

RAMPS resource allocation in multi-project scheduling (컴퓨터) 복수 프로젝트 계획의 자원 할당.

RAN Royal Australian Navy 호주 해군.

RAND research and development 연구개발.

RAND Corporation Research and Development Corporation 1948 년 미공군의 원조로 설립된 미국 최초의 본격적인 싱크탱크.

RANN Research Applied to National Needs (미) 긴급문제 연구. NSF에 의한 환경·건강·사회문제 연구.

r&o rail and ocean 철도 및 해운.

RAOB radiosonde observation 라디오존데 관측.

RAOC Royal Army Ordnance Corps 영국 육군 군수부.

RAP Rocket Assisted Projectile 보조로켓포탄.

RAPCON radar approach control (항공) 레이더 진입관제. 레이더 스크린을 보고 항공기의 착륙을 유도하는 방식.

RAR radioacoustics ranging 바다에서 선박의 위치를 찾아내는 방법.

R&R ① rest and recuperation 전선에서 기지 또는 도시로 전속하는 것. 전선을 떠난 휴가. ② rock' n' roll 로큰롤.

RARC Regional Administrative Radio Conference 지역 무선통신 주관청회의.

RAREP radar report 레이더 보고.

RAS ① radar advisory service 주요 공항 주변에서 소형기의 움직임을 레이더로 추적하여 충돌의 위험성을 알리는 안전정보 제공시스템. ② refueling at sea 해상급유. ③ reliability availability serviceability (컴퓨터) 신뢰성, 가용성, 보수성. 컴퓨터의 능력 평가의 주요소.

RASIS reliability, availability serviceability, integrity and security 신뢰성, 가용성, 보수성, 확실성, 안전성.

RAT rocket-assisted torpedo 로켓 발사어뢰.

r&t rail & truck 철도와 트럭.

R&T research and technology 연구와 기술.

RATCON radar air traffic control 레이더 항공 교통관제.

RATFOR Rationalized Fortran 프로그램 언어의 일종.

RATO rocket assisted takeoff 로켓 추진 이륙. 이륙할 때의 활주거리를 짧게 하기 위하여 로켓을 사용하는 방식.

RATT radio teletype 무선 텔레타이프.

r&w rail and water 철도와 수편.

RAVC Royal Army Veterinary Corps 영국 육군 수의단.

RAWIN radio wind detection finding 송신기를 단기구에 의한 고층풍(高層風)의 측정.

RAX remote access computing system 원격접근계산 시스템. 원격지정보처리방식.

Rb rubidium 루비듐. 원자번호 37.

RB ① reconnaissance bomber 정찰 폭격기를 나타내는 기호. ② remote batch 원격배치. 원격지에 설치한 단말기에서 통신회선을 통하여 중앙처리 장치에 데이터를 전송하여 중앙에서 일괄처리한 후 그 결과를 단말에 반송하는 방식.
③ return to bias recording 자기테이프 등에 디지털식으로 기록하는 방식의 하나.
④ Ritzaus Bureau(Danish News Agency) (덴) 덴마크 통신.
⑤ Racial Bias 인종편견.
⑥ Race Conflict 인종갈등.

RBA Royal Society of British Artists (영) 왕립 미술가 협회.

RBC red blood cell 적혈구.

RBE relative biological effect (iveness) : relative biological efficiency 생물학적 효과비. X선, 감마선, 전자선의 효과를 1로 하였을 때의 방사선의 흡수선량.

RBI run(s) batted in (야구) 타점.

Rbi. Ruble 루블. 소련의 화폐 단위.

RBS Royal Society of British Sculptors (영) 왕립 조각가 협회.

RC ① radio control 무선조종.
② Red Cross 적십자사.
③ regular chain 지점 또는 동일 자본계열의 연쇄점.
④ reinforced concrete 철근콘크리트.
⑤ remittance check 송금수표.
⑥ remote control 원격조종.

RCA ① RCA Corp. 미국 최대의 전기제품회사.
② The Regional Coopreative Agreement (for Research, Development and Training Related to Nuclear Science and Technology) (원자력과학 기술의 연구, 개발과 훈련을 위한) 지역협력협정. IAEA의 아시아 지구에 있어서의 협력 활동.

RCAF Royal Canadian Air Force 캐나다 공군.

RCAG remote control air/ground communication facility 원격제어 대공통신시설. 항공기와 항공 교통관제부와의 직접 통신을 위한 시설.

RCC ① reinforced carbon carbon (우주공학) 강화 카본재.
② rod cluster control (원자력) 로드 클러스터 제어.
③ Roman Catholic Church 로마 카톨릭 교회.

RCD Regional Cooperation for Development 지역협력개발기구. 터키, 파키스탄, 이란이 1964년에 결성.

RCDS Royal College of Defence Studies (영) 왕립 방위대학.

RCIC reactor core isolation cooling 원자로 격리시 냉각계.

RCM radar countermeasures 레이더 방해.

RCMP Royal Canadian Mounted Police 캐나다 기마 경찰.

RCN Royal Canadian Navy 캐나다 해군.

RCNP Research Center for Nuclear Physics 원자물리학연구센터.

RCO Royal College of Organists (영)왕립 파이프 오르간 전문 학원.

RCOT Rolling Contour Optimization Theory (자동차) 주행시 최적 형상 이론.

RCP Royal College of Physicians (영) 왕립 내과 전문 학원.

RCPB reactor coolant pressure boundary 원자로 냉각재 압력 바운더리.

Rcpt. receipt 영수증.

RCR retina character reader 망막 문자 판독장치. 사람의 망막과 같은 방식으로 문자를 판독하는 장치.

RCRA Resource Conservation and Recovery Act (미) 자원보전재생법.

RCS ① reaction control system (우주개발) 반동자세 제어장치. 스페이스셔틀·오비터의 궤도진입 또는 궤도상 및 궤도에서 재돌입할 때에 자세를 제어한다.
② remote computing service 원격정보처리서비스.

RCTL resistor capacitor transistor logic 저항·용량 결합형 트랜지스터.

RCU respiratory care unit 호흡부전 환자 집중치료실.

RCV remote controlled vehicle 원격조작장치. 유색식(有索式)의 무인 해중관찰(작업) 장치로서 수중 텔레비전을 사용하여 원격조작이 가능하다.

RCY Red Cross Youth 청소년 적십자.

RD ① received data 수신데이터.
② record of discussion 토의의사록.
③ refer to drawer (부도어음 등의) 발행인 반환.
④ research and development 연구개발.
⑤ rubber dam 방습용 고무포.
⑥ Racial Discrimination 인종차별.

R/D refer to drawer = R.D. (어음에서) 발행인 회부.

RDA retail display allowance 별진열 보장금(報奬金). 계약에 의하여 잡지의 표지가 잘 보이도록 진열하였을 때에 소매업자가 받는 보장금.

RD&A research, development and acquisition 연구개발과 조달.

RDC ① rail diesel car (美) 자주식(自走式) 디젤 동력 객차.
② Royal Defence Corps 영국 해군 방비대.

RD&D research, development and demonstration 연구, 개발, 실증.

RDD&D research, development, demonstration and deployment 연구, 개발, 실증(實證), 전개.

RDF ① radio direction finder 무선 방향 탐지기.
② Rapid Deployment Forces (미) 긴급 전개부대. 긴급시에 급파하는 특수부대. 미군이 항구적 거점을 갖고 있지 않은 지역에서의 분쟁에 대처한다.

RDJTF Rapid Deployment Joint Task Forces (미) 긴급전개통합군. 세계의 동란에 대처하기 위하여 항상 대기상태에 있는 공·해·육통합군.

RDP radar data processing system 레이더 정보처리시스템. * 레이더 정보를 근거로 하여 관제에 필요한 비행정보를 표시하는 시스템.

RDS respiratory distress syndrome 신생아 호흡장애 증후군.

RDSS rapid deployment surveillance system 긴급전개(展開) 감시시스템. 적국의 기지부근의 해상에 투하되어 잠수함의 정보를 통신위성에 보내는 시스템.

RDX research department explosive 사이클로 나이트(cyclonite). 폭탄·포탄 등에 사용하는 강력 고성능 폭약.

re. reference 참고, 참조.

Re. rhenium 레늄. 원자번호 75.

RE ① rotary engine 로터리 엔진.
② Royal Exchange (영) 왕립거래소.
③ Retained Earning 이익잉여금.

REA ① Rural Education Association (미) 농촌교육협회.
② Rural electrification Administration (미) 농촌전화국(電話局).

REB relativistic electron beam 상대론적 전자빔. 500KeV이상의 고에너지 전자빔.

rec recreation 오락, 유원지.

rec. ① receipt 영수증.
② receivable 수령할 수 있는.
③ received 수취필, 수령필.

REC recording 녹음.

RECON remote control system 원격조작시스템.

RECOVER remote continual verification (원자력) 상시원격 감시시스템. 핵물질의 병기전용을 방지하기 위하여 비엔나의 본부에서 상시 자동적으로 감시하는 시스템.

Red 2 Red Dye No. 2 적색 2호. 나프탈렌에서 추출되는 인공착색료. 발암성의 이유로 미국에서는 사용이 금지되고 있다.

Red 40 Red Dye No. 40 적색 40호. 인공착색료. 식품, 약품, 화장품에 사용한다.

REGISTER Retrieval System for

General Information of Scientific and Technological Research 과학기술연구정보 검색 시스템.

REGREP registered representative (미) 등록증권판매원. 증권업협회, 거래소의 자격시험에 합격하여 등록된 증권판매원.

rehab rehabilitation 사회복귀.

REINS Real Estate Information Network System (일) 전국적 부동산 정보 유통시스템.

REIT real estate investment trust 부동산투자 신탁 회사.

REM Roentgen equivalent man 인체에 미치는 피해 정도에 의한 방사선량(量)의 단위.

REME Royal Electrical and Mechanical Engineers 영국군 전기 기계 기술부.

RENFE (스) Red Nacional de los Ferrocarriles Espanoles (= National Railway Network of Spain) 스페인 국유 철도.

REO Real Estate Owned 은행 소유 부동산

rep Roentgen equivalent physical 방사능 단위.

Rep. ① Representative (미) 하원의원.
② Republic 공화국.
③ Republican (미) 공화당원.
④ Republican Party 공화당.

REP ① radar evaluation pod 레이더 시험의 전자장치.
② reporting point (항공) 위치 통보점.

rept. [receipt] 인수증.

res. research ; reserve ; residence ; resigned ; resolution

RES reticulo endothelial system (해부학) 세망 내피계(細網 內皮系)

RESPA Real Estate Settlement Procedures Act 은행이 융자 신청인과 관련된 모든 비용에 대한 내역을 HUD Form에 자세히 기록하라는 규정

REST restricted environmental stimulation therapy 제한환경 자극요법. 담배를 끊게 하기 위하여 24시간 방 속에 감금하는 방법.

RETAIN remote technical assistance and information network 원격기술 진단정보망. IBM사가 전 세계의 IBM 컴퓨터시스템의 고장사례, 원인, 수복 방법 등의 데이터베이스를 만들어 각지의 단말에서 정보를 입수할 수 있게 만든 것.

RETECS Register of Toxic Effects of Chemical Substances (미) 화학물질의 독성에 관한 국립의학 도서관의 데이터베이스.

REUS reusable 재사용가능.

Reuters

Reuters commodity indexes Reuters 통신의 상품 시세 지수. (U.K. Commodity Index).

Reuters Reuter's News Agency 영국의 통신사.

rev. revenue 세입, 수입, 수익.

Rev. Reverend 목사에 대한 존칭.

REV reentry vehicle = RV (우주) 재돌입 비상체(飛翔體).

REW rewind 되감기(자기테이프).

REXS radio exploratory satellite (일) 전파탐지위성.

rf radio frequency 무선주파(수). 고주파.

Rf rutherfordium 루테퍼듐. 원자번호 104.

RF ① radio frequency 무선주파수. ② range finder 거리계. ③ Republique Francaise(French Republic) 프랑스 공화국. ④ reserve force 예비군. ⑤ reserve fund 적립금, 예비금.

RFD radio farm director 농사 방송 통신원. 농사문제를 취재하여 방송하는 사람.

RFDC radio frequency discharge cleaning 고주파방전세정(洗淨).

RFI radio frequency interference 무선주파방해.

RFK Robert Francis Kennedy 미국 사법 장관을 지낸 인물. 케네디 대통령의 남동생(1925-68).

RFM regency, frequency, monetary 다이렉트마케팅 수법에 관한 전문 용어.

RFNA red fuming nitric acid (화학) 적연질산.

RFO retro fire officer 우주선 역추진 로켓기술자.

RFP reverse field pinch 역자장 핀치 장치.

RFQ request for quotes 견적서 요구.

RFS remote file system 원격 파일 시스템.

RFSP rigid frame selection program 구조부(構造部) 재료선정 프로그램.

RFU Rugby Football Union (英) 럭비 협회.

RG ① report generator 보고서 작성기. 컴퓨터의 파일의 정보를 일정한 형식으로 출력하는 것. ② Red Guard 홍위대(중국).

RGA rate gyro assembly (우주공학) 레이트 자이로 조립부품.

RGB red, green, blue 삼원색. 3원색 모니터(RGB monitor)는 합성컬러모니터(composite color monitor)보다 해상력(解像力)이 우수하다.

RGI (독) Rote Gewerkschaft Internationale (=International Red

Trade Union) 국제 적색 노조.

RGS Royal Geographical Society (영) 왕립 지리 학회.

Rh rhodium 로듐. 원자번호 45.

Rh(factor) Rhesus factor Rh 적혈구 속에 들어 있는 응혈소.

RH relative humidity 상대습도.

RHA Royal Horse Artillery 영국 기마 포병.

RHC regional holding company (미) ATT의 지역 소유 주식 회사.

RHD The Random House Dictionary of the English Language 랜덤 하우스 영어 대사전.

RHEED reflective high energy electron diffraction 반사 고속 전자 선회절법. 고속전자를 사용하여 전극 표면의 결정구조를 해석하는 방법.

RHG Royal Horse Guards 영국 근위 기병대.

RHI range height indicator 거리 고도지시장치.

RHIO Rank has its obligations 지위에는 그에 따른 의무가 있다.

RHIP Rank has its privileges 지위에는 그에 따른 특권이 있다.

rhm roentgen per hour per meter 1m 거리에서 매시간 1뢴트겐의 선량률(線量率)이 있을 때의 방사선 원(源)의 강도.

RHRS residual heat removal system (원자로) 잔류 열 제거 시스템.

RHS ① Royal Historical Society (영) 왕립 사학회.
② Royal Horticultural Society (영) 왕립 원예 학회.
③ Royal Humane Society (영) 수해 구조회.

RI ① radioactive isotope 방사성 동위원소.
② refractive index 굴절률.
③ Refuges International 국제 난민 구제협회.
④ Rehabilitation International 신체 장애자 갱생국제협회.
⑤ reinsurance 재보험.
⑥ Rotary International 국제 로터리클럽.
⑦ Royal Institution (영) 왕립 과학연구소.
⑧ Research Institute 연구소.

R.I. Rhode Island 로드 아일랜드 주(州).

RIA ① reactivity initiated accident (원자력) 반응도 사고.
② Robot Institute of America 미국 로봇 협회.

RIAA Recording Industry Association of America 미국 레코드 공업회.

RIBA Royal Institute of British Architects (영) 왕립 건축사협회.

RIC Royal Institute of Chemistry

Richter

(영) 왕립 화학 학회.

Richter Scale 리히터지진계.

RICO Racketeer Influenced and Corrupt Organizations Statute (미) 조직 범죄 단속법.

RICS Royal Institute of Chartered Surveyors (영) 왕립 공인 측량사 협회.

RID Remove Intoxicated Drivers (미) 음주 운전자를 추방하는 모임.

RIDAN radioactivity disaster alarm net (일) 핵방사능 재해경보망.

RIF reduction in force 인원삭감, 군비삭감.

RIHE Research Institute of Health and Environment(RIHE) 국립보건환경연구원[美].

RILU Red International of Labor Unions 적색노동조합 인터내셔널.

RIM reaction injection molding 반응사출성형.

RIMPAC Rim of the Pacific exercise 환태평양 제국해군합동연습.

RIN Rassemblement pour IIndependance Nationale (Assembly for National Independence) (프) 국민독립회의. 캐나다·퀘백 주의 분리독립을 요구하는 동주의 프랑스계 캐나다인의 집단.

RIND reversible ischemic neurological deficit 가역성 허혈(虛血)성 신경 증상.

Rio Grande 미국 Colorado州 부에서 시작하여 Mexico灣으로 흐르는 강.

RISC reduced instruction set computer 컴퓨터의 기계적 명령어를 ⅓정도로 줄여 시스템 설계를 단순화하며 비용도 절약하면서 성능을 대폭 향상시킨 새로운 컴퓨터.

RIT rate of information through put 단위 시간내에 정보원으로부터 정보수신기에 전달되는 정보량.

RJE remote job entry (컴퓨터) 원격 잡 입력. 통신회선에 접속된 단말기를 사용하여 원격지의 컴퓨터를 이용하는 방법.

RKO Radio Keith Orpheum 미국의 영화 회사.

RL Rugby League (영) 럭비 연맹.

RLF Redundant Labor Force 잉여 노동력.

RLG ring laser gyro 환상(環狀) 레이저 자이로.

RLO returned letter office (영) 배달 불능 우편물 취급소.

RLS Robert Louis Stevenson 영

국의 작가(1850-94)

RLSS Royal Life Saving Society (영) 왕립 인명 구조 협회.

RM ① record management 기록관리.
② Reichsmark 독일의 화폐단위.
③ reinforced masonry 석조건축이나 벽돌건축에 철근콘크리트로 보강하여 내진성(耐震性) 등을 높이는 건축기법.
④ relationship management 거래선 종합관리.
⑤ risk management 위험관리.
⑥ Raw material 원료, 원자재.

R.M. Royal Marines 영국 해병대.

RMA ① random multiple access 임의다중 동시 교신. 한 개의 통신위성을 통하여 몇 개의 국이 동시에 교신하는 것.
② Rice Millers' Association (미) 정미업자 협회.
③ Rubber Manufacturers' Association (미) 고무 제조업자협회.

RMC regional meteorological center 지역기상중추. WWW의 지역별센터.

RMDS report management and distribution system 보고서관리배포시스템. 컴퓨터에 정보를 기억, 관리하여 각종 형식으로 출력할 수 있게 하는 소프트웨어.

RMI radio magnetic indicator 무선(無線) 자방위(磁方位) 지시기. 항공기에 있어서 자기방위와 무선국의 방위를 동시에 표시하는 장치.

RMR relative metabolic rate 에너지 대사율. 작업에만 소요된 에너지량이 기초대사의 몇 배가 되는가를 나타내는 지수.

RMS ① random music sensor 자기가 원하는 곡을 원하는 순서로 자동적으로 재생시킬 수 있는 센서.
② recovery management support (컴퓨터) 회복관리 프로그램. 컴퓨터의 하드웨어의 이상을 검출하고 정상으로 회복시키는 기능을 가진 프로그램.
③ remote manipulator system 원격조작시스템. 스페이스셔틀오비터의 화물, 기기를 내리거나 조립작업을 하는 원격 조작용 암(arm).

Rn radon 라돈. 원자번호 86.

RN registered nurse (미) 정간호사.

R.N. Royal Navy 영국海軍

RNA ribonucleic acid 리보핵산(核酸). DNA의 유전정보를 전사(轉寫)·번역(飜譯)하여 단백질의 합성에 관여하는 생체물질.

RNAF Royal Naval Air Force 영국 해군 항공대. FAA의 옛 명칭.

RNAS Royal Naval Air Service (or Station) 영국 해군 항공기지.

397

RNC ① Republican National Committee (미) 공화당 전국 위원회.
② Royal Naval College 영국 해군 사관 학교.

RNG radio range 무선항로표식.

RNI (프) Rassemblement National des Independants (=National Independent Assembly) (모로코) 독립 국민 연합.

RNZAF Royal New Zealand Air Force 뉴질랜드 공군.

RNZN Royal New Zealand Navy 뉴질랜드 해군.

RO ① receiving office 수리정부. RCT에 의거한 국제출원을 수리한 관청.
② reverse osmosis operation 역삼투. 미세한 물질을 제거하거나 필요성분을 농축하기 위하여 사용되는 방법.

ROA return on assets 한정된 자산으로 어떻게 최대의 이익을 올리는가 하는 경영개념.

ROBECO Rotterdamsch Belegfings Consortium N.V 네덜란드에 있는 유럽최대의 국제 투자 신탁회사.

ROC Republic of China 중화민국 (대만).

ROD refused on delivery 인수 거절(拒絕).

ROE return on equity 자기자본이익률.

ROF Royal Ordnance Factory (영) 왕실 군수 공장.

ROFOR route forecast 항공로 예보.

ROG ① receipt of goods 상품 수령증.
② Rate of Growth 성장률

ROH Royal Opera House (영) (런던의) 왕립 오페라 하우스. 별명 Covent Garden Theatre.

ROI return on investment 투자수익률. 투자액에 대하여 일정기간내의 이익의 비율.

ROIC Return on operating invested Capital 사업용 투자 자본 운용 이익.

ROK Republic of Korea 대한민국.

ROKA ROK Army 한국 육군.

ROKAF ROK Air Force 한국 공군

ROKMC ROK Marine Corps 한국 해병대

ROKN ROK Navy 한국 해군

ROM ① read only memory (컴퓨터) 읽기 전용 기억 장치. 전원이 끊어져도 그 내용이 지워지지 않고 남아 있는 메모리이다.
② return on management 경영 관리 노력의 결과.

ROP run of paper 철판(凸版) 윤전기에 의한 색조(色調).

ROPME Regional Organization for the Protection of Marine Environment 만안해양환경보호기구. 1978년 페르시아만의 오염방지를 위하여 설립.

RO-RO roll on, roll off 짐을 실은 트럭, 대형기계를 그대로 배에 싣거나 내리는 것.

RORSAT radar ocean reconnaissance satellite 레이더해양 정찰 위성.

ROS ① read only storage 판독 전용 기억 장치.
② run of schedule time 광고주가 아니고 방송국측에서 시간을 선택하여 CM을 방송하는 방식.

ROSA rig of safety assessment (원자로) 냉각제 상실 사고 실험 장치.

ROTC Reserve Officers' Training Corps (미) 예비역 장교 훈련단.

ROTHR Relocatable OTH Radar 재배치가능 OTH레이더. OTH-B 레이더의 원리를 이용한 것이며 1600km이상의 탐지거리를 가지고 있고, 폭격기, 순항미사일 및 함정의 행동을 탐지하는 레이더.

ROTR receive only typing reperforator 수신 전용지(紙) 타이프 천공기.

ROV remotely operated vehicle 원격작업기. 무인식의 해중작업장치의 총칭.

ROW right of way 통행권, 교통상의 우선권.

ROY Republic of Yemen 예멘 공화국. 1990년 5월 예멘 아랍 공화국과 예멘 인민 민주공화국이 통합됨.

RP ① Radiopress (일) 라디오 프레스 통신사.
② rallying point 집합점.
③ received pronunciation (영) 용인발음(容認發音). 상류, 지식계급의 사람의 발음.
④ remote processor 원격 처리 장치.
⑤ repurchase agreement 환매 조건부 채권. 채권을 일정기간 후에 일정가격으로 되사는 것을 조건으로 매각하는 것.

RP 화 reproduction parfaite (프) 실물 그대로의 복제화.

RPC remote procedure call 원격 프로시저 호출.

RPE rotating platinum microelectrode 회전 백금 마이크로 전극.

RPG Report Program Generator (컴퓨터) 보고 작성 프로그램.

rph revolutions per hour 매시 회전수. 회전수·주파수의 단위.

RPI ① retail price index 소매 물가 지수.
② row(s) per inch (컴퓨터) 자

r.p.m.

기 테이프의 기록밀도의 단위.

r.p.m. ① resale price maintenance 재판매가격유지.
② revolution per minute 내연기관의 효율을 나타내는 지표의 하나. 1분간의 회전수를 의미한다.

RPO Royal Philharmonic Orchestra (영) 로열 필하모닉 오케스트라.

RPOA recognized private operating agency 국제전기통신업무를 경영할 수 있는 사기업.

RPR (프) Rassemblement pour la Republique (=Assembly for the Republic) (프랑스) 공화국 연합. 정당명.

RPROM reprogrammable read only memory (컴퓨터) 사용자가 스스로 재프로그램 가능한 읽기전용 기억장치.

rps revolutions per second 매초회(전수). 1초당 주기적 현상의 회수.

Rp's repurchase agreements 되사기 약정.

RPS ① reactor protection system 원자로 보호시스템.
② retail price survey 소매물가조사.

RPT [F] Rassemblement du Peuple Togolais (=Togo People's Assembly) (토고 공화국) 토고 인민 연합.

RPV ① reactor pressure vessel 원자로압력용기.
② remotely piloted vehicle 지상으로부터의 전파로 유도되는 무인항공기. 폭격, 정찰에 사용.

RR ① railroad 철도.
② rates of return 수익률.
③ rear engine, rear drive 후기관 후륜구동.
④ Rolls Royce 롤스로이스. 고급 자동차.
⑤ rural route (미) 지방무료 우편 배달 순회로.

RRC ① Road Racing Club (영) 자전거 로드 레이스 클럽.
② Road Runners Club of America 미국 도로 주자 클럽.
③ Royal Red Cross (英) 적십자 훈장. 여성을 위한 군사 공로장.

RRR reduced residual radiation 잔류방사능저감(低減).

RRR 폭탄 reduced residual radiation bomb (미) 잔류 방사선 감소폭탄.

RS ① radio station 무선국
② real storage 실기억장치.
③ record separator (컴퓨터) 레코드 분리를 표현하는 기능 문자.
④ remote sensing 원격탐사.
⑤ Racial Segregation 인종차별.
⑥ Random Sampling 무작위차출.

3R's reading writing, arithmetic 읽기, 쓰기 셈.

RSA Republic of South Africa 남아프리카공화국.

RSC referee stop contest (권투) 시합이 일방적일 때 주심이 중단시키는 시합.

RSD Royal Society of Dublin (영) 왕립 더블린 학사원.

RSE Royal Society of Edinburgh (영) 왕립 에든버러 학사원.

RSH Royal Society for the Promotion of Health (영) 왕립 건강 증진 협회.

RSJ rolled steel joist 형강(形鋼).

RSK (독) Resktor sicherheits-Kommission (=Reactor Safety Commission) (통일 전 서독) 원자로 안전 위원회.

RSL Royal Society of Literature (영) 왕립 문학 협회.

RSMC Regional Special Meteorological Center 지구 특별 기상 센터. WMO의 구상에 의하여 세계의 6개 지구에 설치된 정보 센터.

RSOS range safety operation software 비행안전소프트웨어. 로켓의 현재위치, 낙하 예측점을 계산하여 안전 확인을 하면서 비행을 계속하게 하는 컴퓨터 프로그램.

RSP responder beacon 응답기.

RSPCA Royal Society for the Prevention of Cruelty to Animals (영) 왕립 동물 애호 협회. → SPCA.

RSR route surveillance radar (항공) 항로 수사 레이더.

RSS Rastriya Samachar Samiti (Nepalese Information Agency) (네팔어) 네팔 국영 통신.

RSSF retrievable surface storage facility (원자력) 회수 가능한 지표저장시설.

RSV research safety vehicle 연구 안전차.

RSVP Repondez s'il vous plait (reply, if you please) (프) 회신을 보내주십시오. 초대장의 끝에 출결을 알리도록 부탁하는 약어.

RSWC right side up with care 천지 무용 취급주의.

RT ① radiographic test (원자력) 방사선 투과(透過)시험.
② radio television 라디오와 텔레비전의 동시방송.

RTA ① ready to assemble 조립식.
② reciprocal trade agreement 호혜통상조약.

RTC Recruit Training Center 신병훈련소(新兵訓練所).

RTCC real time computer complex 즉시 처리 컴퓨터 복합체.

RTE real time executive system (컴퓨터) 실시간실행시스템.

RTF (프) La Radio Dffusion et Television Francaise (=French Radio and Television) 프랑스 (라디오 · TV) 방송협회.

RTG radioisotopic thermoelectric generator 원자력 전지.

RTL register transistor logic 저항 트랜지스터 논리(회로).

RTM realtime monitor 실시간 모니터.

RTO railway transportation office (미) 철도수송사무소. 군을 위한 철도수송을 관리하는 기관.

RTOL reduced takeoff and landing 단거리 이착륙(기).

RTS road test simulator 노상 테스트 시뮬레이터.

RTTY ① radioteletype 무선 텔레타이프.
② radio teletype communication 무선 텔레타이프 통신.

RTW ① ready to wear 기성복.
② round the world 세계일주.

RU Rugby Union (英) 럭비 동맹. 아마추어 팀의 연합.

Ru ruthenium 루테늄. 원자번호 44.

RV ① reactor vessel 원자로 용기.
② recreational vehicle 레크리에이션용자동차.

③ reentry vehicle (우주) 재돌입비상체. 대기권외에서 대기권내로 되돌아오는 우주선.

RVLSI restructurable very large scale integrated circuit 재구성 가능한 VLSI.

RVO receiving only earth station 수신전용지상국.

RVR runway visual range 활주로 시거리. 항공기의 이륙시에 활주개시점, 또는 착륙시의 접지점상 5m 높이에서 진행방향을 보았을 때 시인(視認)할 수 있는 거리.

RW ① radiological warfare 방사능전.
② Right Wing [축구] 우측의 선단자.

RWD ① rear wheel drive 후륜구동.
② rewind 테이프 리코더등의 되돌아 감기.

RWM read write memory (컴퓨터) RAM의 별칭.

RWR radar warning receiver 레이더 경보수신기.

RWS Royal Society of Painters in Water Colours (英) 왕립 수채화가 협회.

RWY runway 활주로.

RZSS Royal Zoological Society of Scotland (英) 왕립 스코틀랜드 동물학회.

S ① sulfur 황. 원자번호 16.
② section 課(S-1 = 人事課, S-2 = 정보과, S-3 = 작전과, S-4 = 軍수課)

S. Saturday 토요일
Sunday 일요일.

3S simplification, standardization, specialization 직업방법의 단순화, 부품이나 제품의 표준화, 노동 또는 직장의 전문화. 생산성 향상 운동을 3S 운동이라고 한다.

S secondary wave (지진)횡파(橫)

SA ① Salvation Army 구세군.
② Seventh Avenue 뉴욕시 7번 가. 의복 산업의 대명사로 사용함.
③ shop automation 작업장의 자동화, 생산계획에 따른 설비나 기계의 자동화.
④ social automation 사회의 자동화. 사회생활에 수반하는 각종 자동화.
⑤ store automation 점포자동화.
⑥ system analysis (컴퓨터) 시스템 분석.
⑦ system analyst (컴퓨터) 시스템 분석자.

S/A special agent 특수요원

SAA ① Society of American Archives 미국문서 보존자 협회.
② System Application Architecture 소프트웨어 개발체계 (體系). IBM사가 1986년 발표한 컴퓨터·소프트웨어 기술의 명칭. IBM사는 범용기, 미니컴퓨터, 개인용 컴퓨터별로 기본 소프트웨어를 구축 제공하고 이것을 사용하여 작성한 프로그램은 호환성이 없다. IBM사 제품간에 이러한 문제를 극복하려는 기술이다.

SAAFA Special Arab Aid Fund for Africa 대아프리카 특별 아랍원조기금.

SAARC South Asia Association for Regional Cooperation 남아시아 지역 협력협회.

SABA Saba News Agency (북예멘) 사바통신.

SABC South African Broadcasting Corporation 남아프리카 방송 협회.

SABENA (프) Societe Anonyme Belge d'Exploitation de la Navigation Aerienne (=Sabena Belgian World Airlines) (벨기에) 사베나 벨기에 항공.

SABER Semi Automatic Business

Environment Research 컴퓨터로 여객의 좌석예약, 관리 등을 하는 시스템.

SABIC Saudi Basic Industries Corporation 사우디 기초산업공사.

Sabin vaccine 소아마비 접종약 이름.

SABMIS sea based anti ballistic missile intercept system 해상 함정 탑재 대탄도 미사일·시스템.

SABRE sales and business reservations done electronically 전자적 판매 예약 시스템.

SAC ① Senate Appropriations Committee (미) 상원세출위원회.
② Space Activities Commission (일) 우주개발위원회.
③ Strategic Air Command (미) 전략공군사령부.

SACEUR Supreme Allied Commander, Europe 유럽연합군 최고사령관.

SACU Southern Africa Custom Union 남부아프리카 관세 동맹.

SAD seasonal affective disorder 계절적 정동(情動)장해. 계절이 바뀜에 따라 기분이 심히 변동하여 여러 가지 증세가 나타난다.

SADARM Search Aense and Destroy Armor 스스로 목표를 탐색하여 공격, 격파하는 신세대의 대전차 병기의 하나.

SADCC Southern African Development Coordination Conference 남부 아프리카 개발 조정회의.

SADD Students Against Drunk Driving (미) 음주 운전 방지 학생 연합.

SADM special atomic demolition munition 휴대용 원자폭탄.

SADR Sahara Arab Democratic Republic 사하라 아랍 민주공화당.

SAE self addressed envelope 회신용 봉투.

SAEC Atomic Energy Commission of Sweden 스웨덴 원자력위원회.

SAEF Spacecraft Assembly and Encapsulation Facility (미) 우주선 조립 시설.

SAF structural adjustment facility 구조조정 융자제도.

SAFCA South East Asian Friendship and Culture Association 동남아시아 문화 우호협회.

SAFE[seif] safety and fitness exchange (美) 호신술 교수(敎授)클럽.

SAFISY Space Agency Forum on ISY 우주기관회의.

SAG Screen Actors' Guild (미) 영화 배우 협회.

SAGE semi-automatic ground

environment (미) 반자동식방공관제조직(管制組織). 대공레이더망과 관제센터를 통신회선으로 연결하여 침입하는 비행기나 미사일을 가급적 속히 탐지할 수 있다.

SAH subarachnoid hemorrhage 지주막(蜘蛛膜) 하출혈.

SAIL Shuttle Avionics Integration Laboratory 셔틀 전자 공학 종합 연구실.

SAINT satellite inspector 미국의 인공위성 추적용 비행체.

SAIS School of Advanced International Studies 고등국제문제연구원.

SAL structural adjustment loan 구조조정 차관. 산업구조개편내지 조정을 위하여 IBRD가 제공하는 차관.

S&L saving and loan association (미) 저축대부조합. 주택금융기관.

SALT Strategic Arms Limitation Talks 전략병기제한교섭. 레이건 정부에 의하여 START로 개칭.

SAM ① scanning acoustic microscope 주사초음파 현미경.
② sequential access method (컴퓨터) 순(順) 액세스법. 파일에서 선두에서 순서대로 데이터를 꺼내는 방법.
③ surface to air missile 지대공 미사일.

S&M ① sadism and masochism 사디즘과 마조히즘.
② sadist and masochist ; sado-masochist 가학피학 성애자.

SAMA Saudi Arabia Monetary Agency 사우디아라비아 통화청.

SAMOS ① satellite anti missile observation system 미국의 정찰위성.
② silicon and aluminum metal oxide semiconductor 실리콘·알루미늄 산화금속 반도체.

SAMX surface to air missile X (일) 차기 주력지 대공 미사일.

SANA Syrian Arab News Agency 시리아 국영 통신.

SANE National Committee for a Sane Nuclear Policy (미) 건전 핵정책 전국 위원회.

SAPA South African Press Association 남아프리카 통신사.

SAPI service access point identifier 서비스 접근 포인트 식별자(識別子).

SAR ① Search and Rescue System 수색 구조 시스템. 미국, 영국, 소련, 캐나다의 4개국이 운영, 인공위성을 사용하여 선박, 항공기 등의 구조 활동을 하는 국제적 시스템.
② synthetic aperture radar 합성개구 레이더. 항공기, 인공위성 등에 탑재하여 사용하는 능동형센서, 마이크로파를 대상영역을 향하여 펄스 송신하

여 그의 반사 신호를 일정시간 간격으로 수신하여 대상의 화상정보를 얻을 수 있다.

SARAH search and rescue and homing 수색 구난 자동유도.

SARC South Asia Regional Cooperation 남아시아지역 협력기구.

SARL societe a responsabilite limitee(limited liability company) (프) 주식회사.

SARSAT ① search and rescue satellite 수색구조위성.
② search and rescue satellite aided tracking 수색 구조용 위성 지원 추적 시스템.

SAS ① Scandinavian Airlines System 스칸디나비아 항공.
② slow adjust screw 슬로 조정 나사못.
③ small astronomical satellite (미) 소형 천문 관측위성.
④ space adaptation syndrome 우주부적응 증후군(宇宙不適應症候群).

SASE self addressed stamped envelope 자기앞 반신용 봉투 (封套).

SASR Special Air Service Regiment (영) 대테러특수부대.

SAT ① Scholastic Aptitude Test (미) 대학진학적성시험. 고교생이 대학에 진학을 희망할 때 수험이 요구되는 일반 교양시험.
② static air temperature (항공)

정지대기온도.

SATB soprano, alto, tenor, bass 소프라노, 알토, 테너, 베이스.

SATCOM satellite communications 위성통신.

SAUDIA Saudi Arabian Airlines 사우디항공.

SAVAK Sazemane Attalat Va Anmiyate Keshvar (페르시아어) 국가 치안 정보국. 이란의 비밀 경찰.

SAVE Society of American Value Engineers 아메리카 우수 기술 자협회.

SAW surface acoustic wave 표면 탄성파. 매질의 표면 또는 계면에 따라 전파되는 탄성파.

SAYE save as you earn (영) 급료 공제 예금.

Sb stibium (=antimony) (라) 안티모니. 원자번호 51.

SB ① short bill 단기어음.
② station break 스테이션 브레이크. 방송프로그램 사이의 짧은 시간.
③ store brand 자점(自店)상표.
④ straight bond 고정금리부채권.

S.B. ① sales book 매상장부.
② savings bank 저축은행.
③ small bond 소액채권.

SB -Spot station break spot 라디오나 텔레비전의 프로 사이에 삽

입되는 스폿광고.

SBA Small Business Administration (미) 중소기업청.

SBC ① single board computer 단일기판 컴퓨터. 한 장의 기판상에 장치된 LSI기타부품만으로 컴퓨터로서의 기능을 갖추고 있는 것.
② small business computer 사무용 소형 컴퓨터.

SBIC small business investment company (미) 중소기업투자회사.

SBN Standard Book Number 표준 도서 번호.

SBP strategic Business planning 전략적 사업계획.

SBR styrene butadiene rubber 합성 고무. 타이어, 신발, 상업용품에 이용.

SBS ① Satellite Business System (미) 상업위성통신 회사.
② styrene butadiene styrene

SBT segregated ballast tank (석유 운송선의) 분리 밸러스트 탱크.

SBU strategic business unit 전략적 사업단위. 경영전략의 입장에서 전략적인 관점에서 중요한 사업단위 즉, 금후에 쓸 제품·사업 분야를 말한다.

Sc scandium 스칸듐. 원자번호 21.

SC ① Security Council = UNSC (유엔) 안전보장이사회.
② shopping center 쇼핑센터.
③ super conductor 초전도체.
④ supreme court 최고재판소.

S.C. South Carolina = SC 캐롤라이나 주(州).

SCA shuttle carrier aircraft 셔틀 운반용 항공기.

SCAAP Special Commonwealth African Assistance Plan (영) 연방 아프리카 특별 원조 계획.

SCAD subsonic cruise armed decoy (미) 아음속 순항 무장바람잡이. 대형폭격기에 탑재하여 상대의 대공포화, 지대공미사일의 사정거리 밖에서 발사하는 소형의 무인폭격기.

SCAMA station conferencing and monitoring arrangement 로켓 발사장 모니터 장치.

SCAP Supreme Commander for the Allied Powers 연합군최고사령관.

SCAPA Society for Checking the Abuses of Public Advertising (영) 광고 남용 방지 협회.

SCAPE self-contained atmospheric pressure ensemble (우주공학) 대기압자급시스템.

SCAR Scientific Committee on Antarctic Research 국제 학술 연합 남극 과학 위원회.

SCARA Selective compliance

407

assembly robot arm 수평면 내의 반력에 대하여 강성(剛性)이 낮고 수직 방향의 반력에 대하여 강성이 높은 산업용 로봇.

SCARAB submersible craft assisting repair and burial 수중 케이블 부설용잠수기계정.

SCAT School and College Ability Test (미) ETS가 실시하는 학생 능력테스트.

SCATS sequentially controlled automatic transmitter start (컴퓨터) 정순위 자동 송신 장치.

ScB (라) scientiae baccalaureus (=bachelor of science) 이학사. = BS, BSc, SB

SCC ① sequential control counter (컴퓨터) 축차제어카운터.
② Spacecraft Control Center (NASA의) 우주선 관제 센터.
③ U.S.-Soviet standing consultative commission 미소 상설 협의 위원회.
④ stress corrosion cracking 재료의 부식과 인장응력(弓張應力)과 상승작용에 의한 균열.

SCCA Sports Car Club of America 미국 스포츠카 클럽.

ScD (라)scientiae doctor (=doctor of science) 이학 박사. =DS, DSc, SD

SCE Scottish Certificate of Education 스코틀랜드 보통 교육 수료 증서.

SCFM sintered ceramic friction material 소결(燒結) 합금 마찰 재료.

schiz schizophrenia 정신 분열증.

SCHWR steam cooled heavy water reactor 증기 냉각 중수 원자로.

SCI Service Civil International 국제시민봉사단. 인종, 종교, 정치 신조를 초월하여 인류평화에 봉사하려하는 국제적 운동 단체.

SCID severe combined immune deficiency 중도 복합 면역 부전증.

sci-fi science fiction = SF 공상 과학 소설.

SCI-IVS Service Civil International - International Voluntary Service 국제시민봉사단 · 국제 의용봉사단.

SCLC ① Securities Coordinating Liquidation Committee (미) 증권처리 조정협력 의회.
② Southern Christian Leadership Conference (미) 남부기독교지도자회의. 1968년 암살된 Martin Luther King이 1957년 설립한 흑인차별 철폐 운동단체.

SCM ROK-USA Security Consultative Meeting 한미안보협의회의.

ScM [L] scientiae magister (= master of science) = MS, MSc,

SM 이학 석사.

SCN self contained navigation (NASA의) 자립 항법, 자립항법. 항공기에 항법장치를 탑재하여 자력으로 항행하는 항법.

SCOR Scientific Committee on Oceanic Research (ICSU의) (의) 해양연구과학위원회.

SCORPIO ① Subject Content Oriented Retriever for Processing Information On Line (미) 의회조사국 회화형(會話型) 온라인 정보검색시스템.
② submersible craft for ocean repair, positioning inspection and observation 유색식무인 잠수작업장치. 수중텔레비전, 매니풀레이터, 추진기를 장비, 해저파이프라인, 해양구조물 설치장소의 조사, 해중기기 설치·회수 등을 실시한다.

SCP single cell protein 미생물 단백, 단세포단백. 효모 또는 세균과 같은 단세포에 포함되어 있는 단백을 가축의 사료로 사용하여 간접적으로 또는 단백을 추출 정제하여 직접적으로 사람의 식량으로 이용하려는 단백자원.

SCPC single channel per carrier 하나의 음성채널에 대하여 한 개의 무선반송(搬送)주파수를 할당하는 방식.

SCR silicon controlled rectifier 실리콘제어정류(整流)소자. 교류를 직류로 변환하는 반도체 소자.

SCRAM Scottish Campaign to Resist Atomic Menace 스코틀랜드 반핵(反核)단체.

SCRAP steel, chemical, oil refining, aluminum, pulp 철강·화학·석유정제·알루미늄·펄프. 사양 산업을 열거한 것.

SCS ① silicon controlled switch 실리콘제어 스위치.
② (미) Soil Conservation Service 토양 보전국.

SCSE State Commission for Space Exploration (구소련) 국가 우주탐사 위원회.

SCST State Committee for Science and Technology 소련국가 과학기술위원회.

SCT ① sentence completion technique (심리학) 문장완성법.
② sentence completion test (심리학) 문장완성테스트.

SCUBA self-contained under water breathing apparatus 자급식(自給式) 수중호흡장치.

SCV Sons of Confederate Veterans (미) 남북전쟁 남부군 유가족 단체.

SCX small diameter coaxial cable 세심(細心)동축 케이블.

SD ① safe driver 안전운전자.
② semantic differential 의미해석(意味解釋). 의미의 내용을 객관적, 적량적으로 측정하는

S.D.

　　방법.
　③ sight draft　일람불(一覽拂) 환(換) 어음.
　④ software design　소프트웨어 설계.
　⑤ space development　등가(等價) 교환방식. 지주의 토지에 개발자가 건축하고 건축후 출자율에 따라 건물의 스페이스를 나누는 것.
　⑥ special delivery　속달우편.
　⑦ stage direction　연출.
　⑨ system dynamics　시간과 같이 변화하는 사회시스템의 움직임을 분석하는 방법.

S.D. South Dakota　(미) 사우스 다코타 주(州).

SDA Scottish Development Agency　(영) 스코틀랜드 개발청.

SDAF Special Development Assistance Fund(OAS)　(미주기구) 특별 개발 원조기금.

S.Dak. South Dakota = S.D., SD 사우스 다코타 주(州).

SDC ① submersible decompression chamber　수중 엘리베이터.
　② System Development Corporation　(미) ORBIT에 의한 기술정보서비스기관.

SDCS satellite digital communication system　위성디지털 통신방식.

SDECE Service de Documentation Exterieure et de Contre Espionage　(프) 국외 정보 방첩부. 미국의 CIA에 상당하는 기관.

SDF Self Defence Forces　(일) 자위대.

SDI ① selective dissemination of information　(컴퓨터) 정보선택제공.
　② Strategic Defense Initiative　(미) 전략방위구상. 우주공간에서 미사일을 파괴하는 전략 병기 계획.

SDIO Strategic Defense Initiative Organization　(미) 전략방위 구상국(局).

SDL Specification and Description Language　프로토콜의 그래프 표현형식의 일종.

SDLC synchronous data link control　(컴퓨터) IBM사가 개발한 데이터 통신의 전달 제어 순서.

SDLP Social Democratic and Labor Party　(북아일랜드) 사회민주 노동당.

SDN System Development Network　(한) 국내학술기관과 연구기관을 중심으로 구성된 컴퓨터망.

SDP self-development program　자기 계발 계획.

SDPC shuttle data processing complex　(우주공학) 셔틀데이터 처리 콤플렉스.

SDR special drawing rights

(IMF)의 특별 인출권.

SDS ① Satellite Data System 위성 데이터시스템.
② Special Deposits Scheme 특별예금제도.
③ special discount sale 특별할인판매.
④ submarine desalting system 수중 탈염(脫鹽)장치.

SDV shuttle derived vehicle 제2세대 셔틀, 셔틀파생형 로켓.

Se selenium 셀렌. 원자번호 34.

SE ① sales engineer 판매 담당 기술자.
② sound effects 음향효과.
③ standard english 표준영어.
④ stock exchange 증권거래소.
⑤ system engineer (컴퓨터) 시스템분석이나 시스템 설계를 하는 사람.
⑥ system engineering 시스템공학.

SEA Science and Education Administration (미) 과학 교육 공단.

Seabee Construction Battalion (미 해군 건설대대)의 머리글자 CB의 발음을 단어화한 것.

SEACEN South East Asian Central Banks Group 동남아시아 중앙은행 총재회의.

SEAL Sea, Air and Land Capability (미) 해군 특공대.

Sealab Sea Laboratory (미) 해군의 해저 실험실.

SEALPA South East Asia Lumber Producers' Association 동남아시아 목재생산자 협회.

SEAMEC Southeast Asian Ministers of Education Council 동남아시아 교육 각료 회의.

SEANZA Southeast Asia, New Zealand and Australia 동남아시아, 뉴질랜드, 오스트레일리아 각국 중앙은행 총재회의.

SEASAT Sea Satellite (NASA의) 해양 관측위성.

SEAT [S] Sociedad Espanola de Automoviles De Turismo S.A. 스페인의 자동차 메이커.

SEATO South East Asia Treaty Organization 동남아시아 조약기구.

SEC ① secondary electron conduction 2차전자전도.
② Securities and Exchange Commission (미) 증권 거래 위원회.

SECAM sequence de couleurs avec memoire(color sequence with memory) (프) 프랑스에서 개발된 텔레비전 표준방식.

SECO secondstage engine cut off (로켓) 제2단엔진연소정지.

SECOM ① security communication 안전정보과학.
② SE-COM(주) (일) 일본 경비

보장주식회사.

SECS SEMI Equipment Communications Standard (미) SEMI가 제정한 소프트웨어 표준규격.

SED ① skin erythema dose 피부 홍반 선량(線量).
② Sozialistische Einheitspartei Deutschlands (= German Socialist Unity Party) (독) (통일 전 동독) 사회주의 통일당.

SEDR system effective data rate (컴퓨터) 시스템 실효 데이터율.

SEF steam energy flow 증기 에너지 유량.

SEIU Service Employees' Internation Union 국제 서비스 종업원조합.

SELA Sistema Economico Lationamericano (Latin America Economic System) (스) 중남미 경제기구.

SELBA soundness evaluation of longrange business activities 기업이 일정액이 이익을 확보하기 위하여 수식(數式)을 사용하여 경영계획을 수립하는 것.

SELCAL selective calling system 선택호출방식. 특정 항공기를 부속호출기에 의한 신호로 호출하는 시스템.

SEM ① scanning electron microscope 주사전자현미경.
② space environment monitor 우주환경 모니터.
③ System Engineering Methodology 시스템 공학기법. 미국 공군이 개발.

SEMAL (포) Sociedade Electro Mecanica de Automoveis Lda. 포루투갈의 자동차 메이커.

SEMATECH Semiconductor Manufacturing Technology Institute (미) 관민 공동 반도체 제조 기술 연구조합.

SEMI Semiconductor Equipment and Materials Institute (미) 반도체 제조장치 재료 협회.

Sen Senator (미) 상원의원.

SEP solar electric propulsion 태양 전기 추진. 태양 전기와 전기 추진으로된 시스템.

Sep(t). September 9월.

SEPAC Space Experiments with Particle Accelerators 입자 가속기에 의한 우주과학실험. 인공 오로라계획.

SEP IRA Self Employment Plan Individual Retirement Account 자영업자 은퇴 연금 계획.

SEPP single ended push pull 전원 직렬 푸시 풀.

SER solar energy resources 태양 에너지 자원.

SERI Solar Energy Research Institute (미)태양에너지연구소.

SERT space electronic rocket test 이온 엔진을 사용한 전기추진 로켓 실험기.

SES ① socioeconomic status 사회 경제적 지위.
② surface effect ship 에어 쿠션정(艇). 지면효과를 이용하여 고속으로 수상을 주행하는 호버크라프트함정.

SET Special Excise Tax 특별 소비세.

SETI Search for Extraterrestrial Intelligence 지구외 지적 생물 탐사 계획.

SEV (러) Soviet Ekonomischeskoy Vzaimopomoschchi (=Soviet Council for Mutual Economic Assistance) 동구 경제 상호 원조 회의. COMECON의 러시아어 호칭.

SF ① science fiction (공상)과학소설.
② secured facility 정보안전추출시설.
③ space fantasy 우주에 관한 환상적 이야기.
④ Special Fund 특별기금.
⑤ Speculative fiction 사변(思辨)소설.
⑥ standard floppy disk 표준 플로피 디스크.

SFA Scottish Football Association 스코틀랜드 축구 협회.

SFC ① sound field control 음장(音場)을 자유로 만드는 것. DSP, DAP등의 기기가 있다.
② specific fuel consumption 연료 소비율.

SFD small for dates 태아기에 비해 출산시의 체중이 평균보다 적은 신생아.

SFF Supplementary Financing Facility (IMF의) 보충적 융자제도

SFRC steel fiber reinforced concrete 강(鋼)섬유강화콘크리트.

S.F.R.C. Senate Foreign Relations Committee 미국 상원 외교 위원회

SFU space flyer unit (일) 우주실험 관측 프리 플라이어. HII로켓으로 궤도상에 쏘아 올려 3개월 후에 스페이스셔틀로 회수하는 무인 우주실험실.

SFX ① sound effects 음향효과.
② special effects cinematography (영화, 텔레비전) 특수촬영.

SG ① Secretary General 사무국장.
② specific gravity 비중.
③ steam generator 증기발생기.
④ Surgeon General 군의총감.
⑤ security guard 경비보초.

S.G. Secretary General (of the United Nations) 유엔사무총장.

SGA ① second generation acrylic adhesive 제2세대 아크릴접착제.
② Special Session of the

General Assembly (유엔) 특별총회.

SGDG (프) sans garantic du gouvernement (=patent issued without government guarantee) 정부의 보증이 없는 특허.

SGEMP system generated electromagnetic pulse 시스템 내부 발생형, 전자 펄스.

SGHWR steam generating heavy water reactor 증기 발생중수 원자로.

SGR sodium graphite reactor 흑연을 감속제로하고 나트륨을 냉각제도 한 원자로.

SH system house 소프트웨어시스템의 수주, 생산, 개발을 하는 회사.

SHA sidereal hour angle (천문) 항성시각(恒星時角).

SHAPE Supreme Headquarters, Allied Powers in Europe 유럽 연합군 최고사령부.

SHED solar heat exchange drive (우주공학) 태양열교환추진. 태양열을 이용하여 우주선을 추진시키는 방법.

SHF super high frequency 극초단파(極超短波), 마이크로파.

Shiite 시이아파(회교의 한 파).

SHIPNETS Shipping Cargo Information Network System (일) 항만화물정보네트워크 · 시스템.

SHM ① ship's heading marker 선수(船首) 마커.
② simple harmonic motion 조화(調和) 운동.

SHORAN short range navigation 자위치(自位置) 측정 장치.

SHP shaft horsepower 축마력.

SHR spontaneous hypertensive rat 자연발병 고혈압 래트.

SHT solution heat treatment (원자력) 용체화(容體化) 열처리. 강(鋼)의 합금성분을 고용체(固容體)로 용해하는 온도이상으로 가열하여 충분히 시간을 보지하고 급냉하여 그의 석출을 저지하는 조작.

SHX submarine helicopter X (일) 차기 대잠수함초계 헬리콥터.

Si silicon 실리콘. 원자번호 14.

SI ① Smithsonian Institution (미) 스미스소니언연구소.
② social indicator 사회 지표. 복지 수준을 측정하는 지표.
③ Socialist International 사회주의 인터내셔널, 국제 사회주의 연맹.
④ Software Initiative (미) 소프트웨어주도. 미국이 소프트웨어 생산성에서 세계의 주도권을 장악하는 것을 목적으로 한 소프트웨어 개발 지원 계획.
⑤ System International d'Unites (프) 국제단위계. 국제도량형총회에서 정한 단위계.

⑥ system integrator 복잡한 대규모의 정보시스템의 기획에서 시스템 운용 개시까지를 일괄하여 청부하는 시스템 개발 서비스.

SIA ① Securities Industry Association (미) 증권업 협회.
② Semiconductor Industry Association (미) 반도체 공업회.
③ Singapore Airlines 싱가포르 항공.

SIAD Society of Industrial Artists and Designers (미) 산업미술·디자이너협회.

SIAM ① Society for Industrial and Applied Mathematics (영) 산업수학·응용 수학회.
② Self initiated Antiaircraft Munition 자동발사 다목적 대공 미사일.

SIAP Statistical Institute for Asia and the Pacitic (유엔) 아시아태평양 통계연구소).

SIBOR Singapore Inter Bank Offered Rate 싱가포르 금융시장에서 은행간 거래에 적용되는 금리.

SIC ① silicon carbonite 탄화규소.
② specific inductive capacity 비유전율(比誘電率)
③ standard industrial classification 표준 산업 분류.

SICBM small ICBM 소형 대륙간 탄도 미사일.

SIDA Swedish International Development Authority 스웨덴 국제 개발청.

SIDS sudden infant death syndrome 유아(乳兒) 돌연사 증후군(症候群).

SIEF Societe Internationale d'Ethnographie et de Folkore (프) 국제민족학·민속학회.

SIF selective identification feature system 선택 식별 장치. 펄스전파에 의한 항공기의 식별장치.

SIG Working Group on Search Information (WIPO의) 서치 정보에 관한 작업오일.

SIGGRAPH Special Interest Group on Computer Graphics (미) 계산기학외의 컴퓨터 그래픽스 분과회.

SIGINT Signals Intelligence (미) 군사 통신 탐자 위성.

SIGMA Software Industrialized Generator and Maintenance Aids 시그마 계획. 미국보다 열세에 있는 소프트웨어 산업을 만회하려는 일본 통산성의 계획.

SIGMET significant meteorology 악천후.

SIGPLAN Special Interest Group on Programming Languages (미 컴퓨터) 프로그램 언어에 관한 특별 이해(利害) 관계자 단체.

SII structural impediments initiative 일미구조문제협의. 일미간의 무역불균형을 시정하기 위하여 양국의 경제구조에 관하여 토의하기 위하여 1989년 9월에 동경에서 열린 협의.

SIIS Shanghai Institute for International Studies 상해국제문제연구소.

SIL speech interference level 회화 방해 레벨.

SIM simultaneous interpretation method 동시통역방식.

SIMD single instruction stream multiple data stream (컴퓨터) 단일명령다중데이터처리.

SIMEX Singapore International Monetary Exchange 싱가포르 국제금융거래소.

SIMS ① secondary ion mass spectrometry 2차이온 질량분석.
② standards information management system 규격에 관한 종합적 정보관리시스템.

SIMSCRIPT simulation scriptor (컴퓨터) RAND사가 개발한 범용 시뮬레이션언어.

SIMULA Simulation Language (컴퓨터) 시뮬레이션용으로 개발한 언어.

SINK single income no kids 한사람(남편이든 부인이든)만이 벌고 어린이가 없는 부부.

SINS ship inertial navigation system 관성항법(慣性航法).

SIO ① serial input output 직렬 입출력.
② start I/O 입출력개시명령.

SIOP Single Integrated Operation Plan (미) 단일통합작전계획. 핵전쟁을 위한 최고 작전계획.

SIPC Securities Investor Protection Corporation (미) 증권 투자자 보호 기관.

SIPRI Stockholm International Peace Research Institute 스톡홀름 국제평화문제 연구소.

SIR ① selective information retrieval (컴퓨터) 선택적 정보 검색.
② semantic information retrieval 의미론(意味論)적 정보검색 시스템.
③ styrene isoprene rubber 합성고무.
④ submarine intermediate reactor 잠수함 탑재 중속(中速) 중성자로.

SIRA Scientific Instrument Research Association (英) 과학기기 연구협회.

SIRIUS scientific information retrieval and integrate utilization system ISAS가 과학위성으로 관측한 데이터를 통일적으로 축적, 관리하기 위한 데이터 베이스 시스템.

SIRS satellite infrared spectro-

meter 외성적외분광계.
SIS ① safety injection system (원자로) 안전주입시스템.
② satellite interceptor system 위성요격시스템.
③ Secret Intelligence Service (영) 비밀정보국.
④ strategic information system 전략적 정보시스템. 컴퓨터를 비롯하여 고도정보기술을 기업전략에 적극적으로 활용하는 것.
⑤ Scientific Intelligence Survey 과학정보조사원

SIT ① special interest travel 특정 목적 여행. 해외어학 연수여행 등과 같이 확실한 목적이나 대상을 가진 여행.
② static induction transistor 정전(靜電) 유도 트랜지스터.

SITA Societe Internationale de Telecommunications Aero nautiques (International Aeronautical Telecommunications Society) 국제 항공 통신 협동 조합.

SITC Standard International Trade Classification 표준 국제 무역 분류.

SITCOM situation comedy (텔레비전의) 연속 코메디.

SITIC static induction transistor IC 저전류 영역에서도 고속 동작하는 특징을 이용한 고속 동작의 집적회로.

SIU Seafarers' International Union of North America 북미해원(海員) 국제 조합.

SJAC Society of Japanese Aerospace Companies, Inc. 일본 항공 우주 공업회.

SJAE steam jet air ejector (원자력) 증기식 공기 추출기.

SJC supreme judicial court (미) 주(州) 최고재판소.

SK Saskarchewan (캐나다) 서스캐처원 주(州).

SKB standard key board 표준 키보드.

SKF (스웨덴어) Svenska Kullagerfabriken 스웨덴의 볼베어링(ball bearing) 제조 회사.

SL ① salvage loss (해상보험)구조손.
② sea level 해면고도 항공기의 성능을 표시할 때 고도를 표시하는 약호(略號)로서 사용함.
③ steam locomotive 증기관차.
④ Shelf Life 유효저장 기간.

SLA ① Special Libraries Association (미) 전용 도서관 협회.
② Symbionese Liberation Army 심바이오니즈 해방군. 미국의 과격파 조직.

SLAC Stanford Linear Acceleration Center (미) 스탠퍼드 선형 가속기센터.

SLAM scanning laser acoustic

microscope 레이저주사 초음파 현미경.

SLAN sine, loco, anno, nominee (라) 장소, 연대 또는 저자명의 기재없이.

SLAR side looking aerial radar 기상측시(側視)레이더. 지형영상을 얻기 위한 레이더.

SLB Siberia Land Bridge 시베리아 철도에 의한 화물 수송.

SLBM submarine launched ballistic missile 잠수함 발사탄도 미사일.

SLB Service Siberia Land Bridge Service 극동에서 시베리아 대륙을 경유, 유럽지역으로 수송하는 해륙복합수송 형태를 말함.

SLC submarine laser communication 잠수함 레이저 통신.

SLCM ① sea launched cruise missile 해상 발사 순항 미사일. 함정에서 발사한다.
② submarine launched cruise missile 해중 발사 순항 미사일. 잠수함에서 발사한다.

SLCSAT submarine laser communication satellite 잠수함레이저 통신위성.

SLE systemic lupus erythematosus (의학) 전신(성) 에리테마토수스. 전신 홍반성(紅斑性) 낭창(狼瘡).

SLEP Service Life Extension Program (미 해군) 군함 인명 구조 계획.

SLF shuttle landing facility 셔틀 착륙 지원 시설.

SLFP Sri Lanka Freedom Party 스리랑카 자유당.

SLIS shared laboratory information system 임상검사실 공동 정보시스템.

SLL Southern Limit Line 남방 한계선.

SLLL synchronous line, low load 저부하(低負荷) 동기(同期)용 회선 접속 기구.

SLM sea launched missile 해상발사 미사일.

SL-MATH subroutine library mathematics 수치계산 라이브러리. IBM사의 소프트웨어.

SLOC sea lanes of communication 유사시(有事時) 해상연락 교통로. 유사시 국가가 생존상 또는 전쟁에서 확보하지 않으면 안 되는 해상 연락 교통로.

SLOOC Seoul Olympic Organizing Committee 서울 올림픽 조직위원회.

SLOP smog, litter, over population, pollution 스모그, 쓰레기, 과잉인구, 오염. 공해의 4대 요소.

SLOT seems like old time 옛날이 그리운 것.

SLP ① (라) sine legitima prole (= without lawful issue) 합법적인 자손이 없는.
② Socialist Labor Party (미) 사회주의 노동당. 877년 결성.
③ super long play 초 LP.

SLR ① satellite laser ranging 위성 레이저측거(測距). 1000km 이상 떨어진 두 지점에서 레이저 광선을 발사하여 인공위성으로부터의 반사 시간을 측정함으로 두 지점의 거리를 측정하는 방법.
② single lens reflex 일안(一眼) 리플렉스 카메라.

SLS space lab simulator 스페이스 랩 시뮬레이터. 우주 비행사 훈련용.

SLSI supper large scale integration 초대규모집적회로.

SLT ① shuttle and loop transit NASA의 셔틀·루프소송. 운행간격이 짧고 단순한 왕복 또는 순환운행을 하는 궤도 수송 시스템.
② single lane transit 자동운전의 궤도 셔틀버스.
③ solid logic technology (컴퓨터) 고체 논리 기술.

SLV satellite launching vehicle 위성 발사용 로켓.

Sm samarium 사마륨. 원자번호 62.

SM ① sadism and masochism 새디즘과 매저키즘.
② semi mat 사진용 인화지의 반광택.
③ service module (달우주선의) 기계선.
④ standard missile (미해군) 함정 방위용 최신장비 표준 미사일.
⑤ strategic missile 전략미사일.
⑥ styrene monomer 폴리스틸렌수지, 합성고무에 사용된다.
⑦ super market 슈퍼마켓.
⑧ synchronous motor 동기전동기.
⑨ systems management (우주공학) 시스템관리.

SMA ① superplastic metal alloy 형상기억합금.
② synthetic milk adapted 모유화(母乳化) 밀크.

SMART Space Maintenance and Repair Techniques (미) 우주보급정비계획.

SMATV satellite master antenna television 방송위성으로부터의 텔레비전 프로그램을 공동 안테나로 수신하여 가입자에게 보내는 방식.

SMAW shield metal arc welding (원자로) 피복 금속 아크 용접.

SMC ① standard mean chord (항공기) 기하 평균 익현(翼弦).
② Safety Management System 안전관리체제

SMD symbol manipulation device

SME

심볼 조작 장치. 컴퓨터의 별칭.

SME stochastic macroeconomics 확률론적 마크로 경제학.

SMF system management facility 시스템 관리기능. 컴퓨터 시스템 내에 각종 사상(事象)을 기록, 관리하는 기능을 가진 프로그램.

SMFM sintered metal friction material 소결(燒結) 합금계 브레이크 재료.

SMG Stroke Mandeville Games 중증신체 장애자 스포츠대회. 통칭 패럴림픽.

SMI systems measurement instrument 시스템 측정 기기.

SMIC Societe Internationale pour la Musique Contemporaine (International Society for Contemporary Music) (프) 국제현대음악협회.

SMIPC Small Industry Promotion Corporation (한) 중소기업 진흥공단

SMIRT Structural Mechanics in Reactor Technology 국제원자로 구조 역학회의.

SML Securities Market Line 증권시장선.

SMM solar maximum mission 태양 관측 위성.

SMMP standard method measuring performance 성능 측정 표준 방법.

SMMT Society of Motor Manufacturers and Traders (영) 자동차 제조 판매 협회.

SMON subacute myelo optico neuropathy 스몬병(아급성 척수시신경 말초 신경증).

SMPTE Society of Motion Picture and Television Engineers (미) 영화·기술자 협회.

SMRT Scheduling Management and Allocating Resources Technique 프로제작에 필요한 시설, 기재, 요원이 자동적으로 할당되는 시스템. 1969년 NHK가 개발.

SMS ① stationary meteorological satellite 정지 기상 위성. ② stationary (synchronous) meteorological satellite 정지(동기형) 기상위성. 태풍이나 폭풍우를 연속적으로 관측하여 30분마다 기상사진을 보내온다.

SMSA standard metropolitan statistical area (미) 표준대도시 지구. 통계의 단위. 수도 워싱턴과 볼티모어를 하나의 도시권으로 취급한 것.

SMSG School Mathematics Study Group (美) 학교 수학 연구회. 1957년 구소련이 세계 최초의 인공위성 발사에 성공했을 때 미국의 지배층들이 그 사실을 위기로 받아 들여 기존 학교 교육에 대한

전면 재검토를 실시하여 그 일환으로 SMSG가 발족하고 수학 교육의 현대화 운동이 일어남.

SMTAS shuttle model test and analysis system 셔틀 모델 시험 해석 시스템.

SMV slow moving vehicle 움직임이 느린 차.

SMW Sheet Metal Workers' International Association (미) 판금공 국제 조합.

SN scope note 주기(注記).

Sn stannum (=tin) (라) 주석. 원자번호 50.

SN service number 軍番 ; serial number 連番號.

S/N ① Shipping note 선적통지.
② signal to noise ration = SNR 신호대 잡음비.

SNA ① System Network Architecture (미) IBM사가 개발한 통신체계.
② System of National Accounts (유엔) 국민소득계산 방식. 기업회계 원리를 응용하여 국민소득 통계의 국제적 통일을 도모하는 것.

SNAP system for nuclear auxiliary power (미) 원자력보조전원. 소형 원자력 발전 장치.

SNC Satellite News Channel (미) 통신위성을 이용한 24시간 텔레비전·뉴스·서비스.

SNCC The Student Nonviolent Coordinating Committee 학생 비폭력 조정 위원회(민권운동 단체).

SNCF (프) Societe Nationale des Chemins de Fer Francais (= National Railway Company of France) 프랑스 국유 철도.

SNEA (프) Societe Nationale Elf Aquitaine 프랑스 국영 석유회사.

SNF short range nuclear forces 단거리 핵전력.

SNG ① satellite news gathering 통신위성을 이용한 텔레비전 중계방송.
② synthetic(or substitute) natural gas 합성천연가스. 석탄의 가스화에 의하여 제조함.

SNM special nuclear material 특정 핵물질.

SNOBOL String Oriented Symbolic Language (컴퓨터) 문자열을 취급하기 위해 만들어진 프로그램 언어의 일종.

SNP Scottish National Party 스코틀랜드 국민당.

SNR signal to noise ratio 신호대 잡음비. 녹음기 등의 성능을 나타내는 잡음 매개 변수비(雜音媒介變數比).

SNU Seoul National University (한) 서울대학교.

SO ① satellite office 출장소.
② staff officer 참모장교.

③ symphony orchestra 교향악단.

S/O Shipping Order 선적 지시서.

SOAP spectrochrmical oil analysis program (미 공군) 윤활유 분광 분석 프로그램.

s.o.b. son of a bitch (미 속어) 개자식, 후레자식. bitch는 [암캐]이지만, 15세기경부터 [음란한 여자]라는 의미로 사용되면서 son of a bitch는 상대를 천하게 비난하는 말이 되었다. 제1차 대전 때 미병사가 [빌어먹을]과 같은 감탄사로 많이 사용하였다.

SOB ① son of the boss 사장의 아들. 사업의 후계자로서의 2세를 말함.
② strap on booster 발사로켓의 제1단 보조로켓.

SOC ① social overhead capital 간접사회자본.
② space Operations Center (미) 유인 우주 스테이션.

SOCAP Society of Consumers Affairs Professionals in Business (미) 기업내 소비자 문제 전문가 회의.

SOCC satellite operation control center (미) 위성 운용 관리 센터.

SOCONY Standard Oil Company of New York (미) 뉴욕 스탠더드 석유 회사.

SOED The Shorter Oxford English Dictionary 옥스퍼드 영어 사전.

SOF ① sound on film 음성이 들어있는 선전용 텔레비전 필름.
② Special Operation Force (미) 특수작전부대. 미국이 제3세계에 발생하는 테러, 폭동, 내란 등을 방지하기 위하여 소규모의 특수임무부대.

SOFA Status of Forces Agreement in Korea 한미 행정 협정.

SOFAR Sound Fixing and Ranging (미해군) 조난 항공기나 선박의 위치를 조사하기 위한 수중 측음(側音)장치.

SOHC single overhead camshaft 싱글 오버헤드 캠샤프트. 실린더마다 흡·배기 밸브가 각 1개씩 달려 있는 엔진구조.

SOHO South of Houston Street 뉴욕시 맨하턴 도(島) 남부 지구로서 전위적인 예술가·음악가·영화인 등이 모이는 곳.

SOI ① silicon on insulator 절연기판위의 실리콘. 실리콘단 결정의 웨이퍼를 사용한 반도체.
② Southern Oscillation Index 남방(南方) 진동지수. 적도서태평양과 적도동태평양의 지상기압은 해수온의 변화가 원인이 되어 시소와 같이 진동하며 이것을 남방진동이라고 한다. 타이티와 다윈의 기압차를 남방진동지수라고 한다.

SOI - substrate Silicon on Insulating - substrate 스피넬이나 사파이어 등의 절연체 결정기판 위에 실리콘의 집적회로를 만든 소자.

SOLAS International Convention for the Safety of Life at Sea 해상에 있어 인명안전을 위한 국제조약.

SOM ① sexually open marriage 부부가 자유로 애인을 만들고 부부는 서로 사랑하는 결혼. ② Senior Officials Meeting 고위 실무자회의.

SOMPA System of Multicultural Pluralistic Assessment (미) 문화적 요인에 의한 편향을 배제한 어린이의 지능 평가법.

SOMS shuttle orbiter medical system 오비터 승무원용 약상자. A형(단기·경증용)과 B형 (장기·중증용)의 두 종류가 있다.

SONAR sound navigation and ranging 수중음향탐지기.

SONNA Somali National News Agency 국영 소말리아 통신.

SOP ① standard(or standing) operating procedure 표준작업규정. 조직의 목적을 다수인원으로 달성하기 위하여 필요한 각자의 맡은 일의 수준을 표준적으로 규정한 것. ② study organization plan (컴퓨터) 연구조직계획. 시스템의 검토·설계의 수법.

SOPECAM (프) Societe de Presse et d'Edition du Cameroun (= Cameroon Press and Publishing Co.) 카메룬 통신.

SOR synchrotron orbital radiation =SR 싱크로트론 방사광. 싱크로트론이란 원형가속기를 말한다.

SORTMICS Sunlit On line Real-time Total Management Information Control System 선라이트 산업의 사내(社內) 전국 온라인 시스템.

SORTO Seoul Olympic Radio and Television Operations 서울 올림픽 방송 운영 본부.

SOS ① 1908년에 제정된 국제 무선 조난신호. save our souls, save our ship, stop other signals, suspend other service 등의 약자라고 하는 것은 속설이며 문자자체에는 의미가 없다. ② Secure Operating System 미국의 DOD에서 연구 개발된 컴퓨터 안전 대책을 위한 OS. ③ silicon on sapphire 사파이어 기판상에 기상화학반응에 의하여 실리콘단 결정을 성장시킨 반도체. ④ sound on sound 독립하여 녹음 재생할 수 있는 2채널 이상의 테이프 리코더에 의하여 재생 음에 다른 음을 겹쳐서 녹음 채널에 녹음하는 것. ⑤ sound over sound 2중 녹음.

SOSUS sound surveillance system (미) 음향감시시스템. 미국 해군이 잠수함 탐지를 위하여 해양에 배치한 음향감시시스템.

SOW Special Operations Wing (미 공군) 긴급 하이테크 공수부대.

Sp. Spain ; Spaniard ; Spanish

SP ① sales promotion 판매촉진.
② Security Police (일) 요인 호위관.
③ Shore patrol 미해군 헌병대.
④ short program 프리 스케이팅 종목의 하나.
⑤ space character (컴퓨터) 간격문자.
⑥ space platform 우주플랫폼.
⑦ Standard & Poor's Corp. 미국의 주가조사회사.
⑧ standard playing record 1분간 78회전의 레코드.
⑨ structured programming (컴퓨터) 구조화 프로그래밍.
⑩ sulphite pulp 아황산펄프.
⑪ supply point 보급소.

SpA (이) Societa per Azioni (= incorporated joint stock company) 주식회사.

SPA Saudi Press Agency 사우디아라비아 국영 통신.

SPAAG self propelled anti aircraft gun 대공(對空) 자주포(自走砲).

SPACE Society for Private and Commercial Earth Station (미) 개인·상업용 지상위성 수신 스테이션 협회.

SPAD soil & plant analyzer development (일) 토양·작 물체 분석기기 개발사업. 토양·작물의 영양 진단 용기기 개발사업.

SPADATS Space Detection and Tracking System 우주탐지추적시스템. NORAD소속.

SPADOC Space Defence Operation Center (미) 우주방위 작전센터.

SPAR (라) semper paratus (= always ready) (미) 연안 경비모토.

SPATG self propelled anti tank gun 대전차(對戰車) 자주포(自走砲).

SPB still picture broadcasting 정지 화상 방송.

SPC ① self polishing copolymers 자기 연마형 공중합체(自己研磨型共重合體). 방오(防汚)도료.
② Solar Power Cruiser 태양전지 발전차. 임시 전원.
③ South Pacific Commission 남태평양 위원회.
④ stored program control (컴퓨터) 내장 프로그램 제어.
⑤ Suicide Prevention Center (미) 자살방지센터.

SPCA Society for Prevention of Cruelty to Animals (미) 동물학대 방지협회.

SPCC ① Society for Prevention of Cruelty to Children (미) 아동학대 방지 협회.
② speech path common controller 디지털교환기.

SPCK Society for Promoting Christian Knowledge (영) 그리스도교 지식 보급회.

SPD supplementary petroleum duty 추가석유세.

SPDPM Subcommission on Prevention of Discrimination and Protection of Minorities (유엔) 차별방지·소수민족보호소위원회.

SPDT single pole double throw 단극(單極) 쌍투접점(雙投接點).

SPE Society for Pure English 영어 순화 협회.

SPEC ① South Pacific Bureau for Economic Cooperation 남태평양 경제 협력국.
② specification 명세서, 시방서.
③ specimen 견본, 표본.
④ speech predictive encoded communications 음성예측부호통신.
⑤ Symposium on Pacific Energy Cooperation 태평양 에너지 협력회의.

SPECT single photon emission CT 단광자 방사 단층 촬영.

SPEEDI system for prediction of environmental emergency dose information 긴급시 환경 선량 (線量) 정보 예측 시스템.

SPF ① Software Protection Fund (미) 소프트웨어 보호기금.
② South Pacific Forum 남태평양 제국회의.
③ System Productivity Facility 시스템 생산성 향상기능.
④ Sun Protection Factor 자외선 차단지수.

SPG ski paraglider 이 착륙시에 스키를 사용하는 패러글라이더.

SPH ① self propelled howitzer 자주(自走) 유탄포.
② standard public housing 표준형 주택.

SPI surface position indicator (우주공학) 지표면 위치 지시계.

SPIDER Subroutine Package for Image Data Enhancement and Recognition 화상처리의 대표적인 알고리즘을 수록한 소프트웨어.

SPIDPO Shuttle Payload Integration and Development Program Office (미) 셔틀 페이로드 조정 개발 계획국.

SPIN ① Searchable Physics Information Notes 물리학 문헌정보 데이터베이스.
② situation, problem, implication, needpay off 상황, 문제, 시시, 해결. 판매원이 손님에게 물건을 권할 때의 질문하는 방법.

SPK (캄보디아어) Saporamean

425

Kampuchea (=Kampuchea Information Agency) 캄보디아 인민공화국 국영 통신.

SPL sound pressure level 음압(音壓) 레벨.

SPLA Sudan People's Liberation Army 수단 인민 해방군.

SPM suspended particulate matter 부유 입자상물질. 입경(粒徑)이 10마이크론 이하의 대기중에 부유하고 있는 입자상 물질.

SPO (독) Sozialistische Partei Osterreichs (=Socialist Party of Austria) 오스트리아 사회당.

SPOC Seoul Paralympic Organizing Committee 서울 장애자 올림픽조직위원회.

SPOE (스) Partido Socialista Obrero Espanol (=Spanish Socialist Labor Party) (스페인) 사회 노동당.

SPOOL simultaneous peripheral operation on line (컴퓨터) 복수 프로그램 동시처리.

SPOT satellite positioning and tracking 인공위성발견추적.

SPQR small profits and quick returns 박리다매.

SPR ① Society for Physical Research (英) 물리 연구 협회.
② Society for Psychophysiological Research (美) 정신생리학 연구 협회.

SPRFA South Pacific Regional Fishing Agency 남태평양 지역 어업기관.

SPS ① service propulsion system 우주선의 궤도 수정용 로켓.
② solar power satellite 우주공간에서의 태양광발전.
③ super proton synchrotron 초대형 양자 가속기.

SPST single pole single throw 단극 단추 접전(單極單投接點).

SQ square 광장.

SQC statistical quality control 통계적 품질관리.

SQG Working Group on the Special Questions WIPO의 특별 문제에 관한 작업부회.

SQUID superconducting quantum interference device 초전도 양자(量子)간섭소자. 자장(磁場)의 강도를 최소의 단위(양자단위 · 量子單位)로 측정할 수 있는 전자소자.

Sr strontium 스트론튬. 원자번호 38.

Sr. Senior 상급자, 연장자, 경력자

SR ① scanning radiometer 주사 방사계(計).
② strategic reconnaissance 전략정찰. 미국의 전략정찰기.
③ synchrotron radiation = SOR 싱크로트론방사광.
④ synthetic rubber 합성고무.

S.R. ship's receipt 화물 수취증.

SR&CC strike, riot and civil commotion = SRCC (보험) 동맹 파업, 소요 및 폭동.

SRAM ① short range attack missile 단거리 공격 미사일. ② static random access memory S램. 충전 없이도 일정기간 기억내용이 지워지지 않는다.

SRB solid rocket booster (우주공학) 고체연료로켓·부스터. 스페이스셔틀을 발사 후, 주엔진을 보조하고 상승시의 추진을 증강하는 두 개의 구체 추진제(推進劑)로켓.

SRBM short range ballistic missile 단사정거리 탄도미사일. 사정거리 800km 이하.

SRC ① solvent refined coal 무기 황화합물을 촉매로 하여 액화한 석탄. ② steel reinforced concrete 철골 철근 콘크리트.

SRCC Risks Strikes, Riots, Civil Commotions Risks (해상보험) 동맹파업, 태업, 쟁의, 폭동, 정치 또는 사회적 요소로 발생되는 손해에 대해서는 보험회사가 책임을 지지 않는 것, 적정한 추가 보험료를 납부함으로써 이로 인한 손해를 보상받을 수 있다.

SRE surveillance radar element 감시 레이더부(部).

SRI International Stanford Research Institute International (미) 스탠퍼드 국제연구소.

SRINF Short Range INF 사정거리 500~1000km의 INF.

SRM solid rocket motor 고체 추진제 로켓 모터.

SRN state registered nurse (英) 정(正)간호사.

SRO ① single room occupancy hotel (미) 노령자나 부랑자가 시의 보조로 장기 체류할 수 있는 뉴욕의 호텔. ② standing room only 입견석 이외 만원.

SRP ① sealift readiness program 긴급 해상 수송 계획. ② state registered physiotherapist (英) 공인 물리 요법사.

SRS ① seat reservation subsystem 좌석예약시스템. ② Statistical Reporting Service (미) (농무성) 통계 보고국.

SRT Special Representative for Trade Negotiations 대통령 통상교섭 특별대표부.

SRTNF short range tactical nuclear force 단거리 전술 핵 미사일.

SRV space rescue vehicle 우주 구조 장치.

SS ① secret service 첩보기관. ② service station 주유소. ③ ship submarine 잠수함.

④ speed sensitive 흑백필름의 감도를 표시하는 계수의 하나.
⑤ steamship 기선.
⑥ surface to surface 소련의 지대지 미사일에 붙인 NATO 의 기
⑦ surveillance station 방공 감시소.
⑧ suspended sentence 집행유예
⑨ suspended solid 물속의 불용성 부유 물질.
⑩ substitute securities 대용증권

SS20 소련의 중거리 탄도미사일.

SSA ① security supporting aid (미) 안전보장확보를 위한 원조.
② Social Security Administration (미) 사회보장국.

SSAFA Soldiers', Sailors' and Airmen's Families Association (英) 국인 가족회.

SSAT Secondary School Admissions Test (미) 중등학교 입학 검정시험.

SSB ① conventional powered ballistic missile submarine 탄도미사일 탑재 통상 추진형 잠수함.
② single side band 단측파(單側波). 장거리 전화에 사용한다.

SSBC sinking, stranding, burning, collision 침몰, 좌초, 화재, 충돌의 약자이다. 해상 고유의 위험을 표현하는 단어이며 주요 해상사고라 부른다.

SSBN nuclear powered fleet ballistic missile submarine 탄도미사일 적재 원자력 잠수함.

SSC ① semi submerged catamaran 반 몰수형쌍동선. 바다가 거칠어도 안정성이 높은 것이 특징.
② shield storage cask, 고레벨 방사성 폐기물의 수용용기.
③ small savers' certificate (미) 소액 저축자 정기 예금 증서.
④ super conducting super collider 차기(次期)대형입자 가속기.

SSCAE Special senate Committee on Atomic Energy (미) 상원 원자력 특별 위원회

SSD ① solid state storage device 고체기억장치.
② Special Session of the United Nations General Assembly on Disarmament 유엔 군축 특별 총회.
③ super Schottky diode 반도체와 초전도체를 접촉시켜 만든 다이오드.

SSDDS self service discount department store 셀프 서비스식 염가 백화점.

SSDS ① self service department store 셀프 서비스 백화점.
② Supplementary Special Deposits Scheme 추가적 특별 예금제도.
③ System of social and demo-

graphic statistics 사회 인구 통계 체계.

SSE ① supply side economics 수요면보다 공급면을 중시하는 경제정책.
② Sydney Stock Exchange 시드니 증권거래소.
③ synthetic secondary effluent 합성2차 처리수(處理水).

S.Sgt. Staff Sergeant 下士.

SSGW strategic surface to surface guided weapon system 전략 지대지 유도병기시스템.

SSI ① small scale integration 소규모 집적회로. 1팁상의 소자 수가 100개 이하의 IC.
② Space Services Inc. of America 미국 우주 서비스 회사. 로켓 발사를 대행하는 민간 회사.

SSIC small scale integrated circuit 소규모 직접 회로.

SSM ① super supermarket 종합 식료품, 생활관련 용품을 판매하는 슈퍼마켓.
② surface to surface missile 지대지 미사일, 함대함 미사일.

SSME space shuttle main engine 스페이스 셔틀의 주엔진.

SSMI Surface to Surface Missile (일) 지대함 유도탄.

SSN ① ship submarine nuclear 원자력 잠수함.
② severely sub normal 대단히 지능이 낮은.
③ Social Security Number (미) 사회 보장 복지 번호.

SSO structure, sequence, organization 구조, 순서, 구성. 저작권 · 지적소유권에 관련하여 사용되며 권리침해의 판단에 중요하다.

SSP static spontaneous potential 정적(靜的) 자연 전위.

SSPE subacute sclerosing panencephalitis (의학) 급성 경화성전뇌염.

SSR solid state record 고체 레코드. 장래출현이 예상되는 등의 반도체 기억소자에 의한 녹음체.

SSRC Social Science Research Council (미 · 영) 사회 과학 연구 협의회.

SSS ① silicon symmetrical switch 실리콘 대칭 스위치.
② super speed sensitive 흑백 필름의 감도표시계수의 일종.

SSSR Soyuz Sovetskikh Sotsialisticheskikh Respublik (러) 소비에트 사회주의 공화국연방.

SST ① solid state technology 고체 기술. 반도체소자와 집적회로의 제조법에 관한 기술.
② supersonic transport 초음속 여객기.
③ Sea Surface Temperature 해수면 온도.

SSTV satellite STV 위성방송에 의한 유료텔레비전 서비스.

SSU Sudan Socialist Union 수단 사회주의 연합.

SSUS spinning solid upper stage 회전형 고체 상단 로켓.

St. Saturday 토요일 ; Saint 성인 Strait 해협 ; Street 가.

ST ① safety toy 안전완구.
② sensitivity training 감수성 훈련.
③ space telescope 우주공간에서 사용하는 텔레스코프.
④ speech therapist 언어 요법사.

STABEX stabilization of Export Earning (EC) 수출소득보상 융자제도.

STAC ① Science and Technology Advisory Committee (NASA의) 과학기술자문위원회.
② spare tool automatic change 예비 공구 자동 보급 교환.

STAR satellite telecommunication with automatic routing 통신 위성 중계의 위성 전화 통신.

STC ① Satellite Television Corporation (미) 위성 텔레비전회사.
② sensitivity time control 레이더의 시간적 감도 조정기.

STD ① sexually transmitted disease 성행위감염증.
② standard 표준, 규격.
③ subscriber trunk dialing 전화 가입자 장기 리다이얼 즉시 통화.
④ Short term External Debt 단기 대외부채. (1년 이내에 지불해야 할 대외부채).

STDN space tracking and data network 우주 추적 데이터망.

STE ① Special Travelling Expense Fund (테니스) 데이비스컵전(戰)의 수입에서 잉여금을 적립하여 팀의 원정 여비의 보조를 충당하기 위한 기금.
② synchronous terminal equipment 동기(同期) 단층(端層) 장치(裝置).

STM scanning tunneling microscope 주사 터널 현미경.

STN science and technology network 과학기술 정보 네트워크.

STOL short takeoff and landing 단거리이착륙(기).

STORET storage and retrieval for water quality data (미) 전국 수질 환경 데이터 파일.

STOs state trading organizations 국영 무역기구.

STOVL short takeoff and vertical landing 단거리 이륙 수직 착륙.

STP ① scientifically treated petroleum 가솔린 첨가제의 상품
② serenity, tranquility, peace 환각제 DOM의 별명.
③ standard temperature and

pressure 표준온도와 기압.

S.T.P. Sea water treating Plant 해수처리공장.

STPD standard temperature and pressure, dry 표준온도, 압력, 건조도.

STR Special Trade Representative (미)특별 무역대표

STRAC Strategic Army Corps (미) 육군 전략 기동군단.

STRAF Strategic Army Forces (미) 전략 육군부대.

STRI-COM Strike Command 전략 출격 사령부. Strategic Air Command (전략 공군 총사령부)와 Tactical Air Command (전술 공군 사령부)를 병합한 것.

STS ① serological test for syphilis 매독 혈청반응 검사. ② space transportation system 우주 정기 왕복 시스템.

STUC Scottish Trades Union Congress 스코틀랜드 노동조합회의.

STV ① scramble TV 송출되는 화상의 동기신호를 가공하여 특정한 디코더가 없으면 계약자 이외에는 시청할 수 없게 한 텔레비전 방송. ② Space Transfer Vehicle 우주간 수송기. ③ subscription television 유료 유선 텔레비전.

STVA Subscription Television Association (미) 유료 텔레비전협회.

STX start of text character (컴퓨터) 텍스트 개시문자, 데이터 통신에서 전송 텍스트의 시작을 나타내는 부호.

STY space-time yield 공시수량 (空時收量).

SU Soviet Union 소비에트연방.

SUAWACS Soviet Union Airborne Warning and Control System 소련의 조기경계 관제기.

SUBROC submarine rocket 대잠 수함 로켓.

SUM surface to underwater missile 함대 수중 미사일.

SUNA Sudan News Agency 수단 국영 통신.

SUNFED Special United Nations Fund for Economic Development 유엔 경제개발특별기금.

SUNY State University of New York (미) 뉴욕 주립 대학.

SV ① space velocity 우주속도. ② speed value 필름 감도지수.

SVCS satellite video communication system 위성 비디오 통신 방식.

S-VHS Super Video Home System VHS비디오 고화질 방식.

SVI Smoke volatility index 연(煙)증발지수. 연료의 연료 잔사 생성(殘渣生成) 경향을 나타내는

431

지수.

SVP senior vice president 상무.

SVR Supply voltage rejection ratio 전원 전압 제거비(比).

SVS slide vanbody system 트럭의 짐받이(vanbody)를 트럭에서 화차로, 또는 화차에서 트럭으로 옮겨 실을 수 있는 트럭과 철도의 협동일관 수송방식.

SW ① scenario writer 시나리오 작가.
② shortwave 단파.
③ software 소프트웨어.
④ switcher (방송) 디렉터의 지시에 의하여 선택스 위치를 다루어 텔레비전 프로그램의 화면을 바꾸는 기술자.

SWAK sealed with a kiss 키스로 봉했습니다. 어린이나 애인이 편지에 쓰는 말. → SWALK.

SWALK sealed with a loving kiss 애정을 담은 키스로 봉했습니다. → SWAK.

SWAPO South west African People's Organization 서남 아프리카 인민 기구.

SWAT Special Weapons and Tactics 또는 Special Weapons Attack Team. (미) 특별기동대. 저격총, 기관총 등의 특수 화기의 사용훈련, 레인저훈련, 인질구출 훈련 등을 받은 특수임무의 경찰부대.

SWATH small waterplane area twin hull 반 몰수형(半沒水型) 쌍동선(双胴船).

SWD/CAP Social Welfare and Development Center for Asia and the Pacific (영) 아시아 태평양 사회복지개발센터.

SWG standard wire gauge 표준 와이어 게이지.

SWIFT Society for Worldwide Interbank Financial Telecommunications 국제 은행간 통신 협회.

SWIS sensitive wildlife information system (미) 야생동물의 생식, 생태에 관한 데이터베이스.

SWISSAIR Swiss Air Transport 스위스 항공.

SWP ① Forschungsinstitut fur internationale Politik und Sicherheit, Stiftung Wissenschaft und Politik (독) 과학정치재단 · 국제정치안전보장 연구소.
② steel wire piano 피아노선.

SWR Swiss Air 스위스 항공.

SWSD still with sound and data 유성(有聲) 정지화(靜止畵) 및 디지털데이터.

SWU separative work unit 분리 작업단위. 천연우라늄에서 농축 우라늄을 만들 때의 작업량의 단위.

SYMAP synagraphic mapping system (컴퓨터) 의사(疑似)지도 작성시스템.

Syn synthesizer 전자음 합성장치, 악기로 사용한다.

sync ① synchronism = synch 동시 진행. 영상과 음성의
② synchronization synch 동기화. 한 조작을 또 하나의 조작에 맞추는 것.

SYNCOM synchronous communication satellite (미) 동기통신위성. 정지통신위성.

SYSOP system operator 시스템·오퍼레이터.

SYSTRAN system translation 컴퓨터에 의한 기계번역시스템.

433

t ton ; teaspoon ; teaspoonful

T ① absolute temperature 절대 온도.
② tablespoon
③ tension 장력.
④ tritium 삼중수소.

T. Tuesday 화요일

Ta tantalum 탄탈륨. 원자번호 73.

TA ① teaching assistant (교원의) 조수.
② technology assessment 신기술평가. 환경을 파괴할 가능성이 있는 신기술을 사전에 점검하는 시스템.
③ transactional analysis 교류분석.

TAA ① Technical Assistance Administration (유엔) 기술원조국.
② television audience assessment 텔레비전 시청자 사정 (査定).

T&A tits and ass (미 속어) (텔레비전 쇼에 나오는) 섹스.

T&AVR Territorial and Army Volunteer Reserve (영) 국방의용 예비군.

TAB ① tax anticipation bills (미) 납세국채. 법인세수를 예측한 4분기마다의 만기의 재무증권. 법인세 납부는 액면으로 지불된다.
② Technical Assistance Board (유엔) 기술 원조 평의회.

TABA the American Book Award 미국 도서상.

TAC ① Tactical Air Command (미) 전술공군(사령부)
② Technical Assistance Committee (유엔)기술원조위원회
③ total allowable catch 어획(漁獲) 허용량.

TACAMO take charge and move out (미해군) 공중 통신 중계기.

TACAN tactical air navigation 전술항법정차. 송신국의 방위(方位)와 거리에 의하여 항공기의 위치를 결정하는 장치.

TACOMSAT tactical communications satellite = TACSAT (미) 전술통신위성. 군사시설 사이의 연락에 사용된다.

TACSAT ① tactical communications satellite =TACOMSAT 전술통신위성.
② tactical satellite communication program (미) 전술위성통신계획 근거리 통신을 목

적으로 하는 군사 통신 위성.

TACTAS tactical towed array sonar (美 해군) 전술 예항 전투 배치 해양 음파 탐지기.

TACV tracked air cushion vehicle 궤도식 공기쿠션차량. 공기쿠션차량(호바크라프트-상품명)은 일반적으로 해상을 항행하는 것이지만 TACV는 같은 원리를 이용하여 지상에 설치한 전용 궤도상을 주행한다.

TADI Temporary Acceptable Daily Intake 잠정 일일 섭취 허용량 (일일섭취허용량을 추정하기 위해 생화학, 독성 혹은 기타 자료를 기본으로 하여 설정한 특정 및 제한된 기간 동안의 일일 섭취 허용량으로 FAO/WHO JECFA에서 분류한 ADI중의 하나).

TAF ① Tactical Air Force 전술공군.
② terminal aerodrome forecast = TAFOR 비행장 기상예보.

TAFOR terminal aerodrome forecast 비행장 기상 예보.

TAM ① tactical air missile 전술항공미사일.
② Television Audience Measurement Limited (영) 텔레비전시청자 조사 회사.

TAN tax anticipation note (미) 납세 지방채. 주, 시 등의 지방자치제가 장래의 세금수입을 예측하여 발행하는 공채.

TANJUG Telegrafska Agencoja Nova Jugoslavija 신유고슬라비아 통신. 국영 국제 통신사.

TANS tactical and air navigation system 전술항법시스템. 도플러 방식을 사용하며 컴퓨터, 레이더, 콘트롤, 디스플레이 장치로 구성되어 있다.

TANU Tanganyika African National Union 탕가니카·디스플레이장치로 구성되어 있다.

Taoism 도교.

TAP Tunis Afrique Presse(Tunis African Press) (프) (튀니지) 국영 통신.

TAPRI Tampere Peace Research Institute 탐페레 평화 연구소.

TAPS Trans Alaska Pipeline System 알래스카 횡단 석유 수송관 망.

TAR ① terminal area surveillance radar 터미널 지역 감시 레이더.
② Tactical Air Reconnaissance 전술 항공정찰.
③ Trains Asian Railway 아시아 횡단철도.

TARAN test and repair as necessary 고장이 확실하지 않으면 수리하지 않는 방식.

TAS ① telephone answering service 전화 응답 서비스.
② texture analysing system 화상 해석 장치.

TASE

TASE thermal application of solar energy 태양광 이용열.

TASF technical assistance fund 기술 원조 기금.

TASI time assignment speech interpolation 시간할당 음성삽입.

TASS ① Telegrafnoe Agentstvo Sovetskovo Soyuza (러) (소련) 타스 통신.
② towed array sonar system 예항(曳航) 어레이소나시스템. 저주파역(域)을 이용하여 잠수함을 탐지한다.

TAT ① thematic apperception test 회화 통각 검사. 어떠한 상황의 그림을 보이며 자유롭게 얘기를 만들어 내게 하여 무의식의 그림을 보이며 자유롭게 얘기를 만들어 내게 하여 무의식이 세계를 분석·해석하는 테스트.
② Transatlantic Telephone 대서양 횡단전화. 광통신 해저케이블에 의함.
③ turnaround time 응답시간. 항공기나 그의 장비가 정비되어 복귀할 때까지의 시간 또 컴퓨터에 정보를 입력하여 처리가 끝나고 출력을 얻을 수 있을 때까지의 시간.

TAT-8 eight transatlantic cable 광섬유에 의한 대서양횡단해저케이블.

TAV trans atmospheric vehicle 대기권내외 비행기. 로켓추진 또는 제트엔진을 병용하여 대기권내에서도 대기권외에서도 비행이 가능한 항공기.

Tb terbium 테르븀. 원자번호 65.

TB ① torpedo boat 어뢰정.
② trial balance 시산표(試算表).
③ Treasury Bill 단기 국채(1년 이하).
④ Treasury Bond 장기 국채(5년 이하).
⑤ tuberculosis 결핵.

TBA to be avoided (미 속어) 피해야 할 사람 또는 물건.

TBC time base corrector 비디오 신호 안정성 개선장치.

TBI Technology Business Incubator 신기술창업보육 (예비창업자 또는 창업1년 이내의 기업에게 기술개발 미치 사업화 자금, 사업장, 기술 및 경영 지도, 각종 정보, 투자 및 연계자금 지원 등을 실시하는 창업보육사업).

TBi Treasury Bill 단기 국채

TBM tera bit memory 1조 비트 메모리.

TBMA Bond Market Association 채권협회[美]

TBO time between overhauls (항공) 점검정비간격.

TBS ① talk between ships 선박간 무선 통화.
② Turner Broadcasting System (미) 뉴스전문 유선텔레비전국.

TBT Technical Barriers to Trade 무역 기술 장벽

TBT Tributyltin 유기주석화합물 (PVC 안정제, 각종 플라스틱 첨가제, 산업용 촉매, 살충제, 살균제, 목조 보존재 등으로 널리 사용되고 있으며 특히 방오제로서 선박용 페인트에 많이 사용되고 있으나 강한 독성을 지니고 있으며 최근에는 내분비계 장애물질로도 추정되고 있는 화합물).

TBTO tributyltin oxide 유기주석화합물. 배와 어망에 해조, 조개류가 부착하는 것을 방지하기 위하여 선저(船底)도료, 양식용어망의 방오제(防汚劑)로 사용하고 있으나 신경에 맹독성이 있다.

TBZ thiaberdazole 오렌지, 바나나, 그레이프 프루츠 등의 곰팡이 방지제.

Tc technetium 테크네튬. 원자번호 43.

TC ① Technical Committee 기술위원회.
② terminal controller 단말제어장치.
③ total communication 청각장애자를 위한 종합 전달법.
④ total cost 총비용.
⑤ Trade Committee (OECD) 무역위원회.
⑥ transmission control (컴퓨터) 전송제어.
⑦ traveler's check 여행용수표.
⑧ Trusteeship Council = UNTC (유엔) 신탁통치이사회.
⑨ type certificate (항공) 형식(型式) 증명.

TCA ① Technical Cooperation Administration (미)(국무성) 기술 협력국.
② terminal control area 최종관제공역(空域). 항공기관제에서 공항근처의 공역을 말한다.
③ total company automation 전사적자동화.

Tcal tetra calorie 1조 열량.

TCAM telecommunications access method (컴퓨터) 통신액세스방식. 컴퓨터의 기억장치와 단말장치와의 사이의 데이터 전송방식.

TCAS ① terminal control address space (컴퓨터) 단말제어어드레스공간.
② traffic alert/collision avoidance system 항공관제충돌 경보 시스템. 지상레이더국의 감시에 의하여 만일 근처에 충돌의 위험성이 있는 타기(他機)가 있을 때 지상으로부터 경고를 받아 이것을 표시하는 시스템.

TCB ① taking care of business (속어) 하려고 하던 것을 하다.
② task control block (컴퓨터) 테스크 제어 블록.

TCBM transcontinental ballistic missile 대륙횡단 탄도미사일.

TCC ① test come clear 원인불명의 시험중 회복

TCD

② transmission control character 전송제어문자.

TCD technical circular directive 내공성(耐空性) 개선통보.

TCDC Technical Cooperation among Developing Countries 발전도상국간의 기술협력.

TCDC/INRES Information Referral System for Technical Cooperation among Developing Countries (유엔) 발전도상국간의 기술협력계획정보 안내시스템.

TCDD tetra chloro dibenzo dioxin 고초제, 제초제.

TCE ton of coal equivalent 석탄 환산톤수. 석탄 1톤당 열량값인 7×10^6 kcal를 말한다. 그러나 영국에서와 같이 최근 수년간의 모든 등급의 석탄이 갖는 톤당 총열량의 평균값을 의미하기도 한다.

TCM thermal conduction module 열전도모듈.

TCMP tightly coupled multiprocessing system 정밀 결합 다중 처리 시스템.

TCR Trans Chinese Railway 중국횡단철도.

TCS ① Telecommunication Control System 증권용 데이터통신제어 시스템.
② tele control system 전화제어시스템. 외출한 곳에서 전화로 목욕탕이나 전기 밥솥 등 전기제품의 스위치를 넣다 끊었다 하는 시스템.
③ transportation control system 수송 관리 시스템.

TCST Technical Committee for Standardization 표준화위원회. ICIREPAT의 하부조직.

TCU transmission control unit 전송 제어 장치. 원격 단말 장치에 대하여 메시지의 송수신을 실행하는 제어장치.

TD ① technical director (방송) 기술스텝의 최고 책임자.
② theoretical density 이론밀도.
③ time draft 일람후 정기지불어음.
④ transmitted data 송신데이터.
⑤ transmitter distributor 자동 송신기.

TDB ① Toxicology Data Bank (미) 독물학 데이터 뱅크.
② Trade and Development Board (유엔) 무역개발이사회.

TDC time division connector (컴퓨터) 시간분할커넥터.

TDCC Transportation Data Coordinating Committee (미) 교통 데이터 협력 위원회.

TDD telecomminications device for the deaf 농아자용 원격 통신장치.

TDE telephone data entry 전화 회선을 통하여 데이터를 컴퓨터 시스템에 입력하는 것.

TDF transborder data flow 국제

간 데이터 유통. 데이터가 국경을 넘어 이동하는 것, 특히 미국에 정보가 집중하는 것.

TDI toluene diso cyanate 유독물질.

TDM time division multiplex (컴퓨터) 시분할다중. 시간을 분할하여 각각 다른 정보를 동시 병행으로 전송하는 통신 방식.

TDMA time division multiple access (컴퓨터) 시분할 다원 접속. 위성통신 등에서 송수신 가능한 시간을 할당하는 방식.

TDN total digestible nutrients 가소화양분총량(可消化養分總量). 사료의 단위중량당 양분의 양.

TDR ① tracking and data relay 추적 데이터 중계.
② transfer of development right (미) 개발권의 이전.

TDRI Thailand Development Research Institute 태국 개발 연구소

TDRS tracking and data relay satellite 추적 데이터 중계 위성. 인공위성의 궤도추적과 위성으로부터의 신호를 지상국에 중계하는 인공위성.

TDRSS tracking and data relay satellite system 추적 데이터 중계 위성시스템.

TDS total dissolved solids 전용(全溶) 함유농도. 전용해고형물.

TDT total development training 종합개발훈련. 영업사원의 스파르타식 특훈.

TDY temporary duty 파견근무.

TDZ touchdown zone (항공) 접지대. 활주로의 입구에서 914m까지의 활주로상의 구역.

Te tellurium 텔루륨. 원자번호 52.

TE ① tariff equivalents 품목별 관세 상당치. 국내와 국제가의 차.
② trade expenses 영업비.
③ transnational enterprise = TNE 다국적 기업.

TEAL Tasman Empire Air Lines 뉴질랜드의 타스만 항공.

Teamsters Union 화물자동차 운전수 노동조합.

TEBO third stage engine burnout 제3단 연소종료. 로켓의 제3단이 연소를 끝마치는 것.

TEC technical college (영) 기술전문학교.

tech technical ; technological ; technology.

TEF ① toronto enterprise fund (캐나다) 사회적 기업지원기관
② Toxic Equivalency Factor 독성등가계수

TECOM terrain contour matching 지형조합(照合).

TEE trans European Express 유럽 횡단 국제 급행 열차.

TEFL Teaching English as a

439

foreign language 외국어로서의 영어교육.

TEFRA Tax Equity and Fiscal Responsibility Act (미) 공평세제 · 재정 책임법.

TEG triethylene glycol.

tel. telegram ; telegraph ; telephone

TEL ① tetraethyl lead 앤티노크제로서 가솔린에 혼합한다. ② transporter erectorlauncher 미사일 운반 · 장가(裝架) · 발사장치.

TELAM Telenoticiosa Americana (스) 델람 통신사. 아르헨티나 국영 통신사.

telecom telecommunication 전기통신.

TELE-DACS television data acquisition and control system 텔레비전 중계방송국 원방(遠方)감시 제어시스템.

TELENET 미국의 TELENET 사의 데이터 통신 네트워크.

TELERAN television radar air navigation 레이더와 텔레비전을 결합한 무선항행 원조시설로서 조종사에게 주위에 있는 다른 비행기의 상황을 알림.

TELEX telegraph exchange, teleprinter exchange, teletypewriter exchange 텔렉스. 다이얼을 돌려 상대를 호출하여 텔레타이프로 통신하는 방식.

telop television opaque projector 합성어. 텔레비전 카메라를 사용하지 않고 사진, 회화, 문자 등을 전송하는 장치 또는 전송된 것.

TELSTAR Telecommunications Star (미) 통신위성. 1962년 12호를 쏘아올림.

TEM transmission electron microscope 투과형(透過型) 전자현미경.

Temperate Zone 溫帶地方. the Frigid Zone = 한대. the Tropical Zone =열대.

TEMPO Technology Management Planning Operation 미국의 싱크탱크.

Tenn. Tennessee 테네시 주.

TENS Telephone Network System 대상자(對象者)와 회의실에 있는 사회자가 전화회선으로 연결하여 인터뷰하는 조사 시스템.

TEPP tetraethyl pyrophosphate 살충 · 살서제.

TERCOM terrain contour matching guidance system 지형조합(照合)미사일유도장치. * 표적지의 지형을 기억시킨 컴퓨터에 의하여 궤도를 수정하면서 나르는 순항미사일의 유도장치.

TEREC tactical electronic reconnaissance 전술전자정찰.

TES total energy system 등유, A

중유, LPG를 연료로 하여 디젤엔진, 가스터빈으로 발전을 하고 배역을, 냉방, 급탕, 난방, 증기의 형태로 이용하는 방식.

TESL teaching English as a second language 제2언어로서의 영어교육.

TESOL ① Teachers of English to Speakers of Other Languages (미) 제2언어로서의 영어교사의회.
② teaching of English to speakers of other language 제2언어로서의 영어 교수법.

TEST thesaurus of engineering and scientific terms (미) 기술·과학용어 어휘집. 동의어(同義語) 검색 시스템.

TeV teraelectron volt 1조 전자볼트.

TEWT Tactical Exercise Without Troops (영) 현지 전술. 사령부, 참모만 참가하는 모의전.

Tex. Texas 텍사스 주.

TEX ① telegraph exchange 텔렉스.
② telex 텔렉스.

TF ① technical fiction, techno fiction, technology fiction 기술미래소설.
② task force 기동부대.

TFA total fatty acids 전(全) 지방산.

TFC Trade Facilitation Committee 일미 통상 원활화 위원회.

TFE tetra fluoro ethylene 불소수지의 원료.

tfr. transfer 대체.

TFR terrain following radar 지형추수(追隨)레이더. 초저공 비행을 하고 있는 항공기가 전방의 지형을 포착하고 그 의지형에 따라 지표에서 일정한 고도를 보지하면서 날으기 위하여 사용하는 레이더.

TFS tin free steel 주석을 사용하지 않은 깡통용 표면처리 강판.

TFT thin film transistor 박막(薄膜) 트랜지스터.

TFTR TOKAMAK Fusion Test Reactor (미) 토커맥형 핵융합시험로.

TGF transforming growth factor 세포 성장인자.

TGI Target Group Index (미) 전국지의 독자조사를 하는 회사.

TGIF Thank God, it's Friday 고맙게도 오늘은 금요일이다. 근로자가 주말이 되어 기쁨을 나타내는 말.

TGIF·OTMWDUM Thank God, it's Friday. Only Two More Work Days Until Monday. 고맙게도 오늘은 금요일이다. 월요일까지 겨우 이틀밖에 근무일이 없구나. 미국 국방성에서 사용되고 있는 모토.

TGP turbulence generating pot 난류(亂流) 생성 포트.

TGS triglycine sulfate 기억소자

TGSCC

와 온도검출기 등에 사용한다.

TGSCC transgranular stress corrosion cracking (原子力) 입내(粒內)응력 부식 크래킹.

TGSM terminally guided submunition 종단(終端) 유도형자탄(子彈). 센서와 유도장치를 가지고 목표를 자가가 발견하여 돌입하며 그 자체는 미사일이나 포탄 등으로 목표지역까지 운반되어 투하되는 것을 말한다. 1발의 미사일이나 포탄은 복수개의 자탄을 가지고 있다.

TGV Tranin a Grands Vitesse (=high speed train) (프) 초고속열차. 파리-리용간을 운행하고 있는 시속 260km의 세계에서 가장 빠른 열차.

TGW terminally guided warhead 종말 유도탄두.

TGWU Transport & General Workers Union (영)운수 일반 노동조합.

Th thorium (화학)토륨. 원자번호 90.

TH ① (독) Technische Hochschule 공과대학.
② true heading (항공) 기수진(眞) 방향.

THAI Thai Airways International 타이 국제 항공. = 17TI

Thanksgiving Day 추수감사절 (11월의 제4목요일).

ThB (라) theologiae baccalaureus (=bachelor of theology) 신학사(神學士).

THC tetrahydrocannabinol 인도 만에서 얻어진 수지 중에 포함된 무색의 액체. 마라화나의 주요 성분.

T.H.E.M. telecommunication, Hackers, Embezzlers, Manipulator (미) 전화선을 사용하는 통신, 횡령자, 조작자. 컴퓨터 정보시스템을 파괴하는 그룹의 명칭.

THF tetrahydrofuran 나일론의 합성 원료.

THI temperature humidity index 온습 지수.

THM trihalomethane 발암물질의 일종. 수돗물의 살균을 위하여 염소를 사용할 때 생성됨.

THP thrust horsepower 추력 마력.

THP·ADM tetrahydro pyranyl adriamycin 복소환식 항암치료제.

Three R's Reading, writing, arithmetic 기초교육.

THY [터키語] Turk Hava Yollari (=Turkish Airlines) 터키항공.

Th(urs) Thursday 목요일.

Ti titanium 티탄. 원자번호 22.

TI ① Transparency International 국제투명성 기구
② Thai Airways International = THAI 타이 항공.
③ Texas instruments, Inc. (미) 반도체 제조회사

TIA Trnas International Airlines

트랜스 인터내셔널항공.

TIAS true indicated air speed (항공) 진대기(眞對氣) 지시속도(指示速度).

TIBC total serum iron binding capacity 총혈청(總血淸) 철(鐵) 결합능철(結合能鐵).

TIBOR Tokyo Interbank Offered Rate (일) 동경의 은행간 거래금리.

TIC Trade and Industry Committee (한)(국회의) 상공 위원회.

t.i.d. (라) ter in die (=three times a day) (처방) 1일 3회.

TIER Taiwan Institute of Economic Research 대만 경제 연구소.

TIH Their Imperial Highnesses 전하(복수).

TIGR treasury investment growth receipts (미) 장기 재무성채권, 성장 투자 증서.

TIM Travel Information Manual 여행 정보 매뉴얼. IATA에 가맹한 14개 항공 회사가 편집한 월간 간행물.

TIO test input output 입출력 테스트(명령).

TIP tax based incomes policy (미) 세제에 의한 소득정책. 임금인상을 억제하고 기업의 비용상승을 경감하여 물가억제에 대한 보상으로서 기업과 노동조합 쌍방에게 세제면의 우대조치를 취하는 것.

TIPS tiny income parents support 젊어서 결혼하여 어린이가 있어 맞벌이를 할 수 없어 부모로부터 원조를 받지 않으면 생활이 안되는 부부.

TIR [F] Transport International Routier (=International Transport of Goods by Road) 국제 도로 수송.

TIROS television and infrared observation satellite (미) NASA가 개발한 기상관측위성.

TIS ① technical information system 기술정보 시스템.
② Trade Information Service 무역 관련 정보 서비스. ESCAP의 지역별 정보서비스 시스템.

Titan 미국 공군의 대륙간강도.

T.J. t.j. talk jockey 사회자. 전화에 의한 청취자 참가 프로그램의.

TKP Trans Korea Pipeline 한국종단송유관. (포항에서 의정부에 이르는 한국종단 송유용 장거리 송유관을 말하며 이는 주한 미 육군에서 설치하여 관할 운영하고 있음).

TKO technical knockout 권투에서 TKO

Tl thallium 탈륨. 원자번호 81.

TL techno lady 시스템엔지니어, 프로그램의 기능이 있는 여자사원.

T.L. total loss 전손.

TLC ① tender, loving care 상냥한 애정이 담긴 배려.

443

TL

② thin layer chromatography 얇은 층 크로마트그래피. 색층분석도.

TL dating thermoluminescent dating 열 루미네슨스 연대(年代) 측정법. 표본을 가열하여 생기는 빛의 강도로 연대를 측정하는 것.

TLF transferable loan facility 양도 가능 론 퍼실리티.

TLO total loss only (해상보험) 전손만 담보.

TLS the Times Literary Supplement (영) 타임즈 지의 문예부록.

TLU table look up (컴퓨터) 테이블조사. 지정된 키와 관계있는 항목의 장소를 찾기 위해 테이블을 검색하는 것. 또는 함수 테이블에서 지정된 인수에 대응하는 함수 값을 꺼내는 방법.

TLX telex = TELEX.

Tm thulium 툴륨. 원자번호 69.

TM ① teaching machine 교육용기계.
② technical manual 기술입문서.
③ theme music 테마 음악.
④ trademark 상표.
⑤ transcendental meditation 초월 명상.

TMA terminal control area 터미널 관제구.

TM dating thermoluminescent dating (고고학) 열(熱) 루미네슨스 연대 측정법.

TMDI Theoretical Maximum Daily Intake 이론적 일일 최대섭취량. (각 농약의 최대 잔류허용기준과 각 식품들의 1인 1일 평균섭취량을 곱한 값).

T men ① traffic men (미) 교통위반 통보원.
② Treasury men (미) 재무성의 탈세 수사관.

TMI Three Mile Island (미) 1979년 3월 28일 이곳에 있는 원자력 발전소에서 방사능누출 사고가 있었다.

TMO telegraphic money order 전신환.

TMP ① test/maintenance program 시험·보수용 프로그램.
② thermo mechanical pulp 기계 펄프의 일종.

TMR Trans Manchurian Railway 만주 통과 철도.

TMS ① telephone management system 전화 관리 시스템.
② time and motion study 시간 및 동작 연구.

TMTD tetra methyl thiuram disulfide 고무가황(加黃) 촉진제, 방비제(防微劑), 농업용 종자 살균제.

TMV tobacco mosaic virus 담배 모자이크 균.

TN ① treasury note (미) 국고 채권. 1~10년의 정부채.
② twisted nematic 액정 디스

플레이용의 액정재료.

TNA Thai News Agency 태국 통신사. 국영 통신사.

TNB trinitrobenzene 기폭제.

TNC ① Trade Negotiations Committee (GATT의) 무역 교섭 위원회.
② Transnational Corporation 다국적 기업.

TNE transnational enterprise = TE 다국적기업.

TNF theater nuclear force 전연 핵전력.

TNIC transmit network identification code 중계망 식별 부호.

TNO Trade Negotiation Organization (GATT의) 무역 교섭기구.

TNR thermal neutron reactor 열중성원자로.

TNT trinitrotoluene 군용폭탄에 사용되는 강력한 화약.

TNW ① tactical nuclear weapon 전술(戰術) 핵 병기.
② theater nuclear weapon 전역(戰域) 핵병기.

TO ① table of organization 인원의 기구표, 편제표, 정원.
② technical order 기술 지령서.
③ turn over = PTO 뒷면에 계속.

T.O. ① turnover 노동이동(勞動移動), 회전율. 자본 투하율.
② Telegraph Office 전신국.

T/O take off 이륙.

TOB ① takeover bid 주식의 공개매입.
② Toxicology Data Bank (미) 독성 데이터 뱅크.

TOC total organic carbon 전유기탄소량. 수중의 유기물 함유량의 지표.

TOCOM Tokyo Commodity Exchange for Industry 동경 공업품 거래소.

TOD ① takeoff distance 이륙 활주 거리.
② total oxygen demand 총산소요구량. 수질오탁을 나타내는 수치.
③ time of delivery 배달시간.

TOE ① table of organization and equipment (군사) 편제 장비표.
② theory of everything 자연계의 네 가지의 기본력(基本力)의 (중력, 전자력, 약한힘, 강한힘)을 통일적으로 설명하고자 하는 궁극의 이론.
③ ton of oil equivalent 석유환산톤수. 석유 1톤당 열량값인 10^7 kcal를 말한다.

TOEBC Test of English for Business Communication 상업 통신 영어 테스트.

TOEFL Testing of English as a Foreign Language 외국어로서의 영어 능력 검정시험.

TOEIC Testing of English for

International Communication 국제 교류를 위한 영어 테스트.

TOFC trailer on flat car 화물수송 방식으로 트레일러 또는 트럭채로 화차에 실은 것.

TOGA tropical ocean and global atmosphere 열대 해양 지구 대기계획. 세계 기후 연구 계획의 subprogram.

TOKAMAK Toroidal Kamera Magnetic 소련에서 개발한 핵융합장치.

TOL Tower of London 런던탑.

TON takeoff noise 이륙소음.

TOP ① technical office protocol OA분야의 LAN의 프로토콜. ② temporarily out of print 일시절판(1時絶版).

TOPEX Typhoon Operational Experiment 태풍재해를 최소한으로 막기 위한 실험.

TOPICS total online program and information control system (일) 프로제작 활동의 기능을 전부 컴퓨터로 관리하는 NHK의 프로편성 시스템.

TOPIX Tokyo Stock Price Index (일) 동경 증권거래소의 주가 지수.

TOPS Thermoelectric outer planet spacecraft 열전식 혹성(惑星)탐사우주선.

TOR terms of reference 조사 사항, 조사범위.

TOS ① tape operating system 테이프 운영체제. ② temporarily out of stock 일시적 재고 품절.

TOT ① time on target 목표시각. ② transfer of technology 기술이전.

TOW ① tube launched, optically tracked, wire guided antitank missile 대전차 유선 유도 미사일. ② tug of war 줄다리기.

TOXLINE Toxicology Information Online (미) 독물학 온라인 정보 데이터베이스.

TP ① teleprocessing 통신 회선으로 연결된 각지의 단말 장치를 통하여 중앙의 시스템에서 처리되는 데이터 처리. ② total productivity 종합 생산성. ③ transparency OHP 투영용 투명판.

TPA terephthalic acid 합성섬유·필름 등의 원료.

TPC ① Trade Promotion Center (ESCAP) 무역 촉진 센터. ② Trans Pacific Cable 태평양 횡단 케이블.

TPHA treponema pallidum hemaglutination test 매독 병원체 적혈구 응집 반응.

TPI ① tracks per inch 플로피 디스크의 기록 밀도를 나타내는 단위. ② treatment of preparatory investment 선행 투자 취급. 심해저(深海低)개발 문제.

TPLF Tigre People's Liberation Front (에티오피아) 티그레 인민 해방 전선.

TPM ① technical performance measurement 기술관리
② total production maintenance 종합생산보전. 현재의 생산시설을 검토하여 능률을 높이기 위하여 개선하는 것.
③ trigger pricing mechanism (미) 트리거가격제도. 수입품에 최저가격을 정하고, 그이하의 가격으로 거래되는 경우 덤핑으로 간주하고 조사를 실시하는 제도.

TPN ① total parenteral nutrition 종합 비경구 영양 수액.
② triphosphopyridine nucleotide 생체 조직에 널리 분포하고 있는 보효소.

TPO time, place, occasion 시간과 장소 그리고 때에 알맞게 옷을 입거나 행동을 하는 것.

TPR thermo plastic rubber 열가소성 고무.

TPRC ① thermophysical Properties Research Center 열적 물성(熱的物性) 연구센터.
② Trade Policy Research Center (영) 무역 정책 연구 센터.

TPS thermal protection system (스페이스셔틀) 내열 타일. 오비터의 전표면에 붙인 내열타일.

TPT triphenyl tin 선저도료(船底塗料)로 사용하였으나 독성이 있어 어류와 수질 등의 환경오염이 문제시되고 있다.

TPU thermo plastic polyurethane 열가소성 폴리우레탄소지.

TQC total quality control 종합적 품질 관리, 전사적 품질 관리.

TR ① Tactical Reconnaissance (미) 전략정찰. 공군의 신형정찰기.
② test responder 시험 응답 장치.
③ total revenue 총수입.
④ track (컴퓨터) 트랙, 테이프의 음대(音帶), 음반의 홈.
⑤ transistor 트랜지스터.
⑥ transmit receive 송수신.
⑦ trust receipt 수입 담보 화물 보관증.
⑧ turning radius (항공) 선회반경.

TRACON terminal radar approach control 공항에 있어서의 레이더 착륙 유도 시스템.

TRAFFIC Trade Records Analysis of Fauna in Commerce 야생동식물 국제 거래 조사기록 특별위원회.

Trans Siberian Railroad 시베리아 횡단철도.

TRF thyrotropin releasing factor = TRH 갑상선 호르몬 방출요인.

TRH ① Their Royal Highnesses 전하(복수).
② thyrotropin releasing hormone 갑상선 자극 호르몬 방출 호르몬.

447

TRIB transfer rate of information bit (컴퓨터) 정보 비트 전송 속도.

Tri·Be·Ca Triangle Below Canal (Street) Canal St., 브로드웨이, 허드슨강으로 둘러싸인 3각지대. 현재 유행의 최첨단을 가고 있는 장소로 알려져 있다.

TRIM Test Rules for Inventory Management 무역관련 투자조치. 투자자에게 일정한 비율의 부품의 현지조달을 의무화하는 요구, 생산량의 일정한 비율을 특정시장에 수출하는 요구, 특정제품을 현지에서 제조하는 것을 강제하는 제조 요구 등이 있다.

TRIPS transformation induced plasticity steel 고강도 강연성 (强延性) 특수강.

TRISNET Transportation Research Information Service Network (미) 교통조사 정보서비스 네트워크.

TRISTAN Transposable Ring Intersecting Accelerator in Nippon (일) 전자·양자 충돌형가속기.

TRMM Tropical Rainfall Measuring Mission 열대강우 관측위성.

TRON계획 the real time operating system nucleus project 1990년대의 컴퓨터의 이용의 호환성을 보증하기 위하여 컴퓨터에 종합적인 신표준을 확립하려는 계획.

TRP time regulated parts (항공) 시간 조정 부품.

TRRS Technical Reports Retrieval System 원자력 관련 기술 보고서 검색 시스템.

TRS Trunked Radio System 주파수 공용 통신.

TRT Trade mark Registration Treaty 상표 등록 조약.

TRU transuranium 초우라늄.

TS ① time sharing 시분할.
② time study 시간연구. 일정한 작업을 재구실을 하는 작업자가 정상적인 노력으로 해내는데 걸리는 시간을 사정하는 것.
③ top secret 극비의.
④ Traffic Safety 교통안전.
⑤ Tax System 조세제도.
⑥ Treasury Stock 의존권이나 배당권이 없는 담보 형식의 주식.

TSB Trustee Savings Bank (영) 신탁 저축 은행.

TSC ① thermally stimulated current 열자극 전류.
② time sharing control task 시분할 제어 태스크.
③ transmitter start code 송신 개시 코드.
④ TV standard converter 텔레비전 표준 변환 장치.

TSCA Toxic Substance Control Act (미) 독성 물질 규제법.

TSCJ Telecommunications Satellite Corporation of Japan (일) 통신·방송위성기구. 통신위성과 방송위성을 운영하며 지상에서 무

선국을 개설하고 있는 이용자에게 각종 서비스를 제공한다. 우정성(체신부) 관할의 인가법인이며 우주에 있어서의 통신의 보급발달과 전파의 유효이용을 목적으로 설립되었다.

TSE ① Tokyo Stock Exchange (일) 동경 증권 거래소.
② trunk signaling equipment 중계선(線)신호장치.

TSFC thrust specific fuel consumption (항공) 추력 연료 소비율.

T.S.H. Their Serene Highness 전하(殿下).

TSIO time shared input/output 시분할 입출력기능.

TSM transportation system management 교통 체제 종합 관리. 교통측면에서만 다루던 교통문제를 건설, 도시계획, 환경 녹지등 각 분야와 연결시켜 종합적으로 운영하는 기법.

TSO time since overhaul (항공) 오버홀후의 사용기간.

tsp teaspoon : teaspoonful.

TSP total suspended particulate 부유분진.

TSPA Traffic Safety Promotion Authority (한) 교통 안전 진흥 공단.

TSR Trans Siberian Railway 시베리아 철도 운송. 극동지역에서 시베리아 횡단철도를 경유하여 유럽 및 중동내륙지점까지 수송

하는 방식.

TSRO topological short range order 기하학적 단범위 규칙성.

TSS ① time sharing system 시분할 시스템. 복수의 이용자가 원격지로부터 단말기를 사용하여 한 대의 컴퓨터를 공동 이용하는 시스템.
② traffic separation scheme 선박 항행 분리 방식.

TSUS(A) Tariff Schedule of United States (of America) 미관세율표.

TT ① technology transfer 기술이전.
② teetotaler 금주자(禁酒者).
③ telegraphic transfer 전신환.
④ teletypewriter 텔레타이프라이터.
⑤ Tidningarnas Telegrambyra 스웨덴 통신사.
⑥ total time 총 사용시간. 엔진 등의 제조시 부터의 누적 사용 시간.

TTB ① telegraphic transfer buying rate 은행이 고객으로부터 외국환을 매입할 때의 가격.
② Test Tube Baby 시험관 아기.

TTBT The Threshold Test Ban Treaty 지하 핵실험 제한 조약.

TTC ① The Telecommunication Technology Committee (일) 전신 전화 기술 위원회. 민간조직.
② total traffic control 열차 운행 종합 제어 장치.

TTFW too tacky for words (미

449

T time

속어) 입 밖에 낼 수 없을 정도로 속된.

T time time for testfiring 실험 발사 시각.

TTL ① through the lens 렌즈 통과. ② transistor-transistor logic 입력측도 출력측도 트랜지스터를 사용하는 논리회로.

TTL through the lens system 방식 렌즈를 통과한 광선을 카메라에 내장한 노출계로 측정하는 시스템.

TTP telegraphic transfer payable 지불전신환.

TTR target tracking radar 목표추적 레이더.

TTS ① taxi telephone shopping 택시내에 포스터·상품리스트를 상비하고 상품의 수주·수부업무를 통판회사(通版會社)를 대신하여 대행하는 것. ② telegraphic transfer selling rate 외환은행이 고객에게 외국환을 팔 때의 가격. ③ temporary threshold shift 일시 청력 손실. 항공기 소음 등에 의하여 일시적으로 청력이 저하하는 것.

TTT time temperature tolerance 허용 온도 시간. 식품이 일정 온도하에서 얼마동안 신선도를 유지하는가를 나타내는 수치.

TTY teletypewriter = TT 텔레타이프라이터.

TU ① 소련의 대형 제트 여객기 이름. ② terminal unit 단말장치. ③ trade union (영) 노동조합.

T.U. Trade(s) 노동조합.

TUAC Trade Union Advisory Committee 노동조합 자문위원회. OECD의 하부기관.

TUC Trades Union Congress (영) 노동 조합 회의.

TULF Tamil United Liberation Front (스리랑카) 타밀 통일 해방 전선.

TUT Typen und Teile (독) 형식(形式)과 부품의 종류를 합리화하여 재료비와 노무비를 제외한 모든 간접비를 삭감하는 것.

TUV (프) Technische Uberwachungs-Verein (=Technical Inspection Association) (통일 전 서독) 기술 검사 협회.

TV ① television 텔레비전. ② tera volt 1조볼트. ③ time value 셔터속도지수. ④ transvestist or transvestite 복장도착자. 이성의 옷을 입으므로 성적만족을 얻는 자.

TVA Tennessee Valley Authority (미) 테네시강 유역 개발공사.

TVC thrust vector control (우주공학) 추력방향제어. 분사가스의 방향을 바꿈으로서 로켓의 추력의 방향을 제어하는 방법.

TVI television interference 텔레비전 전파방해.

TVP textured vegetable protein 식물성 단백질. 콩단백질로 만든 인조고기의 상표.

TVR 영국의 고급스포츠카 전문 제조 회사.

TVRO television receiver only 텔레비전 수신전용.

TVT television typewriter 텔레비전 타자기.

TW tetrawatt 1조 와트.

TWA Trans World Airlines (미) 트랜스월드 항공.

TWI training (of supervisors) within industry 직장내 감독자 훈련. 기업이 실시하고 있는 관리자의 훈련강좌.

TWIF Tug of War International Federation 국제 줄다리기연맹.

TWIMC to whom it may concern 관계자 제위.

TWITS teens with income to spend 가처분소득이 있는 10대 어린이.

TWOV transit without visa 무사증 통과.

TWX teletype wire exchange 텔레타이프교환.

TWY taxiway (항공) 유도로.

TYMNET 미국 TYMSHARE사의 상용(商用) 데이터 통신네트워크.

T-zero 발사시각.
T-plus = 발사~후의.
T-minus = 발사 ~전의.

U ① unit 단위.
② universal or unrestricted (영) 일반대상영화.
③ upper class 상류계급.
④ uranium 우라늄. 원자번호 92.

U-2 Utility-2 (미국의) 고공 정찰 비행기 이름.

UA ① ultra audible (sound) 초음파.
② underwriting account 보험 계정.
③ Unit Account (유럽) 계산단위.
④ United Air Lines (미) 유나이티드항공.

UAA United Arab Airlines 아랍 연합 항공.

UAAC Un-American Activities Committee (미하원의) 비미(非美) 활동 (조사)위원회.

UAB Unemployment Assistance Board (미) 실업 구제국.

UAE United Arab Emirates 아랍에미리트국 연합국.

UAI Unio Academique International (프) 국제학사원연합.

UAL United Air Line = UA (미) 유나이티드 항공.

UAM underwater to air missile 수중 대공 미사일.

UANC United African National Council (짐바브웨) 통일 아프리카 민족 평의회.

UAP Universal Availability of Publication 세계출판물 입수이용. IFLA(국제도서관협회연맹)에 의한 세계 어디서나 누구나 필요로 하는 자료를 입수할 수 있게 하려는 운동.

UAPSP Utility Acid Precipitation Study Program 공익 사업 산성우연구 계획.

U.A.R., UAR United Arab Republic (Syria가 독립하기 전의 Egypt와의 통합국명).

UART universal asynchronous receiver transmitter 직열병열 및 병열직열의 변환 기능을 가진 비동기(非同期)데이터 전소용 인터페이스.

UAS uniform accounting system 통일회계방식.

UATI Union des Associations Techniques Internationales (프) 국제공학단체연합.

UATP Universal Air Travel Plan

세계 공통의 항공권 등의 신용판매제도.

UAV Unmaned Aerial Vehicle 무인 항공기(無人航空機).

UAW United Automobile Workers 전미 자동차 노동조합. 정식명은 United Automobile, Aerospace and Agricultural Workers of America (전미 자동차 항공 우주 농업인계노조)이다.

UB upback (미식축구) 업백.

UBAG unaccompanied baggage 별송 수하물.

UBC University of British Columbia (캐나다) 브리티시 컬럼비아 대학.

U.B.S. Union Bank of Switzerland 스위스 연방 은행.

UC unire de compte (=common unit) = EUA (프) 의 공통 계산 단위.

UCB University of California at Berkeley (미) 캘리포니아 대학 버클리교.

UCC ① Universal Copyright Convention 국제 저작권 협정.
② Universal Copyright Convention 만국[국제] 저작권 조약
③ Uniform Commercial Code 통일 상법전. (각각의 주가 독자적인 입장에서 정했던 상거래 관습의 통일화를 목표로 연방전부에 의해 1950년대 제정된 법률로 미국 상거래의 근간을 이루는 법률).
④ User Created Content 사용자 제작 동영상.

UCCA Universities Central Council on Admissions (英) 대학 입학 중앙 평의회.

UCD (스) Union de Centro Democratioc (=Democratic Central Union) 민주 중도 연합.

UCI Union Cycliste Internationale (International Cycling Union) (프) 국제 사이클리스트 연맹.

UCLA University of California at Los Angeles 캘리포니아 로스 엔젤레스 대학.

UCP Uniform Customs and Practice for Documentary Credits 신용장 통일 규칙.

UCR unconditional response 무조건 반사.

UCS Union of Concerned Scientists (미) 우려하는 과학자동맹. 원자력·핵병기 개발에 반대하는 미국의 과학자의 연합.

UCSD University of California at San Diego (미) 캘리포니아 샌디에이고 대학교.

UDA ① Ulster Defence Association (북아일랜드) 신교도 과격파그룹. IRA에 대항하는 정치조직.

② **Ulster Defence Association** 얼스터 방위동맹. 북아일랜드의 신교도 과격파.

UDAG Urban Development Action Grant (미) 도시 개발 조성계획.

UDC Universal Decimal Classification 국제 10진 분류법. 도서 정리법의 하나.

UDEAC (프) Union Douaniere et Economique de L'Afrique Centrale (=Central African Economic and Customs Union) 중앙 아프리카 관세 동맹.

UDF United Democratic Front (남아프리카) 합법적 반아파르트헤이트 세력 중의 최대의 조직.

UDHR Universal Declaration of Human Rights 세계 인권 선언

UDI Unilateral Declaration of Independence 일방적 독립선언. 1965년 11월, 남 로디지아(현재의 짐바브웨)의 백인 소수파가 행한 영국으로부터의 독립 선언.

UDMH unsymmetrical dimethylhyrazine 액체 로켓 연료. Apollo의 달착륙선 등에 사용.

UDP ① (스) Union Democratica Popular (= Democratic People's Union) (페루, 볼리비아) 인민 민주 연합.
② uridine diphosphate 우리딘이인산.

UDPG uridine diphosphoglucose 우리딘 이인산글루코스.

UDPM (프) Union Democratique du Peuple Malien (= Mali People's Democratic Union) 말리 인민 민주 연합.

U-drive you drive 렌터카.

UDT underwater demolition team 수중 파괴 부대.

UEA Universala Esperanto Asocio (에스) 만국 에스페란토 협회.

UEAC Union des Etats de I' Afrique Centrale (프) 중부아프리카 제국 동맹.

UED Universal Dictionary of the English Language 유니버설 영어사전.

UEFA Union of European Football Association 유럽 축구 연합.

UEP Uranium Enriched Program 우라늄 농축 프로그램.

UER Union Europeene de Radiodiffusion = EUB (프) 유럽방송연합.

UF ① United Force (가이아나) 통일 세력. 정당명.
② urethan foam 우레탄 폼.

UFA unesterified fatty acid 유리지방산.

UFCW United Food and Commercial Workers International Union 국제 식물 상업 조합.

U.F.O., UFO, ufo unidentified

flying object 미 확인 비행물체 (비행접시라고도 함).

UFORA Unidentified Flying Objects Research Association (영) UFO조사 협회.

UFT United Federation of Teachers (미) 미국 교원 연맹.

UFTAA Universal Federation of Travel Agents' Associations 여행업자 협회 세계 연맹.

UFWA United Farm Workers of America 아메리카 농장 노동자 조합.

UGC University Grants Committee (영) 대학 육성 위원회.

UGM underwater to ground (surface) missile 수중 발사대 지 (해상) 미사일.

UGPA Undergraduate Grade Point Average (미) 대학생 성적 평균점.

UGTT [F] Union Generale des Travaillers Tunisiens (= Tunisian General Labor Union) 튀니지 노동 총동맹.

UGW United Garment Workers of America 아메리카 의류 노조 연합회.

UHF, U.H.F, uhf, u.h.f. ultra high frequency 초고주파.

UHG ultra high grade 초고급.

UHMW-HDPE ultra high molecular weight, high density polyethylene 초고분자량 고밀도 폴리에틸렌.

UHMW-PE ultra high molecular weight polyethylene 초고 분자량 폴리에틸렌.

UHT ultra heat tested (우유) 초고온 처리된 UHT 우유. - 75~85℃로 6분, 120~132℃로 2초 살균한 것.

UHV ultra high voltage 초고압.

UI unite internationale = IU (프) 국제단위.

UIA Union Internationale des Architectes (프) 국제 건축가 연맹.

UIBC unsaturated serum iron binding capacity 불포화 혈청 철분 결합 능력.

UIC uncompensated ionization chamber (원자력) 비보상형 전리상(霜)

UICC Unio Internationalis Contra Cancrum (라) 국제 대암 연합.

UIL (이) Unione Italiana del Lavoro (=Italian Union of Labor) 이탈리아 노동 연합.

UIPM Union Internationale de Pentathlon Moderne (프) 국제 근대 5종 경기 연합.

UIPMB Union Internationale de Pentathlon et Biathlon (프) 국

UIR

제 근대 5종 바이아슬론 연합.

UIR upper flight information region (항공) 상층 비행 정보구역.

UIT Union Internationale de Tir = ISU (프) 국제 사격 연합.

UITP (프) Union Internationale des Transports Publics (=International Union of Public Transports) 국제 공공 수송 연합.

UJT uni junction transistor 단접합(單接合) 트렌지스터.

UK United Kingdom 연합왕국, 영국. 정식명은 United Kingdom of Great Britain and Northern Ireland

UKAEA United Kingdom Atomic Energy Authority 영국 원자력 공사.

UKC under keel clearance 선저(船底)간격. 선저와 해저와의 간격.

UL Underwriters Laboratories, Inc. (미) 보험업자 연구소.

ULCC ultra large crude carrier 초대형 탱커. 30만중량톤 이상의 것.

ULD unitized load device 항공기에 의한 화물수송에 사용하는 컨테이너류의 총칭.

ULF ultra low frequency 극저주파.

ULI Urban Land Institute (미) 도시 지역 연구소.

ULL uncomfortable loudness level 불쾌음 레벨.

ULMS underwater launched missile system 수중 발사 미사일 시스템. 수중에서 발사되는 미사일의 총칭.

ULN upper limit of normal 정상치 상한.

ULP ultra light plane 초경량 비행기.

UL ratings (미) US Listed ratings 플라스틱·가정용품·내장품, 건재등의 착화성·연소성 등에 관한 기준이다.

ULSI ultra large scale integrated circuit 초대형 집적회로.

ult. ultimate ; ultimately ; ultimo

ULV ultra low volume 극미량.

UM unaccompanied minor 딸린 사람이 없는 미성년자.

UMC ① Underwater Medical Center 잠수 의학 실험대. ② User Modified contents 사용자 가공 콘텐츠. (=UCC)

UMIS urban management information system 도시 행정 관리 정보 시스템.

UMNO United Malay National Organization (말레이시아) 통일 말레이 국민 조직.

UMP upper mantle project 지구

내부개발계획. 지각과 맨틀 상부의 구조를 탐사하는 계획.

UMR usual marketing requirement 통상 판매 필요량, 통상 무역 필요량.

UMSN Union Mondial de Ski Nautique (World Water Ski Union) (프) 세계 수상스키 연합.

UMT Universal Military Training (美) 일반 국민 군사 교련.

UMW United Mine Workers (of America) 전미 광산 노동자 연합.

UMWA United Mine Workers of America 전미(全美) 탄광 노동자 조합.

UN, U.N. United Nations 국제 연합.

UNA United Nations Association 유엔협회.

UNAC United Nations Atomic Commission 유엔원자력위원회.

UNAFEI United Nations Asia and Far East Institute for the Prevention of Crime and the Treatment of Offenders 유엔 아시아 극동 범죄 방지 연구소.

UNA-USA United Nations Association of the United States of America 미국 유엔 협회.

UNBIS United Nations Bibliographic Information System 유엔 서지(書誌) 정보 시스템. 유엔이 간행 또는 접수한 자료의 서지 관리를 한다.

UNC ① United Nations Charter 유엔 헌장.
② United Nations Command 유엔군.
③ United Nations Congress 유엔 회의.

UNCA United Nations Correspondents Association 유엔 기자 협회.

UNCC United Nations Compensation Commission 국제연합 보상 위원회. (Switzerland Geneva 소재)

UNCD United Nations Conference on Desertification 유엔 사막 회의.

UNCDF United Nations Capital Development Fund 유엔 자본 개발 기금.

UNCHE United Nations Conference on the Human Environment 유엔 인간 환경 회의.

UNCHS ① United Nations Center for Human Settlements 유엔 인간 거주 센터.
② United Nations Commission on Human Settlements 유엔 인간 거주 위원회.

UNCIO United Nations Conference on International Organization 유엔 국제 기구 회의.

UNCITRAL

1945년 샌프란시스코에서 개최된 유엔성립까지의 준비회의.

UNCITRAL United Nations Commission on International Trade Law 유엔 국제 상거래법 위원회.

UNCLOS United Nations Conference on the Law of the Sea 유엔 해양법 회의.

UNCMAC United Nations Cmmand Military Armistice Commission 유엔군 군사 정전위원회.

UNCPUOS United Nations Committee on the Peaceful Uses of Outer Space 유엔 대기권외 평화 이용 위원회.

UNCSTD United Nations Conference on Science and Technology for Development 유엔 과학 기술 개발 회의.

UNCTAD United Nations Conference on Trade and Development 유엔 통상개발회의.

UNCTD United Nations Conference on Trade and Development 유엔 통상무역개발회의

UNCURK United Nations Committee for the Unification and Rehabilitation of Korea 유엔 한국 통일 부흥 위원회.

UND University of National Defence (미) 국방대학.

UNDA United Nations Development Agency 유엔 개발기관.

UNDC United Nations Disarmament Commission 유엔 군축 위원회.

UNDD United Nations Development Decade 유엔개발의 10年

UNDESA United Nations Department of Economic and Social Affairs 유엔 경제 사회부.

UNDEX United Nations Documents Index 유엔 출판물 색인.

UNDIS United Nations Documentation Information System 유엔 문서 정보 시스템. 유엔의 기록·공문서의 관리 시스템.

UNDOF United Nations Disengagement Observer Force 국제 연합 병력 격리 감시군. 1974년 이스라엘과 시리아 병력 격리를 위해 설치.

UNDP United Nations Development Program 유엔 개발 계획.

UNDRO United Nations Disaster Relief Organization 유엔 재해 구제 기관.

UNEDA United Nations Economic Development Administration 유엔 경제 개발국.

UNEF ① United Nationale d' Eudianus de France (프) 프랑스 전학년.
② United Nations Emergency Forces 유엔 긴급군.

UNEP United Nations Environment Program 유엔 환경계획.

UNEPTA United Nations Expanded Program of Technical Assistance 유엔 확대 기술 원조 계획.

UNESCO, Unesco United Nations Educational, Scientific, and Cultural Organization 유엔 교육과학 문화기구.

UNF ① United Nations Forces 유엔군.
② United Nations Foundation 국제 연합 재단.

UNFAO United Nations Food and Agriculture Organization 유엔 식량 농업 기구.

UNFC United Nation Food Council 유엔 식량 이사회.

UNFDAC United Nations Fund for Drug Abuse Control 유엔 마약 통제기금.

UNFP [F] Union Nationale des Forces Populaires (=National Union of People's Forces) (모르코) 인민 세력 사회주의 동맹.

UNFPA United Nations Fund for Population Activities 유엔 인구활동기금.

UNGA United Nations General Assembly 유엔총회.

UNGC The United Nations Global Compact 유엔 글로벌 컴팩트

UNHCHR Office of the United Nations High Commissioner for Human Rights 국제 연합 인권 고등 판무관실. (스위스 제네바 소재).

UNHCR Office of the United Nations High Commissioner for Refugees 유엔 난민 고등 법무관 사무소.

UNHHSF United Nations Habitant and Human Settlement Foundation 유엔 인간 거주 재단.

UNI United News of India UNI 통신사. 인도의 통신사의 하나.

UNIC United Nations Information Center 유엔 홍보센터.

UNICE Uniona des Industries de la Communaute Europeene (프) 유럽 공동체 산업연맹.

UNICEF United Nations International Children's Emergency Fund 유엔 아동기금<유니세프>. 1953년에 United Nations Children's Fund로 개칭, 약칭의 UNICEF는 그대로 사용.

UNICON university computer network (한국) 대학 전산망.

UNIDIR United Nations Institute for Disarmament Research (Geneva, Switzerland) 국제군축연구소.

UNIDO United Nations Industrial Development Organization 유엔 공업 개발 기구.

UNIDROIT International Associ-

UNIFEM

ation for Unification of Roman Private Law 로마 사법 통일 국제 협회.

UNIFEM UN Development Fund for Women 유엔 여성 개발 기금.

UNIFIL United Nations Interim Force in Lebanon 국제 연합 레바논 잠정 주둔군.

UNIMA Union International de Ia Marionnete (International Puppeteers Union) 국제 인형극 연맹.

UNIMARC Universal MARC Format 만국 MARC 포맷

UNI-SAT United Satellite 1986년6월 영국이 쏘아올린 방송용 위성.

UNISCAN United Kingdom and Scandinavia 영국 스칸디나비아 경제 동맹.

UNISIST United Nations International System of Information in Science and Technology 유엔 과학 기술 교류기관.

UNISPACE United Nations Conference on Exploration and Peaceful Uses of Outer Space 유엔 우주 평화 이용 회의.

UNITA (포) Uniao National PraraIndependencia of Angola) National Union for the Complete Independence of Angloa 앙골라 완전 독립 민족 동맹.

UNITAR United Nations Institute for Training and Research 유엔 훈련 조사 연구소.

UNIVAC Universal Automatic Computer Sperry Corp가 제조 판매하고 있는 컴퓨터.

Universiade universite + olympiade 국제 학생스포츠 대회.

UNKRA United Nations Korean Reconstruction Agency 유엔 한국 부흥기관.

UNLF Uganda National Liberation Front 우간다 민족 해방전선.

UNMOGIP United Nations Military Observer Group in India and Pakistan 국제 연합 인도·파키스탄 군사 감시단.

UNO, U.N.O. United Nations Organization 유엔 기구.

UNOS United Network for Organ Sharing 미국 장기 이식 정보 센터. (미국의 장기이식을 종합적으로 관리하고 있는 비영리기관).

UNP United Nations Party (스리랑카) 통일 국민당.

UNPC United Nations Peace Corps 유엔 평화부대.

UNREF United Nations Refugee Fund 유엔 난민 기금.

UNRISD United Nations Research Institute for Social Development 유엔 사회 개발 연구소.

UNRRA United Nations Relief and

Rehabilitation Administration 유엔 구제 회복 사무국.

UNRWA United Nations Relief and Works Agency for Palestine Refugees in the Near East 유엔 팔레스티나 난민 구제 사업 기관.

UNSC United Nations Security Council 유엔 안전 보장 이사회.

UNSCC United Nations Standards Coordinating Committee 유엔 규격 조정 위원회

UNSCEAR United Nations Scientific Committee on the Effects of Atomic Radiation 원자방사선의 영향에 관한 유엔 과학 위원회.

UNSF ① United Nations Security Force 유엔 평화군.
② United Nations Special Fund 유엔 특별기금.

UNSGA United Nations Special General Assembly 유엔 특별 총회.

UNSM United Nations Service Medal 국제 연합 종군 무공 훈장.

UNSSOD United Nations Special Session on Disarmament 유엔 군축 총회.

UNTAG United Nations Transition Assistance Group 국제 연합 나미비아(Namibia) 독립 지원 그룹.

UNTC United Nations Trusteeship Council 유엔 신탁통치 이사회.

UNTDB United Nations Trade and Development Board 유엔 무역 개발 이사회.

UNTSO United Nations Truce Supervision Organization in Palestine 유엔 팔레스티나 휴전 감시기구.

UNU United Nations University 유엔 대학.

UNV United Nations Volunteers 유엔 평화 부대.

UNWC United Nations Water Conference 유엔 수자원 회의.

UOD ultimate oxygen demand (수질의) 구극(究極) 산소 요구량.

UP ① unbleached pulp 표백되지 않은 펄프.
② unsaturated polyester resin 불포화폴리에스테르수지.

UPC Universal Product Code (미) 만국 제품 코드. 통일 상품 코드. 슈퍼마켓 등에서 상품의 가격·재고 등을 관리하기 위하여 제품의 포장에 인쇄된 짧은 흑선의 집합 무늬, 전자식으로 판독하게 되어있다. bar code의 일종.

UPF ① Uganda Popular Front 우간다 인민 전선.
② United People's Front (싱가포르) 통일 인민 전선.

UPI ① United Press International

UPI 통신사.
② universal peripheral interface 범용 단말 인터페이스.

UPIS Uranium Price Information System 우라늄 가격 정보 시스템.

UPLI United Poets Laureate International 국제 계관 시인 연합.

UPM Uganda Patriotic Movement 우간다 애국 운동. 정당명.

UPN Unity Party of Nigeria 나이지리아 통일당.

UPOV L'Union Internationale pour Ia Protection des Obtentions Vegetables (프) 신품종 보호 국제동맹.

UPOV조약 United Protection of Vegetation Act 식물 신품종 보호에 관한 국제조약.

UPOW Union of Post Office Workers (영) 우체국 노동조합.

UPRONA (프) Union pour le Progres National (=Union for National Progress) (부룬디 공화국) 민족 진보 연합.

UPS ① uninterrupted power supply 보조전원, 무정전(無停電)전원장치.
② United Parcel Service 미국 최대의 소화물 수송 회사.

UPU Universal Postal Union 만국 우편 연합.

UPVC unplasticized polyvinyl chloride 경질염화비닐수지.

UR Uruguay Round multilateral trade negotiations 우루과이라운드. 가트의 새로운 다각적 무역교섭. 서비스 무역의 자유화, 농업문제, 긴급수입 제한 등의 교섭. 1986~1990년.

Ur uranium [화] 우라늄의 화학기호.

URI upper respiratory infection 상기도(上氣道) 감염.

URL unrequited love (미 속어) 짝사랑.

URNG (스) Unidad Revolucionaria Nacional Guatemalteca (=National Revolutionary Union of Guatemala) 과테말라 민족 혁명 연합.

URPE Union of Radical Political Economics (미) 급진적 정치 경제학 연합.

URSI Union Radio Scientifique Internationale (프) 국제 전파 과학 연합.

URTNA (프) Union des Radiodiffusion et Television Nationales Africaines (=Union of National Radio and Television Organization of Africa) 아프리카 방송 연합.

US United States 미국.

USA ① United States Army 미육군.
② United States of America 아메리카 합중국.

③ United Steelworkers of America 전미 철강노동자 합동조합.

USAC United States Auto Club 미국 자동차 클럽.

USAEC United States Atomic Energy Commission 미국 원자력위원회.

USAF United States Air Force 미공군.

USAFA United States Air Force Academy 미국 공군 사관 학교.

USAFE United States Air Force, Europe 재유럽 미국공군.

USAFI United States Armed Forces Institute 미군 교육기관.

USAFPAC United States Armed Forces, Pacific 태평양 방면 주재미군.

USAFR United States Air Force Reserves 미국 공군 예비 부대.

USANG United States Air National Guard 미국 주(州) 공군.

USAR United States Army Reserves 미 육군 예비 부대.

USAREUR United States Army, Europe 유럽 주둔 미 육군.

USARPAC United States Army, Pacific 아메리카 태평양 육군 총군.

USASCII United States of America Standard Code for Information Interchange 정보교환용 미국 표준 코드.

USASI United States of America Standards Institute 미국규격협회. 현재는 ANSI로 개칭.

USB ① upper side band 상측파대 (上側波帶).
② Universal Serial Bus PC 주변기기 포트 규격.

USBAI United States Boxing Association International 미국 국제 복싱 협회.

USBN universal standard book number 국제 표준 도서번호.

USC ① United State Code 합중국 연방 법규집.
② University of Southern California 남캘리포니아 대학.

USCA United States Code Annotated 주해 미 연방 법규집.

USCAB United States Civil Aeronautics Board 미국 민간 항공 위원회.

UISCENTCOM United States Central Command 미국 중앙군. 남서아시아 지역 방위의 통합군 기구.

USCF United States Chess Federation 미국 체스 연맹.

USCG United States Cost Guard 미국 연안 경비대.

USCI United Satellite Communications, Inc. (미) 위성방송회사.

USCS United States Commercial Standard 미국 상업 표준.

USDA United States Department of Agriculture 미국 농무성.

USDAW Union of Shop, Distribution and Allied Workers (영) 상점, 배급 및 관련사업 노동자 조합.

USERID user identification 이용자 식별.

USES United States Employment Service (미) 노동성 고용국.

USFJ United States Forces, Japan 재일 미군.

USFK United States Forces, Korea 주한 미군.

USFL United States Football League 미국 축구 연맹.

USFPL United States Forest Products Laboratory 미국 임산물 연구소.

USGA United States Golf Association 전미 골프 협회.

USGI U.S. Government Report Index 미국 정부 리포트 색인.

USGPO United States Government Printing Office 미국 인쇄국.

USGS United States Geological Survey 미국 지질 조사소.

USIA United States Information Agency = USIS 미국 홍보 문화 교류청.

USIB United States Intelligence Board 미국 정보 연락 위원회. CIA의 일부문.

USICA United States International Communication Agency 미국 국제 교류청.

USIS United States Information Service 미국 홍보 · 문화 교류국. USIA의 해외 현지 기관.

USJSP U.S. Japan Security Pact [Treaty] 미일안전보장조약.

USM ① underwater to surface missile 수중대지 미사일. ② United States Mail 미국 우편. ③ United States Marines = USMC 미국 해병대. ④ United States Mint 미국 조폐국.

USMA United States Military Academy 미국 육군 사관 학교.

USMC ① United States Marine Corps 미국 해병대. ② United States Maritime Commission 미국 해사 위원회.

USMCR United States Marine Corps Reserves 미국 해병대 예비 부대.

USMM United States Merchant Marine 미국 상선대.

USN United States Navy 미국 해군.

USNA ① United States National Army 미국군대.
② United States Naval Academy 미국 해군 사관 학교.

USNFK U.S. Naval Forces, Korea 주한미해군.

USNG United States National Guard 미국 국방군.

USNO United Sabah National Organization (말레이시아) 통일 사바 국민 조직. 정당명.

USNR United States Navel Reserve 미 해군 예비 부대.

USO ① United Service Organization 미군 서비스 기관. 군대 위문활동을 하는 민간 비영리조직.
② unknown swimming object 미지의 수영 물체.

USOC United States Olympic Committee 미국 올림픽 위원회.

USOM United States Operations Mission 미국 경제 원조 실시 사절단.

USP ① United States Patent 미국 특허.
② United States Pharmacopoeia 미국 약국방.
③ unique selling Proposition unique (그 상품밖에 없는), selling (팔릴 수 있는), proposition (제안)의 머리글자를 딴 것이며 미국의 유명한 카피라이터가 제창한 광고원리.

USPA United States Polo Association 미국 폴로 협회.

USPG United Society for the Propagation or the Gospel 통일 복음 전파 협회.→ SPG

U.S.P.O. United States Post Office 미국 체신부.

USPS United States Postal Service 미국 우정 공사.

USPSD United States Political Science Documents 미국 정치학 문헌.

USRT universal synchronous receiver/transmitter 범용 동기 리시버·트랜스미터.

USS ① United States Senate 미국 상원.
② United States Standard 미국 표준규격.
③ United States Ship 미국 국적선.

USSC United States Supreme Court 미국 최고 재판소.

USSOCOM United States Special Operation Command = USSOC 특별 작전 사령부.

USSR United of Soviet Socialist Republics 소비에트 사회주의 공화국연방.

USTA United States Tennis Association 미국 테니스 협회.

USTC United States Tariff

USTOL

Commission 미국 관세위원회.

USTOL ① ultra short takeoff and landing 초단거리 이착륙.
② ultra short takeoff and landing aircraft 초단거리 이착륙기.

USTR United States Trade Representative 미국 통상 대표부

USTS United States Travel Service 미국 정부 관광국.

USTTA United States Travel and Tourism Administration (미) 상무성) 미국 여행·관광국.

USV United States Volunteers 미국 의용병단.

USW ultra short wave 초단파.

USWA United Steelworkers of America 미국강당노동조합.

Ut. Utah = UT 유타 주.

UT universal time 세계시. GMT 의 별칭.

UTA ① (프) Union de Transports Aeriens 유티에이 프랑스항공.
② upper control area (항공) 상층 관제구.

UTC ① Universal Time Coordinated 협정세계시. GMT대신 방송에서 사용되는 표준시.
② under the counter 부정한.

UTLAS University of Toronto Library Automation System 토론토 대학 도서 목록 데이터 뱅크.

UTM universal transverse mercator's projection 유니버설횡(橫) 메르카토르도법(圖法).

UTO United Towns Organization 자매 도시 단체 연합.

UTP uridine triphosphate 우리딘 삼인산염.

UTT Utility Tactical Transport 다용도 전술 수송. 아일랜드 Shorts Brothers Co.의 비행기.

UTTAS utility tactical transport aircraft system helicopter 다용도 전술 수송 헬리콥터.

UUM underwater to underwater missile 잠수함대 잠수함 미사일.

UV ① ultra high vacuum 초고 진공.
② ultra violet rays 자외선.
③ unemployment and vacancy 실업과결원, 구직과 구인.

UVA ultra violet A 장파장 자외선.

UVB ultra violet B 중파장 자외선.

UVC ultra violet C 단파장 자외선.

UVM universal vender mark (미) 통일 상품 코드. UPC로는 불충분하여 개발된 상품 코드.

UW underwriter 보험업자.

U/W, u/w underwriter 보험업자. (회사)

UXB unexploded bomb 불발폭탄.

v ① verb 동사.
② volt 볼트.

V ① value 가치.
② vanadium 바나듐. 원자번호 23.
③ version 판(版).
④ victory 승리.
⑤ volume 용량, 용적, 권.
⑥ V Series V시리즈. 기존의 전화망에 모뎀을 개재시켜 데이터 전송을 하기 위한 단말 인터페이스로서 CCITT가 권고하는 표준 규격.
⑦ 로마숫자의 5.
⑧ versus …대(對).

Va viola (음악) 비올라.

Va. Virginia = VA 버지니아 주.

VA ① value added 부가가치.
② value analysis 가치분석.
③ Veterans Administration (미) 퇴역군인 관리국.
④ visual aid 시각교재.
⑤ volt ampere 볼트 암페어.

VAB vehicle assembly building 우주 왕복선 조립 공장.

vac vacuum cleaner 진공 소제기.

VAC ① value added carrier 부가 가치 통신 사업자.
② Verified Audit Circulation (미) 발행 부수 공사(公査)기관.

VAD value added dealer 원제품에 부가가치를 붙여 판매하는 중간업자.

VAFB Vandenberg Air Force Base (미) 반덴버그 공군 기지.

VAKA (플라망어) Vlaams Aktiekomittee tegen Atomwapens (=Flemish Action Group against Atomic Weapons) (벨기에) 플라망계 반핵 단체.

VAL ① Villeneuve d' Ascq Lille (프) 전자동(全自動) 무인 지하철.
② Voiture Automatique Legere (프) 자동 운전의 경차량 시스템.

VALS value and life style 가치관과 생활 양식. 소비자 분류의 기준.

VAN value added network 부가가치 통신망.

VANB Value Added Network Bank 부가가치 은행(금융 EDI 및 전자상거래 도입이 활성화되면서 개방 네트워크 상에서 결제

467

VAR

서비스 및 정보의 가공·제공 등을 위주로 영업을 하는 은행).

VAR ① vacuum arc remelting 진공 아크 재용해.
② value added retailer 부가가치소매업자. 제조원의 제품에 부가가치를 붙여 판매하는 소매업자.
③ visual aural range (항공) 가시 가청식 무선 항로 표식.

VAGIG Viacao Aerea Rio Grandense (포) 바리그 브라질항공.

VAS value added service 부가가치 서비스.

VASCAR Visual Average Speed Computer and Recorder 자동차 속도 위반 단속용 계속장치.

VASI visual approach slope indicator 진입각(進入角) 지시등.

VAT value added tax 부가가치세.

V&T vodka and tonic 보트카에 키니네수(탄산수)를 탄 것.

Vatican 로마 교황청.

VATC Vatican City Italy의 Rom에 있는 로마 교황이 지배하는 독립국가.

VAZ Volzhsky Avtomibilny Zavod 소련의 국영 자동차 제조 회사.

VB ① valence bond method 원자가(原子價) 결합법(結合法).
② venture business 벤처기업. 연구 개발형의 중소 중견 기업.

VBL vertical blanking line (문자·도형방송) 수직 폐선 제거기간.

VC ① venture capital 벤처비지니스를 대상으로 금융·투융자를 전문으로 하는 기업 또는 이러한 기업의 자본 자체를 말한다.
② Vietcong 베트콩.
③ vinyl chloride 염화비닐.
④ virtual call 상대선택 접속기능.
⑤ vital capacity 폐활량.
⑥ voluntary chain stores 임의 연쇄점.

VCA voltage controlled amplifier 전압 제어 증폭기.

VCB Vacuum Circuit Breaker 진공 차단기(眞空遮斷機).

VCI volatile corrosion inhibitor 휘발성 부식 방지제.

VCM ① video coding machine 바코드를 찍는 영상적인 봉서(封書) 예비 구분기.
② vinyl chloride monomer 염화비닐 모노머(불포화 결합체) PVC의 원료.

VCO voltage controlled oscillator 전압 제어 발진기.

VCP video cassette player 비디오 카세트 플레이어.

VCR video cassette recorder 비디오 카세트 리코더.

VCT voice code translation 음성

코드 번역.

VCX Video Cassette X-Rated Film, Inc. (미) 성인영화 비디오 카세트 판매 회사.

VD ① vapor density 증기 밀도.
② venereal disease 성병.
③ video disk (일) 음성신호와 영상신호가 기록된 원반 또는 그의 재생장치.

V-Day Victor Day 전승 기념일.

VDB virtual data base 가상 데이터 베이스.

VDFC variable diode function character 가변 2극관식 함수 발생기.

VDFG variable diode function character 가변 2극관식 함수 발생기.

VDH valvular disease of the heart 심장 판막증.

VDI (독) Verein Deutscher Ingenieure (= Society of German Engineers) 독일 기술자 협회.

VDP ① video disc player VD의 재생기.
② video display processor 화상표시용 프로세서.

VDR video disk recorder 비디오 디스크 리코더.

VDRL Venereal Disease Research Laboratory (美) 성병 연구소.

VDS variable depth sonar 가변심도(深度)음파탐지기.

VDT visual(or video) display terminal (컴퓨터) 표시단말기, 단말표시장치.

VDU ① video display unit =VDT.
② visual display unit (컴퓨터) 출력정보를 문자 · 도형으로 브라운관에 표시하는 장치.

VE ① value engineering 가치 공학. 기술 관리와 경영의 효율화를 도모하는 기법.
② video engineer 텔레비전 영상효과 기술자.

VEAP Veterans Educational Assistance Program (美) 복원[퇴역]군인 교육 원조 계획.

V-E Day Victory in Europe Day 제2차대전 연합군 유럽전승 기념일.

Veep Vice President 부통령, 부총재, 부사장.

VENUS Valuable and Efficient Network Utility Service (일) 국제 전신전화 주식회사의 국제 공중 데이터 전송 서비스.

VER ① voluntary export restraint 자유수출 규제.
② Visual Flight Rule 유시계 비행 방식.

VERA vision electronic recording apparatus 텔레비전 프로그램 수록장치.

vet ① veteran (미 구어) 재향 군

인.
② veterinarian 수의사.
③ veterinary 수의사의

VETS Veterans' Employment and Training Service (미) (노동성) 재향 군인 고용·훈련국.

VF ① very fair 쾌청.
② video frequency 화상 주파수.
③ visual field 시야.
④ voice frequency 음성 주파수.
⑤ voltage to frequency converter 전 압 주파수 변환기.

VFET vertical field effect transistor 종형 전계 효과 트랜지스터.

VFO variable frequency oscillator 가변 주파수 발진기.

VFP variable factor programming (컴퓨터) 변동요인 프로그래밍.

VFR visual flight rules 유시계 비행 규칙.

VFT Very Fast Train (오스트레일리아) 초고속 열차.

VFW Veterans of Foreign Wars of the United States (미) 해외 종군 재향 군인회.

v.g. =verbi gratia =for example. 예

VG ① variable geometry (비행기) 가변 후퇴익(後退翼).
② variable-grade record 장시간 레코드의 일종. SP반과 같은 1분간 78회전, 연주시간은 배(倍).

③ very good.
④ videpterminal glass 눈을 보호하기 위하여 표시 단말기에 부착하는 착색 글라스.
⑤ voltage generator 전압 발생기.

VGC viscosity gravity constant 점도 비중정수. 원유의 화학조성의 지표.

VHC very highly commended 대호평.

VHD video high density 일본 비크타가 개발한 흠이 없는 정전(靜電) 용량방식(비디오디스크).

VHDL very high density lipoprotein 초고밀도 리포단백.

VHF, V.H.F., vhf, v.h.f. very high frequency 초단파.

VHLL very high level language 초고급 프로그램 언어.

VHPR vertical temperature profile radiometer 수직온도 분포용 방사계.

VHRR very high resolution radiometer 초고 해상도(解像度) 방사계.

VHS video home system 일본 비크타가 개발한 가정용 비디오 테이프 리코더.

VHSIC very high speed integrated circuit (컴퓨터) 초고속 집적회로.

VHSV volumetric hourly space velocity 단위 시간당 체적 공간 속도.

VHTR very high temperature reactor 초고온 가스 원자로.

VI ① viscosity index 점수지도
② virginium [화] 배지늄의 화학기호.

VIC very important city (공격목표로서의) 최중요 도시.

VID vide(see) (라) 참조하라.

vidicon video iconoscope 비디콘. 광전도효과(光傳導效果)를 이용한 텔레비전 용 소형카메라의 저속형(低速型) 촬상관의 일종.

VIM ① vacuum induction melting 진공 유도 용해.
② Vertical Improved Mail (미) 고층빌딩용 우편물 집배 시스템.

VIN vehicle identification number 자동차 고유 번호.

VIP very important person 중요 인물.

VIS ① visibility (항공) 시정.
② voice information system 음성 정보 시스템.

VISSR Visible (or Visual) and Infrared Spin Scan Radiometer (미) 가시 적외 주사 방사계.

VISTA Volunteers in Service to America (미) 빈민 구제 봉사단.

VITA Volunteers for International Technical Assistance 해외 기술 원조 봉사대.

viz. videlicet (라) 즉.

VJ ① victory over Japan 대일전 (對日戰) 승리.
② video jockey 텔레비전에서 음악비디오 프로를 담당하고 음악사이에 짬짬이 얘기하는 사람.

V-J Day Victory over Japan Day 제2차 대전 연합군. 대일 전승일.

VLA ① very large array (미국 국립 전파 천문 관측소의) 전파 망원경망.
② very low altitude 초저공.

VLBI ① very long baseline interferometer 초장기 선전파 간섭계.
② very long baseline interferometry 초장기 선전파 간섭 관측법. 준성(準星)으로부터 오는 전파를 2점에서 포착하고 그의 도달 시간의 차와 별의 방위(方位)를 측정하여 2점간의 거리를 산출한다.

VLCC very large crude carrier 대형탱커. 16~30만 중량톤.

VLCD very low calorie diet 감식 요법, 반기아 요법.

VLDL very low density lipoprotein 초저밀도 리포단백.

VLF very low freguency 초장파.

471

VLG village 마을.

VLSI very large scale integrated circuit (컴퓨터) 초대규모 집적회로. 수밀리 평방의 실리콘 기판 위에 10만 개~ 100만개의 트랜지스터가 늘어서 있는 집적회로.

VM ① value management 가치관리.
② variable micrograde 1분간 78회전의 장시간 레코드.
③ visual merchandising 시각에 호소하는 상품판매정책. 종래의 단순한 진열에서 탈피하여 새로운 방향을 지향하는 것.

VMC visual meteorological condition (항공) 유시계 기상 상태. 목시(目視) 비행이 가능한 기상상태.

VMD (라) veterinariae medicinae doctor (=doctor of veterinary medicine) 수의학 박사.

VMI Video Music International (미)비디오 주크박스 발매원(發賣元).

VMOS vertical MOS 수직 MOS. 단위면적내의 소자 밀도를 향상시킬 수 있다.

VMS Voice Mail Service 음성전달 서비스.

VMX Voice Mail Box (일) 음성 메일 복스. 전화회선과 컴퓨터를 연결하여 음성 메세지를 전달하는 시스템.

VNA vietnam News Agency 베트남 통신사.

VO very old 포도주, 위스키 등의 저장연수가 10~12년 경과한 것.

V.O. voice over 나레이터의 목소리.

VOA Voice of America 미국의 소리 방송. 미국 정부의 해외방송.

VOC volatile organic compound 휘발성 유기화합물. 도료의 용제로 사용되며, 자동차 등의 도장으로 환경에 배출된 위험이 있으므로 미국에서는 1980년 12월에 VOC규제를 제정하였다.

VOIR venus orbiting imaging radar 금성주회(周回) 탐사기.

VOIS voice input system 음성 입력 시스템.

VOKS Vsesojuznoe Obshchestvo Kuljturnoj Svjaziss Zagranitsej (러) 전 소련 대외 문화교류 협회.

VOL volume 음량. 라디오 등의 음의 크기.

VOLAR voluntary army : volunteer army 의용군.

VOLMET meteorological information aircraft in flight 대항공기 기상통보. 프랑스어의 vol(비행)과 meteorologic(기상)의 합성어.

VOM volt ohm milliammeter 전

압저항 전류계.

VOP valued as in original policy (보험) 협정 보험 가격은 원래 증권대로.

VOR very high frequency omnidirectional range 초단파 전방향식 무선 표식. VOR국에서 전방향으로 위상(位相)이 일정한 기준신호의방위에 따라 위상이 변하는 가변(可變)위상신호의 두 가지를 포함한 전파를 방사하여 항공기는 이 두 가지 신호의 위상차(差)에서 방위를 알 수 있으며 국(局)으로부터는 비행코스를 연속적으로 지시할 수 있다.

VOS vitality, originality, service 활력·독창성·봉사.

VP ① Vice-President 부통령, 부총재, 부사장.
② video package 비디오 테이프에 영상과 음성을 기록한 것.

VPA vote profile analysis (미) 선거 개표 동향 추정법. CBS방송과 IBM사가 협력하여 개발한 선거의 득표동향을 분석하는 방법, 컴퓨터를 사용하여 적은 개표수로 분석할 수 있다.

VPE vapor phase epitaxy 기상성장.

VPF vertical processing facility 종형(縱型)로켓 정비탑.

VPI vapor phase inhibitor 기상방청제. 기화성의 방청제.

VR ① variable reluctance 가변자기 저항.
② vocal resonance 성대 공명.
③ volume ratio (증권) 볼륨 레이쇼. 일정기간동안의 주가 상승일의 거래량과 주가 하락일의 거래량을 누적계수가 아닌 비율로 분석한 것. 보통 과거 1개월간의 주가 상승일의 거래량 합계를 주가 하락의 거래량 합계로 나눈 것이다.
④ Virtual Reality 가상현실

VRA voluntary restraint agreement 자주 규제 협정.

VRAM video RAM 비디오 임의 접근 기억 장치.

VRBM variable range ballistic missile 가변사정(可變射程) 탄도 미사일.

VRC vertical redundancy check (컴퓨터) 수직 용장(冗長)검사.

VRD Royal Naval Volunteer Reserve Officers's Decoration (영) 해군 의용 예비 장교 훈장.

VRM ① variable rate mortgage 변동 저당 증권.
② Venus radar mapper 금성 레이더 탐사기.

VRP Variety Reduction Program 부품반감화(半減化)계획.

VRS ① video response system (일) 화상 응답 시스템.
② voice recognition system (컴퓨터) 음성 인식 장치.

vs. versus (라). …에 대하여.

VS ① vein shot (속어) 정맥 주사.
② veterinary surgeon 수의사.
③ (이) volti subito (=turn quickly) (음악) 빠르게 페이지를 넘겨라.
④ Versus 대

VSA variable stability aircraft 가변 특성기(特性機). 연구 개발용 모의기.

VSAM virtural storage access method 가상(假想) 기억 액세스법.

VSAT very small aperture terminal 초소형지구국. 소형의 안테나를 사용하여 통신위성을 통하여 다지점간(多地點間)에서 데이터 등을 송수신할 수 있다. 전국에 산재하는 지점이나 계열점에 설치하여 데이터 통신이나 팩시밀리 통신 등에 사용한다.

VSB vestigoal side band (컴퓨터) 잔류측파대(殘留側派帶).

VSBC very small business computer 업무용 초소형컴퓨터.

VSM vestigial side band modulation (컴퓨터) 잔류 측파대 변조(變造).

VSO very superior (or special) old 브랜디의 특급. 12~17년 저장의 것.

VSOE Venice Simplon Orient-Express 런던과 베니스간 약 1500km의 국제 열차 정기편.

VSOP ① very superior(or special) old pale 브랜디의 특상급. 18~25년 저장의 것.
② vitality sensitivity, originality, personality 활력, 감수성, 독창성, 인격. 면접시 중요한 것.

VSP vehicle scheduling program 배송(配送)계획을 위한 수법으로 절약법(節約法)의 대표적인 컴퓨터 프로그램.

VSS ① variable stability system = VSA 현유기(現有機)의 자동 제어장치의 제어정수(正數)를 변경시킴으로써 신형기(新型氣)의 운동을 모의하는 방식.
② volatile suspended solid (폐수 등의) 휘발성 부유고형물.

VSTOL vertical and short take-off and landing 수직 단거리 착륙기.

VSWR voltage standing wave ratio 전압 정재파비(電壓定在破比).

VSTNC vertical synchronizing signal (텔레비전의) 수직동기신호. 텔레비전 화상의 종방향의 위치를 정하는 신호.

Vt. Vermont = VT 버몬트 주(州).

VT ① vacuum tube 진공관.
② video tape 비디오 테이프.

VTAM virtual telecommunication access method 가상 기억 통신

액세스 방식.

VTO vertical take off 수직이륙.

VTOC volume table of contents (컴퓨터) 볼륨 목록.

VTOL vertical takeoff and landing 수직 이착륙(기).

VTP video tape player 비디오 테이프 플레이어.

VTR ① video tape recorder 비디오 테이프 녹화·재생장치.
② video tape recording 비디오 테이프 녹화.

VTVM vacuum tube voltmeter 진공관 전압계.

VTX video telex 비디오 텍스.

VU ① voice unit 음성단위.
② volume unit 음량단위. * 음성이나 음악에 대한 전기 신호의 강약을 나타내는 단위.

VUMMIES very upwardly mobile mothers 향상심(向上心)이 강한 어머니.

VUV vacuum ultraviolet rays 진공 자외선.

V.V. vice versa 반대의 경우도 마찬가지.

VVA Vietnam Veterans of America (미) 베트남 전쟁 참가 퇴역 군인.

VVD (네덜란드어) Volkspartij voor Vrijheid en Democratie (= People's Party for Freedom and Democracy) 자유 민주당.

VVSDP very very superior old pale 25~40년 저장의 브랜디.

VVVF variable voltage variable frequency 가변 전압 가변주파수.

VW Volkswagen (자동차) 폴크스바겐.

VWD (독) Vereinigte Wirtschaftdienst (독일) 경제 통신사.

VWP Visa Waiver Program 비자 면제 제도

VX venom toxic 독가스의 하나.

V.y. various year 간년(刊年). 일정치 않음.

w. ① double 이중(二重).
② watt 와트.

W wolfram (라) 텅스텐. 원자번호 74

W. ① warehouse 창고
② Wednesday 수요일.(Wed).

WA with average (해상보험) 단독해손담보.

WAA World Assembly on Aging 유엔 고령자 문제 세계 회의.

WAAS world Academy of Arts and Science 세계 예술 과학 아카데미.

WABT wait before transmit (컴퓨터) 송신 일시 정지요구.

WAC ① Women's Army Corps (미) 육군 여성부대.
② World Aeronautical Chart 국제 민간 항공도.

WACC Weighed Average Cost of Capital 가중 평균 자본 비용.

WACH West African Clearing House 서아프리카 결제동맹.

WACK wait before transmit positive acknowledgement (컴퓨터) 송신 대기 요구.

WACL world Anti-Communist League 세계반공연맹.

WAEC West African Economic Community 서아프리카 경제 공동체.

WAES workshop alternative energy strategy 대체 에너지 전략 워크숍.

WAF Women in the Air Force (미) 공군 여성부대.

WAFA Wakalit Anba Filistin Althawrah 팔레스티나 해방통신.

WAGC world Amateur Golf Council 국제 골프 평의회.

WAIS Wechsler Adult Intelligence Scale 웩슬러 성인용 지능 검사법.

WAM ① Emirates News Agency 아랍 토후국 통신사.
② walking around management 현장중시 경영관리.

WAN ① wide area network 광역통신망.
② world Association of Newspapers 세계 신문 협회. (언론 자유 창달과 회원 간 교류 증대를 통한 세계 신문업계의

발전을 기본목표로 1948 창설된 단체. 1백 13개국 1만 8천여 개의 신문·통신사 및 언론관련 기관을 회원으로 보유.

WANO world Association of Nuclear Operators 세계 원자력 발전 사업자 협회.

WAP ① work analysis program 작업 분석 계획.
② Wireless Application Protocol 무선 어플리케이션 프로토콜

WAPOR world Association for Public Opinion Research 세계 여론 조사 협회.

WAR Wasserman Antigen Reaction (매독의) 바세르만 반응. = WR

WARC world Administrative Radio Conference 세계 무선 통신 주관청 회의. ITU의 주요기관의 하나.

Wash. Washington = WA 워싱턴 주(州).

WASME world Association for Small & Medium 세계 중소 기업 연맹.

WASP ① White, Anglo Saxon, Protestant (미) 앵글로색슨계 백인 신교도. 미국에 있어서 상류계급의 조건.
② William Aerial System Platform 신비행물체.
③ Women's Airforce Service Pilots (미) 육군 항공부대 여성 조종사.

Watergate 워터게이트 사건. 1972년 대통령 선거시, 민주당 전국위원회본부가 있던 종합건물. 민주당 전당대회 계획이 도청되어 문제가 된 후 그 사건의 고유명사가 됨.

WATS wide area telephone service (미) 광역 전화 서비스.
① inward WATS 지역 지정 착신 과금 서비스. 전화의 통화요금을 자동적으로 착신자가 지불하는 서비스.
② outward WATS지역 지정 정액과금 서비스. 통화지역을 정하고 매월 정액 요금으로 몇 번이고 장거리 전화를 할 수 있는 서비스.

WAVES Women Accepted for Volunteer Emergency Service 미국 해군 여자 예비 부대. 1948년 정규 해군 부대로 편입.

WAVPM Women Against Violence in Pornography and Media 포르노와 매스미디어에 있어서 여성에 대한 폭력에 반대하는 여성의회.

WAWF world Association of world Federalists 세계 연방주의자 세계협회.

WAY world Assembly of Youth 세계 청년회의.

WB ① bond with warrant 신주

WBA

　인수건부 사채.
② waybill 화물운송장.
③ wet bulb temperature 습구(濕球)온도.
④ world Bank 세계 은행.

WBA world Boxing Association 세계 권투 연맹.

WBC world Boxing council 세계 권투 평의회.

WBS work breakdown structures 업무분석표.

WBSJ Wild Bird Society of Japan 일본 야조(野鳥)의회.

WC ① water closet 화장실.
② wheel chair 휠체어.

WCA ① Women's Christian Association 여성 기독교협회.
② Workers' Compensation Act (미) 노동자 재해보상법.

WCC ① War Crimes Commission 전쟁범죄 위원회.
② World Council of Churches 세계 교회 협의회.

WCCF West Coast Computer Fair 미국 서해안 컴퓨터 전시회.

WCD Webster's Ninth New Collegiate Dictionary 웹스터 신대학 사전 제9판.

WCED world Commission on Environment and Development (유엔) 환경과 개발에 관한 세계 위원회. 유엔환경특별위원회.

WCEE world Conference of Earthquake Engineering 세계 지진 공학 회의.

WCES Winter Consumer Electronics Show (미) 매년 1월에 서 개최되는 전자 기기 전시회.

WCGA world Computer Graphics Association 세계 컴퓨터 그래픽 협회.

WCH world Congress of the Humanities 세계 인문 과학 학회.

WCI ① world Council on Isotopes 세계동위 원소기구
② Windchill Index 바람 냉각 지수.

WCL World Confederation of Labor 국제 노동조합 연합.

WCO World Custom Organization 세계 관세 기구

WCOTP World Confederation of Organizations of the Teaching profession 세계 교육자 연맹.

WCP ① world Climate Program 세계기후계획.
② world Council of Peace 세계 평화 평의회.

WCPC world Coffee Promotion Committee 세계 커피 진흥위원회.

WCPP world Congress of Partisans of peace 세계 평화협의회.

WCRP ① world Climate Research Program 세계 기후연구계획. ② world Conference on Religion and Peace 세계 종교자 평화 회의.

WCS ① waste collection system (우주공학) 오물수집시스템. ② world Conservation Strategy 세계 자연 자원 보전 전략. 국제 자연 보호 연합이 작성한 지구의 자원을 보호하는 행동계획.

WCT world Championship Tennis 세계 테니스 선수권 대회주체 단체.

WCTU Women's Christian Temperance Union 기독교 여성 금주 동맹.

WCWB world Council for the Welfare of the Blind 세계 맹인 복지 협의회.

WCY world Communications Year 세계 커뮤니케이션 년. 1983년

WD well developed 발육 양호.

4WD 4 wheel driving 전후 4륜 구동.

WDC World Date Center 세계데이터 센터. 세계의 미생물, 세포, 유전자 자원의 정보수집과 제공 활동을 하는 센터.

WDI wind direction indicator 풍향 지시기.

WDM world Development Movement 세계 개발 운동.

WE war engineering 전쟁 공학.

WEA Workers' Educational Association (미) 노동자 교육 협회.

WEAL Women's Equit Action League (미) 여성 평등 행동 연맹.

WEC world Energy Conference 세계 에너지 회의.

WECPNL weighted equivalent continuous perceived noise level 가중등가(加重等價) 감각 소음기준. 항공기 소음의 국제적 평가단위.

WEFA Wharton Economic Forecasting Associates (미) 1981년 펜실베이나 대학에서 분리 독립한 경제 예측 회사.

WEO where economy originates 박리다매 방식의 뜻.

WEOWESTPAC Western Pacific Missile Defense Architectures Study 서태평양 미사일 방위 구상.

Web Sie 한권의 책처럼 하나의 묶음으로 공개되어 있는 Web 페이지 장소

WEU Western European Union 서유럽 동맹.

WF work factor method 동작분석에 의하여 표준작업시간을 정하

는 방법의 하나.

WFB World Fellowship of Buddhists 세계 불교도 연맹.

WFC World Food Council (유엔) 세계 식량 평의회.

WFCL World Food Council 세계 식량 이사회.

WFDY World Federation of Democratic Youth 세계 민주주의 청년동맹. 공산주의 제국이 청년단체의 국제적인 조직.

WFEO World Federation of Engineering Organizations 세계 공학 단체 연맹.

WFLOE Women for Life on Earth (영) 지구 보존 여성회.

WFMH World Federation for Mental Health 세계 정신 위생 연맹.

WFOT World Federation of Occupational Therapists 세계 직업 요법사 연맹.

WFP World Food Program 세계 식량계획. 유엔 전문기관의 하나.

WFSF World Future Studies Federation 국제 미래학회.

WFSW World Federation of Scientific Workers 세계 과학 노동자 연합.

WFTU World Federation of Trade Unions 세계 노동조합 연맹.

WFUNA World Federation of United Nations Associations 유엔 협회 세계 연맹.

WG ① water gauge 수위계.
② wire gauge 와이어 게이지.
③ working group 작업그룹.

WGA Writers' Guild of America 미국 작가 길드.

WH White House 미국 대통령 관저.

WHA ① Wikalat al Magherb al Arabi 마그레브·아라비아통신사. 모로코의 국영통신사.
② World Hockey Association 세계 하키 협회.

WHNS Wartime Host Nation Support 전시 구원하기 위하여 온 동맹군에 대하여 받아들인 나라가 지원하는 것. 동맹군을 받아들인 나라가 전력, 시설, 물자 등을 지원하는 것.

WHNSA Wartime Host Nation Support Agreement 전시(戰時) 주류국(駐留國) 지원협정.

WHO World Health Organization (유엔) 세계보건기구.

WHP Water horsepower 수마력.

WHSV weight hourly space velocity 단위 시간당 중량 공간 속도.

WI warning index (일) 소비자 피

해 조기 경계 시스템.

WIA wounded in action 전상.

WIBC Women's International Bowling Congress 국제 여성 볼링 협회.

WIDER World Institute for Development of Economics Research (유엔) 세계 개발 경제 연구소.

WIG wing in ground effect aircraft 지표 효과형 주익(主翼) 항공기.

Wiki Web 브라우저에서 간단히 Web 페이지 발행, 편집 등을 할 수 있는 Web 켄텐츠 관리 시스템.

WIL Women's International League = WILPE (미) 여성 국제평화 자유 연맹.

WILPE Women's International League for Peace and Freedom = WIL (미) 여성 국제 평화 자유연맹.

WIMS Worldwide Intratheater Mobility Study (미) 세계 전역내(戰役內) 병력 이동 연구. 1988년에 시작한 해외에서의 긴급시의 병력 투입 계획의 개선에 관한 연구.

WIN ① Work Incentive Program (미) 근로 장려책. 생활보호수급자에 일을 제공하는 방책.
② Whip Inflation Now = Ford 美 大統領이 제창한 인플레 퇴치운동.

WINS Wide Information Network Services 종합 정보망.

WIPO World Intellectual Property Organization (유엔) 세계 지적 소유권 기구. 상표, 의장(意匠)등의 보호.

Wis. Wisconsin = Wisc. 위스콘신 주(州).

WISC Wechsler Intelligence Scale for Children 웩슬러 아동 지능 검사법.

WISH Women in Self Help (미) 여성을 위한 무료전화 상담 서비스.

WJC World Jewish Conference 세계 유태인회의.

WJL water jet loom 워터 제트 직기(織機).

WL water line 수선(水線). 배의 표면과 수면이 닿는 선.

WLM Women's Liberation Movement = Women's Lib 여성해방운동.

WMA World Medical Association 세계 의사회.

WMC ① World Meteorological Center 세계 기상중추.
② World Muslim Congress 세계 회교 협의회.

WMD ① weather merchandising

제조업, 유통업을 위한 부가가치를 붙인 기상정보.
② Weapons of Mass Destruction 대량살상무기.
③ World Meteological Organization 세계기상기구.

WMO World Meteological Organization 세계 기상 기구.

WMSF World Masters Sports Federation 세계 마스터즈 스포츠 연맹.

WN well nourished 영양 양호.

WNL within normal limits 정상 범위내.

WNWD Webster's New World Dictionary of the American Language 웹스터 신세계 미국어 사전.

WO ① warning order (군사) 준비 명령.
② warrant officer 준위.

W/O water in oil 유중수(油中水).

WOC without compensation 무보수.

WRI ① wage rate index 임금율지수.
② war risk insurance 전쟁보험.

WRL War Resisters' League 전쟁 저항자 동맹. 본부 영국.

WRM war reserve material (군사) 비축자재. 주로 연료, 물자, 희금속 등.

WRNS Women's Royal Naval Service (영) 해군 여성 부대. 통칭 Wrens

WRS war reserve stocks (군사) 비축 재고품. 주로 병기, 레이더, 통신 등의 장치.

WRVS Women's Royal Voluntary Service (영) 여성 자원 봉사대.

WS ① water sports 수상경기.
② wind speed 풍속.
③ workspace (컴퓨터) 작업용으로 할당된 메모리상의 영역.
④ work station 전산기에 입출력할 수 있는 단말장치.
⑤ world scale 탱커의 기준 운임.

4WS 4 wheel steering 4륜 조타. 핸들을 돌리면 전륜 뿐 아니라 후륜도 방향을 바꾸는 방식.

WSAG Washington Special Action Group (미) 워싱턴 특별 행동 그룹.

WSC ① wire spark chamber 다선식 방전실.
② World Sport Prototype car Championship 세계 스포츠 프로터타이프카(모델차) 선수권.
③ Western Summit Conference 서방 진영 정상 회의.

WSI wafer scale integration (전자공학) 웨이퍼규모의 환성.

WSJ Wall Street Journal (미) 월 스트리트 저널 지.

WSLF Western Somali Liberation Front (이디오피아) 서소말리아 해방 전선.

WSP ① Women's strike for Peace 평화를 위한 여성운동. * 미국의 여성의 평화단체. ② work simplification program 작업 단순화 계획.

WSPU Women's Social and Political Union (영) 여성 사회정치 연합.

WSS World Society of Speechology 세계 음성 학회.

WSTS World Semiconductor Trade Statistics 세계 반도체 무역통계.

WT ① walkie talkie 휴대용 무선 전화기. ② watertight 방수의.

WTA Women's Tennis Association 여자 테니스 협회.

WTBS Warner Bros Turner Broadcasting System (미) 애틀랜타의 UHF 텔레비전 방송국.

WTC World Trade Center 세계 무역 센타.

WTF The World Taekwondo Federation 세계 태권도 연맹.

WTI West Texas Intermediate 미국의 대표적인 원유. * NY-MEX 에서 취급되는 표준원유. 1983년 3월 동거래소에서 원유 선물 거래가 개시된 이후 국제원유 시장의 선행지표가 되고 있다.

WTO ① Warsaw Treaty Organization 바르샤바 조약기구. ② World Tourism Organization 세계 관광 동맹. ③ World Trade Organization 세계 무역 기구.

WTT World Team Tennis 세계 팀 테니스.

WOCE World Ocean Circulation Experiment 세계 해양순환 실험계획.

WOIH Council of World Organizations Interested in the Handicapped 세계 신체 장애자기구.

WOM write only memory 기입(記入) 전용 기억 장치.

Women's Lib Women's Liberation movement 여성해방운동.

WOMP World Order Models Project 세계질서모델 연구회. * 평화, 경제복지, 사회적공정, 환경의 네 가지 가치의 균형유지에 의하여 하나의 인간사회 시스템의 구축을 목표로 하고 있다.

WP word processor 문서 작성 집기.

W.P.A. with particular average 단독해손담보.

WPAJ World Patent Abstract Journal 세계 특허 초록지.

WPB wastepaper basket 휴지통.

WPC ① woman police constable (영) 여성경관.
② wood plastic combination 목재·플라스틱 합재.
③ World Peace Council 세계 평화 협의회.
④ world Petroleum Congress 세계 석유회의.
⑤ World Population Conference (유엔) 세계 인구 회의.
⑥ World Power Conference 세계 동력 회의.
⑦ World Product Code 국제 제품 코드.

WPF World Prohibition Federation 세계 금주 연맹.

WPI wholesale price index 도매 물가지수.

WPL word processor language (컴퓨터) 워드프로세서 언어.

wpm word(s) per minute 매분 ~어.

WPO ① Warsaw Pact Organization 바르샤바조약기구.
② World Productivity Organization 세계생산성기구.

WPPSI Wechsler Primary school and Preschool Scale of Intelligence 웩슬러 유아용 지능검사법.

WPPSS Weshington Public Power Supply System (미) 워싱턴 공공 전력 공급 시스템. 별명 Whoops.

WQC water quality criteria 수질 규준(規準).

WQMS water quality monitoring system 수질 감시 장치.

WR ① warehouse receipt 창고 증권.
② wire rod 선재(線材).

WRAAC Women's Royal Australian Army Corps 호주 육군 여성 부대.

WRAAF Women's Royal Australian Air Force 호주 공군여성 부대.

WRAC Women's Royal Army Corps (영) 육군 여성 부대.

WRAF Women's Royal Air Force (영) 공군 여성 부대.

WRANS Women's Royal Australian Naval Service 호주 해군 여성 부대.

WRC World Rally Championships 세계 랠리 선수권.

WRENDA World Request List for Nuclear Data Measurement 핵 데이터의 측정 요청 리스트.

WRESAT Weapons Research Establishment Satellite (호주) 병기 연구국 위성.

WTAS winner takes all system 승자 일괄 득표제.

WSC ① World Student Council 세계 학생 평의회.

② Wire Spark Chamber 다선식 방전실.
③ Washington Secrity Council 워싱턴 국가 안보 회의.

WTUC world Trade Union Congress 세계 노동 조합 회의.

WUS world University Service 세계 학생 봉사단.

WV wind velocity 풍속.

W.Va. West Virginia 서버지니아 주(州).

W.V.F. world Veterans Federation 세계재향군인연맹.

WVR Within visual range 유시계 내에서.

WW ① wash and wear 세탁하여 곧 입을 수 있는 의류, 또 그와 같이 가공한 섬유.
② World War 세계대전.

W/W warehouse warrant 창고증권.

WWF ① wet weather flow 우천 하수량(下水量).
② World Wildlife Fund 세계 야생 생물 기금.
③ world Wrestling Federation 세계 레슬링 연맹.

WMCCS world Military Command Control System (미) 전 세계 군사 지휘 · 통제 시스템. 군사 통신위성을 통하여 전 세계의 미군의 지휘와 통제를 하고 있다.

WWO World War One 제1차 세계 대전.

WWP Wide World Photos 미국이 사진 통신사.

WW II World War Two 제2차 세계 대전.

WWT World Wide Telescope 전 세계 만원경(인터넷 멀티미디어 서비스)

WWW ① World Weather Watch 세계 기상 감시 계획.
② World wide web 인터넷이나 인트라넷에서 표준적으로 이용되는 도큐멘트 시스템. 정보 검색 프로그램.

WX weather 날씨.

Wyo. Wyoming = Wy., WY 와이오밍 주(州).

WYVEA World Youth Visit Exchange Association (일) 세계 청소년 교류 협회.

WZ web zine 인터넷 잡지.

WZC World Zionist Congress 세계 시온주의자 회의.

WZU World Zionist Union 세계 시오니스트 기구.

x ① X-rated movie (미) 18세 미만은 입장금지. 성인 관람용 영화.
② X Series 디지털 데이터망에 접속하는 조건으로 CCITT가 권고하고 있는 일련의 표준규격.
③ X 로마숫자의 10.
④ Christ 그리스도.

X-C skiing cross country skiing 크로스 컨트리 스키.

XCU transmission control unit = TCU 전송제어장치.

XD ex-dividend 배당락(落).

XE xenon 크세논. 원자번호 54.

XING crossing 동물들이 횡단하는 곳. 철도의 건널목, 네거리, 교차점.

Xinhua New China News Agency (중국) 신화사 통신.

XL extra large 특대.

XLPE X-linkaged polyethylene X-연동 폴리에틸렌.

XMA X-ray microanalysis X선 마이크로 아날리시스.

Xmas Christmas 크리스마스.

X-M Bank Export-Import Bank (미) 수출입은행.

XML Extensible Markup Language (1996에서 World Wide Web Consortium 제안한 것으로서, 웹 상에서 구조화된 문서를 전송 가능하도록 설계된 표준화된 텍스트 형식 언어).

XMT transmit 송신.

XO ① exchange order 교환증.
② executive officer 행정관.
③ extra old 저장 50년 이상의 브랜디.

XOR exclusive or 배타적 논리합을 만드는 논리 연산자(演算子).

XPD expedient demise 시기적절한 사망.

XPS X-ray photoelectric spectroscopy X-선 광전자 분광법.

XRD X-ray diffractometry X-선 회석법(回析法).

XRFS X-ray fluorescence spectroscopy 형광 X-선 분석법.

XUR Extreme Ultraviolet Radiation 극자외선.

XUV extreme ultraviolet 극단자외.

XW ex warrants 주식 매입권락 (落).

XX double X 보통 보다 알코올 성분이 많음. ale의 알코올 강도를 나타내는 기호.

XXX ① three x 초고감도필름. ② (미) 본격적인 포르노 영화.

XYZ Examine your Zipper! (미 속어) 지퍼가 열려 있어요.

y Year 년[年, 單位] (시간의 단위, 1y = 365.2422d)

Y2K Year 2000

Y yttrium 이트륨. 원자번호 39.

YA young adult 젊은이, 젊은이에 적합한(책).

YAC Young Astronauts Club 일본 우주소년단.

YAG yttrium aluminum garnet 레이저 발진에 사용한다.

YAK Yakovlev jet fighters (소) 야크. 제트전투기.

Yalu the 압록강

Yangtze Yangtzekuang 양자강

YAP young aspiring professional (미) 출세 지향의 전문직의 젊은이.

YAR Yemen Arab Republic 예멘 아랍 공화국. 1990년 5월 예멘 공화국으로 통합됨.

YAVIS young, attractive, verbal, intelligent, successful 우수한 젊은이. 젊고, 매력적이고, 말 잘하고, 지적이고, 성공적인.

Yb ytterbium 이테르. 원자번호 70.

YB year book 연감, 연보.

yd. yard 야드.

YEEP youthful energetic elderly people 젊고 정력적인 중년의 사람들.

YFP yellow field pea 캐나다산 완두계(系)의 콩의 대용품. 양질의 단백질 함유량이 많다.

Y.H. Youth Hostel 청소년 간이 숙박소.

YHA Youth Hostels Association 유스 호스텔 협회.

YIG yttrium iron garnet 마이크로파용 자성(磁性)재료로 사용된다.

Yippie Youth International Party에서 따온 말 (미) 1960년대 후반 반전주의적인 젊은이 시절.

YL young lady 젊은 여성.

YMCA ① Young Men's Christian Association 기독교 청년회.
② You might come again 또, 오십시오.

YNA Yonhap News Agency (한국) 연합통신.

y.o.b. year of birth 생년(生年).

YOFFIES young out of shaped fat folks 보기 흉하게 뚱뚱한 젊은이.

YPO Young Presidents' Organization 청년 사장 회의.

YSA Young Socialist Alliance (美) 청년 사회주의 동맹.

YSO young stellar object 젊은 항성상(恒星狀) 천체.

YSP Yemen Socialist Party (예멘 인민 민주 공화국) 예멘 사회당. ※ 1990년 5월 예멘 인민 민주 공화국은 예멘 공화국으로 통합됨.

YT Yukon Territory (캐나다) 유콘 준주(準州)

Yumpie young, upwardly mobile, professional (미) 조직이나 사회에서 출세나 성공을 원하는 전문직의 젊은이.

YUP young, urban, professional (미) 1946년 이후 20년간에 태어나 현재 투표권을 가지고 있으며 가난을 모르는 이 세대 가운데 고등교육을 받고 도시근교에서 전문직에 종사자, 산업계에서의 활약, 우아한 사생활을 누리고 있다.

Yuppie YUP.

YWCA Young Women's Christian Association 기독교 여자청년회.

YWCTU Young Women's Christian Temperance Union 크리스트교(敎) 여자 청년 금주 동맹.

YX 차기 민간 제트여객기.

YXX 차차기 민간 제트여객기.

ZANA Zambia News Agency 잠비아 통신.

ZANU Zimbabwe African National Union 짐바브웨 아프리카 민족동맹. 1963년 발족.

ZAPU Zimbabwe African People's Union 짐바브웨 아프리카 인민동맹.

ZAZ (러) Zaporzhsky Avtomobilny Vavod 소련의 국영 자동차 제조 회사.

ZBB zero based budgeting 예산을 제로에서 검토하여 사정하는 방법.

ZD ① zenith distance (천문) 천정(天頂)거리.
② zero defect 무결점. 공장 생산에서 결함문제를 없애자는 것.

ZDF (독) Zweites Deutsches Fernsehen (통일 전 서독) 제2 텔레비전 협회.

ZEG zero economic growth 경제의 제로성장.

ZETA Zero Energy Thermonuclear Assembly (영) 열 핵융합 반응장치.

ZG ① zoological garden 동물원.
② Zero Gravity 무중력 상태.

ZH Zero Hour 공격 개시 예정 시간

ZI Zonta International 국제 존타 클럽. 여성의 로터리 클럽에 유사한 조직.

ZIP+4 ZIP plus four 미국의 우편번호로서 종래의 5자리에 4자리를 더한 9자리로 한 것. 주로 회사나 사무용의 우편물에 사용한다.

ZIP Code zone improvement plan code (미) 우편번호.

Zn zinc 아연. 원자번호 30.

ZOA Zionists Organization of America 재미 시온단(유태인 단체이름)

ZOPFAN Zone of Peace, Freedom and Neutrality 동남아시아 평화·자유·중립지대구상.

ZP zeta potential 계면동전위(界面動電位).

ZPG zero population growth 인구증가를 제로로 하는 계획.

ZQC zero defect quality control 무결점 품질관리 수법.

Zr zirconium 지르코늄. 원자번호 40.

Z.S. Zoological Society 동물학회

ZSL (폴란드어) Zjednoczone Stronnictwo Ludowe (= United Peasants' Party) 통일 농민당.

ZTT zine sulfate turbidity test 황산 아연 혼탁 반응. 간기능 검사의 하나.

ZU ① ZOOM-up 화면 키우기. ②《美속어》(차가) 달려와 멈추다.

ZZ zigzag 지그재그.

참고 및 인용문헌

한미교육연구원, 생활 영어약자사전, 동양서적, 2009
국정원, 최신 시사영어약어사전, 국가정보원, 2005
권영국 외, 영어약어사전, 계명사, 2000
김기령, 최신 의학약어사전, 아카데미아, 2007
김일영, 정보통신산업 약어사전, 덕산기획, 1997
김정필, 엣센스 실용군사영어사전, 민중서림, 2007
노재균, 현대 종합약어사전, 홍익제, 1993
박시우, 정보통신사전 약어집, 홍릉과학출판사, 2005
사서부, 영어 약어 사전, 교학사, 2007
유성렬,지유애, 21C 최신외래어사전, 크로바출판사, 2008
이우주, 영한 한영 의학사전, 아카데미서적, 1992
정재훈, 현대 영어약어사전, 학원출판, 1999
편집부, 뉴우월드 영한대사전, 시사영어사, 1973
편집부, 동아 신콘사이스영한사전, 동아출판사, 1983
편집부, 최신 영어약어사전, 예술문화사, 1994
편집부, 최신 의약약어사전, 현문사, 2001

한미교육연구원 편저서

1. 미국 유학 (우석출판사, 1987)
2. 올바른 자녀교육 (바울서신사, 1987)
3. 차돌이 교육 방랑기 (우석출판사, 1987)
4. 미국 대학 완벽 가이드 (학원사, 1988)
5. 10대 자녀문제 (학원사, 1988)
6. 청소년 그들은 누구인가 (바울서신사, 1988)
7. 미주교포들의 통일의식 구조 (L.A. 평통, 1988)
8. 미국교육의 길잡이 (바울서신사, 1988)
9. 동·서양의 꽃꽂이와 테라리움 (바울서신사, 1990)
10. 꿈나무들을 위한 성교육 (바울서신사, 1990)

11. 미국의 명문 고등학교 (우석출판사, 1989)
12. 미국의 명문 대학 (우석출판사, 1990)
13. 미국의 명문 대학원 (우석출판사, 1990)
14. 성공적인 자녀교육의 비결 (바울서신사, 1990)
15. 미국의 명문고교 입학 유학 최신정보 (학원사, 1990)
16. 일하며 생각하며 (바울서신사, 1990)
17. 미국 속의 한국인 (공저) (유림문화사, 1991)
18. 갈등 그리고 화해 (국민화합해외동포협의회, 1990)
19. 미주 동포들이 보는 조국 (평화문제 연구소, 1992)
20. 백두산, 장백산, 그리고 금강산 (선진문화사, 1992)

21. 지역 갈등과 화해 (차종환, 1993)
22. 반미감정과 태평양시대 (차종환, 1993)
23. 조국을 빛낸 사람들과 미국대학 입시제도 (차종환, 1993)

24. 미국생활 가이드(공저) (중앙일보, 1993)
25. 이중국적 (차종환, 1993)
26. 한반도 통일문제 (차종환, 1994)
27. 마음은 독수리처럼 날개쳐 올라가고 (바울서신사, 1994)
28. 동서양의 길목에서 (바울서신사, 1994)
29. 남북이 잊은 사람들 (바울서신사, 1994)
30. 기적의 역사(공저) (삶과 꿈, 1994)

31. 미국교육제도와 자녀교육 (차종환, 1994)
32. 귀화동포와 이중국적문제 (한국인권문제 연구소, 1994)
33. 미국대학 및 대학원 진학 가이드 (한샘출판사, 1994)
34. 똑똑한 아이! 이렇게 키워라 (삼성출판사, 1994)
35. 미국의 교육제도 (개정판) (바울서신사, 1994)
36. 세계화 시대의 한미관계 (한미교류협회 1995)
37. 재미있는 핵 이야기 (좋은글, 1995)
38. 초등학생의 가정교육 (우석출판사, 1995)
39. 통일로 가는 길(공저) (바울서신사, 1995)
40. 한국의 국력신장을 위한 해외동포들의 역할 (해외동포 문제연구소, 1995)

41. 중·고등학교의 가정교육 (우석출판사, 1996)
42. 베트남의 황금 문이 열리다 (나산출판사, 1996)
43. 발 마사지와 신체 건강법 (오성출판사, 1996)
44. 태교 및 취학 전 아동의 가정교육 (우석출판사, 1996)
45. 꿈나무와 대학정보 (차종환, 1996)
46. 해외 동포 청소년이 통일교육 (평화문제 연구소, 1996)
47. 꼴찌와 일등은 부모가 만든다 (풀잎문학, 1996)

48. 미국을 알고 미국에 가자 (풀잎문학, 1996)
49. 통일로 향하는 마음(공저) (천일인쇄, 1997)
50. 미국인은 배꼽 아래가 길다 (우석출판사, 1997)

51. 우리 모두 통일로 가자 (나산출판사, 1997)
52. 이것이 미국 교육이다 (나산출판사, 1997)
53. 가정은 지상의 천국 (기독교 문화사, 1997)
54. 발 건강과 신체 건강 (태을출판사, 1997)
55. 꿈나무들 및 교육공로자와 대학정보 (차종환, 1997)
56. 21세기의 주인공 EQ (오성출판사, 1997)
57. EQ로 IQ가 휘청거린다 (오성출판사, 1998)
58. 영국의 명소와 명문 대학 (나산출판사, 1998)
59. 불란서의 명소와 명문 대학 (나산출판사, 1998)
60. 이태리의 명소와 명문 대학 (나산출판사, 1998)

61. 백두산의 식물생태 (예문당, 1998)
62. 배꼽 뒤집어 지는 유머 (예가, 1998)
63. 당신의 성공에는 유머가 있다 (나산출판사, 1998)
64. 미국 유학 - 이민교육필독서 (풀잎문학사, 1998)
65. 꿈나무와 페스탈로찌 (차종환, 1998)
66. 지켜야할 문화와 배워야할 문화 (나산출판사, 1998)
67. 묘향산 식물생태 (예문당, 1999)
68. 재외동포의 출입국과 법적지위 (차종환, 1999)
69. 유머백과 (예가, 1999)
70. 한국의 재외동포 정책 (차종환, 1999)

71. 꿈나무 (차종환, 1999)

72. 비무장 지대의 식물생태 (예문당, 2000)
73. 금강산 식물생태 (예문당, 2000)
74. 고사성어 399선 (예가, 2000)
75. 행복 (좋은글, 2000)
76. 건강 장수 백과 (태을출판사, 2000)
77. 스위스의 명소와 명문대학 (나산출판사, 2000)
78. 항로회춘 (나산출판사, 2000)
79. 지구 과학 (예가, 2000)
80. 꿈나무와 교육자 (차종환, 2000)

81. 독일의 명소와 명문대학 (나산출판사, 2000)
82. 재미있는 동물의 세계로(감수) (예문당, 1999)
83. 재미있는 곤충의 세계로(감수) (예문당, 1999)
84. 재미있는 식물의 세계로(감수) (예문당, 1999)
85. 재미있는 공룡의 세계로(감수) (예문당, 2000)
86. 재미있는 지구의 세계로(감수) (예문당, 2000)
87. 재미있는 우주의 세계로(감수) (예문당, 2000)
88. 재미있는 과학자의 세계로(감수) (예문당, 2000)
89. 재미있는 인체의 세계로(감수) (예문당, 2000)
90. 재미있는 환경의 세계로(감수) (예문당, 2000)

91. 재미있는 발명의 세계로(감수) (예문당, 2000)
92. 중국의 명소와 명문대학 (나산출판사, 2001)
93. 고향 생각과 자랑 (차종환, 2001)
94. 캐나다의 명소와 명문대학 (나산출판사, 2001)
95. 2000년대의 민족의 선택(공저) (한통연, 2001)
96. 영재들과 교육 공로자 (차종환, 2001)

97. 고사성어 대사전 (예가, 2001)
98. 교회의 갈등 그리고 화해(공저) (계명대학교, 2002)
99. 체코와 슬로바키아의 명소와 명문대학 (나산출판사, 2002)
100. 태교출산백과(공저) (으뜸사, 2002)

101. 남북한 통일정책과 민족교육 (차종환, 2002)
102. 북한의 교육정책과 명문대학 (평화문제연구소, 2002)
103. 전남쌀 줄게 개성 인삼다오(공저) (동진문화사, 2002)
104. 21세기와 조국통일(공저) (한통연, 2002)
105. 남북한의 통일 정책과 통일 장애요인(공저) (한통연, 2002)
106. 재외동포법 개정을 위해 (공저) (한국인권문제연구소, 2002)
107. 오스트리아의 명소와 명문대학 (나산출판사, 2002)
108. 꿈나무들과 미국의 교육정보 (한교연, 2002)
109. 민간요법보감 (태을출판사, 2002)
110. 캐나다 로키의 명소와 생태 (오성출판사, 2002)

111. 달라진 남한말과 북한말(공저) (예가, 2002)
112. 일본의 명소와 명문대학 (나산출판사, 2002)
113. 미주 한인 이민 100년사 (공저) (한미동포재단, 2002)
114. 배꼽이 뒤집어지는 유머 ② (예가, 2002)
115. L.A 4.29 폭동과 장학재단 (차종환, 2003)
116. 유머 해학 대사전 (예가, 2003)
117. L.A 4.29 폭동의 실상 (밝은 미래 재단, 2003)
118. 호주의 명소와 명문대학 (나산출판사, 2003)
119. 통일 이야기(초급) (L.A 민주 평통, 2003)
120. 인도네시아의 명소와 명문대학 (나산출판사, 2003)

121. 한국부자 미국부자 (도서출판 사사연, 2003)
122. 오직 올바르게 살자(공저) (나산출판사, 2003)
123. 6.15 공동선언과 조국통일(편저) (한통연, 2003)
124. 꿈나무들과 교육선구자 (한교연, 2003)
125. 미주한인사회와 독립운동(공편저) (미주한인 100주년 남가주 기념사업회, 2003)
126. 미주동포의 민주화 및 통일운동 (나산출판사, 2004)
127. 나는 샐러드보다 파김치를 더 좋아한다(감수) (예가, 2004)
128. 구월산, 장수산 식물생태 (예문당, 2004)
129. 청소년을 위한 통일 이야기 (예가, 2004)
130. 신세대를 위한 통일 이야기 (예가, 2004)

131. 사진으로 본 미주 한인 100년사 (박영사, 2004)
132. 꿈나무와 교육정보 (한미교육연구원, 2004)
133. 조선향토 대백과 (제1권) 평양시 감수, 평화문제연구소 및 조선과학백과사전 출판사, 2003
134. 조선향토 대백과 (제2권) 남포, 개성, 나선시 감수, 평화문제연구소 및 조선과학백과사전 출판사, 2004
135. 조선향토 대백과 (제3권) 평안남도 I 감수, 평화문제연구소 및 조선과학백과사전 출판사, 2004
136. 조선향토 대백과 (제4권) 평안남도 II 감수, 평화문제연구소 및 조선과학백과사전 출판사, 2004
137. 조선향토 대백과 (제5권) 평안북도 I 감수, 평화문제연구소 및 조선과학백과사전 출판사, 2004
138. 조선향토 대백과 (제6권) 평안북도 II 감수, 평화문제연구소 및 조선과학백과사전 출판사, 2004

139. 조선향토 대백과 (제7권) 자강도 감수, 평화문제연구소 및 조선과학백과사전 출판사, 2004
140. 조선향토 대백과 (제8권) 황해남도Ⅰ 감수, 평화문제연구소 및 조선과학백과사전 출판사, 2004
141. 조선향토 대백과 (제9권) 황해남도Ⅱ 감수, 평화문제연구소 및 조선과학백과사전 출판사, 2004
142. 조선향토 대백과 (제10권) 황해북도 감수, 평화문제연구소 및 조선과학백과사전 출판사, 2004
143. 조선향토 대백과 (제11권) 강원도 감수, 평화문제연구소 및 조선과학백과사전 출판사, 2004
144. 조선향토 대백과 (제12권) 함경남도Ⅰ 감수, 평화문제연구소 및 조선과학백과사전 출판사, 2003
145. 조선향토 대백과 (제13권) 함경남도Ⅱ 감수, 평화문제연구소 및 조선과학백과사전 출판사, 2003
146. 조선향토 대백과 (제14권) 함경북도Ⅰ 감수, 평화문제연구소 및 조선과학백과사전 출판사, 2003
147. 조선향토 대백과 (제15권) 함경북도Ⅱ 감수, 평화문제연구소 및 조선과학백과사전 출판사, 2003
148. 조선향토 대백과 (제16권) 량강도 감수, 평화문제연구소 및 조선과학백과사전 출판사, 2004
149. 재외동포들의 권익을 위한 법률 (한미인권연구소, 2005)
150. 북한의 현실과 변화 (나산출판사, 2005)

151. 남북분단과 통일 및 국가안보 (나산출판사, 2005)
152. 남북통일과 평화교육 (나산출판사, 2005)
153. 21세기를 맞는 오늘의 북한 (양동출판사, 2005)

154. 조선향토 대백과 (제17권) 인물 (평화문제연구, 2005)
155. 조선향토 대백과 (제18권) 민속 (평화문제연구, 2005)
156. 조선향토 대백과 (제19권) 색인 (가가거리 - 새지골), (평화문제연구, 2005)
157. 조선향토 대백과 (제20권) 색인 (새지네골 - 힘샌골), (평화문제연구, 2005)
158. 미주 동포들의 인권 및 민권운동 (나산출판사, 2005)
159. 남북한 사회와 통일이야기 (LA 민주 평통, 2005)
160. 수재들과 교육 공로자 (차종환, 2005)

161. 어린이 통일교육 이야기 (동양서적, 2006)
162. 청소년 통일교육이야기 (동양서적, 2006)
163. 최신 피부미용 요법 (동양서적, 2006)
164. 최신 육체미용 요법 (동양서적, 2006)
165. 대마도는 한국 땅 (동양서적, 2006)
166. 한미관계 170년사 (동양서적, 2006)
167. 미리가본 북한 산천 (동양서적, 2007)
168. 독도의 영유권 논쟁과 대책 (동양서적, 2007)
169. 멕시코의 명소와 명문 대학 (나산출판사, 2008)
170. 이것이 북한교육이다 (나산출판사, 2009)
171. 글로벌 영어약자 대사전 (동양서적, 2009)
172. 생활 영어약자사전 (동양서적, 2009)
173. 글로벌 외래어사전 (동양서적, 2009)

글로벌 영어약자 대사전

편찬위원

차종환 : 한미교육연구원 원장
정태연 : 전 THE KOREA TIMES 사장
이태형 : 제일종합보험회사 대표이사
김재익 : 우리말 바로쓰기운동 이사장
장관진 : 전 성균관대학교 동창회장
우인근 : WOORI.COM 대표

글로벌英語略字大辭典

값 17,000원

| 판 권 |
| 본 사 |

인쇄　2009년　6월　20일
발행　2009년　6월　25일

편 찬 처 : 한미교육연구원
편찬위원 : 차종환, 정태연, 이태형, 김재익, 장관진, 우인근

발행인 : 안영동
발행처 : 출판사 동양서적
　　　　　경기도 파주시 광탄면 용미리 251-2
　　　　　전화(031)957-4767 FAX(031)957-4768
등록일 : 1976년 9월 6일
번 　호 : 제6-11호
www.orientbooks.co.kr

ISBN 97889-7262-164-5   13710